Game of Gods

The Temple of Man in the Age of Re-Enchantment

Carl Teichrib

Whitemud House Publishing

Whitemud House Publishing

Teichrib, Carl.
Game of Gods: The Temple of Man in the Age of Re-Enchantment

Includes bibliographical references and index.

ISBN: 978-1-9994929-0-8 (Trade Paperback)

Cover design: Justen Faull.

Table of Contents

I

Dedication

To my mother who instilled the love of reading and learning, who questioned the status quo, and who encouraged our individual gifts within the context of a Christian faith.

As she reminded her children on different occasions: "You were born an original, don't die a copy."

It is in the memory of Janet Teichrib (1944-2011) that I dedicate this book.

Acknowledgements

I am deeply and profoundly grateful for my wife Leanne, and our son and daughter – Scott and Austin – as they personally shouldered the weight of this four-year project. Without their incredible fortitude, understanding and love, this would not have come to fruition. Thank you. To my father and extended family, wondering if son, brother, or uncle would ever emerge from what must have seemed a far-off land, you have been more than patient.

Like everyone else, life challenges are continual, and to tell the story of what transpired during the writing of this book would be a task unto itself. That said, we have been incredibly blessed as family and friends and strangers kept us, and this project, in prayer. Many also reached out with deeds of support and assistance, amazing acts of generosity and kindness that allowed this book to see completion – including the infrastructure required to make it happen. To Mark and Misty Luxmore, who graciously gave me an office space in a spare bedroom for over a year: your hospitality was amazing! To Sheldon Chartier, Don and Tanya Kunzelmann, and Joanne Neufeld – who went above and beyond on so many occasions – you were Godsends, helping us move forward when things looked insurmountable. So many names could be mentioned; brothers-and-sisters in Christ who made research trips happen, standing in the gap when things went unexpectedly sideways, and celebrating with us along the way. Thank you.

To Justen Faull for his cover design, and for those who volunteered to proof read; who offered constructive criticism; who indexed; and who backed up my work with supporting documentation – you have each played an important role, bettering this book in so many ways. Thank you.

In all of this, and more, I give thanks to God my Savior, for without His grace and mercy I would be undone.

III

Scope, Structure, Approach

Game of Gods is a comprehensive investigation into the changing nature of Western civilization, the replacement of the Judeo-Christian framework with a new, yet ancient paradigm. It is a journey into the cracks and crevices of big history; an expedition into the expanding realm of transformational movements and influential ideas – forces of change that are shifting how we think, behave, and relate.

Juxtaposed is a different and contrasting paradigm, a reality claim that emanates from beyond time, space, and matter. We are compelled to ultimately consider two options, *Oneness* or *Otherness*.

Game of Gods is structured with five independent and interlocking parts, implying a degree of thematic overlap. The book can be read end-to-end or in its individual sections, keeping in mind that each part and chapter adds to the unfolding panorama. In a sense, Part 3 offers a mid-point conclusion. Part 4, on the other hand, steps back to consider how the new paradigm manifests in four significant areas: global governance, interfaithism, transhumanism, and evolutionary culture. Each chapter in Part 4 is a self-contained mini-book, independent entries that, together, stand as a documented body of evidence; we are building the Temple of Man in the Age of Re-Enchantment.

"Keep the cookies on the lower shelf," I have heard it said, for reader's attention spans have shortened in our age of information overload. Implied is a lower expectation, a sense that we are incapable of nuanced thought. *Game of Gods*, on the other hand, is written with the belief that we – author and reader – must reach for higher treasures of knowledge and understanding, that we *are* capable of wrestling with big ideas. With that in mind, *Game of Gods* is written as a robust work, treating topics with a serious tone and analytical style. Much of it is survey oriented, having a reference quality – a text you can return to in your own studies. But it is more: Interspersed are excerpts of my own personal story, a journey of exploring and weighing worldviews, observing the interplay of global agendas, and being a witness to the tides of visionary ideas and grand movements.

Game of Gods is meant to be a bulwark, an island fortress in a sea of chaotic information.

Introduction

Two young ladies wearing eclectic costumes, powdered white by the ever-present alkali dust of the Black Rock Desert, slowed their bicycles near our camp before calling out.

"Where are we?" It was an innocent question, for the streets of Black Rock City – the famous Burning Man gathering in northwest Nevada – can be disorienting if one is not paying attention to the road markers.

"5 and Kundalini," I answered, indicating our spot on the city's street grid.

With a quick *thank-you* they peddled off, disappearing into the ethereal blur of sensory overload, a pulsing ocean of light and sound and movement. Robert Worley, my friend and Burning Man companion, quietly mirrored their simple query, adding, "now *that's* quite the existential question."

It is, indeed: *Where are we?*

Imposing this inquiry upon Western civilization, we find ourselves pondering our location on the overlapping grids of religion, philosophy, and ideology. Helping us to better grasp our position, *Game of Gods* takes us on an intense journey wherein the road markers point to a new era. And where the roads intersect, new edifices of religion, politics, technology, and culture are being constructed. The Judeo-Christian structures are being dismantled and replaced; we are witnessing the creation of a new global neighborhood. Its builders anticipate a coming synthesis, and Oneness becomes the banner under which they work.

As we consider what this entails – at its core, a truth claim in conflict with another truth claim – we will begin to comprehend the nature and scope of our changing times, coming face-to-face with the transformation of the Western soul. Much of our attention, therefore, will be on the features that have re-set the Western heart and mind.

To help navigate our journey of discovery, *Game of Gods* has been separated into five sections. The first is comprised of two chapters exploring the concept of Oneness, a theme running throughout the book. Part two is a progressive survey outlining the history of Western thought and social change, touching on the rise and fall of Christendom, the exploration of Modernity and Postmodernism, and the emergence of New Spirituality and Re-Enchantment. The third section tackles Biblical approaches to the topic, necessary for a rounded perspective: God as separate and unique from creation, the recurring spirit of the first deception, and the concept of collective rebellion. Part four contains a series of mini-books, expanded essays on the political, religious, technological, and cultural aspects of Oneness. The book's conclusion – Part Five – is a single chapter meant to spur our thinking as we contemplate responses.

Although this book is content rich, it is by no means exhaustive. Many relevant personalities and historical developments have been excluded. Little is said of Islam or Catholicism, sexuality, pop culture, current affairs, or international security concerns. At one point I considered adding a chapter on world monetary issues, a tangible part of the larger question. At first glance this seemed like a shoe-in as I was published in the field. However, because of ongoing developments in crypto-currencies and distributed ledger technologies, I chose to refrain. That said; this book is research saturated.

With that in mind, a few words on research preferences are in order. For those with an eye to the footnotes, it will become apparent that relatively few Internet sources are cited. Even though I was an early adopter of the World Wide Web, it is only one item in the toolbox – a multi-use implement, to be sure, but not the single or primary means of conducting investigation. Electronic documents are sourced, but references to hardcopies are the norm: books, reports, and journals. Most are publicly obtainable, but I do use papers from archives and private holdings. Personally conducted interviews and surveys – important for digging below the surface – are occasionally employed, as are surveys done by others. The most valuable research method I have found, however, is to be there: to literally put boots-on-the ground, observing and interacting, taking notes and collecting data, and otherwise documenting the event in question.

Another consideration is that this is primarily a critique of big ideas and grand visions. Personalities are mentioned, but care is taken to focus on concepts and beliefs more than individuals. We can scrutinize, criticize, probe, and reveal without resorting to depreciating someone's character. At times this can be a fine line, one that I have crossed in my own life. Nevertheless, as Christians we are to love our neighbors, including those who fundamentally disagree with us. This does not mean sugarcoating uncomfortable topics, but neither does it mean acting disrespectfully or bearing false witness.

It is my sincere desire to be as accurate as possible, a difficult task when covering so many subjects with such brevity.

To my friends who are globalists, transhumanists, atheists and agnostics, who are Burners and spiritual explorers and those of other religions, I am thankful you are willing to read my book. To my friends who are socialist leaning, Christian and otherwise, I am grateful you are willing to consider what I have to say. For the many Christians who are concerned about the direction of church and society, who know something is amiss but find it difficult to grasp *where we are*, I trust this book will be of value. To those who cherish liberty, may this reinforce the seriousness of freedom, and thus turn our hearts to the only one who can truly set us free.

Obviously I have biases. We all do. Allow mine to be transparent: I embrace a Christian worldview with an evangelical point of reference. This will be evident in the text. I am pro-liberty and pro-individualistic, versus politically directed equality and socially generated collectivism. Economically I am pro-free market, the voluntary and consensual exchange of goods and services. On the left-right spectrum, with left being understood as maximum government and minimum personal responsibility, as opposed to minimal government and maximum personal responsibility, I am right of center.

In many respects, *Game of Gods* is an historical overview. For to understand tomorrow's context today, we need to have some idea as to where we are now. To do this we must investigate yesterday, for the present did not emerge from a vacuum. Along the way, we will travel to more recent events of world transformation: closed meetings like the United Nations Millennium Forum, and open-source experiments in social engineering, like Burning Man. If you are interested in the connecting points of religion and philosophy, ideology and history, belief and action – then this book is for you. Agree or disagree with my thoughts or findings: but either way, challenge yourself to consider *why*, and to work through the implications.

Some may be asking: Why? What might be gained by digging into complex worldview issues? A number of thoughts come to mind.

First, so we are not uninformed as to the direction and character of culture and society, seeing past the hype, rumor, and sensationalism. Second, to connect the dots of our own life experiences; the main themes in this book are foundational, being relevant irrespective of demographic or social identifiers. Third, to take heed of the revolutionary transformation in play, and therefore mentally and spiritually equip ourselves – and our families, churches, and communities – so as not to become gullible participants.

For the Christian specifically, to know how the Biblical message is being challenged, and primarily those truth claims central to the faith. Then, to recognize how the culture is preaching to us, seeing past the packaging in order to spot the pitch. In doing so, we become responsible in at least two ways: 1) to wisely inform, exhort and uphold those we are responsible to: family and friends, youth groups, and church congregations, 2) to recognize opportunities in bringing Biblical truths into the conversation, taking the approach of the Apostle Paul in Acts 17 – knowing, recognizing, and leveraging the dominant worldview to share a more sure answer.

In other words: *To become effective Ambassadors for Christ.*

Game of Gods does more than just position us on the grid. It explores the essence of the human story, reflected in each of us, and it offers a panoramic picture of our changing landscape.

Welcome to the Age of Re-Enchantment, reads the sign-of-our-times, pointing to our reconstructed neighborhood. And there, at the crossroads of politics and religion, technology and culture, myth and meaning, a familiar yet distinct tower arises, wrapped in the mist of ages while beckoning with the promise of a new future.

The *Temple of Man* looms before us.

Humanity has three Great Desires: To be as God, to be Masters of Meaning and Destiny, to build Heaven on Earth – *this is that story*.

Part I

Preaching Oneness

How holy, how sinful, how everything hot and cold flows into one another! Madness and reason want to be married, the lamb and the wolf graze peacefully side by side. It is all yes and no. The opposites embrace each other, see eye to eye, and intermingle. They recognize their oneness in agonizing pleasure.
– Carl G. Jung, *The Red Book*.

...all modern trends point to the specter of a terrifying, bigger and more pitiless conformity.
– Erik von Kuehnelt-Leddihn, *Leftism*.

Chapter 1

Visions of One

> The supreme motivating concept of the future is synergy: men and women of all nations coming together under leaders of great vision, who see that the pursuit of a common ideal, one world, one Earth, one people, is the reason for all existence. – Desmond E. Berghofer.[1]
>
> ...you will all one day melt into the Oneness. – Neale D. Walsch.[2]

"Welcome, global citizens!"

Those energetic words of unity and affirmation were given on the threshold of the one-thousandth day before the dawning of the New Millennium. Excitement was in the air, for this greeting-of-oneness resonated with those who had come to envision a new world. The event was the Global Citizenship 2000 Youth Congress, held in the mountain-framed city of Vancouver, British Columbia, April 1997. It was a time for dreaming, for anticipating, for visioneering.[3] It was a call to embed a planetary philosophy, as expressed through the World Core Curriculum, into Canada's education system and thus shape a generation of "global citizens."

We came to assert *Oneness*.

With some trepidation I found myself attending this unique gathering. Granted, I had been studying global unity concepts for a number of years prior, but embedding oneself into a paradigm-shifting event is something different. Physically stepping into the operational environment of *one world* is

---

1 Desmond E. Berghofer, *The Visioneers: A Courage Story about Belief in the Future* (Creating Learning International Press, 1992), p.289.

2 Neal Donald Walsch, *Communion With God* (Berkley Books, 2000), p.165.

3 "Visioneering" was the word used by Desmond Berghofer, an organizer of the Global Citizenship 2000 Youth Congress. Visioneering is the task of dreaming potential futures.

not the same as academic book study, with its comfortable distance between the reader and the action. I was entering new territory.

The opening ceremony, held in the Coliseum-styled promenade of Vancouver's Public Library, grandly proclaimed our oneness through music and a parade of thematic banners. We are interconnected was the message; to the Earth, to the energy of the universe, to each other.

As an expression of this unity we each received a symbolic Global Citizenship passport, inspired by the work of famed world-government advocate, Garry Davis.[4] The words on the inside back-page encapsulated the purpose of our Congress: "A good inhabitant of the planet Earth, a member of the great human family... You are the Earth become conscious of herself... Unite, global citizens, to save and heal planet Earth."[5]

The following day was about putting oneness into practice as we considered global citizenship and the role of education. Teams comprised of school children and teachers, university students, and community organizers brainstormed a better world. Urging us to "always think of the Earth" was the grandfatherly figure, Robert Muller, who as former United Nations Assistant Secretary-General had been a confidant to world leaders.[6]

As the author of the *World Core Curriculum* and one who had a personal hand in the creation of eleven UN agencies, Muller was in an unparalleled position to motivate planetary action. Our task, inspired by Muller's enthusiasm and life story, was to flesh out tangible expressions of unity as we focused on his *Curriculum*,

> A new world morality and world ethics... global management... [to] become again what we were always meant to be: universal, total beings... [a] vast synthesis... to make each human being proud to be a member of a transformed species.[7]

---

4 Garry Davis was the founder of the World Service Authority, which issues "world citizen" passports. Applicants have to sign an Affirmation: "As a World Citizen, I affirm my planetary civic commitment to WORLD GOVERNMENT, founded on three universal principles of One Absolute Value, One World, and One Humanity..." (capitals in original).

5 The quote comes from Robert Muller's poem, "Decide to be a Global Citizen," reprinted inside the Global Citizenship 2000 Youth Congress *Passport*.

6 Muller was the United Nations Director of Budget and UN Assistant Secretary-General. Upon retirement he became Chancellor of the UN University of Peace in Costa Rica. In 1989 his *World Core Curriculum* earned him the UNESCO Peace Education Prize.

7 A copy of the *World Core Curriculum* is on file with the author.

Selling A Feeling

To consider oneself part of a grand synthesis, a transformed species, may have seemed like a fringe idea to many Christians back in 1997. Such thinking, however, was firmly embedded in the soil of our culture. Of course, the seed of ideas come from somewhere, and we should have noticed the new flowers scattered across the social and spiritual landscape. Eleven years later, an Oprah event revealed the intensity of the bloom.

The public response to the 10-part webcast hosted by Oprah Winfrey and Eckhart Tolle, *Oprah and Eckhart: A New Earth*, was nothing short of astonishing. In the initial minutes of the first broadcast, Oprah announced that 139 nations were represented; people from around the world had joined the online seminar based on Tolle's book, *A New Earth*. On the third week 11 million had logged in,[8] and by the fall of 2009 the series had been accessed 35 million times.[9] It has been called "one of the ten largest spiritual 'gatherings' in recorded history."[10] Book sales skyrocketed.

But Tolle was doing more than selling merchandise. He was an evangelist, spreading the message of human potential through your personal awakening to *non-separation*. It was an enticing vision of oneness and transformation.

"A new species is arising on the planet," Tolle concluded in his bestseller. "It is arising now, and you are it!"[11]

Oprah had embraced the message, and the world was buying: We are interdependent, we are in the timelessness of *Now* – and *we feel it*. As Tolle explained in his previous, Oprah-endorsed bestseller, *The Power of Now*, to be enlightened is "simply your natural state of *felt* oneness with Being."[12]

Call it a transformative sensation; this feeling is a palpable impression that re-orients a person's inner placement, a *state of consciousness* that produces a *change of consciousness*. Words such as connection and synchronicity,

---

8 Ether Walker, "Eckhart Tolle: This man could change your life," *Independent*, Friday, 20 June 2008, online edition [www.independent.co.uk/news/people/profiles/eckhart-tolle-this-man-could-change-your-life-850872.html].

9 Ken MacQueen, "Eckhart Tolle vs. God," *Maclean's*, October 22, 2009, online edition [www.macleans.ca/culture/eckhart-tolle-vs-god].

10 Steven Kotler and Jamie Wheal, *Stealing Fire: How Silicon Valley, the Navy SEALs, and Maverick Scientists Are Revolutionizing the Way We Live and Work* (Dey St., 2017), p.75.

11 Eckhart Tolle, *A New Earth: Awakening to Your Life's Purpose* (Plume, 2006), p.309.

12 Eckhart Tolle, *The Power of Now: A Guide to Spiritual Enlightenment* (Hodder Australia, 2004), p.12, italics in original.

expansion, and transcendental have been used to describe it. The *numinous* and "the sublime *kairos*" are other ways this inner shift has been referenced.[13] The ancient Greeks identified its full flowering as *ekstasis* or ecstasy, to be "standing outside of oneself."[14] Within the Islamic mystical tradition of Sufism it is considered the annihilation of the individual ego, an "inner dimension of experience," altering the mind and bringing new action.[15] Psychedelic and soundscape explorer, James Jesso, described the experience as the "self and social awareness of oneness."[16]

Analyzing variants of the phenomena, performance entrepreneurs Steven Kotler and Jamie Wheal noticed that four qualities often manifest: the feelings of selflessness, timelessness, perceptional richness, and effortlessness.[17] These four facets, the duo discovered, are primarily triggered by neurochemical responses to sensory stimulation, often resulting in a changed psychological frame of reference. The saying, "it's all in your head," has some merit.

An array of activities can induce non-ordinary states: contemplative spiritual practices and postures, extreme sports or combat action, and in the taking of psychedelic substances. *Communitas* – the energy of community flow – can arise through the structured orchestration of group emotions, or when structure gives way to organic movement and freeing creativity. Both can invoke feelings of collective deep meaning; the "Utopia of We."[18] Sensory overload and overwhelming awe can induce sensations of unity and wholeness; this can be encountered in the pulsing energy of a rave, or in the visual grandeur of a panoramic sunset. Virtual reality with its disembodying properties has the ability to stimulate non-ordinary states. Manipulated sexual activity is another route.

---

13 For "sublime kairos," see Tom Wolf, *The Electric Kool-Aid Acid Test* (Picador, 1968/2008), p.231, italics in original. Rudolf Otto was an early user of the word; see his book, *The Idea of the Holy: An Inquiry into the Non-Rational Factor in the Idea of the Divine, and its Relation to the Rational* (Oxford University Press, 1923).

14 See Theodor H. Gaster's note #152 in James George Frazer's *The New Golden Bough: A New Abridgment of the Classic Work* (Criterion Books, 1959), p.215, in "Part II: Taboo and the Perils of the Soul."

15 Carl W. Ernst, *Sufism: An Introduction to the Mystical Tradition of Islam* (Shambhala Publications, 2011), pp.114-119.

16 James W. Jesso, *Soundscapes and Psychedelics: Exploring Electronic Mind Expansion* (SoulsLantern Publishing, 2014), p.41.

17 Kotler and Wheal, *Stealing Fire*, 37-46.

18 Ibid., p.69.

The dopamine spike from a favorable check of your social media is but a miniscule reflection of the *feel*.

The quest to "get out of our skin" is big business. In calculating the financial side of the "Altered States Economy," broadly interpreted and categorized under "drugs, therapy, media and recreation," Kotler and Wheal estimated that *$4 trillion* annually goes to the "Church of the Ecstatic."[19] We are willing to pay handsomely for temporary bliss, often incurring costs that go far beyond the monetary.

However, we are far more than just biology and chemical reactions. We are creatures of flesh *and* spirit. We are also creatures of emotion and logic, incapable of living on either alone. Belief, creativity, compassion, sacrifice, and forgiveness – these are attributes and values that point to something other than pure, materialistic existence. The question, "what is consciousness?" remains a question. We are integrated beings: mind, body, and soul.

While mystical sensations may be conjured by manipulating neurobiology through breathwork and body movement[20] – or psychedelic drugs[21] – a spiritual dimension is also acknowledged. Transpersonal psychiatrist Stanislav Grof describes this as *first form* spirituality,

> A person having this form of spiritual experience sees people, animals, and inanimate objects in the environment as radiant manifestations of a unified field of cosmic creative energy and realizes that the boundaries between them are illusory and unreal. This is a direct experience of nature as god…[22]

---

[19] Ibid., p.31. See also note 28, running from pages 238-243.

[20] Ibid., pp.95-114.

[21] In 1962, twenty Protestant seminary students took part in the Good Friday Experiment. Ten of the volunteer subjects were given psilocybin, and the other ten were administered a placebo. The purpose: to see if mystical states could be reproduced in a controlled setting. Walter Pahnke, a graduate of Harvard Divinity School – with Timothy Leary acting as academic advisor – conducted the experiment at Boston University's Marsh Chapel. The findings ignited a controversy over "authentic" spirituality versus chemical imitation or "instant" mysticism. See Rick Doblin, "Pahnke's 'Good Friday Experiment': A Long-Term Follow-up and Methodological Critique," *The Journal of Transpersonal Psychology*, 1991, Vol. 23, No. 1, pp.2-28. See also, Martin A. Lee and Bruce Shlain, *Acid Dream: The Complete Social History of LSD: The CIA, The Sixties, and Beyond* (Grove Press, 1992), pp.76-77, and Kotler and Wheal, *Stealing Fire*, 58-59.

[22] Stanislav Grof, *Psychology of the Future: Lessons from Modern Consciousness Research* (State University of New York Press, 2000), p.210.

Outer and inner merges, boundaries liquefy, and the universal becomes sacred: Grof is portraying a spirituality based on the blurring of distinctions.

It is Oneness.

In a similar way, Franciscan mystic Richard Rohr talks about the Divine Flow: "We'll begin to experience God almost like a force field... And we're *all already* inside this force field, whether we know it or not, alongside Hindus and Buddhists and every race and nationality."[23]

This is more than selling a feeling: Grof and Rohr and Tolle are pointing to a cosmological paradigm, a claim on reality. Beliefs and values change in correspondence to the paradigm, and we cross the bridge into the realm of worldview. "Oneness" thus becomes capitalized as a central concept – a core principle – shaping philosophy and ideology, religion, and culture. The feeling is now secondary to the worldview.

Is there a danger in taking a concept like Oneness and engaging in a type of general reductionism? Absolutely. To claim that it alone provides the total substance of a complex ideology, religion, movement or idea would be inaccurate. A better perspective would be to see it as a foundation upon which complex structures are built. Like most foundations, it remains assumed and seldom considered after the edifice is finished. But the planners and architects; they remember and refer to it.

How important is this foundation? Upon it are claims of divinity, the meaning of being human, and future salvation.

Robert Muller[24] brings this together,

> We must feel part of all space and time, of the greatness and wonders of the universe... We must stand in awe before the beauty and miracle of creation. Perhaps this will be the new spiritual ideology which will bind the human race. We must lift again our spirits and hearts into the infinite bliss and mystery of the universe... We are

---

23 Richard Rohr and Mike Morrell, *The Divine Dance: The Trinity and Your Transformation* (Whitaker House, 2016), p.111, italics in original. Note: This book sells an alternative spirituality, another version of Oneness.

24 Robert Muller – raised Roman Catholic – was spiritually influenced as an adult by the quiet Buddhism of UN Secretary-General, U Thant, and the writings of Catholic mystic, Pierre Teilhard de Chardin. For more on the role of Chardin's ideas and Thant's influence on Muller, see Robert Muller, *New Genesis: Shaping a Global Spirituality* (World Happiness and Cooperation, 1989, originally published in 1982), pp.159-171.

too heavy, too earthbound. We must elevate ourselves again as light, cosmic beings in deep communion with the universe and eternity. We must re-establish the unity of our planet and of our beings with the universe and divinity.[25]

Global Oneness

Becoming "universal, total beings" – a unity of collective divinity – is the heartbeat of Oneness. In one branch of Hindu cosmology this is expressed as *Advaita*, literally "non-secondness" or "not-two," and is contextually placed as the "Planetary Experience."[26] Advaita thus assigns cosmic unity to diversity: "On the basis of our common experience we can infer that the diversity of the world as a whole is reducible to a unity… being dependent upon universal consciousness for its revelation."[27]

When considering the broad theme of Oneness, it is important to note that this is not about an imposed cultural sameness or the crushing of expression or creativity. Tolerance and openness exists for cultural, ethnic, social, personal, sexual and religious identities. Diversity is encouraged, so long as *divisive exclusivity* – "separateness" or *two-ness* – does not threaten the fabric of anticipated harmony. In fact, distinctive cultural sensitivities and personal tastes are respected so long as they remain within the mosaic.

Unity in diversity is celebrated, recognizing stylistic uniqueness while consciously feeling the sense of union. Everyone participates in the cosmic script of transformation; we are all just colorful images in the universe's movie.

Noted emergence thinker Barbara Marx Hubbard calls this *synergy*, the energy of "conscious evolution,"[28] subsuming the parts in its whole. That is, a grand synthesis is taking place and once a critical mass is achieved to that end, this shared experience will birth a new planetary reality. We will move beyond individual humanity and, as a group united in a vision of ascension, expand ourselves and awaken the cosmos. The famed personal-growth motivator, Ken Keys, Jr., described this as a tipping point that unleashes our

[25] Robert Muller, *New Genesis: Shaping a Global Spirituality* (World Happiness and Cooperation, 1989, originally published in 1992), p.37.

[26] *Preceptors of Advaita* (Sri Kanchi Kamakoti Sankara Mandir, 1968), p.xi.

[27] Ibid., p.209.

[28] See Barbara M. Hubbard, *Conscious Evolution: Awakening the Power of Our Social Potential* (New World Library, 1998).

"collective conscious."[29] Human potential guru Willis Harman coined it as a "global mind change."[30] The Temple of Understanding, an organization dedicated to inter-spirituality, couched this as "interdependence" and "communion" – humanity reaching for "an ever expanding realization of Divinity"[31]

The Urantia Book, a text claiming to be scribed by celestial beings, says something similar: To accept "cosmic citizenship" through an "awareness of the interdependence of evolutionary man and evolving Deity... the birth of cosmic morality and the dawning of universal duty."[32]

Mystic philosopher and practitioner, David Spangler of the Findhorn Foundation, simply said: "We are one. Wholeness is our oneness in action."[33]

New York Times bestselling author, Neale Donald Walsch, a celebrated modern prophet of Oneness, describes this as the New Spirituality and the awakening of "Tomorrow's God." It is "perhaps the single most important message"[34] – All is God and God is All. Everything is divine. Our conception of "Yesterday's God" was couched in destructive *separateness*, an exclusivist deity standing outside of creation. Tomorrow's evolutionary-oriented God will emerge through a revolution in spiritual and social interconnection. Like a sleeper jolted from the shadows of dreams and illusions, we will open our eyes to Ultimate Reality and rise as One. This is the heartbeat of the quasi-official *Global Oneness Day* – GOD – celebrated at the same time as United Nations Day on October 24.[35]

This is the message of Oneness: nature is God, we are God, the energy of the universe is God. It is the rootstock of the New Age movement, and

---

[29] Ken Keyes, Jr. was a personal growth instructor and teacher of New Age consciousness. His books were popular during the 1970s and 1980s, with his *Handbook to Higher Consciousness* selling over one million copies. His tipping point concept was described as the "Hundredth Monkey" effect.

[30] See Willis Harman, *Global Mind Change: The Promise of the Last Years of the Twentieth Century* (Knowledge Systems/Institute of Noetic Sciences, 1988).

[31] Temple of Understanding, www.templeofunderstanding.org/wwa_Faith_Ecology.html. Note: the website has changed. This text comes from a July 25, 2009 screenshot.

[32] *The Urantia Book* (Urantia Foundation, 2010 edition), Paper 110: Section 3, p.1206.

[33] David Spangler, *Reflections on the Christ* (Findhorn Foundation, 1977), pp.127-128.

[34] Neale Donald Walsch, *Tomorrow's God: Our Greatest Spiritual Challenge* (Atria Books, 2004), p.34.

[35] In 2008, Walsch and his organization – Humanity's Team – went to the UN with 50,000 signatures and requested the formation of "Global Oneness Day." Humanity's Team was encouraged to proceed before the UN came to a consensus.

finds expression in a multitude of terms and labels, as former New Ager and now Christian author, Warren Smith, reminded me in a recent conversation.[36] Phrases like New Paradigm, New Worldview, New Consciousness, New Gospel and New Spirituality punctuate the culture.

Christian apologist and social historian, Dr. Peter Jones, critically expressed this worldview as a spiritual-oriented *ideology*: "One-ism."

"In One-ism, everything shares the same essence," Dr. Jones writes. "In a word, everything is a piece of the divine."[37]

The Biblical view, as Jones explains in his study of the topic, is categorically different: *Two-ism* – the God who is *separate*, and then everything else.

Although advocates of world unity tout this revolutionary shift as a "new paradigm," it is anything but. Peter Jones asserts that the One-ist worldview "eagerly resuscitates the ancient worlds of pagan philosophies and priests."[38]

The use of *pagan* is provocative, causing us to ask: What is paganism?

The word pagan is rooted within the ancient Roman concept of *pagus,* a tract of agricultural land with familial guardianship and attached spiritual meaning.[39] Pagus also carries a communal flavor. One British Druid defines pagus this way: "a village community, one that was reliant upon the cycles of nature for its wealth and well-being."[40] A modern *relational* perspective may look like this: A human reflection of immanence[41] with *Nature*, placed within a shared spiritual experience.

In the past, paganism has also been associated with anyone outside of the Christian framework, including philosophers and thinkers and cultural elites who espoused views antithetical to Christianity. This association was derived from ancient times when Roman soldiers disparaged non-combatants.

---

36 Warren Smith is the author of *The Light That Was Dark: From the New Age to Amazing Grace* (Mountain Stream Press, 2006), *Deceived on Purpose: The New Age Implications of the Purpose-Driven Church* (Mountain Stream Press, 2006), *A Wonderful Deception* (Mountain Stream Press, 2011), *False Christs Coming: Does Anybody Care?* (Mountain Stream Press, 2011), and *Another Jesus Calling* (Lighthouse Trails Publishing, 2013).

37 Peter Jones, *One or Two: Seeing a World of Difference* (Main Entry Editions, 2010), p.17.

38 Ibid., p.13.

39 Prudence Jones and Nigel Pennick, *A History of Pagan Europe* (Routledge, 1995), p.33-34.

40 Emma Restall Orr, "The Ethics of Paganism: The Value and Power of Sacred Relationship," *Pagan Visions for a Sustainable Future* (Llewellyn Publishing, 2005), p.10.

41 Immanence refers to a staying-within or indwelling. Pagan immanence places the sacred within creation: soil, trees, mountains, rivers, blood, etc.

Comparatively, early Christians referred to those outside the faith as "stay-at-homes, *pagani*."[42] This definition, unfortunately, lent itself to a dismissive or derogatory posture. This has been a mistake, for in adopting these characteristics, Christians risked denigrating neighbors and becoming blinded to the seriousness of what paganism is.

For the purpose of this book, paganism with a *small-p* is a general worldview that affirms interconnection and interdependence in *essence*. Immanence is therefore experienced through a *communion* of Nature and spirit, group and self, emotion and action, will and power. The pagan assertion can be articulated this way: The idea of a transcendent God is illusionary and alienating, whereas the pagan expression of deity is discovered in what is tangible, organic, and unifying. Paganism with a *large-P* refers to the *religious* expression of the pagan ideal, and those who fall under that category as representatives of this spiritual tradition.

The general and religious meaning allows for a range of diversity. Digging into the core of the ancient mythic cults with their anthropomorphic deities to the present context of Cosmic Humanism, the essence of what paganism is was succinctly expressed by Professor of Old Testament, John N. Oswalt, in his consideration of the meaning of myth – *continuity*,

> This is the idea that all things that exist are part of each other. Thus, there are no fundamental distinctions between the three realms: humanity, nature and the divine... all things that exist are physically and spiritually part of one another.[43]

Famous New Age author, Marilyn Ferguson, described this in the telling of a young boy who watched his little sister drink milk. "All of a sudden I saw that she was God and the milk was God. I mean… all she was doing was pouring God into God."[44] This is continuity, also known as monism: All is contained in the One. It is the grand mythos of unity.

Oneness is thus paganism in practical belief, and myth is its communicable representation – a *personified connection* to the All. Wicca, the tradition of witchcraft, falls under this Pagan umbrella as a religion of deified creation.

---

[42] Jones and Pennick, *A History of Pagan Europe*, p.1, italics in original.

[43] John N. Oswalt, *The Bible Among the Myths* (Zondervan, 2009), pp.48,49.

[44] The boy in the story was J.D. Salinger. Marilyn Ferguson, *The Aquarian Conspiracy: Personal and Social Transformation in the 1980s* (J.P. Tarcher, 1980), p.382.

"That perhaps is at the core of Wicca – it is joyous union with nature," explained Scott Cunningham in his hugely popular book, *Wicca: A Guide for the Solitary Practitioner*. "The Earth is a manifestation of divine energy… When we lose touch with our blessed planet, we lose touch with Deity."[45]

Recounting prayer in *Living Wicca*, Cunningham wove myth and continuity within meditative contemplation,

> *O Goddess Within, O God Within*… Wiccan prayer, then, isn't addressed to some distant deities who reside in alien cloud palaces. We needn't use a bullhorn to call to the Goddess and God. Rather, we need only become newly aware of Them within us. This is the secret.[46]

One Pagan who established a nature-spiritual community in the virtual world of Second Life put it this way, "I see nature (including all things within it, us too) as connected, we are all part of the greater spirit. We each perceive in our own ways, and use Gods and Goddesses to focus on it, but ultimately we are all one." Robert M. Geraci, author of *Virtually Sacred*, reminds us that "pantheistic nature religions... have become commonplace in twentieth- and twenty-first-century life."[47]

In considering myth, whether ancient or fashioned in today's New Spirituality, what we are witnessing is not simply a cultural "bedtime story," religious folklore or fantasy, but an observable "ancient-future" worldview. The nuances may be complex, wrapped in differing experiences and customs and techniques, but a common paradigm unfolds, even as a multitude of labels are attached to it. Humanity's impending perfection and ascension, it is hoped, will be realized when we actualize the *vision of one*.

Myth as a meta-narrative of *continuity* has been the clothing of ancient Paganism, and it acts as the backdrop for the general worldview, threaded into the compelling ideas of nature and community, security, progress and order – our experiential story of one world. The fact remains that as the

---

[45] Scott Cunningham, *Wicca: A Guide for the Solitary Practitioner* (One Spirit, 2003, reprint edition), p.6.

[46] Scott Cunningham, *Living Wicca: A Further Guide to the Solitary Practitioner* (Llewellyn, 2001), p.55, italics in original.

[47] Robert M. Geraci, *Virtually Sacred: Myth and Meaning in World of Warcraft and Second Life* (Oxford University Press, 2014), p.122.

garments of Christianity are culturally discarded, a new wardrobe is being fashioned from an ancient loom. Professor John Oswalt explains,

> ...when we talk about the common worldview of myth, we are not talking about a quaint, outgrown idea without relevance to the present. Myth is not the thought of primitives who cannot think of reality in abstract terms. It is simply a way of thinking about reality different from the one that shaped Western thought... this understanding of reality is increasingly common in the modern, technological world. We dress it differently, but beneath the new clothes, it is the same body as that which has existed for thousands of years.[48]

Capturing the Whole

From the murky past to the glittering present, continuity – Oneness – is the paradigm framing our world.

If this analysis is correct, then our era will be marked by the culturally accepted resurrection of Paganism and the embracement of Oneness in *practical application* and *celebration*. Furthermore, because this "revolution of consciousness" is about *wholeness*, this thread must weave through every facet of life, including politics and education. Lewis Mumford, the famed American sociologist and historian, preached this very thing in his 1951 book, *The Conduct of Life*,

> ...there must be a change in values, and further a change so central that all the other activities that rotate around this axis will be affected by it... The new philosophy will treat every part of the human experience, from the enduring structure of the physical world to the briefest incarnation of divinity, as an aspect of an inter-related and progressively integrating whole.[49]

Not long after Mumford penned those telling words, the West was rocked by waves of cultural insurrection.

The splash of the 1960s was more than just Apollo 11 returning to Earth, it was the change-over from Modernity to Postmodernism, and with it, the emerging acceptance of Eastern spirituality in the West. A generation eager

[48] Oswalt, *The Bible Among the Myths*, p.47.

[49] Lewis Mumford, *The Conduct of Life* (Harcourt, Brace and Company, 1951), p.226.

to drop their parent's "square thinking" and embrace enticing dreams of wholeness was animated: The New Left's hip-Marxism raised its fist in the spirit of solidarity; "world peace" became the battle-hymn for social integration; the "sacrament of LSD"[50] tuned-in the self to a larger unity; Hindu gurus won hearts and minds as Maharishi Mahesh Yogi flew in on the wings of The Beatles; and the International Society for Krishna Consciousness introduced the "ideals of spiritual communism... the oneness of the entire society, nay, of the entire energy of living beings."[51]

Western society was being re-wired by cultural shock and Eastern awe. It created a soul-level dissonance that now, roughly half a century later, is being accepted as an evolutionary finality.

"The true aftermath of that earthquake wasn't experienced at the time," penned Roger B. Neill in his autobiography. "We are experiencing it now." Neill, a former Marxist of that era who had a *revolutionary heart change*, reminds us that in the 1960s, "a revolution had indeed taken place – a revolution in mind and praxis – that changed the course of modern history."[52]

By the 1980s, the upward swell of a worldview tsunami could be discerned. Mumford's hope of a "progressively integrated whole" was clearly visible. A new way of thinking was cresting on the shores of Western thought and soon every aspect of life, from business and education to healthcare and Hollywood, was swimming in the *new consciousness*.

Douglas Groothuis, a Christian philosopher, described this "revolution of consciousness" as a meta-movement; "the One." Groothuis' words, written in 1986, compelled Christians to understand the shift *already taking place*,

> A new world view is in the offing; a revolution in consciousness beckons. All is one – both good and evil. We are all god – and our first-graders should know it. The mind controls all – if we only use it. These are ideas – potent ideas – that have consequences for the whole of life.[53]

---

[50] Lysergic acid diethylamide (LSD). For an interesting, first-hand narrative of the LSD counter-culture of the 1960s, see Charles W. Slack, *Timothy Leary, the Madness of the Sixties and Me* (Peter H. Wyden, 1974).

[51] A.C. Bhaktivedanta Swami Prabhupada, *Srimad Bhagavatam, First Canto – Creation* (International Society for Krishna Consciousness/Bhaktivedanta Book Trust, 1972), p.xv.

[52] Roger Brian Neill, *Revolution in Mind: An Autobiography* (Word Alive Press, 2014), p.xi.

[53] Douglas R. Groothuis, *Unmasking the New Age* (Inter-Varsity Press, 1986), pp.15-16.

Groothuis wrote, "The whole society must be brought into harmony with the One as the New Consciousness produces the New Age."[54]

Oneness must capture all spheres of human activity – politics, economics, religious sentiment, cultural expressions, and technological development – for greater interconnectivity. All must work to bend the arc of history and advance the "Age of One." It must shape our self image and lodge itself in the framework of our collective thinking; moreover, it must energize the emotional will of the masses. In this arousal of emotional will,[55] realized in group-generated experiences, there is an undeniable appeal; we *feel* ourselves becoming part of something larger. We grope for and seek a new reality, and in working towards it, we affirm our greatness and boast in our empowerment. Collective community compels us, shapes our identity and ethos, and presents a higher purpose: "Welcome, global citizens."

World Minded

This "vision of the anointed," our modern salvation message given by the self-appointed priesthood of experts and gurus and academics,[56] must become globally animated; advanced by the wizards of technology, implemented in the halls of politics, embedded in education from cradle-to-grave, shouted by the preachers of the entertainment industry, pushed by emergent theologians, and accepted by the masses, who – conditioned by democratic behaviorism[57] – claim Oneness as their own. When acceptance turns to celebration, as evidenced by the tremendous rise of transformational festivals,

---

[54] Ibid., p.111.

[55] An almost forgotten book propagating the idea of "emotional will" for collective integration is *The Science of Power*, by Benjamin Kidd (Methuen & Co., 1918). Note: Kidd used the concept of "pagan" in its reversed form – the individual and the State whose standards do not extend past self interests, and advises that *this* must bend to the Universal.

[56] The term "vision of the anointed" is taken from Thomas Sowell, who describes this in the context of political and cultural engineering through social visionaries – self avowed saviors of society. See his books, *The Vision of the Anointed: Self-Congratulation as a Basis for Social Policy* (BasicBooks, 1995) and *Intellectuals and Society* (BasicBooks, 2011, revised and enlarged edition).

[57] To help understand the role of democracy as a process of conditioning, see Alexis de Tocqueville, *Democracy in America* (this was published in two volumes, first: 1835, second: 1840). Other works which critically examine aspects of democracy are: J.L. Talmon, *The Origins of Totalitarian Democracy* (Frederick A. Praeger, 1960), Erik von Kuehnelt-Leddihn, *Liberty or Equality: The Challenge of Our Time* (Christendom Press,

we are then witness to the social triumph of integration. Capture the mind, own the heart, direct the future.

Writing in the early 1960s, social futurist W. Warren Wagar relished what other "prophets of world order" had long envisioned, "a unified world culture." Allowing for a range of expressions, global society would be qualitatively and emotionally enabled through this "metaphysical starting point... the organic coherence of the cosmos." And those involved in facilitating this massive ideological and spiritual shift, Wagar pointed out, inevitably build from this presupposition: "They are all monists: for them, the universe, all reality, all being, is ultimately one."[58]

An organic, planetary-aware citizenry will materialize as the technical, philosophical, religious, and intellectual branches coalesce around the Oneness model. We are becoming *re-enchanted* with the allure of a magic-like connection to *everything*, animating the gospel of interdependence with a new sense of reason and duty – a new spiritual aesthetic, a re-born myth to follow.

"The unity of purpose and direction necessary to the spiritual health of a society is achieved by coordinating all the elements in its culture," explained Wagar.[59] Thus we become "world minded."

Groothuis rightly discerned the scope of propagation,

> But if the transformation is to be complete, it must permeate and overtake the Western mindset. This means nothing less than the infiltration and revision of the major intellectual disciplines as well as the common world view of the person on the street. The One must move from the avant-garde fringe to the very heart and mind of society.[60]

Professor Philip C. Bom of Regent University described the institutional meme that Oneness assigns as *Commonism*; a "political religion which creates and

---

1993 edition), Arthur Seldon, *The Dilemma of Democracy: The Political Economics of Over-Government* (Institute of Economic Affairs, 1998 – provides a British critique of political-economic problems linked with democracy), Hans-Hermann Hoppe, *Democracy: The God That Failed* (Transaction Publishers, 2001/2007), and Frank Karsten and Karel Beckman, *Beyond Democracy* (BeyondDemocracy.net/CreateSpace, 2012).

58 W. Warren Wagar, *The City of Man* (Houghton Mifflin Company, 1963), pp.175-176.

59 Ibid., p.132.

60 Groothuis, *Unmasking the New Age*, p.51.

evaluates standards and goals in line with the principle that man governs the universe."[61]

This plays out as *device*: common security, common global values, and the management of the global commons through global governance. Bom correctly perceived the device and doctrine of Commonism as a "new ideological age of global spiritual politics." It is a structural revolution that defines individual human purpose and identity within the cosmology of Oneness, "the building of a whole new man for a whole new world."[62]

A New Enlightenment is dawning; a neo-Renaissance is upon us.

Wholeness expressed and emotionally activated was the driving desire of the Global Citizenship 2000 Youth Congress. It was up to us, we were told, to manifest Oneness in practical and far-reaching ways. Evolution was in our hands.

We would be the change.

---

[61] Philip C. Bom, *The Coming Century of Commonism: The Beauty and the Beast of Global Governance* (Policy Books Inc., 1992), p.4.

[62] Ibid., p.302 for "spiritual politics" and 352 for "whole new world."

Chapter 2

The Planetized Generation

> A global democracy of children... The first place to organize is in our schools. – Youth of the World.[1]

> Global Citizenship Education should strive to be a holistic and transformative experience. – UNESCO.[2]

"If we're going to shift the foundation of the way things are done on this planet, people have to shift the way they think," wrote Desmond Berghofer, co-convener of the Global Citizenship 2000 Youth Congress, in his novel *The Visioneers*. "The battlefront is now at the level of the mind. The ultimate force is mindpower."[3]

To shift the way we think, from archaic traditionalism to progressive futurism, was a primary goal of the Congress. With our minds remade and emotions stirred, our Saturday afternoon assignment was to use our collective mind-power and collaborate for action. Breaking into working groups, each cell brainstormed "Millennium Projects" via "hold fire and think" exercises: a game meant to expand on previously accepted outcomes, but with no room to critically analyze the fundamental nature of our quest. "Valid concerns" and "gut feelings" could be raised about specific *ideas*, overcome through

1 "Youth of the World" represents the "10,000 children in 200 groups in 75 countries" that participated in the *Rescue Mission* project. *Rescue Mission Planet Earth: A Youth Edition of Agenda 21*, (Kingfisher Books/Peace Child International, 1994, in association with the United Nations, UNESCO, UNEP, UNICEF, UNDP, and Government of Canada), p.84.

2 *Final Report - Second UNESCO Forum on Global Citizenship Education: Building Peaceful and Sustainable Societies* (United Nations Educational, Scientific and Cultural Organization, 28-30 January 2015), p.6, paragraph 13.

3 Desmond E. Berghofer, *The Visioneers: A Courage Story about Belief in the Future* (Creating Learning International Press, 1992), p.34-35.

group dialogue and consensus, but the *dogma* of Oneness and global unity was beyond question.

However, there was little concern that Congress participants would challenge the underlying assumptions. After all, the elixir of positive reinforcement – that we were enlightened members of a "transformed species" poised to change the world – was too heady to resist. Educators and students alike saw themselves as ambassadors of Oneness. As our symbolic Global Citizenship 2000 *Passports* read, "You are the Earth become conscious of herself."

In reality, we were play-acting the script of Berghofer's 1992 *Visioneering* novel. In its pages a diverse group of illuminated youth recognize and respond to the Earth-destroying chaos of separation, leading the way to a planetary synthesis through their interconnected visioneering. From beginning to end, the book *preached*.

Geraldine Schwartz, the other Congress co-convener, reminded us that "our minds, our consciousness has got to be equal to the task of the future..." And what a task! As Berghofer's epic novel imparted,

> We begin by understanding that the world can and does have a mind. It's a manifestation of the collective conscious of all the minds existing on the planet. The great project in the 21st century will be the gathering of these minds into a single, resolute purpose for the betterment of Earth and everyone on it. The nation state that we have designed is an imperfect concept. At best it's a stepping stone to the place where we must now go: planetary stewardship. And we can't get there unless we turn five and a half billion minds from a multitude of cultural ignorances into a unified mindframe. They must see that human fellowship in union with the life systems of the planet is the only possible way for a decent future life.
>
> Creating that mindscape is the momentous task of our band of Visioneers. They must seek out the pressure points and touch them to move the power levers of politics and wealth and military might with a new more powerful force: enlightened visions of human destiny... That's the mission of our Visioneers.[4]

Engaging in "visioneering" that Saturday afternoon, each Congress team offered up dreams and ideas reflecting planetary loyalties.

---

4 Ibid., p.37.

Suggestions included the launching of a youth-based United Nations, setting up international student conferences to show the adult world what needs to be done, starting SCREAM clubs ("Students Concerned Regarding Environment and Mother Earth"), and developing school-based interfaith groups and global citizenship cells. Others talked of establishing a Global Citizenship Day and fostering Earth Pride. Another suggestion was to lobby for the creation of a Global Ministry of Planetary Preservation. A participating Bahá'í school recommended a Youth Communications Network to coordinate student-directed global citizenship programs. One team called to zero-out world debt, abolish money, and issue everyone a biometric card with a points-system based on your occupation and its value to the planet. Health care, access to education, and daily food and shelter would be tied to your positive contribution to the "common good."

At the table next to mine, a group of junior-high girls exemplified the new paradigm in a one-act play. "Mother Earth" sat on a round table with pine boughs held aloft, then, one after another, students laid hands on Mother and made confession: "I'm guilty... of wasting water... wasting electricity... killing animals by wearing leather sandals... polluting the environment when I'm fully aware of the oil leak in my dad's car."[5] In turn Mother Earth forgave each child as they vowed to redeem their eco-sins.

Robert Muller, the UN "prophet of hope," spurred us on by sharing his many achievements. He told us about planting the seed of the United Religions Initiative during the 1993 Parliament of the World's Religions and then again, in 1995, at the 50th anniversary of the United Nations in San Francisco.

"I almost cannot believe they listened to me," he beamed. "I will be the father of the United Religions!"[6]

Muller elaborated on his vision for a politically managed planet. He suggested different approaches to world order, encouraging the pursuit of each: Empower the United Nations into a "United States of the World," form a constitutional World Federation, integrate continental regions – creating an American Union and an African Union – and then bring these together with the European Union into a "World Union," establish communities around dominant terrestrial features such as a Pacific Community, an Atlantic Com-

[5] All Congress dialogues in this chapter are taken from notes and recordings of the event.

[6] At the time, the United Religions Initiative (URI) was still in development. It was not until the year 2000 that the URI was officially chartered.

munity, an Arctic Community – even a Desert Community, uniting countries around a shared arid landscape – and the "great rivers of Amazon should be practically one region where the people should be with nature."

Muller pressed the need to "acquire new values and behavior." If we didn't change for the global good then "all life on this planet will extinguish." The weight of the world's salvation was placed on our shoulders. It was an emotionally charged call-of-duty. "Either you change your values, or you don't," explained the Prophet of Hope. "If you change, if you consider the Earth as being number one, your Mother, then it will change."

The flip side was that if we continued to consume and express the wrong values, "you will be the responsible generation of having to put an end to all life on this planet." Students responded; one 14-year old, with tears running down her face, called for an end to children. Reproduction was a sin.

The spiritual outlook required to save the world was to recognize the "basic truth" as given by "Jesus, by Mohammad, by these emissaries from outer space." What was this basic truth? The cosmos incarnating itself through our collective divinity,

> You are not children of Canada, you are really living units of the cosmos because the Earth is a cosmic phenomena... we are all cosmic units. This is why religions tell you, you are divine. We are divine energy... it is in your hands whether evolution on this planet continues or not...

This paralleled what Muller wrote in his book, *New Genesis: Shaping a Global Spirituality*, published while he was UN Assistant-Secretary-General,

> ...humankind is seeking no less than its reunion with the 'divine,' its transcendence into ever higher forms of life. Hindus call our earth Brahma, or God, for they rightly see no difference between our earth and the divine. This ancient simple truth is slowly dawning upon humanity. Its full flowering will be the real, great new story of humanity, as we are about to enter our cosmic age and to become what we were always meant to be: the planet of God.[7]

[7] Robert Muller, *New Genesis: Shaping a Global Spirituality* (World Happiness and Cooperation, 1982/1989), p.49.

As an independent attendee of the Global Citizenship congress I was assigned to a team of university students who hoped to become educators. This group was focused on tangible ways to integrate Muller's *World Core Curriculum* in the classroom. *How?* was the question.

Recognizing the spiritual nature of Muller's worldview, and that our mission of global citizenship had entered the arena of beliefs and values modification, the talk turned to traditionally held parental convictions and how to "deal with parental pessimism." It was noted that if a child's values could be changed in the classroom, then family attitudes would shift also. This, the future teachers acknowledged, was a worthy goal.

After some discussion it was agreed that creatively placing global citizenship values into all subject areas was the most important way to influence young minds. International problems requiring global solutions – such as overpopulation – would be embedded into literature, history, and mathematics. Planetary awareness would be emphasized, along with calls for collective action. By entrenching emotionally-charged global concerns into the lifespan of formal education, and in-turn facilitating the responsive values, the correct Oneness philosophy would become profoundly infused within the fabric of society. We would create social justice warriors.

As one student said, "*make it a virus, no inoculation, infect everyone*."

Muller was ecstatic with each team's presentation and encouraged the Congress leaders to send reports of what had transpired to agencies around the world. As a former UN official, he told us the organizers would be given a list of who to contact, including the UN Secretary-General's office, UNICEF, UNESCO, UNEP,[8] and the Earth Council in Costa Rica. The mayor of Vancouver, who earlier had sent personal greetings to the Congress, would be notified of our important work. We had engaged in an astonishing vision with scalable applications, and this needed to be shared.

Muller gushed, "I do not know if you realize that you're doing something here which is probably being done in the first time in the entire human history… very practical proposals… communicate them to other authorities, to other schools, to UNESCO… And you will be the first example given by UNESCO of how to [save the world]. So this is very, very important what you have done today."

---

[8] UNICEF: United Nations Children's Fund. UNESCO: United Nations Educational, Scientific and Cultural Organization. UNEP: United Nations Environment Programme.

Berghofer was visibly pleased. For as the youth in his novel informed and shaped the minds of world leaders to accept planetization, so too our ideas would be channeled to people of influence.

The Congress ended a little past midnight as we slipped from April 5th to the 6th, the one-thousandth day before January 1, 2000. Our conclusion was an expression of illumination; we were now Enlightened beings.

Like the previous activities, the closing ceremony was to be a transformational experience. It started with a "festival of lights" as a parade of children marched in the darkened concourse while excitedly waving flashlights: "because light is the primary energy of the universe." It was a time of songs, speeches, and self-congratulations.

Just before midnight the elephant-headed, six-armed Hindu deity Ganesha entered the stage as part of a theatrical drama. Ganesha explained his power and purpose to the youth,

> I have been around for thousands and thousands of years. And you can call on me anytime to remove your thoughts of any obstacles. If you should ever worry or anguish... or if life gets you down... whisper an Aum. Call on loving Ganesha who always is there, for Ganesha is none other than you.

This too fit with the script of Berghofer's novel, for at one point in his story a great spiritual teacher from India tells the visioneering youth that they are all part of *Atma*, the universal consciousness,

> Because everyone is *Atma* we are all of one being, one spirit, and that one spirit is God… That's the truth I've come to teach, and it's the truth that underlies what you call visioneering.[9]

In the post-Congress report, Berghofer and Schwartz emphasized the mounting epoch change associated with their vision: "The important thing is to understand that this is a time of transition. We can view the beginning of the third millennium as a time of passage… This is a time of passage from nationhood to planethood."[10]

---

[9] Berghofer, *The Visioneers*, p.94.

[10] Desmond Berghofer and Geraldine Schwartz, *When the Earth Still Had 1000 Days: Facilitator's Guide* (International Foundation of Learning/Open Learning Agency, May 1999), p.25.

Collective Ideal

The children who took part in the Congress left with the feeling of connecting into something bigger; the planetary community and Mother Earth. Aroused and empowered by a manufactured social purpose, they now viewed themselves as visioneers – emboldened to move forward as influencers and activists – accepting responsibility as future leaders. Teachers and administrators returned to their schools as proselytizers, "change agents" facilitating a shift in values and attitudes. This higher calling put a new spring in their step. To those who organized the Congress, it was an affirmation of how collective evolution could be engineered and actualized; minds can be motivated to embrace the cosmic gospel of Oneness.

Moreover, as demonstrated by each school team's dream projects, this new crop of young people had *already* been conditioned to accept revolutionary integration on all fronts. Going forward, the only solution to impending destruction would be planetary unification – a mantra that would be endlessly repeated in classrooms throughout North America and Europe. What I had witnessed in Vancouver was simply a snap-shot of a larger panorama. The Millennial generation was being set up for the Great Emergence,[11] a guided response to the *forces of change*.

As a Christian researcher on worldview trends, I walked away from the Congress with a fresh appreciation as to the speed of social and spiritual transformation. I had personally witnessed a powerful demonstration of the collective ideal in action. Looking back, I am reminded of what British social thinker Benjamin Kidd wrote approximately one century ago: "The influence of a collective ideal imposed on the minds of the young under conditions of emotion is incalculable."[12]

---

[11] The "Great Emergence" is a term used by New Age futurist, Barbara Marx Hubbard, to describe a particular time-period when humanity is being consciously transformed into a planetary society. In a similar way, Phyllis Tickle used the concept of a "Great Emergence" to flesh out her argument that Christianity is at a transition point – a shift into an emergent theology in-tune with the current epoch change. Both Hubbard and Tickle expressed this as the Great Transition. See Barbara Marx Hubbard, *Conscious Evolution: Awakening the Power of Our Social Potential* (New World Library, 1998) and *Emergence: The Shift from Ego to Essence* (Hampton Roads Publishing/Foundation for Conscious Evolution, 2001/2012). See also, Phyllis Tickle, *The Great Emergence: How Christianity is Changing and Why* (Baker Books, 2008).

[12] Benjamin Kidd, *The Science of Power* (Methuen & Company, 1918/1919), p.295.

An epoch change was in the air. The last riggings of the traditional Judeo-Christian framework that had informed the Western[13] mind were being cut away. Scientific materialism, the high calling of Modernity, was likewise being hacked and tossed overboard. Postmodernism, a distrust of secular materialism and a rejection of Christian convention, sailed the cultural ocean.

But the Global Citizenship congress represented *something different* than Postmodernism. A new guiding story was being written into our civilization. A future was unfolding, scribed from an ancient vision and repackaged for today. Like the passenger on a ship who has taken a tour through the inner workings of the vessel, I, too, was given a glimpse into the bowels of Oneness. What I had seen, and what I have since witnessed, has convinced me that Postmodernism is passing.

Another age is upon us; *the era of Re-Enchantment*.

However, if we want to understand this other narrative – and we better, for it is shaping our children and ourselves – then we need to consider how society arrived at this point. Hence, the next section of this book will briefly and progressively detail the intellectual and cultural back-story, even at the risk of causing historians to cringe at our brevity. Along the way it will become evident that revolutions-in-thinking transpire in response to the rejection of authority, especially claims of ultimate authority.

What humanity seeks is another source of meaning and Truth.

---

[13] Geographically, the Judeo-Christian framework is grounded in the Middle East and Meditation region, not the West in the sense of Western Europe and the Americas. However, Europe – including Eastern Europe – and later the Americas, were unquestionably and overwhelmingly shaped by Judeo-Christian influences, providing the structure for academic thought, civil discourse, economic activity, social structure, and theological life. Today, the Eastern and Southern parts of the world have experienced a surge in Christian growth, but the historical association in terms of impact and development is generally understood as a Western phenomena.

Part II

Changing Epochs

As the Christian consensus fades into the shadows, the stage is set for a global sea change of unprecedented magnitude.
– Patrick M. Wood, *Technocracy Rising*.

He had become a player in a game of gods, and must learn the rules as he went along.
– Arthur C. Clarke, *2010: Odyssey Two*.

Chapter 3

Shifting Faiths

> Western civilization without Christianity is like a beef broth without beef. – Robert W. Keyserlingk.[1]

> ...a 'revolutionary situation' exists when, in every cultural area of a society, old values are in the process of being rejected, and new values have been prepared, or are being prepared, to replace them. – Jean-Francois Revel.[2]

The human story is a turbulent quest for knowledge and meaning.

Attempting to follow paths of self-mastery, we have been striving for some way to verify our divine impulse.[3] Our notions of how this *should be* has resulted in a constant splintering of ideas and the fragmenting of order, expressed in religious beliefs and philosophical arguments, scientific interpretations, social experiments, and personal behavior. Innumerable and diverse shards of thought have thus lodged into the construction of civilization, and our present paradigm flows out of an abundance of competing, contradicting, and consuming narratives. Ideas have consequences.

The Christian milieu itself has been challenged and shaped by this flux, and not always for the better. In fact, much of the New Testament is an admonition to early Christian communities to stay true to the message of Jesus Christ as counter-claims and errant teachings arise. The book of First John fits this pattern, as do the letters of the Apostle Paul. Consider the strong language Paul used when he wrote to the Galatians: "But even if we,

---

1 Robert W. Keyserlingk, *Unfinished History* (Robert Hale Limited, 1948), p.175.

2 Jean-Francois Revel, *Without Marx or Jesus: The New American Revolution Has Begun* (Doubleday and Company, 1971), p.9.

3 Genesis 3:5.

or an angel from heaven, preach any other gospel to you than what we have preached to you, let him be accursed."[4]

Moreover, as early Christianity integrated into a cultural and civil framework, politically adopted for its stabilizing value, it found itself becoming increasingly institutionalized. Arguments have been made for the positive and negative influences this has had on Western civilization. Nevertheless, it opened up the Pre-modern epoch, the first of three broad stages of Western intellectual and social development.

Today's transformation and tomorrow's realities, the fourth broad phase of Western change, has not been without foreshadowing.

The Pre-Modern Backdrop

Pre-modernism, or Pre-modernity, can have various starting points. However, as our interest lies in the progress of civilization *Anno Domini*, we need to stay within the bounds of Christianity's socio-political development. Constantine's *Edict of Milan* in AD 313 could thus be considered a beginning, for the Emperor's decree granted toleration to Christianity and allowed it to enter the mainstream of the Roman Empire. The *Edict of Thessalonica* in AD 380 is a contender as it made Christianity the official Roman religion, and the 607 decree by Byzantine Emperor Phocus could be included for it elevated the Roman church as "head of all churches."[5] Another possible starting point is Charlemagne's imperial crowning on Christmas Day, 800 AD, wedding the papal office with "sacred kingship" – establishing "the Holy Roman Empire in fact."[6] Whichever starting line you choose, Pre-modernity is rooted in the rise of the Roman Church as a political culture.

Pre-modernity, beginning in 313 for the sake of argument and ending at the close of the 18th century, can also be called the Age of Faith or *Christendom*. It was a time when European social mores and intellectual thought were grounded in a Christian-conscious sense of order, scripted first by Romanism and then re-shaped by the Protestant Reformation. Religious con-

---

4 Galatians 1:8.

5 This was not the first time such a decree was issued. Justinian I had passed a similar edict many decades earlier. The importance of the Phocus declaration, however, was its lasting effect in cementing the idea of papal authority.

6 Will Durant, *The Age of Faith* (Simon and Schuster, 1950), p.469.

cepts informed the customs and traditions of local communities and broader regions, providing a common ethos for social life.

But the governing religious agencies were far from perfect. Erroneous justification for papal authority,[7] combined with politicking and economic interests, often led to authoritarian impulses and opulence. The Biblical commandments to "love the Lord your God with all your heart, with all your soul, and with all your mind," and to "love your neighbor as yourself,"[8] had in too many cases been subverted for illicit gain. Unease and distrust stirred under the surface of Western civilization.

For example, in the mid-1150s, Pope Adrian IV asked his friend, John of Salisbury, what the common man thought of the pope and the Roman Church. John, a secretary to the Archbishop of Canterbury, frankly expressed the feelings of citizens and local clergy. His bold comments – critical, first, of the princely class – could only have made Adrian shudder,

> Scribes and Pharisees sit in her seats, and place on the shoulders of men unbearable burdens which they themselves do not deign to touch with even the tip of their finger. They lord it over the clergy instead of making their own lives an example to lead the flock to life by

---

7 The Catholic position of papal authority stems from a problematic interpretation of Matthew 16:18-19. Here we read the words of Jesus Christ: "And I also say to you that you are Peter, and on this rock I will build My church, and the gates of Hades shall not prevail against it. And I will give you the keys of the kingdom of heaven, and whatever you bind on earth will be bound in heaven, and whatever you loose on earth will be loosed in heaven." Catholicism holds that Peter was thus given apostolic headship to be passed to a papal office. However, this is not Scripturally sound. A similar promise was made in Matthew 18:18 to *all* Jesus' disciples, and in the fuller Biblical context, the Catholic assertion of Peter's primacy cannot be found. Instead, we read in Isaiah 44:8 that God is the only Rock, and in 1 Peter 2:6-8, Peter himself writes that Christ is the *petra* or "rock." If the Catholic notion of apostolic authority is wrong, then the papal claim of mandated guidance and authority is in error. Indeed, Scripture reveals that God guides through His Word (2 Timothy 3:15-17), the power of the Holy Spirit (John 16:12-14), and through *Jesus Christ* as high priest (Hebrews 7:22-28). For rebuttals to the Catholic plank of Petrine authority, see the following: Norman Geisler and Ralph E. MacKenzie, *Roman Catholics and Evangelicals: Agreements and Differences* (Baker Books, 1995), pp.207-210; James G. McCarthy, *The Gospel According to Rome: Comparing Catholic Tradition and the Word of God* (Harvest House Publishers, 1995), pp.237-248; and Dave Hunt, *A Woman Rides the Beast* (Harvest House Publishers, 1994), pp.145-150.

8 Matthew 22:37-39.

> the straight and narrow path; they pile up costly furniture, they load their tables with gold and silver... They oppress the churches with extortion, stir up strife, bring the clergy and people into conflict, never take compassion on the sufferings and misery of the afflicted, rejoice in the spoils of churches, and count all gain as godliness. They give judgment not for the truth but for money. For money you can get anything done today, and without waiting; but you will not get it done even tomorrow if you do not pay a price. Too often they commit injury, and imitate the demons in thinking that they are doing good when they merely refrain from doing evil; except a few of them who fulfil the name and duties of a shepherd. Even the Roman pontiff himself is a grievous and almost intolerable burden to all; the complaint is everywhere made that while the churches which were built by the devotion of the fathers are falling into ruin and collapsing, he has built for himself palaces, and walks abroad not merely in purple but in gold. The palaces of priests dazzle the eye, and meanwhile in their hands the Church of Christ is defiled.[9]

John of Salisbury continued, "Truly the mouth of God has promised that by what judgment they have judged, they shall themselves be judged, and that with their own good measure it shall be meted out to them again. The Ancient of Days cannot lie."

He later admonished his friend: "Father, you are wandering in the trackless wilderness and have strayed from the true way."[10]

Renaissance

Turbulent political and religious waves were lapping on the shores of Western civilization by the 13th century.

Roman Catholicism, the gatekeeper of faith and academic life, found its cultural position weakening. With this backdrop, a rebirth – literally a *renaissance* – in ancient literature and artistic expression emerged, first in Italy, and then in other parts of the continent. This exploration of alternative models allowed a new humanism to flourish. However, unlike today's

---

[9] *The Statesman's Book of John of Salisbury: Being the Fourth, Fifth, and Sixth Books, and Selections from the Seventh and Eighth Books of the Policraticus* (Russell & Russell, 1963, translated by John Dickinson), pp.252-253. [*Policraticus*, Book 6, Chapter 24].

[10] Ibid., p.253, 255.

secularist movements it was not an outright rejection of religion, as many clerics participated in its development. Nevertheless, such a shift in intellectual inquiry resulted in a new emphasis. "Renaissance Man" sought knowledge and articulation beyond the bounds of traditional parameters, and as historian Will Durant explained, this turned "from religion to philosophy, from heaven to earth, and revealed to an astonished generation the riches of pagan thought and art."[11]

Philosophical and theoretical ideas gained traction, and an openness to outside experiences and technical concepts – innovation and invention – moved the knowledge base away from ecclesiastical norms. Mysticism, too, came into vogue, including the introduction of a written Kabbalah. Humanity was being repositioned to a "natural" state of affairs.

"The proper study of mankind was now to be man," expounded Durant, "in all the potential strength and beauty of his body, in all the joy and pain of his senses and feelings, in all the frail majesty of his reason."[12]

Artist and mathematician, Leonardo da Vinci – a true polymath – expressed the human-centered ideal in his famous drawing, *Vitruvian Man*. Here, superimposed within a circle and a square, man touches the "limits of the universe" and his proportions correspond to the measurement of all things.[13] Although da Vinci's *The Last Supper* is an iconic piece resonating with generations of Christians, the artist himself was not devoted "to Church or Christ." Rather, he upheld causality and unity in naturalism, with science and experience as the guiding principle. "Science is the captain," he penned in his philosophical maxims, "and practice the soldiers."[14]

---

[11] Will Durant, *The Renaissance: The History of Civilization in Italy from 1304-1576 A.D.* (Simon and Schuster, 1953), p.77.

[12] Ibid., p.77.

[13] On the "limits of the universe," see Peter Conrad, *Creation: Artists, Gods & Origins* (Thames & Hudson, 2007), p.171.

[14] For "Church or Christ," see Daniel J. Boorstin, *The Creators: A History of Heroes of the Imagination* (Random House, 1992), p.401. Pages 398-407 give a brief survey of the artist. Regarding Leonardo da Vinci's view of Nature as causality, see *The Literary Works of Leonardo da Vinci*, in two volumes, compiled by Jean P. Richter (Sampson Low, Marston, Searle & Rivington, 1883). For the philosophical maxim, see *The Literary Works of Leonardo da Vinci*, Volume 2, p.290 (section 1160). An older but interesting view of the artist can be found in *Leonardo da Vinci and His Works*, compiled by Mary Margaret Heaton, (Macmillan and Company, 1874). Durant described his religion as "mystic pantheism," *The Renaissance* (Simon and Schuster, 1953), p.226.

The rediscovery and recapturing of the high nature of Man, the pagan impulse, was important to this period. Pico della Mirandola, a young scholar and traveller, sought this divine-human outcome by attempting to synthesize Christianity, Greek paganism, Jewish Kabbalism, Arab and Persian beliefs, and scientific concepts into a unity of truth – a perennial philosophy, or *theosophy*. Redeemed by Christ, Pico believed, humanity's dignified soul and mind could thus move upward.[15] Man, the *effect* of God as *Cause*, could "recollect himself into the center of his own unity, he will there, become one spirit with God."[16] Pico wrote,

> God is all things and most eminently and most perfectly all things... It follows that God being perfect has in Him neither any defect nor any particularity, but is the abstract universal unity of all things in their perfection.[17]

Hand-in-glove with the elevation of Man came the symbolic resurrection of pagan deities.

The enchanted worldview emerged in art, architecture, garden spaces, and public celebrations. One humanist described a festival in 1434 wherein costumed deities entered by procession: Apollo, Bacchus, Mars, Mercury, Venus, Cupid, Hercules – "ranks of higher and lower beings taking over the Savior's place."[18] Wedding celebrations witnessed dramatized pageants of gods and goddesses, with parades of chariots decorated to expound mythical themes. Esoteric historian, Joscelyn Godwin, described one such event as a "living encyclopedia of pagan theology."[19]

The Renaissance, with its focus on humanism and celebratory paganism, was the harbinger of a time to come. But it was the Reformation, more than the Renaissance, that upset Europe's tradition of papal authority in matters of state and theology.

---

15 Russell Kirk, in his introduction to *Oration on the Dignity of Man*, by Giovanni Pico della Mirandola (Henry Regnery Company/Gateway, 1956), p.xvii.

16 Giovanni Pico della Mirandola, *Oration on the Dignity of Man* (Henry Regnery Company/Gateway, 1956), p.9.

17 Pico della Mirandola, as quoted in *Giovanni Pico Della Mirandola: His Life by His Nephew Giovanni Francesco Pico*, translated by Thomas More, and with introductory notes by J.M. Rigg (David Nutt, 1890), p.xxii.

18 Joscelyn Godwin, *The Pagan Dream of the Renaissance* (WeiserBooks, 2002/2005), p.3.

19 Ibid., p.198.

Reformation

Roman Christendom, the political and economic institution tying the European continent together, found itself in a crisis of its own making. The concerns expressed by John of Salisbury many years earlier had continued without remedy. Nor could these problems be rectified easily as they stemmed from the Church's inception. The privileges affixed by Emperor Constantine had caused a central rot, compounded by centuries of ill-gotten gain.[20]

Medieval banking and money lending, part of the fascinating backstory of Western civilization, was inseparable from the political clout and economic interests of church officers. Usury and extravagance and overreach had seeded unrest and discontent. Historian Rodney Stark tells us,

> Bishops and cardinals were among the very best clients of usurers. That is not surprising since nearly everyone holding an elite church position had purchased his office as an investment, anticipating a substantial return from church revenues. Indeed, men often were able to buy appointments as bishops or even cardinals without having held any prior church positions, sometimes before they were ordained, or even baptized! This aspect of the medieval church was an endless source of scandal and conflict, spawning many heretical mass sect movements and culminating in the Reformation.[21]

Pushback against the Catholic Church, therefore, was not merely a challenge to prevailing theology and claims of ecclesiastical duty, but a threat to political dynasties and economic powers. By the last years of the 12th century, religious groups rejecting Catholic teachings and offices had experienced persecution in France, Germany, and northern Italy. During the year 1400, Oxford and two other universities "wrote against the apostasy of the Roman church, and demanded a reformation."[22]

In 1517, Martin Luther nailed his *Ninety-Five Theses* to a Wittenberg church door, protesting Catholic positions and calling for a purer understanding of Christianity: "The true treasure of the church is the most holy gospel of the

---

[20] Rodney Stark, *The Victory of Reason: How Christianity Led to Freedom, Capitalism, and Western Success* (Random House, 2005), pp.202-203.

[21] Ibid., p.67.

[22] *Martyrs Mirror*, compiled by Thieleman J. van Braght (Herald Press, 1990 printing, originally published in 1660), p.327.

glory and grace of God."[23] Luther's *Thesis* was the spark that ignited the fuel of change.

The Reformation would recast Christianity by awakening individual's religious consciousness, spurring personal responsibly in matters of faith. Believers could judge spiritual and ethical concerns with recourse to the Word of God *apart* from Roman Catholicism. Diversity flowed from this liberty, and a surge in denominations and congregations ensued; from newly constituted state-and-city churches to underground movements to independent bodies. The Roman tradition was being critiqued and new freedoms were gradually unfolding, with flaws and improvements.

Whereas the Renaissance elevated humanism and paganism, the Reformation sought a Biblical approach to authority – an emphasis on Scripture instead of human agency. Christian historian, Francis A. Schaeffer, described the latter's stance in relationship to the Roman office,

> To the Reformation thinkers, authority was not divided between the Bible and the church. The church was *under* the teachings of the Bible – not above it and not equal to it.[24]

But as Schaeffer noted, this time of immense change was "not a golden age." Religiously charged conflicts and revolts took place as cities and powers were shaken. Secretive groups like the Society of Jesus, better known as the Jesuit Order, worked to counter the Reformation. Civil rule and ecclesiastic authority were interlocked, and church-state capital punishment allowed for Catholic agents to execute Protestants, for Protestants to execute Catholics, and for both to kill Anabaptists. Convictions could be costly.

In 1887, English legislator and Catholic historian, Lord Acton, famously wrote his criticism of the inquisitions and papal governance,

> Power tends to corrupt and absolute power corrupts absolutely. Great men are almost always bad men, even when they exercise influence and not authority... There is no worse heresy than that the office sanctifies the holder of it.[25]

---

[23] Point 62 of Luther's *Ninety-Five Thesis*, as taken from *The Protestant Reformation*, edited by Lewis W. Spitz (Prentice-Hall, 1966), p.48.

[24] Francis A. Schaeffer, *How Should We Then Live? The Rise and Decline of Western Thought and Culture* (Fleming H. Revell Company, 1976), p.82, italics in original.

[25] Lord Acton, *Essays on Freedom and Power* (Meridian Books, 1955), pp.335-336.

Lord Acton's point was valid, and could easily – and rightly – be extended past his immediate context.

The Reformation shook papal authority, spurring a revolution in mind and spirit. No longer was a particular Roman office the arbitrator of truth or salvation. Instead, the protesting side of Christendom put the Bible into the hands of common people, and with this came the realization that Jesus Christ – "the Word made flesh"[26] – is truth personified. A temporal and expensive priest-ruler sitting in a far-off city was unnecessary, for an eternal High Priest[27] had made salvation freely available.

The salvation of souls and the significance of the individual rested in a Personality beyond ecclesiastical and political control, even as church-and-state *acted to the contrary*. Fundamental value, identity, and purpose was not to be found in the hands of kings and clerics.[28] To those who trusted in Christ alone through faith alone, true citizenship rested in the kingdom of God.

Scottish minister, William Stevenson, reminds us that the ultimate concern of the Reformation was theological in character,

> Though the Protestant Reformation has influenced human life as a whole in all its various branches, it cannot be too strongly emphasized that it was primarily a religious movement. Its true concern was God's will for men, men's relation to God, and the salvation of the human soul.[29]

Although negative sides to Christendom existed, including mistakes made through colonial activities,[30] the positive impact of the Christian ethos has

---

26 John 1:14.

27 See the book of *Hebrews* in the New Testament.

28 This, however, did not give license for disobedience over civil issues, but as the secular rulers often fronted for religious powers, a person could be hauled before magistrates over theological differences – as this would be an affront to state/church unity. Such was the case with Hans Knevel in 1572. A citizen of Antwerp, Hans was arrested as an Anabaptist. After being tortured for many days, he was told it was because he did not "obey the authorities." Hans responded, "We will gladly obey the authorities in all taxes, customs and excises…" But to change his Christian convictions in order to align with the magistrate, that he would not do. Hans was executed by being burned alive. See *Martyrs Mirror*, compiled by Thieleman J. van Braght, pp.945-947.

29 William Stevenson, *The Story of the Reformation* (John Knox Press, 1959), p.178.

30 An example of this was the Indian residential school system in Canada. The program was orchestrated by the federal government but the task of education and residential housing

been vast. We are still benefiting from how it shaped civilization. Indeed, the Christian milieu affirmed concepts of law and justice and liberty, higher learning, science and development, and produced a rich heritage of community care in the form of orphanages, hospitals, chaplaincy work, and humanitarian aid.[31] Civil benefits emerged from both Catholic and Protestant thinkers, molding the West in ways unforeseen in other parts of the world. *Reason* as an extension of Christian theology produced a faith-generating rationality that encouraged growth and betterment.[32] As such, a generally accepted and culturally stabilizing Christian consensus remained during much of the 20th century. Today's society appropriates the blessings while despising the very ethos that created them.

The Protestant Reformation indelibly altered Christendom. Theology was repositioned, as was the relationship between church and state and society. Moreover, with the loosening of papal authority and new attitudes of intellectual permission, alternative philosophical arguments and ideas were also finding a voice.

In the Dutch Republic, Baruch Spinoza followed the Rationalist path – a naturalist view of reason – arguing that God is an impersonal Being. The universe, Spinoza contended, was permeated and unified by a single *Substance*, an active force whereby God and natural processes are one and the same. Everything exists and *strives* within a mechanical cosmos. This monism operates without passion or emotion and our "love toward God" comes from immovable reason: "The intellectual love of the mind toward God is that very love of God whereby God loves himself…"[33] Everything is unified.

---

was administered by Catholic, Anglican, and Presbyterian churches. Documented physical and sexual abuses, cultural prohibitions, and the removal of children from families to attend the schools have resulted in historical grievances. It has also created a general backlash against Christianity. Unfortunately, the fact that this topic now carries a politicized narrative means that a balanced history is hard to establish, for positive experiences – voiced by other attendees of residential schools – are not politically popular.

31 For an overview of benefits to civilization, see Alvin Schmidt, *How Christianity Changed the World* (Zondervan Publishing, 2004). Re: Liberty. Erik von Kuehnelt-Leddihn writes in his book, *Leftism: From de Sade and Marx to Hitler and Marcuse* (Arlington House, 1974), that "[personal liberty] makes its appearance in the Western World – and solely in the Western World – only with the advent of Christianity." (p.48).

32 For a discussion on this topic, see Stark, *The Victory of Reason* (Random House, 2005).

33 Baruch Spinoza, *Ethics* in *Philosophy of Benedict de Spinoza* (Tudor Publishing, 1933, translated by R.H.M. Elwes), p.272, Proposition XXXVI.

Spinoza shaped a new order of thinkers, including the German philosophers Hegel and Nietzsche.[34] He also pressed toward Biblical higher criticism with its view of Scripture as allegory, and his impact on scientific thought was substantial. Will Durant writes,

> Science itself, which so superciliously scorns metaphysics, assumes a metaphysic in its every thought. It happens that the metaphysic which it assumes is the metaphysic of Spinoza.[35]

New Orthodoxy

Bursting through the Renaissance and paralleling the Reformation came an upsurge in natural discoveries and technical advances.

Mathematical breakthroughs, the printing press, findings in astronomy and physics: the Scientific Revolution was ignited. Experimental trailblazers such as Kepler, Galileo, and Newton still connected their work to Christian parameters.[36] In fact, the modern conception of scientific inquiry was rooted in the Scholastic tradition, an exercising of intellectual exploration and the pursuit of knowledge – including Greek philosophy – under a banner of Catholic culture and the Christian belief in a God who is creative and knowable. Professor Stark points out that "because God is a rational being and the universe his personal creation, it necessarily has a rational, lawful, stable structure, *awaiting increased human comprehension*."[37] This worldview,

---

[34] Georg Wilhelm Friedrich Hegel (1770-1831), envisioning a new spirit or *Geist*, worked to find unity within the dialectical process of thesis, antithesis, and synthesis. Friedrich Nietzsche (1844-1900) rejected the notion of objective truth and proclaimed, "God is dead." His "will to power" has parallels to the "striving" of Spinoza.

[35] Will Durant, *The Story of Philosophy: The Lives and Opinions of the Greater Philosophers* (Simon and Schuster, 1926), p.187.

[36] James Nickel, *Mathematics: Is God Silent?* (Ross House Books, 2001), surveys the Christian influence upon mathematical philosophy. See pp.108-128 re: Napier, Copernicus, Kepler, Galileo, and Newton. On the connection between Christendom and scientific development in the Medieval period, see James Hannam, *The Genesis of Science: How the Christian Middle Ages Launched the Scientific Revolution* (Regnery Publishing, 2011). Hannam approaches this topic through a Catholic lens. Historian and secularist, David F. Noble, provides an overview of Christian interaction with science and its impact on Western development in his book, *The Religion of Technology: The Divinity of Man and the Spirit of Invention* (Penguin Books, 1999).

[37] Stark, *The Victory of Reason*, p.12, italics in original.

he explains, framed the theological backdrop through which the Scientific Revolution could take place.

Secularizing perspectives, however, were coming into play. Galileo and the English statesman, Francis Bacon, argued for an independent approach to the study of nature. Contrary to some of the talking points found in today's popular atheism, this plea to break from Church involvement was not an assault on Christianity. Yale professor Franklin Baumer relates that, "Bacon and Galileo meant no harm to Christian theology, far from it; but they were determined to free science from theological control."[38]

Like the ecclesiastical break experienced during the Reformation, Catholic offices no longer dominated scientific scholarship. This shift resulted in the growing acceptance of a Modernist attitude, a quickening to see the world through a naturalistic lens. Could the universe be a mechanical thing devoid of an outside and personal Intelligence? *Naturalism*, the idea that nothing exists outside of Nature, was becoming an accepted position. Rational Man with his ability to calculate the cosmos, and not a transcendent God who bestowed humanity with capacity, would thus be the "measure of all things."

Men's minds were being re-oriented to a "new orthodoxy" – "a belief in progress and the power of human reason."[39] Professor Baumer outlined how mid-Seventeenth Century thinkers were conceptualizing this new faith. Belief in God's Providence was less fashionable; talk of human providence was in vogue. With this came a new psychological tone, "the sense of new beginnings, almost of salvation by human works."[40]

Baumer writes,

> By means of his power man could establish a veritable utopia on earth, not the sort of utopia or millennium foretold by the Book of Revelation, but a utilitarian 'kingdom' or 'empire of man over things' in which the emphasis was on the relief of man's worldly estate.[41]

The Age of Faith was slipping into the shadows of a rising and imposing edifice; the Great Secularization – the Temple of Man.

---

[38] Franklin L. Baumer, *Religion and the Rise of Scepticism* (Harcourt, Brace & Company, 1960), p.114.

[39] Robin Briggs, *The Scientific Revolution of the Seventeenth Century* (Longman Group, 1969), p.89.

[40] Baumer, *Religion and the Rise of Scepticism*, p.127.

[41] Ibid., p.126.

Chapter 4

The Temple of Man

> Science is a religion, science alone will henceforth make the creeds, science alone can solve for men the eternal problems, the solution of which his nature imperatively demands. – Ernest Renan.[1]

> Yes, we are going to destroy everything, and on the ruins we will build our temple! – V.I. Lenin.[2]

Christianity, "that infamous thing," was to vanish in revolutionary fervor. Politicized Christendom would be overthrown by the enlightened masses who, armed with reason and guided by passion, were themselves led by men of conviction. Churches were vandalized, mounds of hymn books burned, and "ceremonies of mockery" witnessed priests denouncing their faith. Even the Gregorian calendar was dissolved, with its seven-day week replaced by a ten-day cycle dedicated to the veneration of nature. And as each month was structured with an even thirty days, the year would end with an extra five-day block set aside for humanist festivals.[3]

Fraternity, liberty, and equality: The citizen's Republic would replace the monarchy and aristocracy. Catholicism would be pushed out, not to be replaced by Protestantism – itself having been expelled years earlier[4] – but with a devotion to rationalism, naturalism, and civic patriotism. France was "enlightened," and the world would never be the same.

---

1 Ernest Renan, *The Future of Science* (Chapman and Hall, 1891), pp.90-91.

2 Quoted by Robert Payne, *The Life and Death of Lenin* (Simon and Schuster, 1964), p.419.

3 Simon Schama, *Citizens: A Chronicle of the French Revolution* (Alfred A. Knopf, 1989), pp.767-779.

4 The Protestant Huguenots were driven out of France after being militarily defeated by the Catholic aristocracy. A nationally-stable Protestant base never took hold. Will and Ariel Durant write, "France bypassed the Reformation, and went directly from the Renaissance to the Enlightenment." *Rousseau and Revolution* (Simon and Schuster, 1967), p.881.

On November 10, 1793, this new *faith* was celebrated through the Festival of Liberty and Reason, held in the "liberated" and re-purposed Cathedral of Notre Dame. Yale professor Franklin Baumer described the spectacle,

> [As the spectators] entered the cathedral, they saw, some doubtless with astonishment, the insignia of Christianity covered up and their place taken by the symbols of a strange new religion. Rising up in the nave was an improvised mountain, at the top of which perched a small Greek temple dedicated 'To Philosophy' and adorned on both sides by the busts of philosophers... Halfway down the side of the mountain a torch of Truth burned before an altar of Reason. Then ensued a bizarre ceremony which culminated in the emergence from the temple of a beautiful woman, an actress of the Paris Opera, dressed in red, white, and blue garments, who personified Liberty. The spectators proceeded to render homage to Liberty by stretching out their arms to her and singing a hymn... 'Come, holy Liberty, inhabit this temple, Become the goddess of the French people.'[5]

The liberty of Reason was costly. Heads rolled, for this was the Terror and the guillotines chopped daily. Paris was the epicenter of total transformation, and society's evolution required a revolution to birth the New Man.

Long before the uprising, Renaissance voices like Pico and the Italian diplomat, Machiavelli – whose book, *The Prince*, illustrated a secular and amoral pragmatism – contributed to Enlightenment thinking. More immediate personalities such as Voltaire and Rousseau, England's John Locke, Scotland's David Hume and Prussia's Immanuel Kant, had and were changing the way European intellectuals viewed the world. But if a starting line is to be drawn for the era of Modernity, the French Revolution is a logical choice.[6]

The Paris uprising would become a beacon illuminating the path for future revolutionary experiments.

---

5 Franklin L. Baumer, *Religion and the Rise of Scepticism* (Harcourt, Brace & Company, 1960), pp.35-36.

6 Why not the American Revolution instead of the French? Professor J.L Talmon neatly compares: "The French Revolution compared with the American Revolution had been an event on quite a different plane. It had been a total revolution in the sense that it had left no sphere and no aspect of human existence untouched, whereas the American Revolution had been a purely political change-over." Talmon, *The Origins of Totalitarian Democracy* (Frederick A. Praeger, 1960), p.27.

Prelude to Planning

Modernity is an umbrella label for an epoch that witnessed a number of movements and ideas expressing a similar outcome – the humanist progression of society, wherein authentic knowledge and meaning are discovered by *naturalistic* determination and not Christian revelation. In general, Modernity, often used interchangeably with *Modernism*,[7] upheld humanist rationalism as the arbitrator of truth. Reason, therefore, proclaimed the goodness of Man over the Christian teaching of original sin, celebrated individual autonomy without moral guilt, worked through industry to harness the beast of nature, and looked to naturalism for social guidance.[8] Man became the center of the universe.

Science, the testable exploration of creation – an honorable quest reflecting a Biblical worldview[9] – became saddled with a naturalistic outlook: *Nothing exists outside of Nature, and Man is the measure of all things*.

Unlike Christendom during the Pre-modern era, lasting approximately 1500 years, the lifespan of Modernity was short, diminishing and morphing by the late 1960s.[10] Granted, we still experience aspects of Modernity today just as we have carry-over from the previous period. There will always be fluidity and flux in the shifting of cultures and values, and Modernity's impact was too profound to just drop away.

The trendsetters of Modernity were many. However, two French citizens, the teacher-student duo of Henri de Saint-Simon and Auguste Comte, deserve special mention. As the fathers of sociology, literally the *science of society*, their ideas formed the seedbed for the technically ordered and managed state – the planned society of *collectivism* and *socialism*.

In the planned society, economic and civic life are directed to achieving social targets: Equality, racial harmony, social justice, or the classless state. Assurances of peace and prosperity dangle before the toiling masses, for so-

[7] Modernism is generally associated with the artistic and literary movements that correspond to Modernity.

[8] Stewart E. Kelly lays out a number of conditions in respect to Modernism. See his book, *Truth Considered and Applied: Examining Postmodernism, History and Christian Faith* (B&H Publishing Group, 2011).

[9] "The works of the Lord are great, studied by all who have pleasure in them." – Psalm 111:2.

[10] Some scholars place Modernity's end at the Fall of the Berlin Wall in 1989, and others position it at the collapse of the Soviet Union in 1991.

cial and economic problems – so the promise goes – may be overcome by technically attuning community life through economic structuring, regulations, and social management.

It is true that in all nations and societies a certain measure of administrative planning is necessary, *within limits*. Today it is practically impossible to find a country that does not incorporate socialist elements. Differences in how this is arranged can be seen from place to place, and each nation's history, social environment, and culture-of-elites plays a role in setting the tone. Nevertheless, there is an observable history of negative consequences.

With state socialism the difficult and honorable road of free enterprise is softened through group solutions, and the slower-to-come social benefits of capitalism[11] are apparently accelerated through the promise of planning. But there are costs. Private property and the means of production are interfered with, including the ability to dispose of assets. In full state control of production, private ownership becomes moot – you are an owner in *name only*, at best. Socialism's history of property management is abysmal.

The expense is not just the damage to private ownership in the name of the "general good," nor the price tag for supporting larger government,[12]but a host of important civilizing characteristics are ultimately devalued: Personal incentive and responsibility, ethics and morality, and the mindset of personal liberty – requirements for civilization to flourish. Each are eroded in time, representing hidden costs that, in a generation or two, exhibit themselves in social, civil, and economic decline.[13]

---

[11] Works to consider in the study of economic systems: Thomas Sowell, *Basic Economics: A Common Sense Guide to the Economy* (Basic Books, 2007); Hernando de Soto, *The Mystery of Capital: Why Capitalism Triumphs in the West and Fails Everywhere Else* (Basic Books, 2000); *The Freedom Philosophy* (Foundation for Economic Education, 1988); Milton Friedman, *Capitalism and Freedom* (The University of Chicago Press, 1962); Ludwig von Mises, *Socialism* (Liberty Fund, 1981); Hans-Hermann Hoppe, *Democracy: The God That Failed – The Economics and Politics of Monarchy, Democracy, and Natural Order* (Transaction Publishers, 2001/2007). The *Champions of Freedom* series by Hillsdale College Press has a wealth of knowledge regarding associated topics.

[12] In socialist economies, the primary and largest welfare recipient is the government.

[13] Rarely is it recognized that cultural decline stems from collective endeavors. For by the time society experiences the hidden costs, the solutions are almost always couched in the need for *more* socialism. Occasionally governments see the futility of their previous collective actions and make corrective measures, but usually it takes a massive economic crisis – or a series of crises – to recognize the need for reform.

Not surprisingly, the poor remain locked in poverty as society is gutted and property ownership displaced – slowly or quickly – for the "common good," or the "public interest," or the other "gods that collectivists worship."[14]

Organizing begets more organization, and expenses and complications arise, intensifying as "collective solutions" impede or nullify promised benefits.[15] But the solution can only be *more organization*, for the centrally planned civilization assumes that the social organ is of higher value than the individual. It inherently declares the person to be made in *its* likeness. This becomes more troubling when the organizing party, the *director*, emotionally fuels the masses to encourage planned uniformity.[16]

During Modernity and continuing today, such planning has been expressed as Progressivism, Socialism and Fascism, Communism, and Technocracy. Each are related, have variations, and are often in competition; the common thread is a technically driven collective ideal.

American Progressive, Stuart Chase, in comparing systems of central planning, favorably classified this trend as *Leftism*.[17]One could call it a form of socio-political *monism*. It is the *Positivism* of Saint Simon and Auguste Comte applied to politics and social order.

---

[14] For other "gods," see Robert Formaini, "Laissez-Faire: Let Each Individual Choose," *Between Power and Liberty: Economics and the Law* (Hillsdale College Press, 1998), p.103. To expand on the overall costs of socialism, see Thomas Sowell, *Intellectuals and Society* (Basic Books, 201). See also, *American Perestroika: The Demise of the Welfare State* (Hillsdale College Press, 1995). On the issue of poverty and economics, see E. Calvin Beisner, *Prosperity and Poverty: The Compassionate Use of Resources in a World of Scarcity* (Wipf and Stock Publishers, 2001); D. Eric Schansberg, *How Poor Government Policy Harms the Poor* (WestView Press, 1996); Arthur C. Brooks, *Who Really Cares: The Surprising Truth About Compassionate Conservatism* (Basic Books, 2006). See also, Ludwig von Mises, *Socialism* (Liberty Fund, 1981).

[15] A fantastic book on the growth and problems of the organizing principle is *Haga's Law: Why Nothing Works and No One Can Fix It and the More We Try the Worse It Gets*, by William J. Haga and Nicholas Acocella (William Morrow and Company, 1980).

[16] See F.A. Hayek, *The Road to Serfdom: Text and Documents* (The University of Chicago Press, 2007, edited by Bruce Caldwell). Hayek's consideration of a world federation at the end of his book is, I believe, misguided. He is correct in that an association or voluntary organization for international discussion is needed, but to grant it legislative and moral power to ensure "world peace" is problematic and potentially dangerous.

[17] Stuart Chase, *A New Deal* (The Macmillan Company, 1932), pp.154-155. Chase was not the first to have used the term, but as a leading Progressive and the intellectual father of America's New Deal, his argumentation for it is of special importance.

Simon and Comte

In 1803, Saint-Simon recommended that twenty-one men of science and industry, armed with wealth and prestige and influence, should manage humanity's development. Civilization, he argued, must be structured around three classes: Scientists, industrialists, and the masses. "Spiritual power" would lie in the hands of scientists while temporal clout would be given to men of industry, whom he called the "property owners." Together, these two classes would have but "one interest common to the whole of humanity, the progress of the sciences." The task of the masses was to nominate mankind's esteemed leaders.[18]

Later, Saint-Simon described his ideal "religion" as "New Christianity."

Divorced from traditional modes, New Christianity would be a universal and positive worship – a faith in utilitarian systems – and it would encourage a serviceable brotherhood devoted to science and progress,

> This rejuvenated religion is called upon to organize all peoples in a state of perpetual peace, by allying them all against the nation which tries to gain its own advantage at the expense of the good of the whole human race... It is called upon to link together the scientists, artists, and industrialists, and to make them the managing directors of the human race, as well as of the particular interests of each individual people. It is called upon to put the arts, experimental sciences and industry in the front rank of sacred studies...
>
> Finally, New Christianity is called upon to pronounce anathema upon theology, and to condemn as unholy any doctrine trying to teach men that there is any other way of obtaining eternal life, except that of working with all their might for the improvement of the conditions of life of their fellow men.[19]

New Christianity was envisioned as the sole and universal civic religion. It was believed that with the acceptance of this materialist faith, the traditional Christian emphasis – worship of God and Bible study – would be recalibrated for the public good. Longing for such a day, Saint Simon explained

---

[18] Henri de Saint-Simon, "Letters from an Inhabitant of Geneva," *Social Organization, The Science of Man and Other Writings* (Harper Torchbooks, 1952), pp.9-11.

[19] Saint-Simon, "New Christianity," *Social Organization, The Science of Man and Other Writings* (Harper Torchbooks, 1952) p.105.

that "worship should be regarded only as a means of reminding men, on the day of rest, of philanthropic feelings and ideas." Bible study was seen as damaging: "The study of the Bible draws attention to political motives contrary to the public welfare... It prevents the Protestants from working for a political system in which common interests will be managed by the ablest men in science, art, and industry..."[20]

Auguste Comte, a protégé of Saint-Simon, expanded naturalism into a secularist "Religion of Humanity." This creed was built around a model he called Positivism, described by historian Jacques Barzun as "the most powerful doctrine of the century."[21] Comte's work applied biological evolution to human social systems, interconnecting "the humblest vegetative existence with the noblest social life through a long succession."[22]

For Comte, knowledge went through three historical phases: 1) *Theological*, with humanity looking to God as the explanation of causes, 2) *Metaphysical*, in which it is perceived that an inner essence moves natural phenomena, 3) *Positivism*, declaring that authentic knowledge is only understood and explained empirically.

In Positivism, what is measurable and observable – science – is the singular mechanism for knowing reality. Values and experiences must be legitimized through empirical means. Translated into the social sphere, this thinking held that as the universe was governed by mechanical laws, humanity, too, could be technically managed. Positivism was therefore a "regenerating doctrine," an "all-embracing creed" that would lead society out of ignorance and into the light of science-based reason. Scientism, that is, the application of the scientific method as an authoritative worldview, flowed naturally from Comte's philosophy. Order and Progress would follow.[23]

"The primary object... of Positivism is two-fold," he explained. "To generalize scientific conceptions, and to systematize the art of social life. These are but two aspects of one and the same problem."[24]

---

20 Ibid., pp.106-107.

21 Jacques Barzun, *Darwin, Marx, Wagner* (Doubleday Anchor, 1941/1958), p.49.

22 Auguste Comte, *The Positive Philosophy*, Volume III (George Bell & Sons, 1896 English edition, translated by Harriet Martineau), p.399.

23 Brazil's motto, Order and Progress, is adapted from Comte's philosophy.

24 Auguste Comte, "Introductory Remarks," *A General View of Positivism* (George Routledge & Sons, 1848/1908), p.3.

What was the problem to overcome? The "great problem of human Unity."[25] Such a synthesis of science and society, Comte noted, would bring about "social reconstruction."

Understanding the importance of manufacturing an emotional spirit to ensure social cohesion, the philosopher organized Positivism into a religion of Order and Living. *Order* would appeal to the male character. "Live for Others," conversely, would be a motto "especially adapted to women, who are thus invited to participate in these public manifestations of social feeling."[26] Pure reason needed emotion to energize activity, and the female spirit represented that power. Thus, his symbol of Humanity personified would be a "woman of thirty years of age, bearing her son in her arms."[27]

Comte's religion of good works and progress would be a deeply *humanist faith*, and he called for people to make a distinct choice: Positivism or Theology. As science moved into what he called the "synthetic state," that is, science as a "high mission" inspiring human action, the old faiths would wither. In 1858 he published a lengthy catechism with the Preface declaring that Roman Catholicism and Islam "must put aside all theology and all metaphysics" and unite under science, or decay.[28]

His secular, replacement religion – a faith without appeal to a transcendent Personality, a religion without revelation – was not without form; rather, it was built around systems of order and dynamic experiences. Appointing himself "High Priest of Humanity" and the "Founder of Universal Religion," he created a series of rituals to mark the stages of life "from birth to 'incorporation' and 'transformation' into the Great Being." Activities included "positivist marriage ceremonies" and a "system of group worship designed to reinforce social feelings."[29] Enlightened humanity would be the "only true Great Being," the highest intelligence.

Temples of Humanity – the churches of Comte's religion – still exist in Paris and three Brazilian cities: Rio de Janeiro, Curitiba, and Porto Alegre.

---

[25] Ibid., p.23, capital in original.

[26] Ibid., p.431.

[27] Ibid., p.431.

[28] Auguste Comte, *The Catechism of Positivism; or, Summary Exposition of the Universal Religion in Thirteen Systematic Conversations Between a Woman and a Priest of Humanity* (John Chapman, 1858), pp.8-10.

[29] Dante Germino, *Machiavelli to Marx: Modern Western Political Thought* (University of Chicago Press, 1972), pp.289-296.

"We are invincible"[30]

Comte's "group worship" brings up the subject of individualism.

Liberated from "oppressive" Christian morality, Modernist individuality had an appealing factor. Man was now unbound, an "intelligent animal" free to choose without God. To Comte, morality would follow a Positive path of science and order. For others who looked to naturalism, morality was more nebulous. An irony exists, of course, in that naturalism and *determinism* go hand-in-hand: You are just the product of chemicals and energy, a mechanical cause-and-effect without escape or intervention or *free will.*

But where, then, would purpose and worth come from? Certainly not from having personal value as an exceptional creation of God. And to think of ourselves as meaningless atoms in a pointless universe is defeating. Purpose, then, must come through group experiences – the synthesis of Rationalism and Emotions, the individual and the community. Value would be grasped by placing the self in the collection of other selves; we will all feel good about ourselves in the self-congratulating structure of the herd. It is in the group where alienation and separation gives way to a feeling of Oneness.

British socialist, Sidney Webb, put it this way,

> Though the social organism has itself evolved from the union of individual men, the individual is now created by the social organism of which he forms a part: his life is born of the larger life; his attributes are moulded by the social pressure; his activities, inextricably interwoven with others, belong to the activity of the whole.[31]

Another British social theorist, Benjamin Kidd, eagerly described the group integration process,

> Once effectively imposed, this idealism becomes the expression of the living soul of a people. Its influence cannot be estimated. It subordinates everything. It becomes Power incarnate.[32]

Somewhat similar to Comte, Kidd believed a community psyche or spirit would move the individual into an energized whole. His emphasis, however,

---

30 *The Political Thought of Mao Tse-tung* (Praeger Publishers, 1971), p.438.

31 Sidney Webb, "History," *Fabian Essays in Socialism* (The Fabian Society, 1920 edition, originally published in 1889), pp.56-57.

32 Benjamin Kidd, *The Science of Power* (Methuen and Company, 1918/1919), p.296.

was on the power of harnessed emotion – what he described as the *emotion of the ideal* – and the ability to mobilize these feelings for social evolution: "*The great secret of the coming age of the world is that civilization rests not on Reason but on Emotion,*"[33]

> It is clearly in evidence that the science of creating and transmitting public opinion under the influence of collective emotion is about to become the principal science of civilization to the mastery of which all governments and all powerful interests will in the future address themselves with every resource at their command.[34]

Journalist Robert Keyserlingk witnessed the consequences of such revolutionary thinking. While in Berlin, 1930, he watched in astonishment as "several hundred young men and young women were being 'confirmed' into the 'Socialist Faith'." This, Keyserlingk noted, was indicative of the spiritual vacuum created in the West by its explicit rejection of Christian principles,

> Having negated personal creation and therefore individual salvation, but finding it impossible to live as a senseless atom in a cruel world, men filled the spiritual vacuum by the ideal of primitive mankind: the group worship of itself.[35]

Three years later the newly appointed Reich Chancellor of Germany, Adolf Hitler, made it clear that value is bound in the will of the community,

> Man as an individual, whatever power he may have in himself, will be incapable of higher achievements unless he can place the powers of many in the service of a single idea, a single conception, a single will, and can unite them for a single action.[36]

Modernity, while claiming freedom through naturalistic philosophy and messianic secularism, bound the person to an imposed vision of social order. The political extension of Modernity attempted to integrate the individual through an appeal to nationalistic or ideological "rationalism" and the power

---

[33] Ibid., p.118.

[34] Ibid., p.124.

[35] Robert W. Keyserlingk, *Unfinished History* (Robert Hale Limited, 1948), pp.175-176.

[36] Adolf Hitler, "Speech of September 3, 1933, Nuremberg," *My New Order* (Reynal & Hitchcok, 1941), p.199. *My New Order* is a collection of Hitler's speeches.

of the group emotion, yet chained the person to structures of *systems thinking*.[37] Rugged individualism would have to go.

Individualism properly understood allows for personal striving *and* responsibility. Rugged individualism, the ability to establish oneself without making undue demands on state or society, was once considered a virtue. Persons who exemplified this attitude were viewed as the bedrock of a community – hardworking, someone who could be reasoned with, respectful of neighbors, and often the first to help others in times of need. The "rugged individual" was a person who reflected an ethic higher than the aggregate; he or she would do the "right thing," even if unpopular. Such a person is not easily herded into a system, either by coercion or consensus. Does such individualism still exist? Yes. I just described many of my neighbors, friends, and family. This spirit is alive, even in today's culture.

Systems thinking, oriented to group planning, crushes this independent spirit. Human value, rather, is discovered and expressed in a pre-determined vision of wholeness, and techniques of social engineering – psychological conditioning – reinforce this theme to ensure compliance and unity.

"There is more psychiatry than surgery in planning," wrote political behaviorist and Progressive intellectual, Charles E. Merriam.[38] Men's minds must be molded for social efficiency.

Comte himself said, "Man indeed, as an individual cannot properly be said to exist, except in the exaggerated abstractions of modern metaphysicians. Existence in the true sense can only be predicated of Humanity."[39]

In other words, individualism is illusionary and the value of your existence is relative to the larger unit. The ideal of social cohesion, powered by emotions and lodged in our minds, is the path to evolutionary integration.

---

[37] An older book advocating systems thinking is, *The Era of the System: How the Systems Approach Can Help Solve Society's Problems*, by Gerald Rabow (Philosophical Library, 1969). For a critical review of systems thinking, see Neil Postman, *Technopoly: The Surrender of Culture to Technology* (Vintage Books, 1993). To better understand technique and national planning, see James C. Scott, *Seeing Like a State: How Certain Schemes to Improve the Human Condition Have Failed* (Yale University Press, 1998).

[38] Charles E. Merriam, *The Role of Politics in Social Change* (New York University Press, 1936), p.110. Merriam was the first political science faculty member at the University of Chicago, a federal planner, and helped organize the Social Science Research Council.

[39] Comte, *A General View of Positivism*, p.370. Some may question the wording choice "of Humanity." This is how it is found in the translated text.

Integration, of course, needs an *integrator*.

J.L Talmon recognized this fact in his book, *The Origins of Totalitarian Democracy*, as he considered where naturalistic ideals placed the person,

> Although prima facie [at first sight] the individual is the beginning and the end of everything, in fact the Legislator is decisive. He is called upon to shape man in accordance to a definite image. The aim is not to enable men as they are to express themselves as freely and as fully as possible, to assert their uniqueness. It is to create the right objective conditions and to educate men so that they would fit into the pattern of the virtuous society.[40]

Follow a path other than what "visionary intellectuals" ordain? Live by a set of values and ethics higher than the prescribed system? Acknowledge individual worth beyond the group context? Consider private property to be exclusive to its possessor? How dare you!

Comte foretold: "Men are not allowed to think freely about chemistry and biology, why should they think freely about political philosophy?"[41]

For that matter, why should "men think freely" about anything if mechanical naturalism is the guiding force of the universe? Just trust the secular priesthood as they interpret the movements of energy and matter, and abide by their applications upon *human matter*.

Commenting on the Positivist worldview, Herbert E. Cushman wrote,

> Science alone must be the new foundation – a science of facts. The age of freedom of conscience will cease when indubitable science rules man in his ethics, psychology, and government as it now rules in the natural sciences.[42]

---

40 J.L. Talmon, *The Origins of Totalitarian Democracy* (Frederick A. Praeger, 1960), p.37. Alfred M. Bingham said the following in *The Techniques of Democracy* (Duell, Sloan and Pearce, 1942): "The genius that has given man mastery of his physical environment, is now, in sociology and psychology, being applied to man's mastery of himself and his social environment. Not only does democracy foster science and science foster democracy, but democracy is becoming a science." (p.272)

41 As quoted by W.H.G. Armytage, *The Rise of the Technocrats: A Social History* (Routledge and Kegan Paul, 1965), p.298.

42 Herbert Ernest Cushman, *A Beginner's History of Philosophy*, Volume 2 (Houghton Mifflin Company, 1920), p.384.

Evolving Positivism

Although the French duo never became household names and Comte's "Religion of Humanity" was a flop, their concepts opened vistas of thought. In the decades to follow, their insights were studied, debated, criticized and ridiculed, modified and assimilated within other competing arguments. The authors of *The Communist Manifesto* – Karl Marx and Friedrich Engels – while indebted to German philosopher Georg Hegel, nevertheless acknowledged Saint Simon's influence and absorbed some of his principles.[43] In 1902, Vladimir Lenin called Saint Simon a genius whose social theories were being proven correct.[44] On the other hand, Marx was disparaging of Comte.

Comte, too, was critical of "the programme of Communism." Nevertheless, he acknowledged that Positivism and Communism were not so far apart,

> The errors of Communism must be rectified; but there is no necessity for giving up the name, which is a simple assertion of the paramount importance of Social Feeling... Positivism, then, has nothing to fear from Communism; on the contrary, it will probably be accepted by most Communists among the working classes, especially in France where abstractions have but little influence on minds thoroughly emancipated from theology.[45]

Positivism impacted other notable personalities. Charles Darwin wrote that Comte made him "think deeply" with his "grand ideas."[46] Thomas Huxley, Darwin's friend and "Bulldog," offered a sharper analysis,

> That a man should determine to devote himself to the service of humanity – including intellectual and moral self-culture under that

---

[43] Karl Marx and Friedrich Engels, *The Communist Manifesto* (Penguin Books, 1985), p.115. See also, David McLellan, *The Thought of Karl Marx: An Introduction* (Harper Torchbooks, 1974), pp.7, 25, 212-213. Marx was also critical of the monetary theory derived from the followers of Saint Simon. See Karl Marx, *Early Writings* (Penguin Books, 1992), p.263.

[44] V.I. Lenin, *What Is To Be Done?* (International Publishers, 1902/1969), pp.27-28. See also, Armytage, *The Rise of the Technocrats*, p.65 (and chapter 14).

[45] Comte, *A General View of Positivism*, p.169.

[46] Charles Darwin, *Notebook M* (1838), and *Notebook N* (1838-1839) [*Darwin Online*, http://darwin-online.org.uk], accessed February 13, 2016. Stephen Jay Gould briefly acknowledged the impact of Comte on Darwin in *The Panda's Thumb: More Reflections in Natural History* (W.W. Norton & Company, 1980), p.65.

> name; that this should be, in the proper sense of the word, his religion – is not only an intelligible, but, I think, a laudable resolution... But when the positivist asks me to worship 'Humanity' – that is to say, to adore the generalized conception of men as they ever have been and probably ever will be – I must reply that I could just as soon bow down and worship the generalized conception of a 'wilderness of apes.' Surely we are not going back to the days of paganism...[47]

Huxley added, "His works are repulsive on account of the dull diffuseness of their style, and a certain air, as of a superior person, which characterizes them; but, nevertheless, they contain good things here and there."[48]

Huxley's support for Darwin's theory of evolution was substantial, and not just because of their friendship. Far more important was the recognition that evolution via natural selection was the "working hypothesis" to which men of science would be freed from the dilemma of refusing the "Creation hypothesis."[49] It was a shift in thinking with massive implications.

"I look forward to a great revolution being effected," Huxley wrote to a friend. "Depend upon it, in natural history, as in everything else..."[50]

Comte's influence upon scientific thought, however unnerving his humanist religion was to Huxley and others, acted as a stepping stone. Jacques Barzun tells us that Comte's effort in creating an "orthodoxy for science" was important to evolutionary thinking: "He minutely set forth the relations of the sciences to one another, making a 'positive' hierarchy of their methods and contents. This is where his influence... made directly for a revival of materialistic mechanism and paved the way for Darwinism."[51]

Darwin's model, like the Biblical record it countered, became a cornerstone for constructing worldviews. It informed theories on everything from psychology to politics to ecology. And it added another layer to naturalism,

---

[47] Thomas Huxley, "Agnosticism," *Christianity and Agnosticism: A Controversy*, by Henry Wace, Thomas Huxley, et al. (The Humboldt Publishing Company, 1889), p.27.

[48] Ibid., p.29.

[49] Sir William Cecil Dampier, *A History of Science and Its Relations with Religion and Philosophy* (Cambridge University Press, 1944, third edition), p.299.

[50] Ronald W. Clark, *The Survival of Charles Darwin: A Biography of a Man and an Idea* (Random House, 1984), p.111.

[51] Barzun, *Darwin, Marx, Wagner*, p.50.

a "deeper continuity" in which nature and "the fate of the single individual" became "interwoven in the great web binding the life of the species with nature as a whole."[52]

Humanist concepts of evolution predated Darwin, but the Englishman was the first to formulate an accepted hypothesis. His model quickly gained popularity as it addressed the issue of origins within the bounds of naturalism. Important challenges to the assumptions of Darwinian evolution have since risen,[53] but today, as in Darwin's time, naturalism is the "cultural authority" that defines scientific argument.[54] In his bestselling book on evolution, Professor Jerry A. Coyne defined and asserted the dominant position,

> Naturalism is the view that the only way to understand our universe is through the scientific method. Materialism is the idea that the only reality is the physical matter of the universe, and that everything else, including thoughts, will, and emotions, comes from physical laws acting on that matter. The message of evolution, and all of science, is one of naturalistic materialism.[55]

Darwinism offered the hope of progress without the need for God; as biology evolved, all else must move upward by natural means. Human society itself evolves and as Man now understands the natural world, so the argument goes, our communities can be planned for optimal existence. Social evolution represented a new synthesis. The technical management of communal life could produce a "oneness of man and nature."[56]

The Temple of Man would thus arise.

---

[52] H. Hoffding, "The Influence of the Conception of Evolution on Modern Philosophy," as printed by A.C. Seward, *Darwin and Modern Science: Essays in Commemoration of the Centenary of the Birth of Charles Darwin and of the Fiftieth Anniversary of The Origin of Species* (Cambridge at the University Press, 1909), p.450.

[53] Works critical of evolution and written from a Christian perspective incorporating scientific arguments (technical and layman), include: *Evolution's Achilles' Heels* (Creation Book Publishers, 2014, edited by Robert Carter); Jay Seegert, *Let There Be Light: Making Sense of the Creation/Evolution Controversy* (Icon Publishing Group, 2012); Marvin L. Lubenow, *Bones of Contention: A Creationist Assessment of Human Fossils* (Baker Books, 1992); Jack Cuozzo, *Buried Alive* (Master Books, 1998).

[54] See Phillip E. Johnson, *Reason in the Balance* (InterVarsity Press, 1995), pp.105-107.

[55] Jerry A. Coyne, *Why Evolution is True* (Penguin Books, 2209), p.224.

[56] Eric Fromm described the socialist aim of Karl Marx as the "oneness of man and nature." See Eric Fromm, *Marx's Concept of Man* (Frederick Ungar Publishing, 1966/1976), p.38.

Engineering Unity

The intellectual impact of Positivism, naturalism and evolution – scientific materialism – was predictable. Christianity could no longer be tenable for the "educated man." A mind switch in academics took place. Profound changes within the arts demonstrated the cultural acceptance of naturalism, and at the same time, pointed to the internal struggle for meaning.[57] And churches and seminaries attempted to reconcile Biblical positions with naturalistic theories. Unable to grasp the difference between scientific claims and naturalistic philosophy, or uninterested in rocking that boat, they found themselves compromising in order to be accepted.

Politically, the ramifications of Modernity had a profound effect. Materialist revolutions in state and society shook nations and the world. Vladimir Lenin, Joseph Stalin, and Leon Trotsky burned Russia to the ground, erecting a colossal temple to scientific materialism – the Soviet Union. Christianity, that "infamous thing," was driven underground. Instead of prosperity and peace and equality, Christians experienced repression and direct persecution. Contrary to what New Atheist and best-selling author Richard Dawkins claims, a tangible connection existed between official atheism and Soviet brutality. The Party *enforced* its atheistic worldview.[58]

---

[57] See H.R. Rookmaaker, *Modern Art and the Death of Culture* (Inter-Varsity Press, 1970).

[58] Richard Dawkins claims there is no link between acts of despotism, atheistic leaders, and their atheistic worldview. In *The God Delusion* (Houghton Mifflin, 2006), Dawkins references Stalin and says, "individual atheists may do evil things but they don't do evil things in the name of atheism" (p.278). Evidence is to the contrary. There is a connection between many of the horrors of the Soviet Union and its atheist platform. See Paul Gabel, *And God Created Lenin: Marxism vs. Religion in Russia, 1917-1929* (Prometheus Books, 2005); Paul Froese, *The Plot to Kill God: Findings from the Soviet Experiment in Secularization* (University of California Press, 2008); Daniel Peris, *Storming the Heavens: The Soviet League of the Militant Godless* (Cornell University Press, 1998). See also the sections written by Solzhenitsyn on religious persecution in *The Gulag Archipelago* series, (Harper and Row Publishers). Consider too the words of E.E. Yaroslavsky, a member of Soviet Agitprop and later head of the Militant Atheists: "Is the communist movement anti-religious? Yes... Must our party wage a war with religion? Yes. It must conduct a war with religion by means of propaganda, agitation, the preaching of atheism, the uncovering of ties between religion and the exploiting ruling classes..." Yaroslavsky, reprinted in *Bolshevik Visions: First Phase of the Cultural Revolution in Soviet Russia, Part 1* (The University of Michigan Press, 1990), p.242. Mikhail Gorbachev, the last Soviet President, explained that "after the civil war ended, in time of peace, they [Lenin, Stalin, Trotsky,

Leading revolutionist, Leon Trotsky, wrote the following: "Religiousness is irreconcilable with the Marxian standpoint. We are of opinion that Atheism, as an inseparable element of the materialist view of life, is a necessary condition for the theoretical education of the revolutionist."[59]

Former atheist, Peter Hitchens, reminds us that "Soviet power was – as it was intended to be – the opposite of faith in God. It was faith in the greatness of humanity and in the perfectibility of human society."[60]

In this "worker's paradise," Christians could expect to be ostracized and marginalized, if they were so fortunate. Many had their property confiscated, found themselves imprisoned, forced into hard labour, or executed. But that is what Lenin said he would do! In a speech during the Russian Revolution, he promised that a priority would be "ruthlessly suppressing by military methods yesterday's slave-owners (capitalists) and their hordes of lackeys." Lackeys to be suppressed included priests and church leaders.[61] Once in power, Lenin asked to be daily notified as to the number of priests being executed, and if religious leaders opposed the state seizer of church property, they were to be shot, "the more the better."[62]

But the Soviet Union was more than just militantly anti-God. As the first national state-system in the 20th century to be built upon Modernity's foundation, *everything* was measured against the *Plan*. Consider the account of Maurice Hindus, a correspondent who witnessed the Kremlin's management of the Russian peoples,

> The Plan... envisages the recasting of society into a new mold. Man's 'I' is no longer the center of things. It is an organic part of the aggregate – or, as the Russians say, of the mass. In the basic things of life the individual cannot sunder himself from the mass without

etc] continued to tear down churches, arrest clergymen, and destroy them... Atheism took rather savage forms in our country at the time." Gorbachev, *On My Country and the World* (Columbia University Press, 2000), pp.20-21.

59 Published in *The Communist Review*, June 1924. [accessed via www.marxists.org].

60 Peter Hitchens, *The Rage Against God: How Atheism Led Me To Faith* (Zondervan, 2010), p.138.

61 V.I. Lenin, "How to Organise Competition," *The Russian Revolution: Writings and Speeches from the February Revolution to the October Revolution, 1917* (Lawrence and Wishart, 1938, with speeches and texts from Joseph Stalin included), p.291.

62 See *The Unknown Lenin*, edited by Richard Pipes (Yale University Press, 1996), p.11 and footnote #17.

> inviting disaster and even destruction. In the chief calculations of the government it is the mass that counts, and everything that man as an individual needs… comes to him by the grace and the force of the Plan for the mass…
>
> The Plan is the life-blood of everything and everybody. Everything you do is part of the Plan. You dig a ditch, you plant potatoes, you heave bricks, you blast rock, you study medicine – it is all part of the Plan: you buy shoes, you decorate a house with pictures, you install a telephone, you eat canned tomatoes – it is all the result of the Plan…
>
> There is no schoolhouse, co-operative farm, or factory that has not a plan of its own which fits into some other plan and which, like a rivulet that flows into a river on its way to the ocean, does not in the end become part of the one Plan. I have seen dances and songs and games and plays that center in the idea and the emotion of the Plan.[63]

"If the Soviets were to fall today," wrote Hindus in 1933, "the one idea that would be sure to survive them is that of national planning."[64]

Russia was not alone. In time, China too became the planned society.

In 1949, after more than two decades of warfare and civil strife, Mao Tse-tung became the leader of the People's Republic of China. Twelve days after gaining office he acknowledged the role of his revolutionary heroes: "We are indebted to Marx, Engels, Lenin and Stalin for giving us a weapon. The weapon is not a machine-gun, but Marxism-Leninism." China became "a people's democratic dictatorship," and the nation collectivized around principles of technical management.[65]

That Mao advanced industry and productivity is without question, moving rapidly into the modern era. But the People's Republic also witnessed bizarre and extreme expressions of planning: The Great Leap Forward.

From 1959 to 1962, China underwent an episode of Modernity gone wild, an era when materialism and irrationality produced a deadly bureaucratic insanity. As the nation was looking to raise itself up as an industrial power-

---

63 Maurice Hindus, *The Great Offensive* (Harrison Smith and Robert Haas, 1933), pp.60-61.

64 Ibid., p.55.

65 Mao Tse-tung, *On People's Democratic Dictatorship* (Foreign Language Press, 1959, written July 1, 1949), see p.2 for "machine-gun" and p.11 for "democratic dictatorship."

house, the Chinese countryside was turned into a giant machine. Everything was collectivized; pots and pans, rakes and shovels, farm animals and homes. The masses were mobilized into brigades of worker bees.[66]

"Rank and file, we are all the same," said Chairman Mao. "A real spirit of communism comes when your raise a giant people's army."[67]

But they were not all the same. Mao placed upon himself the mantle of a messiah: "What is wrong with worship? The truth is in our hands, why should we not worship it?... Each group must worship its leader, it cannot but worship its leader."[68] Humanity was sacrificed on the Chairman's altar.

Men and women – like wheat and lumber and iron – were a material resource to be used. Villages and farms were collectivized into labor camps where all of life could be directed. Gigantic construction projects were tackled. Mountains were moved, rivers dammed.

The Great Leap Forward only lasted a handful of years, but the outcome was astonishing. Productivity reached miraculous levels. Agricultural output and metal production was up – way up! Bureaucrats armed with charts and graphs proved that an engineered paradise was happening; it was a planned economy overflowing with milk and honey. So said the functionaries.

Reality was something else. Charts and memos said one thing – unprecedented growth – but people were dying. In the end it was discovered that the miraculous increase was mainly illusionary, propped up by cadres fabricating numbers to appease higher officials, who, in turn, made their own false projections and fed this up the political food chain. Grossly unrealistic forecasts were met with impossible demands to increase even more.

To meet such miraculous growth benchmarks, political managers devised new and impossible farming techniques, such as "deep plowing" – overturning the soil to a depth of six feet, by hand – and massive over-fertilization. To maximize efficiency and productivity, farms and villages were forced into communal units. Collectivization, however, destroyed any semblance of property ownership, wiped out incentive, and shattered the social fabric. Famine soon stalked the land, and centrally planned food redistribution schemes funneled away what little was being produced.

---

66 Information gleaned from Frank Dikotter, *Mao's Great Famine: The History of China's Most Devastating Catastrophe, 1958-1962* (Walker & Company, 2010).

67 Quoted by Frank Dikotter, *Mao's Great Famine*, p.50.

68 Ibid., p.19.

Industry and trade suffered too with inferior products and waste, and steel production goals forced farmers to smelt down essential tools and implements, along with household cooking pots and other metal objects. Building materials were requested for government projects, so houses were dismantled for their lumber. Mud-and-straw peasant homes were reclaimed as "soil nutrients." Buildings were used for collective needs, and others were "torn down to make way for a vision of modernity that never quite managed to migrate from paper to the village."[69]

Historian Frank Dikotter describes the Great Leap Forward as the "greatest demolition of property in human history."[70] Millions of Chinese were displaced and untold scores were worked to ruin. In five years, approximately 45 million people died from starvation and other causes related to the Plan.

Mao's vision of Modernity had reduced humanity to a collective resource.

The Anguish of Modernity

Communism, "the most colossal case of political carnage in history,"[71] was an extension of Modernity's birth via the French Revolution. The Temple of Man had produced a deadly lineage of Marxist priests: Lenin, Stalin, Tito, Mao, Pol Pot, Che Guevara and Castro, Mengistu and Samora Machel, and Kim Il-sung. These and other Red tyrants were responsible for some of the most heinous acts of repression and *democide*[72] in the 20th century. The German National Socialism of Adolf Hitler, while struggling against the competition of Soviet communism, was an ideological cousin that followed the revolutionary tradition of death and destruction.[73]

---

69 Ibid., p.168.

70 Ibid., p.169.

71 Martin Malia, "Forward: The Uses of Atrocity," *The Black Book of Communism: Crimes, Terror, Repression* (Harvard University Press, 1999), p.x.

72 "Democide" is a term referring to the mass murder of civilians by their own government. To better understand the scope of democide in the 20th century, see R.J. Rummel, *Death By Government* (Transaction Publishers, 1994).

73 Major differences existed between Nazism and Communism in terms of domestic outlook and function, and in economic interests and operations, but both shared core similarities in terms of collective will, central planning, leadership style and one-party rule, and mass technique. When Robert W. Keyserlingk asked Alfred Rosenberg, the prominent Nazi theorist, what the basic difference was "between Communism and National Socialism," Rosenberg replied: "We are Germans and they are Russians and that is all

Both systems were constructed around collective technique.[74]

But Modernity in the 20th century was also wrapped up in *warfare*, and it exploded for all the world to feel in 1914.

World War I, then known as the Great War, offered a grave vision of technical and collective progress – "the conversion of a hundred million combatively individualistic people into a vast cooperative effort in which the good of the unit was sacrificed to the good of the whole, and of how the entire industrial power and machinery of the Nation were focused on war ends."[75]

Prior to war's start, science and industry were heralded as a mechanical horn of plenty, the provider of many wonderful gifts. Civilization prospered. But as nation rose against nation, millions of people experienced the dark extremes of Modernity.

Amazingly, the opening battles witnessed French infantrymen marching across fields in "blue breaches and red coats," and artillery officers in bold black and gold dress, throwbacks to an age of chivalry and pageantry. This, however, was the era of *science* and *mechanization*, and France, like the other countries involved, adjusted patterns to meet this new reality. Samuel P. Wilson, an explosives chemist for the US Navy during World War I, observed the following,

> ...the highest degree of training and skill in the physical sciences is now being brought to bear upon improving and controlling the paraphernalia of war. Present campaigns are between opposing forces of technicians, and battle-fields are their laboratories.[76]

Verdun, Vimy, the Somme, Ypres and the many other battlefields of the Great War witnessed new technologies of annihilation: machine guns, tanks, advanced artillery techniques, and poison gas. Killing had been mechanized.

---

the difference I need." Keyserlingk, *Unfinished History*, p.295. French social historian and theologian, Jacques Ellul, wrote that "Hitler's methods stem directly from Lenin's precepts; and conversely, Stalinism learned certain lessons about technique from the Nazis." Ellul, *The Technological Society* (Vintage Books, 1964), p.290.

[74] See Jacques Ellul, *The Technological Society* (Vintage Books, 1964), pp.290-291.

[75] Grosvenor Clarkson, *Industrial America in the World War: The Strategy Behind the Line, 1917-1918* (Houghton Mifflin Company, 1923), pp.3-4.

[76] Winston Groom, *A Storm in Flanders – The Ypres Salient, 1914-1918: Tragedy and Triumph on the Western Front* (Atlantic Moody Press, 2002), pp.18-19. See also, John Keegan, *The First World War* (Alfred A. Knopf, 1999), p.755.

Almost a century after the War, one professional bomb sweeper working in France had this to say regarding the gas shells and shrapnel bombs,

> ....with these two weapons, whole armies could be killed without their opponents ever seeing them. When the power to destroy faceless men came into our hands, men learned that God can abandon them. With these weapons, a religion without God had arrived.[77]

Britain took over 50,000 casualties on the first day at the Battle of the Somme. At Verdun, France and Germany lost over 500,000 lives in less than a year. The Flanders region became one of the largest graveyards on earth, with more British killed in Flanders "than the entire number of Americans killed in action during all of World War II."[78]

But it was not just technology and science that set this war apart; the thinking of the day allowed for a Modernist justification. The Darwinian struggle and a sense of ***ultimate nationalism***[79] gave license to think of war as part of an upward progression; naturalism applied to the evolutionary impulse of civilization. Speaking of the Darwinian "struggle for life" as linked to the Great War, historian Ian Ousby wrote, "it served to justify precisely the code of warrior values – disciplined brutality and disciplined sacrifice..."[80] Conflict was the norm in nature, so too the evolutionary path for Mankind was force and combat. ***Might was right***.

Helmuth von Moltke, Chief of the German General Staff from 1906 to 1914, viewed the war through this lens, as did many other Germans of his day.[81] Elites in France and Britain likewise gravitated to this perspective.[82]

Benjamin Kidd wrote, "the state of war became spoken of again among men not as a shame and a rebuke to civilization but as a state of nature."[83]

---

77 Quoted by Donovan Webster, *Aftermath: The Remnants of War* (Pantheon, 1996), p.53.

78 Winston Groom, *A Storm in Flanders*, p.260.

79 This represents the idea of one's nation being the primary source of identity and value, taking upon itself a state-based, salvific quality: "My country, right or wrong."

80 Ian Ousby, *The Road to Verdun: World War I's Most Momentous Battle and the Folly of Nationalism* (Doubleday, 2002), p.245.

81 Richard F. Hamilton and Holger H. Herwig (editors), *The Origins of World War I* (Cambridge University Press, 2003), pp.164f, 186.

82 Leonard V. Smith, Stephane Audoin-Rouzeau, and Annette Becker, *France and the Great War, 1914-1918* (Cambridge University Press, 2003), pp.58-59. See also, Ian Ousby, *The Road to Verdun*, pp.243-248.

83 Kidd, *The Science of Power*, p.12.

"The Darwinian thesis," Kidd explained, "had a remarkable effect on civilization. It presented to the masters of force in the West a conception of the world which they rendered exclusively in terms of force and struggle."

Writing during the Great War, Kidd made the following observation,

> Darwin's theories came to be openly set out in political and military textbooks as the full justification for war and highly organized schemes of national policy in which the doctrine of Force became the doctrine of Right... As the prestige of Darwinism increased and as the new ideas became entrenched in the handbooks of popular science and in systems of revolutionary criticism, it was almost as if the desert and the jungle had begun to voice themselves in human thought. The world beheld the champions of force gradually becoming again in their own right the Supermen of systems of popular philosophy. In solemn treatises of social science it saw them emerging as 'efficients'... The doctrine of the supremacy and the omnipotence of force became the doctrine of absolute Right expounded as the law of 'biological necessity'... [84]

The Great War wiped out 7000 men *per day* for 220 weeks. When the ashes and artillery barrels cooled, the world had irreversibly changed.

The six century-old Turkic-Islamic Ottoman Empire collapsed, and a reconfigured Middle East emerged under French and British control.[85] Hope for a Jewish homeland gained steam.[86] The mighty Habsburg Dynasty with its centuries of influence over central Europe was swept away. The Russian Empire, eviscerated before the War, buckled as Lenin animated Karl Marx's theories of scientific materialism and the "dictatorship of the proletariat." Inside Germany a red revolution erupted and the monarchy abdicated.[87]

---

84 Ibid., "force and struggle," p.9, "state-craft and war-craft," p.47.

85 In the spring of 1916, Britain and France – with Russia's assent – concluded a secret treaty known as the *Sykes-Picot Agreement*, set to go into effect after the war. This plan granted the British and French administrative control over great swaths of the Middle East, and allowed for the division of lands and the drawing of boundaries.

86 See Chaim Weizmann, *Trail and Error* (Harper and Brothers, 1949), chapter 16.

87 In early November 1918, Communist-backed German sailors, soldiers, and workers formed revolutionary councils and revolted. The result: "Their uprising toppled the German Empire on November 9 and brought Germany's participation in the war to an abrupt end..." See *The German Revolution and the Debate on Soviet Power: Documents,*

Historical dominoes fell, and collective political movements rose in response. Benito Mussolini introduced Fascism to Italy: "Outside of our principles there is no salvation for individuals and far less for nations."[88] Soviet Russia promised a better world through revolution: "Without revolutionary measures there can be *no* salvation."[89] The National Socialist German Worker's Party, commonly referred to as the Nazis, soon emerged with their radical worldview: *"May Reason be our leader, Will our might."*[90]

Modernity had become the midwife to the Great Evils of the 20th century. Erik von Kuehnelt-Leddihn soberly reminds us of our recent history,

> If one were to take paper and pencil to make an estimate of how many people were murdered or killed in battle because of the ideas of the French Revolution in their various stages, guises, and evolutionary forms, because of the ideas of equality, ethnic or racist identity, a 'classless society,' a 'world safe for democracy,' a 'racially pure people,' 'true social justice achieved by social engineering' – one would arrive at simply staggering sums. Even the Jewish holocaust offered by the National Socialists with five or six million dead would seem almost a drop in the bucket. There must have been at least 120 or 150 million victims, perhaps even 300 million. The victims of the French Revolution were relatively few, but sadistic bestiality had entered Western Civilization through that door...[91]

Modernity demonstrated that when mankind is reduced to a soulless animal in an accidental universe, humanity becomes expendable as Rational Man – the "scientifically" organized Party and State – *plays God.*

1918-1919 – Preparing the Founding Congress (Anchor Foundation, 1986, edited by John Riddle), p.ix. For more on the German Communist movement and the post-war German Revolution, along with the workings of international Marxism, see Jan Valtin's book, *Out of the Night* (Alliance Book Corporation, 1941).

88 Quoted by Ethan Colton, *Four Patterns of Revolution* (Association Press, 1935), p.141. Or, "All within the State, nothing outside the State, nothing against the State" (p.123).

89 V.I. Lenin, "The Proletarian Party at the District Council Elections," *Collected Works*, Volume 24 (Progress Publishers, 1964/74, and digitally reprinted in 2011), p.391, italics in original. This statement was made in early 1917, before Lenin took power in Russia, but nevertheless reflects a theme found in the broad scope of Soviet thought.

90 Adolf Hitler, *Mein Kampf* (Reynal & Hitchock, 1925/1939/1941), p.932, italics original.

91 Erik von Kuehnelt-Leddihn, *Leftism: From de Sade and Marx to Hitler and Marcuse* (Arlington House Publishers, 1970), pp.418-419.

Whittaker Chambers, a former member of the Communist Party USA, expressed something similar in a letter to his children. Revealing that the real appeal behind Marxism was not "workers of the world unite," but "philosophers have explained the world; it is necessary to change the world," Chambers penned the following,

> It is the vision of man's mind displacing God as the creative intelligence of the world. It is the vision of man's liberated mind, by the sole force of its rational intelligence, redirecting man's destiny and reorganizing man's life and the world. It is the vision of man, once more the central figure of the Creation, not because God made man in His image, but because man's mind makes him the most intelligent of the animals.[92]

Western Materialism

The war experience had a profound effect on Western society, yet most of the West did not take on the Communist persona that streamed from the long-running cracks caused by the Great War. The specter of the Red Star was a constant source of tension, and in some circles the Communist ideal made great headway, but it never ruled Western culture as it did in Russia or China. Part of the reason, I believe, is that the Christian ethos was still generally valued – holding a place in the hearts of the public, regardless of what humanists in ivory towers pontificated.

This dovetails with Peter Hitchens observation,

> If God is not dethroned and his laws not revoked, he represents an important rival to the despot's authority, living in millions of hearts. If he cannot be driven out of hearts, total control by the state is impossible. This may seem trivial to us in our secularized societies still benefiting from the freedoms that flowed from centuries of Christianity. We have forgotten how we arrived at our civilized state.[93]

Hitchens, a journalist who experienced Moscow in the final years of the Soviet Union, reminds us that early on the Marxists' brand could not be adopted in Western Europe. Why? Because the citizens were "well-informed about

[92] Whittaker Chambers, *Witness* (Regnery Publishing, 1952/1980), p.9.

[93] Hitchens, *The Rage Against God*, pp.211-212.

revolution, were too much in love with Christianity, liberty, and legality to believe in any utopia."[94] A warning for today is discernible.

For most of Western Europe, the Commonwealth nations and the United States, a softer form of Modernity played out. Instead of falling prey to the dictatorship of "scientific socialism," we followed a path of *production*. Our boast was in our accomplishments; the acceleration of mechanical *technology* instead of social *technique*. The yearning to remake humanity was masked by the desire to make *things*.

Benefits were and are obvious. A major part of human flourishing is the ability to creatively fill a material need and receive a return for the investment of labor, time, and capital. Work and reward and private property are Biblical principles, and its fruit extends our capacity for acts of utility, compassion, and creativity.[95] But a fatal flaw comes when productivity and wealth become our security and measure of success: Mammon becomes our master. We are correctly told that "where your treasure is, there your heart will be also" (Matthew 6:21). And 1 Timothy 6:9 reminds us that our desire to become rich is a temptation and snare. The attitude of our heart is telling.

Modernity revealed that attitude. We became enamored with the works of our hands and believed we could *purchase* our destiny.

However, when society constructs a God substitute we become entangled with systems of imposition. Good intentions notwithstanding, we demand the mitigation of risk and seek to take from others via *redistribution*. Government, a Biblically mandated instrument for justice, turns into an overlord as greed and the need for security drives us deeper into its arms.

In the 19th century the Western heart swelled with the greatness of our industrial and national accomplishments. We could manufacture a new Eden. Few noticed the foreshadowing of a looming, bureaucratic machinery.

This celebrated grandeur in human progress was the energy behind the great technical expositions. Starting as industrial trade fairs in the 1790s, by the 1850s such exhibitions became international showcases for science, art,

---

[94] Ibid., p.212.

[95] Some passages on work and reward: Exodus 34:21, Deuteronomy 24:14-15, Proverbs 21:20, Ecclesiastes 9:10, Colossians 3:23-24, 2 Thessalonians 3:10, and 1 Timothy 5:8. The concept of private property is visible in the Ten Commandments (Exodus 20:1-17). Howard Dayton's book, *Your Money Counts* (Crown Financial Ministries, 2007), offers important perspectives on the Biblical role of money, possessions, work, and attitude.

and the advancement of knowledge. Indeed, Britain's 1851 Great Exhibition raised the bar as a true World Fair, collecting under one roof the "industrial production… of every nation."[96]

Over the course of 164 days, six million people visited London's vast conservatory, the Crystal Palace. Under its canopy of glass, men of industry rubbed shoulders with an awe-inspired public. The marvels of Man were displayed for all to see; wonderful inventions, exotic cultural displays, and magnificent works of art. Tying this together was the meme of humanity's unifying efforts through science and industry.

Prayers to God and calls to Christian brotherhood were made during the event's ceremonies, but the underlying spirit was a confidence in materialism. Recognizing this Modernist thrust, one historian portrayed the Great Exhibition as a "secular faith in progress, and a secular faith that human beings – through their own endeavor – could improve society."[97]

Such a faith was visible during its opening: "As the clocks in the Exhibition struck nine, the gates were thrown open, and the temple of industry was, in a short space, more crowded with living beings than was ever the temple of the sun of old, in its day of dedication to idolatry."[98]

Since the Great Exhibition of 1851, international celebrations focusing on technology, culture and knowledge, national branding and human unity, have been held on a near annual basis. In 2017, Astana, Kazakhstan hosted a world Expo on *Future Energy* and in 2020, Dubai will hold its "festival of human ingenuity" with the theme: *Connecting Minds, Creating Futures*. From London to New York to Rio de Janeiro and Shanghai, World Fairs and Expos have been spectacular showcases of achievement.

The 1893 Chicago World Columbian Exposition, however, stands as extra special. Considered the opening act of the 20th century, "the greatest event of modern times,"[99] the Chicago Exposition was an undertaking of gigantic

---

96 *The Industry of Nations, as Exemplified in The Great Exhibition of 1851: The Materials of Industry* (Society for Promoting Christian Knowledge, 1852), p.21.

97 This was said during an interview on BBC Radio 4, *In Our Time*, "The Great Exhibition of 1851," broadcast on Thursday, 27 April, 2006. Archived online at www.bbc.co.uk/programmes/p003c19x

98 *The Industry of Nations, as Exemplified in The Great Exhibition of 1851*, p.157.

99 *The World's Fair, Being a Pictorial History of The Columbian Exposition* (P.D. Farrell & Company, 1893), p.3.

proportions. Its planning and construction were feats in themselves.[100] For the six-month event, approximately twenty-seven million people visited the White City, a complex of almost 200 structures built of wood-and-plaster to give the appearance of neoclassical stonework. Adorned with canals, promenades and arches and colonnades, oversized statues and castings, fountains, and thousands of exhibits – along with George Ferris' massive upright wheel moving over 2,100 people per twenty minute rotation – the Chicago "World Fair" was a modern marvel. An Art Palace, "a temple dedicated to all that is most refined and elevating in life," beaconed the worship of beauty.[101] The Manufacturing Building, measuring 1,687 feet by 787 feet, was described as the Temple of Industry. It was a testimony to the power of imagination and the will to achieve.

A materialist spirituality pulsed within the Exposition. At the same time, classical cultic imagery was on display: Greco-Roman goddesses, the Hawaiian Goddess of Fire, and a distinctly American divinity – a 65-foot statue called *The Republic*, "an American goddess… with golden hair, clothed in shimmering draperies and by night a halo of stars around her head."[102] In one hand she held a globe with an eagle resting on it, in the other was a staff "crowned by a Phrygian cap, a symbol of the French Revolution."[103]

Special congresses were convened on technical and social topics: civil law and government, the insurance industry, public health, chemistry, banking and profit sharing, and more. Electrical lighting was a highlight, and for the first time the public was able to see Hollerith tabulators, the precursor to large computation machines and, much later, the personal computer.[104] A lavish feast of innovation and production was set before the world, the likes of which had never been seen before.

The 1893 Exposition unquestionably elevated the public mood for material capacity. A new and exhilarating age was dawning: *Consumerism*. Our personal sense of security, value and identity became increasingly wrapped

---

[100] A popular overview of the Chicago Exposition is Erik Larson's *The Devil in the White City: Murder, Magic, and Madness at the Fair that Changed America* (Vintage, 2004).

[101] Ibid., p.283.

[102] See the Landmark Designation Report, *Statue of the Republic: Jackson Park at Hayes and Richards Drs* (Dept. of Planning and Development, City of Chicago, 2002), p.6.

[103] A scaled-down model of the statue was erected afterwards, without the Phrygian cap.

[104] For more on tabulators at the Exposition, see David Alan Grier, *When Computers Where Human* (Princeton University Press, 2005), pp.96-101.

in our products. Likewise, our sense of national importance was mirrored in our ability to achieve on a grand scale.

For the consuming West, Modernity screamed of Man's industrial might; from the Empire State Building to the *Titanic* and the Hoover Dam. Along the way, man-made lighting illuminated the darkness, and distance was diminished with the telegraph and telephone. Steam power was applied to ships and rails, and then the internal combustion engine revolutionized everything again. Gravity was overcome, and eventually the bounds of Earth itself were breached.

Admiring the feat of carving the Panama Canal, travel writer Richard Halliburton wrote: "One has the feeling that this is the work of gods, not men."[105]

Divine sentimentality was exhibited with the splitting of the atom and the Space Age.[106] It was visible in the "scientific management" of manufacturing, prescribed by Frederick Taylor and Henry Ford. In his book, *My Philosophy of Industry*, Ford's first chapter was titled "Machinery, the New Messiah."

Such a faith would need its own priests and popes and clerics devoted to the vision. It would need doctrines, edicts, and regulations to affect values and behavior. And it would need community response – participation in the materialist dream. We would worship with our wallets.

If the Western materialist society was going to work as a well-oiled instrument, it would need to be managed. This was a lesson taken from the Great War. Visionaries of the day looked upon the techniques of wartime planning as the "way of the future." Historian William Akin offers the following context in his treatise, *Technocracy and the American Dream,*

> By the end of World War I a cluster of 'progressive' ideas about technology and the industrial state, planning and expertise, efficiency and social engineering had become current... Progressives tended to see centralized direction as the only method of abolishing the economic hardships and class conflict associated with industrialization,

---

[105] Richard Halliburton, *New Worlds to Conquer* (The Bobbs-Merrill Company, 1929), p.128. Halliburton is the only person to swim the canal *and* lock system, requiring him to legally register as an ocean vessel: *S.S. Richard Halliburton*. For being a "ship" and using the locks, he had to pay the calculated tonnage fee of thirty-six cents.

[106] Re: Atom splitting – see David F. Noble, *The Religion of Technology* (Penguin Books, 1999), p.107. Re: Space age – see Marina Benjamin, *Rocket Dreams: How the Space Age Shaped Our Vision of a World Beyond* (Free Press, 2003).

> of achieving social justice, and of assuring that the industrial machine met the needs of society. Planning required the use of experts who alone possessed the professional training, technical skills, and scientific rationality to understand the complex modern industrial machine. Rational planning demanded that experts be freed from partisan politics in order to bring their ideologically neutral rationality and efficient scientific methods to bear on the engineering of social problems.[107]

Efficiency and cooperation became buzz words. Technical agencies would thus be organized around industries, natural resources, and the needs of the nation. Planning and research councils were established, foundations and institutions gave experts a platform, study groups and advisory committees shaped government priorities, and bureaus – armed with the latest data and legislative decisions – enforced regulations in order to reach social and economic targets. Risk in all forms must be mitigated, and competition would be guided by well-intentioned administrators. Free-enterprise was thus bent to the forces of planning.[108] *Nothing can be left to chance*: "A craving for control beats in the collective heart of mankind."[109]

Political scientist, James C. Scott, captured the mood in his book, *Seeing Like A State*: "Order and harmony that once seemed the function of a unitary God had been replaced by a similar faith in the idea of progress vouchsafed by scientists, engineers, and planners."[110] And a faith it was and *is*.

Technocracy, a belief that engineers must direct society for maximum efficiency – supplanting politicians if needed, and forming a new economy around energy use – was a popular notion from 1900 to the early 1940s. Committees and alliances to lobby for a technocracy popped up in Canada, England, and the United States.[111] The Soviet Union had technocratic aspi-

---

[107] William E. Akin, *Technocracy and the American Dream* (University of California Press, 1977), pp.4-5.

[108] When a nation attempts to juggle free-enterprise and socialist planning at the same time it is known as a "mixed economy."

[109] William J. Haga and Nicholas Acocella, *Haga's Law*, p.33.

[110] James C. Scott, *Seeing Like a State: How Certain Schemes to Improve the Human Condition Have Failed* (Yale University Press, 1998), p.342.

[111] An important study of American technocracy and its connection to global management is Patrick M. Wood, *Technocracy Rising: The Trojan Horse of Global Transformation* (Coherent Publishing, 2015). For an older overview of the technocratic mindset, see John

rations, for Lenin himself believed the final revolutionary phase would see the political state replaced by technical managers.[112] Nazi Germany also had a strong technocratic element in its ranks.[113] And in the early 1930s, technocrat and progressive, Stuart Chase, showed affinity to dictatorial regimes as models for the scientific management of America.[114] To Progressives, the Soviet system offered a glimmer of hope.

A line from the 1936 movie, *Things to Come*, based on H.G. Wells' book by the same name, gives us a glimpse into the technocratic mindset: "[We're] the brotherhood of efficiency, the Freemasonry of science. We're the last trustees of civilization when everything else has failed."

The message was clear: *Your salvation is found in the cult of experts.*

Writing on the history of technocratic planning, W.H.G. Armytage recounts the growth of British "scientific service" committees attached to government ministries: "The number of specialist advisory committees increased from 200 in 1939 to 700 by 1949, and to 850 by 1958."[115]

L. Reed, *The Newest Whore of Babylon: The Emergence of Technocracy – A Study in the Mechanization of Man* (Branden Press, 1975). On the history of the American technocrat movement, see William E. Akin, *Technocracy and the American Dream: The Technocrat Movement, 1900-1941* (University of California Press, 1977). And on technocracy as a social meta-movement, see W.H.G. Armytage, *The Rise of the Technocrats: A Social History* (Routledge and Kegan Paul, 1965). Works by technocrat thinkers: Thorstein Veblen, *The Engineers and the Price System* (Batoche Books, 2001, originally published in 1921); *Technocracy Study Course* (Technocracy Inc., 1945, fifth edition); Harold Loeb, *Life in a Technocracy: What It Might Be Like* (Syracuse University Press, 1933/1996); and, Graham A. Laing, *Towards Technocracy* (The Angelus Press, 1933).

[112] V.I. Lenin, *State and Revolution* (International Publishers, 1917/1969), pp.42-44. For an academic study on the technocratic shift in the Soviet Union, see Don K. Rowney, *Transition to Technocracy: The Structural Origins of the Soviet Administrative State* (Cornell University Press, 1999).

[113] See Monika Renneberg and Mark Walker (editors), *Science, Technology and National Socialism* (Cambridge University Press, 1994); Albert Speer, *Infiltration: How Heinrich Himmler Schemed to Build an SS Industrial Empire* (Macmillan Publishing, 1981); and, Gotz Aly and Susanne Heim, *Architects of Annihilation: Auschwitz and the Logic of Destruction* (Princeton University Press, 2002). For the disturbing role of punch cards and Nazi technocratic designs connected to the Jewish holocaust, see Edwin Black, *IBM and the Holocaust: The Strategic Alliance Between NAZI Germany and America's Most Powerful Corporation* (Crown Publishers, 2001).

[114] Stuart Chase, *Men and Machines* (The Macmillan Company, 1929), pp.346-348; and, *A New Deal*, chapter 8.

[115] Armytage, *The Rise of the Technocrats*, p.278.

The United States witnessed a surge in projects dedicated to social management. Franklin Delano Roosevelt's "New Deal" had a foundation in technocratic thinking.[116] Its intellectual father, Stuart Chase, understood the broader theme of efficiently controlling the consumer machine. To Chase, non-conforming individualism was "a cancer," and capitalism would give way to a scientific economy as investors existed only to serve the nation,

> The state, despite the hard names you habitually apply to it, is your spiritual father; that Zeus whose final word is law even among gods. The state is the embodiment of the whole community, and its rule of action, in theory at least, 'the public interest.'[117]

Chase openly wished for a revolution to remake America into a technocracy. Comparing the Red and Black roads of total power – the Communist and the Fascist paths – he suggested a "third way," an American version where *technique* would dictate economic and social life. "Basically it is the road of science," he wrote. To Chase, the "new regime" would proscribe its economic system "by firing squad if necessary."[118]

> I am not seriously alarmed by the sufferings of the creditor class, the troubles which the church is bound to encounter, the restrictions on certain kinds of freedom which must result, nor even the bloodshed of the transition period. A better economic order is worth a little bloodshed.[119]

Follow and support the new technocratic planners, he exhorted in his influential book, *A New Deal*: "Watch them. They will bear watching. If occasion arises, join them." Chase closed with these words, "Why should Russians have all the fun of remaking a world?"[120]

FDR's New Deal never carried through to the extent Chase hoped, but it introduced a well-intended program, Social Security. In the process, however, a Modernist outcome emerged: *Everyone became a number*. And decade after decade we have added more organizing structures; more rules, more requirements, more numbers.

---

[116] Ibid., p.240.

[117] See Stuart Chase, *A New Deal*, page 221 for the topic of investors.

[118] Ibid., on "road to science" see p.179-180, on "firing squad" see p.163.

[119] Ibid., p.156.

[120] Ibid., p.252.

In the early 1960s, Columbia University professor, Amitai Etzioni, remarked that "Modern society is to a large degree a bureaucratic society... The most powerful social units which make up modern society are bureaucracies."[121]

Certainly we must operate with law and order. I do not deny this, nor would I wish to live otherwise. But we have moved far from the transcendent nature of *true law*, which supersedes class distinctions and generations, remaining anchored in a reality that surpasses politics. In the West this was the Ten Commandments, which gave us liberty with responsibility.

In the technically managed society, however, law is replaced with *regulation*. The result is a constant state of flux as new approaches are necessary to modify public and private behavior. "Rules," therefore, change with cultural whims and lobbying pressures and the never ending demands of political bureaucracy. It is the soft-Modernist machinery of the West. Everything needs to be ordered and categorized; everything must be numbered, even as the regulations themselves are counted in the tens of thousands.

For example, at the end of 2016 the US *Federal Register* – a listing of regulations and notices added or amended by the federal government – topped out at 97,110 pages *for that year alone*.[122] This number does not include the mountain of state, city, municipal and county regulations, nor the multitude of other rules and codes we regularly bind ourselves with. And everywhere it is the same: The hallmark of Western civilization is micro-management.

We have become saturated in the numerical organization of life, from birth to school to profession to grave. But it makes sense. When naturalism is our basis for reality and scientific materialism our source of authority, when consumerism becomes our purpose and product our identity, then what is Man but a number?

Humanity simply turns into another *thing* to be engineered, another statistic to be catalogued. We become a human resource.

Modernity in the West celebrated the building of great and marvelous things, but it did something to the soul.

---

[121] Amitai Etzioni (editor), *Complex Organization: A Sociological Reader* (Holt, Rinehart and Winston, 1961), p.257. Responding to problem of self and society, Etzioni fashioned a Communitarian approach in the 1980s and later created The Communitarian Network. Currently he is the Director of the Institute for Communitarian Policy Studies at George Washington University.

[122] Office of Federal Register, *Federal Register*, Vol. 81, Num. 251, December 30, 2016.

Worshiping Man

For all the talk of rationalism and naturalism and the end of Christianity, Modernity revealed the inescapability of religion. Reject the transcendent God who created the universe, and humanity worships itself. We fashion a "God substitute" formed in the image of what we think is best.

In 1872, Winwood Reade celebrated this exalted humanity in his book, *The Martyrdom of Man*, which made him famous as a freethinker,

> Thus Man has taken into his service, and modified to his use, the animals and plants, the earths and stones, the waters and the winds... By means of his inventions and discoveries, by means of his arts and trades, by means of the industry resulting from them, he has raised himself from the condition of a serf to the condition of a lord. His triumph, indeed, is incomplete; his kingdom is not yet come... Earth, which is now a purgatory, will be made a paradise, not by idle prayers and supplications, but by the efforts of man himself... When we have ascertained, by means of Science, the method of nature's operations, we shall be able to take her place and perform them for ourselves. When we understand the laws which regulate the complex phenomena of life, we shall be able to predict the future...
>
> Hunger and starvation will then be unknown... Population will mightily increase, and the earth will be a garden. Governments will be conducted with the quietude and regularity of club committees. The interest which is now felt in politics will be transferred to science... Not only will Man subdue the forces of evil that are without; he will also subdue those that are within... he will obey the laws that are written in his heart; he will worship the divinity within him... Man then will be perfect; he will then be a creator; he will therefore be what the vulgar worship as a god.[123]

And we will glorify in power. That "God is Love" is illusionary, said Reade. The "Book of Nature" teaches something else, something more fitting with the Darwinian impulse of evolutionary survival: "Murder is the law of Growth. Life is one long tragedy; creation is one great crime."[124]

---

[123] Winwood Reade, *The Martyrdom of Man* (Trubner & Company, 1887, twelfth edition), pp.512-515.

[124] Ibid., pp.519-520.

"There is only One Man upon earth" explained Reade, "what we call men are not individuals but components; what we call death is merely the bursting of a cell; wars and epidemics are merely inflammatory phenomena incident on certain stages of growth…"[125]

It is in such cruelty that the Temple of Man could be erected,

> If we take the life on a single atom, that is to say of a single man, or if we look only at a single group, all appears to be cruelty and confusion; but when we survey mankind as One, we find it becoming more and more noble, more and more divine, slowly ripening towards perfection.[126]

"Supernatural Christianity is false," Reade penned. "God-worship is idolatry. Prayer is useless. The soul is not immortal…"[127]

The spiritual heartbeat of secular Man, what Julian Huxley – the grandson of Thomas Huxley – once proposed as a "religion without revelation," throbbed and longed for the day when Christianity would finally die,

> It is obvious that any religion which lays primary emphasis on salvation in the next world will be something of an obstacle towards getting the best out of this world as speedily as possible… Once we have rid ourselves of this doctrine of a Divine Power external to ourselves, we can get busy with the real task of dealing with our inner forces.[128]

Although Huxley was critical of all "supernatural religions," his antagonism was directed toward Christianity with its "mental disease" of sin and "belief in personal supernatural beings." The coming "religion without revelation" would have no need for such Christian hang-ups. Instead, our search for meaning and authority and purpose would emerge from the illumined minds of humanist thinkers, poets, philosophers, and historians,

> *The Origin of Species* is to-day a good deal more profitable as theology than the first chapter of Genesis, and William James's *Principles of Psychology* will be a better commentary on the Decalogue

[125] Ibid., p.522.
[126] Ibid., p.522.
[127] Ibid., p.523.
[128] Julian Huxley, *Religion Without Revelation* (Watts & Company, 1941/1945), p.vii.

> than any hortatory sermon... Trevelyan's *History of England* is likely to be a more salutary history lesson, because nearer home, than the historical books of the Old Testament; Whitehead's *Science and the Modern World* is more likely to help the perplexed mind of a twentieth-century Englishman than the apocalyptic visions of Revelation or the neo-Platonic philosophy of the Fourth Gospel; to sacrifice a score of Sundays to making acquaintance with the ideas of other great religions like Buddhism would be very much preferable, even from the purely religious point of view, to continuance in the familiar round and the familiar narrowness of one's own church.[129]

Christian beliefs, Huxley explained, "need to be destroyed like other idols."[130]

Modernity did not crush that "infamous thing." But it did give rise to spiritual secularism, that "religion without revelation" – our faith in naturalism and collectivism and science. And along the way we formed codes and creeds and rituals, fashioned false messiahs, and elevated atheism and materialism to a new theology. We even sacrificed others to appease the gods made in our image. Matter became deified.

"Science is being daily more and more personified and anthropomorphised into a god," acknowledged the Victorian-era novelist, Samuel Butler. "By and by they will say that science took our nature upon him, and sent down his only begotten son, Charles Darwin, or Huxley, into the world so that those who believe in him, etc."[131]

Industry and science, the material achievements of Modernity, brought great blessings and curses. But Modernity did more. It realigned our thinking to accept a secular paganism: *Man is the measure of all things, therefore Man is God.*

Woe unto us.

---

[129] Ibid., pp.79-80.

[130] Ibid., pp.103-104.

[131] Samuel Butler, *The Note-Books of Samuel Butler* (E.P. Dutton and Comp., 1917), p. 339.

Chapter 5

Fuzzy Daze

> Our age is characterized by non-meaning. – Jacques Ellul.[1]
>
> 'What's right is what feels right,' has no basis for personal ethics, much less a foundation for a free society. – Lloyd Billingsley.[2]

Epic music was cued to an iconic scene of Washington DC. A panoply of psychologically stimulating images met the viewer's eyes; satellites and data downloads, marching soldiers, explosions and doors being kicked-in, drones, and spooky government agents.

"Like yourself," a serious voice intoned, "I'm a true believer."

The official video trailer for the 2016 release of the revamped FOX television show, *The X-Files*, was a tantalizing promise of mystery and shadows. As the trailer concluded, the words that flashed across millions of TV screens during the last decade of the 20th century came to life, but with one small twist: "The Truth... Is *Still*... Out There..."

If ever a television program epitomized Postmodernism, it was the hit series *The X-Files*. Opening each episode was the haunting tagline that, in 1993 when it originally aired, hinted at deeper questions lurking beneath the surface: *The Truth is Out There*. To the post-modern mind the truth may be "out there" in a taunting sort of way, but it is incapable of being discovered through the Christian message or the authority paradigm of Modernity.

The X-Files was, in many respects, the quintessential program of the Questioning Age. It was critical of establishment institutions, mistrustful of government, wary of scientific certainty, and agnostic to religion. Introspective

---

1 Jacques Ellul, *The Ethics of Freedom* (William B. Eerdmans Publishing Company, 1976), p.461.

2 Lloyd Billingsley, *The Absence of Tyranny: Recovering Freedom in Our Time* (Multnomah Press, 1986), p.35.

enquiries regarding "belief" and "faith" persistently played out between the main actors. Show after show blurred the lines between science and religion and philosophy. Even the roles of the characters – FBI Special Agents Fox Mulder and Dana Scully – often reversed or blended. Aesthetically moody, the images and scripting touched a nerve with a generation raised to believe "you can be anything you want to be," yet unsure of ***believability***.

Similar to other law-and-crime programs, cases would be solved and investigations wrapped up, but a disproportionate number of shows left the audience hanging. The drama would come to an end, but nagging uncertainties often remained: "I guess we'll never know" was a standard line. Unsolvable mysteries fed the imagination.

Around the perplexing scenarios swirled other questions: What is the meaning of life? Are we alone in the universe? Is there a God? Can truth be known? While Mulder and Skully were investigating crimes, searching for ***what is true***, their experiences inevitably bumped into those looming thoughts of ultimate reality. Always, the big answers remained aloof. Final authority, true meaning, and life-purpose dangled just beyond reach.

Pondering Postmodernism

Today, we find ourselves steeped in the post-modern environment, even as Modernity remains entrenched in scientific philosophy and is actively promoted via the New Atheists.[3]

Postmodernism, better labeled as Postmodernity[4] – but we will stick to the more popular expression – is a mindset and cultural mood that can be difficult to describe. Debate swirls over what it is, how it manifests, and where it could be going. A variety of thought exists behind the label. Defining Postmodernism has been likened to "nailing jelly to a wall."

---

3 The New Atheists are those intellectuals who have played a major role in contemporary atheism: Richard Dawkins, Sam Harris, Daniel Dennett, and Christopher Hitchens. These authors became famously known as the "Four Horsemen" after an informal table-talk took place between them in September, 2007. This conversation was recorded and then released for public purchase under the title, *The Four Horsemen*.

4 Postmodernism is the more popular way of expressing the age after Modernity, and the term is often used interchangeably with Postmodernity. However, there are differences. Properly considered, Postmodernism is a form of artistic and literary criticism in response to Modernity's interpretation. Postmodernity, on the other hand, is equated with a social condition that questions and/or opposes Modernity's authority claims.

Upfront, I believe Postmodernism is a transitional phase. It is true that Postmodernism powerfully exhibits itself in today's culture, especially as a mask for ideologically driven politics, but an eclipsing process is observable in the search for a new meaning.

Fundamentally, Postmodernism was and is a *reaction to* and *rejection of* foundational truth claims and the narratives supporting them – first in terms of Modernity, but also the assertions of Christian revelation. Biblical doctrine had been overshadowed by materialist dogma, but now both were being pushed aside. How truth was measured and considered by other generations no longer applied. Past approaches were and are viewed as too narrow and associated with *oppression*, linking knowledge with power and the placing of gatekeepers to bar the way for others. Therefore, historical truth claims remain as *claim only* and are treated with suspicion. Grand narratives and their related worldviews are no longer relevant to the post-modern mind.

We are left with questions but no defining answers, and no tangible framework to develop a coherent worldview.

The slope immediately becomes slippery. Judgments resting on previously held truth claims melt away. History fades into oblivion. The meaning of language bends. Tolerance *without definition* becomes the new norm. Inclusion and broad interpretations represent the progressive path, and personal transformation means conforming to ever changing cultural cues. Traditional standards are diluted as society attempts to scrub out reminders of "privileged" exclusivity. What was once virtuous is vilified, and what was morally shameful is celebrated. Truth and falsehood are no longer discernible, and what is known to be factual becomes blurred and distorted – including biology, identity, and sexuality. Higher values are lost in the fuzzy daze of a wandering culture. Does this sound like today?

In such a milieu there is an almost irresistible pull to elevate *self*. Certainly, self-actualization and experiments in self-identity are lauded within the post-modern context. Our personal reality is fashioned in the image of our felt needs. The psychological cult of *Selfism*, a "form of secular humanism based on worship of the self,"[5] attempts to fill the vacuum of lost value. Yes, mankind has always struggled with pride and hubris, but Selfism elevates vice to virtue and packages it as illumined personal discovery. Selfism,

[5] Paul C. Vitz, *Psychology as Religion: The Cult of Self-Worship* (William B. Eerdmans Publishing Company, 1977), p.9.

a product of the human potential movement, feeds our desire for meaning while stroking our ego. The Self rises as a divine spark. We are *each* divine selves, masters of destiny and voices of self-authority.

This is manifestly different from the Christian approach to the individual. Stanly Grenz, author of *A Primer on Postmodernism*, reminds us that the Biblical position recognizes "God's concern for each person, the responsibility of every human before God, and the individual orientation that lies within the salvation message."[6] It was also different than Modernity with its tendency to integrate the person into state-directed systems of meaning. The cult of Selfism, rather, is a "horizontal heresy, with its emphasis only on the present, and on self-centered ethics."[7]

And how could this not be? For decades, public education and mental health services have washed our brains in the "holy waters" of the human potential movement: the theories of Erich Fromm, Carl Rogers, and Abraham Maslow.[8] Following Sigmund Freud's guilt-based theory of human development and B.F. Skinner's behavioral models, Maslow's teachings on self-actualization – the "third force" in psychology – saturated Western thinking. From the experiential encounters at the Esalen Institute[9] to your neighborhood clinic, from daytime television to church pulpits, the feel-good mantra of Selfism rang across the land: "Express thyself, Accept thyself, and Esteem thyself."[10]

---

6 Stanley J. Grenz, *A Primer on Postmodernism* (William B. Eerdmans Publishing Company, 1996), pp.167-168.

7 Vitz, *Psychology as Religion*, pp.95-96.

8 Erich Fromm celebrated humanity's independence from God and described Man as intrinsically good. Carl Rogers focused on experiencing oneself and encouraged therapists to sense what client's feel. The highest ideal of the self is for the person to become unified as an experiential flow or movement. Maslow introduced a hierarchy of felt human needs and believed that the greatest achievement was an enlightened self-actualization.

9 The Esalen Institute was a primary vehicle for Gestalt techniques in whole-person self awareness, and was an important point of contact for Maslow's human potential movement. Educators, psychologists, cultural leaders, and clergy from liberal churches would gather at Esalen in the 1960s and 1970s, looking to experientially raise personal consciousness, advance self-awareness, explore alternative religious practices, and engage in sexual discovery. See Marion Goldman, *The American Soul Rush: Esalen and the Rise of Spiritual Privilege* (New York University Press, 2012).

10 Christina Hoff Sommers and Sally Satel, *One Nation Under Therapy: How the Helping Culture is Eroding Self-Reliance* (St. Martin's Press, 2005), p.56.

In an eerie symbiosis the celebrated Self and the materialistic consumer walk hand-in-hand. We line up for the hottest deals on Black Friday and then, armed with our wireless devices, proclaim moral indignation and denounce the "evils of corporations." A universe of selfies are snapped with our smartphones and posted on social media. Seated in the third row of the concert hall we watch the live-performance through a three-inch wide screen, digitally capturing the experience of "being there" while living through our technology. We are consumed with the image itself. We are the symbol of our things.

A fitting analysis was given over two decades before Web 2.0 existed,

> Selfist psychology emphasizes the human capacity for change to the point of almost totally ignoring the idea that life has limits and that knowledge of them is the basis of wisdom. For selfists there seem to be no acceptable duties, denials, inhibitions, or restraints. Instead, there are only rights and opportunities for change. An overwhelming number of the selfists assume that there are no unvarying moral or interpersonal relationships, no permanent aspects to individuals. All is written in sand by a self in flux.[11]

But the need for a connection to something larger, a foundation of truth, tugs at the human heart. Where do we turn now that we have rejected a relationship with the transcendent Creator? And in rightly criticizing the application of naturalism to society, we distanced ourselves from the suffocating structures of Modernity. With what now will we clothe ourselves?

We stand naked and we know it.

Relativism, therefore, becomes our covering, and subjective social markers and experiences act as our guide. Because of this we constantly seek reinforcing "safe spaces" with others who share similar sentiments – an "organic community" – a location, flexible in orientation to meet our changing convictions, where we can emulate each other and call this truth.

Stanley J. Grenz put it this way,

> The postmodern worldview operates with a community-based understanding of truth. It affirms that whatever we accept as truth and even the way we envision truth are dependent on the commu-

---

[11] Vitz, *Psychology as Religion*, p.38.

> nity in which we participate. Further, and far more radically, the postmodern worldview affirms that this relativity extends beyond our perceptions of truth to its essence: there is no absolute truth; rather, truth is relative to the community in which we participate.[12]

Truth is discovered through personal experience as you *feel* yourself part of a culturally transforming group, and identity and meaning exist in social emotions and sub-cultural expressions. Everyone becomes a back-seat driver as we navigate by social consensus. What else could there be if the other ways to measure truth are no longer accepted?

Reality, therefore, is what we *encounter* and can only be *subjective*, for each person experiences differently. No wonder history becomes an object of question, truth ever changing, morality moveable, definitions indefinable, and language remade to fit the fads of the day. This is to be expected when our convictions are dictated by our emotions, and our feelings conditioned by the loudest mob – itself moved by voices of influence. However, if *you* challenge the mob, watch out! Since everyone is a backseat driver on the road to some indefinable destiny, you will be shouted out of the car.

In our age of fuzzy thinking, truth is defined by sub-cultures pushing an agenda. Hence, the post-modern claim of being untainted by "narratives of power" is artificial.

"While postmodernism did open a larger space for cultural critique," explains Christian academic Mary Poplin, "in its purest form it is the ultimate rejection of any universal story that connects us to one another and to the world (metanarrative). There can be no truth claims, except of course this one."[13]

Postmodernism thus sets up its own gatekeepers.

Not unlike Modernity, "Post-modern Man" still views himself as behind the steering wheel of destiny, moving civilization down the road of progress. There is a difference, however. During late Modernity, political and technocratic elites obsessed over subsuming individual autonomy into a narrow and technical efficiency. Postmodernism loses this flavor of a *tightly closed order*, but the desire for transformation and unity is nevertheless invoked.

---

12 Grenz, *A Primer on Postmodernism*, p.8.

13 Mary Poplin, *Is Reality Secular? Testing the Assumptions of Four Global Worldviews* (IVP Books, 2014), p.134.

Tolerance-in-diversity is the song, and the dance of harmony is found in the acceptance of accelerating changes.

This does not mean the authority systems of the past have disappeared. Political influence remains a compelling force in the post-modern environment – a reality in every age – and today's information technologies have lured and pushed us into the arms of Big Data.[14] Our world is wrapped in a web of technocratic governance,[15] demonstrating the ongoing influence of modernist structuring. But the post-modern mind is nudged by something more emotional – the *narratives* of special interests groups, often with goals embodying cultural leftism.[16] Moreover, these narratives are powerfully leveraged in political circles, resulting in office holders catering to and often running on socially approved messages.

Voices of special interests associated with the post-modern mood now represent the sentinels of civilization. After deconstructing traditional "narratives of oppression," these new gatekeepers issue social license, energize "grassroots" movements, enable political actors, and establish networks of new privilege. Political correctness is their assertion of moral authority, and for you to question or criticize the *correct narrative* is to court disaster. Disagree with the powerful LGBTQ[17] meme and you might lose your job or have your business boycotted, or worse. Offer a public criticism of Islam's

---

[14] Big Data is a term used to describe the accumulation and acceleration of mass data collection, both structured and unstructured, through social media, online purchases, and a host of other interconnected mediums.

[15] A contemporary overview of technocratic-based global governance can be found in *Technocracy Rising: The Trojan Horse of Global Transformation*, by Patrick M. Wood (Coherent Publishing, 2015).

[16] The list of post-modern special interests seems to grow daily: LGBTQ demands (Lesbian, Gay, Bisexual, Trans and Questioning), anthropogenic global warming, a long list of *environmental justice* issues, wealth redistribution and massive taxation of the 1%, official gender parity, a myriad of social justice concerns, animal rights, demands for free college tuition, legalizing marijuana, mandated "safe space" zones on college campuses, radical feminism, sanctioned religious tolerance, and a host of other demands and sub-narratives under the heading of human rights (sadly, real human rights issues have often been overshadowed by social agendas masked in human rights language). Usually lurking behind the social/political curtain is a reaction against conservative values and past-norms of morality; traditional families, free-enterprise economics, Christian-identified individual autonomy, and commodity-based industries – energy, agriculture, forestry, fishing, mining, etc.

[17] LGBTQ: Lesbian, Gay, Bisexual, Trans and Questioning.

prophet Mohammad or challenge the inroad of Sharia law, and you may be facing a Human Rights Commission. Are you a politician or noted personality who disputes the doctrine of "manmade global warming"? Be on guard, some public figures think you should be criminally prosecuted.[18]

Gender differences? Depending on the source there are 3, 6, 58, or possibly 63 different gender expressions to be celebrated. At the same time we are told that the *idea* of male and female is just a social construct, a hang-on from a bygone era. Today we find ourselves in a contradicting world of limitless possibilities, even as we scramble to erase distinctions. Of course, the animal kingdom operates in a male-female binary. We, however, are at war with all forms of otherness. *Never mind what is natural or factual.*

Transgender pronouns? The New York City Commission on Human Rights stated the following in a 2015 Legal Enforcement document: "Some transgender and gender non-conforming people prefer to use pronouns other than he/him/his or she/her/hers, such as they/them/theirs or ze/hir." If you have a business or rental property in New York City and transgress the "preferred pronouns," you could receive a hefty fine: "The Commission can impose civil penalties up to $125,000 for violations, and up to $250,000 for violations that are the result of willful, wanton, or malicious conduct."[19]

Thought crimes? Cultural gatekeepers? Penalties for pronouns?

A heavy blanket of political correctness smothers Western civilization. Postmodernism, which forces us to embrace opposites in the quest for illusionary meaning, descends into absurdity. Consider a personal example.

One of my friends was looking at university options in the province of Ontario. He sent letters of admission to different schools, listing his credentials

---

[18] David Suzuki, a leading voice in Canada on environmental issues, called for the imprisonment of former Prime Minister, Stephen Harper. *Rolling Stone* magazine, February 2016, Australian ed., (http://rollingstoneaus.com/culture/post/david-suzuki-encounter/3089). Robert F. Kennedy, Jr., son of "Bobby" Kennedy, made similar statements regarding petroleum executives and politicians who have sold out the "public trust" by denying manmade climate change. See Craig Bannister, "RFK, Jr.: Climate Skeptics 'Should Be at the Hague with All the Other War Criminals'." *CNS News*, September 22, 2014 (www.cnsnews.com/mrctv-blog/craig-bannister/rfk-jr-climate-skeptics-should-be-hague-all-other-war-criminals).

[19] *NYC Commission on Human Rights Legal Enforcement Guidance on the Discrimination on the Basis of Gender Identity or Expression* (New York City Commission on Human Rights, December 21, 2015, as pursuant to Local Law No.3, 2002; NYC Admin. Code § 8-102[23]), pp.4, 10.

and background, including a Masters Degree from a distinguished American institution. After receiving a less than enthusiastic reply from one particular school, he decided to try the same university again, but with a more socially conscious approach. He drafted and sent a letter of fiction: A one-page note dripping with an over-the-top tale of politically correct feelings, aspirations, and felt needs. Saturated with buzz-phrases and entirely made-up words that sounded culturally plausible, the last sentence closed to the effect of *I'll be the bearded person on campus wearing a dress*.

The reply from the school was acceptance! The door swings open when you are perceived as exemplifying the celebrated narrative.

My friend chose a different university.

Percolating Change

The forces of thought and culture that brought about this change in social attitude are multifaceted. That being the case, we need to briefly consider a few of the early road markers that pointed to the post-modern shift. In so doing we can better learn to discern the patterns of today and the trajectory of tomorrow.

Fine Art:

The revolutionary development of Modern art, a complex subject with "a bewildering list of isms,"[20] served as a vanguard to the post-modern setting. It pointed to something important; the internal struggle for meaning and the search for value. In this way fine art acted as a warning bell sounding over the rolling waves of culture.

A storm was brewing in the Modern mind.

Art is an important aspect of what it means to be human. It is an intentional and creative integration of movement and emotion, an aesthetic experience in which the thinker is expressively connected to the medium – it may be beautiful, but it does not need to be so. Moreover, the artisan is energized by an inward passion and need for outward release. There is a drive to create at a conceptual level, but art is more than that; it is a way of asking questions and exploring thoughts, allowing for and encouraging introspection

20 As described by Advanced Placement art teacher, Mary McConnell, in her online lecture, *Expressionism*, published on YouTube (https://youtu.be/DKnRrhYOsJY), March 26, 2014.

and analysis. It is a search for perception. Because of this, fine art communicates indwelling values and acts to interpret and convey presuppositions in three fundamental areas: humanity, nature, and God.

Peter Conrad, in his critique of religious themes within classical art, wrote that "any investigation of art has to ponder the notion of God's creation, although it will probably soon reach its own heterodox conclusions."[21]

Fine art historian H.R. Rookmaaker offers this worldview insight while discussing the work of Jan van Goyen,

> Those who think that a painting must be a copy of nature to be realistic are mistaken: art never copies nature, but always portrays reality in a human way. That means that this painting does not copy nature as a camera would, but depicts a human experience, a human understanding, an insight and emotion into what the truth about reality is. It speaks in an artistic way about reality, as have all paintings ever made.[22]

American architect Louis Kahn once penned, "Art is the making of a life."[23]

Sadly, the thoughtful participation of Christians – particularly evangelical believers – within the broader discussion of fine art is lacking. We have long ignored this essential aspect of humanity's special-creation, and in so doing, diminished our voice.[24]

Art is also a barometer revealing latent pressures behind cultural and intellectual change. Knowing this intimately, Rookmaaker lamented, "Too many have bypassed modern art with a shrug of the shoulder, failing to see that it is one of the keys to an understanding of our times."[25]

By the end of the 19th and into the 20th century, what is known as Modern art underwent a revolution as painters and sculptors wrestled with questions of meaning and aesthetic criticism. Realism, a style depicted through the

---

[21] Peter Conrad, *Creation: Artists, Gods and Origins* (Thames and Hudson, 2007), p.15.

[22] H.R. Rookmaaker, *Modern Art and the Death of a Culture* (Inter-Varsity Press, 1973/1978), p.21.

[23] Louis I. Kahn, "Architecture," *On the Future of Art* (The Viking Press, 1970), p.34.

[24] Rookmaaker suggests, "It could well be that the arts are indeed 'avant-garde' – in the sense that they are ahead of the rest in the quest for a non-Christian way of spirituality. Why? Because for so long Christians have taken no part in artistic discussion or activity." H.R. Rookmaaker, *Modern Art and the Death of a Culture*, p.32.

[25] Rookmaaker, *Modern Art and the Death of a Culture*, p.135.

lens of naturalism, attempted to portray life in a humanistic truthfulness; communicating only what could be seen by the eye of the painter, often rendering a photo-like illustration of ordinary existence. Missing was the depth of drama, the themes of grandeur and higher meaning. Life is more than just three men meeting on a road, or girls sifting grain.[26]

Other styles followed as artists explored colors and shapes and textures in new ways. Perceptions of reality were being reconsidered, world-views challenged. Major themes from the Enlightenment era – especially Positivism – were being pushed against and materialism was being questioned. Speaking to these changes and its future impact, Rookmaaker noted,

> If we put on exhibition all the most important works of modern art up to 1920, we would already be able to see almost all the different aspects of twentieth-century art. Expressionism, abstract art, cubism, Dada, with their new methods of depicting reality, the collages, the particular styles, the use of colour, the search both for the absolute and for absurdity, their negation of all values, their pan-eroticism, we would see all the best and the worst features of the art of our century...
>
> But the spirit spread. While the modern movement was previously the work of a restricted group of artists and their public, it now influenced the minds and way of life of an ever-increasing number of people. In fact it is not too much to say that a new era in cultural history was inaugurated...
>
> So art played a vital part in giving form to a whole new mentality, a new spirit. It was one of the main agents for spreading the new thinking, the new ideas. Modern art is not neutral (art never was!). Its message is a new age, a new culture, a new world.[27]

But the new thinking, still wrapped in humanism, faced the persistent questions of Modernity. Is there purpose in a naturalistic universe? What does it mean to be human? Can beauty exist? Followed to its *rationalistic* end, hopelessness and vanity overshadows the human experience. Despair beckons us into its dark embrace, and damnation pursues us in our desperate groping for mirages of meaning.

---

[26] David Courbet, the French artist who birthed Realism, painted only "what he could see."

[27] Rookmaaker, *Modern Art and the Death of a Culture*, p.131. "(art...)" in original.

If, however, there is a transcendent God who composes structure and bestows value, then art seeks something noble: an aesthetic expression of ultimate truth, a richness in life, a sense of awe in the grandeur of creation, hope in pain and suffering, a higher analysis of good and evil, and the knowledge of love and grace. There is significance in being human.

The revolution in Modern art represented many things, including the breakdown in authentic human meaning. Questions devoid of liberating answers loomed, for true Truth had been abandoned.

Science:

Modern science is historically steeped in naturalistic philosophy, being linked to humanist interpretations of Newtonian physics. Professor of philosophy, Alex Rosenberg, offers this consideration,

> Newtonian mechanics gave strong grounds for determinism about everything in nature. Given only the position and momentum of a body, no matter how large or small, Newton's laws governed its entire future and past trajectories – paths through time and space. If the laws hold for all physical objects, including all living things, including us, then our behavior is determined as strictly as that of the planets in their paths around the Sun. In so far as everything that happens to us consists in the interaction of corpuscles within and at the boundaries of our bodies, all of our behavior is determined as well.[28]

In this manner the *mechanical view* presented an all-encompassing narrative, producing an inflexible view of human nature. The Nobel Prize winner in physics, Werner Heisenberg, recognized this problem and wrote the following in 1958,

> ...natural science proceeded to get a clearer and wider picture of the material world... The world consisted of things in space and time, the things consist of matter, and matter can produce and can be acted upon by forces. The events follow from the interplay between matter and forces; every event is the result and the cause of

[28] Alex Rosenberg, *Philosophy of Science: A Contemporary Introduction* (Routledge, 2012, third edition), p.132.

> other events. At the same time the human attitude toward nature changed from a contemplative one to the pragmatic one. One was not so much interested in nature as it is; one rather asked what one could do with it. Therefore, natural science turned into technical science...
>
> In this way... the nineteenth century developed an extremely rigid frame for natural science which formed not only science but the general outlook of great masses of people... Matter was the primary reality. The progress of science was pictured as a crusade of conquest into the material world. Utility was the watchword...
>
> On the other hand, this frame was so narrow and rigid that it was difficult to find a place in it for many concepts of our language that had always belonged to its very substance, for instance, the concepts of mind, of the human soul or of life.[29]

Newton's discoveries initiated the mechanical worldview, and 20th century physics called this into question.

Quantum Theory, Albert Einstein's Special and General Relativity, and Werner Heisenberg's Uncertainty Principle undermined the claims of mechanical and positivist certainty. Said theories and subsequent findings were important in changing long-held views of knowledge and science. Matter was far more complex than previously thought, and ideas of time, space, energy, and their observation were being reconsidered. The rigid principles of the Enlightenment softened under the heavy blow of advanced physics.

The new physics had a ripple effect as possibilities and speculations captivated scientists and philosophers. Academic fields of study opened, and new ways of looking at technical problems allowed for the engineering of advanced technologies, enriching our lives.[30] Intellectuals debated. Mystics talked of "quantum spirituality" and "quantum theology."

Hard-and-fast mechanistic views were shaken by new theories manifesting paradox and contradiction. As the new science filtered into the population, trust in the certitude of singular claims diminished; narrow assertions may be pragmatically useful or constructive, but not necessarily true.

[29] Werner Heisenberg, *Physics and Philosophy: The Revolution in Modern Science* (Prometheus Books, 1958/1999), pp.196-197.

[30] Computers, smart-phones, lasers, global positioning systems, and advanced medical devices are products of quantum science.

Postmodernism, surfacing in the mainstream decades after quantum theory was articulated, floated on the philosophical ripples caused by the splashdown of quantum physics.

Intellectuals:

The post-modern mood was influenced by more than just scientific theory. Modern philosophers, too, had greatly contributed to the new attitude.

Long before the phrase "post-modern" was uttered, intellectuals like Søren Kierkegaard and Georg Hegel introduced ideas that would lodge into the post-modern mind-frame.[31] Friedrich Nietzsche, an erudite and sophisticated German thinker noted for his sharp analysis of art and culture,[32] was also an important frontrunner. His arousal of moral skepticism and his critiques of reason and knowledge contributed to an atmosphere of questioning. Since his death in 1900, Nietzsche's perspective on the "modern ideas" of truth, science, religion, and the limits of being all-too-human, have become powerful points of academic debate and discussion.

Nietzsche's popular legacy, however, was the Übermensch, an allegorical Superman freed of Christian bonds and charting a new course through the *will to power* – the fierce desire for self-mastery and self-existence. Man as a construct of the stifling past will be superseded,

> Man is something that shall be overcome...
>
> What is ape to man? A laughing-stock or a painful embarrassment. And just the same shall man be to the Übermensch...
>
> The Übermensch is the meaning of the earth. Let your will say: The Übermensch *shall be* the meaning of the earth!
>
> ...*remain true the earth*, and do not believe those who speak to you of otherworldly hopes! They are poison-mixers...[33]

---

[31] A discussion on "Kierkegaard, Mass Society and the Road to the Postmodern" is found in *The Postmodern Turn* by Steven Best and Douglas Kellner (The Guilford Press, 1997), p.40ff. For the role of Hegel, see Nancy Pearcey, *Finding Truth: 5 Principles for Unmaking Atheism, Secularism, and Other God Substitutes* (David C. Cook, 2015), p.118.

[32] For examples of Nietzsche's thoughts on art, poetry, the writing of books and other aspects of culture – in a pithy and at times playful manner of speaking – see Friedrich Nietzsche, *Human, All Too Human: A Book For Free Spirits* (George Allen & Unwin Ltd., 1911, translated by Paul V. Cohn), p.54ff (aphorism 99 and beyond).

[33] Friedrich Nietzsche, *Thus Spoke Zarathustra* (Barnes & Noble Classics, 2005, originally published in the 1880s), p.9-10, italics in original.

As Zarathustra, the main character in Nietzsche's philosophical novel, said: "Dead are all gods: Now we want the Übermensch to live."[34]

It was a boast that echoed through the 20th century,

> God is dead! God remains dead! And we have killed him! How can we console ourselves, the murderer of all murderers! The holiest and the mightiest thing the world has ever possessed has bled to death under our knives: who will wipe this blood from us? With what water could we cleanse ourselves? What festivals of atonement, what holy games will we have to invent for ourselves? Is the magnitude of this deed not too great for us? Do we not ourselves have to become gods merely to appear worthy of it? There was never a greater deed – and whoever is born after us will on account of this deed belong to a higher history than all history up to now![35]

Stewart E. Kelly, a Christian professor of Philosophy at Minot State University, bridges Nietzsche and Postmodernism: "Nietzsche called for a new worldview that sloughed off the dead skin of Christianity and replaced it with the *will to power, truth as a mobile army of metaphors*, and a world where God is no longer even relevant."[36]

Another 20th century thinker, the esteemed Spanish writer and philosopher José Ortega y Gasset, foreshadowed Postmodernism in his critique of the rationalist point of view: "But reality happens to be, like a landscape, possessed of an infinite number of perspectives, all equally veracious and authentic. The sole false perspective is that which claims to be the only one there is."[37]

Albert Einstein's theory of Relativity was important to Ortega's conception: "The theory of Einstein is a marvelous proof of the harmonious multiplicity of all possible points of view. If the idea is extended to morals and aesthetics, we shall come to experience history and life in a new way."[38]

---

[34] Ibid., p.69.

[35] Friedrich Nietzsche, *The Gay Science* (Cambridge University Press, 2001/2008), p.120.

[36] Stewart E. Kelly, *Truth Considered and Applied: Examining Postmodernism, History, and Christian Ethics* (B&H Publishing Group, 2011), p.2, italics in original. Kelly is professor of Philosophy at Minot State University.

[37] José Ortega y Gasset, *The Modern Theme* (Harper Torchbooks, 1961, originally published in 1931), pp.91-92.

[38] Ibid., p.143.

Ortega wrote, "Each individual is an essential point of view in the chain. By setting everyone's fragmentary visions side-by-side it would be possible to achieve a complete panorama of absolute and universally valid truth." This panorama, he postulated, is "God's point of view" as God sees through the "medium of mankind" – "mankind is the visual organ of divinity."[39]

Such an idea imparts that God's knowledge is dependent upon Man. This may be the case if God is nothing more than a postulate of humanity, a deity inseparable from the material cosmos. But the God revealed to the ancient Hebrew people stands apart, a Being *different* than what the mind of Man constructs – nor *would* or *could* we construct this Being, for our self-mastery is immediately challenged and ultimately dismantled by the Judge whose standards are higher than human council.

The Old Testament book of Isaiah asked a rhetorical question fitting to our discussion: "Who has directed the Spirit of the LORD, or as His counselors has taught Him? With whom did He take counsel, and who instructed Him, and taught Him in the path of justice? Who taught Him knowledge, and showed Him the way of understanding?"[40]

The New Testament book of Romans offers this parallel: "Oh, the depth of the riches both of the wisdom and knowledge of God! How unsearchable are His judgments and His ways past finding out! 'For who has known the mind of the LORD? Or who has become His counselor?'"[41]

Other intellectuals in the 20th century who contributed to the post-modern mood included the German and French philosophers, Martin Heidegger and Michel Foucault. Both had controversial political histories: Heidegger was a member of the Nazi Party from 1933 until the end of World War II, and Foucault held a brief membership in the French Communist Party.

Heidegger wrestled with the idea of *Being*, a "they-self" construct in which authenticity is experienced in the community of all. Everyone is an instrument of Being and has meaning in the tasks furthering its interlocking nature. Existence is in wholeness. Stanley Grenz explains: "His goal is to dislodge such traditional dichotomies as mind and body, self and world, subject and object, self and other."[42]

---

39 Ibid., p.95.

40 Isaiah 40:13-14.

41 Romans 11:33-34.

42 Grenz, *A Primer on Postmodernism*, p.105.

In August 1934, the Nazi intellectual delivered a speech highlighting the "spirit of the community" found in National Socialism, a "new configuration of the people," and an "inner reeducation of the entire people toward the goal of wanting its own unity and oneness."[43]

James Phillips, author of *Heidegger's Volk*, commenting on the speech asks a perplexing question: "Can a people, as authentic Being-with-one-another, want, without contradiction, its own unity and oneness?" The answer: "the people simply *wills* its own oneness."[44] *Das Man* is therefore the soul of the living community, mythically connected in a symbiosis of the past, present and future, and rooted in the sacredness of the land – *blood and soil.*

Influenced by Nietzsche, Heidegger likewise celebrated the "death of God" and the "will to power." And he reoriented knowledge; "questioning itself becomes the highest form of knowing."[45] Professor of Literature and cultural critic, Gene Edward Veith, notes the intellectual fallout,

> Heidegger's conclusion has become accepted to the point of becoming a commonplace of contemporary thought, *that knowledge is a matter of process, not content.* With the death of God, there is no longer a set of absolutes or abstract ideals by which existence must be ordered. Such 'essentialism' is an illusion; knowledge in the sense of objective, absolute truth must be challenged. The scholar is not the one who knows or searches for some absolute truth, but the one who questions everything that pretends to be true.[46]

To *inquire* is an amazing human attribute, reflecting the pursuit of some area of knowledge or understanding. It is an action we take for granted, yet it is a gateway to growth, creativity, and problem solving – a portal to know truth. Rhetorical questions, on the other hand, are given by the *holder* of knowledge and reveal introspection, experience, and authority. In either instance the use of the *question* is a profound thing.

The Bible is laced with questions, both inquisitive and explanatory: the anguished queries of the Psalmist, "Has God forgotten to be gracious? Has

---

[43] Martin Heidegger, as quoted by James Phillips, *Heidegger's Volk: Between National Socialism and Poetry* (Stanford University Press, 2005), p.50.

[44] Ibid., p.51, italics in original.

[45] As quoted by Gene Edward Veith, Jr., *Modern Fascism: Liquidating the Judeo-Christian Worldview* (Concordia Publishing House, 1993), p.85.

[46] Ibid., p.85, italics in original.

He in anger shut up His tender mercies?"[47] And in the soul-search for lasting meaning: "For who knows what is good for man in life, all the days of his vain life which he passes like a shadow?"[48] Or God's answer to the wounded cries of Job, a man who knew intense anguish and pain – yet who still trusted in God as Redeemer – even though Job brought a charge against Him: "What have I done to You, O watcher of men? Why have You set me as Your target?"[49] God responds with round after round of rhetorical questions that display His grandeur, a cross-examination placing Job's suffering – indeed, all of our existence – into a context far larger than ourselves. Job is left metaphorically stripped naked, as we are, in the realization that God's purposes are greater than we can truly comprehend.

"Therefore I have uttered what I did not understand," Job acknowledges in humility. "Things too wonderful for me, which I did not know."[50]

There is tremendous good in asking questions. It can signal a search for Wisdom. But in the post-modern context wherein questions are an end to themselves, a masquerade for knowledge – a justification for the abandonment of truth – then the only thing left is absurdity and despair.

Finally, we will consider Michel Foucault, a leftist French intellectual who was influenced by Nietzsche's thoughts on power and existence.[51] In fact, he has been described as living the "great Nietzschean quest."[52]

Foucault, a provocative writer who took an experiential approach, explored a range of topics from the meaning of knowledge and power to criminality to madness to sexuality.[53] In France he became an academic celebrity noted for his style of teaching, his participation in student demonstrations, and his public activism to empower socially oppressed sub-groups.[54]

---

[47] Psalm 77: 9-10.

[48] Ecclesiastes 6:12a.

[49] Job 7:20.

[50] Job 42:3.

[51] Michael Mahon, *Foucault's Nietzschean Genealogy: Truth, Power, and the Subject* (State University of New York Press, 1992), p.2.

[52] James Miller, *The Passion of Michel Foucault* (Simon and Schuster, 1993), p.183.

[53] Some of Foucault's books include, *Madness and Civilization: A History of Insanity in the Age of Reason* (Vintage, 1988); *Discipline and Punish: The Birth of the Prison* (Vintage, 1995); *The History of Sexuality*, 3 Volumes (Vintage 1990); and, *Power/Knowledge* (Vintage, 1980).

[54] The social liberation of prisoners and homosexuals were lightning rods for his activism.

His views on power and oppression struck a cord with the burgeoning post-modern mindset of the late 1960s. However, it was while traveling in the United States during the 1970s that Foucault pushed new personal limits; experimenting with LSD, and participated in the San Francisco bathhouse and gay bar scene. Drugs and sadomasochism dangerously fed his drive for new experiential realities.

Death too, which fascinated him from a young age, was an encounter to feel and embrace as a mystical pleasure. His 1978 brush with death in Paris was revealing,

> Once I was struck by a car in the street. I was walking. And for maybe two seconds I had the impression I was dying and it was really a very, very intense pleasure. The weather was wonderful. It was seven o'clock during the summer. The sun was descending. The sky was very wonderful and blue and so on. It was, it still is now, one of my best memories.[55]

Foucault sought after what Nietzsche conveyed as the *Dionysian element*: A transformational encounter through the chaos of raw, emotive, and ecstatic experience. Old norms would have to be transgressed, and personal feelings and social limits experientially pushed. As moral claims and truth statements were institutional constructs associated with oppression, he believed, they must be contravened in the search for the lived life.

Stanley Grenz writes: "Foucault asserts that every interpretation of reality is an assertion of power... every assertion of knowledge is an act of power."[56]

Freed from what Foucault believed to be oppressive bonds and moral limitations, a new human could be created, unencumbered by the restraints of labels and categories and histories. The painter's canvas was open for new colors. Foucault himself, it could be argued, was attempting to become the expression of a living artwork.

Postmodernism did not appear out of thin air. Rather, a long genealogy of intellectuals left their mark on a society ripe for change. While the average person toiled and worked, built businesses and went to church, from the time of Nietzsche until Foucault – and continuing today – branches of academia have wrestled with the post-modern outlook. What is real? How is

---

[55] As quoted by Miller, *The Passion of Michel Foucault*, p.306.

[56] Grenz, *A Primer on Postmodernism*, p.6.

knowledge knowable? Can it be separated from power? Does anything exist outside of our experiences? What is true?

If traditional sources of certainty are rejected, what will be our foundation?

The Last War of Modernity

Sex, drugs, and rock-n-roll. The counter-culture of the 1960s and early 1970s was epitomized by this bold phrase. The message was clear: Traditional lines of authority and their narratives of truth were no longer accepted. It was supposed to be the "end of ideology."[57]

The decade of the 1960s was marked by turmoil and change. Consider some of the features of the time: the Space Race and the placing of man on the moon, the Civil Rights movement, broad acceptance of the television, new music styles, and the growing use of psychedelic substances.

In California the Black Panthers waved guns and demanded "justice and peace."[58] The US Supreme Court said "no" to public prayer in school. America's fabric was torn by domestic assassinations, and the "political truth" of the JFK inquiry undermined public confidence.[59] Paul Ehrlich was selling population control: "We can no longer afford merely to treat the symptoms of the cancer of population growth; the cancer itself must be cut out."[60]

"Hip Marxism" – the New Left – promised an end to oppression; a bright future of social equality and cultural transformation. Radical student movements made the evening news.

At the Esalen Institute a "religion without religion" was being birthed, combining psychedelics, yoga, sex, psychology and liberal theology into a new humanist spirituality – adjustable to one's felt needs. In San Francisco, Anton LaVey formalized a pragmatic, anti-Christian religion – the Church of Satan – "a temple of glorious indulgence" that would "recapture man's mind

[57] David Toolan, *Facing West From California's Shores: A Jesuit's Journey into New Age Consciousness* (Crossroad Publishing Company, 1987), p.4.

[58] This was point 10 in the Ten-Point Program of the Black Panther Party, 1966. Besides "justice and peace," point 10 included "land, bread, housing, education, clothing."

[59] Edward Epstein described the Warren Commission, charged with investigating the assassination of John F. Kennedy, as engaging in "political truth." Edward Jay Epstein, *Inquest: The Warren Commission and the Establishment of Truth* (The Viking Press, 1966).

[60] Paul Ehrlich, *The Population Bomb: Population Control or Race to Oblivion?* (Ballantine Books/Sierra Club, 1968), Prologue.

and carnal desires as objects of celebration."[61] To LaVey, his Church was the real counter-culture.[62] It certainly embodied the spirit of the age.

Closer to Los Angeles, members of Elysium were shedding their clothes "for the well-being and advancement of the public."[63] In Laurel Canyon, a new music scene was churning out anthems for America's Cultural Revolution; leaving a trail of personal wreckage.[64] Colorado's Drop City became an artistic vortex for "a new society in which the individual may fill both his spiritual and physical needs while doing just what he wants."[65] On a farm in New York, 400,000 people danced and frolicked in the mud and rain. Woodstock, "An Aquarian Exposition," celebrated "love and peace."

Dreams of sexual freedom, social and political utopia, and a world imagining itself into a new reality flittered in the minds of millions. It was in this milieu that Postmodernism exhibited itself and entered the mainstream. Dissatisfaction with Modernity had percolated to the surface within the intellectual and cultural sphere. But something more was happening than just artistic influences, scientific theories, and intellectual discontent. A fresh generation prepped by post-modern thinking and energized by leftist rhetoric found itself under the shadows of war. And it moved them to action.

It is important to remember that an overriding feature of Modernity had

---

[61] Anton Szandor LaVey, *The Satanic Bible* (Avon Books, 1969), "temple" quote on the inside front page, attributed to LaVey. The "temple" quote was part of the original introduction used in the 1969 edition up until 1972. The other section, "recapture man's mind" is taken from Burton H. Wolfe's Introduction to *The Satanic Bible*.

[62] "I considered the 60's and 70's a barren, aesthetically destructive era. America, especially San Francisco, was a mire of ignorance, stupidity and egalitarianism. I created my own world – the Church of Satan. That's the only way I could survive. It turned out to be a real cudgel on the head of mainstream society at the time. Without us there would have been no counterculture. All the Ken Keseys and Timothy Learys did was attach great importance to the worthless." – Anton LaVey, quoted by Blanche Barton, *The Secret Life of a Satanist: The Authorize Biography of Anton LaVey* (Feral House, 1992), p.115.

[63] Editorial by-line from *ANKH*, Volume 1, Number 4 (1968), inside cover. *ANKH* was the official magazine of Elysium, the popular and controversial nudist camp and center. Elysium was noted for its pornographic interests and alternative sexual/social lifestyles.

[64] A strange and troubling survey of the Laurel Canyon music scene is David McGowan's book, *Weird Scenes Inside the Canyon: Laurel Canyon, Covert Ops & the Dark Heart of the Hippie Dream* (Headpress, 2014).

[65] K. Drescher and M. Lamb, "What Hath LSD/God/LSD Wrought?" *ANKH*, Volume 1, Number 4 (1968), p.9.

been its amplification of our ability to destroy. Two times the world plunged into industrial-sized infernos, scalable to the science of the day, with the Second World War (WWII) giving us an iconic Modernist symbol: The menacing image of the mushroom cloud.

This stark reality undermined the Modernist vision of a perfected society guided by enlightened authority, even as the war sparked interest in World Federalism.[66] H.G. Wells found his long-held optimism in a humanist world order cracking. In his 1940 edition of *The Outline of History*, Wells ended with pronouncements of world federalism and universal social justice: "Nothing is needed but collective effort and mutual toleration... the final achievement of world-wide political and social unity." His last sentence radiated confidence in Modernity,

> Gathering together at last under the leadership of man, the student-teacher of the universe, unified, disciplined, armed with the secret powers of the atom, and with knowledge as yet beyond dreaming, Life, for ever dying to be born afresh, for ever young and eager, will presently stand upon the earth as upon a footstool, and stretch out its realm amidst the stars.[67]

Post-war editions of his book, on the other hand, removed the above hubris and ended with dark doubts about "the terrible potential dangers of Man's recent advances in knowledge and power."[68] As his son G.P. Wells pointed out: "Man's powers of destruction are too great, and wisdom in using them that man has shown is too small, for us to have any confidence."[69]

Modernity had wounded itself with its own "powers of destruction."

For the 1960s college generation the specter of warfare was unshakable. Their grandparents had lived through the Great War. World War II was their

[66] World Federalism is a movement to create a world government based on federalist lines.

[67] H.G. Wells, *The Outline of History*, Volume III – Modern History (Triangle Books, 1940). On "collective effort," see page 1195. On "political and social unity," see page 1197. Final sentence, see page 1197. "Life" is capitalized in original.

[68] H.G. Wells, *The Outline of History*, Volume II. Note: Later editions were two volumes instead of three (Doubleday & Company, 1971), p.995 for "knowledge and power." Wells passed away in 1946, and subsequent editions of *Outline* included editorialized material that fit with his post-war outlook.

[69] G.P. Wells and Raymond Postgate revised and updated the post-war editions of H.G. Wells' *Outline*. Ibid., p.1045.

parent's time and it had an overshadowing effect. Uncles and older siblings experienced the horrors of the Korean War. Colonial end-game conflicts often became proxy matches between Eastern and Western powers; wars and rumors of wars abounded.[70] The memory of the Cuban Missile Crisis was still fresh. Hanging over everybody was *the bomb*.

And then there was Vietnam, the trigger event for the post-modern shift.

Following the French defeat at Dien Bien Phu in 1954,[71] America found itself increasingly committed to the extremely complex struggle in Indochina. Under US President Lyndon Johnson the war effort accelerated and by 1968 over half a million American servicemen were involved overseas. It was a strategically important year, with the Tet Offensive exacting a heavy toll on the attacking North Vietnamese forces and at the same time, shaking up the South Vietnamese government and gravely eroding the will of the American people at home.[72] One of the outcomes was Robert McNamara resigning as US Secretary of Defense, a position he held since 1961.

Vietnam was the *over-managed* war. McNamara, a bombing analyst from WWII and the first non-family president of Ford Motor Company, was noted for his technocratic prowess.[73] His statistical work during WWII increased bombing efficiencies against Japanese cities and his analytics at Ford boosted the company's performance. One biographer described McNamara "as a

---

[70] Colonial conflict zones included the Congo, Angola, Mozambique, Guinea-Bissau, Algeria, Sudan, and Vietnam. Other tensions included Maoists activity in Bangladesh, the Indo-Pakistani War, Argentina's revolution, civil war in Nigeria, unrest in Laos, the regrouping of the IRA in Northern Ireland, and the Six Day War in the Middle East.

[71] The cultural impact of Dien Bien Phu, and then the loss of Algeria almost a decade later, added to French discontent. Postmodernism in France owes much to the social stresses caused by its defeats in Vietnam and Algeria. For a detailed account of the military confrontation at Dien Bien Phu, see Martin Windrow, *The Last Valley: Dien Bien Phu and the French Defeat in Vietnam* (Da Capo Press, 2004).

[72] Alexander Kendrick wrote, "The Tet offensive staggered the Johnson administration and dumbfounded American opinion, wiping out whatever optimism had been created by official statements that the war was going well." Alexander Kendrick, *The Wound Within: America in the Vietnam Years, 1945-1974* (Little, Brown and Company, 1974), p.249.

[73] McNamara wrote in 1968: "The challenge of the Department of Defense is compelling. It is the greatest single management complex in history; it supervises the greatest aggregation of raw power ever assembled by man." Robert McNamara, *The Essence of Security: Reflections in Office* (Harper & Row, 1968), p.87. For a short recount of McNamara's managerial approach, see Ronald H. Spector, *After Tet: The Bloodiest Year in Vietnam* (The Free Press, 1993), pp.219-222.

kind of postwar technocratic hubristic fable. He was an extraordinary impressive person, almost a new Adam, who abused his trust..."[74]

Reliance on technocratic methods has a way of masking reality, especially in the fluidity of a combat theater.[75] Technocratic logic can produce a blinder effect, the inability to empathize and appreciate an opponent's creativity. Moreover, it tends to diminish an understanding of *the why* as it focuses on *the how*. The result can be a dangerous loss of meaning, inevitably followed by pointless action. When the long-tail of directives, orders, regulations, and rules of engagement ends with micro-management, then the focus inevitably becomes appeasing the political upstream. Although the goal of engineered efficiency sounds good, it can destroy spontaneity and moral responsibility. In the military, an environment already brimming with hierarchy and protocol, such an approach mired down front-line men.

War historian Christopher Robbins tells of the regulations endured by Air Force personnel,

> The rules were impossible to memorize in their entirety, and sometimes even to understand, and were open to different interpretations. Huge sanctuary areas were granted to the enemy. A fighter pilot could not attack a North Vietnamese MiG sitting on a runway until it was in flight, identified, and showing hostile intentions (the possible peaceful intention of an enemy MiG were left undefined). In some regions enemy trucks could avoid attack by simply driving off the road. SAM [Surface-to-Air] missile sites could not be struck while under construction, but only after they became operational. Limited extensions of target areas would be arbitrarily declared, only to be unexpectedly cancelled and withdrawn later...[76]

---

[74] Paul Hendrickson, *The Living and the Dead: Robert McNamara and Five Lives of a Lost War* (Alfred A. Knopf, 1996), p.356.

[75] Example: McNamara's choice of determining battle victory through the body-count of enemy dead. Reports of confirmed kills were submitted up the military chain, and a metrics applied. In a war with no clear boundaries, this might have been the only measuring stick. But this system resulted in problems: fudging numbers, and because of this, the risk of false justification. Worse, it produced an illusion of winning. North Vietnam, on the other hand, used an entirely different standard for victory – one with clear targets and goals, even as it threw men into the fire like sacrificial animals.

[76] Christopher Robbins, *The Ravens: The Men Who Flew in America's Secret War in Laos* (Crown Publishers, 1987), p.17. For more on the regulatory insanity of the Vietnam War,

Robins explains: "The realities of the battlefield demanded again and again that the rules be broken."[77]

Washington's disconnect from the realities of Vietnam not only damaged the ability of its own forces to act in a measured manner,[78] it left policy makers ill-equipped to understand the bigger picture.[79] The Beltway's confusion became Hanoi's strength. At the international bargaining table, diplomatic political games traded lives for slogans and signatures. Lies and half-truths became an industry. America wandered in a maze of moral dilemmas.[80]

Domestically, trust broke down and society frayed. The post-modern attitude, bubbling under the surface for decades, found angry release at the national level. Universities became lightning rods for discontent.

On American campuses with vocal, leftist professors, the narrative of *power equals oppression* was trumpeted. *Two, Three... Many Vietnams*, a book of essays from leftist intellectuals, compiled by David Horowitz – then a Marxist student agitator, now the editor of *FrontPage Magazine* – equated the US

---

see Ed Gaydos, *Seven in a Jeep* (Columbus Press, 2013). See also, "Size-Twelve Boot, Size-Ten War," *Everything We Had: An Oral History of the Vietnam War by Thirty-Three American Soldiers Who Fought It* (Ballantine, 1981, edited by Al Santoli), pp.87-99. This section contains a gritty comparison of frontline life with rear support experiences.

77 Robbins, *The Ravens*, p.19.

78 For an interesting analysis of how this disconnect impacted Special Operations Groups, America's forerunner to Special Forces, see Richard H. Shultz, Jr., *The Secret War Against Hanoi: Kennedy's and Johnson's Use of Spies, Saboteurs, and Covert Warriors in North Vietnam* (HarperCollins, 1999).

79 Because of this, working battle strategies were stopped and obvious steps to defeat the enemy were ignored or politicized beyond effectiveness. A captured Vietcong commander said the following regarding the halting of America's bombing campaign: "When I first heard of the complete bombing halt I thought it must be a joke, and I laughed. But when I realized the United States was serious, I was dumbfounded by the stupidity." See Louis A. Fanning, *Betrayal In Vietnam* (Arlington House Publishers, 1976), p.21.

80 It is important to recognize that the North Vietnamese Army (NVA), the Viet Cong (VC), and associated political actors were not morally superior, a position inferred by Marxist commentators such as Jean-Paul Sartre. See his essay, "On Genocide," *Two, Three... Many Vietnams: A Radical Reader on the Wars in Southeast Asia and the Conflicts at Home* (Canfield Press, 1971). For example, when NVA and VC forces overran the city of Hue in 1968 they liquidated "civil servants, school teachers, university professors, men, women, children – in fact, anyone who could be remotely classified as an anti-Communist." For a short description of the Hue Massacre which killed between 4,000 to 6,000 civilians, depending on sources, see Louis A. Fanning, *Betrayal In Vietnam* (Arlington House Publishers, 1976), p.49.

Government to Hitler, saying America was liquidating the Vietnamese while portraying Communist forces as the "consciousness of humanity."[81] Leftist movements such as Students for a Democratic Society and Marxist groups like the Young Socialist Alliance engaged in campus agitation. The Western world was increasingly framed as immoral and repressive.

"Instead of an effort to preserve the freedom of the Vietnamese people," explains professor David Levy, "the war was seen by the intellectuals of the left as nothing more than the latest chapter in the long and bloody story of American imperialism."[82]

However, as Levy points out, scores of colleges and thousands of students did not participate in anti-war activities. A sizable number of youth actually supported the war effort and, conversely, a large percentage of older citizens opposed it. Nevertheless, the explosive encounters on select campuses turned on the public spotlight.[83]

Other factors contributed to the unease. For the first time in television history, raw battle images streamed into American households, producing a "profound emotional effect."[84] Politically, an inept Congress enlarged public resentment, and the *Pentagon Papers* revealed misjudgment and contradictions at the highest levels of office. Republicans and Democrats, incapable of seeing through the fog, waffled in support and then opposition. As one author said: "It was not the Hanoi Communists who won the war, but rather the American Congress that lost it."[85]

Mistrust and anger marked the domestic spirit. Mass demonstrations tore at the nation's fabric. Troops were not just being sent to the jungles of Asia, they were marching on the streets of Detroit, Chicago, and Washington DC.

---

81 *Two, Three... Many Vietnams: A Radical Reader on the Wars in Southeast Asia and the Conflicts at Home* (Canfield Press, 1971). *Ramparts* magazine, of which Horowitz was editor, commissioned the book and edited it with the assistance of Banning Garrett and Katherine Barkley. Horowitz wrote the Preface. The title was inspired by the Cuban communist, Che Guevara.

82 David W. Levy, *The Debate Over Vietnam* (The John Hopkins University Press, 1995), p.84.

83 For more on the complexities of generational support and opposition, and university issues, see Levy, *The Debate Over Vietnam*, pp.102-109.

84 Michael Charlton and Anthony Moncrieff, *Many Reasons Why: The American Involvement in Vietnam* (Hill and Wang, 1978/1989), pp.150-157. General Westmoreland was the one to utter "profound emotional effect." See page 151.

85 Louis A. Fanning, *Betrayal In Vietnam* (Arlington House Publishers, 1976), p.11.

At Kent State University, members of the Ohio National Guard shot and killed four students. America wandered in a daze of lost meaning.

Historian David Levy writes,

> Who could look at the country in the late 1960s and not recognize that the debate over the war – over its necessity, its morality, its wisdom – had poisoned the society, had made many doubt the credibility of their government, had filled America with suspicions about the motives and values and ideals of one another?[86]

This paralleled what famed journalist and broadcaster, Alexander Kendrick, explained in 1974,

> The Vietnam War was disruptive and destructive to the fiber of American life and society. It helped create the amoral climate that nurtured Watergate. It brought into question the quality of national leadership, the uses of national power, the validity of national aims and values, the order of national priorities, the process of decision-making, the nature of the American governmental structure, the pretensions of American world 'leadership,' the constitutional freedoms of press and assemblage, the effectiveness of political democracy, the consequence of technology, even the sacrosanct rule of law.[87]

On January 23, 1973, US President Nixon signed a peace treaty with North Vietnam. At the end of April 1975, tanks from the communist North pressed against the Southern capital of Saigon. During those closing days, US helicopters airlifted personnel and South Vietnamese allies from the besieged city. Crowds of American supporters, many with direct ties to US military operations and in danger of communist retaliations, desperately pushed against the gates of the American Embassy – hoping against hope to be on the final flight. Early in the morning of April 30, the US Ambassador to South Vietnam was lifted out. Hours later Saigon fell.

America's last war of Modernity came to a close, symbolized by a lone Huey helicopter perched on a Saigon rooftop, making ready to leave.

---

[86] Levy, *The Debate Over Vietnam*, p.75.
[87] Kendrick, *The Wound Within*, p.4.

Pointing Somewhere?

For the United States, the Vietnam War was the seminal event that shook the post-modern fruit from its exalted tree of intellectualism. The outcome was a "revolution in mind."[88] Today's post-modern mood is the child of that broader revolution.

Using another metaphor, Alexander Kendrick described the Vietnam experience as "the label on the bottle of tumult, alienation and readjustment that represented the decade," even as the war itself "was a kind of last gasp of old policies and methods."[89]

This "bottle of tumult" spilled far and wide. Roger Neill, a Canadian friend, described his experience during that time period,

> My cynical, bitter, guilty, self-loathing, capitalist-loathing, government-loathing, prosperity-loathing self had no expectations. My professors had taught me that we were overpopulating and polluting the earth and that an apocalypse was inevitable. It was very religious, all the while claiming that it was anti-religious.[90]

Modernity had been questioned and left wanting, yet the post-modern environment was incapable of laying a meaningful foundation. The New Left wished to achieve structural transformation, but as a movement it was too splintered to be an effective and permanent political force. Bitterness and disappointment followed. However, the Marxist/leftist push had been successful in changing the social and cultural mindset, and in this way it became an important part of the post-modern story.

Thanks to the work of Nietzsche and other intellectuals, Western thinking had been opened up to relativism and subjectivism. Generations of war undermined Modernity's potency, and a mishandled conflict triggered mistrust in government and anger towards authority. Postmodernism soaked into the nervous, sweating skin of society.

But could anything lasting be built on shifting sand? Could non-meaning provide purpose and non-reason bring guidance? Could questions refusing answers exhibit wisdom?

What was left?

---

88 This is the phrase my friend, Roger Neill, used as the title for his book. An apt motto.

89 Kendrick, *The Wound Within*, pp.15-16.

90 Roger Brian Neill, *Revolution in Mind: An Autobiography* (Word Alive Press, 2014), p.65.

Chapter 6

Enchanting Ourselves

> We must be bold to say, that an Earthly man, is a mortal God; and that the heavenly God, is an immortal Man. – Trismegistus.[1]

> ...the new God would be in the relative. – Carl G. Jung.[2]

Kirtan music floated in the background. Colorful silk *saris* and white arched windows and exotic pictures of an ancient culture greeted my eyes. Miniature deity statues stared amidst the peacock feathers and souvenir trinkets. A small but tempting buffet beckoned, filling the air with the rich aroma of curry and cloves, and the subtle notes of cardamom.

I made a beeline for the food.

After my second helping of *palak paneer* – a savory dish of spinach and paneer cheese – and far too much *mango lassi*, the guru beckoned me to join him in a cozy alcove under a white staircase. A painting hung on the back wall; adoring women and cows watching Krishna playing a flute. The staircase ascending above our heads, I correctly assumed, was the inside access to the temple space.

"When you came in," my host gestured with an exaggerated sweep of an arm, "the smells and sights caught your attention, yes?"

"Yes," I answered, "and the food was *very* tasty."[3]

His wife and assistant quietly joined us in a mostly one-sided conversation. English was not my host's native tongue, and he had much to say.

"Why here?" I interjected. "Why Utah?"

---

1 Hermes Mercurius Trismegistus, *Divine Pymander* (Yogi Publication Society, no date), p.56 – Fourth Book (*The Key*), verse 93.

2 Carl G. Jung, *The Red Book: Liber Novus* (W.W. Norton & Company, 2009), p.166.

3 Later I discovered the buffet is blessed twice a day by the Hindu deity, Lord Krishna. The situation reminded me of 1 Corinthians 8 with its discussion of food offered to idols.

"Krishna directed us to this place."

Since 1998, the Sri Sri Radha Krishna Temple – also known as the Lotus Temple – has been a landmark in the predominantly Mormon community of Spanish Fork, located approximately 50 miles south of Salt Lake City. The Temple is comprised of gleaming white domes, over 100 arches and columns, a grand outdoor staircase guarded by two bronze elephants, and a spacious upper level walk-around patio. This remarkable edifice, set against a mountain backdrop, is visible from Interstate 15.

Established as part of the ISKCON network – the International Society of Krishna Consciousness, also known as the Hare Krishna Movement – the Lotus Temple's heritage is built on the teachings of the late A.C. Bhaktivedanta Swami Prabhupada. Thirty-nine other ISKCON temples and Vedic centers currently dot the United States, each advancing the mission of Prabhupada.

Renowned for his volumes of Hindu commentary and influence upon Western spiritual change, Swami Prabhupada's message was one of religious universalism and conscious transformation.

"Actually, it doesn't matter – *Krisna* or *Christ* – the name is the same," he told Benedictine monk, Emmanuel Jungclaussen, during their notable 1974 meeting. "The main point is to follow the injunctions of the Vedic scriptures that recommend chanting the name of God in this age."[4]

The name chanted is *Krishna*, avatar of the Hindu deity, Vishnu. In reciting the Hare Krishna mantra and through the practice of Bhakti yoga – devotion through yoga – the follower embraces the unity of religions. Prabhupada explained it this way as he walked with Father Jungclaussen,

> To practice *bhakti-yoga* means to become free from designations like 'Hindu,' 'Muslim,' 'Christian,' this or that, and simply to serve God. We have created Christian, Hindu, and Mohammedan religions, but when we come to a religion without designations, in which we don't think we are Hindus or Christians or Mohammedans, then we can speak of pure religion, or *bhakti*.[5]

While I was at the Lotus Temple, the resident teacher told me that Hinduism has been evangelizing the West through yoga, and to a lesser but growing

---

4 A.C. Bhaktivedanta Swami Prabhupada, *The Science of Self-Realization* (The Bhaktivedanta Book Trust, 2006), p.107, italics in original. Krishna can also be spelled Krisna.

5 Ibid., p.107, italics in original.

extent the Holi Festival of Colors.[6] The thought struck me: *The West is being Hinduized in-fact but not in-name.* We are not converting to an organized form of the Eastern religion; rather, we are embracing its thinking and spirit as we mimic its religious practices. We are enchanting ourselves.

Referring to Spanish Fork, the guru boasted: "Every Sunday, 100 to 150 Mormons come to the temple for yoga and the Maha Mantra."[7]

Hare Krishna, Hare Krishna, Krishna Krishna...

Motioning I was free to go-and-explore, I climbed the stairs and entered the temple proper. To my right was a life-like statue of Swami Prabhupada sitting in meditation, on my left was a staging area for speakers and musicians, and to my front was an elaborate, hand-carved teakwood altar with the mounted figures of Krishna and Radha. Squatting in the wide windowsill to the immediate right of Krishna's altar was Ganesha, "the elephant-headed god of wisdom."[8]

I had seen Ganesha represented many times before. But this encounter in the Lotus Temple sparked a particular memory; the closing hours of the Global Citizenship 2000 Youth Congress and the words of oneness uttered to the delight of school children – *Ganesha is none other than you.*

My experience at the Lotus Temple and the Global Citizenship 2000 Youth Congress may not be the norm for most people, but both represent a monumental shift. Not too far back in the annals of history, Western civilization was primarily grounded in a Christian context, with associated blessings and responsibilities. That has changed; now we live in a global age with new influences and different expectations.[9]

In fact, earlier in my own lifetime the likeness of these two experiences would have only been found in distant corners: tight-knit communities, specialized academic circles, or little-known retreat centers. Not any more.

Today we interact with an array of religions, ideologies and competing worldviews, often mixed together in a postmodern mash up. Multiple Hindu and Buddhist temples are likely found in your province or state or city, and

---

6 Its more consumer-oriented expressions are the popular 5k color runs and associated color festivals.

7 Each Sunday, the temple puts on a Hare Krishna Love Feast. It is a time for lectures, worship and yoga, and a fellowship meal.

8 Margaret and James Stutley, *Harper's Dictionary of Hinduism: Its Mythology, Folklore, Philosophy, Literature, and History* (Harper & Row Publishers, 1977), p.91.

9 This does not negate other historical influences. See chapters 3 to 5.

the Eastern practice of yoga is commonplace. Shrines and mosques point to the fact that the religious makeup of our society is changing, and with this come fresh challenges and opportunities. Global citizenship themes are embedded in public school curriculum and popular culture, and a new generation expresses itself in global terms. What was once understood as New Age techniques are now routinely employed in the fields of education and healthcare, and integrated into Christian institutions and churches. Mysticism has become a salable commodity. Annual Pagan Pride Day events take place in approximately 100 US cities, and paying homage to the Earth is an act of international diplomacy and personal priority – a spiritual *politik*.

But we did not arrive at this social, cultural, and religious environment overnight. The enchanted worldview has been simmering for generations.

Modernity and Religious Diversity

Contrary to what many humanists had hoped, Modernity did not subdue or dismantle religion.[10] Rather, it seeded a materialist faith in systems. Nor did the commanding bulwark of naturalistic philosophy create permanent barricades to spirituality.

Religion was not disappearing. It was diversifying.

A variety of metaphysical beliefs were clearly evident throughout Modernity, including in its early stages. As the 19th century moved forward, an outpouring of philosophical, religious, and spiritual developments excited laymen and elites alike.

Consider a small sampling.

---

[10] Hope for a humanist world order without recourse to supernatural religion was celebrated in the science fiction of Arthur C. Clarke. His novel, *The Songs of Distant Earth* (Del Rey/Ballantine Books, 1986), presented a utopian world "completely free from the threat of supernatural restraints." In his book, *Childhood's End* (Harcourt, Brace & World, 1953), religions collapse when a race of demonic-looking space beings called Overlords – complete with "leathery wings, the little horns, and barbed tail" – arrive on Earth to assist humanity. Clarke preaches: "Within a few days, all mankind's multitudinous messiahs had lost their divinity. Beneath the fierce and passionless light of truth, faiths that had sustained millions for twice a thousand years vanished like morning dew. All the good and all the evil they had wrought were swept suddenly into the past, and could touch the minds of men no more. Humanity had lost its ancient gods: now it was old enough to have no need for new ones." (p.73). At the same time Clarke presented mystical themes of conscious evolution.

Romanticism:

Dubbed as the "rebellion of feeling against reason" – a push against the sterility of the mechanical worldview – Romanticism was an aesthetic, literary, and philosophical movement stressing the artistic interpretation of nature, science, and community. Variations existed between the American, British, French and German approaches, but in the aggregate it stressed immanence and connection.[11] Passionate visions of an animated relationship between nature and humanity aroused feelings of wholeness, inviting a mythical return to the land, to folk belief, and to organic social interactions. Instead of the individual being a utility substance in a materialist universe, persons were accorded meaning in the community and the greater consciousness of life, the "being of all."

Professor Keren Gorodeisky captured the Romantic heartbeat: "Natural phenomena and human beings are simply different manifestations of an encompassing nature, which is therefore nothing other than Spirit."[12]

In terms of identity it tended to stress two aspects: the Over-soul and the national soul. The first encompassed all of humanity and nature; the *soul of life*. The second characterized the *general will*, often wrapped in ethnic and cultural ideals. Long before Adolf Hitler was born, German Romanticism planted the seeds that would later blossom and bear his rotten fruit.[13]

The Francophone father of Romanticism, Jean-Jacques Rousseau – known for his idea of the *social contract* – greatly influenced the French Revolution

[11] For a survey of Romanticism, see *European Romanticism: A Reader* (Bloomsbury Academic, 2010, edited by Stephen Prickett). A short and approachable overview is Tim Blanning's book, *The Romantic Revolution: A History* (Modern Library Chronicles, 2012). On French Romanticism and the role of Jean Jacques Rousseau, see Will and Ariel Durant, *Rousseau and Revolution: The Story of Civilization*, Volume 10 (Simon and Schuster, 1967), pp. 887-892. A text of interest is *The Origins of French Romanticism*, by M.B. Finch and W. Allison Peers (Constable and Company, 1920). For an older book on German Romanticism, see A.W. Porterfield, *An Outline of German Romanticism: 1766-1866* (Gin and Company, 1941). A contemporary offering is *Romanticism: A German Affair*, by Rudiger Safranski (Northwest University Press, 2015).

[12] Keren Gorodeisky, "19th Century Romantic Aesthetics," *The Stanford Encyclopedia of Philosophy* (Fall 2016 Edition), Edward N. Zalta, editor, (http://plato.stanford.edu/archives/fall2016/entries/aesthetics-19th-romantic).

[13] See Robert G.L. Waite, *The Psychopathic God: Adolf Hitler* (Basic Books, 1977), pp.299-305. See R. Mark Musser, *Nazi Oaks: The Green Sacrifice of the Judeo-Christian Worldview in the Holocaust* (Advantage Books, 2013, third edition).

with his dream of "collective liberty." To Rousseau, men are free individuals and must rule themselves by converting liberties into a conscious social order: "A sacred right which serves as a basis for all other rights."[14] The *general will*, the total of social energy applied to political action and civic behavior, would govern in solidarity: "Each to all and all to each."[15] A new social spirit would thus be evident in the union of persons, and a compelling civic religion would be birthed in which man's freedom was dependent upon being knitted into the group. Collective relationships would become the framework for individual freedom.

Rousseau wrote: "Whoever refuses to obey the general will shall be constrained to do so by the whole body... he shall be forced to be free."[16] Everything that undermines social unity, the "civil religion," should be destroyed. Intolerance would be anathema: "Intolerance is something which belongs to the religions we have rejected."[17]

Romanticism awakened an image of Man and Nature in a spirit of monism, and Rousseau excited dreams of community wholeness – what Erik von Kuehnelt-Leddihn described as a "new society of obedient nonentities ready to be submerged in the mass."[18]

New Religions:

Nineteenth century America was hailed as a land of expansion and opportunity. It was also fertile ground for novel religious movements.

Living in New York State, the young Joseph Smith received a visitation from an angelic host called Moroni. By 1830 he published *The Book of Mormon* and established a religious society, later known as the Church of Jesus Christ of Latter-day Saints (LDS). Mormonism, a progressive faith – that is, it claims to receive updated revelations – established hierarchies of church order and systems for the attainment of *exultation*.

Smith, in his 1844 King Follett Sermon, taught that God was an exulted

---

[14] Jean-Jacques Rousseau, *The Social Contract* (Penguin Classics, 1968), p.50.

[15] Ibid., p.77.

[16] Ibid., p.64.

[17] Ibid., p.186.

[18] Erik von Kuehnelt-Leddihn, *Leftism: From de Sade and Marx to Hitler and Marcuse* (Arlington House Publishers, 1974), p.87.

man and that the Mormon goal was "to learn how to be gods yourself... the same as all gods have done before you."[19]

"God" would thus be a materialist deity and subject to the same laws of nature as other men. Parley Pratt, the "Apostle Paul of Mormonism,"[20] said as much in his book, *Key to the Science of Theology,*

> Each of these Gods, including Jesus Christ and His Father, being in possession of not merely organized spirit, but a glorious immortal body of flesh and bones, is subject to the laws which govern, out of necessity, even the most refined order of physical existence.[21]

Mormonism therefore presents a naturalistic theology wherein the LDS deity acts as a master engineer. Such a God could not engage in creation *ex nihilo* – creation out of nothing – for that would require a different kind of deity, a spirit-personality not subject to the physical limitations of matter or time or space. An interesting consideration emerges. As the Mormon version of God is an exalted man bound to physical matter, "full salvation" or exaltation requires a naturalistic or humanistic mechanism. Good works and obligations, coupled with faith, fills that role.[22]

Other "made in America" religions cropped up during Modernity. The teachings of Mary Eddie Baker, known as Christian Science; the Watch Tower Bible and Tract Society, today recognized as the Jehovah's Witnesses; and the Unity Church and New Thought Movement.

Starting in the mid-1800s, Spiritism – also labeled Spiritualism – became an exciting and controversial movement, a "scientific" demonstration of the existence and survivability of the human soul.[23] Table rapping, séances, excretions of ectoplasm, levitations, telekinesis and apparitions; throngs of

---

[19] Quoted by Bruce R. McConkie, *Mormon Doctrine* (Bookcraft, 1979), p.321.

[20] See Terryl L. Givens and Matthew J. Grow, *Parley P. Pratt: The Apostle Paul of Mormonism* (Oxford University Press, 2011).

[21] *Parley P. Pratt, Key to the Science of Theology* (Dessert News, 1915), p.42. *Doctrine and Covenants* 131:7 states, "There is no such thing as immaterial matter. All spirit is matter, but it is more fine or pure, and can only be discerned by purer eyes."

[22] For a detailed list of what is required, see Bruce R. McConkie, *Mormon Doctrine* (Bookcraft, 1979), pp. 669-670.

[23] Bruce F. Campbell writes of its historical context in the 19th century: "Spiritualism was part of the movement away from Puritan Christianity in America, which has been termed the revolt against Calvinism." Bruce F. Campbell, *Ancient Wisdom Revealed: A History of the Theosophical Movement* (University of California Press, 1980), p.9.

people in the United States, England, France, and later Brazil[24] gravitated to the paranormal experiences of Spiritism. An ancient practice, and one forbidden in the Bible,[25] communicating with the dead became a religious fad. Scores of home circles and hundreds of congregations came together to encounter psychic phenomena, and Spiritualism was touted as Christianity's replacement and the "basis of all religion."[26]

Sir Arthur Conan Doyle of Sherlock Holmes fame converted to Spiritualism and, in 1923, traveled to Winnipeg, Manitoba to proselytize its cause and to connect with prominent citizens engaged in psychic activity. Doyle noted: "I came away with the conclusion that Winnipeg stands very high among the places we have visited for its psychic possibilities."[27]

Spiritism preached a message of self-perfection through reincarnation of the soul: To evolve toward God.[28] In 1921, psychic researcher Gustave Ge-

---

[24] Brazil's 2010 census revealed 2 million of its citizens are Spiritists. See *Censo Demografico 2010*, Instituto Brasileiro de Geografia e Estatistica, June 29, 2012, p.11.

[25] The Bible warns against spiritualist activities. I believe the admonition is in place not because spiritualist activities are always fraudulent (the Spiritualist movement certainly has had frauds and con-artists), but because a supernatural reality does exist and it is a dangerous environment for human interaction. Consider the warning given to Israel in Deuteronomy 18:9-14. "When you come into the land which the Lord your God is giving you, you shall not learn to follow the abominations of those nations. There shall not be found among you anyone who makes his son or his daughter pass through the fire, or one who practices witchcraft, or a soothsayer, or one who interprets omens, or a sorcerer, or one who conjures spells, or a medium, or a spiritist, or one who calls up the dead. For all who do these things are an abomination to the Lord, and because of these abominations the Lord your God drives them out from before you. You shall be blameless before the Lord your God. For these nations which you will dispossess listened to soothsayers and diviners; but as for you, the Lord your God has not appointed such for you." Galatians 1:8 also warns that supernatural entities may bring a deceptive message: "But even if we, or an angel from heaven, preach any other gospel to you than what we have preached to you, let him be accursed."

[26] G.K. Nelson, "Spiritualism," *Man, Myth and Magic*, Volume 19 (Marshall Cavendish Corporation, 1970, edited by Richard Cavendish), p.2659.

[27] "Arthur Conan Doyle's Adventures in Winnipeg," *Manitoba History*, Nu. 25, Spr. 1993.

[28] Allan Kardec, *The Spirits' Book* (International Spiritist Council, 2010, originally published in 1857), p.168. Kardec mixed Christian terms and concepts with his Spiritism. In fact, the movement itself had a strong but erroneous Christian flavor. Kardec described Spiritism as the "third revelation of God's Law" after Christ and Moses: Allan Kardec, *The Gospel According to Spiritism* (International Spiritist Council, 2011, originally published in 1864), p.51.

ley described what he believed to be the future of the individual, *collective evolution* into *cosmic consciousness,*

> At what we call the summit of evolution... the apparent separation and the temporary scission between the conscious and the subconscious will no longer exist... The subconscious being will have disappeared and only the conscious being will remain. Then, but only then, the essential dynamo-psychism will deserve the name of Will... each individual consciousness will be expanded to total consciousness; it will have become the total Consciousness Itself. The 'summit' of evolution may then be imaged as a kind of 'conscious nirvana.'[29]

Alfred Russel Wallace, the co-founder of Darwinian evolution,[30] was a strong proponent of Spiritualism and wrote: "Spiritualism is an experimental science, and affords the only sure foundation for a true philosophy and a pure religion."[31] Sir Francis Galton, the father of eugenics and Charles Darwin's cousin, also dabbled in Spiritualism and sent letters to Darwin about his séances.[32]

Religious changes happened in other parts of the world too. In Persia, a claim was made that God was manifesting through an Islamic offshoot, soon to be known as the Bahá'í faith. Syncretistic in nature, the Bahá'í aimed then and now to be a unifying system, drawing mankind into a political and religious order of global harmony[33] – what the faith's founder, Bahá'u'lláh, described as a "new World Order... this wondrous System."[34] Since the late 1940s, the Bahá'í International Community has been an active participant within the United Nations, which it sees as a manifestation of its prophesied "new world order."

---

[29] Gustave Geley, *From the Unconscious to the Conscious* (Harper & Brothers Publishers, 1921), p.241.

[30] At one time the theory of evolution was called the Darwin-Wallace theory.

[31] Alfred R. Wallace, *A Defence of Modern Spiritualism* (Colby and Rich, 1874), p.62.

[32] Karl Pearson, *The Life, Letters and Labours of Francis Galton*, Volume II (Cambridge at the University Press, 1924), pp.62-67.

[33] See John Ferraby, *All Things Made New: A Comprehensive Outline of the Bahá'í Faith* (Bahá'í Publishing Trust, 1975).

[34] "Writings of Bahá'u'lláh," *Bahá'í World Faith: Selected Writings of Bahá'u'lláh and 'Abdu'l-Bahá'* (Bahá'í Publishing Committee, 1943), p.35. Note: Bahá'u'lláh wrote about the "new world order" in *The Kitáb-i-Aqdas* in 1873.

The Bahá'í spiritual-political vision has been described as "the oneness of the world of humanity," and the faith itself has been portrayed as "the divine religion of oneness."[35] *One World* is the hope.

Modernity, with its hard materialism, was an era of religious enthusiasm.

Esotericism:

A renewed interest in the occult and esoteric took place during Modernity: "The search for a single key that would solve the mysteries of the universe."[36]

Freemasonry, with its older history and layers of meaning, became a lightening rod for questions of occult interaction – and this was from within the Craft itself.[37] Masonic philosopher Albert Pike, the Sovereign Grand Commander of the Scottish Rite's Southern Jurisdiction, published his magnum opus, *Morals and Dogma*. In it, Pike wove a complex narrative of comparative Masonic knowledge with interpretations from ancient mystery schools and religions. He concluded with the "Secret of the Universal Equilibrium," wherein Man gains perfection, and everything – human and divine, light and darkness, good and evil – culminates in a point of balance.[38] Other Masonic thinkers and esoteric philosophers paraded mystical interpretations.[39]

A swath of arcane societies cropped up. Some came-and-went like shadows on the wall, others lingered in obscurity, and a few profoundly energized the growing interest in occultism.[40]

---

35 "Writings of 'Abdu'l-Bahá'," *Bahá'í World Faith*, p.218, 237.

36 Peter Washington, *Madame Blavatsky's Baboon: A History of the Mystics, Mediums, and Misfits Who Brought Spiritualism to America* (Schocken Books, 1993/1995), p.9.

37 Speaking to the controversy, Albert Mackey noted that a favored theory is to "trace the origin of Freemasonry to the Mysteries of Paganism," while others who deny this claim still find the comparisons remarkable. See Albert Mackey with Robert I. Clegg, *Mackey's History of Freemasonry*, Volume 1 (The Masonic History Company, 1898/1921), p.196.

38 Albert Pike, *Morals and Dogma of the Ancient and Accepted Scottish Rite of Freemasonry* (Supreme Council of the Southern Jurisdiction, A.A.S.R., USA, 1871/1944), pp.859-861.

39 Later examples include C.W. Leadbeater, *Ancient Mystic Rites* (Quest Books, 1995, originally published 1926); Manly P. Hall, *The Lost Keys of Freemasonry* (Macoy Publishing and Masonic Supply Company, 1951, originally published 1923, before Hall became a Mason of influence); and Henry C. Clausen, *Emergence of the Mystical* (The Supreme Council, 33, Ancient and Accepted Scottish Rite of Freemasonry, 1981).

40 A list of Western esoteric societies arising during the 19th and early 20th centuries (not exhaustive and in no particular order): Co-Freemasonry, The Druid Order, Rites of Mizraim and Memphis, Societas Rosicruciana in Anglia (only Master Masons could join), United

Organized Theosophy, a blending of Hinduism and Buddhism entwined with strands of Western occultism, was one of the new approaches to spirituality. Co-founded by the Russian-born Helena Petrovna Blavatsky, who was introduced to Spiritualism in the United States,[41] Theosophy quickly gained traction in America, India, England, and Germany. Drawing to itself an array of personalities including Thomas Edison[42] and the famed poet W.B. Yeats,[43] Theosophy captured the minds of the social upper crust.

Commenting on the 19th century context, historian Cherry Gilchrist explains Theosophy's rise from her favorable point of view,

> If we can think ourselves back to nineteenth-century Europe and America, the limitations on vision that existed become very apparent, for materialist science was gaining the upper hand, and Christianity was in a straight-jacketed phase where believers were not expected to think for themselves, or try to find their own way into the sacred mysteries. Spiritually speaking, Western civilization was grasping for fresh air. Today, we take for granted our access to esoteric and religious studies of all kinds, but this openness owes a lot to the advent of Theosophy. Blavatsky burst like a primal force onto the European scene, and though her teachings came like a howling winter wind to the orthodox, to those eager for new horizons, they blew open a door to other worlds.[44]

Ancient Order of Druids, Edda Society, Hermetic Order of the Golden Dawn, Ancient and Mystical Order Rosæ Crucis, Armanen-Orden, Rosicrucian Fellowship, Ordo Templi Orientis, Lectorium Rosicrucianum, Anthroposophical Society, Martinist Order, Thule Society, Fraternitas Saturni, Order of the Temple of the Rosy Cross, Order of the Rising Sun, Germanenorden, Fratres Lucis, and Ordo Novi Templi.

[41] Bruce Campbell, *Ancient Wisdom Revived: A History of the Theosophical Movement* (University of California Press, 1980), pp.20-26. A Theosophical text dedicated to spiritualist practices and experiences is *The Other Side of Death: Scientifically Examined and Carefully Described*, by C.W. Leadbeater (Theosophical Publishing Society, 1904). Leadbeater noted that Theosophy and Spiritualism have much in common and that "we each have our part to fill in the great work of the future." (p.399).

[42] Washington, *Madame Blavatsky's Baboon*, p.68. Washington lists Alfred R. Wallace, Darwin's collaborator, as a Theosophist. Although Wallace was interested in Theosophy, his membership in the Theosophical Society is questionable. Campbell writes that Wallace "practiced his religiosity outside Christianity and later gravitated to Theosophy" (p.18).

[43] Campbell, *Ancient Wisdom Revived.*, p.168.

[44] Cherry Gilchrist, *Theosophy: The Wisdom of the Ages* (HarperSanFrancisco, 1996), p.13.

Theosophy described itself as "Divine Knowledge or Science" and the "Wisdom of the gods."[45] The Theosophical Society motto was and remains, "there is no religion higher than truth."[46] As another Theosophist put it: "Theosophy is a scientific religion and a religious science."[47] It taught that Man could be perfected, and human evolution was now being guided by already Perfected Men known under a variety of names – "Adepts or Supermen," the "Great White Brotherhood," Planetary Spirits, Great Angels, and Masters.[48] Theosophy's secret, like the worldview of the East it mirrored, was the union of Man and God and Nature. Blavatsky described this in three words: *All in all*. This "all in all," she explained, is the basic concept "on which the Secret Doctrine rests."[49]

David Morris in his review of Theosophy's impact on literature and culture described the movement this way,

> Its novelty lay in that it sought to replace the belief system of the Christian religion and the knowledge system of modern science, replacing both with a spiritual knowledge that was free from associations of guilt and which did not carry within it a moral imperative. Theosophy transmuted scientific knowledge into an echo of spiritual knowledge.[50]

Theosophy would, in turn, stimulate other esoteric schools of thought. Lucis Trust, an occult group founded by Alice Bailey – herself a personality in the Theosophy movement – and Benjamin Crème's Share International, are two of the bodies birthed through Blavatsky's work. Both Lucis and Share look for a coming World Teacher who will inaugurate planetary oneness. And here we come full circle, for the main speaker at the Global Citizenship 2000 Youth Congress, Robert Muller, had ties to Lucis Trust. His World Core Curriculum was soaked in Theosophical thinking.[51]

---

45 H.P. Blavatsky, *The Key to Theosophy* (Theosophical University Press, 1889/1995), p.1.

46 Ibid., p.2.

47 William Q. Judge, *The Ocean of Theosophy* (The Theosophy Company, 1893/1947), p.1.

48 C.W. Leadbeater's book, *The Masters and the Path* (The Theosophical Press, 1925), is devoted to exploring the Theosophical theme of Ascended Masters.

49 H.P. Blavatsky, *The Secret Doctrine*, Vo.1 (Theosophical University Pr., 1888/1988), p.20.

50 David Morris, *The Masks of Lucifer: Technology and the Occult in Twentieth-Century Popular Literature* (B.T. Batsford, 1992), p.24.

51 In 1979, Muller spoke to Lucis Trust's Arcane School Conference in New York City. The

The impression of Theosophy on religious thought was profound. Gilchrist was correct when she said: "It is the impetus of Theosophy that has enabled the whole New Age movement to come into being."[52]

Esoteric philosophy blossomed during the height of Modernity. Scores of books and pamphlets were published and distributed, including *The Aquarian Gospel of Jesus the Christ*: "The universal God is one, yet he is more than one; all things are God; all things are one."[53] The first English translation of the Jewish mystical text, the *Kabbalah*, was published and released.[54] Other books of mysticism, collections of grimoires,[55] and works of general magic began to circulate.[56]

Occultism flourished during the Age of Science.

Parliament of Religions:

Writing on the upsurge of interest in religion and spirituality, historian Peter Washington tells us: "It was becoming clear that an enormous and enduring public appetite existed in the West for new and exotic forms of religion."[57]

---

transcript of Muller's address is found in his book, *New Genesis: Shaping a Global Spirituality* (World Happiness and Cooperation, 1989), pp.117-127. Christian researcher Berit Kjos describes in *Brave New Schools* (Harvest House Publishers, 1995) a personal encounter at The Robert Muller School in Arlington, Texas, in which Muller's *World Core Curriculum* was openly connected to Alice Bailey's thinking.

52 Gilchrist, *Theosophy*, p.4.

53 Levi H. Dowling, *The Aquarian Gospel of Jesus the Christ: The Philosophic and Practical Basis of the Religion of the Aquarian Age of the World* (De Vorss & Company, 1982, originally published 1907), chapter 28, verse 4.

54 S.L. MacGregor Mathers, a Freemason and leading occultist, translated and released part of the *Kabbalah* in 1887. See Mathers, *The Kabbalah Unveiled* (Samuel Weiser, 1970, originally published 1887/1888). In 1926, Mathers' wife wrote a preface, saying "The whole aim and object of the teaching is to bring a man to the knowledge of his higher self... that he may ultimately regain union with the Divine Man latent in himself." (p.ix). Mathers also translated and published *The Key of Solomon the King* (Weiser Books, 2002, originally published in 1889), an occult text of importance.

55 A grimoire is a textbook on spell casting and summoning.

56 Two examples: Eliphas Levi, *Transcendental Magic: Its Doctrine and Ritual* (Bracken Books, 1995, originally published in two parts, 1854 and 1856); Arthur Edward Waite, *The Book of Black Magic: Including the Rites and Mysteries of Goetic Theurgy, Sorcery, and Infernal Necromancy* (Samuel Weiser, 1998, originally published 1890).

57 Washington, *Madame Blavatsky's Baboon*, p.25.

The 1893 World's Parliament of Religions was the place to taste the new and exotic. An official part of the World's Columbian Exposition in Chicago, the Parliament started on September 11 and ended on the 27th. Between 3,000 and 7,000 people attended, depending on the day. Seventy-eight percent of the speakers came from Protestant, Catholic and Orthodox backgrounds, marking this as an historic ecumenical event.[58] But it was more. The Parliament was a global interfaith gathering, the first of its kind, as an array of other religions and spiritual systems were represented: Buddhism and Zen, Hinduism, Confucianism, Islam, Judaism, Taoism, Zoroastrianism, Jainism, Spiritualism and Theosophy. It was from this event that the modern interfaith movement springs.

Speaking of its significance in America's religious history, one interfaith commentator noted that, "the Parliament took place when the USA was ceasing to be just a Protestant Christian nation. Indeed, the Parliament symbolized the coming change to a religiously plural society."[59]

A new era of unity was promised at the Parliament, as the following quote from an 1893 speech demonstrates,

> The religion of the future will be universal in every sense. It will embody all the thought and aspiration and virtue and emotion of all humanity; it will draw together all lands and people and kindreds and tongues into a universal brotherhood of love and service; it will establish upon earth a heavenly order.[60]

Excited crowds filled the halls and galleries, eager to sample exotic spiritual flavors. The appetite displayed for Theosophy was telling.

Organizers first gave the Theosophical Society a room with seating capacity for 250 people. The public response, however, surpassed expectations. Next a space for 1,500 was arranged, but this was likewise inadequate. Organizers

---

[58] Diana L. Eck, "Forward," *The Dawn of Religious Pluralism: Voices from the World's Parliament of Religions, 1893* (Open Court/The Council for a Parliament of the World's Religions, 1993, edited by Richard H. Seager), p.xv.

[59] Marcus Braybrooke, *Pilgrimage of Hope: One Hundred Years of Global Interfaith Dialogue* (SCM Press, 1992), p.8.

[60] Merwin-Marie Snell, "Future of Religion," *The Dawn of Religious Pluralism: Voices from the World's Parliament of Religions, 1893* (Open Court/The Council for a Parliament of the World's Religions, 1993, edited by Richard H. Seager), p.174.

had to quickly adjust by preparing a hall for 3,000, which was soon packed.[61] Hindu cosmology and Eastern philosophy were major Theosophical talking points, and the public was hungry. Attendees, be they Christian ministers or university professors or the American press, savored the oneness message of the "Divine Human."[62]

The 1893 Parliament also introduced the *personalities* of the East to the West. Swami Vivekananda, a disciple of the Indian mystic Sri Ramakrishna, was unquestionably the star of the Parliament,

> No sooner had he addressed the assembly as 'Sisters and Brothers of America' than a great wave of enthusiasm went through the audience. They rose to their feet with shouts of applause, as if they had gone mad. Everyone was cheering, cheering, and cheering. The Swami was bewildered. For two full minutes he attempted to speak, but the wild enthusiasm of the audience would not allow it.[63]

The *Boston Evening Transcript* wrote, "He is a great favourite of the Parliament… If he merely crosses the platform he is applauded."[64]

Vivekananda wowed the crowd. "Man is to become divine by realizing the divine," he told the assembly.[65] To call someone a "sinner," then, would be an act of *defamation*,

> 'Children of immortal bliss' – what a sweet, what a hopeful name! Allow me to call you, brethren, by that sweet name – heirs of immortal bliss – yea, the Hindu refuses to call you sinners. Ye are the Children of God, the sharers of immortal bliss, holy and perfect beings. Ye divinities on earth – sinners! It is a sin to call a man so; it is a standing libel on human nature.[66]

---

[61] Joy Mills, *100 Years of Theosophy: A History of the Theosophical Society in America* (The Theosophical Publishing House, 1987), pp.18-19.

[62] *The Theosophical Congress, Held by the Theosophical Society at the Parliament of Religions: Report of Proceedings and Documents* (American Section Headquarters, Theosophical Society, 1893). See page 31 for "oneness" and the Divine Human.

[63] Swami Vivekananda, *Chicago Addresses* (Advaita Ashrama, 49th reprint, 2013), pp.16-17, "The Background Story."

[64] Ibid., p.62.

[65] Ibid., p.44.

[66] Ibid., p.34.

Vivekananda's overall impact has been described as a "turning point" in modern history.[67] So profound was his influence in bringing the East to the West that his legacy was repeatedly acknowledged at the 2015 Parliament of the World's Religions.[68]

After his Chicago debut, the swami embarked on a nation-wide lecture tour, spreading his progressive Hindu message across America. His spiritual persona[69] and his teachings on "Oneness – the Unity of all," the "Divine Self," coupled to "relative truths" – struck a cord with a receptive public and social elites.[70] He described his Western approach as "dry, hard reason, seasoned in the sweetest syrup of love and made spicy with intense work, and cooked in the kitchen of Yoga."[71] Swami Vivekananda's influence went far beyond the 1893 Parliament, inspiring the creation of Vedanta Societies in New York, Hollywood, Berkeley, and San Francisco.[72]

The Chicago Parliament, however, was not the first time the East and West touched.[73] Trade and colonialism, missionary activity, and Jesuit interac-

---

67 See *Vivekananda as the Turning Point: The Rise of the New Spiritual Wave* (Advaita Ashrama, 2013, published on behalf of the Committee for the Celebration of 150th Birth Anniversary of Swami Vivekananda, edited by Swami Shuddhidananda).

68 From personal observations at the 2015 Parliament in Salt Lake City. Vivekananda was acknowledged during the opening and closing ceremonies of the Parliament, and workshops specifically explored his impact on Western society and religious life.

69 One New York City devotee described Vivekananda this way: "We recognized in him a power that no other teacher possessed. It was he alone who was shaping our thoughts and conviction. Even my dog – an Irish setter – felt this. He would stand perfectly still and a quiver would run through his body whenever Swamiji would lay his hand on his head and tell him he was a true *yogi*" [italics in original]. See *Reminiscences of Swami Vivekananda: His Eastern and Western Admirers* (Advaita Ahrama, fourth edition, 2004), p.124.

70 To read a collection of personal memories regarding Vivekananda and his teachings in the West, see *Reminiscences of Swami Vivekananda: His Eastern and Western Admirers* (Advaita Ahrama, fourth edition, 2004).

71 *Vivekananda as the Turning Point*, p.616.

72 Today approximately 180 Vedanta centers dot the planet. Advaita Ashrama is the umbrella entity serving the global Vedanta community.

73 Some of the earliest American personalities shaped by Hindu philosophy were Ralph Waldo Emerson, Henry David Thoreau, and Walt Whitman. See Philip Goldberg's book, *American Veda: From Emerson and the Beatles to Yoga and Meditation – How Indian Spirituality Changed the West* (Three Rivers Press, 2010). In England, famed author Edwin Arnold was engrossed in Eastern spirituality, and his book *The Light of Asia*, found an audience in America and Great Britain.

tions in India had been the source of earlier contact. It has been contended that Western Enlightenment and Romanticism were inspired, in part, by the complexity of the Hindu worldview. Sutapas Bhattacharya, who promotes oneness and an East/West synthesis, tells us that the rootstock – Vedantic Brahmanism – was inspirational to early Westerners visiting the subcontinent. Noting this historic interplay between Europe and India, and the interest in Vedic philosophy, he explains that "the Jesuits had hopes of applying such ideas to Christianity and indeed such ideas from India played a key role in the development of European Deism during the Enlightenment (e.g. the Cult of the Supreme Being in revolutionary France)."[74]

Philip Goldberg, author of *American Veda* and an authority on the Eastern influence upon the West, notes a similar relationship,

> To many educated Europeans, knowledge of India and its dominant religion came as a revelation. Most powerfully affected were the philosophers and poets associated with Romanticism... who saw in Eastern philosophy a possible antidote to materialism and the cult of reason.[75]

Surging behind the imposing barrier of Modernity was an ocean of religion.

Religious Ripples

In the preceding years, before Postmodernism cemented itself in the "cultural decade,"[76] voices of mystery and imagination stirred the waters of religion, causing ripples in spiritual and social attitudes.

Stimulated by Theosophy, Canadian-born Manly P. Hall excited luminaries with his books and lectures on occult philosophy.[77] Pierre Teilhard de

---

[74] Sutapas Bhattacharya, *The Oneness/Otherness Mystery: The Synthesis of Science and Mysticism* (Motilal Banarsidass Publishers, 1999), p.34. The example given of the Cult of the Supreme Being is in the original text.

[75] Philip Goldberg, *American Veda: From Emerson and the Beatles to Yoga and Meditation – How Indian Spirituality Changed the West* (Three Rivers Press, 2010), pp.29-30. Goldberg also recounts Jesuit interest in Hindu cosmology, see page 28 in his book.

[76] Approximately 1963 to 1974.

[77] Manly P. Hall (1901-1990) was renowned for his knowledge of esoteric subjects, mythology, and religion. He founded the Philosophical Research Society, gave more than 8,000 lectures, and his many books included *The Secret Teachings of All Ages* (Philosophical Research Society, 1928), *Lectures on Ancient Philosophy* (Philosophical Research Soci-

Chardin, a Jesuit mystic, proclaimed the gospel of cosmic evolution and planetary consciousness.[78] Psychologist Carl G. Jung, touched by the teachings of Vivekananda, wove tales of ancient meaning through symbolism and archetypes, projecting myth and continuity into popular thought.[79] Aldous Huxley, inspired by the Vedanta Society in Hollywood, preached the *perennial philosophy* – that all religions share a common truth, expressing an inner mystical divinity – and then, through psychedelic substances, ventured into the experience of chemically induced oneness.[80]

Paramahansa Yogananda moved from India to the United States, establishing the Self-Realization Fellowship,

> To teach that the purpose of life is the evolution, through self-effort, of man's limited mortal consciousness into God Consciousness... To reveal the complete harmony and basic oneness of original Christianity as taught by Jesus Christ and original Yoga as taught by Bha-

---

ety, 1929/1984), *The Lost Keys of Freemasonry* (Macoy Publishing and Masonic Supply Company, 1923/1951), and *The Mystical Christ* (Philosophical Research Society, 1951).

78 Pierre Teilhard de Chardin (1881-1955) viewed Christ as the agency of cosmic/human ascension, moving us to an Omega Point – the evolutionary rise of neo-humanity and an awakened planetary consciousness, what he called the Noosphere. His books included *The Phenomenon of Man* (HarperPerennial, 1959/1976), *The Future of Man* (Harper, 1964), and *The Divine Milieu* (Harper Torchbooks, 1960). Although ostracized by the Roman Catholic Church during his lifetime, a broader acceptance of Chardin has been visible in the past few decades. Chardin's ideas intersected science and spirituality, and played an important role in the New Age movement and Transhumanism.

79 A contemporary and colleague of Sigmund Freud, the influence of Carl G. Jung (1875-1961) upon modern psychology and consciousness thinking has been astounding, inserting into everyday language such words as "archetype," "collective unconscious," and "introvert" and "extravert." Beyond depth psychology, he opened new avenues for comparative religious studies, inter-spiritual exploration, and the meaning of myth in relationship to the broader human story. Jung was influenced by Swami Vivekananda, and in 1932 he gave lectures on the "Psychology of Kundalini Yoga." It has also been suggested that Jung did research in Manly P. Hall's library.

80 Literary and cultural trendsetter, Aldous Huxley (1894-1963), is probably best noted for his 1932 book, *Brave New World*. Less known, but of equal weight in terms of intellectual influence, was his work on mysticism and spirituality, *The Perennial Philosophy* (1945). And his experiments with psychedelic substances led him to publish *The Doors of Perception* (1954) and *Heaven and Hell* (1956). Regarding the Vedanta Society and perennial philosophy, see *Aldous Huxley, 1894-1963: A Memorial Volume* (Chatto & Windus, 1965), p.158.

> gavan Krishna; and to show that these principles of truth are the common scientific foundation of all true religions... To unite science and religion through realization of the unity of their underlying principles... To serve mankind as one's larger Self.[81]

Different *systems* of religion also popped up along the ragged edges where Modernity and Postmodernism met: the Unification Church with its messianic leader Sun Myung Moon, L. Ron Hubbard's Dianetics and Scientology, and the Eastern universalism of Ananda Marga.

The Japanese Buddhist movement known as Soka Gakkai preached oneness. Daisaku Ikeda, the third president of Soka Gakkai International (SGI), extended a version of Buddhist harmony: "The life-space of the Buddha becomes united and fused with the universe. The self becomes the cosmos, and in a single instant the life-flow stretches out to encompass all that is past and all that is future."[82]

To Ikeda, time itself is in the flow of oneness, just as everything is interconnected. Such was the implication of an SGI brochure I was given while attending a World Federalist event in Washington DC,

> Our core philosophy is rooted in the concept of 'human revolution,' a process of inner transformation that centers on the idea that each act we take has an influence that extends beyond its immediate context to affect the vast and complex web of life... a concept of interrelatedness where nothing, whether in the realm of human society or of nature, exists in isolation.[83]

Presently, the number of adherents to Soka Gakkai is slightly smaller yet comparable to the membership of Mormonism worldwide.[84] Like the Bahá'í International Community, SGI works to advance the cause of global governance. Oneness, by its nature, demands a political recalibration.

---

81 *Aims and Ideals of Self-Realization Fellowship: As Set Forth by Paramahansa Yogananada*, points 2, 3, 9, 11. A copy of the Aims and Ideals can be found on the website of the Self-Realization Fellowship (www.yogananda-srf.org/Aims_and_Ideals.aspx).

82 As quoted by Richard Causton, *The Buddha in Daily Life: An Introduction to the Buddhism of Nichiren Daishonin* (Rider, 1995), p.75.

83 *SGI-USA: A Buddhist Movement for Peace, Culture and Education* (SGI-USA, 1996).

84 By "Mormonism" I am referring to The Church of Jesus Christ of Latter-day Saints, which has a membership of approximately 15.6 million worldwide. Soka Gakkai has over 12 million members.

Anticipating the unity of "one world" and the demise of previously accepted beliefs, Lancelot Law Whyte composed the following in 1950,

> Today the West cannot but admit its ugly failure. Measured by the Eastern criterion of unity and harmony the West has not merely failed to succeed, it has failed even to try. Unitary man recognizes this and accepts from Asia its deeper aim of harmony as proper to all men. Enriched by the grand failure of Christianity, static reason, and quantitative science, a new type of man emerges combining the unity of the East with the differentiation of the West. The separation of East and West is over...[85]

Religious ripples portended a spiritual riptide.

Psychedelic Spirituality

Aldous Huxley, psychedelic pioneer and literary legend, believed that a revival in religion was quickly approaching. Forecasting the earthquake about to begin, he penned the following in 1958: "Religion will be transformed into an activity concerned mainly with experience and intuition."[86]

A mind-trip spiritual experience would be unleashed through the biochemical door. Moving from the lab to the Central Intelligence Agency and into the culture, its public face was Huxley's friend, Timothy Leary.[87]

A clinical psychologist at Harvard, Leary, along with psychologists Ralph Metzner and Richard Alpert[88] – with input from Huxley – formed the Harvard Psilocybin Project. It was the spark of an inner revolution that fanned into a social and spiritual wildfire, and it is burning stronger now than before.

"In the 1960s," Leary tells us, "we promiscuously started raising questions about cosmic consciousness and alternative realities and declaring God lost and found: in a pill, a grain of sand, love, or an Eric Clapton guitar solo."[89]

---

85 Lancelot L. Whyte, *The Next Development in Man* (A Mentor Book, 1950), p.244.

86 Aldous Huxley, "Drugs That Shape Men's Minds," essay republished in his modern two volume reprint, *The Doors of Perception* and *Heaven and Hell* (HarperPerennial Modern Classics, 2009), p.16 in back section.

87 One history, with some criticism, is Martin A. Lee and Bruce Shlain, *Acid Dream: The Complete Social History of LSD: The CIA, The Sixties, and Beyond* (Grove Press, 1992).

88 Alpert traveled to India in 1967 and returned to America as Ram Dass, a metaphysical explorer who helped fuel the West's interest in Eastern spirituality.

89 Timothy Leary, *Design For Dying* (HarperEdge, 1997), pp.14-15.

Contextually linked to the Postmodern setting, the "new spirituality" being projected was nevertheless different. Whereas the Postmodern mood was a rejection of meta-narratives, the new spirituality – a seemingly disjointed collage of experiences and beliefs and ideas – pointed to a *universal narrative*: Everything is One.

Leary, Metzner, and Alpert claimed this path to oneness was found in LSD. Analyzing the psychedelic experience through the lens of Carl Jung and the death rituals in *The Tibetan Book of the Dead* – which Jung attributes to his fundamental insights[90] – the trio pontificated cosmic spirituality: "Remember the unity of all beings... Jettison your ego program and float back to the radiant bliss of at-one-ness."[91]

We find this depiction in their famed manual, *The Psychedelic Experience,*

> A sense of profound one-ness, a feeling of the unity of all energy. Superficial differences of role, cast, status, sex, species, form, power, size, beauty, even the distinctions between inorganic and living energy, disappear before the ecstatic union of all in one. All gestures, words, acts and events are equivalent in value – all are manifestations of the one consciousness which pervades everything. 'You,' 'I' and 'he' are gone, 'my' thoughts are 'ours,' 'your' feelings are 'mine.' Bodies melt into waves. Objects in the environment – lights, trees, plants, flowers – seem to open and welcome you: they are part of you. You are both simply different pulses of the same vibration. A pure feeling of ecstatic harmony with all beings is the keynote of this vision... You suddenly wake up from the delusion of separate form and hook up to the cosmic dance.[92]

Mimicking the *bardo* – the supposed transition between the final breath and the next birth, the intermediate state described in Tibetan Buddhism – the psychedelic encounter was portrayed as a *mirroring* experience: "This is

---

90 In Carl Jung's introduction to *The Tibetan Book of the Dead*, he says the following: "For years, ever since it was first published, the Bardo Thodol [aka *Tibetan Book of the Dead*] has been my constant companion, and to it I owe not only many stimulating ideas and discoveries, but also many fundamental insights." See Jung "Psychological Commentary," *The Tibetan Book of the Dead* (Oxford University Press, 1960), p.xxxvi.

91 Timothy Leary, Ralph Metzner and Richard Alpert, *The Psychedelic Experience: A Manual Based on the Tibetan Book of the Dead* (Citadel Press, 1964/1992), p.32

92 Ibid., p.49.

now the hour of death and rebirth; Take advantage of this temporary death to obtain the perfect state – Enlightenment. Concentrate on the unity of all living beings."[93]

Jesuit priest David Toolan, who found himself at the Esalen Institute studying meditation, tells of his LSD *birthing* encounter,

> After about a half hour, the walls of the room and house where two friends and I were experimenting simply fell away – I was navigating about in a space something like Stanley Kubrick explored at the end of *2001: A Space Odyssey*. It was a wonderland of sensory distortion and synesthesia, solid objects turning liquid, colors and sounds vibrating and fusing; the ordinary empirical world assumed all the charged panpsychism of a Van Gogh painting. But I didn't spend long with this epicurean feast. Before I knew quite what was happening, I felt my body shrinking. With all the physical sensations of it, I was catapulted back to infancy; further, into the womb. I had to get born again...[94]

With the help of his friends simulating a birth canal, Toolan "pushed and shoved" his way from "uterine darkness" into the light. The encounter was unifying, interweaving the psychological and spiritual, blending and combining and transforming – "it rendered worlds soluble."[95]

Quantum unity was to be found in a dosage, where nothing is real and everything appears to be true. It is a state of *hyper-suggestibility* predicated on what Leary, Metzner, and Alpert called *set-and-setting*.

"Listen! Wake up!" screamed Leary in his book, *High Priest*. "You are God! You have the Divine plan engraved in cellular script within you. Listen! Take this sacrament! You'll see! You'll get the revelation! It will change your life! You will be reborn!"[96]

Commenting on the psychedelic experience, Dr. Charles Slack, a friend of Leary and an experimenter himself, wrote about the response LSD invoked: "The first time you take LSD, it makes you think you are God. This is certainly

---

[93] Ibid., p.97.

[94] David Toolan, *Facing West from California's Shores: A Jesuit's Journey into New Age Consciousness* (Crossroad, 1987), pp.58-59.

[95] Ibid., p.64.

[96] Timothy Leary, *High Priest* (Ronin Publishing, 1995, originally published 1968 by The New American Library), p.285.

one of the most common reactions to the drug. Proselytizing is likely to follow – with little success among those who have't had any of the drug."[97]

"I knew the truth of being one with God, one with His Power," explained Slack after a psychedelic trip in the presence of a Swami companion. "I had within me at that time a power. I knew I did. It seemed quite reasonable… All the superman myths of the ages were recreated for real in me."[98]

Slack, however, recognized the *problem of interpretation*. When talking to another person "goofed-up" on LSD who also claimed to be God, how was this situation handled? Which one is God? In the Oneness view of cosmology, everyone and everything is infused with deity, but Slack also grasped that there was something unrealistic in the claim.

Speaking to Leary's motto that "two acid-heads are better than one," Slack made an interesting confession,

> Each tends to support the other's delusion… A mutual conspiracy of non-criticism, an I-won't-break-your-euphoria-if-you-won't-break-mine agreement, unspoken and the stronger for being silent, takes place. As a consequence of LSD, there was a lot of ego-involved spiritual rap… [99]

Slack writes, "LSD had become a social movement, an art style, a religious belief, a revolutionary political philosophy and a way of life for thousands. We were all participating in the cultural and artistic (and criminal) aspects of the revolution."[100]

A more recent psychedelic proponent described the spiritual awakening as a "non-dual experience, a 'merger with the white light' type experience… one sees the larger currents of information relative to human self-awareness manifesting as things like visions of the Christ, or Buddha."[101]

Manifesting "religious figures" seems to be a common theme. For *psychonauts*, the chemical-directed "inner revolution" stimulates mystical feelings and spiritual visions. But as Slack discovered, it is a grand delusion.

---

[97] Charles W. Slack, *Timothy Leary, the Madness of the Sixties and Me* (Peter H. Wyden, 1974), p.7.

[98] Ibid., pp.123-124.

[99] Ibid., p.7.

[100] Ibid., p.65.

[101] James W. Jesso, *Soundscapes and Psychedelics* (SoulsLantern Publishing, 2014), p.35, see note #16 on the bottom of the page.

For Leary, his trip into Hinduism corresponded with visits to a Vedanta ashram in 1962, where he guided worshippers in a psychedelic session,

> I came to the ashram... and joined the meditating-chanting service. Then, those who were to take the trip remained for more prayers and contemplation. The LSD had been placed in chalices on the altar. Incense and flowers adorned it. The LSD sacrament was mixed with holy water from the Ganges, blessed, and drunk...
>
> ...I was high too and overcome by the power of the ashram and the shrine and the ancient rituals. We were all caught in Hindu mythologies...
>
> ...I looked around the room. Ramakrishna's statue breathed and his eyes twinkled the message. Vivekananda's brown face beamed and winked. Christ grinned to be joined again with his celestial brothers. The rare-wood walls breathed. The sacred kundalini serpent uncoiled up the bronzed candelabra to the thousand-petaled lotus blossom. This was the fulcrum moment of eternity. The exact second of consciousness, fragile, omniscient. God was present and spoke to us in silence...
>
> I was a Hindu from that moment on. No, that's not the way to say it. I recognized that day in the temple that we are all Hindus in our essence. We are all Hindu Gods and Goddesses. Laughing Krishna. Immutable Brahma... That day in the temple I discovered my Hindu-ness.[102]

Eastern interests and psychedelic spirituality correlated. Dr. Rick Strassman, a medical researcher who specialized in psychiatry, tells of attending a Zen Buddhist monastery in the US Midwest for a multi-week meditation retreat in 1974. He questioned the resident monks: "Did you take psychedelics before becoming a monk? How important were they in your decision?"

Strassman's findings are noteworthy,

> Most interesting was that most of them had gained their first view of the spiritual path while on psychedelic drugs... The overwhelming majority had taken them and had experienced their first glimpse of the enlightened state of the mind with their assistance.[103]

---

[102] Leary, *High Priest*, pp.297-298.

[103] Rick Strassman, *DMT: The Spirit Molecule* (Park Street Press, 2001), p.296.

The Western psychedelic wave floated Eastern beliefs to a new high. From Harvard to Hollywood, American culture was tripping on experiential spirituality – *advaita* in a pill. But there was something else lurking.

During the early 1990s, Strassman received US government approval to conduct clinically controlled DMT[104] experiments on voluntary human subjects. One of the more troubling aspects of his research was subject contact with other entities: mental interactions with nonmaterial life-forms. Test patients described encounters with angelic beings and alien creatures. Strassman had previously heard of strange life-forms seen in psychedelic visions, but the doctor was unprepared for their level of involvement. These beings were communicating with and manipulating his subjects.

"Their 'business' appeared to be testing, examining, probing, and even modifying the volunteer's mind and body," he reported.

One patient described it this way: "It's more like being possessed. During the experience there is a sense of someone, or something else, there taking control. It's like you have to defend yourself against them, whoever they are, but they certainly are there. I'm aware of them and they're aware of me. It's like they have an agenda."[105]

Strassman tried to understand these experiences through a scientific framework, chalking it up to brain chemistry and psychological conditioning. But the visitations were too interactive and the experiences too invasive, strongly hinting that a threshold had been crossed between drug-induced imagination and *something else*.

The entities promised to open vistas of spirituality and inter-connection.

Left with little choice, Strassman hypothesized that DMT unlocked a *different level of reality*, creating a passing-through-the-veil effect whereby his subjects had made contact with its inhabitants – entities that exhibited a *special intelligence*. Others before Strassman had intentionally used DMT for religious revelations. In the Amazon basin, the plant derived mixture known as *ayahuasca* naturally releases the properties of DMT. Ingested as a tea, ayahuasca provides "soul access to other worlds."[106] Ceremonies and rituals have been created around its use, and in Brazil the religion of *Santo Daime* combines Spiritism, Roman Catholic traditions, and the "plant teachings" of

---

[104] DMT = Dimethyltryptamine.

[105] Strassman, *DMT*, p.189.

[106] Ibid., p.331.

ayahuasca. Today ayahuasca has international exposure, and was introduced at the 2015 Parliament of the World's Religions as an "effective catalyst of religious and spiritual awakening."[107] Seeking wisdom from "plant spirits" is popular in San Francisco's tech industry, and with cultural elites.[108]

Dr. Strassman described DMT as the "spirit molecule."

Could it be that psychedelics open some kind of mind-and-soul portal to the supernatural? It certainly appears that way. Are psychedelics a possible gateway to encounter what the Apostle Paul described as "seducing spirits and doctrines of demons"?[109] I believe a good argument could be made to that end. Paul reminds us that Satan, in his acts of deception, transforms himself into an "angel of light."[110] Ironically, as the chemical user claims a new and personal revelation of inner divinity, it is simply the mirroring of an ancient ruse: "Your eyes will be opened, and you will be like God..."[111]

There *is* a spiritual realm, a supernatural reality – and like other known techniques, it appears psychedelic usage can be a tool for gaining access to this other dimension. The forbidden fruit shines with inner light.

The connection between Eastern philosophy and mind-altering substances, however, runs much deeper than what transpired during the cultural revolution of the 1960s and early 1970s.

In *The Rigveda*, a collection of hymns foundational to Hindu lore, we read of *Soma* and its "juice for thee to drink."[112] The purpose?

"We have drunk Soma and become immortal; we have attained the light, the gods discovered… Soma, thou art our life-giver: aim of all eyes, light-finder, come within us."[113] Hymn after hymn is given to Soma, which provides mental power "to make us better than we are."[114]

---

[107] "Introducing Ayahuasca Religion," workshop at the 2015 Parliament of the World's Religions, Monday, October 19, 2015. Taken from the Parliament *Program Schedule*, p.235.

[108] This was borne out for me at Burning Man 2017, where I attended lectures and workshops on modern shamanism, psychedelics, and entrepreneurial visioning.

[109] 1 Timothy 4:1.

[110] 2 Corinthians 11:13-14.

[111] Genesis 3:5.

[112] *The Rigveda*, 8:45:22, page 255 of the Ralph T. H. Griffith translation, *The Hymns of the Rigveda*, Volume 3 (E.J. Lazarus and Company, 1891). Troy Wilson Organ touches on Soma in *The Hindu Quest for the Perfection of Man* (Ohio University, 1970), p.117.

[113] *The Rigveda*, 8:48:3 and 15, pp.265-266 of the Griffith translation.

[114] *The Rigveda*, 9:4:1-10, p.365 of the Griffith translation. The *Valakhilya Hymns* are noted for their many references to Soma.

Shrouded in questions of interpretation, the knowledge of precisely what Soma was – a drink of some kind, a life giver, a spiritual fire – has been lost in time. Suggestions have been made that it was a plant substance whose refined juices were ritually offered to the gods,[115] and inner light was granted to those who consumed the elixir. According to one source, it had "strong intoxicating or more probably hallucinogenic properties."[116] Another commentator explained it this way: "A drink made from a plant, and produced hallucinations of the kind made familiar by modern experiments with a variety of drugs and herbs."[117]

So important was this juice that Soma was made an object of worship and a ritualistic portal for mystical experience. Soma became a personified deity.

Hindu's ancient story may be the result of a psychedelic trip.

Religious Riptide

Ashrams and yoga and LSD – Eastern oneness blossomed with Western psychedelic wholeness. But the religious message was not limited to chemical experimenters.

In the 1960s, Maharishi Mahesh Yogi traveled around the world lecturing on Hindu beliefs and Transcendental Meditation (TM). His tours took him into the lofty towers of academia and within the esteemed halls of political power, including a meeting with UN Secretary General U Thant. In the United States his technique of meditation, TM, soon became a sensation.

"It wasn't hipsters who gravitated to him at first," explained Philip Goldberg. "His earliest supporters, drawn by invitations from friends or small ads in local newspapers, were... clean-shaven dads with neat haircuts and good jobs, and apron-wearing moms..."[118]

Sold as a way to find "infinite inner happiness," Maharishi was endorsed by The Beatles, sending the guru's popularity soaring. And although The Beatles soon distanced themselves from the guru, other notables such as Mike Love of the Beach Boys and television host Merv Griffin embraced his

[115] Terence McKenna discusses Soma in *Food of the Gods: A Radical History of Plants, Drugs and Human Evolution* (Rider, 1992).

[116] Stutley, *Harper's Dictionary of Hinduism*, p.282.

[117] Ainslie T. Embree, *The Hindu Tradition: Readings in Oriental Thought* (The Modern Library, 1966), p.21.

[118] Goldberg, *American Veda*, p.155.

message. Pulitzer Prize-winning author, Alice Walker, recalls her experience with TM: "I was in that state of oneness with creation, and it was as if I didn't exist except as a part of everything."[119]

Others from the East traveled to Europe and America. Yogi Bhajan packaged a syncretistic version of Sikhism, teaching Kundalini Yoga and preaching an immanent shift in global consciousness. Sri Chinmoy, arriving in America in 1964, attracted the attention of musicians and politicians with his brand of meditation. Invited by U Thant, Sri Chinmoy convened twice-weekly meditation meetings at the United Nations in New York City. But it was not just the East coming west, affluent and searching Westerners departed for India.

Michael Murphy, a Stanford University student who traveled to the Sri Aurobindo Ashram in India during the early days of spiritual tourism,[120] returned and co-founded the California-based Esalen Institute in 1962. Here, nestled among pine trees and redwoods in the Big Sur region south of San Francisco, visitors and residents could soak in the hot springs, bask in ocean vistas, and explore conscious development through chemical substances, integrated yoga, humanistic psychology, and sensual pleasures. A stream of Hollywood insiders and influential personalities embraced the blending of LSD, group play and Gestalt therapy, sexual adventurism and Eastern philosophy. Over the decades, a steady stream of diverse workshops have covered everything from "Modern Shamanic Initiation" to "Spiritual Psychology" to "Yoga Works" to "Deep Mythology" and "Spiritual Democracy."[121]

From transformational art to energy healing to leadership development and relationship building, Esalen became the go-to-place to acquire tools for personal transformation and social change.[122]

[119] As quoted by Jack Forem, *Transcendental Meditation: The Essential Teachings of Maharishi Mahesh Yogi* (Hay House, 2012, revised edition), p.62.

[120] Murphy was in India from 1956 to 1957, and in 1960 joined the Cultural Integration Fellowship – also known as Asia House – a San Francisco group dedicated to the teachings of Sri Aurobindo. For a retracing of spiritual tourism, see Roy Maclean, *Magic Bus: On the Hippie Trail from Istanbul to India* (Viking, 2006). For a Christian review and testimony, see Caryl Matrisciana, *Gods of the New Age* (Harvest House Publishers, 1985).

[121] Taken from *The Esalen Catalog*, January-June 1993 edition.

[122] For more on Esalen, see Marion Goldman, *The American Soul Rush: Esalen and the Rise of Spiritual Privilege* (New York University Press, 2012); Jeffrey J. Kripal, *Esalen: America and the Religion of No Religion* (The University of Chicago Press, 2007); and Walter Truett Anderson, *The Upstart Spring: Esalen and the American Awakening* (Addison-Wesley Publishing Company, 1983).

Early lecturers at the Institute demonstrated the uniqueness and importance of what was transpiring under the pines and in the hot springs. Teachers included Alan Watts, Arnold Toynbee, Timothy Leary, Aldous Huxley, Fritz Perls, Carl Rogers, Abraham Maslow, Buckminster Fuller, Terence McKenna, Joseph Campbell, B.F. Skinner, Stanislav Grof, George Leonard, and Will Schultz. Notable church leaders also contributed. Bishop James Pike of San Francisco's Grace Cathedral Episcopal Church was a bridge between the Institute and other "theological mavericks." Pike's Episcopal colleague, Robert Cromey, lectured at Esalen on homosexual enlightenment.

"By the late 1960s," explains the Institute's chairperson Jeffrey Kripal, "Esalen, through Cromey, had helped open up a cultural space to address the intersection of sexual orientation, spirituality, and social justice."[123]

Pike ended up repudiating Christian tenets and "saw the historical Jesus as a kind of political revolutionary or social critic."[124] Today these same themes resonate in *progressive Christian* circles.

Professor Marion Goldman comments on the "sweeping impact on American religion" that emerged through the Esalen experience, opening up spiritual options that were previously in the shadows of culture,

> "Esalen played a critical role in introducing and promoting esoteric spirituality so that it flowed into mainstream culture...
>
> Innovative approaches to spiritual growth and personal transformation did not spring up suddenly like magic mushrooms in the cultural forests of the 1960s. Instead, they were cultivated on Esalen's 120 acres in Big Sur, California, and introduced to middle-class Americans through media and word of mouth."[125]

Ken Wilber described it this way: "There is nothing like Esalen anywhere in the world. I truly believe it has changed the course of human history."[126]

Laced throughout the Institute's many activities was the Eastern reminder of human perfection: "Esalen promoted the growth and spread of spiritual

---

[123] Jeffrey J. Kripal, *Esalen: America and the Religion of No Religion* (The University of Chicago Press, 2007), p.183.

[124] Ibid., p.185.

[125] Marion Goldman, *The American Soul Rush: Esalen and the Rise of Spiritual Privilege* (New York University Press, 2012), pp.1-2.

[126] Quoted in *Esalen Media Kit*, "Celebrating 50 Years of Pioneering Leadership in Personal and Social Transformation," p.1. Wilber is a psychologist and founder of Integral Theory.

privilege because its foundational doctrine held that everyone had sparks of divinity that could be connected to a benevolent, distant cosmic force."[127]

Academic and public interest in Esalen increased and then rocketed. During its 50th anniversary in 2012, the Institute reported that approximately 17,000 people per year had participated in its workshops. Roughly 900,000 people had visited the California location since 1962.[128]

Money interests, too, were watching and participating. Lawrence Rockefeller, whose Baptist father had reportedly been influenced by Vivekananda and whose mother showed interest in Zen Buddhism, provided special funding to Esalen and other related organizations.[129] In fact, Murphy related in a 2012 public conversation that "[Lawrence] has seeded so much, I mean, he's the single biggest donor we've ever had at Esalen."[130]

"From the early 1970s until his death, in 2004," elaborated Marion Goldman, "Rockefeller donated millions of dollars to Esalen and three related organizations that promote inclusive spirituality and synthesize Asian and Western traditions: the San Francisco Zen Center, the Lindisfarne Association, and the California Institute for Integral Studies."[131]

Each of these institutions connected with one another. Each advanced the work of spiritual enterprise and transformation.

---

[127] Goldman, *The American Soul Rush*, p.3.

[128] *Esalen Media Kit*, "Celebrating 50 Years of Pioneering Leadership in Personal and Social Transformation," p.5.

[129] According to *Vivekananda as the Turning Point* (Advaita Ashrama, 2013), Lawrence's father, John D. Rockefeller, visited the swami and was challenged to channel his money to the betterment of the world. "Rockefeller was annoyed and left, but a week later he came and threw on Swamiji's desk a paper containing his plans to donate an enormous sum of money towards philanthropy and said to Swamiji that he should thank him. Swamiji did not even lift his eyes. He quietly read the paper and said, 'It is for you to thank me'." (p.407). "Abby" Aldrich Rockefeller, Lawrence's mother, was an international art collector and had a special interest in Asian culture. Marion Goldman writes that it was because of his mother's interest in Zen that Lawrence explored alternative spirituality. After being introduced in the 1960s, Michael Murphy became a trusted spiritual and personal advisor to Lawrence. See Goldman, *The American Soul Rush*, pp.143-144.

[130] "Esalen and CIIS," a conversation between Esalen co-founder Michael Murphy and Robert McDermott of the California Institute of Integral Studies, June 1, 2012. Held at the CIIS Main Campus, Namaste Hall, 1453 Mission Street, San Francisco, CA. The video of the conversation has been placed on YouTube at https://youtu.be/uKkSJU4Qpeo.

[131] Goldman, *The American Soul Rush*, p.143.

By the late 1960s and early '70s, this religious riptide was pulling at popular culture. A post-secular mash-up of Eastern devotion and experiential consciousness was put to music. Floating over radio waves from San Diego to London to Saigon came the melodic hit, *My Sweet Lord*, a tune of affection to Krishna with its overlay of *hallelujah* and *Hare Krishna*. The 5th Dimension sang of planetary peace and "mystical crystal revelation," the dawning of the *Age of Aquarius*. Moody Blues' *Legend of a Mind* toasted Timothy Leary, enticing you to take an astral trip. Jefferson Airplane chased the *White Rabbit* and Three Dog Night invited everyone to the "halls of Shambala." John Lennon imagined the world as one.

The spiritual vision initiated by Vivekananda, packaged in a pill and pushed by Leary, and then experienced and externalized at Esalen, had spread far and wide. A revolution-in-mind was taking place.

Philip Goldberg tells of his moment,

> My own story is typical. As a college student in the Sixties, I was a political radical, a determined seeker of truth, and a confused mess who couldn't figure out how to live happily in society, much less comprehend any higher meaning or purpose. I had no use for religion, but I was disillusioned with Marx and Freud too. As the era's social tension grew, so did my craving for fulfillment and relief. The descriptions of enlightened yogis and the sublime faces of Buddhist statuary made me think, *I want what those guys had*. I wanted bliss. I wanted wisdom, infinite love, and union with the cosmos.[132]

Goldberg's account is similar to so many others who came of age during that era. Roger Neill's story touches some of these same themes, but with a different outcome,

> Aimless, morally confused, culturally relative youth like myself found that the socialist revolution didn't come immediately, as we expected. Evil capitalism didn't collapse with our dope-smoking, fornicating, Age-of-Aquarius attack on it. The revolution must have been taking place in the empty space between our navel-gazing ears. Over one generation, we retreated from the unsuccessful socialist revolution into the psycho spiritual 'garden of earthly delights,' brought about

[132] Goldberg, *American Veda*, p.13, italics in original.

> by the products of modern drug labs, eastern religion, and psychological technology.[133]

Victor Marshall, later to be a Christian chaplain inside Ohio's correctional services, relates his experience and the emptiness it presented,

> The Beatles made their journey through drugs and Hinduism, and so eventually, would I. From 1970 to 1983, I was immersed in a longhaired culture of psychedelic rock, drugs, New Age theosophy, Eastern religion, pseudo-science, UFOs, and the occult... Psychotropic substances, like the forbidden fruit, promised an enlightened revelation of my 'god' nature. Instead, it only produced a terrible nakedness of the soul...
>
> A study of the Bagavad Gita, the Rig Veda, the Upanishads, the writings of Confucius and Lao Tsu, the sayings of Buddha, the life of Muhammad, I Ching, Tai Chi, Kung Fu, pyramid power, astrology, astral projection, Zen Buddhism, the Egyptian and Tibetan books of the dead, primitive tribal religion, shamanism, spiritualism, Greek mythology, Greek philosophy, and a host of lesser dabblings brought me no closer to peace of mind or health of soul.[134]

Whereas Goldberg turned to the East with its elevated Self, Neill and Marshall saw through the façade and bowed to the Creator of the cosmos – the God who is separate and distinct from creation.

Many more interactions between the religions of the East and the minds of the West demonstrated the growing power of this spiritual riptide. Bhagwan Shree Rajneesh established a frightening and bizarre "dynamic meditation" sex-cult in Oregon. TM made its way into the corporate world, becoming a business in its own rite. Yoga, a technique to realize the *universal* – "all the potencies of the All" – and a quest for the "Perfection of Man," was sold as physical fitness and health.[135] The West ate it like candy.

---

[133] Roger Brian Neill, *Revolution in Mind: An Autobiography* (Word Alive Press, 2014), p.67.

[134] Victor Marshall, "From New Age to New Creation," *Persuaded by the Evidence: True Stories of Faith, Science, and the Power of a Creator* (Master Books, 2008, edited by Doug Sharp and Jerry Bergman), pp.164-165.

[135] See Troy Wilson Organ, *The Hindu Quest for the Perfection of Man* (Ohio University, 1980), pp.315-332. For a Christian criticism of yoga, see Dave Hunt, *Yoga and the Body of Christ* (The Berean Call, 2006). Hindu sources: *The Bhagavad Gita* (Penguin Books,

Today's acceptance of yoga and Buddhist-based mindfulness are popular facets of Eastern importation. Speaking on behalf of the International Day of Yoga – for it has become a global phenomenon – India's Prime Minister Modi told the United Nations in 2014 that, "Yoga is not about exercise but to discover the sense of oneness with ourselves, the world and Nature."[136]

From the gleaming white marble-mountain of India's Oneness Temple, known as the Temple of the Golden Orb – inaugurated in 2008 – to the hundreds of Krishna centers scattered around the world, to the West's appropriation of Eastern practices, we face a global, spiritually charged context.

Do you live in the United States? Eastern spiritual communities are no longer a feature of the Orient only. For Buddhism, the picturesque City of Ten Thousand Buddhas is located 110 miles north of San Francisco. Or you can visit the Great Stupa of Dharmakaya at the Shambhala Mountain Center, fifty miles outside of Fort Collins, Colorado. Bloomington, Indiana is home to the Tibetan Culture Center,[137] founded by the Dalai Lama's brother. Or you can go to the Catskill Mountains above Woodstock, NY, and visit the Karma Triyana Dharmachakra.

For Hinduism, you can travel to the Mahalakshmi Temple in Delaware or the sprawling Radha Madhav Dham complex near Austin, Texas, or the Malibu Temple devoted to Venkateswara and Shiva. One of the largest temples in North America, at 43,000 square feet, is just outside of Minneapolis. Temples and communities can be found coast-to-coast.

Of far more importance is that millions of souls embrace the philosophies of Eastern spirituality, often naively blending flavors of Oneness with Christian ideas. Just talk to your neighbors or family.

We are being swept into a vast ocean of *advaita*.

Maybe *Newsweek* was right when it suggested in 2009 that Americans are becoming "more like Hindus and less like traditional Christians."[138]

Namaste.

1962), and, *Bhagavad-Gita: As It Is*, by A.C. Bhaktivedanta Swami Prabhupada (The Bhaktivedanta Book Trust, 1972). See also, A. Avalon, *The Serpent Power: Being the Sat-Cakra-Nirupana and Paduka-Pancaka* (The Lost Library, orig. published 1918).

[136] As printed in *Common Yoga Protocol: International Day of Yoga* (Government of India, Ministry of AYUSH, no date), p.1. Adopted by UN resolution on December 11, 2014.

[137] It was renamed The Tibetan Mongolian Buddhist Cultural Center in 2007.

[138] Lisa Miller, "U.S. Views On God And Life Are Turning Hindu," *Newsweek*, August 14, 2009 [www.newsweek.com/us-views-god-and-life-are-turning-hindu-79073].

New Age Shift

The nebulous nature of the New Age movement makes defining it tricky.

Religious sociologist Christopher Partridge positions the New Age milieu as an *internalizing of spiritual authority*, wherein "personal experience is the final arbiter of truth."[139] In this sense the New Age can be considered an individualistic search for inward affirmation. This is the opposite of the Biblical approach to spiritual understanding whereupon the individual rests on the *outward authority* of an eternal and unchanging God. One is Self-aggrandizing, the latter acknowledges our sinful character and the need for a Redeemer who is *other* than nature. Partridge sets up the contrast,

> "New Age belief systems teach... a religion of divine-human *continuity* presupposing the innate goodness of humanity, not a religion of divine-human *discontinuity*, supported by a doctrine of sin."[140]

The New Age can be viewed as a culture of personal spirituality, one that dovetails with the Postmodern attitude. No wonder a vast marketplace catering to every whim of spirituality has developed; Eastern offerings, metaphysical lore, mystical techniques, and the cultural repackaging of occultism; what Partridge calls *occulture*. Society thus echoes what it absorbs,

> Hence, terms and ideas such as Gaia, reincarnation, *feng shui*, *chakra*, karma, *prana*, *chi*, *yin*, *yang*, and *tao* are not only entering mainstream Western thinking, but are being reinterpreted and owned by Westerners seeking to develop their own spiritualities. Whatever is going on here, it is not secularization.[141]

A jumble of beliefs and spiritual pursuits entered the mainstream, even as the New Age movement appeared to be nothing more than a subgroup. Nevertheless, a collective theme was evident: The evolving divinity of Man within a cosmic paradigm. In other words, Self arises with other Selves, each blending into a unified Great Being of consciousness.

The New Age movement and human potential psychology are, no surprise, fellow travelers: "Turn within and seek and find and know the only Presence,

---

[139] Christopher Partridge, *The Re-Enchantment of the West: Volume 1 – Alternative Spiritualities, Sacralization, Popular Culture and Occulture* (T&T Clark, 2004), p.32.

[140] Ibid., p.32, italics in original.

[141] Ibid., p.57, italics in original.

the only Power, the only Cause, the only Activity of your eternal life. Be a totally open channel for the glorious expression of this infinite YOU!"[142]

Wrapped in a veneer of Christian terminology, *A Course in Miracles* exemplified the New Age message of "self salvation." Professor of Medical Psychology, Helen Schucman of Columbia University, penned the *Course* through the transmission of an "inner voice" claiming to be "Jesus." Lesson 57 in the *Course* taught "the holiness of all living things, including myself, and their oneness with me." Lesson 70 said, "my salvation comes from me and only from me." Sales of the book rocketed in the early 1990s when New Thought guru, Marianne Williamson, praised it on *The Oprah Winfrey Show*.

Millions of people have embraced the *Course* since its release in 1976. Warren and Joy Smith were counted in that mix.

Warren's spiritual story started with a rooftop prayer to "all you on the other side." Soon afterwards he gravitated to the teachings of Bhagwan Shree Rajneesh and then pursued the guidance offered through *A Course in Miracles*. Embracing the new spirituality and looking for the "light," they nevertheless found *something else*, a palpable darkness. Unable to shake themselves from a malevolent spiritual grip, they turned to the only Savior who could set them free – and this was not the "Jesus" of Schucman, but the one and only Jesus Christ who, in John 14:6, spoke words of *exclusivity*: "I am the way and the truth and the life. No one comes to the Father except through Me."

Warren tells of his realization in *The Light That Was Dark*,

> I realized now that, although I was made in the image of God, I was not God or a part of God in any way. God was God, and I was me. I wasn't Christ or a part of Christ, and neither was Buddha or anyone else. Jesus was the Christ, and there was no other. And, in spite of what anyone else tried to say, He *had* won an amazing victory on the cross of Calvary…
>
> ...It was the 'victory in Jesus' that *A Course in Miracles* desperately tried to redefine and explain away. It was the 'amazing grace' that had saved the likes of Joy and me.[143]

---

[142] John Randolph Price, *The Planetary Commission* (Quartus Foundation, 1984), p.31, capitals in original.

[143] Warren Smith, *The Light That Was Dark: From the New Age to Amazing Grace* (Mountain Stream Press, 1992/2005), pp.146-147, italics in original.

By the early 1970s, a spiritually hungry public was poised to buy the New Age message. Tapping into the growing post-modern emptiness and the swelling interest in Eastern spirituality, a gush of literature flooded the market.

Jeremy Tarcher, a student of Vedanta who spent time at Esalen – later becoming a trustee – established a publishing venture catering to this burgeoning market. Tarcher has been described as "one of the first publishers to cultivate mass markets for books about yoga, tarot cards, meditation, alternative religions, and human potential psychology."[144] In time, J.P. Tarcher entered a distribution agreement with St. Martin's Press before being absorbed into Penguin, where it remains as an imprint on spiritual self-improvement.

TM advocate Peter Russell called for a "spiritual renaissance" via "psychotechnology." His eyebrow-raising book, *The Global Brain*: *Speculations on the Evolutionary Leap to Planetary Consciousness*, published by Tarcher and endorsed by Leary, drew on the work of Maharishi Mahesh Yogi, Teilhard de Chardin, and Sri Aurobindo. His thesis was a coming super-organism of connected humanity, a oneness-operating platform to network the planet and awaken consciousness. If this happened, he believed, a grander spiral could be imagined. The universe itself would cycle in a cosmic reincarnation, universe upon universe, evolving into the sum of all beings. Russell called this "the enlightenment of Brahman: the perfect cosmos."[145]

Russell's idea of a planetary nervous system became a metaphor pointing to the budding global knowledge network, the World Wide Web.[146]

In 1980, Tarcher published Marilyn Ferguson's text, *The Aquarian Conspiracy*. Ferguson, a TM practitioner and producer of the *Brain/Mind Bulletin* – a newsletter of spirituality and psychology – quickly became renowned as a trailblazer in social transformation. Endorsed by Carl Rogers and George Leonard, and praised by the *Globe and Mail* and *Baltimore Evening Sun*, Ferguson's book celebrated a "leaderless but powerful network" of individuals and organizations working hard to shift humanity into the New Age,

> Broader than reform, deeper than revolution, this benign conspiracy for a new human agenda has triggered the most rapid cultural

[144] Goldman, *The American Soul Rush*, p.159.

[145] Peter Russell, *The Global Brain: Speculations on the Evolutionary Leap to Planetary Consciousness* (J.P. Tarcher, Inc., 1983), p.218.

[146] James Hughes, *Citizen Cyborg: Why Democratic Societies Must Respond to the Redesigned Human of the Future* (Westview Press, 2004), p.174.

> realignment in history. The great shuddering, irrevocable shift overtaking us is not a new political, religious, or philosophical system. It is a new mind – the ascendance of a startling worldview that gathers into its framework breakthrough science and insights from earliest recorded thought.[147]

This ancient-future worldview was supported by *legions of conspirators*,

> The Aquarian Conspirators range across all levels of income and education, from the humblest to the highest. There are schoolteachers and office workers, famous scientists, government officials and lawmakers, artists and millionaires, taxi drivers and celebrities, leaders in medicine, education, law psychology. Some are open in their advocacy, and their names may be familiar. Others are quiet about their involvement, believing they can be more effective if they are not identified with ideas that have all too often been misunderstood.[148]

Human potential guru and New Age activist, Dick Sutphen, fleshed out the scheme a few years after Ferguson's book was released,

> One of the biggest advantages we have as New Agers is, once the occult, metaphysical and New Age terminology is removed, we have concepts and techniques that are very acceptable to the general public. So we can change the names and demonstrate the power. In so doing, we open the New Age door to millions who normally would not be receptive... New Age Activists encourages you as an individual to network with your family, friend and associates, and to infuse New Age concepts and awareness into every area of your personal world, from the office to the bridge club, from the schoolroom to the Little League.[149]

The Aquarian Conspiracy became a bestseller with multiple language translations. Its message of a new consciousness was coupled with a call to action, preaching that all fields of human endeavor were to be impacted; and now it

---

[147] Marilyn Ferguson, *The Aquarian Conspiracy: Personal and Social Transformation in the 1980s* (J.P. Tarcher, 1980), p.23.

[148] Ibid., pp.23-24.

[149] Dick Sutphen, "Infiltrating the New Age into Society," *What Is*, Summer 1986, Vol.1, No.1, pp.14-15 (published by Reincarnationists, Inc., with Sutphen as president).

was your turn to become an agent of change. Remembering Ferguson after her death in 2008, Deepak Chopra recalled her influence on himself and others: "Ferguson helped make possible a new style of politician like Barack Obama and ecological activists like Al Gore."[150]

The year Tarcher published *The Aquarian Conspiracy*, Allen Michael – born Allen Noonan – self-released his galactic testament, a 457-page mish-mash of channeled dissonance: "Christ Communism" and "group tantric natural selection" and the Elders of Zion and UFO Astral Beings and a "World Wide Work Stoppage karma yoga exercise." Through the ramblings emerged a consistent two-fold calling: the "absolute, unlimited God Mind – our higher mind," and "we are all the Christ for whom we seek."[151]

Extraterrestrials would usher in the New World Order, Michael promised Charles Slack in 1968 during a psychedelic encounter in a Krishna meditation room. He told Slack of the mission given to him by these alien overlords,

> I was interviewed by several of the Higher Extraterrestrial Beings, who told me that they were the same as angels in the Bible. [They] asked me in the form of my astral self if I would like to be the Messiah of Mankind. As Messiah or Messenger of Mankind, it would be my duty and responsibility to bring the true vision of the New World Order to the planet Earth. The New World Order would then replace the Old World Order with all its negative hang-ups.[152]

Dr. Slack, although stoned, recalls his gut reaction,

> The words of the Holy Messenger Allen rapped right into the pit of my stomach. I was listening to a dope-head talk about being appointed Messiah by the Saucer People... This was an insane asylum. These people were nuts. They were out of their minds and I was going along with their insanity and being a part of it all, *condoning* this madness, lending my ear to a goof spout off and nearly believing it. Lemmeoutahere.[153]

[150] Deepak Chopra, "Marilyn Ferguson: An Appreciation," *Beliefnet*, [www.beliefnet.com/columnists/intentchopra/2008/11/marilyn-ferguson-an-appreciati.html].

[151] Allen Michael, *GOD – Ultimate Unlimited Mind – Speaks* (Starmast Publications, 1982), pp.xv, 377.

[152] Slack, *Timothy Leary, the Madness of the Sixties and Me*, p.82.

[153] Ibid., p.83, italics in original.

There is a reason I chose to tell of Allen Michael.

The eclectic nature of the New Age – spirit channeling, oracles and divinations, astrology, vibration energy in rocks and crystals, communication from supposed space-brothers and a host of other activities and beliefs – has caused many Christians to dismiss the movement as so much nonsense. This is somewhat understandable as tracking the New Age can feel like a journey to the outer edges of culture.

Three points, however, need to be considered:

1. Regardless of what we think of New Age beliefs and practices, the spiritual worldview is serious – with eternal, personal ramifications and profound social consequences.
2. That a supernatural environment exists is Biblically understood, and in this we are to be cautious. Concerning deceptive and malevolent spiritual forces, the Apostle Paul writes, "Put on the whole armor of God, that you may be able to stand against the wiles of the devil. For we do not wrestle against flesh and blood, but against principalities, against powers, against the rulers of the darkness of this age, against spiritual hosts of wickedness in the heavenly places."[154] Admittedly tapping into a spiritual/supernatural reality, the New Age embraces teachings and religious techniques that consistently counter the God who is *other*.
3. Susceptibility exists for Christians on two fronts: A) Human potential thinking, packaged in the garb of self-help, is sold to a Christian audience that has – often unconsciously – accepted a secular view of human nature, B) Mystical, contemplative and Eastern approaches – re-fashioned for mainstream Christianity – promises *spiritual formation* to those earnestly desiring a deeper "God experience." The believer's intention may be noble, yet spiritual syncretism is the actuality.

The New Age may seem unusual to those looking in, *but it is not marginal.*

Willis Harman, a human potential leader whose connections to government agencies allowed him to warn Esalen of drug raids,[155] understood that by the late 1980s, the New Age was inculcating a transforming worldview,

> We are already well into the mind change. It is altering the way we interpret science; it is drastically modifying our concepts of health

[154] Ephesians 6:11-12.
[155] Kripal, *Esalen*, p.133.

> care; it is revolutionizing our concepts of education; it is causing major changes in the world of business and finance; it is in the process of delegitimating war and causing a total rethinking of the means of achieving national and global security.[156]

The corporate world took notice of the New Age and embraced it.

Pacific Bell, Proctor & Gamble, Ford Motor Company, Polaroid, Boeing, General Mills, and Scott Paper were some of the corporations attaching early significance to New Age concepts. Eastern spirituality and human potential teachings were being tailored to meet company needs. *Newsweek* reported in 1987: "By one estimate, their programs accounted for about $4 billion in corporate spending each year."[157]

America's defense community was interested too.

During the late 1970s, Lt. Col. Jim Channon was part of Task Force Delta, a US Army War College project exploring novel ideas for human potential. Channon headed to the Esalen Institute, investigating non-ordinary states and experiencing "esoteric technology."[158] He was the first *Be All You Can Be* soldier. The result? An operations manual for a theoretical combat unit, the First Earth Battalion, with the recommendation to develop Warrior Monks in "harmony with planetary evolution." These mind-soldiers would be spiritually and psychologically attuned to wholeness, engaging the enemy at the psychic level. The manual offered an Earth Prayer,

> Mother Earth... my life support system.. as a soldier.. I must drink your blue water.. live inside your red clay and eat your green skin. I pray... my boots will always kiss your face and my footsteps match your heartbeat... carry my body thru space and time.. you are my connection to the Universe.. and all that comes after. I am yours and you are mine, I salute you.[159]

---

[156] Willis Harman, *Global Mind Change: The Promise of the Last Years of the Twentieth Century* (Knowledge Systems and the Institute of Noetic Science, 1988), Introduction.

[157] Annetta Miller with Pamela Abramson, "Corporate Mind Control," *Newsweek*, May 4, 1987, p.38.

[158] Steven Kotler and Jamie Wheal, *Stealing Fire: How Silicon Valley, the Navy SEALs, and Maverick Scientists Are Revolutionizing the Way We Live and Work* (HarerCollins/Dey St., 2017), p.190.

[159] Jim Channon, *Evolutionary Tactics: First Earth Battalion Operations Manual*, OM-1, 1982, "Section 3 – Evolutionary Teamwork." The triple-double dots are in the original.

In the Pentagon, a Meditation Club formed "in a cooperative effort to build mentally a shield of radiance, focused through the Pentagon, incorporating the city of Washington DC, the nation and ultimately the world."

Self-labeled as the Spiritual Defense Initiative (SDI), the Club started with Transcendental Meditation and added Masonic symbolism to visualization sessions. Technically under the jurisdiction of the Pentagon Chaplain, SDI was an independent body of individuals interested in new consciousness. However, in light of the 1988 Soviet-American Citizens' Summit, the Club was officially called upon to escort the Soviet Central Peace Commission to the Pentagon's annual prayer breakfast. The evening before, SDI led the Commission in a twenty-minute visualization exercise.[160]

The New Age was especially intriguing to the Soviets.

Spiritual Perestroika

An unusual meeting took place in Alexandria, Virginia in February 1988: The Soviet-American Citizens' Summit.

Remember, this was during the Cold War and the Soviet Union was a closed society, restricting travel abroad and careful about managing what ideas entered its space. The New Spirituality, nevertheless, found a solid foothold in the last years of the USSR.[161]

Chaired by futurist Barbara Marx Hubbard, the Summit brought together Soviet officials and cultural figures with "new consciousness" thinkers from the West. The purpose: to "facilitate the new way of thinking and acting" in response to the "awakening going on across the planet."[162] It was a "conver-

---

[160] Ruth C. Clark, "Pentagon Meditation Club," *Meditation*, Fall 1988, pp.6-8, on Masonic symbols, see p.12. The article lists the summit as the Reagan-Gorbachev Summit from the previous February. However, no Reagan-Gorbachev Summit took place in February 1988. That said, the Soviet-American Citizens' Summit did take place in February 1988, and I have listed it as such in my text.

[161] Russian interest in esoteric subjects is longstanding. For Russian Cosmism, a spiritual-technological belief, see George M. Young, *The Russian Cosmists: The Esoteric Futurism of Nikolai Fedorov and his Followers* (Oxford University Press, 2012). Regarding metaphysical topics in the USSR, see *Psychic Discoveries Behind the Iron Curtain*, by Sheila Ostrander and Lynn Schroeder (Prentice-Hall, 1970). Note: Kripal described the findings of Ostrander and Schroeder as real but flavored with sensationalism.

[162] *Welcome to the Soviet-American Citizens' Summit: Social Inventions for the Third Millennium* [sic], February 1-5, 1988, Alexandria, VA, official agenda, p.1.

gence process" with Task Forces overseeing themes of politics, education, business, religion and spirituality, psychology and social change, and other mutual concerns.

Organized by the Center for Soviet-American Dialogue (CSAD) in cooperation with the Soviet Peace Committee, a state-sponsored agency engaged in "active measures," the Summit pulled together approximately 100 attendees from the Soviet Union and another 300 from the United States. Western participants included former UN official Robert Muller, astronaut Brian O'Leary, Willis Harman, Hazel Henderson, US Ambassador John McDonald and other personalities associated with the US security and foreign affairs establishment, and Ted Turner of CNN fame.[163]

Mikhail Gorbachev, General Secretary of the Soviet Union, sent an appreciative message to the gathering. A few months later he would personally meet with some of these same "peace delegates."[164]

---

[163] Some of the security establishment participants included Marcus Raskin, co-founder of the Institute for Policy Studies and former National Security Council Assistant for Disarmament; Theodore Taylor, former Weapons Director at Los Alamos; Robert Legvold, former Director of the Soviet Studies Project at the Council on Foreign Relations; Stephen H. Rhinesmith, President Reagan's coordinator for US-Soviet exchanges; Geoffrey Kemp, Carnegie Endowment fellow and former staff member with the National Security Council; Helmut Sonnenfeldt, member of the Brookings Institute and former State Department Counselor and advisor to Henry Kissinger; Arthur M. Cox, former member of the Central Intelligence Agency and specialist with the State Department and Brookings Institute; Toby Gati, Vice President of the United Nations Association USA, member of the Council on Foreign Relations, and later made Assistant Secretary Of State For Intelligence And Research by President Bill Clinton; Amory Lovins, Rocky Mountain Institute and formerly with the U.S. Department of Energy's Energy Research Advisory Board (Amory would later be named by *Time* magazine as one of the world's 100 most influential people); and Carol Rosin, former Corporate Manager of Fairchild Industries (an aerospace company that designed the A-10) and confidant to Wernher Von Braun during his last years. Rosin was a space-and-missile defense consultant, and founder of the Institute for Security and Cooperation in Outer Space, which included Astronaut Edgar Mitchell.

[164] On Gorbachev's message, see "Summit Breaks New Ground for US-USSR," *Soviet-American News*, Center for Soviet-American Dialogue, Vol.1, No.1, Spring 1988, p.1. About the later meeting, see "Gorbachev Speaks to World Peace Leaders," *Soviet-American News*, Vol.1, No.2, Winter 1988-1989, p.2. Two important resources on Soviet peace programs are: Philip C. Bom, *The Coming Century of Commonism* (Policy Books, 1992), which examines the role of peace movements during the Gorbachev era; and Frederick C. Barghoorn, *Soviet Foreign Propaganda* (Princeton University Press, 1964), which gives an overview of active measures associated with the early peace movement.

Global Family, a networking group co-founded by Barbara Marx Hubbard with the motto "connecting to celebrate our oneness," headed up the Summit's Convergence Center, a clearinghouse for Task Force outcomes. "In this convergence process," Global Family reported, "the relationship between ourselves and the Soviets will not only expand, but will begin to shift global consciousness."[165]

Global Family described the Summit as moving "the energy of 'Harmonic Convergence' from sacred sites in nature to a conference center."[166]

"This is New Age," Robert Muller told the distinguished delegates in his opening speech: "We need a new cosmology, a new cosmic paradigm for the future of this planet. I think that the religions together with the scientists can produce such [a] cosmology."[167]

The Summit was groundbreaking on a number of levels, but it was not the first interaction between Western New Agers and the Soviets. CSAD already had an interesting connection with the Soviet Union.

In 1985, Rama Vernon, a pioneering yoga instructor and co-founder of *Yoga Journal*, established CSAD as a way to bridge the divide between the two superpowers. Over the life of the organization it sponsored dozens of Soviet-American awareness projects, including a new teaching program in Moscow and Leningrad. The announcement read in part: "In March of 1986, we will, as citizen diplomats, take *A Course in Miracles* to Russia, as we apply the principles of the *Course* into our meetings and interactions with Soviet officials, theologians, artists, writers, actors and physicians."[168]

Other Soviet-based events included a Planetary Healing Pilgrimage, a meeting of the International New Thought Alliance, and a Global Family conference with the leader of the Pentagon Mediation Club. CSAD arranged "the first official Yoga demonstration in the Soviet Union," sponsoring Swami Satchidananda to lecture in Prague, Moscow, Leningrad, and Odessa. On

---

[165] "Building Convergence at the Citizens' Summit," *Global Family: Connecting to Celebrate our Oneness*, Special Summit Edition, February 1988, p.1.

[166] "The Soviet-American Citizens' Summit: Harmonic Convergence Revisited," *Global Family: Connecting to Celebrate our Oneness*, April 1988, p.1.

[167] "Muller Asks For New Set of Ten Commandments," *NRI Trumpet*, March 1988, p.7. Three days after the Summit closed, a meeting was held at the United Nations for the purpose of introducing the event's outcomes to senior American and Soviet officials.

[168] *A Course in Miracles Goes to Russia*, promotional flyer, Center for Soviet-American Dialogue (CSAD), March 2-16, 1986.

the Black Sea, participants meditated and discussed consciousness and "interspecies communication" with dolphins. Later in 1989, 250 Soviets participated in a CSAD Yoga and Meditation Conference. Speakers included the Soviet Minister of Health and "TM teacher," Deepak Chopra.[169]

Barbara Marx Hubbard also hosted CSAD projects in the Soviet Union. Bringing together "Soviet officials, educators, psychologists, foreign relations specialists, scientists, journalists, theologians and healers," her 1986 *Positive Future* dialogue asked the following questions: "What is the Communist dream that has not yet been fulfilled? What is the American hope of a New Order of the Ages? What might the Soviet and American people be able to create together?"[170] In response, Radio Moscow and Soviet National Television interviewed Hubbard.

Hubbard, who had been placed in nomination for the US Vice-Presidency on the 1984 Democratic ticket, sat on the CSAD executive board. Willis Harman did as well. Swami Satchidananda was on its advisory board, along with James Garrison of the Esalen Institute.

It should be no surprise that Esalen already had a foothold in Moscow.

Back in the mid-1960s, Michael Murphy had "put feelers out" to Soviet scientists working in the field of parapsychology. Murphy was fascinated by psychic possibilities, and the publishing of *Psychic Discoveries Behind the Iron Curtain* fueled his interest in what lay behind Russia's dark doors.[171] On a Soviet research trip in 1979, he and his colleagues connected to an eclectic spirituality far outside the norm of secular Marxism: Theosophy, yoga, shamanism, psychics, spiritualism, and Christian mysticism.

Murphy explained: "[At] Ismailov Park, Moscow we would get together with psychics and physicists and groups of singers who sang pagan, pre-Christian songs… Everywhere we've been in the Soviet Union, we've met people who are interested in the 'new age'."[172]

---

[169] As taken from *Citizen Diplomacy Trips to the Soviet Union, 1986-1987*, CSAD, brochure; *International Citizens Diplomacy Missions to the Soviet Union, China, Africa & Central America, 1989*, CSAD, fact sheet; *History of CSAD Trips: May 1985 through November 1990*, CSAD, fact sheet.

[170] *In Search for a Positive Future*, CSAD, January 19 to February 2, 1986, invitation sheet.

[171] *Psychic Discoveries Behind the Iron Curtain* was written by Sheila Ostrander and Lynn Schroeder (Prentice-Hall, 1970).

[172] As quoted by David Landau, "Citizens Diplomacy," *The Guide to New Age Living*, pp.77-78. For more on Murphy's Soviet experience, see Kripal, *Esalen*, chapter 14.

Esalen entered a special relationship with the Russians in 1980. Leveraging the political ties already made by the Institute, the organization established a bi-national Exchange Program,

> Like Americans, the Soviets are beginning to yearn for some spiritual dimension that has been missing in their organized, rational lives. It was this common interest in self-improvement and personal growth that led to the creation of Esalen's Soviet-American Exchange Program.[173]

Seed money came from the "Rockefeller Family Fund, Apple Computer Inc., the American Express Foundation and the MacArthur Foundations." As Murphy reminded potential supporters in a fund raising letter, "being a good citizen these days requires being a global citizen... the world has grown truly interdependent."[174]

Spirituality and human potential entailed one aspect of the Program. More concretely, Esalen was a vehicle for the new field of "citizen diplomacy," becoming a conduit – a back channel – for American and Soviet officials, cosmonauts and astronauts, academic and business leaders, and members of the intelligence community.[175] Esalen had entered a complicated field of work, becoming a mentor and bridge for personnel connected to the KGB, CIA, the State Department, and the Kremlin.

According to a 1982 Esalen document: "The project management is committed to continuing this program with a policy of openness and disclosure about its activities to all interested parties while maintaining a low public and media profile."[176] Esalen was playing in the world of spooks and spies.

Cultural exchanges, too, were important. Jeffrey Kripal tells us,

> In 1982... Esalen employed satellite communication technology to pioneer the first spacebridge communications between Americans and Soviets... described in the Esalen catalog as a 'Satellite Rock-and-Roll

---

[173] *The Esalen Institute Soviet-American Exchange Program: An Interim Report*, September 1982, p.1. Document on file.

[174] Letter with supporting corporations and foundations on file.

[175] "Citizens diplomacy" was coined as Track II diplomacy by Joseph Montville of the US State Department. As an Esalen personality, he was considered the Institute's unofficial State Department representative.

[176] *The Esalen Institute Soviet-American Exchange Program: An Interim Report*, p.2.

> Fest.' American and Russian bands and ecstatic youth in San Bernardino, California, and Moscow screamed, grinned, and danced to each other's music as they watched one another on large screens.[177]

A "Global Gestalt," an emotional and psychologically moving encounter – a unifying of opposites – it was thought, was needed for planetary wholeness.

Central to the Soviet-American complex was James "Jim" Garrison, the son of Baptist missionaries who served in China. Turning from his parent's faith and adopting an antinomial view of God, Garrison – introspective and generous with a catching personality – met Murphy at Cambridge in 1982. By the mid-1980s he was the Executive Director of the Soviet-American Exchange Program, a position held until the early 1990s.[178]

One highlight was securing the Institute's hosting rights for Boris Yeltsin's 1989 trip to the United States. Fifteen other organizations were vying for the opportunity, including the Rockefeller and Ford Foundations, along with the Council on Foreign Relations.[179] Garrison was put in charge.

Face-to-face with the daily affluence we take for granted in a society built on free enterprise, Yeltsin was overwhelmed by America, concluding the Iron Curtain was meant to keep Soviets unaware of the truth. His Soviet-instilled illusions had been shattered like glass. "We were told fables!" he said to his assistant. The experience of Yeltsin's trip was a factor in his later break from the Party. And while his on-tour drinking problem was a public embarrassment, stressful for Garrison, the venture was largely successful. But there were concerns. Yeltsin could be overbearing in sensitive meetings, hinting at a power complex. Garrison sent Mikhail Gorbachev a memo.[180]

Esalen favored Gorbachev. He had become a political celebrity and was the public face of *perestroika*, the concept of restructuring the economic and civic framework of the USSR. It would also have an inward dimension.

---

[177] Kripal, *Esalen*, p.334.

[178] Garrison's personality is gleaned from my conversations with his siblings and a life-long friend. Regarding his early interaction with Murphy and other Esalen members, and his view on God, see Kripal, *Esalen*, pp.393-394. For more on his antinomial position, the belief that God has a light and dark side – good and evil – see Jim Garrison, *The Darkness of God: Theology After Hiroshima* (Eerdmans Publishing Company, 1983).

[179] Kripal, *Esalen*, p.393.

[180] Ibid., pp.394-397. For extra details on Yeltsin's trip, see Conor O'Clery, *Moscow, December 25, 1991: The Last Day of the Soviet Union* (Public Affairs, 2011), pp.79-80.

"Perestroika is to provide a melting pot for society and, above all, the individual himself," explained the General Secretary. The new society would be "a shining temple on a green hill."[181]

"It will be a renovated society." Gorbachev continued. "Today our main job is to lift the individual spiritually, respecting the inner world and giving him moral strength."[182]

But restructuring was not to be divorced from the past,

> The essence of perestroika lies in the fact that it unites socialism with democracy and revives the Leninist concept of socialist construction both in theory and practice. Such is the essence of perestroika, which accounts for its genuine revolutionary spirit and its all-embracing scope.[183]

At the 19th All-Union Conference, Gorbachev invoked Karl Marx and Vladimir Lenin in "building a society of social justice." These pillars of Communism would guide "us in our revolutionary perestroika."[184]

Appeals to Marx and Lenin notwithstanding, the communist system could not be reformed. But the economic, social and political lid on the long-closed box had opened too far to shut. The Soviet situation rapidly moved in complex and unforeseen ways. Gorbachev's "new thinking," an internationalist approach, also morphed within the shifting domestic and global context. Something extraordinary was happening in Russia.[185]

---

[181] Mikhail Gorbachev, *Perestroika: New Thinking for Our Country and the World* (Harper and Row Publishers, 1987), p.29

[182] Ibid., p.30.

[183] Ibid., p.35. On July 1, 1988, during the 19th All-Union Conference of the CPSU, Gorbachev said: "Every Communist must become a fighter for perestroika, for the revolutionary renewal of society. Let that be the chief mandate of our Conference."

[184] *Documents and Materials: Report and Speeches by Mikhail Gorbachev*, 19th All-Union Conference of the CPSU (Soviet Life/Embassy of the USSR, 1988), p.93.

[185] Perestroika and what Gorbachev called the "new thinking" always had international implications. An early and important set of interpretations is found in *Perestroika: Global Challenge* (Spokesman/Russell Press Ltd., 1988, edited by Ken Coates). For more on perestroika see the following: Mikhail Gorbachev, *Perestroika: New Thinking for Our Country and the World* (Harper and Row Publishers, 1987); Mikhail Gorbachev, *Socialism, Peace and Democracy: Writings, Speeches and Reports* (Zwan Publications, 1987); *Documents and Materials: Report and Speeches by Mikhail Gorbachev*, 19th All-Union Conference of the CPSU (Soviet Life/Embassy of the USSR, 1988); Baruch A. Hazan, *Gor-*

In late December 1991, days before the USSR's dissolution, Garrison was brought into the Kremlin and told about Gorbachev's secret resignation plan. Approximately one month later with Yeltsin as Russia's president, Garrison found himself back in Moscow. This time he was meeting with Gorbachev at his new headquarters, the International Foundation for Socio-Economic and Political Studies. Here, at this session, it was agreed to establish an outpost in the United States of America: the Gorbachev Foundation/USA.

A new game was in play.

Armed with immense political and social capital, Gorbachev could export his "new thinking" through an American non-profit entity. The Gorbachev Foundation/USA would be the first non-military organization to be housed at the Presidio of San Francisco, an historic Army base in the process of closing.[186] Garrison became its president.

At the heartbeat of the Foundation was the "Revisioning Global Priorities" agenda.[187] This was the body's larger mission, and to that end it set up the State of the World Forum in 1995, an event that became its own organization. Another Gorbachev Foundation office had already opened in Calgary, Alberta and in 1997, a North American branch was announced for Boston's

---

bachev's Gamble: The 19th All-Union Party Conference (Westview Press, 1990); Stephen F. Cohen and Katrina vanden Heuvel, *Voices of Glasnost: Interviews with Gorbachev's Reformers* (W.W. Norton & Company, 1989); Judith B. Sedaitis and Jim Butterfield, *Perestroika From Below: Social Movements in the Soviet Union* (Westview Press, 1991); Robert G. Kaiser, *Why Gorbachev Happened: His Triumphs and His Failures* (Simon & Schuster, 1991). Post-Soviet interviews and analysis can be found in *Demokratizatsiya: The Journal of Post-Soviet Democratization* (Institute for European, Russian, and Eurasian Studies, Elliott School of International Affairs).

[186] The April 17, 1993 edition of *The Kansas City Star* reported: "His foundation is considered a desirable tenant because it may attract other prestigious organizations with an international focus, a theme the Park Service is promoting." (Article title: "Gorbachev's office is on military post," p.2, first published in the *Los Angeles Times*). Eventually a number of diverse organizations would take up residency in the Presidio: Aspen Group, Tides Foundation, Bright Minds Institute, The Wilderness Society, United Religions Initiative, All Species Foundation, Panchamama Alliance, EcoTalk, Guild for Psychological Studies, Consultative Group on Biodiversity, International Forum on Globalization, Thoreau Center for Sustainability, Interfaith Center, Rudolf Steiner Foundation, World Wildlife Fund, and the Association for Transpersonal Psychology (to name just a few).

[187] "Revisioning Global Priorities" was taken from a Gorbachev Foundation/USA letter. The letter laid out key areas of work, two of note: The creation of the State of the World Forum, and a project called *Redefining Global Security*. Letter has no date; copy on file.

Northeastern University. At the Presidio, the Foundation folded into the new project and Garrison became president of the State of the World Forum, with Gorbachev as chairman.

"We are giving birth to the first global civilization," proclaimed the Mission Statement of the Forum.

A "global brain trust" was to be established. From 1995 until 2010, Garrison advanced the "new thinking" through a series of high-level networking events and dialogues around the world. The first Forum gathering took place in San Francisco during late September 1995.

Officially titled *Toward a New Civilization*, the Forum was a who's who of world influencers. Forum "Fellows" included George H.W. Bush, Nelson Mandela, Brian Mulroney, Carl Sagan, Maurice Strong, Sonia Gandhi, and Ted Turner. Willis Harman of the Institute of Noetic Sciences and Esalen's Michael Murphy were Fellows also.[188] Actor and New Age author Shirley McLaine attended, as did Barbara Marx Hubbard and Robert Muller. Buddhists leaders from Southeast Asia were the main religious representatives.

"We must reinvent the world together," Gorbachev informed the participants. "We need unity in diversity." In a debate between the Soviet politician, Bush and Margaret Thatcher, it was evident that divisions of opinion over the role of the United Nations existed.[189] However, a general consensus was in the air. Global governance and collective measures were repeated themes.

"The universe is seeking to fulfill itself through us," Deepak Chopra, another Fellow, reminded the audience. "Are we up to the responsibility?"[190]

Noticing the emphasis on Buddhism and New Age thinking, some members of the press questioned why Christian leaders were not represented. Former National Security Advisor and co-founder of the Trilateral Commission, Zbigniew Brzezinski, tried to answer: "I happen to know that President Gorbachev is a very good friend of the Pope – and I am too."[191]

It was a weak response.

---

[188] Taken from two different State of the World Forum documents: a "confidential" pre-event Fellows and Participants list (no date), and a preliminary *Toward a New Civilization* agenda package (May 10, 1995). Both documents on file.

[189] Quoted by Samantha Smith, "Gorbachev Forum Highlights World Government," *Hope For The World Update*, Fall 1995, p.2. Smith attended as a member of the press.

[190] Quoted by Berit Kjos, "Gorbachev's Global Conference," *The Christian Conscious*, November 1995, p.36.

[191] Ibid., p.37.

Christian author Berit Kjos, who attended with press credentials, commented later on the Forum's religious situation: "Looking at reality through the utopian filter of the new global paradigm, they have no idea what Christians believe nor the value of the liberty we treasure."[192]

The 1995 Forum was the first in a line of similar "new civilization" events hosted by Garrison and Gorbachev.

During the year 2000, the Forum focused its attention on the Millennium gatherings in New York City. Garrison sat on the steering committee for the United Nations Millennium Forum, an event I participated in, and his office coordinated with the Interfaith Center of New York in anticipation of the UN Millennium Peace Summit of Religious and Spiritual Leaders.[193]

The main show for Gorbachev and Garrison, however, was Forum 2000.

Cooperating with the UN Secretary General's office, Garrison positioned his event to run concurrently with the most important high-level meeting of the year, the United Nations Millennium Summit. Together, the Summit and Forum 2000 would constitute a "global town meeting," highlighting issues of governance, UN empowerment, and planetary loyalty.[194] Heads-of-state attending the Summit traveled the few blocks to the Forum, which had its own contingent of world-known personalities and ranking officials. These sister events became revolving doors of power and prestige.

Appealing to the inner dimension, Forum 2000 also explored religion and spirituality, cosmology, and the "Evolution of Human Consciousness."[195] Each day a different spiritual teacher opened with meditations. One morning it was a rabbi "whose belief in the universality of spiritual truth led him to study with Sufi Masters, Buddhist teachers, Native American elders, Catholic monks, and humanistic and transpersonal psychologists." On September 7th

---

[192] Ibid., p.37.

[193] Known as the World Peace Summit, 1,000 religious leaders gathered in the cause of global unity. At a 1999 World Federalist event, Maurice Strong told me how the forthcoming World Peace Summit was conceived. Ted Turner woke up one day with the thought, *what would happen if all the religions could work together?* Ted phoned Strong, then Special Advisor to the UN Secretary General, and told him of his idea. The rest is history.

[194] The Summit adopted the *United Nations Millennium Declaration* (A/RES/552), containing a number of empowerment provisions. It also birthed the UN Millennium Development Goals. Re: Forum 2000. According to the event's *Executive Summary*, Gorbachev's opening plenary was themed, "Globalization and the New World Order."

[195] Taken from the Forum 2000 daily agenda, September 6, 2000. Document on file.

it was Audrey Kitagawa, a well-spoken and passionate devotee of the Divine Mother who was said to embody the teachings of Sri Ramakrishna. Deepak Chopra led meditations the following day.[196]

The Forums hosted by Gorbachev and Garrison, and the corresponding Millennium meetings, were instrumental in projecting a global *spiritual politics*. Enchanted by a sense of human grandeur in planetary service, the millennium changeover anticipated a political future in-step with the metaphysical ideal of Oneness. It is a dream that continues.

In 2006 the former Soviet leader wrote: "Nowadays humanity, so multifarious within its oneness, needs a new philosophy of life, a new ethic that can shape the fundamental values which are common to all religions and which rest upon the consensus of all the peoples of the earth."[197]

As demonstrated by the above statement, Mikhail Gorbachev's worldview had moved a long way since his time in the Kremlin. *Or maybe not*.

Recounting the final years of the Soviet Union, Gorbachev noted that perestroika – his esteemed "new thinking" – was firmly situated in Oneness,

> What are the basic postulates of the new thinking? Its starting point is the recognition that despite their dissimilarities all the nations of the world are interdependent. We speak of recognition because this interdependence, which is the form of unity or oneness, had been taking shape for decades… interdependence was a tangible reality, impossible to disregard, and by the mid-1980s it had become the foremost tendency in world relations.[198]

The former Soviet leader continued,

> The recognition that interdependence was the real state of affairs in the world meant that the foremost trend of development was not one of ever deepening division but one of ever greater unity in the worldwide system. And the Soviet Union – as part of this system – should search for and find its new place within this framework.[199]

---

196 Biographies and meditation schedule, Forum 2000 booklet. Document on file.

197 Mikhail Gorbachev, *Manifesto for the Earth: Action Now for Peace, Global Justice and a Sustainable Future* (Clairview Books, 2006), p.100.

198 Mikhail Gorbachev, *On My Country and the World* (Columbia University Press, 2000), pp.187-188.

199 Ibid., pp.188-189.

"A new revolution in consciousness is needed," he had said in 1989. "Only on this basis will a new culture and a new politics adequate to the challenge of our times be created."[200]

Keep in mind that the above statement was given when Gorbachev was the avowed Communist leader of the USSR. And yet the recipe he presented then, and at other times, sounds familiar: ingredients from the human potential movement, a dash of Eastern wholeness and New Age spirituality, all baked into the cake of global interdependence. Where did the Marxist politician find such a well-stocked pantry of new thought?

Esalen.

That the Institute and its affiliated networks played a part in fostering such thinking is clear. Exactly how much influence is difficult to verify, and to put too much emphasis on one group runs the risk of oversimplification and inaccuracy. Nevertheless, there is an important correlation between Gorbachev's evolutionary thinking and the concepts that emanated from the retreat center on California's shore. Jim Garrison himself has cautiously acknowledged Esalen's participatory role in glasnost and perestroika.[201]

But there are hints of something more.

Remember, Esalen was a diplomatic back-channel for the two countries. It would then make sense that Moscow had a secret listening device on location. Jeffrey Kripal relates an interesting story of what was thought to be confidential discussions in an Esalen building known as the Big House,

> ...in the late 1980s, Esalen figure and career diplomat Joe Montville became increasingly convinced that the Gorbachev administration was actually taking some of its ideological cues from that very room... He couldn't help but notice how they would explore a particular theme at a gathering, and then a few weeks later Gorbachev would be saying more or less the same thing in his public speeches. At the first symposium held at the Gorbachev Foundation, Montville decided to ask Gorbachev about his theory. Gorbachev simply smiled, as he pointed to the ceiling in the traditional Russian sign of 'you were bugged.'[202]

---

[200] Ibid., pp.192-193.

[201] Kripal, *Esalen*, p.399.

[202] Ibid., p.399.

In Your Neighborhood

By the year 2000 the United States public was, conscious of it or not, becoming more accepting of Oneness. This was reflected in a survey conducted by Positive Future Consulting. The company was unabashedly New Age in its worldview, which raises the question of bias. However, its methodology was transparent and its findings were comparable to surveys conducted by Gallup and other research groups.

Titled, *In Our Own Words 2000 Research Program*, the study was built upon a 210-point questionnaire which was completed by 1,600 representative households. Following a methodology resulting in an overall margin error of +/– 1.5% to 2.4% at a confidence level of 95%, it produced some remarkable findings:

- 90% of respondents believed in "God or a higher spiritual consciousness," however this may be defined.
- 83% agreed to the statement, "we all just want to connect to God or a higher spiritual consciousness."
- 61% said that religion and spirituality are not the same thing, and 86% felt their lives needed more spiritual growth.
- 55% responded favorably to the following question: "Have you ever experienced a sense of the sacred in everything around you or perceived everything as being spiritually connected together as one?"
- 43% agreed that God "is something separate from me," which is a Biblical position. At the same time, an incredible 85% of Americans affirmed that, "underneath it all, we're all connected as one."
- 81% confirmed the following statement: "Our earth is a unique kind of living organism and as a whole system is fundamentally alive."[203]

"The research supports the observation that we are in the midst of a shift in consciousness of unprecedented proportions," stated the final report.[204]

Since then other polls have confirmed America's transformation. In a 2009 survey by Pew Forum, 24% of Americans affirmed belief in reincarnation and 26% declared that spiritual energy is "located in things like mountains, trees,

[203] *What Brings Us Together: A Presentation of the IOOW 2000 Research Program – Executive Briefing and Summary of Results* (Fund For Global Awakening, 2001), p.27.

[204] Ibid., p.2.

crystals." At the time, Pew found that approximately one-in-ten evangelical Protestants accepted Eastern and New Age beliefs.[205]

Then in May 2017, Summit Ministries and the Barna Group reported the findings of their jointly conducted worldview survey: 61% of *practicing Christians* "agree with ideas rooted in New Spirituality." Breaking this down further, 28% of professing Christians strongly agreed that "all people pray to the same god or spirit," and 27% said that "meaning and purpose come from becoming one with all that is."[206]

Bookstores too have affirmed the worldview transformation.

I enjoy perusing the shelves at Half Price Books (HPB), a used-book chain scattered across 17 American states. At each HPB store, residents in the surrounding community exchange their used books for cash, and the items are re-shelved and re-sold back to the public. In this way HPB presents us with a picture of what the neighborhood is reading.

During a visit to a Minneapolis HPB in 2013, I did some counting of cases and shelves in the religion and spirituality sections. Each bookcase held seven shelves: One shelf was dedicated to Atheism, Islam had three and Judaism was allotted five shelves. Eastern religions made up a case-and-a-half. The New Age/Occult section had five cases, with the vast majority of items being non-fiction. Seven cases were dedicated to Christianity, broadly speaking, including a sizable amount of fiction.[207]

Over the years I have repeated my shelf-counting experiment, including stores that only sell new books. My general observation is not surprising: Christian stock has decreased while space for New Age and Eastern literature has increased. In the fall of 2015 I stopped at a chain bookseller in a small

---

[205] *Many Americans Mix Multiple Faiths: Eastern, New Age Beliefs Widespread* (Pew Forum on Religion and Public Life, December 2009), p.7. For more data on religious changes in America, see *"Nones" on the Rise: One-in-Five Adults Have No Religious Affiliation* (Pew Forum on Religion and Public Life, October 2015). To read a detailed survey on oneness as an accepted paradigm, see *Spirituality in the 21st Century: Journeys Beyond Entrenched Boundaries* (Inter-Disciplinary Press, 2013).

[206] *Competing Worldviews Influence Today's Christians*, Barna Group, Research Releases in Culture and Media, May 9, 2017, www.barna.com/research/competing-worldviews-influence-todays-christians/

[207] I am not opposed to Christian fiction, for it is an effective way to explore truth themes using an entertaining and often faster-flowing medium. However, when fiction takes a dominant place in a specialized, non-fiction subject area, it often signals a general shift away from educational reading.

Saskatchewan city; the Christian selection was a fraction of what was offered in the New Age section.

This is not just a North American phenomenon.

Christian researcher and author, Ray Yungen, told me of some counting he did during a 2014 European trip. Visiting major book sellers in Ireland, Germany and England, Ray discovered that secular Europe was very spiritual. Going to three major bookstores in three cities, his shelf count was this: Dublin, Ireland – 80 shelves dedicated to literature on New Age themes; Dusseldorf, Germany – 88 shelves; Birmingham, England – 100 shelves. Ray was a perceptive individual, and in our conversation he stressed that he did not count books from the Self-Help section or other overlapping categories. His conclusion: "The New Age is the religion of Europe."

This does not diminish other religious developments in Europe. Islam is numerically growing while Christianity struggles, and followers of Eastern religions and those who identify as "unaffiliated" are on the rise.[208]

Australia's religious landscape is transforming. New Zealand as well. Even as secular voices are becoming louder, a chorus of religious pluralism rises. Meanwhile, the drums of Oneness pound.

Postmodernism is giving way to a new story.

New Age Re-Focus

The New Age movement has been turning over. As mentioned earlier, in the 1980s and 1990s the New Spirituality appealed to the market-driven *you*. In his "conversations with God," a discourse between Neale Donald Walsch and a *force* animating his pen who claimed to be God – *telling Neal he was God* – we read that "God" recommends "you put yourself first."[209]

Although not as loud, the message of *We* was also being communicated.

Shirley MacLaine wove *Me* and *We*: "Since there is no separation, we are each Godlike, and God is in each of us. We experience God and God experiences through us. We are literally made up of God energy."[210]

---

[208] *The Future of World Religions: Population Growth Projections, 2010-2050* (Pew Research Center, 2015), p.147.

[209] Neal Donald Walsch, *Conversations With God: An Uncommon Dialogue*, Book 1 (G.P. Putnam's Sons, 1995/1996), p.132 on self first, p.202 on already being God.

[210] Shirley MacLaine, *Going Within: A Guide for Inner Transformation* (Bantam Books, 1989), p.66.

Self and *We* were always to be interconnected and interdependent, but the heavy focus on human potential tended to obscure the intended group shift. With the millennium change, however, the *We* component was re-stressed. Awakening the Self was still advertised, but *social space* was taking place.

A combination of factors contributed to this shift. The Millennium events offered a common vision through the UN Millennium Development Goals, providing social targets backed by political agency. The internet enabled instant access to information and connectivity. Public education stressing global citizenship implanted a new consciousness – the Millennial Generation and Gen Z found their emotional energies being channeled towards social activism and service to the Earth. Everywhere the post-modern attitude of "socially constructed truths" de-emphasized traditional standards. New Age beliefs and Eastern practices became more accepted, losing their social taboos – and even their labels – under the banner of spirituality and tolerance. Unifying narratives were assumed as a *common good*.

The prayer at the opening ceremony of the Millennium Peace Summit of Religious and Spiritual Leaders demonstrated a spiritual transformation almost beyond recognition. It was an enchanted invocation,

> I offer this prayer of peace, not to any one god, nor to many gods; not to the Christian god, nor to the Jewish god, nor the Buddhist god, nor the Islamic god, not even to the indigenous gods of many nations, but to the divinity within us all, that makes us brothers and sisters: To make us truly One Family in the name of humanity. I offer this prayer of peace to the cosmic Oneness that is our birthright, our privilege, and our strength…[211]

Envisioning world peace after the terror attacks of September 11, 2001, New Thought minister Dr. Angelo Pizelo wrote,

> We are activities of God and when we come to full awareness and realization of this, we transform our lives and thereby transform our world. Then we will all collectively experience the awesome reality that everything is good and everything is God.[212]

[211] Ilchi Lee, "Prayer of Peace" given on August 28, 2000, and reprinted in *Peaceology For Healing Society* (Healing Society, 2003), pp.1-2. Punctuation added.

[212] Angelo Pizelo, "God Within," *Peaceful Earth: Spiritual Perspectives on Inner Peace and World Peace* (Hold the Vision, 2003), p.72.

If "everything is good and everything is God," then tragedy and conflict are only *perceived*, the result of illusionary constructs. Not only does this fly in the face of evidence, it begs the question: Why bother? If tragedy is only perceived, then peace is only perceived – and none of it is true. *There is no right or wrong...*

"Tomorrow's God" would be fashioned by the *We*, and so we will determine our own right and wrong, our own good and evil.

"We need a new God," claimed Neal Donald Walsch. "The old God isn't working anymore."[213]

Tomorrow's God will have to be a god-in-community, one that extends beyond democracy and creed and class and gender and individuality. *All* will be embraced in an experiential spirituality. This is the god Walsch anticipates: Everything is God, and so even belief will no longer be necessary.

"Tomorrow's God," he explained, "does not require anyone to believe in God." Rather, everyone will talk *with* God and *for* God; an ever-changing, "unconditionally loving, non-judgmental, noncondemning, and nonpunishing" *experience of living*. Nothing will be separate from the "All in All," for "Tomorrow's God is not a singular Super Being, but the extraordinary process called Life."[214]

As visionary futurist Philip Comella expressed in 2014: "No more proofs of God's existence will be necessary because there will be no doubt, based on the success of the united dreaming effort, that we are God... Our fates are intertwined, and so we find salvation in each other."[215]

Modernity's Temple of Man forced a change in thinking. In response we embraced the post-modern vacuum of meaning. In return, a wave of spirituality swept into the void. From Vivekananda to psychedelic visions to the Kremlin to your town, and maybe even closer to home, the evidence is before us: *we are enchanted by the image of ourselves*.

However, as humanity chases self-divinity through New Age enlightenment, we find ourselves betrayed by our soul's haunting emptiness. Or like Warren Smith, we encounter spiritual darkness and discover that malevolent

213 Neal Donald Walsch, *Tomorrows God: Our Greatest Spiritual Challenge* (Atria Books, 2004), p.3.

214 Ibid., p.386.

215 Philip Comella, *The Collapse of Materialism: Visions of Science, Dreams of God* (Rainbow Ridge Books, 2013/2014), p.282.

supernatural entities actually exist. Held in spiritual bondage yet thinking we are free, we can only wrap each other in collective barbed wire. *Shambhala never materializes*.

But something more is going on. Western civilization is turning back. No, this is not a return to Christianity with its message of sin and salvation, nor to Materialism with its hollowing of life and spirit, and not Postmodernism with its intellectual quicksand.

Pushing past rationality and facts, the next phase of civilization will gravitate to imagination and myth. In the search for wisdom and cohesion and meaning, humanity will acknowledge the primal and seek the archaic. Ritual will emerge and celebration will have a magical quality; experience will be super-charged. Spiritual technology will promise connection and purpose, and *occulture* will constantly feed our dreams and stories. We will be enamored with Mystery and solicit its communion. Nature and non-human intelligences will be embraced as kin.

The road ahead will be discovered by *what lies behind us*.

Like all futures we can only see it dimly, but as we have already been dragged over its threshold we can begin to discern its composition. A profile is coming into view; *an ancient landscape frames our new story*.

Chapter 7

Magical Re-Enchantment

> ...for the new decade is seeing a remarkable revival of interest in magic, witchcraft, alchemy, astrology and mythology which is invading even the universities and creating the suspicion that the world-view of modern science may itself have been a peculiar form of myth. – Alan Watts.[1]

> The only hope, or so it seems to me, lies in a reenchantment of the world. – Morris Berman.[2]

An imposing goddess stood before my young family, bold and commanding, dressed in glistening gold. Around her wrists were bracelets made of delicate snakes, a hideous gorgon head was visible between her breasts, and she wore a lavishly decorated helmet with three combs. Protected by the goddess's battle shield was an ominous looking serpent; head erect, body coiled, its tail slithered behind her feet. Against her left arm rested a spear almost as long as she was tall. In the palm of her extended right hand was a winged, figurine-like character. The room she stood in was impressive, too; ancient looking statues and sculptures lined the walls, and the high ceiling was held in place by vaulted colonnades.

It was a setting that invoked a sense of awe.

My wife and son had entered the majestic room first, immediately catching sight of the diva. Our five-year-old daughter, holding my hand, noticed her as well. How could you not? She was the center of attention, and her deadpan gaze rested on all who approached.

---

1 Alan Watts, *In My Own Way: An Autobiography, 1915-1965* (Pantheon Books, 1972), p.323.

2 Morris Berman, *The Reenchantment of the World* (Bantam, 1981), p.10.

"Daddy," my daughter's voice sounded distant in the expansive space. "Why are we looking at a false god?"

How perceptive.

There we stood, the four of us, in the grandeur of Athena's Temple – the Parthenon – staring at a 42-foot tall, gold gilded image of the Goddess of War. No, we had not been magically transported to ancient Greece. We were in Nashville, Tennessee.[3]

Put away the idea of needing a time machine to encounter the images of ancient, pagan deities. You can see them today.

In Chicago, the Roman goddess of grain and fertility is perched atop the Board of Trade Building. At one time, Ceres' blank face beheld the entire city, then taller skyscrapers hemmed her in. Ceres also stands on the Missouri state capital building, and a striking statue of Nike is poised on Arizona's capital dome. Nike, the Goddess of Victory,[4] caps the Soldiers' Monument in Worcester, Massachusetts, as she does at the Solders' and Sailors' Monument in downtown Indianapolis.

Vulcan, the Roman deity of fire and the forge, overlooks Birmingham, Alabama. Originally built to represent the state's mineral resources for the 1904 St. Louis World Fair, it remains the largest cast iron statue in the world at 56-feet. Standing atop Red Mountain, the ridge separating Homewood[5] from Birmingham, and perched on a stone pedestal twice its height, Vulcan has a commanding view of the University of Alabama and the city beyond.

At 92-feet, Venus – wrapping in twisting robes of silvery steel – is currently the tallest statue in San Francisco. Opened to the public in the spring of 2017, the goddess of love, sex and fertility, arises in the tucked-away courtyard of Trinity Place. In the same city you will find Minerva, the wife of Jupiter who is affiliated with war, wisdom and commerce, as she stands atop the Pioneer Monument. Minerva is featured on California's state seal.[6]

Stationed at Rockefeller Center, New York City, is a bronze, 18-foot high, Prometheus. In Greek mythology this Titan stole fire from Zeus and gave

---

3 The Nashville Parthenon can be found at 2500 West End Ave, Nashville, TN.

4 The figure in Athena's hand in Nashville is Nike.

5 Before being repositioned on his pedestal, Vulcan's bare bottom was angled toward the Homewood district, earning the affectionate phrase, "moon over Homewood."

6 Other official seals with Greco-Roman goddess symbolism includes South Carolina, New Jersey, New York, and Virginia.

it to Mankind, thus becoming a symbol of human progression. Of course, the Roman goddess Libertas on Liberty Island in Upper New York Bay is world-renowned as a beacon of freedom.

A plethora of smaller, cultic images dot the American landscape.

Persephone can be found on the grounds of Butler University in Indianapolis; a colorful Sun God is perched at the University of California, San Diego; Minerva is displayed at the University of Albany; *The Great God Pan* rests at Columbia University, a short distance from the *Alma Mater* monument depicting Athena; *Isis, Goddess of Life*, is seated on a throne at President Herbert Hoover's birthplace near Iowa City; and the Mesoamerican deity Quetzalcoatl is coiled in downtown San José, California.

America's capital is awash in classical opulence. Greco-Roman themes and deity portrayals are displayed throughout Washington DC, including the nation's homegrown goddess, Columbia. Amidst the backdrop of its daily political drama, the ancient past comes to life in the symbolic detail of the city's monuments and sculptures, engravings, paintings, and architecture. Egyptian motifs are found too.[7] Washington's Monument, the largest structure in the city, was intentionally erected in the style of an Egyptian obelisk.[8] At the time of completion in 1884 it was the tallest structure in the world.[9]

Canada, too, has similar cultic depictions, but nothing like the volume of the United States. Toronto's remarkable Princes' Gates, a triumphal arch flanked by grand colonnades, is watched over by Nike. A modernist interpretation of the goddess stands in downtown Vancouver, a gift from Olympia's mayor to commemorate the 2010 Winter Olympics. The Manitoba Legislative Building in Winnipeg is capped with a gold gilded statue of Mercury, a deity in the Roman pantheon connected to commerce, magic, and the underworld. To the ancient Greeks he was understood as Hermes, but to Manitobans he is known as Golden Boy.[10]

As North America is now a religious melting pot, images highlighting Eastern spirituality are becoming more prevalent.

---

7 Egyptian themes include sphinxes and the all-seeing eye, associated with Ra and Horus.

8 Obelisks are associated with solar worship. The structure also has phallic connotations.

9 Historic Preservation Review Board, *Application for Historic Landmark or History District Designation* (Gov. of the District of Columbia/National Park Service, 2016), p.23.

10 Manitoba's Legislative Building is famed for its esoteric symbolism. Masonic and Rosicrucian themes are found throughout the structure. See *The Hermetic Code: Unlocking One of Manitoba's Greatest Secrets* (Winnipeg Free Press, 2007).

A golden, 50-foot tall Hanuman *murti* – an embodiment of the popular Hindu deity – can be viewed at the Vishnu Mandir in the Greater Toronto Area. In the Chicago suburb of Glenview stands a 22-foot Lord Hanuman in the recently constructed Hanuman temple.[11] Embassy Row in Washington DC boasts a gleaming white statue of the Hindu goddess, Saraswati.[12] And inside the Chuang Yen Monastery near Carmel, New York, you can gaze upon a 37-foot statue of the Great Buddha Vairocana – the largest Buddhist statue in the Western Hemisphere. Of course, American examples of Eastern representations are small in size and number compared to Asian counterparts.

It seems to be an ironic concurrence: In the West, and particularly the United States, classic pagan pageantry has been used to symbolize democratic ideals in a land sprinkled with Christian crosses. During the nation's first two hundred years its citizenry lived within a culturally accepted Christian ethos, yet at the same time, cultic imagery was used to display Enlightenment principles and the spiritual aesthetics of Romanticism. It is a testament to the lasting power of myth, and the *sacred secularism* that underscored Modernity.

What does this all mean? *Nothing* and *something*.

Nothing in that like many of the days of the week and months of the year, named after pagan divinities, we go about our busy lives without giving it any thought. That this historical milieu exists as part of our culture's habit is not something to become unduly excited about. It is an unchangeable piece of our social fabric. *It just is*.

Something in that we have a glimpse of the past in the present: We can properly see these representations as reminders of the ancient worldview. These quiet heralds of stone and metal, often standing in our high places, whisper to us that the pagan past is not so far removed.

In the case of newer inclusions such as Hanuman or Ganesha or Shiva, these can be likened to memos announcing the contemporary shift in spiritual attitudes. In a way similar to the Renaissance when garden deity statues and private shrines acted as harbingers of major societal change,[13] we can

---

11 The Hanuman Mandir of Greater Chicago is located at 3623 W Lake Ave, Glenview, IL.

12 Saraswati is located on the grounds of the Indonesian Embassy.

13 See Joscelyn Godwin, *The Pagan Dream of the Renaissance* (WeiserBooks, 2002/2005). See also, Prudence Jones and Nigel Pennick, *A History of Pagan Europe* (Routledge, 1995), pp.200-203.

look upon these images as way-markers; physical symbols of our transforming culture and reminders of an active, supernatural setting.

Putting aside the Hindu and Buddhist depictions, I wonder what first century Christians would think if they could be transported to America for the intent of gazing upon the nation's display of classical paganism. How would they respond?

Not with shock, but the familiar recognition of a pagan enchantment.

Disenchantment and Myth

In his 1917 lecture, "Science as a Vocation," German sociologist Max Weber noted that the ever-progressive nature of modern science and rationalism had created a condition of *disenchantment*,

> ...principally there are no mysterious incalculable forces that come into play, but rather that one can, in principle, master all things by calculation. This means the world is disenchanted. One need no longer have recourse to magical means in order to master or implore the spirits, as did the savage, for whom such mysterious powers existed. Technical means and calculations perform the service.[14]

Weber had used the phrase "disenchantment of the world" in previous essays on religion. It was language he borrowed from the German Romanticist, Friedrich Schiller,[15] adapting it to highlight the tension between scientific rationalism and the historic role of belief. Weber also recognized that the bureaucratic trend, everywhere evident, was clearly derived from technique and the pragmatic character: "rules, means, ends, and matter-of-factness dominates its bearing."[16] Specialization and bureaucracy, he noted, are at odds with traditional cultural moods and aesthetic qualities.

Science had disconnected humanity from mystery and the materialist outlook had eroded the sense of spirit. Thanks to industrialization and technology and urbanization, the masses were increasingly distanced from the toil

---

[14] Max Weber, From Max Weber: *Essays in Sociology* (Oxford University Press, 1946, translated and edited by H.H. Gerth and C. Wright Mills), p.139.

[15] Ibid., p.51, introductory remarks by Gerth and Mills on the role of Schiller. Friedrich Schiller was a playwright, poet, and aesthetic philosopher, forming an important link in the chain of German Romanticism.

[16] Ibid., p.244. See his entire essay, "Bureaucracy," which makes up chapter 8.

of fields and forests. Natural struggles and processes were moving into the background. Modernity and secularism had replaced the mythic, displacing wonder and stripping the imagination. We had become disenchanted.

Weber, born in 1864, had lived through the intellectual high tide of Modernity. But as explored in previous chapters, the Enlightenment era and the Modernist epoch also witnessed the inner revolution of Romanticism, new religious movements, and an upsurge in esoteric interests. Secularity had the appearance of social ascension, and it made incredible strides to that end, but spiritual winds were blowing. Disenchantment sets in motion the desire to replace lost purpose.

Rejecting Modernity's claim that science is the "one true description of reality,"[17] and unwilling to re-consider the Christian worldview, the postmodern mind found itself drifting in a sea of conflicting currents. At the same time, the need for alternative answers to the question of human meaning resulted in a growth market of novel ideas. Postmodernism and the New Age walked hand-in-hand. However, the New Age movement with its spiritualized, Self-focused human potential and its tendency to feast at a thinly-spread spiritual smorgasbord – while profoundly impacting the social landscape with its message of Oneness – was incapable of providing a base narrative that impelled global action.

This does not mean Postmodernism has simmered; the pressure cooker seems to be getting hotter. Nor has the New Age movement disappeared; acceptance is closer to the norm. And the allure of Self-ism, the product of human potential thinking, continues to psychologically validate the pursuit of our own desires; a sign of perilous times – "for men will be lovers of themselves."[18] None of these attributes have dissipated, and yet they failed to offer a path forward – a perceived justification for the re-ordering of a global civilization.

Could something more primal hold the key?

---

[17] Berman, *The Reenchantment of the World*, p.190. Berman equates scientific dogma with the prior-held medieval Catholic system.

[18] "But know this, that in the last days perilous times will come: For men will be lovers of themselves, lovers of money, boasters, proud, blasphemers, disobedient to parents, unthankful, unholy, unloving, unforgiving, slanderers, without self-control, brutal, despisers of good, traitors, headstrong, haughty, lovers of pleasure rather than lovers of God, having a form of godliness but denying its power. And from such people turn away!" – 2 Timothy 3:1-5.

A new context was about to be shaped through an archaic lens, one paralleling Postmodernism and the New Age, yet offering a more robust setting for change. It would recognize the technical while affirming the spiritual, merging Modernism into mystery and the human with the natural. It would be essentially religious, or better said, *mythic* – powerfully transforming the psyche of Western civilization through a new *framing story*. However, before considering the scope and role of such an integrating mythology, we need to consider the meaning of myth. Upfront, it is acknowledged that interpretations of what myth *is* are varied, but for the sake of this discussion, one explanation will be extracted and applied.

Different than, but related to the epic tale, myth explains and exemplifies aspects of perceived reality through the use of symbolic narrative and imagery. Carl G. Jung offers this analysis,

> The need for mythic statements is satisfied when we frame a view of the world which adequately explains the meaning of human existence in the cosmos, a view which springs from our psychic wholeness... No science will ever replace myth, and myth cannot be made out of any science. For it is not that 'God' is a myth, but that myth is the revelation of the divine life in man...[19]

Eminent scientist and humanist, René Dubos, connected the archaic to the modern in his 1972 book, *A God Within*,

> The myths of ancient peoples are still meaningful to us because they express preoccupations and moods which are universal and eternal... myths change their external appearance when they are adopted by a new culture, but their core of fundamental truth is not thereby altered.[20]

The "fundamental truth" that Dubos alluded to is continuity. Old Testament scholar John N. Oswalt describes the relationship between myth and continuity this way: "Myth depends for its whole rationale on the idea that all things in the cosmos are continuous with each other. Furthermore, myth exists to actualize that continuity."[21] Thus, the deities of myth are depicted

[19] Carl G. Jung, *Memories, Dreams, Reflections* (Vintage Books, 1989), p.340.

[20] Rene Dubos, *A God Within* (Charles Scribner's Sons, 1972), p.251.

[21] John N. Oswalt, *The Bible Among The Myths* (Zondervan, 2009), p.45.

as being dependent on material existence, are driven by necessity, and are bound to external forces.[22] Mythic gods and goddesses, contained within the cosmos, reflected the jurisdictions they were associated with – a community of beings existing within and acting upon the cycles and processes of nature. Interdependence was a given.

However, the Biblical narrative, as Oswalt noted, does not qualify as myth for it presents an understanding of reality that is antithetical to continuity. Mythic *thinking* within the Bible is undeniably evident – the existence of an overarching narrative, the layering of meaning, symbolic richness, supernatural assignments, and ancient themes of physical cosmology ascribed to cultural perspectives – but its *essence* remains distinct.[23] Whereas myth communicates an interconnected, *cyclical* view of time – that events in the past have a repeatable quality, and "all that humanity is, the gods are"[24] – the Bible presents an atypical paradigm: "a completely different understanding of existence and of the relationship among the realms."[25]

God, as revealed in the Bible, is utterly unique and separate from creation and matter. All other spiritual personalities – angelic figures and demonic powers and yes, human beings – are ultimately subject to His laws, and Mankind holds a situational value higher than the animal and plant kingdoms. Time itself is the result of, and is subject to, God's action upon space and matter; it is therefore *linear*.

Israeli scholar Yehezkel Kaufmann explained that the Biblical theme of monotheism points to a deity "who is the source of all being, not subject to a cosmic order, and not emergent from a pre-existent realm; a god free of the limitations of magic and mythology."[26]

---

[22] See Yehezkel Kaufmann, *The Religion of Israel: From Its Beginnings to the Babylonian Exile* (The University of Chicago Press, 1960, translated and abridged by Moshe Greenberg), pp.24-44.

[23] Regarding the issue of myth and literary similarities found in the Bible, Oswalt writes: "Are there striking similarities between the Bible and the religion it describes and the ancient Near Eastern literature and the religions found therein? There certainly are, and we should be surprised to find it otherwise. Israel is described in the Bible as a full participant in its world. But what we find is that those similarities are not the defining features of the Bible or of biblical religion. This is unmistakably evident to anyone who takes the Bible as a whole." *The Bible Among The Myths*, p.192.

[24] Ibid., p.45.

[25] Ibid., p.46.

[26] Kaufmann, *The Religion of Israel*, p.29.

From the perspective of myth, the three realms – Nature, Humanity, and Deity – operate within a shared reality in which all are mystically bound and interrelated. When this worldview is enacted via *ritual*, the practitioner is embarking on a trans-personal journey meant to shift one's sense of time and space, to induce an altered state of mind, and to magically interact with cosmic cycles. Ritual, which can be related to but different than ceremony, is "a sacred drama in which you are the audience as well as the participant."[27] It allows one to "*identify* with the thing, not sit back and analyze it."[28]

The renowned Witch, Starhawk, associates ritual with opening consciousness and connecting to the Divine within.[29] It is a psychic and spiritual theater where the *All-Self* is experienced, stirring the soul as distinctions dissolve and meaning is imparted. Ritual fuses the abstract and tangible, the past and present, the material and ethereal – and it may facilitate communion with supernatural entities, including the gods and goddesses of myth.[30]

Nels and Judy Linde, respected ritual designers in the neo-Pagan community, tell us that, "Ritual is sacred theater, evoking the principles of belief or faith, reenacting tales of the gods or of myths."[31] Adapting a Jungian perspective, referenced because of Jung's tremendous impact on Western thinking, their interpretation of myth and ritual links the ancient to the modern,

> Ancient myths that have entered into our common psyche carry the power of the archetypical characters and story inside them, even when we modify the story to suit our ritual purpose. Mythic reference can prepare us to experience spiritual mystery. Even with a

---

[27] Sharon Devlin, as interviewed by Margot Adler, *Drawing Down the Moon: Witches, Druids, Goddess-Worshippers, and Other Pagans in America Today* (The Viking Press, 1979), p.138.

[28] Orrin E. Klapp, *Ritual and Cult: A Sociological Interpretation* (Public Affairs Press, 1956), p.16, italics in original.

[29] Starhawk, *The Spiral Dance: A Rebirth of the Ancient Religion of the Great Goddess* (HarperOne, 1999, 20th Anniversary Edition), p.72.

[30] Famed Wiccans, Janet Farrar and Gavin Bone, bring this out in their book, *Lifting the Veil: A Witches' Guide to Trance-Prophecy, Drawing Down the Moon, and Ecstatic Ritual* (Acorn Guild Press, 2016). For example, in one interview regarding trance-prophecy, Witch Gede Parma described it thus: "Any vessel who hopes to partner with a deity or spirit in possessory work must know this: both parties must treat the experience as a holy communion – the temple of flesh meeting with the mantle of spirit" (p.54).

[31] Nels and Judy Linde, *Taking Sacred Back: The Complete Guide to Designing and Sharing Group Ritual* (Llewellyn Publications, 2016), p.19.

> different storyline the strength of the original myth can empower the presented symbology.[32]

Jungian psychologist Stephen Larsen writes: "Myths emerge from, or are contained by, rituals. Rituals are the embodiment of myths."[33]

Although the role of ritual in relation to myth is important, it is the aspect of *reality narrative* we need to consider. In this way, myth serves as a tool to disseminate ideas, embed values, shape worldviews, and emotively position grand themes as representing something sacred and unifying. Myth, understood as an *information technology*, takes upon itself a propaganda quality and becomes a powerful actor for social transformation.[34] It functions as a framing story, not as a tale or fable, but as a way to think and behave.

"The mythic, like any statement," writes Bill Kinser and Neil Kleinman, "organizes meaning by highlighting and shaping details and by arranging them into a declarative plot."[35]

Kinser and Kleinman were describing myth in the context of Nazi Germany. Their overall analysis bears consideration. Take note of the link between narrative, social acceptance, and the development of policy,

> Events and situations require explanation. Explanations – universalized, generalized and given imaginative flesh – become myths. Myths shape perception. Perceptions produce policies. Policies cause events and situations. And (to begin again at the beginning) events and situations require explanation. How can one separate the beginning of the circle from the end, the mythic invention from the archetypal situation, or the fabrication from the candid recognition of a geopolitical fact? They share a self-perpetuating cycle. The first feeds the last, and the last vindicates – and reinstates – the first.[36]

---

32 Ibid., p.62.

33 Stephen Larsen, *The Mythic Imagination: Your Quest for Meaning Through Personal Mythology* (Bantam Books, 1990), p.31. Larsen was a friend to and sat under the teachings of Joseph Campbell, and trained with Stanislav Grof.

34 See Jacques Ellul, *Propaganda: The Formation of Men's Attitudes* (Vintage Books, 1973, originally published in 1965).

35 Bill Kinser and Neil Kleinman, *The Dream That Was No More a Dream: A Search for Aesthetic Reality in Germany, 1890-1945* (Harper and Row, 1969), p.12.

36 Ibid., p.13.

Myth, symbol, theater and drama: Kinser and Kleinman remind us that the power of persuasion, wrapped in a connecting narrative, can refashion social order and *remake Man's image of himself.*

In the 1970s, Ervin Laszlo, a renowned systems theorist directing a Club of Rome research project, firmly articulated that a psychological restructuring – the sculpting of minds – was crucially needed in light of world transformation.[37] Although the Club of Rome was known for their technocratic modeling, the *Goals in a Global Community* research report stressed the reshaping of *values* and *beliefs*. One contributor emphasized the creation of overarching social narratives: "New images or myths are needed that will be able to act as guiding images of social change."[38]

Cultural targeting would be critical,

> Western, developed countries, are among the best initial candidates for the mythmaking project. The countries of this area will be required to make some significant, and sometimes drastic, shifts of perception in order for the 'new international order' to be fulfilled. Thus it is very important for these societies to make changes in their value systems. In addition, a shift in values in these societies should have a great impact on the rest of the world... The Western countries, therefore, appear to be very good candidates for the reception of myths about a global society.[39]

The Stanford Research Institute (SRI), located on the southwest side of San Francisco Bay and recognized as one of America's leading research centers, was considering new images, too.

During the 1970s, SRI explored models for social evolution as part of a program initiated by the US Office of Education.[40] Willis W. Harman – an

---

[37] Ervin Laszlo, "The Inadequacy of Contemporary Goals – Some Conclusions," *Goals in a Global Community: The Original Background Studies for the Goals for Mankind – A Report to the Club of Rome, Volume II – The International Values and Goals Studies* (Pergamon, 1977, edited by Ervin Laszlo and Judah Bierman), p.551.

[38] Anne Corrigan, "Science and Myth: Two Proposals to the Club of Rome," *Goals in a Global Community: The Original Background Studies for the Goals for Mankind – A Report to the Club of Rome, Volume I – Studies on the Conceptual Foundations* (Pergamon, 1977, edited by Ervin Laszlo and Judah Bierman), p.305.

[39] Ibid., p.306. The US Office of Education made the request in 1968.

[40] O.W. Markley and Willis W. Harman, *Changing Images of Man: Prepared by the Center*

early LSD researcher[41] and the first official lecturer at Esalen[42] – was the SRI project supervisor, and visionary professor Oliver W. Markley its director. Reviewers and advisors included Ervin Laszlo, mythologist Joseph Campbell, René Dubos, Margaret Mead, Carl R. Rogers, John White from the Institute of Noetic Sciences, and Timothy Leary's collaborator in *The Psychedelic Experience*, Ralph Metzner.[43] Each contributor had "a deep appreciation for the profound ways in which myths and images affect the perceptions and actions of humankind in the universe..."[44]

The project report was publicly released as *Changing Images of Man*, and it claimed that a fresh vision was coming into focus. Humanity was tipping toward a perennial perspective. The new story of civilization would be interdependence and global community, the cultivating of spirituality and higher consciousness, and a restored relationship with nature. The boundaries of science would expand, producing a "new science of consciousness and ecological systems not limited by manipulative rationality."[45]

Similar to Max Weber, the SRI team acknowledged that science had displaced faith, but this had created other issues and concerns. Although science "now performs the cosmological function," the general public had "little comprehension *how* scientific knowledge defines the world."[46]

---

for the Study of Social Policy/SRI International (Pergamon Press, 1982), p.xvii. Note: This report was completed in 1974 but was not published in a widely distributed format until Pergamon released it in 1982. It was through Ervin Laszlo's work as editor of the *Systems Science and World Order Library: Explorations of World Order*, a series under the Pergamon label, that *Changing Images of Man* was considered for a larger audience.

41 Harman was introduced to LSD in the late 1950s through Captain Al Hubbard, a renowned figure in the American intelligence community who has been described as the "Johnny Appleseed of LSD." In the 1960s, Harman was engaged in LSD therapy research via the International Federation for Advanced Studies. See Martin A. Lee and Bruce Shlain, *Acid Dreams: The Complete Social History of LSD: The CIA, the Sixties, and Beyond* (Grove Press, 1992), p.198.

42 According to Walter Truett Anderson, Harman was the first to give an official lecture at Esalen. See Walter T. Anderson, *The Upstart Spring: Esalen and the American Awakening* (Addison-Wesley Publishing Company, 1983), p.68. Anderson details the connection between Esalen and Stanford via Michael Murphy's experiences at the university, saying, "Much of the credit (or blame) for the birth of Esalen goes to Stanford." (p.26).

43 Markley and Harman, *Changing Images of Man*, pp.vii,xv.

44 Ibid., p.xix.

45 Ibid., p.203.

46 Ibid., p.8, italics in original.

Furthermore, scientific materialism had an effect on civil structures, empowering a rigid set of gatekeepers to determine values: universities generated knowledge and granted status, industry provided economic reason, government fashioned context, and bureaucracy became enforcers of social order. Humanity was being squeezed into something monetized and managed, and this, the SRI report noted, was a mismatch to the new and emerging image: "disenchantment with the technocratic elite, [and] the decreasing trust and confidence in governments" was evident in the survey data.[47] The budding, post-industrial image would be nestled within an organic and networked environment, and institutions would have to adapt to the new paradigm. It was a message that was euphoric, yet controversial.[48]

The venerated new image would adopt "an *ecological ethic*, emphasizing the total community of life-in-nature and the oneness of the human race," and it would entail a "*self-realization ethic*" focusing on selfhood and human development. Man's new image must be "*multi-leveled*, *multi-faceted*, and *integrative*," embracing cultural and personal diversity. Social balance would be key, yet the overall project must remain "*experimental*, *open-ended*, and *evolutionary*."[49] The SRI team affirmed that the new image was itself an *old image*, stemming back thousands of years, "in the core experiences underlying the world's many religious doctrines, as reported through myth and symbols, holy writings, and esoteric teachings."[50]

Conspicuously absent from *Changing Images of Man* was a roadmap on how to achieve the celebrated paradigm, although the new image can "be hastened or slowed by deliberate choice," pointing to crisis and social disruption as drivers of change.[51]

---

47 Ibid., p.185.

48 For extra details on SRI, see Art Kleiner, *The Age of Heretics: A History of the Radical Thinkers Who Reinvented Corporate Management* (Wiley, 2008, second edition).

49 Markley and Harman, *Changing Images of Man*, p.202, italics in original.

50 Ibid., p.184. The report equated the new vision as "true Freemasonry," saying there is "one lodge – the universe, and one brotherhood, everything that exists. Each person has the 'privilege of labor,' of joining with the 'Great Architect' in building more noble structures and thus serving in the divine plan." The authors believed that by adopting this as a social norm, compatible with "more indigenous" versions from other parts of the world, Americans might discover a renewed sense of meaning in their "technological-industrial thrust" (p.185).

51 Ibid., p.160.

But its lack of a blueprint was not a weakness, for a comprehensive plan would have relegated the project to just another utopian expectation. The strength of their approach, instead, was to encourage adaptations and cultural points of entry, producing an evolutionary transformation on multiple levels. Furthermore, the very fact that an institute of this caliber sponsored such a project lent credibility to the social and spiritual revolution already in motion – a revolution fueled, in large part, by the very personalities who contributed to the report.

The bourgeoning New Age community latched on. Mark Satin's influential book, *New Age Politics*, referenced the SRI document in making the case for a new ethics.[52] Marilyn Ferguson praised the work of Harman and the SRI team, recognizing that their project had "laid the groundwork for a paradigm shift in understanding how individual and social transformation might be accomplished."[53] Her massively influential book, *The Aquarian Conspiracy*, was simply a repackaging of SRI and Esalen.[54]

The SRI team had validated a nebulous idea, a mythic transformation.

Disenchantment portended a new framing story.

Re-Enchantment

French theologian and social thinker, Jacques Ellul, said the following on the heels of the Cultural Revolution in the West: "Secularization is always an intermediate stage between a religious society on the way out and the appearance of a new religious structuring."[55]

If the 1960s and 1970s represented the revolutionary seedbed for a new spiritual outlook, the 1980s and 1990s were the decades of blossoming. In my view, this 40-year window was a critical time for the Christian church in the West. Alas, the year 2000 and onward would see both a harvest and re-seeding of spiritual alternatives; fresh shoots are flourishing in what is now established soil.

We have entered the Age of Re-enchantment.

---

[52] Mark Satin, *New Age Politics: Healing Self and Society* (A Delta Book/Dell Publishing, 1979), p.104.

[53] Marilyn Ferguson, *The Aquarian Conspiracy: Personal and Social Transformation in the 1980s* (J.P. Tarcher, 1980), p.61.

[54] This is my own analysis of Ferguson's book.

[55] Jacques Ellul, *The New Demons* (The Seabury Press, 1975), p.219.

What is Re-enchantment? The assembly of meaning and purpose within a matrix of wonder and mystery, aesthetic expressions, symbolism and sentiment, all pointing to a paradigm of holism; whereas disenchantment produced an *I-it* relationship – with the person as *I*, and the Earth and cosmos as *it* – re-enchantment emphasizes an *I-thou* perspective. Everything is in community. Humanity is sublimely connected to a wider sense of being.

That nuances and interpretations exist regarding Re-enchantment is evident in the literature. How could this not be? The term itself is vague.

Professor Morris Berman's 1984 book, *The Reenchantment of the World*, was an early, contemporary call to an enchanted worldview. Scientific certainty, he outlined, had been the "integrating mythology of industrial society." This one-sided reality had produced a dysfunction in our structures of knowledge, values, and relationships. Our hope was to be found in "a very different sort of integrating mythology."[56] We needed a magical reunion with the cosmos, with nature, and ourselves.

Finding our new foundation would thus necessitate a realignment of knowledge. Science was not superior, nor was the occult worldview inferior.[57] The same mental universe holds both; therefore, science and *participatory consciousness* would need to find an alchemical synthesis. Holism is reality and destiny. Re-enchantment would be a return to the mystery made manifest in *shamanism* – the animistic bonding to Nature – specifically, "the God within, and the ecosystem that reflects it."[58]

Twenty years after Berman's book was released, Christopher Partridge, a professor of Contemporary Religion, published the first of his two-volume series, *The Re-Enchantment of the West*.[59] When both volumes were made available, they painted a remarkable picture of a new situation.

In Europe, the historic and traditional Christian base for culture had collapsed. North America's foundational Christian ethos was fading. Secularism was rising, yet it could not claim ascendency: "Another religio-cultural milieu has taken its place."[60]

---

56 Berman, *The Reenchantment of the World*, p.187.

57 Ibid., p.127.

58 Ibid., p.300.

59 Christopher Partridge, *The Re-Enchantment of the West: Alternative Spiritualities, Sacralization, Popular Culture and Occulture*, 2 Volumes (T&T Clark International, 2004, 2005).

60 Partridge, *The Re-Enchantment of the West: Volume 1*, p.4.

Partridge cataloged the West's new spiritual environment: Eastern philosophy and the New Age are accepted. Popular literature, movies, and music continuously reinforce the already occurring shift; Christian models are out, alternatives are in. Cyberspace has animated techno-paganism, and archaic spirituality flows from a renewed interest in psychedelics. Paranormal subjects have mass appeal, and public interest in the UFO phenomena is undeniable; society is *enchanted by extraterrestrials*. Interestingly, the channeled messages received from apparent aliens – and much of the associated literature on the subject of UFOs – delivers an unmistakable, New Age worldview. Who knew that extraterrestrial are Theosophists from outer space?[61]

A renaissance in occultism was evident.

Whereas Berman *advocated*, Partridge *analyzed*.

Surveying a range of socio-religious indicators, Partridge observed that a central characteristic of Re-enchantment was *occulture*. Used as a general heading, occulture could be considered this way: The social acceptance of esoteric and supernatural sub-themes percolating within popular culture, often unnoticed by the general population, yet cultivating new norms. Themes within occulture may be diverse,[62] but together they express a change in religious attitudes,

> When thinking of 'occulture'... foundational understanding of the occult should be broadened to include a vast spectrum of beliefs and practices sourced by Eastern spirituality, Paganism, Spiritualism, theosophy, alternative science and medicine, popular psychology

---

[61] See Partridge, *The Re-Enchantment of the West: Volume 2*, chapter 5. For an older text, see David Morris, *The Masks of Lucifer: Technology and the Occult in Twentieth-Century Popular Literature* (B.T. Batsford Ltd., 1992). One striking example of Theosophy within the UFO context comes from the channeled writings of Benjamin Crème, *The Reappearance of the Christ and the Masters of Wisdom* (TARA Press, 1980), p.205ff.

[62] Partridge explores an array of subjects: trance festivals, popular literature, psychedelics, UFOs, demonology and Satanism, healthcare and wellness, and deep ecology. His final chapter in volume 2 is on eschatology and the appeal of apocalyptic themes. In this he explores pseudo-Christian cults such as the Jehovah's Witnesses, and gives space to evangelical Christians. Regarding the latter, Partridge discusses the *Left Behind* series, conspiracy theories, secret societies, and anti-Semitism. I have some criticism regarding his approach, but my general and practical take-away as a Christian researcher is this: We must strive for accuracy in specifics and generalities, being attentive to sources, and cautious when speculating (speculation is useful in exploring ideas, if handled properly).

> (usually Jungian), and a range of beliefs emanating out of the general cultural interest in the paranormal.[63]

Occulture and Re-enchantment draws from the mythic past,

> Whether drawing on Eastern spirituality or Gnosticism, there is broad occultural agreement that the key to vibrant, authentic contemporary spirituality is the resurgence of ancient traditions. Whether one worships the Goddess, studies the rites of ancient orders, charts the stars, channels messages from those who once walked the streets of Atlantis, explores the secrets of the Mayan civilization, or even attempts to translate the ancient Enochian angelic tongue revealed during the crystal-gazing experiments of the Elizabethan occultists... there is a sense of continuity with the ancients.[64]

Similar to Berman, Partridge documented Re-enchantment as a movement of holism, one with the capacity to embrace the *sacred* and *secular*, together representing a "non-Christian religio-cultural milieu."[65]

But not everyone holds to a mythic-religious reading, seeing this, instead, as a secular-technical process. Philosopher Bernard Stiegler – influenced by Marx, Nietzsche, Freud and Heidegger – referred to Re-enchantment as an "industrial economy of spirit," a new post-capitalist order. Such a re-purposed political economy would rest on a *technology of spirit*, a raised level of "individual and collective intelligence," acting through a "*new form of public power, itself resting upon a new form of political will*."[66] Stiegler looked forward to "new cultural, educational, scientific, and industrial politics capable of *taking care of the world*."[67]

Through an economy of contribution, we all would partake in a technically enlightened future. Stiegler's version of Re-enchantment was a secular trust in the dynamics of technique, placing and identifying humanity within systems of technological change.

---

[63] Partridge, *The Re-Enchantment of the West: Volume 1*, pp.69-70.

[64] Ibid., p.77.

[65] Partridge, *The Re-Enchantment of the West: Volume 2*, p.2.

[66] Bernard Stiegler, *The Re-Enchantment of the World: The Value of Spirit Against Industrial Populism* (Bloomsbury Academic, 2014, originally published in French in 2006, translated by Trevor Arthur), p.7, italics in original.

[67] Ibid., p.18, italics in original.

Humanistic interpretations were also argued in *The Re-Enchantment of the World: Secular Magic in a Rational Age*. This anthology investigated a range of motions "held together by their common aim of filling a God-shaped void."[68] Threads of commonality wove within a diversity of subjects, from literature to sports and language, for the God-replacement – referencing Nietzsche – would need to serve "multiple functions simultaneously."[69]

An interesting observation was expressed in the Introduction,

> If the world is to be re-enchanted, it must accordingly be reimbued not only with *mystery* and *wonder* but also with order, perhaps even with *purpose*; there must be a hierarchy of *significance* attaching to objects and events encountered, individual lives, and moments within those lives, must be susceptible again to *redemption*; there must be a new, intelligible locus for the *infinite*; there must be a way of carving out, within the fully profane world, a set of spaces which somehow possess the allure of the *sacred*; there must be everyday *miracles*, exceptional events which go against (and perhaps even alter) the accepted order of things; and there must be secular *epiphanies*, moments of being in which, for a brief instant, the center appears to hold, and the promise is held out of a quasi-mystical union with something larger than oneself.[70]

This is sacred secularity.

What was being elucidated is a humanistic spirituality, an emotive sense of meaning and belonging – higher values, sublime qualities – without reliance on traditional religion and theological truth claims, or appeals to a transcendent God. This non-supernatural magic unfolds as philosophy and art and technique reintegrates experientially, as the individual inwardly connects with the energy of the group, and as the group finds beauty and validity and purpose in a grander vision.

Sacred secularity is the placing of awe, wonder, and reverence within the creativity of humanity, often associated with a rationalized, sacredness of Nature. It is worship in the Temple of Man.

---

68 Joshua Landy and Michael Saler, "Introduction," *The Re-Enchantment of the World: Secular Magic in a Rational Age* (Stanford University Press, 2009), p.2.

69 Ibid., p.2.

70 Ibid., p.2, italics in original.

Consider this troika of holism – spirit, science, and nature – as prepared for the American Institute of Planners' Fiftieth Year Consultation, a visioning process that started during the mid-1960s in contemplation of the year 2000. Ralph G.H. Siu, then Deputy Director of Development at the US Army Material Command, wrote that the "present age of materialism seems to be giving way to a new age." He called this the Age of Holistic Humanism: "a harmony of things spiritual and intangible with the cornucopia of material abundance... Man and Nature are to be one. This is the tenor of the new age."[71] Technology would be nudged by "the grandeur of Art and Spirit," and humanity would no longer be viewed as separate, but as "an intuitive whole with Nature."[72]

Beat poet, Richard Brautigan, offered an enchanted dream – the vision of a techno-natural paradise – in his 1967 poem, *All Watched Over by Machines of Loving Grace*. This three-stanza composition spoke of a "cybernetic meadow" wherein computers and animals live in harmony. Forests of electronics would be at peace with nature, carefully managed by "machines of loving grace" in a perfect, "cybernetic ecology." Humanity, freed of toil by technology, would thus return to a holistic garden.[73]

Both examples correspond to the notion of sacred secularity.

Burning Man, the massive, celebratory gathering in northern Nevada, exhibits a similar flavor; *spiritual secularism*. Likewise, the transhuman impartation of sacredness to technology dovetails this theme. The quest for world order, with its search for meaning and unity within a political technique, has the making of a secular enchantment. These three subjects will be covered in upcoming chapters.

But Re-enchantment, as outlined by Partridge, can be more than just imbuing a sense of the sacred upon secular attitudes. It is frequently swathed in a *religiously spiritual context*. This includes our contemporary fascination with what he calls "dark occulture,"

> This reliance on the monstrous other, the demonic foil... lies close to the heart of contemporary Western occulture and re-enchantment. Indeed, the demonic has become iconic. The satanic other, flourish-

---

71 Ralph G.H. Siu, "Role of Technology in Creating the Environment Fifty Years Hence," *Environment and Change: The Next Fifty Years* (Indiana University Press, 1968), p.95.

72 Ibid., p.98.

73 As printed in the text book, *I Am a Sensation* (McClelland and Stewart Ltd., 1971), p.11.

> ing beyond the boundaries of institutional religion and respectable culture, is becoming increasingly attractive to many contemporary Westerners.[74]

In the Modernist presentation of secularism and materialism, belief in malicious spiritual entities faded as just another form of superstition, and yet, "interest in the demonic is experiencing something of a revival."[75]

Partridge highlighted a few contemporary examples of dark inspiration; the influence of Aleister Crowley on the Western Cultural Revolution, Anton LaVey's Church of Satan with its self-centered philosophy and vicious brand of Darwinism, and the Temple of Set with its ceremonial magic.[76] He also commented on the influx of demonic themes within the entertainment industry and related subcultures, and the reaction of Christians to these modern developments.[77] After examining a variety of dark expressions, Partridge observed "that occulture turns East for much of its self-spirituality and West for its demonology."[78]

The Biblical message of the Apostle Paul to his young friend, Timothy, written two millennium ago, rings clear and true: "Now the Spirit expressly says that in latter times some will depart from the faith, giving heed to deceiving spirits and doctrines of demons."[79]

Enchantment as a phenomenon of holistic integration, including a dark embrace, is not without precedence. Last century, one nation in particular

---

[74] Partridge, *The Re-Enchantment of the West: Volume 2*, p.208.

[75] Ibid., p.216.

[76] Aleister Crowley (1875-1947) was a mystic and occultist of great influence. For a glimpse of Crowley's impact on the Cultural Revolution, see Robert Anton Wilson's autobiographical journey, *Cosmic Trigger: The Final Secrets of the Illuminati* (Kangaroo/Pocket Books, 1977). Re: LaVey and his satanic Darwinism – "Blessed are the strong, for they shall possess the earth – Cursed are the weak, for they shall inherit the yoke! Blessed are the powerful, for they shall be reverenced among men – Cursed are the feeble, for they shall be blotted out!" Anton Szandor LaVey, *The Satanic Bible* (Avon Books, 1969), p.34. Re: The Temple of Set – a spin-off from LaVey's Church of Satan – the Temple of Set claims a Satanic lineage from ancient Egypt.

[77] Partridge, *The Re-Enchantment of the West: Volume 2*, chapter 6. Partridge is critical of Christian reactions, describing certain responses – especially to popular rumors – as "Satanic Panic." Furthermore, he draws parallels and convergences with extraterrestrial themes and demonism, and comments on Christian responses.

[78] Ibid., pp.277-278.

[79] 1 Timothy 4:1.

ventured down paths of Re-enchantment, albeit with its own flavoring. This was a country where the mythic and the present combined to birth a new future in a grotesque, theater of experience: Nazi Germany.

So much of the popular interest around Nazi Germany is centered on World War II. Far less attention is given to the domestic-spiritual milieu of the National Socialist state. Of importance is the development of myth and meaning as put forward by Party leadership, and by those intellectuals who fashioned the underlying context. Keep in mind, however, that in dealing with National Socialism there are layers of complexity, nuance, and paradox.

On one hand we see what Hermann Rauschning called the "opportunist policy" of direct action and pragmatism.[80] In this there is an element of modernity and disenchantment: The behemoth of Nazi bureaucracy enforcing Party plans – be they rational or irrational – and the organizing of technical solutions to pressing problems. Technocratic attitudes were visible in the interplay between State goals, science, and industry. Racial science, an accepted discipline in the Western world at the time, married the *will to power* with biological determinism, justifying a Darwinian license for experiments in racial purity.[81] By war's end, technocracy was "one of the most powerful and last pillars of the National Socialist state."[82]

Techniques of domination, industries of extermination, and the science of misery turned Europe into a living nightmare.

On the other hand, the Third Reich was mesmerized by an aesthetic way of seeing itself. Mythic meaning was woven into art and literature and film, in its new way of looking at religion, in its emphasis on youth and vitality, and in the stirring of mass mood.[83] Nazi education stressed total integration

---

80 Hermann Rauschning, *The Revolution of Nihilism: Warning to the West* (Alliance Book Corporation, 1939), p.23. Rauschning was a member of the National Socialist party, but renounced his position in 1934.

81 See Richard Weikart, *From Darwin to Hitler: Evolutionary Ethics, Eugenics, and Racism in Germany* (Palgrave Macmillan, 2004). See also, Robert N. Proctor, *Racial Hygiene: Medicine Under the Nazis* (Harvard University Press, 1988), and Marc Hillel and Clarissa Henry, *Of Pure Blood* (Ferni Publishing House, 1979).

82 Monika Renneberg and Mark Walker, "Scientists, engineers and National Socialism," *Science, Technology and National Socialism* (Cambridge University Press, 1994), p.9. For a specific example related to the Nazi concentration camp system, see Edwin Black, *IBM and the Holocaust: The Strategic Alliance Between Nazi Germany and America's Most Powerful Corporation* (Crown Publishers, 2001).

83 See Bill Kinser and Neil Kleinman, *The Dream That Was No More a Dream: A Search for*

and "we-consciousness," creating an emotional experience that bound the heart of the student to the spirit of the nation.[84] Farming practices became models of naturalistic holism, following the Germanic paganism of Walther Darré, the Reich Minister of Food and Agriculture.[85] National Socialism was the first *green* state, instituting land preservation laws and emphasizing a romanticized version of nature.[86] Green members of the Party wedded ecology with racial biology and Social Darwinism.[87] It was a secular religion framed around a Pagan worldview, preaching a sacred duty.

Three national themes instilled mystery, myth, and meaning: *Führer*, the leader-messiah who is absorbed into the fate of his people, a mystical incarnation of the national soul[88] – *Volk*, the authentic and pure community, an ethnic-spiritual identity in which the individual is consumed within the Germanic ideal[89] – *Blut und Boden*, "blood and soil," the life-force which drives purpose, connecting the fluid of sacrifice and toil to the sacredness of the land.[90]

None of this emerged in a vacuum.

Before the Nazis came to power, influential segments of the German population were exploring a range of pagan expressions: Nordic mythology, folklorism, Theosophy, and Aryan cultic doctrines.[91] In his bestselling book, *The Myth of the Twentieth Century*, Germanic theorist Alfred Rosenberg explained that society, because of the Great War, had turned away from abso-

---

Aesthetic Reality in Germany, 1890-1945 (Harper and Row, 1969); and Richard Grunberger, *The 12-Year Reich: A Social History of Nazi Germany, 1933-1945* (Holt, Rinehart and Winston, 1971).

84 Claudia Koonz, *The Nazi Conscience* (Harvard University Press, 2003), p.161.

85 See Anna Bramwell, *Blood and Soil: Richard Walther Darré and Hitler's 'Green Party'* (The Kensal Press, 1985).

86 See Mark Musser, *Nazi Oaks: The Green Sacrifice of the Judeo-Christian Worldview in the Holocaust* (Advantage Books, 2010/2013).

87 Musser, *Nazi Oaks*, see especially chapter 4, and 258ff.

88 Robert G. L. Waite, *The Psychopathic God: Adolf Hitler* (Basic Books, 1977), pp.90-94.

89 Ibid., p.95-97. Volk associates the peasant farmer, whose blood is indistinguishable from his ancestors, with land and culture. For an interesting comparison of folk within German National Socialism and its Russian-Stalinist counterpart, see Michaela Pohl, *Ideologies of Identity: Volk and Narod in Nazi and Stalinist Folkloristics* (Indiana Center on Global Change and World Peace, Indiana University, Occasional Paper No.28, 1995).

90 See Bramwell, *Blood and Soil* and Musser, *Nazi Oaks*.

91 See Nicholas Goodrick-Clarke, *The Occult Roots of Nazism: Secret Aryan Cults and Their Influence on Nazi Ideology* (New York University Press, 1992).

lute values. Christianity and materialism were being rejected. However, by re-orienting via ancient myths, a new spiritual worldview would guide the nation.[92] Rosenberg spun an Aryan story while referencing Nordic deities, Hindu oneness, and simultaneously disparaging Jews even as he argued for a re-configured Christianity. In 1937 he was given the National Prize for Art and Science, receiving an official commendation approved by Adolf Hitler,

> Alfred Rosenberg distinguished himself because he helped establish and stabilize the worldview of National Socialism both scientifically and intuitively. He especially distinguished himself because he fought untiringly to maintain the purity of the National Socialist worldview.[93]

Hitler understood the necessity of a national-ethnic framing narrative.

The Führer himself talked of religion and the life force of nature, promoting a racial-pagan "Positive Christianity."[94] But as a man of political action, he

---

[92] Alfred Rosenberg, *The Myth of the Twentieth Century: An Evaluation of the Spiritual-Intellectual Confrontations of Our Age* (Invictus Books, 2011, originally published in 1930), p.17ff. Note: Invictus Press, which produces the only English-language copy of Rosenberg's book that I am aware of, is sympathetic to Aryan nationalism.

[93] As quoted by I. Hexham, "The Mythic Foundation of National Socialism and the Contemporary Claim that the Nazis were Christians," *Koers: Bulletin for Christian Scholarship*, Volume 76, Number 1, 2011, P.159.

[94] Themes of life force and religion are evident in Hitler's collection of speeches: Adolf Hitler, *My New Order* (Reynal & Hitchcock, 1941, edited with commentary by Raoul de Roussy de Sales). Folk as a form of ethnic spirituality is discussed in his primary work, *Mein Kampf* (Houghton Mifflin Company, 1971, originally published 1925), pp.378-384. Another source of interest – extolling science while condemning Christianity – is *Hitler's Table Talk: 1941-1944 – His Private Conversations* (Enigma Books, 2000, translated by Norman Cameron and R.H. Stevens). One of the most comprehensive overviews of Nazi dealings with Christianity and the vexing role of churches, with discussions of Hitler's motivations, is Ernst Christian Helmriech, *The German Churches Under Hitler: Background, Struggle, and Epilogue* (Wayne State University Press, 1979). For a brief but informative review of religion, see Richard Grunberger, *The 12-Year Reich: A Social History of Nazi Germany, 1933-1945* (Holt, Rinehart and Winston, 1971), chapter 29. Finally, as an aid in understanding the Nazi mindset to Christianity – particularly what Hitler called "Positive Christianity" – see, the following two documents; Artur Dinter, with commentary by James Parkes, *The Completion of the Protestant Reformation* (Friends of Europe, No.51, no date), and Bishop Ludwig Müller and Bishop Weidemann, with commentary by H.C. Robbins, *The Germanisation of the New Testament* (Friends of Europe, No.64, no date). From my own analysis, the Nazi relationship with Christianity followed this

took a more pragmatic attitude, even chastising the cultic side of the National Socialist movement.[95]

Meanwhile, Heinrich Himmler – Reichsführer of the Schutzstaffel – was enthralled with mysticism and esoteric philosophy. He was drawn to the occult mythology of Karl Maria Wiligut, a mystic claiming ancestral-clairvoyant powers.[96] Hindu lore was of interest, chiefly the *Bhagavad-Gita*.[97] Otto Rahn's pagan adventures, too, captured the Reichsführer's attention. Rahn's quest to find the light of Lucifer – Baldr to the Norse, and Apollo to the Greeks[98] – as outlined in his book, *Lucifer's Court*, was of keen consideration. In fact, Himmler ordered the printing of 5,000 leather-bound copies.[99] Himmler also established the Ahnenerbe, a Nazi research agency with teams traveling to Tibet and Nordic lands in search of Aryan clues: runes and deity myths and cultic artifacts.[100]

Two brief examples from Otto Rahn's work help us to see the enchanted worldview that excited German laymen and luminaries alike.

In *Lucifer's Court,* Rahn recounts his wanderings in southern Germany. After stopping under an apple tree, he felt compelled to write the heretical

---

pattern: 1) theorize a Positive Christianity devoid of the Old Testament and the Jewishness of Jesus Christ, 2) openly court German churches for political gain, 3) attempt to assimilate German churches into a unified State organ, 4) largely ignore the churches during the war years, while persecuting pastors who speak against the new order, 5) after the anticipated Nazi war victory, allow for private superstitions while celebrating the annihilation of Christianity.

[95] See Adolf Hitler's speech of September 6, 1938 as found in Adolf Hitler, *My New Order* (Reynal & Hitchcock, 1941, edited with commentary by Raoul de Roussy de Sales), pp.499-500.

[96] Goodrick-Clarke, *The Occult Roots of Nazism*, pp.183-190. See also Heather Pringle, *The Master Plan: Himmler's Scholars and the Holocaust* (Hyperion, 2006), pp.48-50, 83-85.

[97] Peter Padfield, *Himmler* (MJF Books, 1990), pp.401-403.

[98] See Otto Rahn, *Lucifer's Court: A Heretic's Journey in Search of the Light Bringers* (Inner Traditions, 2008, originally published in 1937). Little is written of Rahn that is available in English. Nigel Graddon's biography, *Otto Rahn and the Quest for the Holy Grail: The Amazing Life of the Real "Indiana Jones"* (Adventures Unlimited Press, 2008), offers investigative details. Graddon writes, "Rahn's published works were required reading for all principle Nazi dignitaries, thereby attaining the status of Nazi gospel" (p.105).

[99] Christopher Jones, "Translator's Forward: Prolegomenon," *Lucifer's Court*, p.ix. The 5,000 copies of Himmler's special edition were destroyed in an Allied bombing raid.

[100] For information on the Ahnenerbe, see Heather Pringle, *The Master Plan: Himmler's Scholars and the Holocaust* (Hyperion, 2006).

thoughts of traveling spirits from centuries ago: "Jesus is not Christ... What is God?... Lucifer is nature as you see it in you, around you, above you."[101]

Soon a scout patrol came into view, and Rahn joined in a song of solidarity,

> If one of us becomes tired,
> The others are awake for him.
> If one of us wants to doubt,
> The others who believe laugh.
> If one of us is to fall,
> The others stand for two,
> Because each fighter is a God,
> The comrades together.[102]

Rahn also described when he and a friend were in Iceland, researching the island's pagan past.

On the night of the summer solstice, the two found themselves on a mountain slope, transfixed by the beauty of the raw landscape under the light of the Midnight Sun. Hours passed, and who talked first is unknown, but Rahn's friend broke the spell with a monologue on myth and meaning,

> Ancient myths are inseparable from the power of gods. This spiritual association is part of a blood bond that gives a people their inner strength...
>
> ...the divine did not reside in an unfathomable Paradise that was attainable only through faith... Instead, nature was the all-powerful and ever-present countenance of divine reality. Above all other peoples, the Germanic tribes encountered their deepest spirituality in nature. Their gods were natural gods, their mysteries were the mysteries of nature. The Germanic soul was immersed in the sunny and innocent dream of the spiritual revelation of nature...
>
> This mythological prehistory becomes understandable only when we recognize that our modern concept of the individual was nonexistent. Ancestral order dwelled in the deep subconscious, not in individual thoughts and desires. Nature is not only populated with gods, it is filled with the souls of the departed.[103]

[101] Rahn, *Lucifer's Court*, p.135.
[102] Ibid., p.138.
[103] Ibid., p.230-231.

The connection between myth and the Nazi mindset is profound. Germanic enchantment offered meaning to the purpose of National Socialism.

Christian professor and cultural historian, Gene Edward Veith, in his critique of Nazi fascism, reminds us of the worldview ramifications,

> The fascists aligned themselves not only against the Jews but against what the Jews contributed to Western civilization. A transcendent God, who reveals a transcendent moral law, was anathema to the fascists. Such transcendence, they argued, alienates human beings from nature and from themselves. Fascist intellectuals sought to forge a new spirituality of immanence, focused upon nature, human emotions, and the community. The fascists sought to restore the ancient pre-Christian consciousness, the ancient mythic sensibility, in which individuals experience unity with nature, with each other, and with their own deepest impulses.
>
> Fascism was essentially a spiritual movement. It was a revolt against the Judeo-Christian tradition, that is to say, against the Bible.[104]

Germany was the epicenter of transformation: an explosive collision at the crossroads of Modernity and Myth, so violent it set the world on fire.

The Third Reich was Re-enchanted.

However, to claim that today's milieu of enchantment is akin to Nazism would be a mistake, for National Socialism had features unique to its era. Our epoch, which is still being shaped, has perspectives and approaches fitting of our time. Remarkable similarities nevertheless exist; appeals to continuity, animosity to the Biblical message of God as separate from creation, and the energizing power of group emotion to shape social dynamics.

One primary theme of Re-enchantment stands out. In fact, it is the foundation of myth and, regardless of historical era and cultural setting, remains central to the enchanted worldview. It synthesizes the ancient and future, and projects the primal and archaic into the present. Man must be placed into its service, for this reflects the baseness of cosmic unity, the starting point of evolutionary oneness.

It is the framing story of our time, as it is the narrative of past epochs: *Nature deified.*

---

[104] Gene Edward Veith, Jr., *Modern Fascism: Liquidating the Judeo-Christian Worldview* (Concordia Publishing House, 1993), pp.13-14.

Mythic Green

General interest in ecology emerged after Rachael Carson's 1962 book, *The Silent Spring*, catapulted environmental concerns onto the public stage.[105] But it was eight years later when the energy of youth and emotion, combined, projected *green* as a mechanism to reshape society. Other developments, too, reinforced and expanded a new version of Man's relationship to nature. A meta-myth was soaking into the marrow of Western civilization.

There is no denying the influence of the modern environmental movement. Political life and national economies are enmeshed in its narrative. Agencies of global governance have been organized in response. Business and trade and commerce are profoundly affected by decisions emanating from environmental assumptions. Forests of regulations and oceans of policies have feverishly been written, dismantling and creating and re-destroying industries. Our educational institutions are saturated with a green ethos. Revolutionary and radical ideas are part of the mix, and have been since its contemporary inception; schemes for social engineering – from population control to global taxation proposals – have been touted as necessary measures to meet the challenges of a supposedly degrading planet.[106]

To be fair, some good has resulted. Harmful industrial practices from the past have been nullified or rectified, better agricultural techniques have emerged, mining operations take land reclamation into consideration, and energy production is more efficient.[107] On a personal level we are more cognitive of our waste.

But there is much more to the narrative than blue, recycling boxes.

---

[105] Carson was not the first to bring environmental concerns forward, but *The Silent Spring* was remarkable in how it generated public interest and political action. Her book, a bestseller, effectively demonized DDT – Dichlorodiphenyltrichloroethane, a chemical compound manufactured as an insecticide – and while the product was overused, its subsequent banning was ultimately disastrous to human health. For a brief discussion of Carson's book and DDT, see Michael S. Coffman, *Saviors of the Earth? The Politics and Religion of the Environmental Movement* (Northfield Publishing, 1994), pp.34-37.

[106] Some examples can be found in the following reports: Paul R. Ehrlich and Anne H. Ehrlich, *Population, Resources, Environment: Issues in Human Ecology* (W.H. Freeman and Company, 1972, second edition); *Reshaping the International Order: A Report to the Club of Rome* (E.P. Dutton, 1976); *Our Global Neighborhood: The Report of The Commission on Global Governance* (Oxford University Press, 1995).

[107] Marketplace competitiveness and other mechanisms also play into these benefits.

A social and spiritual message is preached, higher purpose and meaning are assigned, and we marvel at the ancient-future wheel of life: *holism*, *continuity*, *oneness*.

We are enamored with the *sacred Earth*.

Spaceship Earth:[108]

"Our planet is a lonely speck in the great enveloping cosmic dark," wrote the astronomer, Carl Sagan. "In our obscurity, in all this vastness, there is no hint that help will come from elsewhere to save us from ourselves."[109]

In his book, *Pale Blue Dot*, Sagan walked a tightrope of guarded despair and open wonderment. On one hand he highlighted the apparent insignificance of humanity in relationship to the known universe, on the other he marveled at the splendor beyond this planet – reminding us, at the same time, that this *pale blue dot* is all we have. What is the Earth but a speck of dust, and what is Man but an evolutionary accident?

On one level I can empathize with Sagan. When I consider creation it is easy to be overwhelmed by its magnitude. Who am I compared to the ocean, to the Sun and Moon, to all the starry hosts?

There is a Biblical parallel, but with a conclusion far more hopeful than what Sagan offered, and fundamentally different than the One-ist worldview. Acknowledging the Creator – "O Lord, our Lord, how excellent is Your name in all the earth, who have set Your glory above the heavens!"[110] – King David praised and proclaimed,

> When I consider Your heavens, the work of Your fingers,
> The moon and the stars, which You have ordained,
> What is man that You are mindful of him,
> And the son of man that You visit him?
> For You have made him a little lower than the angels,
> And You have crowned him with glory and honor.
> You have made him to have dominion over the works of Your hands;
> You have put all things under his feet.[111]

---

[108] The term, "Spaceship Earth," was popularized by R. Buckminster Fuller.

[109] Carl Sagan, *Pale Blue Dot: A Visions of the Human Future in Space* (Random House, 1994), p.9.

[110] Psalm 8:1.

[111] Psalm 8:3-6.

Sagan's outlook was different. He marveled at creation but denied its Maker.

"The evidence, so far at least and laws of Nature aside, does not require a Designer," he said. "Maybe there is one hiding, maddeningly unwilling to be revealed."[112]

Sagan's humanist approach immediately raised questions of meaning and purpose, to which the astronomer chimed: "The significance of our lives and our fragile planet is then determined only by our wisdom and courage. We are the custodians of life's meaning."

There is no one to "forgive us our errors," he continued. Reassuring fables of a God who created the universe must be discarded. It is up to us now: "If we crave some cosmic purpose, then let us find ourselves a worthy goal."[113]

Like so many of his generation captivated by the promises of the Space Age, it was, ironically, the images of Earth-from-space that captivated us. Looking from our elevated position, we had suddenly discovered our "worthy goal." Highlighting this obscure yet interesting aspect of the Space Age, author Marina Benjamin gives us a literary glimpse into the power of the Earth's image,

> The American program never got past the Moon's first base – a feeble effort by cosmic standards, like chucking tin cans across the backyard – and even then homesickness prevailed over the imperative to press onward and upward. Images of our lush fragile globe beamed back from afar made cooing, protective converts of the most forward-thinking rationalists, and before long many of these had swaddled themselves in Gaia and environmentalism. Exploration was out and conservation was in. Worse still (at least for those of my generation who had imbibed Space Age dreams along with our mothers' milk), space itself was internalized, its dark brooking depths becoming little more than a poetic analogue for the uncharted continents of the human mind. Within less than a decade of landing on the Moon, all our outward-bound aspirations had more or less turned in on themselves.
>
> To add to this irony, the principle people we have to thank for this unexpected legacy are none other than the astronauts.[114]

[112] Sagan, *Pale Blue Dot*, p.57.

[113] Ibid., p.57.

[114] Marina Benjamin, *Rocket Dreams: How the Space Age Shaped Our Vision of a World Beyond* (Free Press, 2003), p.47.

Astronaut Dick Gordon told Benjamin: "People are always asking what we discovered when we went to the Moon: what we discovered was the Earth."[115]

Edgar Mitchell of Apollo 14 fame was so enchanted that he founded the Institute of Noetic Sciences (IONS), an organization focusing on global peace, parapsychology, and holism. From an IONS document we read,

> On his journey back to the planet of his birth, Mitchell saw the Earth rise on the horizon and was profoundly moved. His striking vision of life's interconnectedness, of the inherent link between science and spirituality, was the spark of inspiration that created IONS.[116]

Looking for "a new story to answer the questions in the space age of who we are, how we got here and where we're going,"[117] Mitchell gravitated to Willis Harman and the SRI *Changing Images of Man* program. Harman joined the IONS board of directors.[118] Located in the San Francisco region, the Institute became a conduit for transformational research. It quickly connected with Esalen and became an integral part of the budding, New Age network.[119]

To the renowned astronaut, the most important aspect of the entire Apollo program was how it changed consciousness; *all are interconnected*, and this should be viewed as a "living, thinking, intelligent organism on the cosmic scale."[120] Mitchell described his space-revelation in the context of bonding

---

[115] Ibid., p.49.

[116] Stephen Villano, *IONS Noetic Post: Special 40th Anniversary Edition*, Autumn 2012, p.1.

[117] Edgar Mitchell, as quoted by Benjamin, *Rocket Dreams*, p.53.

[118] *IONS Noetic Post: Special 40th Anniversary Edition*, p.3. Willis Harman became a board member in 1976 and was its president from 1978 until 1997, the year he passed away.

[119] Esalen Trustee and scholar, Jeffrey Kripal, explains: "Esalen and Mitchell's Noetics Institute, it turns out, would go on to form numerous institutional and close personal connections that continue to this day." Jeffrey Kripal, *Esalen: America and the Religion of No Religion* (The University of Chicago Press, 2007), pp.340-341. In 1982, IONS sponsored a Soviet-American astronaut dialogue as part of the Esalen Soviet-American exchange program. See *IONS Sponsored Projects Program*, brochure, 1982, document on file. On New Age connections: *The New Age Catalogue* prominently details IONS in its section on New Physics. See *The New Age Catalogue: Access to Information and Sources* (Dolphin Doubleday, 1988), p.76. For an overview of IONS and its history of cultural influence, see *IONS Noetic Post: Special 40th Anniversary Edition*, Autumn 2012.

[120] *Spaceline* interview with Edgar D. Mitchell, *Spaceline*, Fall 1987, p.1. *Spaceline* was the quarterly newsletter of the Institute for Security and Cooperation in Outer Space (ISCOS), organized by Carol S. Rosin. Mitchell was the chairman of the ISCOS Advisory Board at the time of this interview's publication.

science and religion, bringing Eastern spirituality and Western traditions together as a divine body compatible with science, and "to change science in a way that made it compatible with divine ideas."[121]

This spiritual-material symbiosis was all part of "Gaia... mother Earth."[122]

Earth Day:

The First National Environmental Teach-In, April 22, 1970, became a "defining moment in the modern environmental movement."[123]

Styled after the anti-Vietnam war demonstrations on American campuses, this Teach-In, initiated by Senator Gaylord Nelson, was meant to create a revolutionary ethic.[124] Young people across the country were questioning and rejecting what were considered to be traditional, American values. Nelson believed the Teach-In would empower this wandering generation with a new sense of purpose. As a politician, the Senator also understood that if young people identified as environmental citizens, then the federal government could take vital first steps toward a system of far-reaching regulations. He envisioned a National Land Use Policy, a National Policy on Air and Water, an Ocean Policy, a Policy for Resource Management, and a National Policy on Population. Nelson was aware that these initiatives would interfere with American livelihoods, more-or-less saying as much in a *Look* article published the day before the Teach-In.[125] But so what? The future of the planet was at stake, or so everyone was told.

On that day, the 22nd of April, approximately 20 million Americans participated in rallies, marches, and demonstrations: "the event included local beach cleanups, tree plantings, horseback rides down interstate highways, parades of gas-masked marchers in urban centers, open-air campus teach-ins on ecology, and a thousand other innovations on a theme."[126]

Leading environmentalist, Barry Commoner, described it as an "enthusias-

---

[121] Ibid., p.1.

[122] Ibid., p.1.

[123] Bill Christofferson, *The Man From Clear Lake: Earth Day Founder Senator Gaylord Nelson* (The University of Wisconsin Press, 2004), p.175.

[124] Ibid., p.7.

[125] Senator Gaylord Nelson, *Look*, April 21, 1970, p.33.

[126] David Helvarg, *The War Against the Greens: The "Wise Use" Movement, the New Right, and Anti-Environmental Violence* (Sierra Club Books, 1994), p.59.

tic outburst," saying it was the impetus for the US Environmental Protection Agency to begin its work.[127]

"On Earth Day," explained Nelson the following month, "it was estimated that 2,000 college campuses, 2,000 community groups and 10,000 elementary and secondary schools were holding events."[128] An entire generation was awakening to the idea of being Earth citizens.

To facilitate this Green Revolution – aligning itself with the Religious Revolution and Cultural Revolution already in motion – Friends of the Earth published *The Environmental Handbook*, a resource prepared ahead of time for the Teach-In. Thousands of students across the country, and beyond, receive copies; my high school in rural Manitoba used it as a textbook. The *Handbook* offered a radical vision, as displayed in its opening pages with a Smokey the Bear Sutra,

> With a halo of smoke and flame behind, the forest fires of the kali-yuga, fires caused by the stupidity of those who think things can be gained and lost whereas in truth all is contained vast and free in the Blue Sky and Green Earth of One Mind; Round-bellied to show his kind nature and that the great earth has food enough for everyone who loves and trusts her; Trampling underfoot wasteful freeways and needless suburbs; smashing the worms of capitalism and totalitarianism... Wrathful but Calm, Austere but Comic, Smokey the Bear will Illuminate those who would help him; but for those who would hinder or slander him, HE WILL PUT THEM OUT... And he will protect those who love woods and rivers, Gods and animals... Now those who recite this Sutra... Will enter the age of harmony of man and nature... AND IN THE END WILL WIN HIGHEST PERFECT ENLIGHTENMENT.[129]

Lynne White Jr's famous essay, "The Historical Roots of Our Ecological Cri-

[127] Barry Commoner, *Making Peace With The Planet* (The New Press, 1975/1992), p.20 for "outburst," p.181 for "Environmental Protection Agency."

[128] "Earth Day – 1970," *The Gaylord Nelson Newsletter*, May 1970. A digital version can be accessed here: www.nelsonearthday.net/images/nelson_newsletter_may70.jpg

[129] "The Meaning of Ecology: Five Views – Smokey the Bear Sutra," *The Environmental Handbook: Prepared for the Fist National Teach-In, April 22, 1970* (Ballantine Books/Friends of the Earth, edited by Garrett de Bell), pp.2-3, capitals in original.

sis," first published by *Science* magazine in 1967, was printed near the front of the *Handbook*. Christianity was to blame, so a new religion was needed,

> Christianity, in absolute contrast to ancient paganism and Asia's religions... not only established a dualism of man and nature but also insisted that it is God's will that man exploit nature for his proper ends.
>
> At the level of the common people this worked out in an interesting way. In antiquity every tree, every spring, every stream, every hill had its own genius loci, its guardian spirit. These spirits were accessible to men... Before one cut a tree, mined a mountain, or dammed a brook, it was important to placate the spirit in charge of that particular situation, and to keep it placated. By destroying pagan animism, Christianity made it possible to exploit nature in a mood of indifference to the feelings of natural objects.[130]

> What we do about ecology depends on our ideas of the man-nature relationship. More science and more technology are not going to get us out of our present ecological crisis until we find a new religion, or rethink our old one...[131]

> No new set of basic values has been accepted in our society to displace those of Christianity. Hence we shall continue to have a worsening ecologic crisis until we reject the Christian axiom that nature has no reason for existence save to serve man.[132]

> Both our present science and our present technology are so tinctured with orthodox Christian arrogance toward nature that no solution for our ecologic crisis can be expected from them alone. Since the roots of our trouble are so largely religious, the remedy must also be essentially religious, whether we call it that or not.[133]

Everything, however, must change: "total transformation."[134]

---

[130] Lynn White Jr., "The Historical Roots of Our Ecologic Crisis," *The Environmental Handbook*, pp.20-21.

[131] Ibid., p.24.

[132] Ibid., p.25.

[133] Ibid., p.26.

[134] "Four Changes," *The Environmental Handbook*, p.330.

A reduced and optimal human population was envisioned, employing "sophisticated and unobtrusive technology" in harmony with an environment "left natural." Humanity in diversity would be "unified by a type of world tribal council," and computer technicians would "run the planet part of the year and walk along with the Elk in their migrations during the rest."[135]

Obviously, this eco-techno-utopianism would require a new spiritual reference. To that end, a list of acceptable worldviews was presented: social and religious forces that are ecologically and culturally enlightened. This list, including one scientific field of study – which I assume was inserted because of its Darwinian approach – along with three ethnicities, probably named for their historic beliefs, offered agreeable patterns for the students to adopt and emulate,

> Let these be encouraged: Gnostics, hip Marxists, Teilhard de Chardin Catholics, Druids, Taoist, Biologists, Witches, Yogins, Bhikkus, Quakers, Sufis, Tibetans, Zens, Shamans, Bushmen, American Indians, Polynesians, Anarchists, Alchemists… the list is long. All primitive cultures, all communal and ashram movements. Since it doesn't seem practical or even desirable to think that direct bloody force will achieve much, it would be best to consider this a continuing 'revolution of consciousness' which will be won not by guns but by seizing the key images, myths, archetypes, eschatologies [sic], and ectasies [sic] so that life won't seem worth living unless one's on the transforming energy's side.[136]

Sex education and family planning, too, would be an integral part of the revolution. With 3.7 billion people alive in 1970, the threat of overpopulation was itself becoming a growth industry. René Dubos articulated that the increasing, world population was exacerbating the ecological crisis.[137] Population alarmist, Paul Ehrlich, painted an apocalyptic scenario of global catastrophes and extinctions; by 1979 all major ocean life would vanish.[138]

In his chapter on eco-survivability and the necessity for new educational priorities, journalist John Fischer wrote: "It has long since become glaringly

---

[135] Ibid., pp.330-331.

[136] Ibid., p.331.

[137] René Dubos, "The Limits of Adaptability," *The Environmental Handbook*, p.29.

[138] Paul R. Ehrlich, "Eco-Catastrophe!" *The Environmental Handbook*, p.174.

evident that unless the earth's cancerous growth of population can be halted, all other problems – poverty, war, racial strife, uninhabitable cities, and the rest – are beyond solution."[139]

"No technical solution can rescue us from the misery of overpopulation," declared the ecologist-philosopher, Garrett Hardin. "Freedom to breed will bring ruin to all."[140]

Suggested solutions were presented,

> Legalize voluntary abortions and sterilization and provide these serves free... Remove all restrictions on the provision of birth control information and devices; provide these services free to all, including minors... Make sex education available to all appropriate levels, stressing birth control practices and the need to stabilize the population... Offer annual bonuses for couples remaining childless and eliminate tax deductions for more than two children.[141]

Marriage, too, must be re-imagined: "Explore other social structures and marriage forms, such as group marriage and polyandrous marriage... Share the pleasure of raising children widely... We must hope that no one woman would give birth to more than one child."[142] The ideologically charged saying, *it takes a village*, seems much more literal.

It could be said that the Religious Revolution, Cultural Revolution, and Green Revolution – a social ménage à trois – birthed the Sexual Revolution. Again, it takes a village.

Not ironically, we were and are repeating, in our own way, the causal relationship found in Romans 1. Refusing to acknowledge God, to glorify Him and give thanks, we claim ourselves to be wise and believe the Lie. Theologian Peter Jones, founder of TruthXChange, explains it thus: "*The truth* consists in the worship and service of *the Creator*, *the lie* consists in the worship and service of *the creation*."[143]

---

[139] John Fischer, "Survival U: Prospects for a Really Relevant University," *The Environmental Handbook*, p.139.

[140] Garrett Hardin, "The Tragedy of the Commons," *The Environmental Handbook*, p.49.

[141] Keith Murray, "Suggestions Toward an Ecological Platform," *The Environmental Handbook*, p.318.

[142] "Four Changes," *The Environmental Handbook*, p.324.

[143] Peter Jones, *One or Two: Seeing a World of Difference* (Main Entry Editions, 2010), p.92, italics in original.

A truth choice is before us; either there is a God who is separate from nature and who is the creator of the universe, or the universe created itself; either God is the utterly unique Other, or everything is One and creation is Divine. When we choose Oneness over the Other, we partake in a *truth exchange*. Dr. Jones breaks this down:

1. We make a *thought* exchange (vs.23);
2. We make a *worship* exchange (vs.25);
3. We make a *sexual* exchange (vs.26).[144]

A shift in sexual mores becomes inevitable. Biblical norms and values – two genders and heterosexual marriage – are patterns reflective of a moral Law Giver. Boundary dissolving beliefs and practices, instead, are exalted as a reflection of the exchange we are now participating in. Morality is less important than an ethics of radical tolerance. One road is narrow and restrictive; the opposite path is broad and holistic. As transcendent values are replaced with cultural dictates and personal whims, general morality itself becomes debased, as indicated in the last part of Romans 1.

It should be no surprise, then, that the Green Revolution undermines the Genesis foundation of the Judeo-Christian worldview. The Genesis mandate to "be fruitful and multiply; fill the earth and subdue it,"[145] can no longer be acceptable in the green world order. Humanity's positional value *cannot* be admitted, and the family unit *must not* be recognized as a primary institution. The Green Gospel demands a total transformation.

On the day before the April 22 Teach-In, *Look* magazine ran a series of articles on Earth Day. Senator Gaylord Nelson wrote, "We must evolve a philosophy emphasizing our interdependence with nature."[146] René Dubos said, "To some overcrowded populations, the bomb may one day no longer seem a threat, but a release."[147] Cultural anthropologist, Margret Mead, called for "a new religious system with science at its very core."[148]

In the immediate wake of that first Earth Day's excitement, French social historian, Jean-Francois Revel, succinctly expressed what happened: "'Earth

[144] Ibid., p.97, italics in original.
[145] Genesis 1:28.
[146] Senator Gaylord Nelson, *Look*, April 21, 1970, p.33.
[147] René Dubos, *Look*, April 21, 1970, p.34.
[148] Margaret Mead, *Look*, April 21, 1970, p.37.

Day' in America was one huge pantheistic feast."[149] Revel understood that a revolution was in motion.

While North America celebrated Earth Day, a little village in Scotland was experimenting with Re-enchantment: Man, Nature, and Spirit in community.

Pan was dancing in a garden.

Findhorn:

Approximately 50 miles east and north of Inverness, on a cold, wind swept sliver of ground on the edge of the North Atlantic, a magic garden was blooming in the vicinity of beach dunes and tidal flats. After visiting the relatively obscure location in the early 1970s, Paul Hawken wrote, "a garden growing in the sand and cold, producing sixty-five different vegetables, forty-two herbs, and twenty-one types of fruit. Even if they could be cultivated in that climate, the reports of 42-pound cabbages and 60-pound broccoli plants made it quite unbelievable."[150]

Something extraordinary was happening. Plants that would not normally survive the harsh climate and nutrient-poor soil were not only growing, but flourishing. Word quickly spread of an enchanted plot near the village of Findhorn, and people flocked to it. Soon, the name Findhorn was less associated with the actual town, becoming synonymous, instead, with the new eco-village and its famed gardens. Something ethereal was at work, something mythical and mysterious.

What was the open secret of Findhorn? The unusual interfacing of Nature Spirits and humans in a symbiotic relationship with plants. Re-enchantment was being experienced in *total community*.

Sprites and fairies and elementals and gnomes, Findhorn became renowned as a place where supernatural entities manifested to the sensitive and attuned. Plant spirits, devas – the word is etymologically linked to the luminous deities in the Vedas[151] – offered advice on gardening while imparting metaphysical messages.[152] Pan, the horned, woodland deity – "ruler

---

[149] Jean-Francois Revel, *Without Marx or Jesus: The New American Revolution Has Begun* (Doubleday and Company, 1971, originally published in French, 1970), p.213.

[150] Paul Hawken, *The Magic of Findhorn* (Harper and Row, 1975), p.5.

[151] Margaret and James Stutley, *Harper's Dictionary of Hinduism: Its Mythology, Folklore, Philosophy, Literature, and History* (Harper & Row, 1977), pp.71-72, 84-85.

[152] *The Findhorn Garden: Pioneering a New Vision of Man and Nature in Cooperation* (Harper & Row, by the Findhorn Community, 1975), pp.7-9, 79-99.

of all Nature spirits, god of male sexuality, animals, fertility… gardening… plants"[153] – and associated with Dionysus, frolicked in the foliage and talked with humans.[154]

A former member of the Findhorn eco-village described one encounter near a grotto,

> As we stepped down into the sunken garden, the energy became more and more powerful, and I was left absolutely speechless. I literally couldn't vocalize or use my tongue. I realized… that there was a living presence there, and I had a very good idea of what that presence was. Already knowing the answer I simply put out mentally, "Who are you?," and the answer, which was not a voice – it was more like a total concept fed into my spirit – came back immediately. The nearest I could get to a verbalization of it was simply, "I AM PAN."[155]

Robert Ogilvie Crombie, one of the first to encounter Pan, relates his walk-in experience with this ancient nature deity,

> I became aware of Pan walking by my side and of a strong bond between us. He stepped behind me and then walked into me so that we became one, and I saw the surroundings through his eyes. At the same time, part of me – the recording, observing part – stood aside. The experience was not a form of possession but of identification, a kind of integration.[156]

Despite shying away from the admittance of spiritual possession, what Crombie described *was* spiritual possession. It is reminiscent of other temporary possessions found within the Pagan experience.[157]

---

[153] D.J. Conway, *Magick of the Gods & Goddesses: How to Invoke Their Powers* (Llewellyn Publications, 1997), p.176.

[154] Hawken, *The Magic of Findhorn*, pp.135-138.

[155] *Faces of Findhorn: Images of a Planetary Family* (Harper & Row, 1980), p.136, capitals in original.

[156] *The Findhorn Garden*, p.119.

[157] One example from the Wiccan path is the Drawing Down the Moon ritual. The result being that the goddess temporarily possesses the practitioner and speaks through the human vessel, then, when the action is complete, the possessing spirit supposedly departs. A contemporary examination of such rituals and possessions, from the perspective

In one conversation, an interesting politics-of-nature took shape. Talking with Crombie, Pan insisted that part of a garden remain off-limits to humans. This would be a *protected area* "for his subjects alone," an undisturbed setting where nature spirits could focus their energies.[158]

Findhorn was touted as a model for global change, a hands-on workshop for the discovery of evolutionary enlightenment. David Spangler, a leading voice of the Findhorn experience, described his eco-community as a locus of planetary transformation,

> It is Findhorn's task to discover and demonstrate for mankind a new vision of the Divine potentialities inherent in each of us. It is a pioneering centre working to fulfil a spiritual hunger and need of man for new ideas, new concepts, new visions...[159]

Social philosopher, William Irwin Thompson, compared the community to the SRI *Changing Images of Man*. Whereas SRI was about human behavior and establishing new values, Findhorn was about human belief and experiencing holism: "At SRI they talk to the important people of the world, but at Findhorn they talk to the plants in the garden."[160]

Thompson understood that what SRI had been discussing, Findhorn was doing.[161] It was evident that a shamanistic technology was being explored in real time.

"Animism and electronics is the landscape of the New Age," Thompson wrote, "and animism and electronics is already the landscape of Findhorn."[162]

Spangler argued that Findhorn was part of a grand, spiritual unfolding. It was here, amidst the gardens, where the cosmic Christ – "a universal Christ, a New Age Christ" – would evolve within the group, and by extension, within the planet.[163] Spangler explained that Lucifer, the "angel of man's evolu-

---

of modern Witchcraft, is Janet Farrar and Gavin Bone, *Lifting the Veil: A Witches' Guide to Trance-Prophecy, Drawing Down the Moon, and Ecstatic Ritual* (Acorn Guild Press, 2016).

[158] *The Findhorn Garden*, p.25

[159] David Spangler, *Vision of Findhorn: Anthology* (Findhorn Foundation, 1976), p.72.

[160] William Irwin Thompson, "Introduction," *The Findhorn Garden*, p.viii.

[161] Ibid., p.viii.

[162] Ibid., p.x.

[163] David Spangler, *Reflections on the Christ* (Findhorn Foundation, 1978), see p.102 for "unfoldment," and p.107 for "New Age Christ."

tion... of man's inner light" and the "angel of experience,"[164] was striving to bring completeness,

> Lucifer comes to give to us the final gift of wholeness. If we accept it then he is free and we are free. That is the Luciferic initiation... it is an initiation into the New Age.[165]

All must be in communion,

> ...man to nature, man's oneness with all the lives of earth, animal, vegetable, mineral; and man to spirit, man's oneness with the more evolved life forms such as the Christ and the Hierarchy, and man's oneness with God... the reality of one humanity, one Earth, one planet, and indeed one life.[166]

This message of communion is what the spirits at Findhorn were preaching. One deva imparted that "Heaven will be brought down to Earth" when humans, nature, and ethereal beings all slip into each other as a unity.[167] On October 6, 1969, the Lord of the Elements whispered: "This concept of oneness is being stressed everywhere, being interpreted everywhere."[168]

The magic remains, but Findhorn is now better known for its applications of sustainable development and mystic knowledge. Each year, thousands of people come for workshops on environmental activism, community building, human potential, contemplative practices, and co-creative spirituality. The Findhorn Ecovillage was given a UN-HABITAT Best Practice Award,[169] and the Findhorn Foundation is represented at the United Nations.[170]

But the devas are never far away.[171]

---

[164] Ibid., p.37 for "angel of evolution... light," and p.41 for "angel of experience."

[165] Ibid., p.45.

[166] Ibid., p.19.

[167] *The Findhorn Garden*, p.80, the Pear Deva message from March 13, 1965.

[168] Ibid., p.94.

[169] Stephen Tinsley and Heather George, *Ecological Footprint of the Findhorn Community* (HIE Moray, 2006), p.5.

[170] The Findhorn Foundation is accredited with of the UN Department of Public Information, and sits on the UN-NGO Spiritual Caucus Coordinating Council, the Values Caucus Council, and the Conference of NGOs Committee on Sustainable Development.

[171] As I write this, the Findhorn Foundation has announced a 6-day conference, *Co-Creative Spirituality: Shaping Our Future with Unseen Worlds*, set to begin on September 22,

Gaia Rising:

Gaia lodged herself in the mind of a NASA consultant in the 1960s. She stayed there, stretching and developing and maturing. Having written a little about her already, this scientist, James Lovelock – partnering with microbiologist Lynn Margulis – fleshed out Gaia as a hypothesis in 1974.[172] It was a value changing experience,

> When I started to write in 1974 in the unspoilt landscape of Western Ireland it was like moving into a house run by Gaia... I began more and more to see things through her eyes and slowly dropped off, like an old coat, my loyalty to the humanist Christian belief in the good of mankind as the only thing that mattered. I began to see ourselves as no more than part of a community of living things that unconsciously kept the Earth a comfortable home, that we humans have no special rights only obligations to the community of Gaia.[173]

Gaia, the Great Mother in Greek mythology, would become a scientific proposition: the planet as an information-based, cybernetic-regulating, total life system. *The Earth was alive*.

Others, too, had previously expressed ideas of a living Earth. Catholic mystic, Pierre Teilhard de Chardin, postulated a co-evolving planet, enveloped in living consciousness, and possessing a universal spirit.[174] And the emerging neo-Pagan community embraced the Earth as Great Mother, recognizing that the "ultimate potential of Gaea [Gaia] was the telepathic unity of consciousness between all parts of the nervous system."[175] Gaia represented an awakening.

2018. From the website: "the Findhorn Foundation invites you to join a uniquely experiential gathering of human and non-human adventurers to explore these new possibilities. Together we will help shape a future of creative partnership." [www.findhorn.org/programmes/co-creative-spirituality].

[172] James E. Lovelock and Lynn Margulis, "Atmospheric homeostasis by and for the biosphere: the gaia hypothesis," *Tellus*, 1974, Volume 26, Issue 1-2, pp.2-10.

[173] James Lovelock, *Gaia: A New Look at Life on Earth* (Oxford University Press, 1979, with a new Preface in 1995), Preface, p.viii.

[174] Chardin's theory of a planetary super-consciousness later played into the New Age movement. His book, *The Phenomenon of Man* (HarperPerennial, 1959), is a key text promoting the hypothesis.

[175] Margot Adler, *Drawing Down the Moon: Witches, Druids, Goddess-Worshippers, and Other Pagans in America Today* (The Viking Press, 1979), pp.282-283.

In Margot Adler's sweeping survey of neo-Paganism in America, she writes,

> The cosmic purpose of Neo-Paganism is to facilitate that increased awareness – to work for it by supporting all ecologically oriented movements, establishing alternative communities, demonstrating alternative possibilities for survival on the planet, and, ultimately, awakening Gaea, the Goddess, the planetary mind.[176]

According to Adler, Tim Zell from the Church of All Worlds – a neo-Pagan body chartered in 1968 – was briefly in correspondence with Lovelock, comparing worldviews.[177]

Lovelock's hypothesis was pushed into the mainstream with the publishing of his 1979 book, *Gaia: A New Look at Life on Earth*. For the first time, an accessible, scientific argument was being made for what had previously been considered an eco-Pagan construct. The hypothesis excited intellectuals; conferences were held, peer reviewed papers submitted, and modifications and counter-arguments were discussed in lectures and journals.

As a scientific hypothesis relating to the environment, Gaia was obviously applied to the field of ecology. However, as a broad theory of planetary life, it acted as a worldview filter for studies on international peace and disarmament, overpopulation and poverty, energy and technology, and other social concerns. *The Gaia Peace Atlas* was an example of applied Gaian principles across the spectrum of world problems. International leaders contributed to the project, and the UN Secretary General penned the foreword.[178]

In the beginning we read,

> …our planet may even, itself, be alive, a self-sustaining entity, Gaia. Human impact now threatens to outweigh the stabilizing capacity of Gaia…

---

[176] Ibid., pp.284-285.

[177] Ibid., p.285.

[178] Contributors: Kenneth E. Boulding (Systems Theorist), Gro Harlem Bruntland (Prime Minister of Norway and Chair of the World Commission on Environment and Development), Johan Galtung (founder of the International Peace Research Institute), Petra Karin Kelly (Co-founder of the German Green Party), M.J.K. Nyerere (former President of Tanzania), Maurice Strong (former Executive Director of the United Nations Environment Program), Inga Thorsson (Minister of Foreign Affairs, Sweden), Archbishop Desmond Tutu (Nobel Peace Prize recipient), and Sir Brian Urquhart (former Assistant Secretary-General to the UN). The foreword was written by UN Secretary General Javier Pérez de Cuéllar.

> The science of Gaia is new, exploring the planet-wide homeostatic processes in which we share. But the concept is old, a rediscovery of what all earlier peoples have known…
>
> In every culture, the power and spirit of nature were the centre of religious feelings. The Earth was a goddess, given many names. But the rational culture of science and politics outlawed such awareness. As we discovered and named the other planets, each after a classical god, we still left our own with no deity. Only since space travel showed us the barreness of Mars and Venus and the unique life of Earth, have we begun to rename our planet Gaia.[179]

Media mogul Ted Turner embraced the idea and, inspired by conversations with Jim Channon – creator of the *First Earth Battalion* – the successful children's cartoon was launched, *Captain Planet and the Planeteers*.

In the television show, Gaia awakens from her slumber and commissions five young people to become "Planeteers," giving them each rings of power to control Earth, Fire, Water, Wind, and Heart. By combining these elements a planetary superhero would emerge, "Captain Planet," and together they battled polluters. Voice actors included David Coburn as "Captain," and Whoopi Goldberg and Margot Kidder as "Gaia." James Coburn was the eco-villain, "Looten Plunder."[180] The program was "syndicated in over 220 U.S. markets and in over 100 countries worldwide," and, time and again, it ranked on top of the Nielsen ratings.[181] The show ran for six years.

Vice President Al Gore was also drawn into Lovelock's hypothesis.

Drawing attention to species die-offs and climate disruption, Al Gore, in his book *Earth in the Balance*, lamented that if we could "understand our own connection to the earth," then we might become truly aware of our ecological impact. Noting that Lovelock himself did not insist on a spiritual interpretation of Gaia, Gore nevertheless viewed the hypothesis within a re-enchanted context, saying, "it evokes a spiritual response in many of those who hear it." The long process of evolution, Gore elucidated, has shaped our

---

[179] *The Gaia Peace Atlas: Survival into the Third Millennium* (Doubleday, 1988, with Frank Barnaby as General Editor), pp.10-11.

[180] Captain Planet and the Planeteers," *IMBD*, www.imdb.com/title/tt0098763, see its list of Creators and Stars, accessed March 31, 2018.

[181] *Our Story: Timeline of the Foundation – Captain Planet 25 Years*, Captain Planet Foundation, www.captainplanetfoundation.org/about/our-story (Accessed April 1, 2018).

complex interrelationships. Lovelock's concept may be considered from a scientific vantage point, but "the simple fact of a living world and our place on it evokes awe, wonder, a sense of mystery – a spiritual response – when one reflects on its deeper meaning."[182]

Gaia's spiritual meaning was not unnoticed. Science reporter, Lawrence E. Joseph, recognized the science-to-spirituality shift initiated by Lovelock,

> Certainly the most colorful and eclectic Gaian phenomenon has been the rebirth of the Earth goddess in the popular imagination. For every scientific symposium and scholarly lecture, there has been at least one festival, workshop, or art exhibition celebrating 'the goddess' as a spiritual or creative inspiration. [183]

"Gaia, Greek goddess of the Earth," Joseph wrote, "has been reborn through modern science."[184]

The real success of Lovelock's hypothesis, in my view, is the depth of its occulture messaging: Earth is not a *thing* but a *thou* – a spirit infused in nature but not a personage, for as one expert on ancient cults tells us, "Gaia reminds us that the divine is transhuman and pre-human."[185] Nevertheless, every school child knows of her, and she is on everyone's lips, for Gaia is the persona of our dominant framing story. The ideal of global citizenship emphasizes Gaian responsibility.[186] Most people, of course, do not use her Greek name, but the more generic epitaph: *Mother Earth*.

She even has a special day, marked by the United Nation as an annual commemoration: International Mother Earth Day. The date? April 22.[187]

Actor James Coburn understood the spiritual significance of Mother Earth. On April 22, 1990, during the Earth Day festival at Malibu Beach, Christian

---

[182] Al Gore, *Earth in the Balance: Ecology and the Human Spirit* (Plume, 1993), p.264.

[183] Lawrence E. Joseph, *Gaia: The Growth of an Idea* (St. Martin's Press, 1990), p.12.

[184] Ibid., p.1.

[185] Christine Downing, *The Goddess: Mythological Images of the Feminine* (Crossroad, 1984), p.140.

[186] For example, the Manitoba curriculum, *Grade 12 Global Issues: Citizenship and Sustainability* (Manitoba Education and Training, 2017), advances the following as an important Area of Inquiry: "Gaia hypothesis, systems thinking, interconnectedness of human and natural systems, living sustainably." p.25.

[187] *Resolution adopted by the General Assembly on 22 April 2009: International Mother Earth Day* (United Nations General Assembly: A/RES/63/278).

documentary producer, Caryl Matrisciana, had the opportunity to ask the Hollywood star a pressing question: "Why should we care about Earth Day or Mother Earth?"

Coburn responded,

> Mother Earth is our Mother! She's the Mother Goddess. She's the one that we should be praising rather than raping. I mean all of these people here today are here for one reason: Because they're concerned about what's happening to the Earth – what Mankind is doing to the Earth. I mean, the negative emotions we carry around, a lot of us, is another contributor to it; it feeds the Moon. What we have to do is be true to ourselves, if we're true to ourselves we'll be true to Mother Earth. Mother Earth's going to be bountiful; she's going to give us everything we need. She has for a long time. We've lost our way. The pagans used to know how to do it. And the Indians, some of them still remember how to do it. The Earth is a living organism. We're killing the one we love the most, and she loves us. We've got to praise our Mother Goddess![188]

Goddess veneration, overtly as demonstrated by Coburn, or in subtle ways and through general acceptance, is a hallmark of Re-enchantment.

What is our expected role? In the parlance of this ancient-future myth, our task is to serve the goddess by co-creatively tending to our divine garden, making Heaven on Earth.

In *total community* we build our planetary Findhorn.

Enchanting Politics:

The 1992 United Nations Earth Summit, held in Rio de Janeiro, was unprecedented in the number of governments participating: 172 nations were officially represented, with 108 heads-of-state attending. Maurice Strong, the event's Secretary-General, called it a "summit to save the world."[189] To that end, governments worked through agreements that would fundamentally re-orient national and global priorities.[190] *Agenda 21*, the *Convention on*

[188] This interview is part of the video documentary, *Earth's Two-Minute Warning* (Jeremiah Films, 1997).

[189] Maurice Strong, *Where on Earth are We Going?* (Alfred A. Knopf Canada, 2000), p.215.

[190] The *Convention on Biological Diversity*, *Framework Convention on Climate Change*, and the *Convention to Combat Desertification* were binding texts. *Agenda 21*, the *Forest*

Biological Diversity, and the *Convention on Climate Change* would each become bedrock documents used to build environmental agendas at global, national, state/provincial, and local levels. More than any other Summit, Rio acted as ground zero for a rippling revolution in green regulations.

Other events happened in conjunction with Rio. These auxiliary gatherings expanded the scope of grassroots influence, bringing other voices to the table. Just prior to the Summit, the Sacred Earth Gathering of Spiritual Leaders issued a *Vision Statement*,

> The crisis is global... We must therefore transform our attitudes and values, and adopt a renewed respect for the superior law of Divine Nature...
>
> Individuals and government need to evolve 'Earth Ethics' with a deeply spiritual orientation or the earth will be cleansed.
>
> We believe that the universe is sacred because all is one.[191]

Paralleling the Earth Summit was the Global Forum, a convergence of 2,400 organizations and 17,000 participants.

Held in Flamingo Park, the Forum has been described as "part soap-opera, part new-age carnival, part human zoo."[192] Opening the event was the arrival of the Viking ship, *Gaia*, carrying messages "to international leaders from children from around the world."[193] Personally addressing the Global Forum, the Dalai Lama told delegates, "Our mother earth is teaching us a lesson in universal responsibility."[194] Over twelve days, Forum attendees

---

Principles, and the *Rio Declaration on Environment and Development* were framework documents to be used as guiding principles for nations to follow.

191 "Vision Statement: The Declaration of the Sacred Earth Gathering, Rio-92," *Who is Who in Service to the Earth: People, Projects, Organizations, Key Words* (VisionLink Education Foundation, 1993, edited by Hans J. Keller), p.ii. Maurice Strong comments on the Sacred Earth Gathering in his book, *Where on Earth are We Going?*, p.217.

192 *Youth Source Book on Sustainable Development* (International Institute for Sustainable Development, 1994), p.75.

193 *Formati on The '92 Global Forum: Rio – Special Edition* (Forum of Brazilian NGOs/International Facilitating Committee, February 1992), p.8.

194 14th Dalai Lama, "Universal Responsibility and Our Global Environment," *Alternative Treaty-Making: A Process in Support of Sustainable Societies and Global Responsibility* (International Non-Governmental Organization Forum/Global Forum, Revised and Pre-Publication Edition, October 1992), p.9, speech given on June 7, 1992, Global Forum.

worked to draft a large collection of *Alternative Treaties*. The Forum's alternative *Earth Charter* called for new social, economic, and spiritual values – for we honor the Earth, and *we are the Earth*.[195]

The *Alternative Treaties* were a mix of holistic spirituality, international socialism, and population control. For it will take nothing less than the "creation of a new civilization" for the "salvation of the Planet."[196]

During the close of the 1992 Rio Earth Summit, Boutros Boutros-Ghali, the United Nations Secretary-General, reminded government leaders of their new political commitments: *Agenda 21*, the *Convention on Climate Change* and *Biological Diversity*. A new international program had been defined, built on "a universal basis by all countries of the world."[197]

He wrapped up his comments with these words of Re-enchantment,

> I should like to conclude by saying that the spirit of Rio must create a new form of good citizenship. After loving his neighbour as the Bible required him to, post-Rio man must also love the world, including the flowers, birds and trees - every part of that natural environment that we are constantly destroying.
>
> Over and above the moral contract with God, over and above the social contract concluded with men, we must now conclude an ethical and political contract with nature, with this Earth to which we owe our very existence and which gives us life.
>
> To the ancients, the Nile was a god to be venerated, as was the Rhine, an infinite source of European myths, or the Amazonian forest, the mother of forests. Throughout the world, nature was the abode of the divinities that gave the forest, the desert or the mountains a personality which commanded worship and respect. The Earth had a soul. To find that soul again, to give it new life, that is the essence of Rio.[198]

After Rio, the arduous task of interpreting and applying the Summit texts began. Governments integrated the *Climate* and *Biodiversity* conventions, and

---

[195] *Earth Charter*, NGO Treaties, Global Forum 1992, Preamble.

[196] *Rio de Janeiro Declaration*, NGO Treaties, Global Forum 1992, paragraph 3.

[197] Boutros Boutros-Ghali, "Statement," *Report of the United Nations Conference on Environment and Development*, United Nations General Assembly, A/CONF.151/26 (Vol.IV), released on 28 September 1992.

[198] Ibid, no applicable page number in the edition I have.

Agenda 21, within federal ministries and national programming. At the international level, the themes presented in the documents became focal points for global agendas. Like national agencies, the world community fleshed out interpretations for implementation.

One of the more interesting examples was the *Convention on Biological Diversity*. The treaty itself is small, fitting onto 18-pages of letter-sized paper. However, when the United Nations Environmental Programme endeavored to interpret and apply the document, it resulted in an oversized, 1100+ page report entitled the *Global Biodiversity Assessment*. Eco-spirituality was included as an asset, and deemed so important that a second interpretation was released, *Cultural and Spiritual Values of Biodiversity*, stretching out to more than 700 pages.

Together, these behemoth-sized reviews painted a spiritual picture: Christianity has been destructive with its worldview of separation – humanity as distinct from nature, and God above creation.[199] Acceptable cultural and spiritual values are those that integrate nature, humanity, and the divine within a holistic framework. "The hope is that we may consciously search for a re-enchantment of the world," explained David Suzuki, a contributor to the second report.[200]

An eco-feminist interpretation in *Cultural and Spiritual Values* suggested,

> A shift from a conception of God as holding all sovereign power outside of and ruling over nature; to a conception of God who is under and around all things, sustaining and renewing nature and humanity together as one creational biotic community.[201]

"We belong to the Webs-of-being – to Earth – to Gaia," said the report. "We belong to Gaia."[202]

---

[199] See the *Global Biodiversity Assessment* (Cambridge University Press/United Nations Environment Programme, 1995), p.839, and *Cultural and Spiritual Values of Biological Diversity: A Complementary Contribution to the Global Biodiversity Assessment* (Intermediate Technology Publications/United Nations Environment Programme, 1999), p.451.

[200] David Suzuki, "Finding a new story," *Cultural and Spiritual Values of Biological Diversity: A Complementary Contribution to the Global Biodiversity Assessment* (Intermediate Technology Publications/United Nations Environment Programme, 1999), p.73.

[201] Rosemary Radford Ruether, "Ecofeminism: domination, healing and world-views," *Cultural and Spiritual Values in Biodiversity*, p.457.

[202] William N. Ellis and Margaret M. Ellis, "All That Is – Is a Web of Being," *Cultural and Spiritual Values in Biodiversity*, p.449.

Four Responses:

How has the Christian community responded to Re-enchantment, and in particular, the Green Revolution? In four general ways.

My own experience has been that for many Christians there is a disassociation. We either disbelieve that the world has or is changing this radically, or we view it as happening "over there" – a phenomenon taking place on the other side of the fence, but not in our living room. This is akin to burying our heads in the sand. Of course, in doing this we intentionally fail to see the challenges and opportunities, and we are unable to navigate the social changes happening in the space around us. Yet, we still feel that something is amiss; there is pain and confusion, like an unseen adversary is kicking us. When we do finally pull our heads free, we are shocked by the cultural animosity aimed at Christianity – and we foolishly wonder, "how did it come to this?"

When our heads are buried, our ass is exposed. Why are we surprised when it gets kicked?[203]

Another response has been to wrestle with a Biblical position in relationship to environmental concerns. I think of Francis A. Schaeffer's book, *Pollution and the Death of Man*, written, in part, as a response to Lynn White's 1967 essay wherein he blamed Christianity for ecological woes.

Schaeffer rightly reminded Christians that nature is beautiful, a marvelous gift from God. Our attitude to the natural world is, to some degree, a reflection of how we consider our Creator; nature is more than just utilitarian in purpose, it has intrinsic value because of who fashioned it. This understanding rips away the false assumption that we can engage in wonton destruction. Yes, we have dominion over the Earth and its creatures – a status presented in Genesis 1, and a fact borne out by reality. This also means we have a responsibility to that which God created.

Part of that responsibility is to acknowledge real, ecological problems – for we live in a fallen world – and then consider how to engage in constructive responses. We are also responsible to question and confront the assumptions and exaggerations that are endemic within the environmental movement – problems, real or perceived – that have been politicized and

[203] On Monday, March 26, 2018 I posted this line in a social media feed. My friend, Eric Wem, quickly fired back, "You stole this line from me (j/k)." Thank you, Eric, for the friendly banter! It brightened my day.

spiritualized for very radical ends. Schaefer was right to challenge the pantheistic worldview he saw emerging through the environmental movement.

Schaeffer reminded us that God is distinct from nature: "From this, we must understand that creation is not an extension of the essence of God. Created things have an existence in themselves. They are really there."[204]

This means creation is not an extension of His essence. Distinctions are a theological reality, and this fact is daily reflected around us. Schaeffer wrote,

> Thus God treats His creation with integrity: each thing in its own order, each thing the way He made it. If God treats His creation in that way, should we not treat our fellow-creature with a similar integrity? If God treats the tree like a tree, the machine like a machine, the man like a man, shouldn't I, as a fellow-creature, do the same – treating each thing in integrity in its own order? And for the highest reason: because I love God – I love the One who has made it! Loving the Lover who has made it, I have respect for the thing He has made.[205]

As Christians, our starting point in understanding the importance of nature is to grasp the greatness of God. The book of Psalms offers powerful examples,

> The heavens declare the glory of God; and the firmament shows His handiwork. Day unto day utters speech, and night unto night reveals knowledge. There is no speech nor language where their voice is not heard.[206]

> Praise the Lord from the earth, you great sea creatures and all the depths; Fire and hail, snow and clouds; Stormy wind, fulfilling His word; Mountains and all hills; Fruitful trees and all cedars; Beasts and all cattle; Creeping things and flying fowl; Kings of the earth and all peoples; Princes and all judges of the earth; Both young men and maidens; Old men and children. Let them praise the name of the Lord, for His name alone is exalted; His glory is above the earth and heaven.[207]

---

[204] Francis A. Schaeffer, *Pollution and the Death of Man: A Christian View of Ecology* (Tyndale House Publishers, 1970), p.47.

[205] Ibid., p.57.

[206] Psalm 19:1-3.

[207] Psalm 148:7-13.

A third response is to accept, often without question or examination, the assertions of the environmental movement, especially those grand themes pushed by special interest groups, media, and governmental agencies. Too frequently, acceptance of the narrative is accompanied by support for the proposed solutions. But if the problem is overblown or proven to be false, or misunderstood, or politicized for some other gain – or if the fix being suggested is detrimental to liberty and human flourishing – then those resolutions need to be reexamined.

For example, in 1973, responding to the imminent and worldwide ecological catastrophe, the Canadian Council of Churches questioned private land holdings, saying "a strong argument can be made for community ownership of all land." Who would own it? The government, and they would administer land resources "for the benefit of all."[208]

Based on the terrifying predictions from eco-alarmists like Paul Ehrlich, such extreme measures may have seemed reasonable to some Christian leaders. And in saying this I am giving them the benefit of the doubt, for what the Canadian Council of Churches suggested was nothing short of Communism.

Not all proposed fixes are this radical, but some, like the Wildlands Project, are indeed extreme to say the least.[209] Other less malevolent solutions, like Canada's Carbon Tax, can be a costly measure to a problem that is highly questionable and politically framed.

The fact remains: Christians need to question the assumptions and solutions. We need to unpack what are provable motives, benign or otherwise, as this reveals context. In other words, it is time to think.

The fourth response is to adopt themes of Re-enchantment. From the first Earth Day onward, the Christian community has found itself struggling with ecology and its place in the world. For some congregations and parachurch organizations, the green worldview has been internalized.

One historically important congregation is the Cathedral of Saint John the Divine, a flagship of the Episcopal Church.

In 1972, James Park Morton became Dean of the Cathedral and surrounded himself with mystical thinkers. He met René Dubos, and as noted in a 1990

208 See John O'Manique, "Values and Goals in Canada," *Goals in a Global Community, Volume II*, p.28

209 The Wildlands Project envisions vast tracts of land devoid of all human use, including private property in the zones designated as Protected Areas.

interview, "He [Dubos] was the one who really turned me upside down... I went through some very serious reconceptualizing of man's relation to the Earth as it had been spelled out in the Judeo-Christian tradition."[210]

Morton worked hard to turn his church into a Green Cathedral,

> I would say, 'Let's talk about the suffering of the Earth, the passion of water. Let's talk about Jesus in Earth – God incarnate in the flesh of the Earth, the flesh of water, the flesh of the elements of creation and how that creation is suffering – the passion of the creation.' And that was very effective.[211]

In 1979 the Cathedral held its first *solar service*, a "Sun Day Celebration." It also hosted an environmental fair, with the highlight being the public release of James Lovelock's book, *Gaia*.

"We had the book party here at the cathedral," Morton reflected, "and his first public exposition of the Gaia Hypothesis was from our pulpit."[212]

Morton's church was a trendsetter of sorts, as was its sister congregation, San Francisco's Grace Cathedral. Today, themes of Re-enchantment are sprinkled across the Christian landscape.

In my country the United Church of Canada, a denomination with a national footprint, offers examples. A line from its annual, Environmental Sunday bulletin, reads: "We are all one and interconnected with one Earth, one Sea, one Sky – God's wonderful gifts for life."[213] This is only true insofar as we are part of creation, but our position and value exceeds this sense of interconnection, which is spiritually implied. And the spiritual is what is being communicated. To sing of creation we open *More Voices*, the hymnal of the United Church, and celebrate with the song, *O Beautiful Gaia*.[214]

Returning to the Rio Earth Summit, the response from the United Church was a declaration on planetary ethics; a recognition of the wholeness of the Earth, the creation of a "just international economic order," and reducing

---

[210] Alan AtKisson interview with James Parks Morton, "The Green Cathedral," *In Context: A Quarterly of Human Sustainable Culture*, Winter, 1990. This article can be found online at, www.context.org/iclib/ic24/morton (Accessed January 28, 2014).

[211] Ibid.

[212] Ibid.

[213] *One Earth, One Sea, One Sky* (United Church of Canada, 2017); official bulletin for use in congregations.

[214] *More Voices* (United Church of Canada, 2005), song number 41.

population growth. We need to move past materialism and "foster the spiritual connection between humanity and nature."[215]

The above brings new meaning to a rendition of the Lord's Prayer I heard while attending a United Church service in 2015: "Our Mother – Father – Holy God who art in heaven, hallowed be thy name…"

The parachurch organization, Mennonite Central Committee (MCC), has also displayed a taste for Re-enchantment. Its *Women's Concerns* report from the summer of 2000 focused on feminine-connecting rituals. The first article expounded on menstruation rituals – "There's Power in the Blood: Women, Christian Ritual and the Blood Mysteries" – saying,

> As women, we are now claiming ritual in our lives. We are creating together what has been left out of our church experiences. We are finding again the importance of our own bodies, whether through the blood of menstruation or the touch of another. We are reclaiming our ties to that great body upon which we dwell, mother earth. We are encountering new ways to connect with the Holy One.[216]

Another *Women's Concerns* writer extrapolated a modern interpretation of the Genesis creation account,

> We are earth creatures, according to this story. We are earth, we are water, we are air, and we are fire… Joni Mitchell and Carl Sagan remind us as well that we are stardust. This is not only true metaphorically, but also physically.[217]

"I find I am moving toward living in earth's rhythms," said this same contributor, admitting to celebrating the solstices and equinoxes.

She described one *earth-conscious ritual* meaningful to her. A small group of friends entered the woods during the fall equinox, opening with music and poetry and Bible readings. Gathering around a fire, they circled with stops taken to do quarter turns, acknowledging the light and darkness. Another turn to embrace the coming winter, and then back to the light.[218]

---

[215] *One Earth Community: Ethical Principles for Environment and Development* (United Church of Canada, Statement of the 34th General Council, August 1992), p.8.

[216] Cynthia A. Lapp, "Women and Ritual," *Women's Concerns* (Mennonite Central Committee, July-August 2000, Report No. 151), p.1.

[217] Karla Kauffman, "Ritual and the earth, *Women's Concerns*, p.2.

[218] Ibid., p.2.

The report also talked of creating your own rituals by borrowing from other traditions: "Writings from Buddhist, Islamic or other world religions also have much to offer Christian worship."[219]

A few years later, *Earth Trek*, a publication commissioned by MCC, asked us to consider the essential interconnection of nature: "The birds, animals, trees, mountains, and rivers are, in a sense, our brothers and sisters."[220]

Meditative quotes from Teilhard de Chardin and other mystics help set the book's mood. Good global citizens, however, must do more than reflect on interdependence. Action is required. Readers are encouraged to write letters on climate change, eat less meat, to hold your city accountable to its environmental policies, to organize church eco-committees, to become a member of a wildlife protection agency, and to integrate ecology into worship. MCC's *Earth Trek* reminds us to consider overpopulation, and to support family planning organizations like the UN Fund for Population Activities.

Near the end of the book a call to action is given. The bold emphasis is in the original: "This week, **make an offering to the earth**, in the form of a prayer or some other gift."[221]

Robert Muller's message to the Global Citizenship 2000 Youth Congress cycles back; "from now on you have to be Earth citizens, you have to be the children of Mother Earth."[222]

Recently I received a copy of *The Green Bible*. Its preface asks a seemingly innocuous question, "is God green?"[223] The query was rhetorical, as this green-letter edition of the Bible infers a positive answer in its title.

I beg to differ. He is *Holy* – divinely situated and set-apart.[224] He is *Exalted* – of highest standing, lifted above all else.[225] God is not green; He is incomparable.[226]

Maybe the real question is: *Are we pagans?*

---

219 Jane Ramseyer Miller, "Music for ritual," *Women's Concerns*, p.15.

220 Joanne Meyer, *Earth Trek: Celebrating and Sustaining God's Creation* (Herald Press/Mennonite Central Committee, 2004), p.114.

221 Ibid., p.190.

222 Robert Muller, as told to the attendees of the Global Citizenship 2000 Youth Congress, Saturday, April 5, 1997, from my notes taken during the event.

223 *The Green Bible* (HarperOne, 2008), p.I-15.

224 Leviticus 20:26, Psalm 22:3, Psalm 99:9, 1 Peter 1:15-16, Revelation 4:8.

225 Psalm 57:11, Psalm 138:2, Isaiah 33:5.

226 Isaiah 40:12-31.

Paganistan

We finished washing our hands at the same time. I walked to the motion-activated blow dryer on my side of the restroom, and the young professional went to his. Nothing happened as I passed my hand under what I thought was the sensor, and his dryer stayed silent. We each crossed to the other machine, his to mine and mine to his, and – surprise! – nothing worked.

Evidently he thought it was time for drastic action. Stepping into the middle of the room and facing the first dryer, he stretched out his hands to create a focal point. His arms trembled from the strain of concentrating invisible energies, but the blow dryer remained unchanged. Turning to my machine he repeated the gesture with the same result.

In frustration he wiped his hands on his pants and matter-of-factly said, "My magic's not working today." And then he walked out.

For a moment I stood in the silence, processing this unusual encounter. Then, with water dripping, I returned to my dryer and thrust my hands deeper under the machine… whoosh! I was in the right place.

The DoubleTree hotel in St. Louis Park, a western suburb of Minneapolis, was bustling with activity as traveling patrons mixed with conference guests. I wondered what those passing through were thinking. All around was a colorful blend of medieval dresses, pixie hoods, capes and cloaks, fairy costumes, dark robes and rich gowns, gnarled walking sticks and deer antler headpieces. Others were wearing shirts with prints of green-man imagery, the Celtic Tree of Life, pentagrams and other symbols. Near the swimming pool was a long room filled with vendors displaying books, clothing items and jewelry, tarot cards, and ritual paraphernalia. The aroma of teas and oils and incense teased the senses. Not far away was another room for divination.

In another part of the hotel a public art show displayed paintings and other pieces depicting mystic themes, Earth spirituality, and goddess imagery. I was stopped in my tracks by a crucifixion sculpture.

Hanging on a wide, red cross – almost as high as the ceiling – was an effigy comprised of a stag head mounted atop a blue human torso equipped with a large, golden phallus. The creature's arms, detached from its body, extended on the crossbeam and ended with hands holding green boughs. At the base of the crucifixion lay a bronzed human skeleton in a fetal position. The piece was titled *Re-membering the God*, and it was partly inspired by the Osiris-Isis myth of ancient Egypt. To the artist it represented "the re-birth and re-assembling of Paganism and Witchcraft today as a literal re-embodiment of the (collective) God."[227]

A plaque offered this explanation,

> The body of the modern God of the Witches rises from the skeletal seed of the past, like a growing plant, yet he is also shown as if in the process of being re-made, a work in progress. Thus rough edges remain. Modern Pagans are still shaping their God.
>
> As the Egyptian Isis searched for the pieces of her slain husband Osiris in order to reassemble them and bring him back to life, so modern Pagans are reassembling the collective body of the God. Parts are found, parts are re-made; the God's body lives again but is changed.[228]

I was at *Paganicon*.

During the weekend of March 17-19, 2017, over 600 Wiccans and Witches, Heathens – drawing from Germanic, Nordic and Celtic lore – Vodouists, and practitioners from other Pagan branches, converged for the seventh annual Paganicon. Hosted by Twin Cities Pagan Pride, an independent organization with ties to Pagan Pride International, Paganicon is a conference that seeks to empower the Pagan community in the US Midwest, with a focus on Minnesota and western Wisconsin. My purpose in attending was to better understand the Pagan milieu in America, for neo-Paganism is the religious expression of Re-enchantment.

How does the Pagan community see itself in the broader, cultural context? What plans are foreseen to expand its footprint? Because modern Paganism is diverse in its forms, are bridges being established amongst differing groups? What are the trends?

The event itself was a smorgasbord of activities: leadership workshops, lectures on the history of Witchcraft, roundtables and panel discussions, rituals and ceremonies, hospitality rooms, book signings, and an Equinox Ball. The children's program included guided meditations to embody Snake – the Egyptian god Apep, the great serpent of the underworld. This fit the overall theme: *A Journey to the Underworld*.

---

[227] Paul B. Rucker, *Re-membering the God*, mixed media, from the posted interpretation, brackets in original.

[228] Ibid.

The weekend's opening ritual began with a processional as hundreds of Pagans moved from the conference hall to the ritual room, a space spiritually prepared ahead of time. For a few minutes I walked with the crowd, keeping pace and listening as they repeated a four-line song on their march to the symbolic underworld,

> Down we go to the world below,
> We bring with us a light to show.
> Up we rise with the dark in our eyes,
> We bring to light the peace of the night.[229]

With only a few feet to go before entering the room, a spiritual container of sorts, I innocuously sidestepped from the processional. *The ritual space was not my place.*

From my position in the hallway, I watched as Wiccans and Heathens paused inside the door where a rose, dipped in sacred waters, was used to mark each practitioner before beginning his or her journey through a series of stations. The closing song venerated the spirits of Nature,

> Spirits of Earth and Sky,
> Spirits of Sun and Sea,
> We've honored you this night,
> And shared your mysteries.[230]

During the weekend, I attended a number of lectures and panel discussions.

On Friday afternoon I took in Jason Mankey's fascinating talk on the history of modern Witchcraft. Tracing its contemporary roots from Theosophy, Co-Masonry, and Rosicrucian orders – and pointedly telling us that Freemasonry gave Wicca its ritualistic and ceremonial concepts – Mankey elaborated on the work of Gerald Gardner[231] before drawing connections to the Cultural Revolution of the 1960s, including the early environmental movement.[232]

---

[229] Opening Ritual, *Draw Near and Fear Not*, processional song by Judy Olson-Linde. Lyric sheet on file.

[230] Closing song to Opening Ritual, *Farewell*, by Judy Olson-Linde. Lyric sheet on file.

[231] Gerald Gardner (1884-1964) was the British father of contemporary Witchcraft, and was instrumental in bringing Wicca into the public arena.

[232] As per my notes from Jason Mankey's lecture titled *From the Wica to Wicca: The Rise and Development of Modern Witchcraft*, given on Friday, March 17, 2017.

Mankey noted that while there were only a few thousand Pagans in the 1970s, their numbers have increased dramatically.

In a group discussion facilitated by the energetic and well-known Witch, Laura Tempest Zakroff, the Masonic tie was again repeated; if your system of Witchcraft has a degree structure, she explained, it emerged from Masonic practices. Her talk was titled *The Authentic Witch: Crafting a Working Tradition*, stressing that what works for you and what you perceive as truth is the bar of authenticity. She also emphasized the importance of having a three-pronged approach when seeking a legitimate experience: Area – connecting to your natural landscape, Heritage – connecting to your folklore, and Calling – connecting to the deity who beckons for your loyalty.[233]

At one point a question was raised as to who in the room had been born into a Pagan household. Of the fifty or so in attendance, only a few hands went up. Next it was asked if anyone came from another faith, and it was clear the reference was to Christianity. The majority of hands shot up. In my vicinity I could hear murmurs of Lutheran, Baptist, Catholic.

A workshop on conscious creation explored the use of labyrinths and gardens as containers for magic work. A shrine garden, we were told, is to be used for "communion with the deity's energies."[234] In a facilitated discussion on the aesthetics of sacred spaces we examined the principles of balance, harmony, focus, and the flow of energy and rhythm. Sacred space was defined as a place "dedicated to sacred purpose and imbued with the presence of the divine."[235]

On Saturday morning I listened to the panel, *Pagans and the Environment: How Faith can Save the Earth*.

Members from different Pagan traditions agreed that their Earth-centric disposition must be the tie that binds them. There was a general consensus, too, that Pagans need to work closer with the general population on ecological issues, for humanity's common bond is the Earth. This would be good for Mother Earth, and good for public relations.

---

[233] As per my notes from Laura Tempest Zakroff's talk, *The Authentic Witch: Crafting a Working Tradition*, given on Friday, March 17, 2017.

[234] As per my notes from Tinnekke Bebout's talk, *Living the Process: Conscious Creation*, given on Saturday, March 18, 2017.

[235] As per my notes from Angela Raincatcher's facilitated discussion, *Aesthetics of Sacred Space*, given on Saturday, March 18, 2017

Regardless of the path one follows, each person was encouraged to be a local and global activist. The program read,

> Join this panel discussion as we explore the ways that Environmental protection can be the unifying factor for many faiths. As Pagans, we honor the sacred essence and power of the earth. This belief unites us with others, and could be the unifying thread in a collective effort to save the earth.[236]

The group discussion, *Off With Their Heads: Curses, Blessings and Words of Power*, was an engrossing conversation on the ethical use of curses.

Witches debated the pros and cons of hexing, with a lively exchange on the mass spell recently directed at President Donald Trump. Only a few weeks prior, a binding ritual – which seeks to metaphysically restrain a targeted person – had been levied against the newly elected President.[237] A public appeal was issued in the lead-up to the event; it was an open call for Pagans everywhere to collectively participate in a ritualistic revolution, and news outlets had picked up the story. Some in the room knew those who had organized this magical activism, but the consensus was not favorable. Many felt that the shared openness of the ritual was potentially destabilizing, and unintended spiritual consequences could materialize in the future. Equally concerning was that from a public relations perspective the event was a failure. Instead of coming across as sophisticated and astute, the Pagan community looked vindictive and desperate.

It was an interesting session.

On Sunday I attended a workshop on *Building and Expanding the Pagan Homeland*, and it dovetailed with a private conversation I had the day before. Chatting with a young man who was a life-long Pagan, I asked him to clarify something: How do you pronounce *Paganicon*, and what does it mean?

Before arriving in the Twin Cities I had supposed it to be pagan-*icon*, as in the context of an image or symbol reflecting some component of pagan belief. This made sense, but I was hearing something different. There was no long "i" sound in the name.

---

[236] The quote is from the Paganicon 2017 official program, p.15.

[237] The binding spell took place on the stroke of midnight, February 24, 2017. This mass ritual was not the first or last curse placed on Trump by the Pagan community, but news stories elevated the public's attention to this hex date.

"It's not *i*con," the young man said.

Recognizing I was not from the United States, he kindly explained the name: "Think of it as a nation, like Pakistan or Afghanistan. Our community in the Upper Midwest is large enough that we call this region Paganistan. So this is our homeland's convention; Paganicon."

This clarification may sound alarming, but he was right. The Minneapolis-Saint Paul area has a substantial Pagan presence, with one 2011 article putting the number of covens and groups at 236 in the Twin Cities region.[238] According to a January 2017 report by City Vision, a Minneapolis-based Christian research ministry, 334 covens and circles have been identified within the state of Minnesota.[239] It is estimated that 20,000 Pagans are in the metro-region, with the predominant tradition being Witchcraft.[240]

Since the 1960s with the local establishment of Llewellyn Publications – the largest independent publishing enterprise on occult subjects – and the Gnosticon events of the 1970s, this part of the US has become a beacon for neo-Pagans.[241] The American Council of Witches was organized in Minneapolis, publishing its *Principles of Wiccan Belief* in 1974.[242] The Wiccan Church of Minnesota was federally registered in 1989.[243] And the Sacred Harvest Festival, an annual highlight for nature-based religions, takes place

[238] Rose French, "Wiccan prisoner sues, claims bias," *StarTribune*, Saturday, 9 April 2011, p.A1, continued on p.A9.

[239] John A. Mayer, *Megachurches, Witch Covens, and Mosques Compared Per State* (City Vision, January 2017). For the sake of clarification, this number includes groves, circles, and other forms of Pagan community.

[240] Tim Miejan, "2018 Paganicon," *The Edge*, March 2018, p.16.

[241] Llewellyn Publications, also known as Llewellyn Worldwide, originally started in the state of Oregon in 1901, and was purchased by Carl Weschcke in 1961. Weschcke relocated Llewellyn to the Twin Cities the year he purchased the company. In the 1970s, Llewellyn hosted a series of local events known as the Gnostic-Aquarian Festivals, or Gnosticons. According to Margot Adler, Weschcke generously ran Gnosticon at a loss. His publishing house, however, was a profitable venture. See Margot Adler, *Drawing Down the Moon: Witches, Druids, Goddess-Worshippers, and Other Pagans in America Today* (The Viking Press, 1979), p.380. Combined, Weschcke's Llewellyn and Gnosticons created the persona of an occult-friendly metro region. Moreover, Gnosticon was influential in spawning a growth-industry of psychic and New Age fairs. To read the history of Pagan development in the Twin Cities, see Murphy Pizza, *Paganistan: Contemporary Pagan Community in Minnesota's Twin Cities* (Ashgate, 2014).

[242] Adler, *Drawing Down the Moon*, pp.99-101.

[243] Murphy Pizza, *Paganistan: Contemporary Pagan Community in Minnesota's Twin Cities*

in a secluded location approximately halfway between Minneapolis and Duluth. The state of Minnesota – and the Twin Cities specifically – *is* Paganistan, a label affectionately used by local Pagans for a long time.[244]

But the shadow of Paganistan extends across the US Midwest. In January 2017, City Vision reported that 848 covens – including groves and circles – could be found in the twelve states making up the region.[245] Besides covens, there is a celebratory aspect that dots the landscape. Pagan Spirit Gathering (PSG), one of America's longest running Pagan festivals, is a Midwest staple. Beginning in 1980, PSG has been held in Wisconsin, Ohio, Missouri, and Illinois. The Starwood Festival, originating in Pennsylvania the year after PSG started, is routinely held in Ohio. Kansas is home to the Heartland Pagan Festival. Many other gatherings can be found throughout the region, like the Beltane celebration near French Lick, Indiana, Iowa's LammasFest, Wisconsin's Summerland Spirit Festival, and the Saint Louis Pagan Picnic.

Paganism is not regionally confined. It is a coast-to-coast movement, and covens are found throughout the nation: Texas, 226; California, 178; Florida, 161; Pennsylvania, 141; North Carolina, 83.[246]

New Orleans has a tradition of Voodoo.[247] Salem, Massachusetts, is noted for its Wiccan presence. San Francisco has an historically important Pagan community. Bookstores and boutiques catering to neo-Paganism are found in small towns and big cities alike. Gatherings and festivals, too, are part of the national mix.

PantheaCon, the "largest indoor Pagan gathering in the world," takes place at the DoubleTree in San José, California.[248] The intimate Fairy and Human Relations Congress in Okanogan County, Washington, claims to rend the veil between the realm of nature spirits and humanity. Colorado's annual Dragonfest goes back to 1985. Tennessee is host to the long-running Pagan Unity

---

(Ashgate, 2014), p.59. This body was formed as result of a schism, of sorts, from within the Minnesota Church of Wicca, organized in the 1970s.

[244] As was explained to myself during the 2017 Paganicon. For more on the name and the region's Pagan community, see Pizza, *Paganistan* (Ashgate, 2014).

[245] Mayer, *Megachurches, Witch Covens, and Mosques Compared Per State*, the 848 figure is the tally of the twelve individual states as given in the report.

[246] Ibid.

[247] Other terms for Voodoo are Vodou and Vaudoux.

[248] John Beckett, "No Pantheacon Envy," *Patheos*, February 12, 2015, [www.patheos.com/blogs/johnbeckett/2015/02/no-need-for-pantheacon-envy.html].

Festival. Near the western edge of New York State is Sirius Rising, a gathering that ritualistically connects Land and Spirit. The Florida Pagan Gathering, originally known as Freedom Fest, has a history dating to 1995. In many American cities, annual Pagan Pride Day events act as community outreach programs; and not just in major centers like San Francisco or Chicago or New York City, but also in places like Kalispell, Montana and Springfield, Missouri.[249] More than 4,000 people attend the Pagan Pride Days Festival in Raleigh, North Carolina.[250]

Knowing that Paganism is a growing feature of America's religious mosaic, I was very interested in attending the workshop, *Building and Expanding the Pagan Homeland*. Our facilitator, Wade Mueller from Deeply Rooted,[251] reminded us that modern Paganism is still a nomadic culture. This, he said, needed to change if a homeland is to be established. But how could such a nomadic spirituality find grounding? Land.

Acknowledging that while Paganism is a nature-based religion, there is little actual landscape devoted to the faith. Real estate is therefore needed for sacred spaces. If permanent temples could be built to honor the gods and goddesses, "Apollo or Thor or The Morrígan," then a homeland might be possible. Established and visible temples, it was explained, would attract a spiritually hungry public while respecting the deities. Real change would settle into the culture.

At the same time, Mueller chastised the Pagan community for its lack of cohesion, its inability to properly elevate the deities, and its *longstanding failure* – a reference to the historical rise of Christianity and the subsequent downfall of the mythic. Because of this, the gods and ancestor spirits "don't respect us... we failed, we turned our backs on them."[252]

"The onus is not on them to reach to us," Mueller said, adding that, "it's on us to reach to them."

---

[249] The original impetus for Pagan Pride Days is the Pagan Pride Project (www.paganpride.org), which serves as a networking and support organization.

[250] As of February 2018, the leadership team for Raleigh's Pagan Pride Day announced that the 17-year-old event would cease, effectively, because of organizational burnout coupled with a difficult venue change. A public call has been made to those who have participated in the past, with the hope that a new offering will take shape.

[251] Deeply Rooted is an intentional Pagan community located near Athens, Wisconsin.

[252] As per my notes from Wade Mueller's talk, *Building and Expanding the Pagan Homeland*, given on Sunday, March 19, 2017.

Gesturing to the room, he rhetorically asked if the god's are pleased. How could they respect such an unnatural setting? The dullness of a hotel conference room is but a poor substitute for a serious place of worship. "Is this serving the gods and goddesses?"

The bottom line: Pagans have failed the gods, for the deities do not have respectable homes in the midst of humanity. Land is needed; permanence is required. Once this problem is rectified, then the gods will respond appropriately – *build it*, and *They will come*. Manifestation and habitation will result, for the temples will be occupied by their presence.

Mueller emphasized that a homeland also requires social infrastructure. Pagan-directed community centers, libraries, retreats and camps – properly tied to sacred spaces and temples – would form nodes in a growing physical-social-spiritual network. If a number of stable communities could take shape, each being a link in a chain of cooperation, then a legitimate, regional organization could evolve. And if a regional model could be established, then it might metastasize into something national.

Mueller was excited about the potential. His ultimate hope, expressed by others in the room, is for generational change. Once permanent space is obtained and temples are built, a foundation will be laid for future generations to reinstate a fully Pagan culture.

I walked away from Paganicon with some observations and thoughts:

— The phenomenal rise of Paganism in America is not without its challenges. New lines of tension are evident, and old, internal divisions are being reconsidered. Modern Paganism is experiencing growing pains.

— Generally speaking, the Pagan community is wrestling with its place in the public domain. Because of the ongoing, worldview revolution – the saturation of Western society with themes of occulture – the public is more accepting of Paganism than at any time in our recent history. This also means more external scrutiny, more questions of the movement, more press coverage, and more social responsibility. Public perception becomes more critical.

— Modern Pagans desire to exercise greater spiritual authority. Repeatedly I heard talk of the deities personally approaching the individual, and how the gap between the human world and the domain of spiritual entities is progressively blurring. The gods and goddesses, evidently,

> desire a scalable interaction with practitioners, offering guidance, accepting veneration, and even making demands. One Witch expressed frustration, telling me he was tired of Wiccans wasting their time on social justice themes; instead, they need to seriously pursue spirit conjuring, for this is where their power comes from. Overall there seemed to be a sense of urgency – a yearning for magical influence at the human level, and for a manifestation from the realm of spirit.

Neo-Paganism has grown and developed in parallel with the cultural accommodation of Re-enchantment. Both are the same in essence. One lives it out religiously, the other is a universal infusion.

How many people in the United States identify as neo-Pagan is difficult to ascertain. Certainly, *far more* Americans claim to be Christians; the Pew Research Center's Religious Landscape Study indicates that 25.4% of the US population falls under the category of Evangelical Protestant.[253] Contrasting the two may be reassuring to some people, giving the impression that neo-Paganism remains a marginal movement.

Pull your head out of the sand: *Wiccans are not the only pagans*.

"What comes after Postmodernism?" asked Christian thinker, Paul Gould, giving the response at the same time. "Answer: Paganism."[254]

Ancient Futures

Deity statues, as this chapter began, remind us that the ancient paradigm of continuity is never far away. Re-enchantment is nothing new, but this does not make it less effective. From the Apollo images to Earth Day, from Findhorn to Rio, from Pan to Gaia, the enchanted worldview has captured our imagination, shaping the way we think and behave.

"Why do I think this re-enchantment of the cosmos is important?" asked systems theorist, Ervin Laszlo, at a World Goodwill meeting in 2005. "Because – Oneness, Wholeness, has been around for thousands of years... a sense of oneness can be recovered."[255]

---

[253] Pew Research Center, *Religious Landscape Study*, published at www.pewforum.org/religious-landscape-study, accessed March 28, 2018.

[254] The quote comes from the title of Paul Gould's article on the future of postmodernism, *What Comes After Postmodernism? Answer: Paganism*, [www.paul-gould.com/2012/04/25/what-comes-after-postmodernism-answer-paganism], accessed August 11, 2015.

[255] Ervin Laszlo, as printed in the *World Goodwill Newsletter*, 2006, No.2, p.3.

Reflecting on the Global Citizenship 2000 Youth Congress, outlined in chapter two, I am reminded that what I witnessed was a tiny flowering of Re-enchantment. Small as it was, it allowed me to see global transformation not as something abstract, but as tangible; a spiritual-ideological movement exhibiting profound subtleties, yet dominating our dreams and visions.

But can we nail down a contemporary starting point for Re-enchantment? Earth Day, 1970, is when the idea was fertilized in the minds of millions. The 1992 Rio Summit is on the shortlist as the premier, post-Cold War re-alignment of priorities. I believe, however, that the Millennium events offer a reasonable base line. The United Nations Millennium Forum, Millennium Summit, and the Summit of Religious and Spiritual Leaders, aggregated, promised a new world order that surpassed Post-modern confusion and the idiosyncrasies of the New Age movement. Oneness was projected onto the world stage, socially, politically, and religiously. We would all be global citizens, saving the Earth by uniting in community. Did this happen? No. But the desire was intensified, the goal magnified.

An unusual, yet highly symbolic gesture should also be considered.

Against the backdrop of the September 11 attacks in 2001, an extraordinary journey was being made. A handcrafted reinterpretation of the *Ark of the Covenant* – the *Ark of Hope* – was physically carried 350 miles from Shelburne Farms, Vermont, into the heart of New York City. Inside the *Ark* was the *Earth Charter*, a document likened to a new Ten Commandments for the planet, the result of a global consultation process that picked up steam after the Rio Earth Summit.[256] Originally it was hoped the Ark would have a resting place at the United Nations, but due to heightened security, it was placed in New York's Interfaith Center. Soon it was traveling around the world, being displayed at UN summits and international events.

The *Ark* and *Charter*, together, was an evocative image of sacred secularity.

Examples of enchantment are inescapable and ubiquitous. When Bolivia passed its *Law of the Rights of Mother Earth* in 2010, and New Zealand's

[256] Maurice Strong, Secretary-General of the Rio Earth Summit, had originally hoped an *Earth Charter* would be a defining outcome of the Summit. It failed to materialize, and although the 1992 Global Forum drafted an initial *Earth Charter*, it was not universally accepted. After Rio, an *Earth Charter* consultation began through the initiative of Maurice Strong, Mikhail Gorbachev, and Steven Rockefeller. Gorbachev, on more than one occasion, referred to the *Charter* as a new type of Ten Commandments.

Whanganui River was recognized in 2017 as having the same legal status as humans, and in the same year Saudi Arabia granted citizenship to a robot, it was clear that a threshold was being crossed. By legal definition we are becoming *one* with *things* – this, too, is a projection of Romans 1: "They exchanged the truth of God for the lie, and worshiped and served created things rather than the Creator."[257]

Sexually, new boundaries are being blurred. When the San Francisco-based Ecosex movement published its *Ecosex Manifesto* in 2011, promoting erotic encounters with nature and contractual marriages with trees and oceans, it was billed as a truly progressive expression of Earth-love. In subtle and flagrant ways, the products of our *truth exchange* are ever more emboldened.

We are in an epoch of revolutionary transformation – *forcing change*.

Peter Jones from TruthXChange is absolutely correct: "The pagan past is our planetary future."[258]

---

[257] Romans 1:25.

[258] Peter Jones, *Capturing the Pagan Mind: Paul's Blueprint for Thinking and Living in the New Global Culture* (Broadman & Holman Publishers, 2003), p.90.

Part III

The Genesis Factor

Man must choose between God and despair. If a person wagers on God and loses, the person loses nothing. But if a person wagers on God and wins, the person wins everything. If, however, one wagers against God there is no hope of winning. If that person wins, he wins nothing. But if one bets against God and loses, he loses everything.
– Phil Fernandes, *The God Who Sits Enthroned.*

If Jesus rose from the grave, then the Christian faith that stands or falls on Jesus' resurrection is true.
– Andy Wrasman, *Contradict: They Can't All Be True*.

Chapter 8

Agonizing Transcendence

> Look to Me, and be saved, All you ends of the earth! For I am God, and there is no other. – Isaiah 45:22.

> Jesus said to him, "I am the way, the truth, and the life. No one comes to the Father except through Me." – John 14:6.

Humanity's "Real Dream," according to visionary futurist, Philip Comella, is to collectively awaken our "God Mind." Once we realize this Oneness, a new Eden will come into existence. *Hope is found in mystical unity*: "Our fates are intertwined, and so we find salvation in each other."[1]

Mystic and author, Frank X. Tuoti, postulated that in "the evolving Mystical Age, humanity will recover the sacred view, which will be not only our salvation but also our freedom and joy." Salvific enchantment would come through the discovery of the "Divine Mother once again."[2]

Emmy award winning actor and eco-mystic, Dennis Weaver, said it plainly: "It is the realization of our oneness that is our salvation."[3]

Implied is that exclusive and separating truth claims are antithetical to collective salvation. *We are all One* infers that *separation is an illusion*.

"You have merely been segregating yourself from *yourself*," was the message given to Neale Donald Walsch by a non-human intelligence. "When you break through the circle of your containment, you will discover that everything is just like you. Not only everyONE else, but everyTHING else."[4]

---

1 Philip Comella, *The Collapse of Materialism: Visions of Science, Dreams of God* (Rainbow Bridge Books, 2014), p.282.

2 Frank X. Tuoti, *The Dawn of the Mystic Age: An Invitation to Enlightenment* (Crossroad Publishing Company, 1997), p.68.

3 Dennis Weaver, *All The World's A Stage* (Hampton Roads Publishing, 2001), p.303.

4 Neale Donald Walsch, *The New Revelations: A Conversation With God* (Atria Books, 2002), p.189, italics and capitals in original.

The voice told Walsch that separation is *the lie*,

> Stop thinking of yourself as separate, and all the true power that comes from the inner strength of unity is yours... to wield as you wish...
>
> Separation from God and from each other is the cause of all your dysfunction and suffering. Still, separation continues to masquerade as strength, and your politics, your economics, and even your religions have perpetuated the lie...
>
> There is no separation. Not from each other, not from God…
>
> This is the *greatest secret of all time*. It is the answer for which man has searched for millennia. It is the solution for which he has worked, the revelation for which he has prayed.[5]

In his book, *Science and the Reenchantment of the Cosmos*, Ervin Laszlo stressed that the universe is not made up of "separate things and events." Matter itself is "not a separate kind of thing, and it doesn't even have a reality of its own."[6] Events, experiences, consciousness and matter – all are part of each other, and the same, in the One-ist paradigm.

"In truth there is no right or wrong," explained the so-called *ancient astronaut*, self-identified as Ra, in a series of channeled messages. "You are every thing, every being, every emotion... You are unity. You are infinity... You are. This is the Law of One."[7]

Dennis Weaver, who said we have to "*feel* God, and then give ourselves over to that feeling," proclaimed that, "we will awaken to the truth that there is no difference. It is all One. There is no separation."[8]

What will this ultimately produce? According to Comella, the goal of Oneness – to be the united mind of God – is to realize the dream of world peace, and thereby "to make a real heaven on earth."[9]

---

5 Neale Donald Walsch, *Conversations with God: An Uncommon Dialogue, Book 3* (Hampton Roads, 1998), pp.43-44, italics in original.

6 Ervin Laszlo, *Science and the Reenchantment of the Cosmos* (Inner Traditions, 2006), p.1.

7 Don Elkins, Carla Rueckert, and James Allen McCarty, *The RA Material: An Ancient Astronaut Speaks* (The Donning Company, 1984), p.67.

8 Weaver, *All The World's A Stage*, p.239, italics in original.

9 Comella, *The Collapse of Materialism*, p.280.

Oneness offers a vision of hope based on an *ideal image* of ourselves, constructing a thought-platform with redemption and salvation in mind. Variations in how this is conceived or implemented exist,[10] but by definition and proclamation, exclusivity and separation are anathema.

To some extent I can empathize. Peace, harmony, and a brighter future are universally desired. We intuitively know things could be better, and the problem of pain and suffering are reminders we live in a broken world. Struggles and trials are part of daily life, and our mortal end is ever before us. Yet, in the shadows and light and darkness of the human experience, *we still hope*. In fact, hope is essential for survival and flourishing.

But hope in what? Nature? Humanity?

Not in Oneness, for events and things and matter are not separate. Everything and everyone is the same, and there is no right or wrong. Pain is an illusion, pleasure is fiction, your cancer is nothing and everything, your joys are fruitless, rape and murder are equal to charity and compassion, to live or die does not matter: The list is endlessly depressing. Oneness cannot offer a better tomorrow, because "better" and "tomorrow" are non-existent. Hope is hopeless, for hope implies being *favorably separated* from a less desirable condition. The dream of peace is pointless, for war is just the same.

In a dimension where distinctions dissolve, any sense of real value is not only lost, but it can never be assigned. Relationships disappear, and love fades to nothingness.

When Theosophist Alice A. Bailey referenced those "old and undesirable" things that must disappear in the coming New Age – "hatred and the spirit of separation"[11] – I am compelled to ask: *Why*? If all is One, then hatred is non-existent *already*. Or maybe the *real* Oneness is hatred? Who can know?

Of course, to determine if something is hateful requires *judgment*, which is predicated on the act of *separating* beliefs, values, and actions. To announce that separation is the lie, or that it is evil or hateful or wrong, means that distinctions have been categorically declared. Value judgments and truth claims have been made known; separation has taken place. A relationship has been established.

---

[10] Western teachings on Oneness seem to accept the premise without questioning contradictions. Eastern paths, on the other hand, have constructed mazes of philosophy, religious practices, and spiritual disciplines in the attempt to embrace One Reality.

[11] Alice A. Bailey, *The Externalisation of the Hierarchy* (Lucis Trust, 1957), p.62.

But according to an angelic presence speaking to the influential futurist, Barbara Marx Hubbard, the problem of separation is one of remembrance and identity. *We have forgotten we are God*, and therefore we live in an illusion of separation. The solution is to realize our divine union. However, if you are incapable of attaining such lofty enlightenment, or are unwilling to participate in the Plan – to become "godlike" – then you will be discarded.

Describing the coming *selection process*, when those who will *not* participate in the Planetary Birth are to be removed, the non-human intelligence said the following to Hubbard,

> My challenge is, how can the illusion of separation of humanity from God be overcome quickly enough to save the world? The solution is, we must realize the union of humanity and God...
>
> The surgeon dare leave no cancer in the body when he closes up the wound after a delicate operation. We dare leave no self- centeredness on Earth after the selecting process. For when we complete the process of the transformation, all who live on will be empowered to be godlike. They will have touched the Tree of Life. The cherubims and flaming sword will be removed forever. The memory of God will be restored to humanity...
>
> Overcome the devil within, overcome your own sense of separation from God, and thereby release within you the power of God, for the good, and you will save the world.[12]

Putting aside the need to "save the world" and the ominous verbiage of being cut-out like cancer, something akin to a spiritual Hitler[13] *separating the undesirables* for the ideal of group conformity, the message of divine awakening begs the question: If our Divine-Human Oneness has to be remembered, is it real? Why, pray tell, do I need to be *reminded* if All is One?

Having to be told we are God discredits the very idea we *are* God.

[12] Barbara Marx Hubbard, *The Revelation: A Message of Hope for the New Millennium* (Nataraj Publishing, 1995), pp.239-240.

[13] Theosophist and occultist, Alice A. Bailey, whose writings influenced the New Age movement, wrote that Adolf Hitler, Stalin and Franco, "are all expressions of the Shamballa force. " These personalities, according to Bailey, are the "agents of destiny, the creators of the new order and the initiators of the new civilization; they are the destroyers of what must be destroyed before humanity can go forward along the Lighted Way." Bailey, *The Externalisation of the Hierarchy*, see pp.133-135.

The fact that mystical moods can be conjured irrespective of religious characteristics and formalities, being evident in Hinduism, Christian mysticism, Sufism, Buddhism – or through a rave experience – indicates that it begins in the *structures of the mind*. In this I am referring to neurochemical responses and the brain's ability to process the experience. Thought is suspended as flow takes over.

There is physicality to the mystical experience, and health and wellness claims are often associated with it. This is not to say it is corporeal only, but that the sensory starting point of mysticism is traceable to a physical reality *before* shifting into personal abstracts. Inner experience becomes philosophy. The mystical mood ventures into religious and ideological waters.

Ideas have consequences, and Oneness is a *very big idea*.

To the purist, however, Oneness is not a concept or belief that can be framed or communicated; it is a realized truth only. Oneness or Monism, by definition, is formless. Words and language, the essential structures through which purpose, value, and understanding are transmitted, runs counter to the spirit of One-ism. Language is both form and function, and words delineate and impart *meaning*. Oneness, therefore, cannot be *described*.

By rejecting divisions, Oneness also renders legal rule and law as pointless constructs. Justice is dependent on gauging what is true or false, and what is morally measurable. Ethics is based on standards and judgments grounded in value distinctions. Established boundaries separating right from wrong are not frivolous fictions, but real and necessary.

No one who espouses Oneness actually lives it out.

Even the One-ist argument for heaven-on-earth cannot be conceived outside the reality of separateness, for it rests on comparison and judgment. Ironically, while Oneness is opposed to exclusivity, in asserting that it is the *only way to salvation* it finds itself in that very category.

Oneness is the illusion.

Otherness

Seventeenth Century philosopher, Baruch Spinoza, contended that the material world and God were indistinguishable. It was an idea that secularized the spiritual, layering a metaphysical meaning on matter.

Spinoza's thinking was instrumental in framing *Process Theology*, the teaching that some aspects of God, like the universe, are ever changing within an "endlessly complex web of unfolding relationships."[14] Spinoza's view of God became the metaphysical foundation for much of our naturalistic and contemporary, scientific outlook.[15]

Albert Einstein himself wrote: "I believe in Spinoza's God who reveals himself in the harmony of all that exists, but not in a God who concerns himself with the fate and action of men."[16]

Not surprisingly, the more we peer into matter itself and the more we study the material universe – from atomic structure to weather patterns to cosmology – the more we realize how complex, connected, and nuanced creation is. The universe displays knowledge, regularity, design and function, and the intentional "fine tuning" for life.[17] Creation is not random, pointing to an Intelligent Designer.[18]

"The heavens declare the glory of God, and the sky above proclaims his handiwork," shouts the Psalmist.[19] Paul writes in Romans 1:20, "for since the creation of the world His invisible attributes are clearly seen, being understood by the things that are made, even His eternal power and Godhead, so that they are without excuse."

An endless variety of distinctions permeate the known universe. It could be said that uniqueness is *so common* as to be *normal*. Events and things, creatures great and small, and people – practically everything and everyone exhibits individual traits, categorical differences, and characteristics demonstrating broad and fine points of separation. Great complexity abounds, and interconnection can only be understood by acknowledging fundamental divisions *and* points of relationship. Distinctions define reality.

---

[14] Edward O. Wilson, *Consilience: The Unity of Knowledge* (Alfred A. Knopf, 1998), p.263.

[15] Will Durant, *The Story of Philosophy: The Lives and Opinions of the Greater Philosophers* (Simon and Schuster, 1926), p.187.

[16] Quoted by Nigel Calder, *Einstein's Universe* (Wings Books, 1979), p.138.

[17] An interesting essay on Fine Tuning, with counter-arguments, is by Del Ratzsch and Jeffrey Koperski, "Teleological Arguments for God's Existence," *Stanford Encyclopedia of Philosophy* (Stanford University, 2016 edition), https://plato.stanford.edu/entries/teleological-arguments (Accessed April 14, 2018).

[18] An enjoyable yet serious examination of the subject is J. Warner Wallace's book, *God's Crime Scene: A Cold-Case Detective Examines the Evidence for a Divinely Created Universe* (David C. Cook, 2015). Another book of interest is by Dave Hunt, *Cosmos, Creator and Human Destiny: Answering Darwin, Dawkins, and the New Atheists* (The Berean Call, 2010).

[19] Psalm 19:1, *English Standard Version*.

This fits the Biblical worldview. Genesis 1 is a telling example:

- God creates the heavens and earth, marking Him from creation (1:1), and He separates light from darkness (1:3-5). Time comes into existence.
- There is a separation from the ground to the expanse above (1:6-8).[20]
- A further demarcation takes place between water and land (1:9-10).
- Vegetation is produced, "according to their various kinds." Plants bearing seeds and trees with fruit, "according to their kinds" (1:11-12).[21]
- Lights in the expanse divide the day from night. The Sun, Moon, and stars "divide the light from the darkness" (1:14-19).
- Birds "according to their kind" take to the expanse above, and sea creatures "according to their kinds" take to the waters (1:20-22).
- Upon the earth, God made beasts and cattle and creeping things, "according to its kind" (1:24-25). The repetitious phrase, "according to its kind," postulates unique family categories, possibly order or class level distinctions. Is this not what we observe in nature? Definable classifications are evident, and while Oneness fits the Darwinian paradigm of life supposedly emerging from a single organism, what we see from the fossil record to the forest, is everything is created "according to its kind."
- God makes Mankind, male and female, in His image (Genesis 1:26-27). That is, we are specifically fashioned as His image bearers, having a status above the animal and plant kingdoms. We are His appointed representation on Earth, physical beings who are to reflect God's goodness and righteousness, both in spirit and in flesh. This is not so much a moral characterization, but a divinely instituted designation that frames our eternal value. One outcome is that individual persons have worth apart from nature or structures, including groupings; human life has intrinsic value because of our special position.

---

[20] There is theological debate over the meaning of this passage, primarily on the Hebrew word raqîa. Does this section of text imply the creation of a general, spatial relationship between the earth and sky, ground and atmosphere? Some claim it refers to a heavenly dome, or that it delineates a vapor canopy. L. Thomas Holdcroft writes, "No special shape or form is here assigned to the firmament; it is portrayed simply as a vast realm extending upward from the earth's surface." *The Pentateuch* (Western Book Company, 1966), p.3. Paul F. Taylor says, "This whole process gives an impression of a God who is active and at work. We see here God putting into place the physical laws that we observe throughout the universe." *The Six Days of Genesis* (Master Books, 2007), p.41.

[21] As worded in the *New International Version*.

The Biblical view, as Peter Jones explains in his comparative study of One-ism, is *Two-ism* – the God who is *separate*, and then everything else.[22]

"He is not within the system, but operates from outside the system," writes John H. Walton, professor of Old Testament. "The cosmic phenomena are not manifestations of his attributes, but instruments of his sovereignty."[23]

Dave Hunt, a Christian author and lecturer, commented on the reality of the cosmos and the question of origins,

> The fact that the cosmos exists, with life and intelligence resident on planet Earth, demands an explanation. *Nothing* cannot produce *anything*. Either some*thing* of infinite potential or *Someone* of infinite power always was, must still exist, and always will. There is no escaping this conclusion.[24]

Something could not create out of nothing, "because things are neither self-existent nor eternal."[25] The God who created is the God who separates.

The Bible continuously speaks to the reality of distinctions, including between spirit and flesh. Ecclesiastes 12:7 tells us, "Then the dust will return to the earth as it was, and the spirit will return to God who gave it." The Apostle Paul even gave a discourse on types of flesh based on ***kind***, death and resurrection, and the difference between the natural body and the spiritual body.[26] Moreover, there is an acknowledged struggle between the flesh and spirit: "For the flesh lusts against the Spirit, and the Spirit against the flesh; and these are contrary to one another, so that you do not do the things that you wish."[27] Spirit *and* flesh are not treated as illusionary, but as reality.

We are even different than the diverse spiritual entities that reside in the supernatural realm, such as ministering angels and demonic beings.[28] Our

---

22 See Peter Jones, *One or Two: Seeing a World of Difference* (Main Entry Editions, 2010).

23 John H. Walton, *Ancient Near Eastern Thought and the Old Testament* (Apollos, 2007), p.98. See the text box, "Comparative Exploration: Yahweh's Place in the Cosmos."

24 Dave Hunt, *Cosmos, Creator and Human Destiny: Answering Darwin, Dawkins, and the New Atheists* (The Berean Call, 2010), p.144, italics in original.

25 Ibid., p.145.

26 1 Corinthians 15:35-58.

27 Galatians 5:17.

28 Regarding ministering spirits, Hebrews 1:14 asks, "Are they not all ministering spirits sent forth to minister for those who will inherit salvation?" Regarding demons: In Matthew 10:1 we see Jesus giving authority to drive out demonic spirits, and in 1 John 4:1 we are

spiritual struggle corresponds to the wickedness that resides in the supernatural world, as stated by Paul, but we are to be set apart from it,

> For we do not wrestle against flesh and blood, but against principalities, against powers, against the rulers of the darkness of this age, against spiritual hosts of wickedness in the heavenly places. Therefore take up the whole armor of God, that you may be able to withstand in the evil day, and having done all, to stand.[29]

Separation is not illusionary, and God's *otherness* is supreme. This is reflected in the word *holy* – to be set apart. Christian intellectual, Peter Jones, offers this understanding,

> But when we say God is holy, we are not only saying he is morally pure (though he is). We are primarily speaking cosmologically. We are saying he is utterly unique and primary in his being, and that, relative to everything else, he is Other. Nowhere does Scripture define God's essential being as found within or defined by the cosmos. In his creating and saving work, by his Spirit, God upholds all things and even dwells *within* believers. But without fail, the God of Scripture is Other – with us, but beyond us and before us.[30]

A commanding example of God's otherness is seen in Isaiah 40. In this passage He is compared within three categories: Power, Person, and Pastoral.[31] Isaiah 40:12-17 rhetorically contrasts God against the panorama of nature, human wisdom, the might of nations, and the majesty of worship,

> Who has measured the waters in the hollow of His hand, measured heaven with a span and calculated the dust of the earth in a measure? Weighed the mountains in scales and the hills in a balance?
>
> Who has directed the Spirit of the Lord, or as His counselor has taught Him? With whom did He take counsel, and who instructed

---

to test the message of spirits. While humans are different than other spiritual beings, there is a relational correspondence (Luke 15:10; 1 Corinthians 6:3; Hebrews 13:2).

[29] Ephesians 6:12-13.

[30] Peter Jones, *The Other Worldview: Exposing Christianity's Greatest Threat* (Kirkdale Press, 2015), p.148, italics in original.

[31] Walter C. Kaiser's book, *The Majesty of God in the Old Testament: A Guide for Preaching and Teaching* (Baker Academic, 2007), was helpful in understanding Isaiah 40.

> Him, and taught Him in the path of justice? Who taught Him knowledge, and showed Him the way of understanding?
>
> Behold, the nations are as a drop in a bucket, and are counted as the small dust on the scales; Look, He lifts up the isles as a very little thing. And Lebanon is not sufficient to burn, nor its beasts sufficient for a burnt offering. All nations before Him are as nothing, and they are counted by Him less than nothing and worthless.

The awesomeness of the cosmos does not compare, and neither do the features of the earth. Nature is not equal to its Maker. Human wisdom, justice, and understanding are not on par. Nations are likened to the fine dust blown off a scale, not because this tips the balance, but because they matter as nothing and can be scattered with complete impunity.

Even our models of worship fail. The imagery of Lebanon is couched within the Old Testament sacrificial system; if we were to construct a super-sized altar mounded-up with all the trees of Lebanon as fuel and all the cattle as the offering, this enormous expression of worship would not compare.

A modern equivalent would be to disassemble every church and cathedral in the world, take all the collected materials, and then build a single, super-House for every believer to gather and worship in. Make it as ornate as you can imagine, a construction of such magnitude it sucks your breath away. Our human response to this grandeur would be, "God *must* be like this! He must be here!" His comparative response: "nothing and worthless."

Worship is an act of love given back to Him who first loved us. It is beautiful, but our models of worship are not equivalent to who He is: "To whom then will you liken God? Or what likeness will you compare to Him?"[32]

Verses 19-24 contrast God's personality to idols, and then to humanity. Idols, which represent foreign deities, are dead images and without personality. People are like grasshoppers, noblemen are as nothing, and His righteousness nullifies all earthly judges: "To whom then will you liken Me, or to whom shall I be equal? says the Holy One."[33]

From verses 26 to 31, we see His pastoral care. As Creator he calls out all things by name, and knows each finite part of His workmanship: "Not one is missing." And when we are overcome with injustice, feeling neglected and

---

32 Isaiah 40:18.

33 Isaiah 40:25.

abandoned, this too is incomparable. Your despondency is not greater than His understanding and everlasting goodness: "He gives power to the weak, and to those who have no might He increases strength."[34]

Even young men – the embodiment of vitality – will succumb to weariness, faltering and fainting. Human strength gives out. God's care supersedes our mortal limitations, and comes with a promised hope: "But those who wait on the Lord shall renew their strength; They shall mount up with wings like eagles, they shall run and not be weary, they shall walk and not faint."[35]

"God is in a class by himself with no competitors," stated Professor of Old Testament, Walter C. Kaiser.[36]

God is not some bearded, old-guy-in-the-sky – a caricature, a figment of our mocking imagination. In fact, God as revealed in the Bible *cannot be imagined*, for we are unable to fathom a Personality beyond time, space, and matter. From our thoughts sublime to the most insane of fantasies, as amazing and perplexing as they may be, we are incapable of conjuring a God who is utterly distinct from creation. It is logically impossible.

But this God is not only different from the material universe, residing in the realm of spirit, He is also distinct within the supernatural, for this, too, is created.[37] Although the magnitude and complexity of nature points to a Creator, this Being must enter our domain to be personally known.

The Biblical narrative is the story of God revealing Himself to humanity through a distinct people group, the Hebrew nation.

First, God made Himself known as the Almighty to Abraham, instructing the patriarch to leave his country and travel to a different land for the purpose of making a promised people,

> I will make you a great nation; I will bless you and make your name great; And you shall be a blessing. I will bless those who bless you, and I will curse him who curses you; And in you all the families of the earth shall be blessed.[38]

---

34 Isaiah 40:29.

35 Isaiah 40:31.

36 Walter C. Kaiser, Jr., *The Majesty of God in the Old Testament: A Guide for Preaching and Teaching* (Baker Academic, 2007), p.24.

37 John 4:24 tells us God is spirit, and Colossians 1:16 declares Christ created all things, "visible and invisible, whether thrones or dominions or principalities or powers."

38 Genesis 12:2-3.

Abraham's son, Isaac, and his grandson, Jacob, also had personal interactions with the Almighty. These three men were variously tested, and Jacob's name was changed in response: "Your name shall no longer be called Jacob, but Israel; for you have struggled with God and with men, and have prevailed."[39]

Abraham's divine promise of a nation eventually took shape. Much later, the God of Abraham, Isaac and Jacob, set up an encounter with a Hebrew fugitive-turned-shepherd, Moses. In this remarkable meeting, God declared His name as the one who transcends time – "I AM WHO I AM"[40] – a title closely translated as Yahweh, and often configured as LORD. Moses becomes the messenger of God's revealed will.

"His [Yahweh's] first appearance was as redeemer and savior, his demand was for an unremitting battle among men for faith in him," said Israeli scholar, Yehezkel Kaufmann. "To initiate this battle is the task of the messenger."[41]

Moses was given a mission to communicate the knowledge of God to the Jewish people, and to lead Israel out of Egypt. During this exodus, Yahweh summoned the nation to Mount Sinai so as to deliver the Decalogue,[42] the Ten Commandments: "Gather the people to Me, and I will let them hear My words, that they may learn to fear Me all the days they live on the earth, and that they may teach their children."[43]

The communicating of the Decalogue, God's code for relationships, was a *public revealing*. This supernatural manifestation was not the result of an inner feeling or a mystical mood; nor was it a privately claimed revelation, something that could be called into question. Rather, it was a public encounter witnessed by the people as a whole. I cannot think of another revelation from any faith tradition that was broadcast, simultaneously and in real-time, to an *entire nation*,

> Did any people ever hear the voice of God speaking out of the midst of the fire, as you have heard, and live? Or did God ever try to go and take for Himself a nation from the midst of another nation, by trials, by signs, by wonders, by war, by a mighty hand and an outstretched

[39] Genesis 32:28.

[40] Exodus 3:14.

[41] Yehezkel Kaufmann, *The Religion of Israel: From Its Beginnings to the Babylonian Exile* (The University of Chicago Press, 1960), p.229.

[42] Decalogue comes from the Greek, *dekalogos*, which corresponds to "ten words."

[43] Deuteronomy 4:10.

> arm, and by great terrors, according to all that the Lord your God did for you in Egypt before your eyes? To you it was shown, that you might know that the Lord Himself is God; there is none other besides Him. Out of heaven He let you hear His voice, that He might instruct you; on earth He showed you His great fire, and you heard His words out of the midst of the fire. And because He loved your fathers, therefore He chose their descendants after them; and He brought you out of Egypt with His Presence, with His mighty power, driving out from before you nations greater and mightier than you, to bring you in, to give you their land as an inheritance, as it is this day. Therefore know this day, and consider it in your heart, that the Lord Himself is God in heaven above and on the earth beneath; there is no other. You shall therefore keep His statutes and His commandments which I command you today, that it may go well with you and with your children after you, and that you may prolong your days in the land which the Lord your God is giving you for all time.[44]

What God did at Sinai was historically exclusive.

In time, Yahweh imparted a codified social and religious system for His people. The list of requirements included dietary laws, purification practices, the making of offerings, and how to build and operate the nation's sacred spaces – the tabernacle and temple. This was not done to merely create an ethnic tradition or sense of identity; rather, it had a practical, theological basis. The Hebrew nation itself was to be a symbol of God's otherness, a living demonstration to the world of Yahweh's uniqueness. This, too, was the foreshadowing of a coming Redeemer, the *exclusive Savior* of the world; *I AM WHO I AM*, in living form – the *Word made flesh*.

The Decalogue and this codified relationship set the Jewish people apart from the surrounding cultures. But more important than the outward action was God's desire for inward change. This is evident in Psalm 51, a poem of contrition by the nation's leader, King David.

Consider his prayer for repentance and restoration, a "clean heart,"

> Have mercy upon me, O God, according to Your lovingkindness; According to the multitude of Your tender mercies, blot out my transgressions. Wash me thoroughly from my iniquity, and cleanse

[44] Deuteronomy 4:33-40.

> me from my sin. For I acknowledge my transgressions, and my sin is always before me. Against You, You only, have I sinned...
>
> For You do not desire sacrifice, or else I would give it; You do not delight in burnt offering. The sacrifices of God are a broken spirit, a broken and a contrite heart – These, O God, You will not despise.[45]

God's desire for relationship – not a romantic notion, but as a loving father longing for the prodigal to return – a restoration of the individual and the Hebrew nation, did not nullify choice. In a real sense, it heightened the tension between having faith in Yahweh or the placing of one's trust in creation.

Would the people align themselves with the pagan gods of nature? Or with the God who called them to be separate? One-ism or Two-ism?

How will you choose? Whom will you follow?

Israel's Pagan Struggle

"You shall have no other gods before me," reads the first of the Ten Commandments. Attached to this is a charge against making any deity images, for this would be the worship of *created things*.[46] And yet, before the ink was dry – so to speak – and while Moses was in the acknowledged presence of God, the people chose to fashion a golden calf for the purpose of worship.[47]

It has been classically thought that this calf was an image of the bull Apis, the reflection of Ptah, one of the early Egyptian gods.[48] Another possibility is that it was the representation of Baal.[49] Regardless of which religious expression of continuity, it was an act of idolatry: "They have made themselves a molded calf, and worshiped it and sacrificed to it, and said, 'This is your god, O Israel, that brought you out of the land of Egypt!'"[50]

---

45 Psalm 51:1-4a, 16-17.

46 Exodus 20:3-5.

47 Exodus 32.

48 Alfed Edersheim, *Bible History: Old Testament* (Hendrickson Publishers, 1995), p.216. See also G.K. Beale, *We Become What We Worship: A Biblical Theology of Idolatry* (IVP Academic, 2008), pp.84-85.

49 Richard S. Hess, *Israelite Religions: An Archaeological and Biblical Survey* (Baker Academics, 2007), pp.155-157

50 Exodus 32:8.

This action has a *syncretistic* flavor. Syncretism, the amalgamation of divergent religious practices with the belief that Yahweh will be glorified, is alluded to in the declaration that the worship of the calf "is a feast to the LORD."[51] One commentator writes, "It is quite evident that Israel did not mean to forsake Jehovah, but only to serve Him under the symbol of Apis."[52]

But how could God share His glory? This would be a self-contradiction.

Religious idolatry, the worshipful trust in anything other than the true God, shares a commonality with syncretism. One fails to give honor to whom it is due – humanity to our Maker – and the other acts in a way that reduces God's holiness to that which is common. Both imply God is a liar; both implicitly lower His status to that of creation. In reality, Yahweh's position does not change, but a falsehood is perpetrated: a *divine slander*.

Historically the Hebrew people vowed to follow Yahweh, but the appeal of pagan cultures remained strong. King Solomon, the builder of God's temple in Jerusalem, eventually worshipped Astarte and erected images to the pagan deities, Molech and Chemosh.[53] Israel's King Ahab constructed a temple for Baal and instituted its priesthood,[54] prompting a deadly showdown between the prophets of Baal and God's spokesman, Elijah. Standing before the assembled people Elijah famously asked: "How long will you falter between two opinions? If the Lord is God, follow Him; but if Baal, follow him."[55]

King Manasseh converted God's temple to a pagan worship center with an altar built "to all the host of heaven." Manasseh also engaged in witchcraft and mediumship, and "made his son pass through the fire" – a reference to the burning-to-death of one's child as a sacrifice to Molech.[56]

In the Book of Jeremiah we find God issuing a warning: "I will utter My judgments against them concerning all their wickedness, because they have forsaken Me, burned incense to other gods, and worshiped the works of their own hands."[57]

But mercy was still available.

---

[51] Exodus 32:5.

[52] Edersheim, *Bible History*, p.216.

[53] 1 Kings 11:7-10.

[54] 1 Kings 16.

[55] 1 Kings 18:21.

[56] 2 Kings 21. See 2 Chronicles 28 for another example of passing through the fire in the Valley of the Son of Hinnom.

[57] Jeremiah 1:16.

In chapter 2 of Jeremiah, God recounts what the southern kingdom of Judah had done, defiling the land by committing "adultery with stones and trees."[58] God's message to the northern kingdom of Israel was a pleading for repentance,

> "Return, backsliding Israel," says the Lord; "I will not cause My anger to fall on you. For I am merciful," says the Lord; "I will not remain angry forever. Only acknowledge your iniquity, that you have transgressed against the Lord your God, and have scattered your charms to alien deities under every green tree, and you have not obeyed My voice," says the Lord.[59]

Later in that same book, the prophet Jeremiah confronts the Jewish people who had returned to Egypt. His message was not one of interfaith acceptance or syncretistic favor. Instead, a sharp accusation of *spiritual adultery* is leveled. Specifically, the people were venerating the Assyro-Babylonian Mother Goddess, Ishtar, known as the Queen of Heaven. The people's response to the charge of worshiping the Great Mother was open rebellion,

> As for the word that you have spoken to us in the name of the Lord, we will not listen to you! But we will certainly do whatever has gone out of our own mouth, to burn incense to the queen of heaven and pour out drink offerings to her, as we have done...[60]

Although the population had the knowledge of the true God, and Yahweh wished to reason with them – to bring the people back to Himself – they chose idolatry over repentance. Part of God's judgment, not so ironically, was that they would remain mired in their idolatrous situation.[61]

Referring to another passage pertinent to the pagan dilemma, G.K. Beale writes, "Unbelieving Israel is being given what they want. They are punished by the means of their own sin."[62]

A final, brief example of idolatry and syncretism worth noting is the vision seen by Ezekiel of what was transpiring in the House of God – the very

[58] Jeremiah 2:9.

[59] Jeremiah 2:12-13.

[60] Jeremiah 44:16-17a.

[61] Jeremiah 44:25.

[62] G.K. Beale, *We Become What We Worship: A Biblical Theology of Idolatry* (IVP Academic, 2008), p.47.

temple of Yahweh. Looking into its courtyard, Ezekiel witnessed seventy elders offering incense to idols stationed along the walls. At the north gate women were weeping for the Sumerian god Tammuz, the lover of Ishtar who descends into the underworld and returns in the spring with new vegetation.

Then Ezekiel saw greater abominations: "And he brought me to the inner courtyard of the house of Yahweh, and look, at the doorway of the temple of Yahweh, between the portico and the altar, there were about twenty-five men with their backs to the temple of Yahweh and their faces toward the east, and they were bowing down toward the east before the sun. [63]

In Isaiah 45:22, Yahweh makes an appeal from out of His love and truth: "Look to Me, and be saved, all you ends of the earth! For I am God, and there is no other."

Will idols save? No, for they are mute blocks of wood and stone, the work of men's hands, "that which their own fingers have made."[64] This does not mean, however, that idols are without meaning. They are representations of a religious cosmology, and are meant to honor and access the spiritual powers and principality ascribed to that domain.[65]

In other words, pagan spiritual entities are not the products of fable and imagination. Nonhuman intelligences ascribed as "new gods" are recognized in the Bible, being connected to the demonic.[66] Yahweh is contrasted against them: "Who is like You, O LORD, among the gods? Who is like You, glorious in holiness, fearful in praises, doing wonders?"[67]

In the New Testament, the Apostle Paul tells us that Israel's struggle is an example, "written for our admonition."[68] We too must take heed, lest we assimilate the pagan worldview of our surrounding culture.

The choice is ever before us: The personal God who is *Other*, or the impersonal *Oneness* – the idol of creation claiming deification.

---

63 Ezekiel 8:16, *Lexham English Bible*.

64 Isaiah 2:8.

65 For more on idols and idolatry, see Beale, *We Become What We Worship*. Two books exploring the supernatural worldview and the Biblical relationship to Mesopotamian and Egyptian cults, are Michael S. Heiser, *The Unseen Realm: Recovering the Supernatural Worldview of the Bible* (Lexham Press, 2015), and Derek P. Gilbert, *The Great Inception: Satan's PSYOPs from Eden to Armageddon* (Defender Publishing, 2017).

66 Deuteronomy 32:17.

67 Exodus 15:11.

68 1 Corinthians 10:1-14.

Agonizing Love

The desire of Yahweh, the God who transcends all things, is for a restored relationship between His image bearers and Himself. It is a longing that would require God to physically enter creation, the Transcendent taking upon Himself immanence through Jesus Christ: "And the Word became flesh and dwelt among us, and we beheld His glory, the glory as of the only begotten of the Father, full of grace and truth."[69]

I AM moved among humanity as the Son of God.[70] This was Divine Love, for Christ knowingly walked a path of anguish; that He, an Innocent Man, would be tried unjustly and executed on a cross, "for the sins of the whole world."[71] Jesus Christ cruelly tasted what every human was cursed with.

God transcendent, in His love for us, experienced the agony of death.

But the grave could not hold down the Author of Life. Three days after His crucifixion, Christ Jesus demonstrated His victory over all things. He alone could thus claim, "I am the way, the truth, and the life. No one comes to the Father except through Me."[72] Paul's writings to the church in Colosse pressed the case,

> He has delivered us from the power of darkness and conveyed us into the kingdom of the Son of His love, in whom we have redemption through His blood, the forgiveness of sins.
>
> He is the image of the invisible God, the firstborn over all creation. For by Him all things were created that are in heaven and that are on earth, visible and invisible, whether thrones or dominions or principalities or powers. All things were created through Him and for Him. And He is before all things, and in Him all things consist. And He is the head of the body, the church, who is the beginning, the firstborn from the dead, that in all things He may have the preeminence.

---

[69] John 1:14.

[70] Jesus used the I AM phrase in seven declarations, thereby pointing to Himself as the Redeemer – God incarnate. I AM the Bread of Life – John 6:35; I AM the Light of the World – John 8:12; I AM the Door – John 10:7; I AM the Good Shepherd – John 10:11; I AM the Resurrection and the Life – John 11:25; I AM the Way, the Truth and the Life – John 14:6; I AM the True Vine – John 15:1.

[71] 1 John 2:2, *Lexham English Bible*.

[72] John 14:6.

> For it pleased the Father that in Him all the fullness should dwell, and by Him to reconcile all things to Himself, by Him, whether things on earth or things in heaven, having made peace through the blood of His cross. [73]

The news of Jesus Christ as the *risen* and *exclusive Savior* quickly spread from Jerusalem, penetrating hearts, and changing lives. The dominant socio-political setting, however, was not favorable to the Christian message.

Rome was the political powerhouse, and the socio-religious situation was a legally accepted environment of Greco-Roman sects, embracing a range of domestic and foreign deities.[74] Temples to the divinities were not only places of veneration but also hubs of economic activity; cultural and political elites were inseparably linked to the religious milieu. In one's own household, ethnicity was garbed in ancestral gods and mystical lineages, adding a familial dynamic to the spiritual world. Mystery schools and oracles, Egyptian and Mithraic influences, public festivals to honor the gods, and imperial cults and Emperor worship – all were part of the mix. Spiritual exports and imports ebbed and flowed across the Empire, re-transmitting cultic traditions and Roman ideals. Civic pragmatism accompanied religious adaptation.[75]

To be a follower of Jesus Christ without giving fidelity to the accepted religious order was considered disruptive to the greater community. Viewed by Roman authorities with mistrust and charged as superstitious, early Christians lived in a vortex of suspicion, contempt, and hostility. Professor Larry W. Hurtado tells of the testing endured by believers: "In addition to suffering 'mockery of ever sort,' they were torn apart by dogs, or nailed to crosses, or set afire to serve as human torches for Nero's nighttime spectacle."[76]

Pliny the Younger, a Roman magistrate, explained in a letter to Emperor Trajan how he handled Christians: They were to renounce Christ by paying homage to the effigies of the gods and offer wine and incense to the image

---

[73] Colossians 1:13-20.

[74] A short survey of the religious environment is found in chapter 3 of *A History of Pagan Europe*, by Prudence Jones and Nigel Pennick (Routledge, 1995). For more information on the context of cultic movements in Biblical times, see Jack Finegan, *Myth and Mystery: An Introduction to the Pagan Religions of the Biblical World* (Baker Book House, 1989).

[75] For an important discussion of this topic, see Larry W. Hurtado, *Destroyer of the gods: Early Christian Distinctiveness in the Roman World* (Baylor University Press, 2016).

[76] Hurtado, *Destroyer of the gods*, p.21.

of the Emperor, *or be executed*. If they were Roman citizens, however, he would foreword the case to Rome.[77]

Pliny was disturbed by the growing number of people choosing to follow Jesus Christ: "Nor are cities only permeated by the contagion of this superstition, but villages and country parts as well; yet it seems possible to stop it and cure it." Temple economies – which directly supported industries and markets – were being negatively impacted, he inferred.[78] The Christian faith was disrupting the social, religious, and economic sensibilities of the polis.

Christ followers no longer fit within Rome's world order. They were rebels, and, as noted by Christian philosopher Francis A. Schaeffer, the implications were far-reaching and deadly,

> We may express the nature of their rebellion in two ways... First, we can say they worshiped Jesus as God and they worshiped the infinite-personal God only. The Caesars would not tolerate this worshiping of the one God *only*. It was counted as treason. Thus their worship became a special threat to the unity of the state... If they had worshiped Jesus *and* Caesar, they would have gone unharmed, but they rejected all forms of syncretism. They worshiped the God who had revealed himself in the Old Testament, through Christ, and in the New Testament which had gradually been written. And they worshiped him as the *only* God. They allowed no mixture: All other Gods were seen as false gods.
>
> We can also express in a second way why the Christians were killed: No totalitarian authority nor authoritarian state can tolerate those who have an absolute by which to judge that state and its actions. The Christians had that absolute in God's revelation. Because the Christians had an absolute, universal standard by which to judge not only personal morals but the state, they were counted as enemies of totalitarian Rome and were thrown to the beasts.[79]

Persecution may devastate the faithful, *but it does not destroy hope*.

---

[77] *The Letters of the Younger Pliny* (Trübner & Company, 1879 – translated by John D. Lewis), 10.96; p.378.

[78] Ibid, p.379.

[79] Francis A. Schaeffer, *How Then Should We Live? The Rise and Decline of Western Thought and Culture* (Fleming H. Revell Company, 1976), pp.24-26, italics in original.

Not the Same

Metaphysical revelations abound.

When considering Islam,[80] we discover that Muhammad's revelation came through a supernatural being, a visiting entity *claiming* to be the Angel Gabriel.[81] In the Islamic faith, Allah is monotheistic, but unlike Yahweh who secures redemption and invites us into a personal relationship with Himself, Allah is portrayed as distant, impersonal, and unknowable. The Islamic *will* nevertheless, is made plain: Muslims are required to follow the Five Pillars,[82] to endeavor in the cause of Allah and do good works,[83] and to wage in struggle.[84] But salvation *is not secure*, for Allah's acceptance is arbitrary.

While Islam proclaims God as separate, it demands a One-ist approach to redemption: *Man striving for acceptability*. This is not a relationship wherein Allah *first* loved humanity regardless of our sinful state, but one in which Allah extends conditional love *only* once the Muslim demonstrates loving obedience. In the Koran we read,

> Say: "If ye do love Allah, follow me: Allah will love you and forgive you your sins: for Allah is Oft-Forgiving, Most Merciful." Say: "Obey Allah and His Messenger": but if they turn back, Allah loveth not those who reject Faith.[85]

---

[80] In working through this small section, sources consulted included, Mohammed Marmaduke Pickthall, *The Meaning of the Glorious Koran* (Mentor Books, 1953/1963); Abdullah Yusuf Ali, *The Meaning of the Illustrious Qur'an* (Al Hasanat Books, 2015); Ulfat Aziz-us-samad, *Islam and Christianity* (International Islamic Federation of Student Organizations); Usama K. Dakdok, *The Generous Quran: An Accurate, Modern English Translation of the Qur'an, Islam's Holiest Book* (Usama Dakdok Publishing, 2009); Don Richardson, *Secrets of the Koran: Revealing Insights into Islam's Holy Book* (Regal, 2003); and Serge Trifkovic, *The Sword of the Prophet: Islam – History, Theology, Impact on the World* (Regina Orthodox Press, 2002).

[81] Mohammed Marmaduke Pickthall, "Introduction" *The Meaning of the Glorious Koran* (Mentor Books, 1953/1963), p.x.

[82] The Five Pillars: 1) Declaration of Faith – "there is no god but Allah, and Muhammad is the messenger of Allah." 2) Prayers, five times a day, toward Mecca. 3) Giving money to charity, "almsgiving," or *Zakat*. 4) Fasting during the month of Ramadan. 5) *Hajj*, the pilgrimage to Mecca.

[83] Abdullah Yusuf Ali, *The Meaning of the Illustrious Qur'an* (Al Hasanat Books, 2015), 2:195.

[84] Ibid., 4:74-77.

[85] Ibid, 3:31-32.

The God of the Bible clearly reveals something entirely different: "But God demonstrates His own love toward us, in that while were still sinners, Christ died for us."[86] And in 1 John 4:19 we read, "We love Him because He first loved us." Yes, the God of the Bible desires our love and obedience, but in true love He *first* reached to us – *the sinner, the undeserving*.

The Koran and the Bible are in contradiction.[87]

And when considered in the light of Sufism, the aesthetic rebellion of mystical Islam, we encounter an undeniable One-ism. So much so, that Sufism could be called "Vedanta in Muslim Dress."[88] As said in the Sufi text, *The Conference of the Birds*, "When I escape the Self I will arise and be as God… To Nothingness and to Eternity."[89] Another Sufi mystic writes, "We must be as nothing, 'I am not.' Then we are in the state of God-Man, Man-God."[90]

Newer revelations proliferate within religious thought. Emerging from an Islamic context, the Bahá'í movement claimed fresh transmissions from God, including visions of the personification known as the Maiden of Heaven: messages of oneness and world unity poured from the new faith. The entity known as Moroni provided the source inspiration for the *Book of Mormon*, resulting in Joseph Smith's teaching that we can become God.[91] A revelation came to Levi H. Dowling, who authored an alternative scripture, *The Aquarian Gospel*: "all things are God; all things are one."[92]

Hinduism, Sikhism, ancient Pagan beliefs, the New Age, and secular faiths such as Zen Buddhism and Humanism; the world is a tapestry of One-ist considerations. Yet the Judeo-Christian worldview is in a different classification.

Here is the point: The distinct and holy God of the Bible – and His message of exclusive redemption – can never be subsumed into *any* One-ist form.

---

86 Romans 5:8.

87 For comparison, see Usama Dakdok, *The Generous Quran: An Accurate, Modern English Translation of the Qur'an, Islam's Holiest Book* (Usama Dakdok Publishing, 2009).

88 See R.C. Zaehner, *Hindu and Muslim Mysticism* (Schocken Books, 1969), chapter 5. For a detailed discussion on Sufism, see Carl We. Ernst, *Sufism: An Introduction to the Mystical Tradition of Islam* (Shambhala, 2011).

89 Farid ud-Din Attar, *The Conference of the Birds* (Penguin Books, 1984), p.205.

90 Bawa Muhaiyaddeen, *Who Is God?* (The Bawa Muhaiyaddeen Fellowship, 2011), p.2.

91 See *Teachings of the Presidents of the Church: Joseph Smith* (The Church of Jesus Christ of Latter-day Saints, 2007), pp.221-222.

92 Levi H. Dowling, *The Aquarian Gospel of Jesus the Christ* (De Vorss & Company, 1907/1982), chapter 28:4b.

Christianity *in its essence* is incapable of submitting to a human-based system of works salvation,[93] such as Islam, or to any claim of God-Human-Nature holism. The very fact that a belief exists which is antithetical to Oneness, and not just opposed it, but standing outside of its claims in every way, is an irreconcilable problem for One-ism. Even if every person loyal to the exclusive Messiah were to disappear, the reality of Otherness would not change.

Otherness can not and will never be absorbed into Oneness.

After Christ's resurrection, faith in the Redeemer rippled outward from Jerusalem, spreading to Judea and Samaria, and going "to the ends of the earth."[94] Unlike Judaism from which it was born, Christianity was not tied to a national identity: Jews became followers of Jesus Christ, as did Greeks and Romans and others. Ancestral, ethnic, and national boundaries were not barriers to the faith. Social categories, too, were radically breached. Salvation was open to princes and paupers, men and women, soldiers and scholars and slaves. God's redemption would be *inclusive* and *exclusive*; inclusive in that He desires "all people to be saved and to come to a knowledge of the truth,"[95] exclusive in that salvation can only be found in Jesus Christ.

Paul beautifully articulated the depth of God's amazing love,

> For I am persuaded that neither death nor life, nor angels nor principalities nor powers, nor things present nor things to come, nor height nor depth, nor any other created thing, shall be able to separate us from the love of God which is in Christ Jesus our Lord.[96]

Christians also lived differently compared to the Roman social milieu. [97]

New patterns of personal and group behavior were evident. Much of Paul's teachings to the early church included exhortations to live within a moral framework distinct, in many ways, from the prevailing pagan norms. Holi-

---

93 This is not to say that works-based systems are detached from the Christian milieu, far from it. The history of the faith is littered with man-based expectations, added requirements, customs, and the like. These attachments have often been part of the traditions of various church groups, or they come-and-go with certain teachings, yet the core of the faith remains distinct and set apart from systems of human-derived salvation.

94 Acts 1:8.

95 1 Timothy 2:3, *Lexham English Bible*.

96 Romans 8:38-39.

97 For a discussion of Christian behavior in the Roman era, including similarities and points of divergence, see Hurtado, *Destroyer of the gods*, chapter 5.

ness was to be cultivated in light of redemption. The New Testament writer, James – likely a brother to Jesus[98] – strongly reinforced doing good works in correlation to the faith. Christians, being renewed in mind and spirit, were to reflect this change in practical measures. Followers of Christ are not to be *hearers of the word only*, but in love, to be "doers of the word."[99]

As Christ loved us first, so too we are to love God and others. This comes through in the Greatest Commandment, given by Jesus Himself,

> 'You shall love the Lord your God with all your heart, with all your soul, and with all your mind.' This is the first and great commandment. And the second is like it: 'You shall love your neighbor as yourself.' On these two commandments hang all the Law and the Prophets.[100]

Feeding the hungry, assisting orphans and widows, helping the poor, bringing comfort to the sick, visiting prisoners, showing love and compassion to those who grieve; the Christian faith, an inward change of the heart and mind, spilled over into practical deeds. It still does.

In his book, *How Christianity Made the Modern World*, Paul Backholer reminds us of the abiding yet seldom considered power of transformation as expressed through the Christian worldview,

> In history, Bible-believing Christians have only been a small proportion of the world population, yet they are credited with an overwhelming number of reforms which have shaped the lives of billions of people on the planet! The presumption based upon the teachings of Christ, that every human being is created equal in God's image has led evangelical Christianity to become a transforming force around the world. The recognition and safeguarding of human rights in Western law is a theme which was often birthed out of Christians reading the Holy Bible, and applying it to the world that they lived in.[101]

---

[98] Douglas J. Moo, *The Letter of James: An Introduction and Commentary* (Inter-Varsity Press, 1985), p.20.

[99] James 1:22.

[100] Matthew 22:37-40.

[101] Paul Backholer, *How Christianity Made the Modern World* (ByFaith Media, 2017, third edition), p.19.

Christianity also opened new ideas of political liberty and human flourishing. Social sciences professor, Rodney Stark, writes thus,

> While the classical world did provide examples of democracy, these were not rooted in any general assumptions concerning equality beyond an equality of the elite. Even when they were ruled by elected bodies, the various Greek city-states and Rome were sustained by huge numbers of slaves. And just as it was Christianity that eliminated the institution of slavery inherited from Greece and Rome, so too does Western democracy owe its essential intellectual origins and legitimacy to Christian ideals, not to any Greco-roman legacy. It all began with the New Testament.[102]

"In an extremely status-conscious Roman world," Stark reminds us, "early Christians strove to embrace a universalistic conception of humanity."[103]

Religious historian, Thomas Cahill, connects the Jewish worldview – which informed the Christian mind and Western culture – to contemporary themes of justice and human worth,

> "Unbelievers might wish to stop for a moment and consider how completely God – this Jewish God of justice and compassion – undergirds all our values and that it is just possible that human effort without this God is doomed to certain failure."[104]

The Judeo-Christian presupposition birthed the Western model of law and judicial order. It provided the foundation for our modern concept of science, even as Spinoza's metaphysics sparked a revolution in naturalistic thinking. Christian concern was the basis for public and secondary education, hospitals, and disaster relief. The importance of the individual within the group context was largely framed through a Judeo-Christian lens.[105]

---

[102] Rodney Stark, *The Victory of Reason: How Christianity Led to Freedom, Capitalism, and Western Success* (Random House, 2005), p.76.

[103] Ibid., p.77.

[104] Thomas Cahill, *The Gift of the Jews: How a Tribe of Desert Nomads Changed the Way Everyone Thinks and Feels* (Nan A. Talese/Doubleday, 1998), p.251.

[105] For more on Judeo-Christian influences upon the Western world, see Alvin J. Schmidt, *How Christianity Changed the World* (Zondervan, 2004); Rodney Stark, *The Victory of Reason* (Random House, 2005); Paul Backholer, *How Christianity Made the Modern World* (ByFaith Media, 2017, third edition); Thomas Cahill, *The Gift of the Jews* (Nan A.

Cahill brings the individual back to the Hebrew experience,

> The *individual* is responsible, not the tribe. As with the spiritualization of the journey and of religious obligation, the idea of the individual – the single spirit – begins to take hold, an idea that makes its way with great difficulty into the world of groups, tribes, and nations, in which all identity and validation comes from solidarity with a larger entity.[106]

Christian community, too, was and remains an important aspect.

Local church fellowship provides opportunities for teaching, worship and prayer, encouragement, exhortation and admonition, and loving compassion. Unity in faith through Jesus Christ is the bedrock; a unity in spirit, bonded in love. Moreover, within the church – the body of believers – individuals join in bringing their spiritual gifts into service. The worth of the person is not dependent on the group, but the community is important in that each believer participates in building up the faithful, together,

> There are diversities of gifts, but the same Spirit. There are differences of ministries, but the same Lord. And there are diversities of activities, but it is the same God who works all in all. But the manifestation of the Spirit is given to each one for the profit of all.[107]

The local church, along with the individual believer, is also a reflection of the larger body – a family that transcends generations and boundaries. Whether the believer is alone or in a crowd, alive or passed, there is the understanding that God's Spirit keeps us in His providence. In Christ we are secure.

From generation to generation, the Christian message offers real transformation of the soul – from sin to salvation, from Selfism to serving others in a newness of love, purpose, and meaning. The Christian message offers hope; not in the illusion of Oneness with its trust in Self and nothing, but in the promises of Him who is Other and Faithful.

For millions of believers, this trust in Jesus Christ is a source of comfort and strength, even in times of sorrow.

Talese/Doubleday, 1998); and Larry Siedentop, *Inventing the Individual: The Origins of Western Liberalism* (The Belknap Press of Harvard University Press, 2014).

[106] Cahill, *The Gift of the Jews*, p.230, italics in original.

[107] 1 Corinthians 12:4-7.

River of Tears

On the evening of August 8, 1995, a pickup truck lost control as it approached a wooden bridge less than a mile from my parent's farm. It had rained late in the afternoon, and the dirt road was slick. Something happened right before the river crossing and the truck kicked sideways onto the bridge, impacting the wooden guardrail.

Who knows how long the old rail planking had been there? It crumbled and broke and shattered in an instant, and the truck tumbled into the river below, landing upside down.

The driver, a young man named Jeff, miraculously survived the accident. The passenger did not. That day Jeff began a new journey in the metaphorical valley of grief, walking, side-by-side, with the Teichrib family. The passenger was my youngest brother.

Bevan was 17 years old.

An hour or so before the tragedy, my wife and I, with our two-month old son, had been at the farm celebrating Jeff's birthday with a family supper. As per the norm, there was a lot of talk and laughter. It was a good day.

After the meal, Jeff and Bevan decided to go see a movie, which meant driving 50 miles to a small city. It was sometime after they left when we received a disturbing phone call; a truck was in the river, and rescue vehicles were on the scene. In this part of the country neighbors are not strangers, so it was very likely someone we knew was in trouble. Dad and I scrambled into his truck and headed for the bridge. A police roadblock at the top of the valley hill, however, prevented us from going further. We sat on the road, watching and wondering, until an officer – prompted by a fireman – reluctantly told us who had been pulled out of the water. The ambulance had already taken them both, we were told.

Racing to the farm we picked up my mother, leaving Leanne to look after the baby – not an ideal situation given the circumstances – and we rushed to the hospital. When we arrived, the paramedics and a few of the firemen, people we know personally, lined the hallway as we walked in. Their heads were bowed in pain and silence.

After seeing the body, making agonizing phone calls, and visiting Jeff in his room, we quietly returned to the farm. The yard was filled with vehicles. News of the death had spread like a prairie fire, and family, friends, and neighbors had flocked to my parent's place.

Needing to clear my head, I hopped on Bevan's motorcycle and rode to the bridge. The air was cool in the dusk, and the light of the near-full moon illuminated the damaged structure. The truck had been pulled out and towed away hours ago, and the river had returned to its tranquil state.

Somebody else was at the crash scene. A fellow I knew from a nearby town was on the bridge, curious about the accident.

"How are you doing, Carl?"

"Not good," I responded factually. "But God will get us through this."

And He did.

Was it difficult? That summer I cried a river of tears. We all did.

Was God our crutch? Yes, and I am so thankful! Although we grieved, it was never without hope.

Life can be very testing. My mother, a remarkable woman of wisdom and courage, battled cancer three times before it took her at the age of 67. My father, a man of conviction and understanding, comes from a farming era when brute strength and sheer toughness was as necessary as food. The first year my parents were married, Dad was in an airplane crash that killed his brother; the physical damage caused by this drop-from-the-sky, compounded with a long list of farm and machinery accidents, has taken a heavy toll. I have never known my father to be without pain.

Life can be trying and hard and short. Every person reading this book will have a story of trials and troubles. No one has a monopoly on suffering, nor is suffering an argument for the non-existence of God. Jesus Himself intimately knew betrayal, pain, suffering, and the sharpness of death: He felt our plight. And if we are honest with ourselves, we too know the sting is never far away. Pain and mortality *are not illusions*. Goodness and righteousness, beauty and kindness, mercy and grace – these, too, are real and marvelous.

Sin is not an illusion either, and thankfully, neither is *forgiveness*.

Leading up to His own execution, Jesus Christ encouraged His disciples with these words,

> These things I have spoken to you, that in Me you may have peace. In the world you will have tribulation; but be of good cheer. I have overcome the world.[108]

Three days after his crucifixion, Christ proved His power over death.

---

[108] John 16:33.

Unlike Oneness with its blending away of relationships and its submergence of love into a nameless void, the resurrection of Christ demonstrated the eternal, relational character of the Godhead:

1. The Spirit raised Christ from the dead: "But if the Spirit of Him who raised Jesus from the dead dwells in you, He who raised Christ from the dead will also give life to your mortal bodies through His Spirit who dwells in you."[109]
2. Jesus raised Himself: "Therefore My Father loves Me, because I lay down My life that I may take it again. No one takes it from Me, but I lay it down of Myself. I have the power to lay it down, and I have power to take it again. This command I have received from My Father."[110]
3. God the Father raised Jesus Christ: "having loosed the pains of death, because it was not possible that He should be held by it,."[111] And, "God both raised up the Lord and will also raise us up by His power."[112]

In this act of overcoming the grave, the hope of humanity was placed on His shoulders alone.

I am reminded of Job, the Old Testament figure who lost his family, possessions, and health. Wracked with grief and misery, the likes of which are beyond my comprehension, Job nevertheless recognized that God's ultimate plan is bigger than our temporary sufferings, no matter how severe. Job knew a resurrection was on the horizon, not fashioned by Man's hands, but completed through God's *living* Messiah.

Job's future is our future for those who hope and trust in the Savior,

> For I know that my Redeemer lives,
> And He shall stand at last on the earth;
> And after my skin is destroyed, this I know,
> That in my flesh I shall see God,
> Whom I shall see for myself,
> And my eyes shall behold, and not another.
> How my heart yearns within me![113]

---

[109] Romans 8:11.
[110] John 10:17-18.
[111] Acts 2:24
[112] 1 Corinthians 6:14.
[113] Job 19:25-27.

Death could not hold Jesus Christ. How would it? *For Christ is the Author of Life*. And in His resurrection, a foretaste is given to those who hope in Him as Redeemer: "In Him was life, and the life was the light of men."[114]

Will you put your hope in nature? In humanism? In the illusion of Oneness? Or will you trust Jesus Christ, in whom "all things were made"?[115]

Paul, "a bondservant of Jesus Christ,"[116] put it simply but elegantly,

> That if you confess with your mouth the Lord Jesus and believe in your heart that God raised Him from the dead, you will be saved. For with the heart one believes unto righteousness, and with the mouth confession is made unto salvation. For the Scripture says, '*Whoever believes on Him will not be put to shame*.' For there is no distinction between Jew and Greek, for the same Lord over all is rich to all who call upon Him. For '*whoever calls on the name of the Lord shall be saved*.'[117]

Yes, we will all answer – one way or another – the life-or-death question asked by Jesus the Messiah,

> I am the resurrection and the life. He who believes in Me, though he may die, he shall live. And whoever lives and believes in Me shall never die. Do you believe this?[118]

---

[114] John 1:4.
[115] John 1:3.
[116] Romans 1:1.
[117] Romans 10:9-13, italics in original.
[118] John 11:25-26.

Chapter 9

Circle of Gods

> When that day comes I shall look upon you all, brothers and sisters, as workers for the Light and engage you in the transforming of our world… Prepare to see yourselves as Gods. – Maitreya.[1]

> The complete man, who has experienced and mastered all things, has vanquished Nature and mounted higher than the heavens. He has reached the centre where man becomes God. The achievement of this is the Great Work. – Richard Cavendish.[2]

"Everybody stand up."

Chairs shuffled as the crowded conference room came alive. "Now take a hand and form a circle," explained our afternoon speaker. Quickly I scanned for an exit, but a hand grabbed mine and pulled me to the edge of the row. Another hand connected. Soon a chain formed, and I was a link.

A respected Broadway vocalist stepped into our giant ring. Earlier in the day our paths crossed, and her eyes twinkled in a smile. Now, standing before us with confidence and poise, she poured out the richness of her voice. Flowing into every corner of the room she melodically imparting well-known themes from the Gospel of John and the Book of Revelation: "I am the Alpha and Omega, the First and the Last… I am the Word of God… I am the King of Kings and Lord of Lords… I am that I am."[3]

Her last note faded into a reverential hush, a solemn silence. The feeling of being in a place of worship was palpable, and the song could have been

1 *Messages from Maitreya the Christ,* Vol.1., as channeled to Benjamin Crème (Tara Press, 1980), p.76. Maitreya is considered a bodhisattva – a Perfected Man on the Buddhist path, an Ascended Master – and is claimed by occultists to be the coming "World Teacher."

2 Richard Cavendish, *The Black Arts* (G.P. Putnam's Sons, 1967), p.6.

3 All quotes from the SUN conference come from my notes and recordings.

performed in a church service. Heads were respectfully bowed and most eyes were closed in profound introspection. Some in the group would have called this a pause in our collective soul.

Breaking the moment, our speaker – now standing in the center – calmly acknowledged the divinity that encircled him: "The Christ within me salutes, honors, and respects the Christ within each and everyone of you."

Hands dropped as men and women, old and young, turned and bowed with veneration to one another. Each was a divine being. I stood statue-still, encircled by mutually affirming "gods and goddess." Then, like everyone else in the room, I returned to my seat.

It was 1999, and humanity was about to enter a new epoch. Looking to the immediate future, this one-day event, hosted by Spiritual Unity of Nations (SUN),[4] was titled *1999: Year of the Covenant*.[5] Participants from across the US Midwest had gathered to assist in the birthing of a new age in conscious evolution. The dawning of Aquarius, we were told, was at hand.

John Davis, Director of SUN, was there to inspire us with visions of millennial mysticism. Earlier he had published the following,

> Each person is in essence a nation. Living many past lives in various nations on Earth, within us we express the vision of unity... 1999 is truly a year to communicate with the inner planes of consciousness to assist with the higher mental healing of the nations.[6]

Anticipation was in the air, for 1999 was a bridge between the old era and an entirely new millennium. Symbolically we would be merging into a collective whole. The age of *Revelation* was upon us.

To help understand the significance of the transition period, Davis had brought copies of his book, *Revelation For Our Time*. Re-interpreting the New Testament's *Revelation* using the occult technique of numerology, a great secret had supposedly been uncovered: "Revelation has elements of Buddha, the Great Pyramid, and King Arthur within its vibration."[7]

---

4 Spiritual Unity of Nations is the offspring of Coptic Fellowship International, a Michigan headquartered learning center for esoteric/occult teachings.

5 This conference was held in Fort Wayne, Indiana, on July 10, 1999.

6 "1999: What is the Significance of the Year 1999?" *SUN UP Newsletter*, Spiritual Unity of Nations, May 11, 1999, p.1-2.

7 John Davis, *Revelation For Our Time: A New Paradigm for the Next Century* (Spiritual Unity of Nations Publishing, 1998), p.13.

His calculations produced a story of Re-enchantment: The return of the divine feminine to a restored balance in nature; the spiritual connection of all within a Planetary Logos; and the evolution of humanity into the Group Avatar – the "Second Coming," a Messiah of our collective making.

Our task would be to shed the old traditions and beliefs associated with separation and fear. Hence, Davis turned the "Anti-Christ" of *Revelation* into a positive group experience, a foreshadowing "*ante*-Christ," in which we participate as heralds of the Universal Awakening.[8] In his numerology, the "Mark of the Beast," 666, turned into a symbol for the responsibility we have as individuals working for planetary oneness.[9]

"World peace can prevail," promised Davis, "as we replace misguided ideas such as the existence of an AntiChrist with the positive vibrations of thoughts of world peace, world sharing and world unity."[10]

Davis predicated a transformation into a new spiritual season,

> We belong to a new humanity born again beyond personality, beyond soul, born again to a Universal Awareness. We should not be concerned with creating a new religion. The new message is one of unity, planetary sister/brotherhood and opportunity for all. We are presently in the transition period between two dispensations. We are at the end of the old Piscean age and not quite ready for the new energies of the Aquarian.[11]

Although Davis wrote the above in his re-interpretation of *Revelation*, this belief nevertheless pulsed as the heartbeat of our conference.

It was an interesting day.

Egyptologist Ahmed Fayed, who had been a personal guide to Shirley MacLaine, Henry Kissinger, Frank Sinatra, Princess Diana and Elizabeth Taylor, talked about the mystical importance of the Year 2000 and the "capstone ceremony" being planned for the Great Pyramid in Egypt.[12]

---

8 Ibid., pp.81-85.

9 Ibid., pp.82-83.

10 Ibid., p.81.

11 Ibid., p.115.

12 The Pyramid Millennium Concert, a music and light-show extravaganza with strong ritualistic overtones, was to culminate in a "capstone ceremony." At midnight, a golden capstone was to be lowered by helicopter onto the top of the Great Pyramid. For some reason this part of the celebration was cancelled.

Energy healer Roger Stair read from the "angelic-inspired" *Aquarian Gospel of Jesus the Christ*.[13] "My personal truth," Stair explained after the reading, "is as changing as my convictions."

I was given a flyer for The Light Party, a "synthesis of the Republican, Democratic, Libertarian, and Green Parities."[14] We had discussions on how the New Age would challenge politics and religion. Social norms and values, it was agreed, will be entering a time of great flux.

In the afternoon an artistic throne was set before us. Constructed of white plaster over a high-backed chair and decoratively arranged, this, we were told, was the result of a channeling session through which the artist received a vision of the "Mercy Seat of the Ark of the Covenant." However, it needed color. We were thus encouraged to quiet ourselves, close our eyes and free our minds, and open a space to make contact with higher intelligences. Many entered a state conducive for channeling, mentally linking themselves with the directed thoughts of otherworldly entities. After a period of silence, eyes opened and people expressed the color visions they had seen. The artist could now complete her work, and the piece could be moved to its new home – some corporation office, we were not told which.

Later, a Reiki Master who employs hypnotherapy lectured on the subject, "From Duality to the Beatitudes." Separateness and its associated guilt tendencies must give way to an era of World Service. Assisting in this break from the old mind to the new thinking, we were led through a ritualistic release of guilt. It started with a collective chanting of the Hindu AUM.[15] Beginning in a low note and slow rhythm, the mystical sound rose and fell in intensity, and with every breath and resonance the chanters moved deeper into themselves. It felt like I was watching an exercise in mass hypnosis.

Expanding and filling the conference room, the sound finished itself in a peaked crescendo. The leader, like other attendees, was visibly spent in the ecstasy of the moment. Breathlessly she said, "let us pray."

In unison the many voices invocated: "Our Father, which art in heaven, Hallowed be thy Name, Thy Kingdom come..."

It was all very spiritual.

---

[13] This text, released in 1907, was channeled to Levi H. Dowling from an "angelic being."

[14] From a handout given at the SUN 1999 event, *The Light Party*. This strange political aspiration was the brainchild of Da Vid, director of The Global Peace Foundation.

[15] Also spelled as Om, a sound that is said to embody the entire cosmos.

The Genesis of Human Deity

What I had witnessed was a reminder of something very ancient: The Genesis account of the "Fall of Man," the *general* fall instigating our ongoing "divine rebellion" and predicating all other falls – individual and collective.[16]

In Genesis 2 we read that the first human couple, Adam and Eve, had an intimate relationship with their Creator. God directly interacted with them, and even more, provided for their physical needs in a place specifically prepared, the Garden of Eden. Purpose, meaning, rest and good pleasure were wrapped in this relational paradigm set in a distinct location. Yet an option was open for the couple to step outside of this design, for as God is the author of love, choice is required if love is to exist. Moreover, choice infers the use of *will*, a requirement if we are to be God's representatives on Earth.

Evangelist Les Woodson offers this insight,

> If man were to share the Creator's likeness, he must be allowed the use of his will. Where there is no choice, will is not only superfluous but nonexistent. Only in the midst of creative tension which provides at least one option can man be other than a non-choosing beast. The continual conflict made possible by the presence of a choice between two alternatives is an essential ingredient in responsible living.[17]

Enter the Tree of the Knowledge of Good and Evil.

---

[16] It can be argued that Genesis 1-11 introduces all evils into the world, showing us the consequences of our continual sin experience: Genesis 3 introduces the base rebellion of Mankind against God's will and order, resulting in death and pain for all. This can be called a *general fall* for it begins the cycle of sin. Genesis 4 showcases moral failure with envy culminating in the murder of Abel. We also see rebellion against God's judgment in Cain's construction of a settlement. Genesis 6 continues this moral theme with the acknowledgment that men's thoughts were continually evil. The passage also introduces a supernatural element, the participation of created, celestial beings in sinful acts. 2 Peter 2:1-10 and Jude 6-7 gives us insight into this situation. Genesis 9 reveals moral failing again, this time pertaining to Noah – demonstrating the impossibility of righteous living and the continuation of sin even after the Flood judgment. And Genesis 11 presents the case for a collective and peak falling away, resulting in the division of nations and God's choice to begin working through one primary people group – the family of Jacob – while allowing others to follow foreign gods (see Deuteronomy 32 for more information).

[17] Les Woodson, *The Beginning: Genesis* (Victor Books, 1974), p.27.

The choice in Genesis 2 is clear: Partake of the fruit of the Tree, or obey God and abstain. With this option comes a strong warning. If you eat of the tree, you will die. The rationality for this seemingly harsh consequence has a logical consideration. As God is Creator and therefore legal holder of life, to intentionally choose a path other than His is to enter the way of death. The human couple understood this *intellectually* but not *experientially*.

In Genesis 3 humanity comes face-to-face with a tempter, variously called Satan or the Devil. Although unnamed in Genesis, we find a correlation in Revelation 12:9 where he is referred to as the "great dragon, that serpent of old, called the Devil and Satan, who deceives the whole world." We also see this entity interacting in the court of God as our *accuser*.[18] While artistic interpretations of this adversary span the gamut from a medieval-inspired monster to a comic-book figure with horns to a well-dressed businessman, 2 Corinthians 11:14 tells us he comes as an "angel of light." In fact, the Hebrew word given in Genesis 3:1 for *serpent* refers to something – or someone – as *luminous* and *shining*.[19]It can also infer *divination*, the impartation of knowledge through a supernatural means.[20]

We further read in Genesis 3:1 that this entity, who some refer to as Lucifer, is *subtle*. The root word used in this passage implies a remarkable intelligence, the application and delivery of knowledge in a tactical fashion: *Crafty*. Discretion and discernment can be linked, as in Proverbs 13:16 where the root is used for prudent: "Every *prudent* man acts with knowledge, but a fool lays open his folly." It is used in Job 5:12 this way: "He frustrates the devices of the *crafty*, so that their hands cannot carry out their plans."

The one before Eve is shrewd and deliberate, showing an exceptional understanding of the human propensity to rationalize. The serpentine-dragon imagery is a powerful expression of his very potent nature. In the Garden he comes to dialogue, to question and test, and to masterfully engage in the salesmanship of self-justification.

It started with a simple yet suggestive question: "Has God indeed said, 'You shall not eat of every tree of the garden'?" The query introduced doubt.

---

[18] Job 1.

[19] See Michael S. Heiser, *The Unseen Realm: Recovering the Supernatural Worldview of the Bible* (Lexham Press, 2015), p.87-88. See also, Victor P. Hamilton, *Handbook on the Pentateuch* (Baker Book House, 1982), pp.42-43.

[20] Heiser, *The Unseen Realm*, p.87. See also Hamilton, *Handbook on the Pentateuch*, p.43.

Eve responded by confirming God's admonition, but a seed had been planted in her mind.

"You will not surely die," was the response given to Eve. "For God knows that in the day you eat of it your eyes will be opened, and you will be like God, knowing good and evil."

The benefits of partaking appeared to surpass the costs: Life would go on, wisdom was to be granted, and the human status would be elevated. This "knowledge," allowing one to apparently become as Yahweh Himself, would achieve a *greater good*. Enlightenment was before them. Following the angelic advice, they engaged in the act of taking and eating, the first *technique* of human-proclaimed self-divinity.

In so doing, they discovered the tempter had wiled them with a *half-truth*. Immortality vanished and the idea of becoming "as God" proved illusionary. Of course, the truth-part was we experientially and spiritually entered the realm of the "knowledge of good and evil." We had now tasted its capability, but as the Garden incident demonstrated and human history shows, we were personally and collectively unable to control its capacity. *It controls us*.

Ecclesiastes 7:20 is a sobering reminder: "For there is not a just man on earth who does good and does not sin." Romans 3:23 says something similar: "For all have sinned and fall short of the glory of God."

True words.

While acts of goodness are open to us, we have nevertheless been plagued by "divine nightmares" – kings and powers and nations "playing God" against one another. Far more mundane but just as eternally damning is the fact that each of us, myself included, has an inner nature in opposition to the true God. We all pulse with the heartbeat of the Fall.

What the "knowledge of good and evil" is has long been debated in theological circles, although the core meaning may rest on something very basic: To experience autonomy without reverence to God, and with it the ability to act upon good *and* evil. Note that Adam and Eve did not lack intellectual aptitude prior to eating the fruit, for they were making knowledgeable choices (Genesis 2:15-25). Moreover, Eve demonstrated understanding prior to intentionally disobeying God's directive (Genesis 3:2-3). Thus, their pre-fall existence was not one of animal-like "ignorant bliss," nor were they innocent of sexual relations as some have suggested, for becoming "one flesh" was instituted in Genesis 1:28 and 2:24. Rather, their pre-fall existence was couched in response to God's loving order. They alone were responsible to choose love and life per God's will, or pursue an alternative.

Are we not all carrying that responsibility? Part of being made in the "image of God" means we *must* respond to our Maker. I believe Emil Brunner, a Swiss theologian, was onto something when he wrote,

> Man is, and remains, responsible, whatever his personal attitude to his Creator may be. He may deny his responsibility, and he may misuse his freedom, but he cannot get rid of his responsibility. Responsibility is part of the unchangeable structure of man's being. That is: the actual existence of man – of every man, not only the man who believes in Christ – consists in the positive fact that he has been made to respond – to God.[21]

Adam and Eve responded in the negative. Fellowship with God was broken and humanity was distanced from true wisdom. We found ourselves in hostility to "God's image" of righteousness. Death was set in motion.

Neither did human-ascended deity, to "be as God," come to fruition. God recognized that they had become "as one of us" in Genesis 3:22, but the context was in the knowledge of good and evil, not in becoming a *higher being*, and certainly not in becoming equal to the *Highest Being*. Indeed, God stated this as a *fait accompli*. In other words, Adam and Eve's fall was not a development leading to something more or better – as taught by Mormonism[22] – but a *completed* act of disobedience. They had deliberately stepped outside of God's order and now sin and death was embedded in humanity's spiritual and physical existence.

The problem of evil was upon us, by our own making.

Old Testament scholar Michael Heiser comments on the role we play as God's created *imagers* on Earth, distinguishing between predestination and foreknowledge, and the problem of evil,

> God is not evil. There is no biblical reason to argue that God predestined the fall, though he foreknew it. There is no biblical reason to assert that God predestined all the evil events throughout human history simply because he foreknew them...

[21] Emil Brunner, "Man and Creation," *Readings in Christian Theology, Volume 2: Man's Need and God's Gift* (Baker Book House, 1976, edited by Millard J. Erickson), p.49.

[22] See *Gospel Principles* (The Church of Jesus Christ of Latter-day Saints, 1997), p.33.

> *God does not need evil as a means to accomplish anything.*
>
> God foreknew the fall. That foreknowledge did not propel the event. God also foreknew a solution to the fall that he himself would guarantee...
>
> Evil does not flow from a first domino that God himself toppled. Rather, evil is the perversion of God's good gift of free will. It arises from the choices made by imperfect imagers, not from God's prompting or predestination. God does not need evil, but he has the power to take the evil that flows from free-will decisions – human or otherwise – and use it to produce good and his glory through the obedience of his loyal imagers, who are his hands and feet on the ground *now*.[23]

God was not selfish or vindictive, as some have popularly claimed. His righteous standards do not cause us to sin. Nor can we say the "Devil made me do it." Temptations abound, along with opportunities to do what is right. Our acts of good and evil rest on our shoulders. But so often we *blame-shift*.

When faced with having to explain to God why he disobeyed, Adam blamed Eve and indirectly, his Maker: "The woman whom You gave to be with me, she gave me of the tree, and I ate." Eve then acknowledged her deception, and imputes fault on the tempter. We too put blame on others, or we point to circumstances or past wrongs. Certainly there are provoking situations; nevertheless, the responsibility to choose how we act and react is on us.

"All of this means that what we choose to do is an important part of how things will turn out," Heiser reminds us. "What we do *matters*."[24]

This does not change the fundamental nature of our rebellion and its effects. The seriousness of our actions are ever before us, as is the gravity of our turning from the Author of Life. We see and experience it daily.

Proverbs 16:25 speaks to the error committed in the heart of Man: "There is a way that seems right to a man, but its end is the way of death." Romans 5:12 fleshes this out with a direct link to the Genesis account: "Wherefore, as by one man sin entered into the world, and death by sin; and so death passed upon all men, for that all have sinned."

The human cry of *I am God* is the first act of identity theft.

---

[23] Heiser, *The Unseen Realm*, p.66, italics in original.

[24] Ibid, p.66, italics in original.

Eating the Fruit

Ever since Genesis 3 we have figuratively been eating the fruit. Occult historian Richard Cavendish writes the following regarding the *black arts*. Note the emphasis on the "wisdom" imparted by the tempter,

> The driving force behind black magic is hunger for power. Its ultimate aim was stated, appropriately enough, by the serpent in the Garden of Eden... 'Ye shall not surely die: for God doth know that in the day ye eat thereof, then your eyes shall be opened and ye shall be as gods, knowing good and evil.' In occultism the serpent is a symbol of wisdom, and for centuries magicians have devoted themselves to the search for the forbidden fruit which would bring fulfillment of the serpent's promise. Carried to its furthest extreme... to make himself a god.[25]

The quest to yoke with "cosmic deity," wrapped in nature and humanity, is a hope and aspiration that spans the spectrum of human experience.

One example can be found in the 1987 European Year of the Environment. To mark the occasion, the Commission of the European Communities and the International Union for Conservation of Nature (IUCN) collaborated on a book, *New Ideas in Environmental Education*. Starting in Chapter One, we discover that "in the case of the planetary ecology... the problem lies in human consciousness."[26] The Genesis Fall was thus presented as an allegory for evolutionary awakening. By disobeying God we became free, setting our feet on the path of progress,

> The source of our planetary problems lies at that point in evolution at which instinct was transformed to intention through the agency of human life. Like so many events, it is recalled in myth and retold down the ages in the legend of the Garden of Eden...
>
> Traditionally, the Serpent is the symbol of Wisdom, and God's messenger on Earth. Hence, the Serpent symbolises consciousness, a point well understood by yogis and those practitioners who know

25 Cavendish, *The Black Arts*, p.1.

26 Mark Braham, "The Ecology of Education," *New Ideas in Environmental Education* (Croom Helm/ International Union for Conservation of Nature and Natural Resources/ Commission of the European Communities, 1988), p.5.

> somewhat of kundalini, the 'serpent power,' that, rising, through the hierarchy of chakras or centers of consciousness, as they are understood to be in Hindu and Buddhist thought, enables the initiate to acquire successively higher stares of awareness.[27]

Keep in mind, this text was used "as a plea for new approaches to environmental education."[28] It was designed to reshape minds and thus re-set our hearts, a sober reminder that our attitude to God is reflected in our worldview. The field of education is of primary importance in this shaping process. As the Preface stated: "What is required is both evolution and radical change, guiding the school system through new avenues."

Chapter one continued,

> The Serpent, as the principle of consciousness, fecundated Eve, the Earth Mother, who in turn, gave rise to a new Adam, a new type of Man… By eating from the Tree of Knowledge of Good and Evil, Adam broke the bounds of instinct and entered the realm of mind, with its potential for reflection and choice.[29]

The text foreshadowed our age of Re-enchantment,

> …our time is one that is marked by a spiritual quest. Although there has been a loss of faith in traditional religious practices, and little satisfaction in the secularity of the past decades, there is a widespread search for meaning that may include, but cannot be satisfied by, ordinary rationality.[30]

To that end, an inventory of spiritual streams were suggested as a validation of the quest: Judeo-Christianity *in spirit but not letter*, Hinduism, Tibetan and Zen Buddhism, Taoism, Sufism, the Mystery Schools, Gnosticism, Catharism, Templarism, Freemasonry, Cabbalism, Rosicrucianism, Anthroposophy, and Theosophy.[31]

Each way offers oneness with God: Hinduism via liberation or *moksha*; Cabbalism – Jewish mysticism – through the emanation of enlightened sym-

---

27 Ibid, p.8-9.
28 Ibid, "Introduction," p.xi.
29 Ibid, p.9.
30 Ibid, p.20.
31 Ibid, p.20.

bolism; Christian mysticism through asceticism and experiential practice;[32] and the way of Sufi unity, the journey into "Nothingness and Eternity."[33]

Wrapping up this "new vision for education," the European Communities/IUCN text celebrated our collective human advancement. Together we can "find completion in a spiritual renovation of the earth."[34]

Together we eat the fruit. Together we seek a return to the Garden.

The God Market

What I witnessed at the SUN conference and the text from the Commission of the European Communities and the IUCN are but small tastes of our declared human deification. Chapter six – indeed, most of this book – is a reflection of the Genesis 3 predicament. In considering the following examples, it will become obvious how pervasive and *similar* the desire for human-divine Oneness is.

New Age Movement:

As mentioned in chapter six, the New Age movement is an eclectic classification of spirituality and self-awareness, incorporating elements from Eastern religions, Perennial Philosophy, channeled teachings, and human potential psychology. Regardless of the Movement's diversity, a common thread runs through it. SUN's John Davis gives us the common vision: "One Humanity, One world, One true expression of divinity, One within the Christos... One Center of Consciousness... Oneness in all things."[35]

American songwriter and New Age icon, John Denver, said it this way: "We hear in the cry of our hearts expressing connectedness and wholeness and the recognition that we are One."[36]

---

[32] For critiques of modern Christian mysticism, see Greg Hammond, *Mystic Seduction: Awakening Christians to a Real and Present Danger* (BeAlertMinistry.com, 2014); Ray Yungen, *A Time of Departing* (Lighthouse Trails Publishing, 2002/2006); and Roger Oakland, *Faith Undone* (Lighthouse Trails Publishing, 2007).

[33] Farid ud-Din Attar, *The Conference of the Birds* (Penguin Books, 1984), p.205.

[34] Mark Braham, *New Ideas in Environmental Education*, p.29.

[35] John Davis and Naomi Rice, *Messiah and the Second Coming* (Coptic Press, 1982), p.21.

[36] John Denver, "It's a Possibility," *Windstar Journal*, Winter 1986, p.6. Denver started the Windstar Foundation in 1976 to promote education on peace and sustainability, personal growth, and New Age spiritual development.

Using Biblical language, albeit with a now familiar twist, Barbara Marx Hubbard conveyed the same message: "We become Alpha and Omega. We are the beginning and the end. We are the whole... There is no death, only every-higher order, consciousness, and union with God..."[37]

Writing of techniques to unlock the inner light of divine consciousness, actor Dennis Weaver tells us: "We, according to the Masters, being made in the image of God, have latent within us the power to become one with God's consciousness. In reality, our human consciousness is an individualized piece of God's consciousness."[38]

"We have to experience God, *feel* God," explained Weaver, "and then give ourselves over to that feeling."[39]

The New Age movement is a modern extension of Genesis 3: same message, same "angel of light," and the same dreams of grandeur.

"Nothing can touch me but the direct action of God and God is my Omnipotent Self," screamed the text of John Randolph Price. "I can do all things through the Strength of the Christ I AM. I AM STRENGTH!"[40]

Rosicrucianism:

Rosicrucianism, also known as the Rosy Cross, is an esoteric school of thought dating back to the 17th century and the legendary figure of German mystic, Christian Rosenkreuz. Over the centuries, various orders and societies inspired by the Rosy Cross – or with claimed Rosicrucian credentials – arose and folded in England, Germany, France and the United States. Some still exist, and new orders have formed in recent years. Nevertheless, the Rosicrucian meme has influenced modern occultism and Western mysticism.

One organization with a professed Rosicrucian pedigree is the Ancient and Mystical Order Rosæ Crucis (AMORC), which was constituted in June 1915 and is headquartered in San Jose, California. Utilizing home study courses, rituals and convocations, this body of mystical travelers partakes in "Spiritual Alchemy" as they journey toward cosmic consciousness. God, it is

---

37 Barbara Marx Hubbard, *The Revelation: A Message of Hope for the New Millennium* (Nataraj Publishing, 1995), p.162.

38 Dennis Weaver, *All the World's a Stage* (Walsch Books, 2001), p.226.

39 Ibid., p.239, italics in original.

40 John Randolph Price, *The Planetary Commission* (The Quartus Foundation, 1984), p.133, capitals in original.

taught, can be seen as the "Creative Universal Force."[41] An AMORC *Master Monograph* tells us: "To find God, we must see Him in all things at once."[42]

The AMORC *Glossary* explains: "It [Divine Mind] is not only the mind of God but also the consciousness and mind of all living beings on the earth plane."[43] Hence, "God" must be ever changing, reacting to the great flow of human thought and consciousnesses. AMORC teaches this very thing,

> The God of today, in our comprehension and consciousness, will not be the God of next year, for God will evolve as the consciousness of the soul evolves. This evolution will continue until man becomes fully conscious of the consciousness of the Cosmic.[44]

Man thus becomes the spiritual measure of all things. AMORC's Imperator, Christian Bernard, put it this way,

> The Temple of the Universe, the Temple of the Earth and the Temple of Life are only one in the Temple of Man. This is why the time has come to work towards rebuilding it, for the Messianic Light must emanate from the Heavenly Jerusalem which vibrates within us.[45]

Mormonism:

Becoming God is the point of Mormonism. Because the religion's history starts with Joseph Smith and his visitations from an angelic messenger, I will simply quote Smith's teachings from his famous King Follett discourse,

> God himself was once as we are now, and is an exalted man, and sits enthroned in yonder heavens! ...Here, then, is eternal life – to know the only wise and true God; *and you have got to learn how to be gods yourselves*, and to be kings and priests to God, the same as all gods have done before you, namely, by going from one small degree to another, and from a small capacity to a great one; from grace to grace, from exaltation to exaltation...[46]

---

41 Christian Bernard, *So Mote It Be!* (Supreme Grand Lodge of AMORC, 1995), p.157.

42 *Master Monograph, Illuminati Section, Degree 12, Monograph 25* (AMORC), p.4.

43 *Rosicrucian Glossary: A Key to Word Meanings* (AMORC, 1975, seventh edition), p.13.

44 *Master Monograph, Temple Section, Degree 9, Preliminary Monograph 3* (AMORC), p.5.

45 Bernard, *So Mote It Be!*, pp.87-88.

46 Joseph Smith, as printed by Bruce R. McConkie, *Mormon Doctrine* (Bookcraft, 1979, second edition), p.321, italics in original.

In addressing his conception of Godhood, Joseph Smith said the following,

> What is it? To inherit the same power, the same glory and the same exaltation, until you arrive at the station of a god, and ascend the throne of eternal power, the same as those who have gone before.[47]

Freemasonry:

My personal starting point in researching global spiritual movements and ideologies started with Freemasonry. I never joined the Lodge, but due to certain encounters I was compelled to study the Craft.

A turning point in my life is well remembered.

The year was 1991, and the setting was a near-empty restaurant in a sleepy prairie town with two respected community members sitting across the table. I knew what they wanted: my involvement in the Masonic Lodge, for I had been approached numerous times about joining. As an energetic young man involved in my community, I was the type of person they were looking for.

Similar to other conversations it was evident my dinner hosts were trying to explain *something* without telling me *anything*. Nudge-nudge, wink-wink, but never getting to the point. It was a sales pitch cloaked in ambiguity.

It would be beneficial for you to join, I was told. *We make good men better*, I was promised. They waxed on about a legacy, doing good work and having a sense of camaraderie, and the importance of regular meetings.

More meetings? Between family, church, and a host of activities attached to my workplace, my life was busy enough without adding more. Yet these men, board members I answered to in my place of employment and individuals I had a good relationship with, truly believed it was important for me to become a Freemason. So I listened as they attempted to convince me with repetitious non-explanations. It was all very awkward.

"Are you political?" I asked, knowing the answer from previous chats. *No*.

"Religious?" *No*.

"Ok, then what is the Lodge about?" My query was an open door.

Chairs shifted, they glanced at each other; the silence was palpable. Then the hammer dropped: "We're not Satanists."

It was said so matter-of-factly, as if it were a normal response when at a loss for something to say. A lightening bolt from the blue could not have been

[47] Ibid., p.321.

more surprising. *Where had this come from?* I had not suggested anything to elicit such a bizarre statement. The thought had never entered my mind and there was nothing I could correlate this to. I was stunned. Our meal quickly ended and I went home, pondering and perplexed.

In retrospect, my dinner colleagues were probably trying to dispel rumors or alleviate fears. Why else would something so outrageous be said? As this was before the public introduction of the internet, and as television documentaries on Freemasonry were nonexistent, any potential misgivings a person would have had, probably would have been viewed as coming from a church context. This was the only thing that made sense.

I could certainly see this being the case if someone examined my home church, a congregation with a constitutional provision stating you cannot be part of a secretive society and a member of the local assembly. Even though this provision was in place, the irony was that Freemasonry had never – as far as I was aware – been mentioned from my church's pulpit.

But now I was compelled to learn about the Lodge, for *something* had elicited this unusual response. Feeling uncomfortable asking my board members for information, I determined to obtain their own writings and materials. I started collecting their rituals, commentaries, and works of philosophy.

Soon I discovered that there is an interpretation of the Craft which is spiritual in nature, advancing an esoteric worldview.[48]

The Sovereign Grand Commander of the Scottish Rite branch, Henry C. Clausen, offered a glimpse in his 1981 text,

> ...science and religion will be welded into a unified exponent of an overriding spiritual power... The theme in essence is that the revelations of Eastern mysticism and the discoveries of modern science support the Masonic and Scottish Rite beliefs and teachings.[49]

---

[48] Re: Interpretations. An observation I have made is that the average Mason typically disavows spiritual interpretations of the Craft. Conversely, men who have achieved significant stature within the system, such as a Sovereign Grand Commander of the Supreme Council, or who are recognized as noted philosophers or historians are quicker to admit a spiritual dimension. Moreover, I have heard it said that every Mason's interpretation should be viewed as his own. In other words, interpretations are subjective. Compelled to accept this, I have chosen to interpret the Craft through the second group, and not the local Mason whose experience has been narrower in orientation.

[49] Henry C. Clausen, *Emergence of the Mystical* (Ancient and Accepted Scottish Rite of Freemasonry, Southern Jurisdiction, 1981), p.xi.

The following readings from Masonic thinkers sounds like so many other repeats of Genesis 3,

> Man is a god in the making, and as in the mystic myths of Egypt, on the potter's wheel he is being molded. When his light shines out to lift and preserve all things, he receives the triple crown of godhood, and joins that throng of Master Masons who, in their robes of Blue and Gold, are seeking to dispel the darkness of night with the triple light of the Masonic Lodge. – Manly P. Hall.[50]
>
> MAN IS IMPELLED TOWARD PERFECTION! There is that within man – his innermost divinity – which informs him of the possibility of attaining completeness of being and urges him on to strive for that attainment. – George H. Steinmetz.[51]
>
> This – the evolution of man into superman – was always the purpose of the ancient Mysteries, and the real purpose behind modern Masonry is, not the social and charitable purpose to which so much attention is paid, but the expediting of the spiritual evolution of those who aspire to perfect their own nature and transform it into a more god-like quality. – W.L. Wilmshurst.[52]
>
> Masonry, therefore, is not only a system of morality, inculcating the highest ethics through which result, if followed, the conscious unfolding of divinity, but it is also a great dramatic presentation of regeneration. It portrays the recovery of man's hidden divinity and its bringing forth into the light… – Foster Bailey.[53]

Henry C. Clausen encouraged Scottish Rite members to find mastery *within,*

> The Scottish Rite teaches its members how to spell 'God' with the right blocks... We teach our initiates there are available for the mind of man vast spiritual forces, vital spiritual powers.

50 Manly P. Hall, *The Lost Keys of Freemasonry* (Macoy Publishing and Masonic Supply Company, 1954, originally published in 1923), p.92. Hall, an esoteric philosopher, became one of the most influential Masons of the Twentieth Century.

51 George H. Steinmetz, *The Royal Arch: Its Hidden Meaning* (Macoy Publishing and Masonic Supply Company, 1946), p.84, capitals in original.

52 W.L. Wilmshurst, *The Meaning of Masonry* (Gramercy Books, 1980), p.47.

53 Foster Bailey, *The Spirit of Masonry* (Lucis Trust, 1957/1996), p.105.

> Similarly, we in the Scottish Rite can find in our inner selves a refuge from external distractions and evils... Put your trust in your own inherent capacities.
>
> Buddha attained his own enlightenment and said to his followers: 'Be a lamp unto your own feet; do not seek outside yourself'.[54]

The above quotes fit the following selection from J.D. Buck, a proponent of spiritual Masonry from a century past. Buck's text drips in the definitive human boast,

> It is far more important that men should strive to become Christs than that they should believe that Jesus was Christ. If the Christ-state can be attained by but one human being during the whole evolution of the race, then the evolution of man is a farce and human perfection an impossibility... Jesus is no less Divine because all men may reach the same Divine perfection.[55]

Alien Encounters:

When I was at the SUN conference in 1999, I encountered people who claimed to be in contact with space-beings. The New Age movement is laced with such assertions. Like other "angelic" messengers who preach a gospel of self-deity, these "extraterrestrials" are peddling the same fruit as found in Genesis 3: *We are imparting special knowledge... you are divine, you are God... you never really will die, but advance from stage to stage before absorption into the cosmos...* or some variation to that effect.

In his "starseed transmissions," channeled messages from entities posing as angels and extraterrestrials, Ken Carey conveyed the following: "You are the Presence of God. God is present on Earth because of you."[56]

Solara, a *star-being* whose channeled communications started a religious movement called the Star-Borne, tells us that we too are star beings. Through "doorway rituals" we can awaken to who we really are, and together discover our destiny in a non-dual reality. Solara reminds us of our Divine Origin; that we are all star-children, Angels on Earth.

---

[54] Clausen, *Emergence of the Mystical*, pp.76-77.

[55] J.D. Buck, *Mystic Masonry and the Greater Mysteries of Antiquity* (Regan Publishing, 1925), p.62.

[56] Ken Carey, *The Starseed Transmissions* (HarperSanFrancisco, 1982/1995), p.51.

Therefore, as star-children, we must "return to the Light of Oneness,"[57]

> We are called to unite together in a group initiation as One, binding the family of humanity into a collective whole. Our primary identifications with ourselves shall be with the One which we truly are – you, me, and everyone else combined.[58]

And there is a broader community within the wholeness. We must return to the Light with the *other* angels, specifically Lucifer, who, according to Solara, came to Earth as a beneficial volunteer – a star-seed traveling on a Golden Beam of Light – to interlock with matter.[59]

Supposedly we arise and take our rightful place in full union,

> Eventually, if we achieve our chosen task on planet Earth to transmute duality into Oneness, then Lucifer, too, with his fallen Angels, must rise up into the Light to once again sit at the right hand of God as one of the brightest of the Angels. For nothing and no one is to remain separate from God. Within the Greater Reality, everything *is* God.[60]

Or as another alien channeled: "The Second Coming is imminent, and you may as well get ready. This is a particularly good idea because you're it. You are the Second Coming... Become your own Messiah."[61]

Amazingly, extraterrestrial messengers from supposedly distant galaxies, traveling billions of light years by technically manipulating complex rifts in space-and-time, do not come to cure the common cold or end cancer. No. Their task is to spread the message of Cosmic Humanism. Let me be blunt: I do not believe these entities come from a "galaxy far, far away." They are sentient, they are intelligent, but their messages expose their identity. They are spiritual beings aligned with the "angel of light" who visited the first human couple in the Garden, and their agenda is to keep you entrapped in the act of divine identity theft.

---

57 Solara, *The Star-Borne: A Remembrance for the Awakened Ones* (Star-Borne Unlimited, 1989), p.151.

58 Ibid., p.279.

59 Ibid., p.136.

60 Ibid., p.138, italics in original.

61 Zoev Jho, *E.T. 101: The Cosmic Instruction Manual for Planetary Evolution* (HarperSanFrancisco, 1995), pp.44-45.

The forbidden fruit extends into the alien abduction phenomena. Abduction researcher John E. Mack[62] explained how many UFO abductees experience a transformational state-of-mind. Re-enchantment follows,

> The altered consciousness that abduction encounters bring about resembles in some ways the trance states of shamans, and like indigenous peoples, abductees are brought closer to a natural world that is alive with spirits of all kinds and is increasingly perceived as sacred.[63]

This, accordingly, reflects what the aliens themselves portray. Mack tells us: "Abductees consistently report that the beings seem closer to the Godhead than we are, acting as messengers, guardian spirits, or angels, intermediaries between us and the Divine Source."[64] Reconnecting to the Source – or as one client of Mack described it, "God-Goddess-All that is" – becomes the new purpose for living.[65]

Moreover, some channeled transmissions describe a coming co-evolution. *Visitors From Within*, a series of alien communications and interactions, describes the work of synthesis and transformation."Zeta beings," a supposedly alien race not too different from our own species, is destined to spiritually co-evolve with enlightened humanity,

> You are, in a sense, two opposite ends of a pole, and you are coming together to form one integrated consciousness. You are learning from each other. You are growing from each other... We are speaking of species evolution on a very basic level all the way through to the spiritual level.[66]

Do I believe actual *Zeta beings* exist? Not at all. Do I believe spiritual entities are masquerading to sell Oneness? That is far more plausible.

The implications are ominous.

---

[62] John Mack was socially connected to the Esalen Institute and received funding from Lawrence Rockefeller. See Marion Goldman, *The American Soul Rush: Esalen and the Rise of Spiritual Privilege* (New York University Press, 2012), p.144.

[63] John E. Mack, *Passport to the Cosmos: Human Transformation and Alien Encounters* (Crown Publishing, 1999), p.154.

[64] Ibid., p.276.

[65] Ibid., p.272.

[66] Lyssa Royal and Keith Priest, *Visitors From Within* (Royal Priest Research Pr., 1992), p.14.

Hardly Coincidental

Do you see a trend? Whether it is *alien entities* or an *angel of light* or a *channeled spirit*, the same doctrine is preached.

A myriad of *god voices* echo this sentiment. Neale Donald Walsch's *Conversations With God* series, with seven of his books making it to the *New York Times* bestseller list, is a case in point. The Jesus-voice talking to Barbara Marx Hubbard is another. Examples abound of god-voices and private messages from "Jesus the Christ," often revealed through Eastern meditation practices and comparable spiritual techniques. Inevitably these voices reinforce the same Oneness paradigm.

Alternatively, the Creator of Heaven and Earth declared a contrarian position: "For I am God, and not man" (Hosea 11:9).

"To whom will you compare me?" asks the true God in His communications to Isaiah. "Or who is my equal?"[67]

In Isaiah 44:6 we read: "Thus says the LORD, the King of Israel, and his Redeemer, the LORD of hosts: 'I am the First and I am the Last; Besides Me there is no God.'"

In the New Testament we discover the Redeemer that Isaiah announced, Jesus Christ, who self-identifies in Revelation 22:13 – "I am the Alpha and the Omega, the Beginning and the End, the First and the Last." As the letter to Colossians tells us, He created all things on heaven and earth, visible and invisible, "whether thrones or dominions or principalities or powers."[68] His claim to be "Alpha and Omega" is thus absolute and indivisible.

There is no comparison. We did not create the cosmos. We have not defeated death. For as much as we have advanced, our limitations are manifest.

But instead of bowing our knees to Jesus Christ, the Holy One who separated light from darkness, who formed the animal kingdom with distinct species boundaries, who elevated humanity as a royal ambassador over all other creatures,[69] we incessantly shout our greatness.

We are determined to redeem ourselves and thus re-make Eden in our own image; but it is a hopeless cause, for it remains intractably locked in the *illusion of Oneness*.

---

[67] Isaiah 40:25 – *New International Version*, 1984 edition.

[68] Colossians 1:16.

[69] See Genesis 1.

Social theorist, Jeremy Rifkin, echoes the boast of humanity,

> Humanity is abandoning the idea that the universe operates by iron-clad truths because it no longer feels the need to be constrained by such fetters. Nature is being made anew, this time by human beings. We no longer feel ourselves to be guests in someone else's home and therefore obliged to make our behavior conform with a set of pre-existing cosmic rules. It is our creation now. We make the rules. We establish the parameters of reality. We create the world, and because we do, we no longer feel beholden to outside forces. We no longer have to justify our behavior, for we are now the architects of the universe. We are responsible to nothing outside ourselves, for we are the kingdom, the power, and the glory for ever and ever.[70]

It is easy to read Mr. Rifkin's hubristic quote and go, "how shameless!" That, however, is hypocritical – at least for me. For if I am honest, I likewise desire to be god-over-my-own life. I want to direct my own steps, create my own order, and proclaim my own wisdom. If I cannot do it via power and prowess, maybe it will come through piety and good works. But surrender to God? Admit He is right and just? I would rather follow my own moral directives and experience the *feeling* of spiritual Oneness as I blend into the crowd. Such a path would be the wide and easy road to travel. *It would be comfortable*, for a mountain of affirming messages bolsters this position.

But who am I fooling? Certainly not the God who is the author of your life and mine; Jesus Christ said, "I am the way, the truth and the life. No one comes to the Father except through me."[71] No matter how hard *I try*, this fallible creature cannot save himself. Salvation is exclusive to the unique and incomparable Redeemer: Jesus Christ.

I am not God, and neither are you.

But even as I admit that *I'm not God*, a vexing truth hangs over my head. My own pride, lust, envy and greed all indict me, for my moral failings and daily "sin struggles" are constant reminders of the root problem. That I, too, harbor and feed on the desire to be my own Master, and this plays out in my thoughts and actions – just as it does in your life.

The taste of the Garden fruit is on all of our lips.

---

[70] Jeremy Rifkin, *Algeny* (The Viking Press, 1983), p.244.

[71] John 14:6.

Chapter 10

Building Cosmopolis

> The city is the place where man is all-powerful, where he establishes his own justice, opposed to God's will. – Jacques Ellul.[1]

> Civilization is absolutely invincible once it realizes the secret of its own unity. – Benjamin Kidd.[2]

It was my fourth drive around the poorly lit neighborhood, and I was baffled. This was where elite world thinkers were meeting, in an old residential section on the north side of Chicago? All I could see were aged homes, brick-clad apartments, and townhouses. Address numbers were practically invisible in the autumn darkness, and I was coming up – once again – to what was supposed to be the location for a Global Peoples Assembly.

I had to be lost.

The date was November 7, 1997, and when it came to big cities I possessed a country-boy naivety. To someone who had grown up on a grain farm in the Canadian prairies, Chicago felt like another planet, and earlier that evening my inexperience had shone through.

Needing to book a room for the night, I found, a dozen or so blocks from my meeting destination, a 1950ish looking motel. A bed is a bed, right?

"How many hours do you want?" asked the elderly female receptionist, barely looking up from the boredom of her newspaper.

This should have been my first clue.

---

1 Jacques Ellul, *The Meaning of the City* (Wipf and Stock, 1970/2003), p. 93.

2 Benjamin Kidd, *The Science of Power* (Methuen & Co., Ltd., 1919, eighth edition), p.295. Kidd was a British sociologist and social evolutionary who was influenced, in part, by the Social Gospel movement of the 1890s. See D.P. Crook, *Benjamin Kidd: Portrait of a Social Darwinist* (Cambridge University Press, 1984).

"All night," I answered, passing the money for the posted rate of a single bed. Scowling at the cash in her hands, the lady piped-up: "Well, how many are going to be using the room?"

Dumbstruck, I stumbled out an apologetic, "Just me."

"Oh..." with a little smile her eyes came up to meet mine. "You want it for sleeping!" Later in the evening I discovered that "sleeping" was not a priority in my chosen establishment.

Dropping off my luggage in a small, grimy room, I left to find the Global Assembly. After driving in circles for twenty minutes, I parked my car and nervously walked up the steps of an empty looking brick building, the only one that seemed plausible in relationship to the directions on my map. There, in the shadows of the door awning, I found the address number and a taped piece of paper with simple type.

Walking in, I was welcomed to "DreamHouse."

Big City Dreaming

Sometimes expectations and reality pleasantly align. Not in this case.

Knowing that representatives from world government advocacy groups would be meeting to formulate a Global Peoples Assembly, variously framed as a World Citizens Assembly or Peoples Assembly – a "peoples world parliament" – I was expecting the event to be held in a modern conference facility. I also anticipated a substantial number of attendees, better allowing myself to blend in. Instead, the meeting was in a disused Salvation Army chapel being converted into an arts theater. Fewer than twenty people were in the building, and practically everyone knew each other.

I stuck out like a country-boy who had just wandered into a hooker hotel.

The next day Lucile Green, the quintessential networker, acknowledged our small group: "We have here a few important people, this is an important event, and we could change the world."

People of importance *were* in the room. Tom Hudgens and Robert Stuart from the Association to Unite the Democracies were speakers that morning. Hudgens and Stuart's group had played a historical role in the North Atlantic Treaty Organization, especially its Parliamentary Assembly.[3] Nari Safavi was

3 Joseph Preston Baratta, *The Politics of World Federation: Volume 2, From World Federalism to Global Governance* (Praeger, 2004), pp.522-526. The Association to Unite

present. Safavi had sat on the national board of the World Federalist Association, the largest pro-world government lobby group in the United States, and was then the president of the Chicago branch.[4] Years later I would run into Safavi at a Chicago Council on Foreign Relations event. I found him to be winsome and engaging.

But arguably the most important person was Lucile Green herself, with world government accolades beyond anyone else's in the room.[5] Years before, Green founded the World Citizens Assembly in San Francisco which issued the *Declaration of Interdependence*.[6] For this she received the Gandhi Medal. Now it was her Action Coalition For Global Change (ACGC) at the forefront of the Global Assembly movement.

Originally organized as a support body for San Francisco's United Nations 50th anniversary in 1995, ACGC at the same time initiated a "model United Peoples Assembly" to demonstrate how such an organ could meet the UN mandate of "We The Peoples." During the 50th, her model Assembly pre-

---

the Democracies was also known as Federal Union, and was birthed through the work of Clarence Streit and his idea to politically unite the European and North American democracies. Historic personalities included Robert Schumann, Owen J. Roberts, Paul Henri-Spaak, James W. Wadsworth, Lester Pearson, and George Marshall.

4 The World Federalist Association is now known as Citizens For Global Solutions.

5 Lucile W. Green passed away in 2004. She was an early member and Vice President of the World Constitution and Parliament Association, founder of the World Citizens Assembly, member of the World Future Society and the American Humanist Association, founder and co-chair of the World Government Organization Coalition, member of the coordinating committee of Women For Peace, involved with the Population and Ecology Commission of the World Constitutional Convention, a founding board member of the World Federalists of Northern California (now named the Democratic World Federalists), leading figure in the Action Coalition for Global Change, worked with the CAMDUN process, and founder of the Citizens for a United Nations People's Assembly, which held a panel discussion during the 60th Anniversary of the UN in 2005. She was connected to the Club of Budapest and a host of other groups.

6 Although the 1975 World Citizens Assembly was the launching pad for the Global Assembly idea, the broader concept is older. In 1947, a conference took place at the New School of Social Research in New York City to consider the formation of an Emergency World People's Congress. Delegates from 35 organizations attended, and it was agreed that the upcoming People's Congress would be built around a union of non-governmental organizations to bring "about adequate world organization, of, by, and for all the people of the earth." *Report of the Joint Organizing Conference of the Advisory Board, Organizing Committee and Council of Co-operating Organizations for the Emergency World People's Congress*, May 17-18, 1947, presided by Dr. Kirtley F. Mather, report on file.

sented their resolutions to the UN Secretary-General as a validating gesture. By 1996 her group had put together an advisory council to move this forward. Robert Muller was honorary chairman of the Council, and members included Tim Barner from the World Federalist Association, Barbara Marx Hubbard, Ervin Laszlo, and Canadian parliamentarian Douglas Roche. It was hoped a permanent body could be established in New York during the year 2000, thereby creating a new international order.

Green became the face of the Global Assembly movement.

Like James Garrison,[7] Green was born to Christian missionaries in China. As a young lady she studied Chinese philosophy at the university level, and later received her Ph.D. from Ohio State University. She quickly gravitated to the world peace movement and worked to incorporate her adopted Eastern worldview into it. Whether Green and Garrison knew each other I cannot say. Their networks certainly overlapped.

For decades she had been advocating a merger of the "new consciousness" with the drive for world government; a blending of East and West. In a 1980 speech she gave the following advice,

> Building deeper channels between the New Age groups that proclaim a wholistic or global perspective, and all those political action groups working for a democratic, federal world government. It is especially important, I think, for the spiritually aware to become politically astute, so that politics is not confined to flat, two-dimensional issues but reflects the full height and depth of human potential.[8]

Moving this forward, the purpose of our meeting in Chicago was to strategize an international, city-based movement that would ultimately culminate in a robust world order. Only a few month's prior, UN Secretary General Kofi Annan announced that a "Companion People's Assembly" would convene alongside major events in the year 2000. World Federalists believed that the proper response to this invitation was to frame a Global Assembly, and to present it as an action point during the UN Millennium gatherings. It was an open door to launch the next evolution of global governance.

---

[7] See chapter 6.

[8] Lucile W. Green, *Journey to a Governed World: Thru 50 Years in the Peace Movement* (The Uniquest Foundation, 1991/1992), p.46. Given at the Festival of the International Cooperation Council, 1980.

Chicago's meeting was part of that process. Similar campaigns were also coming to life in Boston, Los Angeles, Wellington, New Delhi, Paris, Tokyo, New York, Madrid, London, and Bombay. A few weeks before the Chicago event, 10,000 people took part in a walk from Perugia to Assissi, Italy, in support of a Peoples Assembly. Greetings were sent from the Italian organizers to DreamHouse.

Our group recognized that as mega-cities are hubs of immense political power and economic energy, often having more practical maneuverability than nations, these centers could rightly be considered Global Cities and leveraged as such. A list of 94 metro regions ranked by population was handed to us, along with a proposal to identify and target the world's top 1000 urban concentrations. It was explained that if these centers would send delegates to an annual, global town hall meeting on pressing issues – population control, environmental sustainability, terrorism – this campaign could then be steered into becoming a real "world parliament."[9] Mayors, or city-elected "world citizens" would thus form the nucleus of a Global People's Assembly, offering direct democracy to the international community. The only thing needed, it was explained, was twenty-five Global Cities committing to the project and the ball would roll. *Cities could rule the world*.

Consideration was given to the logistics of such an endeavor. How would electoral delegates be nominated? Would they need to provide "evidence of global world citizenship"? How would constituencies be assembled? What function and purpose would the Global Assembly serve? Suggestions included fostering a "new global ethics" and becoming a "legislative body parallel to the UN General Assembly." How would the world body be financed? Ideas included "direct taxation on the world's people," "fees for use of our Common Heritage, including oceans, air, water," and a tax on international currency exchanges.[10]

My time at DreamHouse revealed two things: First, the push for world federalism was real and active. This was not a conspiracy in the classic, Hollywood movie style with shadowy men in smoke filled rooms. Rather, it was the continuation of a big idea involving motivated people with fixed

---

9 Lucile W. Green, *A Modest Proposal: City-Centered People's Assemblies as First Step to a Global People's Assembly* (Action Coalition for Global Change, 1997). On file.

10 Questionnaire presented at the Chicago meeting: *Discussion on Organizing a Permanent Global Peoples Assembly and Establishing a Legitimate Peoples Agenda*. On file.

goals, and it was open for observation. Second, I learned how out-of-place I was. During lunch, Green and Robert Stuart pulled me aside for questioning, insinuating I was an infiltrator. Stumbling for words, I explained I was attending to learn more about the globalization process.

They were right, and I was not wrong.

After lunch the organizer, an intelligent and cordial fellow, noticed my micro-cassette recorder – an aid in my note taking – and had a look of worry. By mid afternoon Green was quietly talking to me in a corner of the theater. Concern was mounting that I was a mole, and the Assembly movement was too fragile to be compromised by an unknown entity. I just listened.

Nearing supper the organizer vocalized his apprehension in front of the group. Face-to-face, I was effectively charged with being a spy. The point had been made and the Global Assembly put itself on pause while I remained in the building. After a few uncomfortable minutes, I gathered my belongings and walked into the cool freshness of an early November evening.

City of Man

Historically the *city* has been equated with humanity's civilizing ascendance. It represents the quest for security, identity, and progress.

When considering the Biblical narrative, the first human community is usually sourced as Babel – the famous city that housed an infamous tower. The first named city, however, was *Enoch*.

In Genesis 4 we read the account of two brothers, Cain and Abel, and the murder of one by the other. God confronts Cain for his crime and pronounces a sentence, a curse of wandering. Cain, to be separated from a stabilized culture and place of sanctuary, cries out: "My punishment is greater than I can bear!"

Three things caused him angst as found in Genesis 4:14. First, he would no longer live in the security of the place he knows. He is driven from his homeland. Second, he realized his relationship with God would be severed. Third, he understood that as a wanderer he would be prone to attack, a possible reference to the fear of vengeance over the murder of Abel. This was too much for Cain, and God responded to his cry by promising protection while he lived out his sentence. Here was a second chance; Cain could choose to place himself in God's trust as he roamed in consequence.

Cain does wander for a time. We find he travels to the land of Nod, a Hebrew name that means *wandering*. But here things change. Cain stops and builds "a city" – a permanent settlement – and his wife gives birth to a son named Enoch. Cain extends this name to his new community.

Cain is not wandering alone. Others are with him, and we can only speculate on the social situation. What were the ages of Cain and Abel when the murder happened? We assume they were young men, but our Sunday school flannel graph images are probably shamefully inaccurate. The Bible speaks of advanced life spans in the pre-Flood period, and producing years were far advanced from our own.[11] How many children did Adam and Eve have, and over how long a time period? Were siblings born between the births of Abel and Cain? There could be multiple generations already living and inter-marrying before the murder takes place. As I said, we are not cognitive of the social setting, but we know Cain is leading a household.

The focus however is on Cain's actions, which concluded in the building of Enoch. The French thinker, Jacques Ellul, communicated the importance of Cain's decisions. I believe his assessment has merit,

> ...he [Cain] will satisfy his desire for security by creating a place belonging to him, a city... The city for Cain is first of all the place where he can be himself – his homeland, the one settled spot in his wanderings. Second, it is a material sign of his security. He is responsible for himself and for his life. He is far from the Lord's face, and so he will shift for himself... The city is the direct consequence of Cain's murderous act and of his refusal to accept God's protection.
>
> Cain has built a city. For God's Eden he substitutes his own, for the goal given to his life by God, he substitutes a goal chosen by himself – just as he substituted his own security for God's. Such is the act by which Cain takes his destiny on his own shoulders, refusing the hand of God in his life.[12]

---

[11] For example, Seth was not born to Adam and Eve until Adam's 130th year. Genesis 5:4 tells us: "After he begot Seth, the days of Adam were eight hundred years; and he had sons and daughters." Another example is the life of Methuselah who begot Lamech at the age of 187 years, and then had more children. How many children Methuselah had before Lamech is not recorded.

[12] Ellul, *The Meaning of the City*, p.5.

Ellul reminds us that a newly secured state of affairs has emerged through the work of Cain's hands. A purposeful, new order emerges,

> Now a start is made, and it is no longer God beginning, but man. And thus Cain, with everything he does, digs a little deeper the abyss between himself and God. There was a solution for his situation, but the solution was in God's hands, and that is what he could absolutely not tolerate. He wants to find alone the remedy for a situation he created, but which he cannot himself repair because it is a situation dependent on God's grace.[13]

Cain's Enoch, his chosen place of stability, thus becomes symbolic of civilizing for the sake of security under Man's own order. The "city" becomes the place of power, of confidence, of humanity's alchemical quest to save itself under the banner of "strength in unity." Lewis Mumford, whose expansive writings on mechanization and urban development generated much thought and debate, recognized the link between "Megalopolis" – the super city at the heartbeat of collective action – and the desire for utopia.[14] In his acclaimed text, *The City in History*, he critically noted that monopolies of power and knowledge emerge in metropolitan culture.[15] The city becomes more than just a place to live, but a technique and an ideal.

W. Warren Wagar elaborated on this concept in *The City of Man*, a book circulated within the World Federalist community.[16] In it he bridged the ancient concept of *cosmopolitanism* with the modern hope of a world civilization,

> Cosmopolis means simply, from the Greek, 'world-city.' The world-city is the inevitably large spiritual and intellectual and administrative capital of a civilization, of the whole known civilized world. Or,

---

[13] Ibid. p.6.

[14] See Lewis Mumford, *The Story of Utopias* (Boni and Liveright, 1922).

[15] Lewis Mumford, *The History of the City: Its Origins, Its Transformations, and Its Prospects* (Harcourt, 1961), p.542.

[16] Clare and Ronald McLaughlin distributed copies to their network during Christmas, 1963, "as a memorial to John F. Kennedy, hoping to further the cause of an ordered world under law." Clare sat on the National Executive of the United World Federalists and was a board member of the Minnesota United Nations Association. She, along with her husband, organized the Minnesota branch of the United World Federalists. Their special Christmas note, titled, "We Are Committed to a Venture of Confidence in Man," was attached to the copy of *The City of Man* in my possession.

> more broadly, it is the quintessence of a civilization, the gathering of all its vital human resources into a living organic unity... Cosmopolis is simply the world in a state of optimal integration.[17]

Professor Wagar, a futurist and expert on H.G. Wells, was aware that Cosmopolis required more than a political alignment-of-purpose. It needed a synthesis in the core aspects of philosophy, ethics, and spiritual thinking. Cosmopolis, he acknowledged, does not require a single, universal creed, the singular confession of an institutionalized faith. Rather, it necessitates a shared value system, a universal worldview that gives license for all creeds and philosophies to find their place within the Whole. When such a worldview finally saturates society, then Cosmopolis can organically arise in the emotion of collective humanity.

Wagar writes,

> Technics pave the way for communication and exchange of ideas, but they cannot alone create a world culture or even a world state. The only permanently viable societies are founded, in the final analysis, on a common spiritual and intellectual culture, which in turn makes possible unity and fraternity in the sphere of practical politics.[18]

"Men must think and feel as one," explained Wagar, "before they can make the leap to cosmopolis."[19]

Back to Babel

In Genesis we have a taste of Cosmopolis. Best remembered for its tiered ziggurat tower,[20] Genesis 11 tells us that this was more than just an upright structure – it was a city with a cause, a city with a meaning.

What is directly known about the city-tower project, built in the post-Flood period, is recorded in nine verses.[21] The first fact we encounter is the people operated through a single, working language. Could it be that the "one

---

[17] W. Warren Wagar, *The City of Man: Prophecies of a World Civilization in Twentieth-Century Thought* (Houghton Mifflin Company, 1963), p.15.

[18] Ibid. p.135.

[19] Ibid. p.134.

[20] It is assumed the tower was in the form of a ziggurat.

[21] Genesis 11:1-9.

speech" of Genesis 11:1 refers to a *lingua franca*, literally an international trade tongue? Possibly, as the preceding chapter mentions differing languages on three separate occasions, yet other options have been given.[22] Regardless, the idea remains that a universal linguistic system enabled the Babel project to commence. Unity requires intelligible communication.

No wonder Babel has been a powerful symbol in the history of the computer industry, especially in terms of global networking.[23] Another interesting side note was a logo created for an Esalen-Russian tour on human potential in which the human mind became the Tower of Babel. Tour topics included telepathy and cybernetics.[24]

We find in the text that like Cain, the people of Babel sought security in community. Although the tower/city is central to the narrative, the chief concern is found in its purpose: renown in unity.

"Come, let us build ourselves a city, and a tower whose top is in the heavens," reads Genesis 11:4. "Let us make a name for ourselves, lest we be

---

[22] For a brief explanation, see Victor P. Hamilton, *Handbook on the Pentateuch: Genesis, Exodus, Leviticus, Numbers, Deuteronomy* (Baker Book House, 1982), pp.81-82. Note: It is possible that Genesis 10 describes the effect of the Babel judgment before the cause, as it says three times the people had differing tongues. If so, then it could be that Genesis 11:1 is describing a single, monolithic language, and not a trade tongue.

[23] Some examples: The January 1961 issue of *Communications of the ACM* (Association for Computer Machinery) used the image of the Tower of Babel on its cover. That edition, a collection of papers given at the ACM Compiler Symposium from the year before, shows a ziggurat tower extending into the clouds, covered with computing terms and acronyms. The base of the tower reads, "Babel 1960." The June 17, 1971 edition of *New Scientist and Science Journal* likewise referenced the Tower of Babel problem regarding computer language development. See "Towards a lingua franca for computers," by Nancy Foy, on page 680. Then in an IBM press release on March 20, 2008, the headline reads, "IBM, Forterra Using Unified Communications in Virtual Worlds to Solve 'Tower of Babel' for Intelligence Agencies," announcing a virtual reality sharing system: "A futuristic unified communications solution code-named 'Babel Bridge' that could allow U.S. intelligence agencies to use a common graphical collaboration system to instantly communicate within a virtual world." And when IBM introduced its Internet of Things Foundation – "internet of things" (IoT) is the networking of connected devices – John R. Thompson, Vice President of the IBM IoT Foundation, described IoT this way: "At the end of the day, it's the Tower of Babel." (See, Thomas Claburn, "IBM Lays Internet of Things Foundation," *InformationWeek*, October 21, 2014, online edition – accessed April 28, 2015). Many other examples could be given.

[24] Jeffrey J. Kripal, *Esalen: America and the Religion of No Religion* (The University of Chicago Press, 2007), p.328.

scattered abroad over the face of the whole earth." And so the city-tower complex arises. How large the community became, and how tall the tower was are really moot points. The real story is the intention of the people and the assumed place of Man in relationship to the Creator. God's order will be usurped by humanity's dream.

Babel becomes synonymous with idolatry.

Historical Jewish interpretations provide some interesting perspectives. In the Targum tradition of Genesis, a translation-commentary used in Aramaic speaking synagogues, we read that the tower was to be capped with a rallying figure: "Let us make us an idol on the top of it and let us put a sword in its hand, and it will make formations of battle."[25] Drawing on ancient texts, Professor Yehezkel Kaufmann described the Babel experience this way: "Man's rebellion reached its peak. He wished to storm heaven, to be 'like God,' to rule the world."[26]

The city-tower of Babel was the first recorded Temple of Man.

Sometime during the building phase God comes down to examine the construction. As Man builds to assert his unifying ascension, God descends and intervenes. He brings judgment, confounding their understanding – "and they ceased building the city" – and He brings grace, saving them from the consequence of greater rebellion. For we read in verse six that Babel, if left to succeed, would set in motion grander acts of idolatry: "Indeed, the people are one and they all have one language, and this is what they begin to do: now nothing that they propose to do will be withheld from them."

An interesting Hebraic language point is the transliteration of "what they begin," ***chalal***, and "be withheld," ***batsar***. Chalal can mean to defile, profane and violate. Batsar has the connotation of gathering, fortifying and making impenetrable. Babel, in triumph, would be the place where collective Man defiles and shuts out the true God so egregiously that a just response from

---

[25] Pseudo Jonathan on Genesis 11. For historical commentary, see John Bowker, *The Targums and Rabbinic Literature: An Introduction to Jewish Interpretations of Scripture* (Cambridge University Press, 1969), p.182.

[26] Yehezkel Kaufmann, *The Religion of Israel: From Its Beginnings to the Babylonian Exile* (The University of Chicago Press, 1960, translated and abridged by Moshe Greenberg), p.294. The statement "to storm heaven, to be like God, to rule the world" is taken from the Jewish pseudo-historical text, *The Book of Jasher*, chapter 9. Different Jewish pseudo literatures add to or embellish aspects of the Babel narrative. These works are helpful in understanding the range of thinking within ancient Hebrew culture.

the Creator would be catastrophic to humanity. By intervening when He does, God saves them from Himself. In response, He divides the nations and chooses a people who will be His own.[27]

God's judgment demonstrates restraint and irony. Ellul writes,

> But God does not smash or destroy. Babel does not crumble under the lightning flash. The problem is a spiritual one, and Babel is only a symbol. To man's desire to make a name for himself, God responds with the confusion of tongues.[28]

Ellul continues, "Babel was to be the place of unity for the human race, the home of human truth. The city – the place of noncommunication among men, the place where the immense irony of God hides."[29]

A wealth of meaning emerges from Genesis 11. It provides an example of solidarity in collective naming, for in the group we define our purpose and boast in it. This declaration, moreover, is a proclaimed independence from God as we pursue our common design. We frame our own security, achieved through power-in-unity. Faith is found in the works of our hands, it is discovered within us instead of relying upon our Creator. And as we commit idolatry at the world level, the exclusive God – who cannot share His glory, for that would be an untruth – ultimately and rightly brings judgment.

All of the above points to something profound: Babel is history's blueprint. It is the spiritual-physical interplay of humanistic empire building, an apt depiction of Mankind's rejection of God and the desire to replace His order with ours. The unforgettable city-tower complex remains unforgettable; it is the never-ending dream – a vision of human deity, to become master of meaning and destiny, an attempt to force Heaven on Earth.

Two points of remembrance emerge from Babel. First, it is a reminder of idolatry and judgment – that God Himself will step-in as Man ultimately oversteps. Second, it is the vision we are incapable of letting go, a tantalizing illusion of human unity. Cosmopolis is the prize of our own making, and we are drawn to it as a moth-to-the-flame.

It is our past, present and future – until God intervenes.

---

[27] Michael S. Heiser explores this aspect and its connection to Deuteronomy 32 in his book, *The Unseen Realm* (Lexham Press, 2015).

[28] Ellul, *The Meaning of the City*, p.17.

[29] Ibid. p.19.

Towers of Progress

Exploring the archives of a US Midwest state a number of years ago, I stumbled onto an old document with a strange sounding title, *World-Conscience: An International Society for the Creation of a World-Centre*. The cover was brittle and the pages fragile. It had the feel of being long forgotten. However, the idea it presented resonated with the Babel meme, an audacious plan to build a world city.

Penned by Hendrik Christian Andersen, an American sculptor living in Rome, this unusual text detailed an architectural wonder: An urban jewel designed to elevate human unity and model "Heaven on Earth." Released in 1913, the same year Andrew Carnegie opened his "Temple of Peace" at The Hague – itself a beacon of world unity[30] – Andersen's vision was embraced by influential personalities around the planet.

President of the Boston World-Peace Foundation, Edwin Ginn,[31] wrote,

> It is hoped the world will advance to a realizing sense of the value of your scheme and put it into practical operation... Unity of action is all that is needed.[32]

Camille Flammarion, President of the Astronomical Society of France, gushed in affirmation: "There is here a magnificent idea... Let us not be citizens of a nation, but of the whole Earth – an atom in the infinite." Norwegian clergyman, Eugen Hanssen, declared that: "With all my heart I will work for this cause." Famous American sociologist, W.E.B. Du Bois, recognized this as advancing "the idea of the equality and essential unity of all mankind." President of Stanford University, David S. Jordan, told Andersen he sympathized with the idea and could use his name as an endorsement. And George

---

[30] Carnegie's Peace Palace, affectionately dubbed the Temple of Peace, today houses the International Court of Justice, the Peace Palace Library, the Permanent Court of Arbitration, The Hague Academy of International Law, and the Carnegie Foundation. The concept and history of the Peace Palace was and is entwined in Andrew Carnegie's goal of global order. It could rightly be called the "house of international law."

[31] A fascinating historical interplay existed between Ginn's World-Peace Foundation, Andrew Carnegie, and the creation of the Carnegie Endowment for International Peace. See, David S. Patterson, "Andrew Carnegie's Quest For World Peace," *Proceedings of the American Philosophical Society*, Volume 114, Number 5, October 1970, p.371ff.

[32] See Hendrik C. Andersen, *World-Conscience: An International Society for the Creation of a World-Centre* (Communication Office of H.C. Andersen, Rome, Italy, 1913), p.36.

W. Nasmyth, a peace activist connected to the International Federation of Students, gave a telling response,

> The trinity of the divine idea, in harmony with the deepest longings of our age toward world unity, the noble architecture in which the idea is embodied, and the beautiful music of the words in which it is expressed, form a fitting trio of heralds announcing that the time for the creation of this Temple of Humanity is [at] hand.[33]

According to the document, which included city plans and street designs, this city would showcase Mankind's harmony and progress. It would host a World Reference Library, an International Bank, an International Hall of Justice – similar to Carnegie's Temple of Peace –International Scientific Congresses on medicine, sociology, agriculture and transport, and a Temple of Religions. These buildings, each grandiose in size and purpose, would encircle the focal point of the city: A colossal, 320-meter Tower of Progress.[34]

"The Tower which will form the chief feature of both Centre and City," wrote Andersen, "was conceived as symbolic of our faith in Unity."[35]

Radiating from the Tower would be boulevards leading to stadiums, centers for learning and physical fitness, museums, and other civic buildings. An Avenue of the Nations was to extend from the Tower to a Temple of Arts, lined with palaces to house government dignitaries and ambassadors.

Andersen drew on Man's deep yearning for centralization,

> Surely the blending of humanity into one complete unity of purpose and desire can but have been foreseen from the beginning, and it is our duty and privilege in life to help bring all human efforts into one grand harmony.[36]

Cosmopolis was on the horizon, and Andersen could sense it,

> A change is now felt throughout the entire world. A divine responsibility governs our actions. As we are one with the past, so must we be one with the future... [Man's] strength can only come through

[33] All letters and notes of endorsement are found at the back of Hendrik's book.

[34] 320 meters equals 1049 feet.

[35] Andersen, *World-Conscience*, p.4. Uppercase "Unity" in original.

[36] Ibid. p.15.

world unification, peace and fellowship – a grander coalescence – a world centralisation.[37]

Andersen's world-city was to be more than just a global gathering place; it was to be a reflection of "*God in man*,"[38]

> ...the eyes of the soul discern the splendid form of Humanity rising in majestic dignity from earth to heaven... the embodiment of the universal soul mounting in appealing harmony towards the divine source of life... Humanity's mission is to realize that Kingdom of Heaven on earth, visioned from within by the spirit of man. Ever nearer Divinity mounts the human race and every increasingly is the fact brought home to man...[39]

The great dream of world harmony and cosmic oneness never materialized. In fact, the year after Andersen released his celebrated blueprint, the earth shook under the Guns of August.[40]

A Palace for Collective Man

By the 1930s, Joseph Stalin, the feared leader of the Soviet Union, set in motion an architectural edifice that would capture the imagination of Marxists everywhere. Moscow, the epicenter of World Revolution, needed a fitting symbol. This structure would need to command the attention of the world, stimulating "Red Builders of all nations" and acting as "a giant magnet, drawing everything into its field of influence."[41]

Conceived in the 1920s with construction beginning the following decade, this project culminated in the building of a massive *swimming pool*.

But before it became a swimming pool it was a bombing target for the German Luftwaffe during World War II, and prior to that it was a vision – the dream of creating the most impressive structure on the planet, a palace that would forever centralize the global fraternity of Communism.

---

[37] Ibid., p.11.

[38] Ibid. p.10. Italics in original.

[39] Ibid., p.15.

[40] The Guns of August is a reference to the opening salvoes of the Great War. Barbara Tuchman's history of World War I is titled *The Guns of August* (Dell Publishing, 1962).

[41] Soviet memo from 1924, as reprinted in Karl Schlögel's book, *Moscow, 1937* (Polity, 2012), p.549-550.

However, before Stalin ever envisioned his grand palace it was Moscow's Cathedral of Christ the Savior.

Four years after the official design was accepted to build the Palace of the Soviets, ground-work started with the dynamiting of the Cathedral, which was located not far from the Kremlin on the bank of the Moskva River. Initiated by Tsar Alexander I in 1812, the Cathedral was built to honor Christ as the Savior of the Russian people in celebration of Napoleon Bonaparte's failed invasion. On December 5, 1937, this national monument – a gigantic structure that took forty years to complete – was reduced to ruble. Karl Schlögel, professor of Eastern European history, described its destruction as a strike against the soul of Christendom: "The detonation... was the sound of the war raging throughout the country, at the heart of the capital... At stake was the spirit of the city and the empire."[42]

The Palace of the Soviets, the new temple of collectivism to replace the now destroyed symbol of Russian Orthodoxy, was *never built*. Foundations were poured, steel and other materials brought in, and girding erected. However, national economic struggles – due in no small part to the failures of Marxism – played a role in retarding the construction. Soil stability problems added to the difficulties.

"When construction began," writes David Shipler in his acclaimed memoir, "the earth that had been beneath the church suddenly turned wet and mushy, and the building kept sinking. Revenge from the heavens? Many like to think so."[43]

If it had been completed the structure would have been a world-wonder. Schlögel gives us a glimpse,

> You entered the foyer via a splendid 100 metre-long staircase. The palace itself led through magnificent corridors to grand solons, reception rooms and suites. The centre of the building was the Great Hall, 140 metres in diameter and 97 metres high, intended to hold 20,000 people seated in gently rising rows in an amphitheatre-like auditorium beneath a mighty dome... The floors above the Great Hall contained offices, but also a variety of museums.[44]

---

[42] Karl Schlögel, *Moscow, 1937* (Polity, 2012), p.548.

[43] David K. Shipler, *Russia: Broken Idols, Solemn Dreams* (Penguin Books, 1983), p.274.

[44] Schlögel, *Moscow*, p.552.

Capping this towering edifice was to be a 75 metre-high, stainless steel statue of Lenin with an arm outstretched in salute, beckoning all "workers of the world" to the revolutionary struggle. Indeed, the Palace was to become the headquarters for the Third Communist International.

Completed, the Palace would have stood 415 metres tall, 88 feet less than Chicago's Willis Tower, minus the antennas. A Soviet writer of the day boasted that the Palace "will become the central ensemble of the new, socialist Moscow. It will be the greatest memorial to the heroic age of Stalin!"[45]

It was to be no less than a Soviet-styled Tower of Babel. "The building was to be a symbol of solidarity," writes Schlögel, "it stood for the centre, for greatness and technical progress. It was a gesture of unbounded power."[46]

Construction of the Palace halted with World War II as steel from the project was used for war purposes. Moreover, after the Soviet-Nazi pact fell apart and Germany invaded Russia, the massive construction site was used by the Luftwaffe as a targeting point for aerial bombing raids. When the war was over, the reconstruction of Russia's leveled cities effectively put the Palace on the back-burner. After Stalin's death in 1952 the dream of a Soviet temple died with Khrushchev's de-Stalinization campaign. The lofty vision of a Communist, cosmopolitan Babel was shattered once-and-for-all.

In 1958 the foundation for the abandoned Palace was converted into an outdoor swimming area. Up until the 1990s, water enthusiasts and Moscow's youth played and swam in the over-chlorinated Moskva Pool. It was so heavily chemicalized that the fumes reportedly degraded the Impressionist paintings in the nearby Pushkin Museum of Fine Arts.[47] Ironically, during the dark days of the Iron Curtain with its entrenched atheism, Moscow's underground Christians used the pool to perform clandestine baptisms.[48]

The pool itself was dismantled in 1994. Starting in November of that year, new foundations were poured for another construction project, one of great physical size and immense meaning. On January 7, 1996, Russia's President Boris Yeltsin and Moscow's Mayor, Yury Luzhkov – both former members of the Communist Party – along with the Russian Orthodox Patriarch, Alexey II,

---

45 G. Grigoryev, May 1937, in the magazine *Ogonek*, as quoted by Schlögel, p.544.

46 Schlögel, *Moscow*, p.545.

47 Svetlana Boym, "Nostalgic Memorials and Postmodern Survival in Russia," *The Postmodern Challenge: Perspectives East and West* (Rodopi Bv Editions, 1999), p.154-155.

48 Shipler, *Russia*, p.274.

ceremonially laid bricks in the entrance to this new edifice. By 1997 the main construction was complete, and in 2000 the artistic touches were finalized.

The Cathedral of Christ the Savior had returned.

Babel Bigger

It was to be a giant drill-bit, boring into the heavens. The Chicago Spire, a 2000-foot high super-tower, elegantly twisting into the clouds, was started in 2007 by digging and pouring a 76-foot deep foundation. Then because of financial problems, the project died an expensive death.

Since the turn of the century a forest of exceptional skyscrapers and super-towers have been constructed. From New York City's dazzling One World Trade Center, built in the footprint of the Twin Towers and soaring almost 1,800 feet, to the "global magnet" of the Shanghai World Financial Center, to the Abraj Al Bait – a colossal structure capped with an enormous Islamic crescent, pushing nearly 2,000 feet above the Kaaba – a new generation of architectural wonders connect earth to sky.

According to the Council on Tall Buildings and Urban Habitat, 2017 was the "tallest year ever" with 35,145 total meters of height constructed,

> More buildings of 200 meters' height or greater were completed in 2017 than in any other year, with a total of 144 completions... This is an increase of 95 percent from 2013, when only 74 buildings of 200 meters or more were completed. The total number of 200-meter buildings in the world is now 1,319, an increase of 12.3 percent from 2016, and a 402 percent increase from 2000, when only 263 existed.[49]

More are on the way.

Saudi Arabia's Kingdom Tower is set to open in 2019 and will stand over 1000 meters, making it the tallest building in the world. Other supertalls are being constructed in China, Malaysia, United Arab Emirates, South Korea, Russia, and elsewhere. Mumbai's "World One" will be the largest *residential* structure on Earth – a trinity-tower design, complete with a Jain Temple "to

---

[49] *CTBUH Year in Review: Tall Trends of 2017* (Council on Tall Buildings and Urban Habitat), p.2.

enrich your religious life. After all... the city's defining landmark should be blessed with divine grace."[50]

Contemplating the tremendous upsurge in global building enterprises and the "meaning of the skyscraper," British journalist Will Self jumped on the symbolic Babel application,

> Any and all skyscrapers are anthropic subversions of the godly perspective – attempts to realise the entirety of human life within the built environment – and hubristic affronts to our Maker and his transcendent Will... Naturally it follows that God's razing of the Tower of Babel recapitulates that earlier toppling from a peak perspective: Lucifer's jump, and its sequel: the apple of knowledge...[51]

Practically speaking, skyscrapers are simply constructions meant to maximize land value and generate economic return – albeit with a prestige factor – but even the Council on Tall Buildings and Urban Habitat recognizes a deeper meaning is associated with our desire to erect structures into the sky.[52] Our towers, like our cities, can be powerful symbols.

Occasionally there is a grand political hope attached to a tower.

Consider Dubai's Burj Khalifa, the tallest building in the world at 2,716 feet. Soon after its doors opened Dubai announced it would be willing to give the United Nations a new home, moving its nerve center from the aging New York headquarters to the youthful energy of this desert super-city.[53] Although the UN switch never materialized, Dubai nevertheless maintains itself as an international beacon, providing space for United Nations agencies through its International Humanitarian City,[54] playing host to major confer-

---

50 From the World Towers website, www.theworldtowers.com, accessed May 5, 2015.

51 Will Self, "Will Self on the Meaning of Skyscrapers – from the Tower of Babel to the Shard," *The Guardian*, March 17, 2015, Book Section; www.theguardian.com/books/2015/mar/27/will-self-on-the-meaning-of-skyscrapers (accessed May 5, 2015).

52 See the debate in the *CTBUH Journal*, 2012, Issue 1. See also Christopher Michaelson, "The Competition for the Tallest Skyscraper: Implications for Global Ethics and Economics," *CTBUH Journal*, 2014, Issue 4.

53 "Who will fill Dubai's new buildings?" *The Globe and Mail*, January 18, 2010, Life Section, online edition, www.theglobeandmail.com/life/home-and-garden/real-estate/who-will-fill-dubais-new-buildings/article4302172.

54 The International Humanitarian City functions as a logistics hub for United Nations agencies and relief organizations. Offices and warehousing, and a complete support struc-

ences on global governance,[55] acting as a voice for world Islamic culture,[56] and offering more than fifteen free trade zones established as "international cities" and special districts. Wealth and knowledge flows into its gates, even as debt restructuring makes the pages of financial newspapers. Dubai and the Burj Khalifa have been likened to a modern Babel.

However, the concept of Babel is not restricted to skyscraper symbolism. Astana, Kazakhstan, with its purposely-designed ancient-futuristic architecture, fits the meme. Nursultan Nazarbayev, the leader of Kazakhstan since 1989 – first coming to power through the Communist Party – has worked hard at making Astana a centerpiece in the Turkic movement and a symbol of global unity. Astana has become a host city for high-level discussions on creating a new international financial system, global governance and collective security, and major interfaith forums – uniting "religious and secular spirituality."[57] Its pyramid-shaped Palace of Peace has become a focal point to inspire spiritual harmony and the quest for a world-embracing culture of oneness: "We present one Earth civilization."[58]

Uniting the "spiritual elite of humanity," according to the Astana World Forum of Spiritual Culture, is essential if a "new architecture" is to take shape, ensuring the "integrity and unity of the world and humanity… the synthesis of the laws of nature and culture."[59]

Yermentay Sultanmurat, of the World Assembly of Turkic Peoples, boasted that, "Astana has every right to be called the spiritual capital of the world."[60]

---

ture, allows international agencies access to Dubai as a strategic partner. Dubai is an important regional connecting point.

[55] Dubai has hosted many international meetings, including the World Economic Forum and the Global Agenda Summit; the 2015 Government Summit; the World Food Security Summit; the World Green Economy Summit, and others.

[56] Example: the $1.5 million dollar World Peace prize, issued via the patronage of Mohammed bin Rashid Al Maktoum, is awarded in accordance with the promotion of Islam as a faith of peace and for building interfaith cooperation.

[57] Tolegen Mukhamejanov, *Opening Remarks*, International Research-to-Practice Conference: Towards World Peace Through Spiritual Culture, Astana, October 29, 2012.

[58] *Resolution of the International Research and Practice Conference, "Spiritual Culture – A Key to Transformation of the World."* World Forum of Spiritual Culture, Republic of Kazakhstan, June 12, 2012. Document on file.

[59] *The World Forum of Spiritual Culture*, Republic of Kazakhstan, June 14, 2012. On file.

[60] Richard Orange, "Kazakhstan president put forward for Nobel Peace Prize," *The Telegraph*, Sept. 23, 2010. www.telegraph.co.uk/news/worldnews/asia/kazakhstan/8020430/

Babel-inspiration can also be discovered in a single building.

The UN headquarters in New York has been referred to as a Tower of Babel, a place where aspirations for world order and the chaos of global disorder happen simultaneously.[61] The Bank for International Settlements in Basil, Switzerland – the infamous and untouchable central bank for world central bankers – has been called a "Tower of Babel." And in my home province of Manitoba, we watched as an outrageously expensive edifice was built on the banks of the Red River.

The Canadian Museum of Human Rights, located near the conflux of the Red and Assiniboine in downtown Winnipeg, is an architectural marvel. Rising as a tiered mountain of stone and steel, this cavernous structure terminates in a 100-meter tower that pushes through enveloping clouds of glass.

Starting at the bottom with its roots in cold stone and cement, visitors walk a ramp to the first gallery. Here you are met with a timeline of 100 "moments in human rights," along with prominent trail blazers of human rights: Zoroaster first, Buddha and Confucius follow, Jesus of Nazareth comes a little later as does Mohammad, and the list goes on. Highlight moments include:

- "Judaism teaches tolerance, collective responsibility and accountability."
- "Jesus of Nazareth teaches virtues of love, compassion and justice."
- "Islamic prophet Muhammad preaches tolerance, charity and equality."
- "Karl Marx publishes *Capital*, arguing for workers' rights."
- "United Nations Charter emphasizes peace and human rights."
- "The Netherlands becomes first country to legalize same-sex marriage."
- "Rights of Mother Earth are proclaimed at World People's Conference."

Crossing ascending bridges of backlit alabaster imported from Spain, the walls glowing with warm light, you move upward from gallery to gallery. Each display touches on historic and contemporary human rights stories, from the Jewish Holocaust to Indigenous perspectives to same-sex themes. The contributions of Canadians to human rights are explained throughout the museum. On one wall was a plaque: "Human rights are ever-changing in our interconnected world. How should we respond?"

Kazakhstan-president-put-forward-for-Nobel-Peace-Prize.html. Sultanmurat's statement was made in the context of Nazarbayev's Nobel Peace Prize nomination.

[61] Former UN Ambassador, Dore Gold, aptly titled his book on UN security issues, *Tower of Babel: How the United Nations has Fueled Global Chaos* (Crown Forum, 2004).

The message: *Inclusivity is growing*. This sounds good on the surface, but if human rights are ever-changing, then a "right" today can be revoked tomorrow, or we may add "rights" based on political expediencies. Rights have to be grounded in something bigger than society, grander than human wisdom, and surpassing generations and cultures. Human rights, connecting to law and ethics, has to be based on a law giver outside of what is temporal, the Judge who is the "same yesterday, today, and forever."[62]

Nearer the top of the museum, we discover the United Nations is a guarantor of human rights. And the final gallery compels us to become activists for social justice and equality. Finally, we climb the Tower of Hope, a symbol of illumination and transformation. We have followed the architect's vision, "From Darkness to Light," and stand gazing upon the city.[63]

One architectural report described the building as "reminiscent of icebergs, tree roots, and the wings of a dove, symbolizing hope for a changed world."[64] Nothing is accidental in this structure, including built-in astrological alignments[65] and its tiered shape, which evokes an ancient context. There is a reason it has been called a "modern Tower of Babel."

"The whole building is more of a ziggurat, a tower," explained a museum committee member.[66]

ArchitectureWeek depicted it as a cathedral where "national law and divine law are reconciled in a peaceable kingdom." The publication elaborated,

> The Museum for Human Rights completes the evolution of this idea by wrapping the stone core with a diaphanous veil of glass, in an image of both transmutation and transcendence as the building rises from earth to heaven, which is to say from an ancestral memory routed in place to a universal ideal found everywhere... its archetype [is] in the biblical Tower of Babel described in the Book of Genesis.[67]

---

62 "Jesus Christ is the same yesterday, today, and forever." – Hebrews 13:8.

63 *Canadian Museum for Human Rights: A Case Study with a Difference* (Architecture 49, with PCL Constructors Canada, Smith Carter Architects and CH2M HILL, no date), p.3.

64 Ibid., p.3.

65 On one of my visits, a museum attendant explained the solstice features in the building.

66 Said by Victor Rabinovitch, former CEO of the Canadian Museum of Civilization and committee member with the Canadian Museum for Human Rights. See Phil Koch, "Rallying Point," *Canada's History*, online edition, September 17, 2014, www.canadashistory.ca/Magazine/Online-Extension/Articles/Rallying-Point.

67 Christopher Curtis Mead, "Predock's Canadian Museum for Human Rights," *Architec-*

Commenting on his design, architect Antoine Predock explained that the structure is rooted in the "fundamental commonality of humankind... a unifying and timeless landmark for all nations and cultures of the world."[68]

Another structure associated with Babel is the European Parliament in Strasbourg, France.

Officially known as the Louise Weiss building, this integrated tower was apparently built to mirror the Coliseum in Rome. It also has an uncanny resemblance to Pieter Bruegel's 1563 painting, *The Tower of Babel* – enough that contemporary correlations have been made.[69] However, it is more than just a passing likeness to a Dutch Renaissance painting that spurs its Babel-ish identity. Years ago the Strasbourg-based Council of Europe released its *Europe: Many Tongues, One Voice* poster, depicting the continental unification project as a rebuilding of Bruegel's tower.[70] Furthermore, the European Parliament's Committee on Culture and Education, operating under the acronym of CULT, intentionally choose Babel imagery for its annual LUX Film Prize. This award is given to cinematographers who have contributed to Europe's integration. LUX, appropriately, means "Light" in Latin.

The CULT prize is a vertically rolled film strip shaped like a ziggurat: "The concept underlying the logo of the LUX Prize is the Tower of Babel, the symbol (also used by the European Parliament) of multilingualism and cultural diversity united in a single place and with a single goal."[71]

The icing on the cake, however, comes not from a logo but from the deeper meaning of the European experiment. Robert Keyserlingk understood the magnitude of the project as conceived by its founders: "Integration into a federated system, along political, economic and military lines, involving the sacrifice of absolute national sovereignty was their objective."[72]

---

tureWeek, August 24, 2011. The article can be read at www.architectureweek.com/2011/0824/building_2-1.html. Article on file.

[68] Antoine Predock, "Canadian Museum for Human Rights," www.predock.com/CMHR/CMHR.html [Accessed May 7, 2015].

[69] I too have compared the painting and EU Parliament in public lectures.

[70] William F. Jasper published this poster in his 1992 book, *Global Tyranny, Step By Step: The United Nations and the Emerging New World Order* (Western Islands, 1992), p.255.

[71] *LUX Prize: The European Parliament is Committed to Culture*, Press Service, Director for the Media, European Parliament, document #20070927BKG10868, page 12.

[72] Robert W. Keyserlingk, *Fathers of Europe: Patrons of Peace* (Palm Publishers Limited, 1972), p.137.

Notwithstanding the political turmoil in the European program, the continent was to be a pathfinder to world federation. Robert Muller expressed this in 1994: "I hope that more regional communities will be created, following the example of the European Union, so that the UN can be transformed soon into a true World Union."[73]

Winston Churchill, the bulldog of England during World War II, advocated for a united Europe as the steppingstone to a global culture. Many of his key speeches after the War had the theme of international fraternity and world governance, what he called the "Temple of Peace."[74]

In 1947 Churchill stressed the need for the one to ensure the other,

> But let there be no mistake upon the main issue. Without a United Europe there is no sure prospect of world government. It is the urgent and indispensable step towards the realisation of that ideal.[75]

Regardless of the ultimate success or failure of European integration, there is little doubt that the aspirations ascribed to it fit the ancient theme. From Babel-to-Babel-to-Babel, humanity has sought power-in-unity. It is the hope of Cain; the dream of Cosmopolis; the quest for Oneness.

Consider Wagar's heady anticipation,

> The world-city is the inevitably large spiritual and intellectual and administrative capital of a civilization, of the whole known civilized world... it is the quintessence of a civilization, the gathering of all its vital human resources into a living organic unity.[76]

---

[73] Robert Muller, *2000 Ideas for a Better World: My Countdown on Dreams on Mt. Rasur to the Year 2000, for Your Thoughts and Action* (University of Peace, no date, fascicle one), p.5, see idea #23.

[74] The Temple of Peace was a term Churchill used in his "Sinews of Peace" talk at Westminster College, Fulton, Missouri, March 5, 1946. In this speech he called for a world order built around the United Nations and a united Europe, and expressed this a "reality and not a sham... and not merely a cockpit in a Tower of Babel." Here Churchill was likening the ineffectiveness of pseudo internationalism to the Tower, but this misses the point; the Tower was about building order, and confusion was the consequence.

[75] Winston Churchill, "United Europe," Albert Hall, London, May 14, 1947. See *Churchill Speaks: 1897-1963 – Collected Speeches in Peace and War* (Barnes and Noble Books, 1998, edited by Robert Rhodes James), p.913.

[76] Wagar, *The City of Man*, p.15.

Urban World

Standing on the promenade of Canada Place, Vancouver's waterfront convention center with its iconic white, sail-topped roof, I was struck by the incredible combination of natural splendor and human achievement. Looking across Burrard Inlet, I gazed upon the majestic mountains so typical of beautiful British Columbia. To my back rose skyscrapers, towers, and construction cranes – a testament to the growth and energy of Vancouver, one of the most concentrated urban zones in North America. All around me, often shoulder-to-shoulder, a sea of humanity flowed.

More than 10,000 participants from over 100 countries had gathered at Canada Place for the third United Nations World Urban Forum (WUFIII), hosted by UN-HABITAT.[77] For myself, it was the second week of a twenty-three day motorcycle tour as I hopped from city-to-city, with WUFIII as a primary research destination. My purpose in attending was to better understand how urban governance and global governance intersected.

Whether in plenary sessions or workshops, we were told it was up to us as activists, mayors and city-planners to lead the way. Stated and implied was that national governments were too slow, too cumbersome, to effectively meet planetary challenges. As global citizens connected to the power-base of cities, large and small, we could incite transformation: "Because the first steps toward global change, starts with us!"[78]

The time for politicking was over, and the UN General Assembly did not want the World Urban Forum to be a debating platform, but "a summit of actions."[79] Anna Tibaijuka, then Executive Director of UN-HABITAT, reminded us we were "planting the city" in the "mainstream of international politics."[80] This dovetailed with her message in the WUFIII edition of *Habitat Debate*, in which she recounted the words of development theorist, Üner Kirdar,

> We must now learn to live with a global perspective. Humanity is part of the complex planetary system and global issues must be the concern of all people and nations. The world community has the

[77] WUFIII took place from June 19-23, 2006.

[78] *Our Future: Sustainable Cities – Turning Ideas into Action, Conference Program* (UN-Habitat, World Urban Forum III), p.48.

[79] H. P. Oberlander, "Living History – A Personal Look at the Conferences and Resolutions that Led to the Creation of UN-HABITAT," *Habitat Debate*, June 2006, Vol.12, Nu.2, p.5.

[80] Anna Tibaijuka, Opening Speech, June 19, 2006, on file.

> ability, the means and the chance to transform the many threats of today into opportunities for human progress tomorrow. But it needs new vision, long-term perspectives and bold leadership.[81]

The UN Secretary-General's welcome letter urged us forward: "Together, we must scale up our efforts, and make our urban planet more just, equitable and sustainable for all its inhabitants."[82]

Discussions to that end integrated the localization of the Millennium Development Goals and *Agenda 21* – the UN framework on environment and development.[83] Urban policies on climate change would need to take shape, resulting in tangible and enforceable action at the local level. Financial ties, too, would have to be deepened between urban players and the international community. Robert Williams, then Mayor of Georgetown, Guyana, stressed the need for the UN to become a fast track partner between cities and world financial institutions. Katherine Sierra, then VP for Infrastructure at the World Bank, revealed how her group was looking to go beyond working with federal governments and provide cities with direct funding and financial services.[84] Both Williams' and Sierra's words struck a cord with attendees, for they were offering alternatives to national politics.

Practical and complex issues were wrestled with, from energy infrastructure to the challenge of slums to disaster mitigation and housing concerns. More philosophical topics were also explored: social cohesion, modeling inclusion, and gender and social equality. A real-world question perplexed me, one not addressed in any of the workshops I attended, so I pitched it to a few people: *How does the rural fit into this urban world?*

---

81 "A Message from the Executive Director," *Habitat Debate*, June 2006, p.2.

82 See his letter in *Our Future: Sustainable Cities – Turning Ideas into Action, Conference Program* (World Urban Forum, 2006), p.2.

83 *Agenda 21* is a sustainable development framework document initiated by the United Nations at the Rio Earth Summit in 1992. It operates as a backbone upon which national and local governments can build environmental policies in accordance with global governance principles. The UN Millennium Development Goals focused on education, poverty, and health as agreed upon by participating member nations. The MDG's have since been replaced by the Sustainable Development Goals as expressed in *Agenda 2030*.

84 The World Bank has had an urban unit for decades, although city-based projects have typically been part of national lending arrangements. Sierra's remarks, however, demonstrated that the financial body was willing to step beyond traditional boundaries and engage in city-level debt operations.

Incredulity met my query. Two people flat out told me, *we don't need the country*. Not one person understood the gravity of the question, but they did when I reminded them of the following: Your food comes from the country, your water source springs from outside city limits, your electrical and fuel energy originates from a non-urban source, your refuse and sewage is moved beyond the city, and much of the commodities used to build your community – wood, iron, cement – have a rural starting point.

The City is a place of tremendous human growth and power and creativity. It is an engine of economy and modernism. Today's global-minded City, however, is much more. A background document from UNESCO, picked up at WUFIII, suggested the "world-city" should be a place of collective assimilation and solidarity, the "terrain where social transformations originate and are managed."[85] Spiritual transformation was a topic the Forum explored.

On Wednesday, June 21, I sat in on the Spirituality Roundtable. Leaders from different religions and interfaith organizations – including the United Religions Initiative – dialogued on urban wellness and the role of spirituality in the city. Michael Hryniuk, specializing in Christian contemplation and spiritual formation, gave a brief explanation before a time of silence,

> At the outset we would like to honor all spiritual traditions here, and their insight – that one of the great ways to make contact with that source of vision within us, between us, and among us is to enter into silence – into a silence that unites, and allows our minds to settle into our hearts and into our spirits so that we can access the deeper intelligence, a deeper sense of imagination, a deeper sense of vision.[86]

A consensus emerged between faith leaders and attending politicians: Cities need to integrate spirituality within civic planning. Zoning regulations *must* incorporate interfaith sensibilities and encourage urban festivals reflecting universal themes. Narrow truth claims are out, and spiritual inclusivity is in. It was time for urban centers to encourage this transition.

That same evening the Forum's arts and cultural festival kicked off with the burning of a 14-foot effigy in the Bali tradition of Randga, the child-eating

---

[85] *Toward the City of Solidarity and Citizenship* (UNESCO, dialogue document prepared for HABITAT II, 1995/1996), p.8.

[86] Audio of the event on file.

demon queen who battles the forces of good. The purpose? To celebrate the summer solstice. After the "Burning Devil," Vancouver residents and Forum attendees could party at the "Get Down to Earth Solstice Dance."[87] This art event was titled, *Earth: World Urban Festival*, and was billed as a place to connect with the energy of the city in celebration of the Earth.

The Forum itself was its own type of political festival: An experiment in unity, and an affirmation that the City will save itself as it saves the World.

Jacques Ellul's thoughts on the City – penned decades ago – are still relevant, for the City remains a symbol of the human heart,

> ...the city is man's greatest work. It is his great attempt to attain autonomy, to exercise will and intelligence. This is where all his efforts are concentrated, where all the powers are born. No other of man's works, technical or philosophical, is equivalent to the city, which is the creation not of an instrument but of the whole world in which man's instruments are conceived and put to work.[88]

As a *constructed hope*, the City takes upon itself symbolic, theoretical, and practical attributes in pursing the utopian dream of world unity. The ideal is inescapable, sparking our imagination. Together we build the City.

A New City

At Babel, God disperses the nations in consequence to Man's collective rebellion. Out of this He chooses a people-group for Himself, beginning a lineage that would bless the world with a God-given Messiah: from the Hebrew patriarchs to Moses, from King David to the Savior, Jesus Christ. Grace is extended far beyond Babel.

Michael Heiser, a scholar in Hebrew Bible and Semitic Languages, relates the Babel event to our human desire to regain what was lost, and to God's higher purpose of redemption,

> But the incident at Babel, foolish and self-willed as it was, shows us that there's an Edenic yearning in the human heart, a desire for utopia and a sense of divine presence. But God would not trade his

[87] *Earth: World Urban Festival 2006, Program Guide*, (World Urban Forum III, 2006), p.1.
[88] Ellul, *The Meaning of the City*, p.154.

> own version of Eden for humanity's. He punished the nations with disinheritance. He would create a new people as his own portion. That inheritance was begun in covenant with Abraham and passed through his family.[89]

Babel is a reminder of God's great mercy, which extends beyond our capacity for sin and rebellion. At the same time, it is an ancient landmark that haunts, intrigues, and beckons us to find our collective voice – for our self-directed, collective salvation.

Cosmopolis, the Temple of Man, is a reflection of our desire to re-build Paradise in our own image. It is a symbol and a hope, a quest and a conquest. It is a thread that weaves its way through the human story, entangling and enchanting. From the shadows of ancient times, Enoch and Babel, the power of the City tantalizes our soul with its promises of security and mastery.

We dream of Babel and build our Enochs. *We are all Cain.*[90]

It can be argued that a second Babel is being built before us, or at least a type of Babel, following traces of a pattern harkening back to Genesis. We can see its shadow growing.

What earth-shaking events will it take for the next Babel to clearly manifest?

We can analyze and speculate. More concretely we can learn to discern how this pattern displays itself in society, and in our own lives. It is a constant reminder of Man's inescapable character; the more we *technique* for transformation and ascension, the more we wrap ourselves in Babel. And this reminder extends to the image reflected in my bathroom mirror.

There is more. As the first Babel proudly displayed itself for a time, the second one will appear to succeed too. But there is a limit to our hubris and triumph. God intervened in the Genesis prototype, and He will do so again. The pattern is before us, a cause animated by rebellion to be met by an effect based in righteousness. We should not be surprised by the response.

Judgment comes. Jesus Christ enters the world stage with overwhelming power (Revelation 19:15), bringing a sword and treading "the winepress of the fierceness and wrath of Almighty God." He overthrows Babel, and has *every right to do so.*

---

89 Michael S. Heiser, *The Unseen Realm: Recovering the Supernatural Worldview of the Bible* (Lexham Press, 2015), p.155.

90 This is a point Jacque Ellul makes in his book, *The Meaning of the City*.

The architects and builders are without excuse.

But grace follows wrath, for His redeemed people encounter a new city with a new meaning. Enter the New Jerusalem, a city of *His* work and *not ours*. It is His delight, His place of dwelling among Men – a truly global city.

Filled with God's light, the gates of this place *remain open*; and the "nations of those who are saved shall walk in its light, and the kings of the earth bring their glory and honor into it."[91]

Ironic? Yes, and good. For out of the city that God constructs will flow beauty and grace. Grace, grace, marvelous grace,

> Now I saw a new heaven and a new earth, for the first heaven and the first earth had passed away. Also there was no more sea. Then I, John, saw the holy city, New Jerusalem, coming down out of heaven from God, prepared as a bride adorned for her husband. And I heard a loud voice from heaven saying, Behold, the tabernacle of God is with men, and He will dwell with them, and they shall be His people. God Himself will be with them and be their God. And God will wipe away every tear from their eyes; there shall be no more death, nor sorrow, nor crying. There shall be no more pain, for the former things have passed away.[92]

91 Revelation 21:24.

92 Revelation 21:1-4.

Part IV

Going Deeper

Fifty years is ample time in which to change the world and its people almost beyond recognition. All that is required for the task are a sound knowledge of social engineering, a clear sight of the intended goal – and power.
– Arthur C. Clarke, *Childhood's End*.

Well, we are gods now, gods in charge of our own destiny, and gods can't be capricious.
– Maurice Strong, *Where On Earth Are We Going?*

Chapter 11

The Cult of World Order

> The old world is dead. Let the new one arise from its ashes! Arise the new world order shall. – Haridas T. Muzumdar.[1]

> World crisis and world chaos cannot be successfully handled in the absence of world authority. – Scott Nearing.[2]

"Which organization are you representing?"

"None," I answered. "I'm individually accredited." The gentleman's eyebrows went up. I was an anomaly.

My surroundings were surreal: Gazing into the domed space above me, it appeared I was sitting in a giant, inverted bowl. The vast ceiling resembled something out of a science fiction movie with its saucer-like center and concentric rings of lights. Along the two sidewalls, double rows of darkened windows looked down on the milling crowd. Immediately to my front, past the two-tiered marble podium, was an iconic gold-leafed wall shimmering with the reflecting glow of overhead lights – an imposing backdrop for the enormous emblem of world unity that hung above us.

There we were, in our suits and ties, sitting together in the middle of the United Nations General Assembly Hall, surrounded by almost 1400 participants from around the world, each – with the exception of a few dozen people – officially representing a civil society organization or international agency. We had gathered under the banner of *We The Peoples*, the title of the UN Secretary-General's rallying report. We had assembled to birth a new order for the new millennium.

---

1 Haridas T. Muzumdar, *The United Nations of the World* (Universal Publishing Company, 1944), p.105.

2 Scott Nearing, *United World* (Island Press, 1945), p.248.

"Do you know anybody here?" I countered, noticing my table partner was representing a governmental entity.

"No. Do you?"

Earlier in the day I had recognized a few faces behind the registration table as members of the World Federalist Association (WFA), and briefly interacted with them. "If you have any problems with your paperwork," explained an attendant I knew to be a World Federalist, "just come back and we'll take care of it." With a reassuring nod he handed me some forms to fill out.

"We're running the show."

After passing security and entering the General Assembly I had noticed other WFA personalities lingering near the front of the great hall. These were people I had encountered at meetings in Washington DC and Chicago, but I could not honestly say I knew them. After all, I was attending the United Nations Millennium Forum (UNMF) as an *independent* participant.

"I recognize a few people," I said to my companion, "but nobody I know."

The gentleman nodded at my answer. There we were; two strangers surrounded by strangers in the symbolic nerve center of global fraternity. But in a matter of seconds I looked to be the liar.

With the words barely out my mouth, a young professional who was familiar to me as a World Federalist marched from the front of the auditorium and stopped at our desk.

"Carl, we have VIP seats up front. There's a spot reserved for you."

What could I say? I gathered my belongings and, under the glare of my now former table partner, made my way to the front of the General Assembly.

Establishing A New Pathway

Attending the United Nations Millennium Forum, May 22-26, 2000, was an opportunity to intimately witness how "world order" was being envisioned for the 21st century.

Setting this event apart from other UN millennial meetings was its composition. Instead of stacking the Forum with governmental representation, it was geared to "civil society" – accredited, non-governmental organizations (NGOs). This was in keeping with the UN Secretary General's 1997 call for a "People's Assembly."

It is important to note that NGOs encompass a range of organizations and interests. Generally, any non-profit and non-governmental body can fit the category of NGO. This can include charity groups, faith-based and humanitarian agencies, special interest societies and associations, foundations and think tanks.

However, in the context of the international community, NGOs usually refer to civil society organizations that are accredited to the United Nations, agree with its principles, and have a stake in the global narrative. Even here differences are observable. Some groups convey a benign platform, like the World Association of Girl Guides and Girl Scouts, which was accredited to the UNMF. On the other hand, entities such as Lucis Trust and the Institute for Planetary Synthesis – financial contributors to the Forum – openly frame global oneness through occult philosophy. Others work to advance political regionalism, like the Union of European Federalists and The Spinelli Group.[3] Some lobby for an even larger change; the World Citizen Foundation is one example. Another is the World Federalist Association, since renamed Citizens For Global Solutions, and its umbrella organization, the World Federalist Movement (WFM).

For our context NGOs are non-governmental *pressure groups*, pushing for national change to follow a prescribed global narrative. They are repositories and activators of ideas that stimulate transformation. As one NGO activist wrote: "Ideas are powerful instruments of change… Ideas precede action, they impel change in attitude and behavior and thus provide the basis for political change."[4]

UN partnering with civil society is an important part of world order development; it allows new voices and visions to permeate into an otherwise bureaucratic environment. Moreover, many NGOs act as apostles for the world body, disseminating the global narrative into national and local dialogues. At the same time NGOs gain stature, visibility, and reach – their special interests are authenticated. It is a mutually reinforcing relationship.

Unlike governments, most NGOs are seen as detached from partisan influences and are portrayed as untainted by party politics and corporate powers. Championed by cultural influencers, a persona emerges: *We hold the moral*

---

3 The Spinelli Group formed in 2010 as a network of parliamentarians, experts, and academics in favor of a federalist European Union.

4 Tom Burke, "Friends of the Earth and the Conservation of Resources," *Pressure Groups in the Global System: The Transnational Relations of Issue-Oriented Non-Governmental Organizations* (St. Martin's Press, 1982, edited by Peter Willetts), p.106.

high ground.[5] The NGO community is thus upheld as an arbitrator of social legitimacy, a voice of the global conscious.

In saying the above it must be noted that mundane and practical consultations between international agencies, governments, and certain NGOs happen on a daily basis. I have friends who have been involved in this capacity, dealing with routine matters of business and diplomacy, and sometimes working through complex situations; there is need for a neutral space where multi-player concerns can be discussed and resolved. We do live in a global world, a fact that should compel national powers to seek sensible, wise, and mutually beneficial exchanges. However, the NGO-UN interplay at the United Nations Millennium Forum was geared to something more transformational, more profound – the *visionary construction of futures*.

We had gathered to remake the world in our image.

In fact, NGOs with world order aspirations oversaw the collaboration of the Millennium Forum's final report.[6] This outcome document, built on the cumulative work of six UNMF sub-theme committees, would be distributed to heads-of-state and global institutions. We were shaping tomorrow.

Techeste Ahderom, the UNMF Co-chair and Principle Representative of the Bahá'í International Community, told us we were consulting on "humanity's common future" and finding our "collective voice."

"The Forum is more than a weeklong meeting at the United Nations," Ahderom explained. "We believe it holds out the prospect of establishing a new pathway." A few moments later he added,

> As this new millennium begins, we are all increasingly coming to realize that, in our diversity, we are one human family. The only way we can survive the challenges ahead is to stand together. In this

---

5 It is no surprise that verbal inflation and self-congratulations are common traits in the global NGO community. Both are symptoms and byproducts of a "prevailing social vision" that is "dangerously close to sealing itself off from any discordant feedback from reality." See Thomas Sowell, *The Vision of the Anointed: Self-Congratulation as a Basis for Social Policy* (Basic Books, 1995). "Prevailing social vision" and "discordant feedback" are taken from page 1. Verbal inflation refers to the overextended language that pervades politically correct speech: to take the meaning of a word and expand its historical definition to include questionable forms for the sake of political/social argument.

6 The World Federalist Movement took the lead during much of the Millennium Forum, including the development of its final report.

> regard, we have no choice but to follow this path of global inclusion and to recognize and affirm our essential oneness.[7]

We *are* one human family, all stemming from an original human couple. Christians therefore should be the least racist group on Earth, for the Biblical position is that we are all one human race, emanating from a common beginning through Adam and Eve. But Ahderom was suggesting something more *planetizing* – political conformity to an idealized enchantment. Referencing UN Secretary-General Kofi Annan's report, *We The Peoples*, Ahderom told the crowd,

> The Secretary General, in his report to the Millennium Assembly, has also clearly appreciated and articulated the need for a bold new vision of global inclusion, based on the recognition of our interdependence and oneness – for this, above all else, we applaud him.

Annan's document did not specify *oneness*, but Ahderom understood the Secretary-General's context. After Ahderom took his seat, Kofi Annan addressed the assembly,

> You have understood that problems without passports requires blueprints without borders. We can in fact safely say that the NGO revolution is one of the happier consequences of what has come to define our age: globalization.[8]

Herein lies an important factor: NGOs can initiate awareness campaigns and social movements, and thus compel national governments to translate global ideas into local action. And when multiple and diverse NGOs all lobby for the same end, pressuring governments and targeting key groups – even employing *strategic exaggeration* as an issue-attention tactic[9] – the perception of "public interest" is politically magnified. A multiplier effect comes into

[7] All quotes by Techeste Ahderom are taken from his speech during the Opening Plenary, UNMF, Monday, 22 May 2000, speech on file.

[8] UN Secretary-General Kofi Annan, Welcome Speech, Opening Plenary, Monday, 22 May 2000, speech on file.

[9] "Strategic exaggeration" is a tactic admitted by environmental activist, Robin Mearns, in his essay "Environmental Entitlements: Towards Empowerment for Sustainable Development," as published in *Empowerment for Sustainable Development: Toward Operational Strategies* (Fernwood Publishing/International Institute for Sustainable Development, 1995, edited by Vangile Titi and Naresh Singh), p.51.

play and the issue moves into an actionable phase. At the UN Millennium Forum, the NGO community celebrated this rising collective power, recognizing themselves as the revolutionary "third force" in shaping society.

It was a heady experience.

The Forum's thematic groups, bastions of "anointed vision," articulated the political applications of oneness. I was part of Subgroup Six, *Strengthening and Democratizing the UN and Other International Organizations*, which was dominated by the World Federalist Movement and its American branch, the WFA.

The following are some of the points we discussed:

- Establish independent funding for the UN by taxing international currency transactions, or through a carbon tax earmarked for the world body. Another idea was to place levies on the use of the *global commons*: special charges for the commercial use of outer space, oceans and international waterways, and a fee for airlines making trans-national flights. Or allow the UN to issue Special Drawing Rights, a global monetary asset based on a basket of national currencies, or perhaps it could draw its own bonds and thus create an exchangeable currency. If the United Nations could secure independent funding, it was believed, then it could transition into an effective global entity.
- Re-focus the UN Trusteeship Council: "To exercise stewardship over the global commons such as oceans, the atmosphere and outer space."
- Develop a UN controlled international police and military force, complete with headquarters and a unified training regimen. Such a move would allow for the creation of a UN Security Insurance Agency. In this scheme, cooperating nations would disarm and the money saved from de-militarization would be transferred to the United Nations. In turn, if an insured country were to be invaded by a hostile entity, the international force would guarantee its physical security.
- Strengthen existing institutions of world law, including the International Court of Justice, and implement and empower the International Criminal Court. National laws and judicial systems, it was agreed, should be re-structured to dovetail with this budding global legal order.[10]

[10] These examples were extracted from *Theme Six Discussion Paper*, Final Version, 5/30/2000, along with Subgroup Six working papers and our internal deliberations.

The most intense gathering of Subgroup Six happened on Thursday afternoon, and with it, an interesting side story.

Each morning and afternoon started with plenary assemblies to help set the tone for our working committees. Early in the week I found myself sitting a few chairs away from a cheerful, young lady who was representing a youth-based organization. Thereafter, we sat in proximity during most of the plenary talks and frequently engaged in a few minutes of conversation before going our separate ways. Following the afternoon plenary on Thursday, she asked which subgroup I was with as her committee had bogged down in trivial matters. I invited her to our next working session: "Citizenship and Governance: From Local to Global Democracy."

On the surface the title sounded dull. "Citizenship and Governance" has all the panache of a high-school class you wished you had skipped. But there was nothing boring about it.

Our job for the afternoon was to flesh out tangible plans for a permanent World Assembly. The UN Millennium Forum was, after all, an experiment along those lines. The room filled quickly; much was riding on this meeting. The two moderators, each representing a world order NGO, started the afternoon by placing *their* organization's action plans on the table. The rest of the session was a whirlwind of debate and contention as differing groups, all wanting similar ends, clashed with the moderators and each other over how to "collectively invent a new type of democracy, a world democracy."[11]

It was a heated meeting.[12]

Two main avenues were explored: the creation of a Global Peoples Assembly and the establishment of a World Parliament. One body would be built around NGO delegates and the election of "world citizens," and the other would be a scaled-up version of the European Parliament at the UN level. Variations on these two models were considered and contrasted.

---

[11] *Proposed New Text for Session 6.7 – Citizenship and Governance: From Local To Global Democracy*, May 25, 2000, first page, first paragraph, last line.

[12] The moderators were Rob Wheeler of the Millennium People's Assembly Network and Troy Davis of the World Citizen Foundation. They began the afternoon with an agenda of how to construct world democracy, and remained steadfast on structural issues and implementation options. Those who wished to voice a different approach did so, but found themselves shut out of the consensus process. Frustrated and upset, a sizable number of people left by midpoint, and in the end, Wheeler and Davis closed the meeting with their agenda largely intact.

Questions arose from the floor: What would these bodies' relationship be to the United Nations? Would they pass enforceable world laws or just make suggestions? How much political power would be entrusted to them? Should another Assembly be attached to the International Monetary Fund? Could regional Assemblies and Parliaments be established on each continent? What mechanisms would ensure national compliance?

As our meeting progressed it became evident that my visitor was growing uneasy; the topic and its implications were obviously distressing. Seeing her growing agitation one of the moderators stopped the discussion and, pointing at her, asked if there was a problem. Catching the seriousness of the moment she quickly composed herself and the moderator, accepting this, resumed the meeting. We stayed until the closing gavel dropped.

"This is the beast," she murmured as we exited the building. "This is the beast..."

Quietly I asked, "Are you a Christian?"

"Yes."

I explained that I too was a believer, telling her my purpose in attending.

She asked what else my group had planned, and I gave her an overview. For someone unfamiliar with the scope and tactics of world order NGOs, Subgroup Six was a staggering experience. She had witnessed the attempted construction of a political Frankenstein dressed up as a global savior.

Expressions of "one world" could be found throughout the Millennium Forum. Steven C. Rockefeller introduced the final version of the *Earth Charter*, which would be officially unveiled at The Hague in late June. Mikhail Gorbachev sent a statement to the Forum reiterating its significance,

> One of the most important things to recognize is that we are all mutually interdependent... Much can be achieved by a shift in human values... As one of the founders of the Earth Charter initiative, I was very gratified to discover the emphasis placed on this important document in the Millennium Forum's draft declaration... I wish to re-assert the Millennium Forum's call for all governments and individuals to read the document very carefully and join the movement to form a global partnership for the sake of preservation of the Earth.[13]

[13] Mikhail Gorbachev, statement dated May 15, 2000.

Cora Weiss, President of The Hague Appeal for Peace, recommended a UN controlled military force and civilian peacekeepers "trained in gender sensitivity." She told us that, "the Secretary General is the world's top moral authority."[14]

A draft document from Subgroup Five said it was time to consider "a world central bank" and "a world environment agency," asking: "Do we need a world government? Does the UN General Assembly need to be transferred into a kind of world parliament?"[15]

One circulated declaration, *Cultural and Spiritual Concerns*, called for "Religious and spiritual dialogues to promote shared ethics and values in service to the United Nations."[16]

The UN Association of Spain provided this statement: "A global world requires global responses and a system of world government."[17]

And the head of the World Assembly of Turkic Peoples, Yermentay Sultanmurat, disseminated a specially prepared booklet, *Transformation of the World*, with his recommendation for a type of planetary king,

> Small doubt, that the world does need a civilized coordinator in international relations and in settling global problems... this coordinator must be a stabilizing factor, actually, the last ditch authority on the Earth. He must win [the] confidence of each man and each nation. People must be stark sure that this coordinator would solve any problem in a just and humane way. And one should be sure that in him he would find understanding and sympathy, that he would treat any nation as his own son and that he is indeed the last resort. And the man should convince his terrestrial brothers therein by his practical deeds... can the world community do without a coordinator? Definitely [it] cannot.[18]

---

[14] Cora Weiss, speech given at the May 23, 2000 UNMF Plenary Session, "Peace, Disarmament and Security."

[15] Draft Millennium Forum Discussion Paper on Major Sub-Theme 5 – *Facing the Challenges of Globalization: Equity, Justice and Diversity.*

[16] *New Directions in Sustainable Development from an NGO Perspective (North and South): Cultural and Spiritual Concerns.* A paper distributed to the subgroup on Sustainable Development and the Environment.

[17] *Statement of the Convenor on Culture at the Millennium Forum*, United Nations Association of Spain to the Millennium Forum, p.3.

[18] Yermentay Sultanmurat, *Transformation of the World*, p.25 (distributed at UNMF).

The Millennium Forum was a powerful demonstration of the political aspirations orbiting around the ideology of "essential oneness." I had been privy to its machinations.

Which brings up my VIP placement.

The year before I had attended a youth-based World Federalist event in Washington DC, a preparation conference for the upcoming Hague Appeal for Peace – a major peace gathering initiated by the World Federalist Movement.[19] Toward the end of this Washington meeting it was announced that everyone in attendance would receive a gratis membership with the World Federalist Association. Presto! I was part of the club. Then, when it came time to register for the Millennium Forum, I listed my WFA membership along with other details. Little did I know that World Federalists held key positions in the Forum's organizational hierarchy, and they were stacking the deck.[20] Even though I was accredited as an independent participant, in reality I was counted as a WFA asset. Other UNMF "independents" were connected to the World Federalists too.[21]

Obviously, the new world order as laid out by the Millennium Forum has not yet come to fruition. Such a monumental shift requires more than just manifestos and declarations of hope and change. It needs broad acceptance across populations and governments, and in all likelihood it necessitates a crisis of magnitude.

But many who attended the Forum knew that already.

---

[19] The Hague Appeal for Peace took place from May 11-15, 1999, at The Hague – almost one century to the day when the First Hague Peace Convention occurred. "Nearly 10,000 delegates from 1000 civil society organizations" attended, along with prominent world figures such as UN Secretary-General Kofi Annan, Archbishop Desmond Tutu, and Queen Noor of Jordan. Initiated by the World Federalist Movement, the Appeal had broad governmental and NGO support. For a brief history of the Appeal, see "A Message from the Secretary-General" by Bill Pace, Secretary-General of the Hague Appeal for Peace, in *Peace Mattes: Newsletter of the Hague Appeal for Peace*, Volume 2, Issue 2 – "Conference Edition" – September 1999, p.3.

[20] Not only were World Federalist strongly represented in an official capacity, a number of "non-Federalist" organizations sent delegates who were also World Federalist members.

[21] At least six of the thirty "independents" from the United States were members of the WFA or WFM, with myself in the mix (I had a US address at the time, hence I was listed under the United States). Another five had known connections to the World Federalists. Finally, many of the attending, non-Federalist NGOs had a friendly working relationship with the WFM/WFA.

Anticipated World Order

On September 11, US President George Bush told Congress that America would "serve together with Arabs, Europeans, Asians and Africans in defense of principle and the dream of a new world order."[22] It was the Persian Gulf crisis of 1990, and George H.W. Bush was in the Oval Office. On January 16, 1991, the day before Operation Desert Storm commenced, he contextually placed this military engagement within the framework of the United Nations,

> We have before us the opportunity to forge for ourselves and for future generations a new world order – a world where the rule of law, not the law of the jungle, governs the conduct of nations. When we are successful – and we will be – we have a real chance at this new world order, an order in which a credible United Nations can use its peacekeeping role to fulfill the promise and vision of the U.N.'s founders.[23]

Thirteen days later he said the following,

> What is at stake is more than one small country; it is a big idea: a new world order, where diverse nations are drawn together in common cause to achieve the universal aspirations of mankind – peace and security, freedom, and the rule of law. Such is a world worthy of our struggle and worthy of our children's future.[24]

Many Americans were perplexed by this repeated phrase, *new world order*. Some commentators erroneously credited Bush as using it first. He certainly said it often, but others had used this phrase too. President Reagan did in 1982, noting that all countries need to "strive together, motivated by the firm determination to build a new world order which guarantees political justice, economic justice, and social justice."[25] In 1977 President Carter said,

---

[22] George H.W. Bush, Address Before a Joint Session of the Congress on the Persian Gulf Crisis and the Federal Budget Deficit, September 11, 1990.

[23] George H.W. Bush, Address to the Nation Announcing Allied Military Action in the Persian Gulf, January 16, 1991.

[24] George H.W. Bush, Address Before a Joint Session of the Congress on the State of the Union, January 29, 1991.

[25] Ronald Reagan, Toasts of President Reagan and President Soeharto of Indonesia at the State Dinner, October 12, 1982.

"the creation of that new world order demands bold initiatives and global solutions."[26] President Franklin D. Roosevelt employed it *in the negative*, describing Adolf Hitler's global aspirations as "his new world order."[27]

For over a century before Bush's presidency, social and political visionaries, diplomats, and heads-of-state have uttered those words. And it nearly always meant the same thing: a new paradigm in international relations with a corresponding change in civilization – a global restructuring couched in some ideal of homogenization and interdependence. This does not mean, however, that all who desire a new world order follow the same pattern or methodology or philosophy. How it is arrived at and what it entails can be nuanced. Nevertheless, it remains "a big idea."

And it is an *old idea*.

In the 1600's, Moravian Bishop Johann Amos Comenius "maintained that all men were citizens of the world" and should assemble "in one community under international law." William Penn called for a European Diet in 1693, in which nations would pool military resources against any state that refused to submit. In 1796, Carl J.A. Hofheim recommended an Assembly of European rulers to meet in a central, neutral city, and form a Perpetual Congress of Nations. Thomas Paine argued for an Association of Neutrals, a grouping of countries using their combined naval strength to sanction aggressors, with ships of the Association sailing under a rainbow colored flag. United States Senator Charles Sumner advocated for "a Congress of Nations with a high court" in 1849. Each was longing for a new world order, even though the phrase was not part of their lexicon.[28]

The desire for a new order is normally associated with political and economic restructuring. This correlation is accurate, but a wider rearrangement is also envisioned. In the 1870s the founder of the Bahá'í faith, Bahá'u'lláh, spoke favorably of a coming new world order.[29] John Ferraby, a respected Bahá'í leader from the last century, fleshed out what this entails: a "world

---

26 Jimmy Carter, Visit of President Perez of Venezuela, at a Dinner Honoring the Venezuelan President, June 28, 1977.

27 Franklin D. Roosevelt, Address for Navy and Total Defense Day, October 27, 1941.

28 See Edith Wynner and Georgia Lloyd, *Searchlight on Peace Plans: Choose Your Road to World Government* (E.P. Dutton and Company, 1944), for Comenius, p.35; Penn, p.36; Hofheim, pp.54-55; Paine, pp.58-59; and Sumner, pp.77-78.

29 *Bahá'í World Faith: Selected Writings of Bahá'u'lláh and 'Abdu'l-Bahá'* (Bahá'í Publishing Committee, 1943), p.35 – a selection from *The Kitáb-i-Aqdas*, 1873, paragraph 181.

executive, backed by an international force," a World Parliament and a global tribunal, "a uniform and universal system of currency," collective security, a universal language, and a worldwide system of inter-communication – "embracing the whole planet, freed from national hindrances and restrictions." Science and faith would merge, religions would harmonize, East and West would unite.[30] A "most great peace" would prevail on Earth.

A managerial city was pictured: "A world metropolis will act as the nerve centre of a world civilization, the focus towards which the unifying forces of life will emerge and from which its energizing influences will radiate."[31]

The Bahá'í International Community, which deliberates with the UN on global governance agendas, understands the connection between world order and the social acceptance of oneness,

> Laying the groundwork for global civilization calls for the creation of laws and institutions that are universal in both character and authority. The effect can begin only when the concept of the oneness of humanity has been wholeheartedly embraced by those in whose hands the responsibility for decision making rests, and when the related principles are propagated through both educational systems and the media of mass communications.[32]

Faith in The Hague

The allure of world order has excited luminaries and pragmatists alike with its promise of administrative salvation. In 1889, the first organizational model was established, the Inter-Parliamentary Union (IPU), bringing together parliamentarians from different nations. International arbitration as the means of securing order was the goal.

At the first Hague Peace Conference in 1899, national governments, enraptured by the prospects of a new century, established the Permanent Court of Arbitration. Confidence soared as international law was on the agenda. Peace would come through judicial decisions, birthing the IPU vision.

---

30 John Ferraby, *All Things Made New* (Bahá'í Publishing Trust, 1975), see chapters 2-5. See also, William D. Hatcher and J. Douglas Martin, *The Bahá'í Faith: The Emerging Global Religion* (Harper and Row, 1985).

31 Ibid., p.83.

32 *The Prosperity of Humankind* (Bahá'í International Community, Universal House of Justice, 2006 ebook edition, originally published in 1995), p.17.

Intensely joyful by what happened at The Hague, Andrew Carnegie,[33] a believer in the directed evolution of society, became a proselytizer for this new faith in world order. At the same time he knew the Court of Arbitration could not stand-alone; it would require a larger political structure and the engagement of civil society. Giving an address at St. Andrew's University in 1905, he proposed a League of Peace and encouraged the students – and all universities and churches and professionals – to unite in this "holy work."[34]

The sure path to peace would come through international arbitration, backed by a League who would isolate offending nations and, if necessary, use collective force to maintain discipline. Social and cultural leaders, enamored by this newfound faith in cooperative human destiny, would need to act as prophets and saints – pointing the way for others to follow and providing moral legitimacy for its broader acceptance.

"Progressive men in the Old World and New are actively supporting the direct movement for the political unity of the world," penned Raymond Bridgman in 1905.[35]

A member of the American Peace Society, Bridgman had petitioned lawmakers for world organization. His was an intoxicating optimism in a vast coalescence, predicting a utopia so grand as to surpass all of history,

> First and greatest, there would be realized the political self- consciousness of mankind, hitherto never achieved. The world, unified and intelligent, would for the first time in human history come to the grandeur of its existence as one, and would feel the thrill of intelligent unity as it first said 'I' of itself... When it shall have been attained the united race, knowing its unlimited powers, looking over the earth and recognizing its directorship amid all the forces of nature and man, feeling its strength and realizing its boundless opportunity, will say 'I will.' Thus and then would be accomplished the grandest revolution in human history. The world would have found itself, would have come into self-consciousness, realized its

---

[33] For an accounting of Carnegie's response to the first Hague conference, see the *Autobiography of Andrew Carnegie* (Houghton Mifflin Company, 1920), pp.283-285.

[34] See Andrew Carnegie, *A League of Peace: A Rectorial Address Delivered to the Students in the University of St. Andrews, 17th October, 1905* (Ginn and Company/International Union, 1906).

[35] Raymond L. Bridgman, *World Organization* (Ginn and Company, 1905), p.146.

> true supremacy, and discerned its opportunity. It would be thenceforth and forever a new being. All the preceding centuries, it is hardly exaggeration to say, would count for almost nothing in the existence of mankind as an organic whole.[36]

Less hubristic but still politically ostentatious was Theodore Roosevelt's advocacy of world federalism during his 1910 Nobel Lecture. His desire too was for a League of Peace, built upon the model of American federalism and the Hague process. Roosevelt ended his lecture by saying: "The ruler or statesman who should bring about such a combination would have earned his place in history for all time and his title to the gratitude of all mankind."[37]

During this same period the US House of Representatives considered a resolution to combine the navies of the world. Congressman Richard Bartholdt notified his colleagues,

> The work of world organization or world federation was auspiciously begun by the creation of the Hague court, and we do not propose to have it stop there, but must insist that modern conditions which impress all with the absolute interdependence of nations imperatively demand its early completion.[38]

And in The Hague, Carnegie erected his magnificent Peace Palace – a "Temple of Peace" – with the resolute belief in a great and glorious universal brotherhood of nations.

Peace on Earth would come at last.

Kingdom by League

When the Great War ripped through Europe, starting in 1914, internationally minded men recognized an opportunity within the crisis. A catastrophe of this magnitude required a post-war restructuring of global proportions.

Nicholas Murray Butler, then President of Columbia University and the person most responsible for convincing Andrew Carnegie to establish his

---

[36] Ibid. p.148.

[37] Theodore Roosevelt's Nobel Lecture, "International Peace," was delivered four years after receiving the 1906 Peace Prize. The full text of his lecture can be found at Nobelprize.org.

[38] Quoted in *War Obviated by an International Police: A Series of Essays, Written in Various Countries* (The Hague: Martinus Nijhoff, 1915) p.181.

Endowment for International Peace, voiced his support for a new order in response to the world conflict. Speaking to the *New York Times* in 1914 on the subject of a "United States of Europe," Butler announced,

> . . .the time will come when each nation will deposit in a world federation some portion of its sovereignty for the general good. When this happens it will be possible to establish an international executive and international police, both devised for the especial purpose of enforcing the decisions of the international court.[39]

Approximately one year later Butler gave an address to the Union League of Philadelphia, highlighting an envisioned new world order,

> The old world order changed when this war-storm broke. The old international order passed away as suddenly, as unexpectedly, and as completely as if it had been wiped out by a gigantic flood, by a great tempest, or by a volcanic eruption. The old world order died with the setting of that day's sun and a new world order is being born while I speak.[40]

Butler, who had personal access to kings and presidents and prime ministers, understood the enormity of the change being forced upon all by the circumstances of the war. "It is essentially a war for a new world," the citizen diplomat wrote. "It is a war for a new international world."[41]

Teddy Roosevelt pontificated on this theme. He recommended that "the efficient civilized nations – those that are efficient in war as well as in peace" band together in a "world league for the peace of righteousness."

"What I propose," he explained, "is a working and realizable Utopia."[42]

In New York City's Century Club a small group of eminent men who regularly dined together came up with an idea: a league to *impose* world peace. In time this fellowship evolved into a committee led by former US President William Taft, a member of the original dinner group. The League to Enforce

---

[39] Nicholas Murray Butler, *A World in Ferment: Interpretations of the War for a New World* (Charles Scribner's Sons, 1918), p.36.

[40] Ibid., p.106.

[41] Ibid., p.5.

[42] Quoted in *War Obviated by an International Police* (Martinus Nijhoff, 1915), p.150.

Peace (LEP) was birthed: "A world organization which will tend to prevent war by forcing its members to try peaceable settlement first."[43]

Essentially the League was to focus on arbitration as a way to resolve disputes between nations. However, if judicial mediation failed to bring resolution, the League would rally its members to engage in collective measures, particularly economic boycotts and blockades. If needed, the League could employ joint military action against a non-compliant country. Prominent editors, lawyers and judges, university presidents and other influencers rallied around the cause. John B. Clark, Professor of Political Economy at Columbia University and a League to Enforce Peace executive member, stated that, "the world demands a league of some kind for preserving peace and, for the first time, much of the world expects to get it."[44]

At the League's 1916 conference, President Woodrow Wilson would not directly commit to the LEP scheme, but avowed a "creed," a "great consummation... when coercion shall be summoned not to the service of political ambition or selfish hostility, but to the service of a common order, a common justice, and a common peace."[45] Wilson ultimately chose a different path of internationalism, the more organic approach of parliamentarianism.

Frederick Lynch, a Social Gospel minister who was part of the dinner group at the Century Club and a figure within Carnegie's Church Peace Union,[46] worked to bring clergy around to the idea of world order as a high Christian duty. Because he was intimately involved with the Federal Council of Churches (FCC), Lynch was effective in raising the FCC's stature as a progressive voice for world federal authority. Taking cues from scientific pragmatism and Positivism, the God-force of Spinoza and Liberal Theology, the Social Gospel movement sought a managed evolution to collective bet-

---

43 Thomas Raeburn White, "The Platform," *Enforced Peace: Proceedings of the First Annual National Assemblage of the League to Enforce Peace, Washington, May 26-27, 1916* (League to Enforce Peace, 1916), p.13.

44 John Bates Clark, "The European Nations and the League Reform," *Enforced Peace*, p.85. Bates was also the Director of the Department of Economics and History with the Carnegie Endowment for International Peace.

45 US President Woodrow Wilson, closing address, League conference, May 27, 1916, *Enforced Peace*, pp.163-164.

46 The Church Peace Union was renamed the Council on Religion and International Affairs in 1961. It was later restructured as the Carnegie Council on Ethics and International Affairs. Then in 2005 it became the Carnegie Council for Ethics in International Affairs.

terment – a *process salvation* leading to a humanized Kingdom of God on Earth. Thus, Lynch's 1916 book, *The Challenge: The Church and the New World Order*, recommended that Christians band together "and form a compact, or league of nations, or some sort of united nations of the world."[47]

Another noted clergyman, American Baptist minister and Social Gospel campaigner, Samuel Zane Batten, likewise pushed for a new civilization. Similar to Lynch, Batten placed this "big idea" within a Christian calling. Consider what he said in his 1919 book, *The New World Order*,

> If there is to be a new world it must come first of all through a new spirit in the nations. There must be created an international mind and conscience; men must learn to think of humanity as one family and to have a world patriotism; they must keep their minds free from jealousy and selfishness, and base their policy and practice upon true and Christian principles; they must be quick to resent injustice by a nation as by an individual. Humanity must become an ideal in order that it may become an actuality. World patriotism must be a faith, a chivalry, before it can be an organization. International peace must become an aspiration, a religion, before it will become a reality... There must be some international organization which shall make the new ideas effective and secure world justice.[48]

Social Gospel ministers believed that the intrinsic goodness of humanity could be democratically unlocked nation-by-nation. The Brotherhood of Man would be realized and empowered through *righteous internationalism*. Heaven on Earth would manifest as mankind embraced political deliverance, for the "fundamental defect is with society itself."[49] Batten therefore called for a "league of free nations, a federation of the world."[50]

The political Temple of Man – a global parliament, an international court, and a world police force[51] – would usher in the Kingdom.

---

[47] Frederick Lynch, *The Challenge: The Church and the New World Order* (Fleming H. Revell Company, 1916), pp.22-23. Lynch would later become a member of the Committee on the League of Nations.

[48] Samuel Zane Batten, *The New World Order* (American Baptist Publication Society, 1919), p.116-117.

[49] Ibid., p.5.

[50] Ibid., p.124.

[51] Ibid., p.124.

League ideas were also circulating elsewhere.[52] In England the Fabian Society was considering a more robust organ than the American League to Enforce Peace. Their League would include an International Council directed by the Great Powers in a permanently organized structure.[53] On December 28, 1917, the British Labour Party – closely aligned with the Fabian socialists[54] – adopted a peace policy calling for "a Super-National Authority, or League of Nations... which every other independent sovereign State in the world should be pressed to join."[55] One British social scientist later described the hoped-for transformation of the League of Nations into "a true international organ" as "the way to salvation."[56]

Lynch was optimistic that the British and American Leagues could amalgamate into a global Federation,

> They could make a sort of United Nations of the World... The League to Enforce Peace and the League of Nations would have the Powers [to] form a sort of federation, each nation pledged to carry its dispute with another nation to a Court of Nations, a World Court... and all the armies and navies being combined into an international army... so this international army will not allow a nation in the League of Federation to break the peace.[57]

The *League of Federation* never materialized, but the League of Nations did organize in Geneva. British journalist Philip Gibbs recounted the mood,

> And something happened to men's minds in Geneva. I saw it happen. Some mental atmosphere there, a contact with former enemies

---

52 After the War the Germans recommending a League-based World Parliament. See Frederick Pollock, *The League of Nations* (Stevens and Sons, 1920), pp.239-250.

53 *Development of the League of Nations Idea: Documents and Correspondence of Theodore Marburg*, Volume II (The Macmillan Company, 1932, edited by John H. Latane), pp.777-779.

54 See Margaret Cole, *The Story of Fabian Socialism* (Science Editions/Stanford University Press, 1961). For more information on the British-American involvement with the League's development and other ventures in internationalism, see Carroll Quigley, *The Anglo-American Establishment: From Rhodes to Cliveden* (Books in Focus, 1981).

55 "Memorandum on War Aims," as published by Arthur Henderson, *The Aims of Labour* (B.W. Huebsch, 1918), p.84.

56 Goldsworthy Lowes Dickinson, *The International Anarchy, 1904-1914* (George Allen and Unwin, 1926/1937), p.493.

57 Lynch, *The Challenge*, pp.136-137.

> and other types of intelligence, perhaps some spiritual vibrations reaching them from the outer world, broadened their vision and enabled them to see beyond their own boundaries. They learned to think internationally.[58]

Hope in the League came from all corners. A 1925 Marxist pamphlet referencing the "primordial cause of war" as human overpopulation, hinted at a higher deliverance through the work of the League: "We scientific pacifists demand a world-wide limitation on births, affected by all nations leagued together in a desire for peace under the leadership of the League of Nations. This is the primary propaganda to be done by pacifists, for humanity's salvation resides in this solution."[59]

The League of Nations ultimately failed to live up to its many expectations. Indecision and the inability to act on major issues plagued the world body. Moreover, the United States remained outside of the League, even though President Wilson took credit for its development.[60]

For H.G. Wells it was a major disappointment,

> I am hostile to the present League of Nations because I desire the Confederation of Mankind... The League we desired was to have been the first loose conference that would have ended in a federal government for the whole earth. It was to have controlled war establishments from the start, constricted or abolished all private armament firms, created and maintained a world standard of currency, of labour legislation, of health and education...[61]

Something *generationally* larger was on Wells' mind,

> The Confederation of Mankind is a task for generations. Tens of thousands of leaderly men and women must serve that idea and live and die for it before it can approach realization. Millions must respond to the service of their leadership. The idea must become the

[58] Philip Gibbs, *Since Then: The Disturbing Story of the World at Peace* (Harper and Brothers Publishers, 1930), p.349.

[59] *The Biological Cause and Prevention of War: Essay in Scientific Pacifism*, London, 1925, reprinted at www.marxists.org/archive/devaldes/1925/prevention-war.htm.

[60] A breakdown occurred between President Wilson and the US Senate, effectively putting a stop to the US entering the League.

[61] H.G. Wells, *A Year of Prophesying* (Ryerson Press, 1924), pp.9-10.

> fundamental political idea of hundreds of millions, ousting kings and flags from men's imaginations. Then we can begin to get together an effective ruling body. A stupendous task, you say, but not an impossible one.[62]

Wells understood that a world order – a "world revolution" – was to be a salvific act: "This is, I declare, the truth and the way of salvation."[63]

Such a messianic end game, he knew, could not be achieved by one group alone. It would require a correlating network of movements and organizations and external pressures. He labeled this the *open conspiracy*, and looked forward to the day when all would assimilate into the Great Work,

> The character of the Open Conspiracy will now be plainly displayed. It will have become a great world movement as widespread and evident as socialism and communism. It will largely have taken the place of these movements. It will be more, it will be a world religion. This large loose assimilatory mass of groups and societies will be definitely and obviously attempting to swallow up the entire population of the world and become the new human community.[64]

Proposals for Peace

Adolf Hitler's quest for a "New European Order"[65] set the Continent on fire, and with the ravages of a Second World War came a fresh cry for international authority. Clearly the League of Nations failed. In the United States, as in other parts of the Western world, proposals for peace competed for attention. World organization *must* bring deliverance and redemption.

---

62 Ibid., p.12.

63 H.G. Wells, *The Open Conspiracy: Blue Prints for a World Revolution* (Doubleday, Doran and Company, 1928), p.ix.

64 Ibid., p.163.

65 Regarding a "New European Order," see Frederic J. Fransen, *The Supranational Politics of Jean Monnet: Ideas and Origins of the European Community* (Greenwood Press, 2001), p.47. John Laughland similarly couches Hitler's actions as a drive for a Germanic-based European Community, a New Order for Europe. See John Laughland, *The Tainted Source: The Undemocratic Origins of the European Idea* (Little, Brown and Company, 1997).

After returning to America from covering the League in Geneva, *New York Times* journalist Clarence Streit delivered a manuscript to the Harper publishing house. Streit's book urged the United States to form an embryonic world government by unifying the free democracies of the North Atlantic. Released in 1939, *Union Now* quickly became a best seller. His sequel, *Union Now With Britain*, acknowledged the role of the US and UK in the "four experiments in world government" – the League of Nations, the International Labor Organization, the World Court, and the World Bank.[66]

Streit reminded his readers: "No others have done so much to bring about world government as we Americans and British have."[67] These two nations, he argued, should partner in constructing the Commonwealth of Man.

The ideas in *Union Now* started an organization, Federal Union, which lobbied for a North Atlantic confederation.[68] But it did more. It whetted the public's appetite for international solutions, cascading into an avalanche of lectures and books and campaigns and pamphlets.

A crop of organizations emerged to advocate for world order.[69] The World

---

66 The World Court referred to was the Permanent Court of International Justice, which existed from 1922 until 1946. The World Bank referred to is the Bank for International Settlements (BIS), which was established as an agency to handle reparation transfers after the Great War. Today the BIS is the "banker for the world's central banks."

67 Clarence K. Streit, *Union Now With Britain* (Harper and Brothers, 1941), p.124.

68 In England, a Federal Union organization formed in 1938 with the goal of uniting Europe, then the Atlantic nations, and finally creating a world federal union. The British group soon cooperated with Streit's American-based Federal Union, which began as the Inter-Democracy Federal Unionists in 1939. The writings of the British Federal Union soon influenced communist politician Altiero Spinelli, who was a prisoner of Mussolini at the time. In turn, Spinelli co-authored the Ventotene Manifesto (*For a Free and United Europe*) – a source of inspiration for resistance fighters battling the Axis powers. Spinelli soon thereafter created the Movimento Federalista Europeo, to be later incorporated into the Union of European Federalists. In 1970 he became a member of the European Commission and in 1980 he founded the Crocodile Club, which drafted a treaty leading to the establishment of the European Union. Today the Spinelli Group, named after Altiero, is a block of pro-EU influencers working to revitalize European federalism.

69 Many world government groups were organized during the war years and immediately after, and it can be hard to keep track of the mergers and re-structuring that took place during this flurry of activity. One close-knit organization predating the popularity of *Union Now* was the Campaign for World Government, founded by Rosika Schwimmer and Lola M. Lloyd in 1937. The Committee to Study the Organization of Peace, of which Clarence Streit was a member with Sumner Welles, Allen Dulles and John W. Davis, was

Federalist community, the one I tapped into at the Millennium Forum, is rooted in this historical milieu.

Church groups, too, joined the chorus.

In 1940 the Federal Council of Churches formed the Commission to Study the Bases of a Just and Durable Peace.[70] John Foster Dulles – later to become the United States Secretary of State – was the Commission's chairperson, working with a board comprised of leaders from Harvard and Yale and Chicago University, seminary presidents and professors, and well-known ministers. Members of the Church Peace Union and the International Missionary Council were part of the board too. The purpose: to clarify church commitments for a new international order, so that the "latent power of Christianity can be galvanized into effective action."[71]

---

founded in 1939. American organizations that arose in the wake of *Union Now* included: World Federalists USA, Student Federalists (started in 1942 under a Federal Union charter), Massachusetts Committee for World Federation, The World Citizenship Movement, Americans United for World Organization and Americans United for World Government, Committee to Frame a World Constitution, Students for Federal World Government, Committee to Win World Peace, Citizens Committee for United Nations Reform, World Union, International Campaign for World Government (split from the earlier Campaign for World Government), World Citizens of Georgia, and the United World Federalists. The Atlantic Union Committee was formed in 1949 as a Federal Union branch, and that same year, Garry Davis – building on his Paris declaration of world citizenship – formed the International Registry of World Citizens. In Canada, the World Government Association came into being in 1945. And in Luxembourg, the World Movement for World Federal Government was launched, becoming very influential in European and American world government circles.

70 Ecclesiastical interest in world order predated the FCC Commission. The 1937 Oxford Conference on Church, Community and State, called for a "new order in international affairs." The following year, the World Missionary Conference – a precursor to the World Council of Churches – acknowledged that, "the Kingdom of God requires both individual conversion and social change," and stated that, "changed individuals alone without collective action will not adequately change the social order." The final report from the World Missionary Conference said in part: "An effective system of international organization is necessary, to provide peaceful and legal means for political and economic change." On the Oxford Conference see, *The Churches Survey Their Task: The Report of the Conference at Oxford, July 1937, On Church, Community, and State* (George Allen & Unwin, 1937), p.174. Regarding the World Missionary Conference, see "Relation of the Christian and the Church to the International Order," 1938, printed in *A Just and Durable Peace: Data Material and Discussion Questions* (Federal Council of Churches, Commission to Study the Bases of a Just and Durable Peace, 1941), pp.37-39.

71 John Foster Dulles, "Forward," *A Just and Durable Peace: Data Material and Discussion*

Searching for a lasting solution to the problem of war, the Commission believed that a world government – either fully functioning or built-up through specialized agencies – offered the best path to peace. The present system of international order was inadequate, a new order was necessary.

Consider the following from a 1942 Commission meeting,

> (1) The ultimate requirement is a duly constituted world government of delegated powers: an international legislative body, an international court with adequate powers and adequate international police forces and provisions for worldwide economic sanctions.
>
> (2) As steps toward, and potential organs of, such world government, there is need for many sorts of international bodies charged with specific duties, such as the International Labor Organization, and various agencies such as those now acting for the United Nations to coordinate natural resources, shipping, and food distribution. Such bodies must be adapted to the service of world order and government, and must not become a substitute therefore. In the operation of these agencies, and in progressing toward full world government, every effort should be made to achieve agreement and voluntary cooperation of all concerned.[72]

Different denominations ramped up the call for global planning.

The Methodist Council of Bishops initiated a "Crusade for a New World Order" and inundated Washington with letters supporting world organization. So overwhelming was the response that President Franklin D. Roosevelt thanked the Bishops for their part in "transforming public opinion." The Northern Baptist Convention too had a "World Order Crusade." The FCC launched a "World Order Day" when churches would specifically pray for and support the cause of international organization.[73]

Questions (Federal Council of Churches, Commission to Study the Bases of a Just and Durable Peace, 1941), p.6.

[72] *A Message from the National Study Conference on The Churches and a Just and Durable Peace* (Federal Council of Churches, The Commission to Study the Bases of a Just and Durable Peace, convened at Ohio Wesleyan University, March 2-5, 1942), p.19.

[73] See Martin Erdmann, *Building the Kingdom of God on Earth: The Churches' Contribution to Marshal Public Support for World Order and Peace, 1919-1945* (Wipf and Stock, 2005), p.267. Dr. Erdmann's book is an essential work on the role of John Foster Dulles and the FCC in promoting an ecumenical approach to world authority.

Professor of Christian Theology at Andover Newton Theological School, Nels F.S. Ferré, wrote that Christians must embrace socialist planning within the context of world unity. "Nothing less than some kind of supra-national government will do," penned Ferré. "The problem boils down to our need for an adequate international organization based on adequate international authority over all common judicial, military, and economic functions."[74]

Modernist preacher Henry E. Fosdick, who was defended by Dulles on church-charges of heresy, decried the individualist thinking of Christians as an "enemy of peace." Global harmony would require new approaches.

"Peace is now a political problem of world organization," Fosdick said in his Armistice Day message of 1942, noting that such an enterprise would require a moral purpose akin to a "world-wide social revolution." He stressed that "a lasting and worthy peace based on new world ideas involves a heavy price," reminding his parishioners that no sacrifice is too costly in the struggle for world unity, including national sovereignty and the lowering of America's standard of living "for the sake of the world's common good."[75]

Catholics also participated in planetary visioning. Promoting "international goodwill," the Catholic Association for International Peace disparaged nationalism, individualism and capitalism – and warned of the Communist threat – while selling the merits of an encompassing global body: "World organization for justice, peace and well-being does not mean governmental organization alone. It means a variety of world organizations – governmental, economic, cultural and religious."[76]

Church groups and liberal ministers were not the only ones preaching

---

[74] Nels F.S. Ferré, *Return to Christianity* (Harper and Brothers, 1943), p.69.

[75] Henry E. Fosdick, *Crying Peace, Peace: When There Is No Peace – An Armistice Day Sermon* (Preached in the Riverside Church, New York, November 8, 1942), distributed nationally as a pamphlet. Fosdick, a graduate of Union Theological Seminary, took a pastoral position at First Baptist Church (Montclair, NJ) before moving to First Presbyterian Church (New York City). It was at First Presbyterian that Fosdick faced denominational discipline for his liberal/modernist views, whereupon Dulles acted as his legal defense. After Fosdick resigned from First Presbyterian, John D. Rockefeller enabled him to become pastor at Park Avenue Baptist Church, New York City. Henry's brother, Raymond Fosdick, was president of the Rockefeller Foundation from 1936 to 1948.

[76] The Catholic Association for International Peace, *A Peace Agenda for the United Nations: A Report of the Post-War World Committee* (The Paulist Press, 1943), p.9, section VI. The Association was formed in 1927 to, in part, "disseminate and apply the principles of natural laws and Christian charity to international problems of the day."

the Temple of Man. People from most every belief system, walk-of-life, and ideology looked favorably toward some kind of global scheme to procure social and political salvation.

Haridas Muzumdar, the "unofficial ambassador of goodwill from India to America," traveled across the United States promoting world government as the political expression of spiritual oneness. His popular book, *The United Nations of the World*, called for world government through an organized United Nations. Reflecting on the Great War and earlier attempts at international authority, Muzumdar wrote, "we dreamed of a new world order but we failed to make ourselves worthy of it spirituality."[77]

What was needed, he said, was what his friend Mahatma Gandhi called Soul Force: "Soul Force is a way of life in tune with the cosmic process. The fundamental oneness of life is the essential aspect of this universe of ours."[78]

Muzumdar's excitement was palpable. Reciting Henry Ford's approval of world federalism, the Hindu scholar proclaimed "A hearty Amen!" He added,

> A new world beckons to us all. Let us devote every ounce of energy we have to the rebuilding of this common world of ours, to the creation of a world society wherein war drums throb no longer and the battle-flags are furled in the Parliament of Man, the Federation of the World![79]

Famous bridge-player Ely Culbertson became an outspoken campaigner for world government. He drafted a detailed constitution, a "Treaty of World Settlement," centered on a global military quota system and the formation of eleven world regions under an international umbrella.

"The World Federation that I propose embodies the ideal of world citizenship," Culbertson announced.[80] His fame ensured a captive audience and the audacity of his scheme guaranteed wide discussion.[81]

---

77 Haridas T. Muzumdar, *The United Nations of the World* (Universal Publishing Company, 1942, second edition 1944), p.192

78 Ibid., p.194.

79 Ibid., p.147.

80 Ely Culbertson, *Total Peace: What Makes Wars and How to Organize Peace* (Doubleday, Doran & Company, 1943), p.239.

81 Culbertson's blueprint was met with fanfare and fright. His supporters viewed the quota system as a step to ensuring world peace, while others – including Federalists – were wary of his ideas. Rosika Schwimmer, co-founder of the Campaign for World Govern-

Scott Nearing, the radical socialist who later became a counter-culture guru, waxed on about "worldizing processes." Earlier, in 1922, he had advocated an "economic world federation" and before that he had called for a new faith, a Social Religion.[82] Now as World War II came to a close he was proselytizing a United World, a synthesis of thought and action inspiring "world men" to remake civilization:

"Their dominant consciousness is world consciousness," wrote Nearing. "Their dominant loyalty is world loyalty."[83]

To Nearing, the new world order would be a technically determined existence, the product of social engineering. *Calamity*, he noted, would push society to its completion in a collective setting: "The rational, scientific answer to world crisis and world chaos is the organized world community."[84]

Crisis equals opportunity. It allows for the leveraging of emotions, unleashing the forces of ideological change. It prompts "calls to action."[85]

"The Second World War, with its appalling losses," wrote Nearing, "will be followed by another series of social revolutions, and will provide a setting still more favorable to world organization. Social crisis are the occasions for deliberative social changes."[86]

Cultural modification would be a response to the social tempest.

"Worldism, as a cultural stage," he explained, "will be reached when the dominant activities of mankind take place on a world scale... The organization of a world society is the next step in deliberative culture change."[87]

---

ment, privately called him "the Hitler of the peace movement." For more on Culbertson and his influence, including a glimpse into his colorful past, see Joseph P. Baratta, *The Politics of World Federation: Volume 1 – United Nations, UN Reform, Atomic Control* (Praeger Publishers, 2004), p.67.

82 For Nearing's views on economic world federation, see Scott Nearing, *The Next Step: A Plan for Economic World Federation* (Nellie Seeds Nearing, 1922). For his ideas on Social Religion, a Social Gospel aimed at alleviating social problems and vices, see Scott Nearing, *Social Religion: An Interpretation of Christianity in Terms of Modern Life* (The Macmillan Company, 1913). Nearing said, "the believer in Social Religion makes effective his belief by an insistence on Social Justice." (p.198).

83 Scott Nearing, *United World* (Island Press, 1945), p.33.

84 Ibid., p.248.

85 An interesting study on mass manipulation, including the crisis-equals-opportunity dynamic, is Edward Bernays' 1928 book, *Propaganda*.

86 Nearing, *United World*, p.233.

87 Ibid., p.218, 221.

With so much interest in post-war possibilities emerging in the early 1940s, the Washington DC-based Brookings Institute published a small report titled *Peace Plans and American Choices*. A dozen ideas were put on the table – all circulating in the policy marketplace – including unilateral America action, joining with England or partnering in a Union of Democracies, setting up world regions, or establishing an international military to keep the peace. Pros and cons were given for each. The bottom line was this: "Something must be done."[88] And something was being done.

The three Great Powers – the United States, the Soviet Union and Great Britain – met over the course of the war, strategizing military responses to the Axis powers, negotiating settlements, and considering a future international system. In 1941 the United States and England signed the *Atlantic Charter*, anticipating a "permanent system of general security." The 1942 *Declaration by United Nations* witnessed the Great Powers in deliberation.

Transcripts of the talk between Joseph Stalin and Franklin D. Roosevelt at the Tehran Conference gives us a glimpse into what the Allied leaders were thinking. FDR imagined a "world organization" established under the principles of the wartime alliance, known then as the United Nations. This body would be comprised of three organs; a general assembly, an Executive Committee made up of "10 or 11 countries," and a Police Committee to oversee the preservation of peace – which would "act swiftly" against violations. After listening to FDR, Stalin remarked, "in that case it would be a coercive organ." Roosevelt explained that if a police action were to happen in Europe, the US would send ships and aircraft while Britain and Russia would commit troops, either to quarantine the offending country or to subject it "to bombardment or even occupation."

Stalin, in turn, suggested two regional assemblies; a European body headed by England, Russia and America, and another for the Far East and the rest of the world. This was closer to Winston Churchill's earlier proposal of dividing the globe into three organizational blocks.[89]

At the conclusion of the Tehran Conference the three leaders signed the *Declaration of the Three Powers*. It promised two things: destroy the Ger-

88 Harold G. Moulton, "Preface," *Peace Plans and American Choices: The Pros and Cons of World Order*, by Arthur C. Millspaugh (The Brookings Institute, 1942).

89 "Transcript of the Talk Between Stalin and Roosevelt, November 29, 1943," *Tehran, Yalta, Potsdam: The Soviet Protocols* (Academic International, 1970), pp.340-343.

man military machine, and then jointly procure a peace "which will command the good will of the overwhelming mass of the peoples of the world and banish the scourge and terror of war for many generations."[90]

By 1944, the US Department of State was working with church agencies, service clubs, and world government groups to flesh out an American response to world organization. The outcome was not clear, but the machinery was firmly in motion.[91] In February 1945, Roosevelt, Stalin and Churchill, invited other nations to convene on creating a "world order under law." This was to be a "Conference on the United Nations... the Establishment of a General International Organization," with the gathering taking place in San Francisco a few months later.[92]

The United Nations we know today was being born.

Persisting Visions

It quickly became apparent that the newly created United Nations was not to be the "federal world government" so many had envisioned. Yet hope remained that some kind of truly global authority would still come to fruition. Calls to support world order continued and public anticipation mounted, especially in the United States.

Take for example the 1946 Southern Baptist Convention annual meeting, with its Special Committee on World Peace making this statement,

> We believe that the goal of peacemakers must be a world organized on the Christian principles of order and justice. We further believe that in the field of international relations, such a goal can be accomplished only by some type of world government. Accordingly, we recommend that Southern Baptists endorse the principle of world federation, and work toward amending and improving the United Nations organization to achieve that end.[93]

---

90 "Declaration of the Three Powers," printed in *Tehran, Yalta, Potsdam: The Soviet Protocols* (Academic International, 1970), p.46.

91 See Dorothy B. Robins, *Experiment in Democracy: The Story of U.S. Citizen Organizations in Forging the Charter of the United Nations* (The Parkside Press, 1971).

92 "Communiqué" and "Invitation," Ibid, pp.127-136.

93 *Annual of the Southern Baptist Convention*, Miami, Florida, May 15-19, 1946 (Executive Committee, Southern Baptist Convention, 1946), p.65. This was the last year the World Peace committee remained functional. During its operation it supported world organi-

The National Conference of Methodist Youth and the newly formed American Baptist Convention each entertained world government resolutions during their annual meetings in 1950. The Methodist's text called "for the relinquishment of sufficient national sovereignty for the establishment of lasting peace and the eventual development of effective international cooperation in the form of democratic federal world government."[94] The American Baptist Convention sought to revise and amend the UN Charter so as to "strengthen the machinery of world government."[95]

Public interest was also demonstrated through the United World Federalists (UWF), a membership-based organization that started in early 1947 when five world order groups amalgamated. Its first president was 26-year-old Cord Meyer, a Pacific war veteran who had lost an eye to a grenade attack in Guam. Because of his battle experiences, Meyer firmly believed that world peace required world government.[96] His energy and enthusiasm was infectious, and his connections to newspaper editors and congressmen enabled the UWF message to resonate with political elites and the public.[97] In under a year the organization grew to 17 branches with 315 chapters and 16,000 members.[98] By 1950 it had expanded to 40,000 members.[99]

Support for the United World Federalists revealed broad interest. Official observers to the 1949 UWF General Assembly included the American Jewish

---

zation, meeting with the US State Department and the Federal Council of Churches, and participating in the San Francisco conference on the United Nations. To its credit, the World Peace committee campaigned for the cause of religious liberty, including the "right to conduct missions, to hold property dedicated to religious uses, to establish schools and printing presses, and to exercise civil rights without discrimination on grounds of religious faith." (p.63).

94 Resolution presented at the Annual Convention of the National Conference of Methodist Youth, Denver, Colorado, August 28 – September 3, 1950; Report of the Committee on the Domestic Situation. A copy, as sent to the United World Federalists, is on file.

95 Resolution by the American Baptist Convention, formerly known as the Northern Baptist Convention, Boston, Massachusetts, May 26, 1950. A copy of the resolution, as forwarded to the United World Federalists, is on file with the author.

96 See Cord Meyer, *Facing Reality: From World Federalism to the CIA* (Harper and Row, 1980). Meyer would become an important figure in the CIA, taking the position of Assistant Deputy Director of Operations and eventually heading-up the Covert Action Staff.

97 For an informed survey of Meyer's activities within the UWF, see Baratta, *The Politics of World Federation: Volume 2*, chapter 17.

98 Baratta, *The Politics of World Federation: Volume 2*, p.350.

99 *WFA Activist Guidebook* (World Federalist Association, 1997), Section 1, p.15.

Committee, American Library Association, American Psychiatric Association, Brotherhood of Railroad Trainmen, Catholic Association for International Peace, Congregational Christian Churches, Junior Chamber of Commerce USA, National Association of Deans of Women, National Association for the Advancement of Colored People,[100] National Education Association, and the US National Student Association, among others.[101]

Dean Rusk, the Deputy Under Secretary of State, attended the 1949 Assembly and gave an "off the record address." His subject: The relationship between world federalism and UN affairs. Attendees to this annual meeting were reminded that Rusk's comments "must not be quoted or attributed."[102]

Political support for world federalism was nonpartisan.

In 1949, the Young Republican National Federation issued a resolution on empowering the United Nations: "It should be a fundamental objective of the foreign policy of the United States to support and strengthen the United Nations and to seek its development into a world federation."[103] Alfred E. Driscoll, the Republican Governor of New Jersey, was sympathetic to the UWF program.[104]And Republican Governor of Minnesota, Luther W. Youngdahl, was on its National Advisory Board.[105]

The Democratic National Committee was corresponding with the United World Federalists, and James Roosevelt – the eldest son of FDR and a prominent Californian Democrat – was on the UWF executive board. Democratic Governor of Michigan, G. Mennen Williams, was a national advisor.[106] Speaking to the UWF 4th general assembly, Supreme Court Justice and Democrat, William O. Douglas, acknowledged the World Federalist role in buttressing the United Nations and "in educating American opinion and in helping to

---

[100] Based on a letter between the UWF and Madison Jones, October 6, 1949, copy on file.

[101] *Official Observers from Outside Organizations Attending*, Third Annual General Assembly, Cleveland, Oct. 28-30, 1949, United World Federalists, copy on file.

[102] *Program of the 3rd Annual General Assembly, United World Federalists*, held in Cleveland, Ohio, October 27-30, 1949. Rusk's talk took place on Saturday, October 29; the off-the-record caveat is printed in the *Program*. The topic of world federalism and the UN is gleaned from associated UWF correspondence on file.

[103] Young Republican National Federation annual meeting, June 23-26, 1949, Salt Lake City, Utah, copy of the resolution on file.

[104] Letter from Governor Alfred E. Driscoll to Alan Cranston, then President of the UWF, October 13, 1950, copy on file.

[105] UWF 1950 Executive Membership list.

[106] Ibid.

influence American legislative action."[107] During this same meeting, which took place under the long shadow of the Korean War, a letter from Senator Hubert H. Humphrey was circulated to attendees,

> It is appropriate that the United World Federalists meets as the second phase of the Korean campaign begins – the campaign to achieve peace and unity under the sponsorship of the United Nations. The United Nations has gained tremendously under its first baptism of fire, but the world needs more. It needs a clear set of goals. In a sense, world government is the symbol of the goal we seek in the ashes of the Korean struggle.[108]

Years later Humphrey became the US Vice-President.

But not everyone was happy. A sizable percentage of Republicans in California were wary of the UWF's agenda.[109] Nevertheless, a concerted effort from both parties to adopt "world organization" existed.

From 1947 until 1950, the US Congress reviewed resolutions promising a European federation, turning the United Nations into a global authority, or otherwise creating some form of world government. Two examples: House Concurrent Resolution 163 with fourteen co-sponsors, including Richard Nixon, sought to revise the United Nations' Charter and empower the Security Council with "an effective world police force."[110] Then on June 7, 1949, House Concurrent Resolution 64 – "World Federation" – had 111 co-sponsors, including Henry Cabot Lodge Jr., John F. Kennedy, Gerald R.

---

[107] Address by Supreme Court Justice William O. Douglas at Fourth General Assembly Banquet, October 14, 1950, copy on file.

[108] As taken from a list of endorsements circulated during the 1950 UWF assembly.

[109] An internal report from the California Council of Republican Women, Southern Division, explains that the 1949 California Council Convention passed a resolution opposing world government as sponsored by the United World Federalists. A copy of the report is on file. Furthermore, in 1949, the Republican State Central Committee asked Congressman Richard Nixon to check with the Committee on Un-American Activities as to potential investigations regarding the UWF. Nixon responded that no files existed supporting the UWF as a Communist front organization. A duplicate of the carbon copy from Nixon's return letter is on file. Cord Meyer addressed concerns regarding Communist subversion in his book, *Facing Reality: From World Federalism to the CIA*.

[110] HCR-163 was called the "Culbertson ABC Plan" and was introduced March 16, 1948. See Joseph P. Baratta, *The Politics of World Federation: Volume 2 – From World Government to Global Governance* (Praeger Publishers, 2004), p.571.

Ford, and Franklin D. Roosevelt Jr. The bill read: "That it is the sense of the Congress that it should be a fundamental objective of the foreign policy of the United States to support and strengthen the United Nations and to seek its development into a world federation."[111]

"We did not confine our efforts to the Congress," explained Cord Meyer in reference to HCR 64. "We also tried to influence the executive, and a group of us met with President Truman in the White House to put our case."[112]

The UWF was also in correspondence with the United Nations, and the UN itself was interested in the question of international organization. In its 1949 Study Kit, the UN Department of Public Information explored the query: "Why not have a proper world government?" The text hinted at future possibilities,

> In the United Nations, Member States have gone further towards setting up a world government than they had done previously with the League of Nations... Although it will probably take some time before a full system of world government can come into being, more and more, questions are being considered on a world basis; not only political questions, but questions concerning food, housing, trade and money, etc... Side by side with this process is the development through the United Nations of new methods of international co-operation which may in time, if Members agree, tend to obscure the dividing line between what decisions are taken nationally and what may be taken internationally.[113]

UWF influence extended beyond political halls of power; religions too were targeted as valuable to the furtherance of the Great Work.

In 1952 the United World Federalists initiated a "World Government Sabbath" and "World Government Sunday." Drawing attention to the "inter-faith support for our objective," a campaign memo expressed hope that religious leaders would join in "relating the basic principles of their faith to the achievement of peace through world government." Along with the memo was a

---

[111] Baratta, *The Politics of World Federation: Volume 2*, p.578. For examples of State and other Congressional resolutions, see Appendix G and H.

[112] Meyer, *Facing Reality*, p.45.

[113] *Questions and Answers on the United Nations* (United Nations Department of Public Information, Research Section, 1949), section 7, pp.7-8. Part of a document package titled *United Nations Study Kit, No.1*.

public-relations package with statements of support from denominations, including sermons and articles in favor of world government. These documents were sent to all UWF branches and chapters with instructions to contact local rabbis and clergymen. Some organizational distance, however, was recommended. The memo advised that publicity for the Sabbath/Sunday *should not* be attributed to the UWF.[114] It would be better if religious ministers appeared unattached.

In Southern California, some 500 church leaders were asked to deliver sermons and distribute literature in support of world federalism. It was also suggested that Sunday-morning bulletins include denominational affirmations of world order.[115]

Another ministerial suggestion was using John 17:21 as a sermon text – "Jesus prayer: that they may all be one." This was to be connected to a unifying thought: "emphasize the need to undergird any attempt of world government with sound faith, etc. etc."[116]

But John 17:21 is not about political ecumenism or aimed at the world in general; it is focused on the positional unity Christian believers have in Jesus Christ, grounded in Himself as Truth. It is a prayer that strengthens Christians from generation to generation as being in the body of Christ, connected to the will of the Father, operating in and through His Sprit. It is not about organizational conformity, political unity, or international order. Nor is it about discovering the essential oneness of all things.

In Europe the World Movement for World Federal Government (WMWFG), the foundation of today's World Federalist Movement, was gaining momentum. The pinnacle event for the WMWFG was its 1951 Rome Congress, bringing together delegates from other world order groups and Euro-federalist organizations. Officials from the Italian government, including its Foreign Minister, offered words of encouragement and congratulations. Members of parliament from Denmark, France, Great Britain, Italy and Sweden attended,

---

[114] Memo Re: World Government Sabbath/World Government Sunday – April 26-27, 1952. From: Helen A. Shuford, Executive Director, UWF, dated March 28, 1952. To: All UWF Branches and Chapters, copy on file.

[115] Letter from Ted R. Leutzinger, State Vice-President, UWF of California, to Southern Chapter Chairman, March 27, 1952, Subject: Plans for World Government Sunday – April 27, 1952; copy on file.

[116] Memo: World Government Sunday, Suggestions to Ministers, April 27, 1952; copy on file.

along with representatives from unions and various associations – including the Socialist Movement for the United States of Europe.[117]

But the highlight was a special meeting between the WMWFG and Pope Pius XII. Hinting at the present conflict in Korea, the Pope told the world government delegates,

> Your movement, Gentlemen, has the task of creating an effective political organization of the world. There is nothing more in keeping with the traditional doctrines of the Church, or better adapted to her teaching on the rightful or unjust war, especially in the present world situation. An organization of this nature must, therefore, be set up, even if only to end the competitive rearming of nations.[118]

At the same time the Pope warned them of "the deadly germs of mechanical totalitarianism." They were encouraged to pursue a world parliament, adhering to federalist principles as a counter to "mechanical unification."

"What a large amount of moral firmness, intelligent foresight and supple adaptation this world authority will have to possess," said the Pope, explaining that people of goodwill have a "need to be supported by authority" when faced with malevolence. In his closing, Pius XII congratulated them on "the courage to give yourself to this cause," and wished them success.

The Pope's warning about the dangers of totalitarianism is noteworthy, for he expressed concerns similar to what others have articulated. What are the safeguards against the rise of a despotic world authority? Those in the unity movement have typically pointed to the following as checks-and-balances: constitutional limitations within a federal system, laws and courts, democracy and parliamentarianism, enshrined ethics and moral constraints, and the principle of subsidiarity. But none of these configurations can sufficiently curtail totalitarian impulses, nor can they safeguard against the more mundane problem of bureaucratic over-reach.

Would an international authority be more self-restrained than national governments? Probably not.

---

[117] See "WMWFG Revitalized by Rome Congress," *For Your Information (FYI)*, Vol.1, No.5, 18 April 1951, United World Federalists, p.1. See also "Report on the Preparatory Conference for the Rome Congress," *Newsletter No.3*, [no date], World Movement for World Federal Government, p.2.

[118] *Address by His Holiness Pope Pius XII*, during an Audience with Delegates of the Fourth Congress of the World Movement for World Federal Government, 6 April 1951.

For the sake of argument, a limited world government – bound by constitutional limitations and democratic offices – could operate without spiraling into authoritarianism. But is this a hypothesis we are willing to bet on? History shows that democratic institutions can be abused and manipulated to the point of enabling dictatorships: "Both Hitler and Mussolini insisted on the democratic character of their political systems."[119]

The haunting words of Lord Acton drifts in from the past, "power tends to corrupt and absolute power corrupts absolutely."[120]

I am reminded of two British supporters of world government. The first, I believe, was convinced that world organization would safeguard the greater good. The second embraced it as pragmatic despotism.

Following the war, Winston Churchill publicly championed a "Temple of Peace," a UN equipped to ensure world order.[121] He expanded this vision while speaking at the inaugural meeting of the United Europe Movement,

> The creation of an authoritative, all-powerful world order is the ultimate aim towards which we must strive. Unless some effective World Super-Government can be set up and brought quickly into action, the prospects for peace and human progress are dark and doubtful.[122]

The other Englishman is the atheistic philosopher Bertrand Russell who postulated that the world's population would have to be controlled by a world government, "completely evident on Darwinian principles."[123] Ranting on the population problem and suggesting a Black Death every generation, Russell told his readers: "The state of affairs might be somewhat unpleasant, but what of that? Really high-minded people are indifferent to happiness, especially other people's."[124]

---

[119] Erik von Keuhnelt-Leddihn, *Liberty or Equality: The Challenge of Our Time* (Christendom Press, 1993), p.45.

[120] Lord Acton, *Essays on Freedom and Power* (Meridian Books, 1955), p.335.

[121] See Winston Churchill's Fulton, Missouri speech, March 5, 1946, as printed in *Churchill Speaks, 1897-1963: Collected Speeches in Peace and War* (Barnes and Noble, 1998).

[122] Winston Churchill, "United Europe," *Churchill Speaks, 1897-1963: Collected Speeches in Peace and War* (Barnes and Noble, 1998), p.913. For more on Churchill's United Europe concepts, see Klaus Larres, *Churchill's Cold War: The Politics of Personal Diplomacy* (Yale University Press, 2002).

[123] Bertrand Russell, *The Impact of Science on Society* (Simon and Schuster, 1953), p.105.

[124] Ibid., pp.103-104.

In his 1959 book, *The Future of Science*, Russell offered a logical conclusion to his technocratic imaginings,

> I believe that, owing to men's folly, a world-government will only be established by force, and will therefore be at first cruel and depotic [sic]. But I believe that it is necessary for the preservation of a scientific civilization, and that, if once realized, it will gradually give rise to the other conditions of a tolerable existence.[125]

No thank you. This is not the kind of society I want my children or grandchildren to endure, or anyone else for that matter.

Peace At Any Cost

As quickly as world federalist groups gained public notice and favor, the movement hit a wall. Cold War realities challenged their grand assertions.

The Soviet-Western divide was more than rhetoric; it was a deadly conflict unleashed on foreign battlefields and encountered in the perilously shifting maze of espionage and diplomacy. With the Soviet Union exporting its brand of internationalism – a collectivism grinding down Eastern Europe and parts of Asia – genuine concern existed that the Kremlin was penetrating Western peace groups, universities, and government agencies. It was not an unfounded fear.[126] Cord Meyer himself recognized the dangers of an overbearing Communist block forming in the United Nations, and noted that the Soviet regime had "its own version of an eventual world government."[127]

This seemingly irreconcilable divide between East and West undermined public hope in a new world order. How could the globe come together if the two superpowers were at odds? The UWF agenda was faltering.

A growing anti-Communist sentiment also undercut the movement, especially as the Korean War intensified. Magazine articles critical of international order began to circulate. UWF leaders – hoping to distance themselves from

---

[125] Bertrand Russell, *The Future of Science* (Philosophical Library, 1959), p.34.

[126] For an important contribution regarding Soviet action and American left-wing denial of said activity, see John E. Haynes and Harvey Klehr's *In Denial: Historians, Communism and Espionage* (Encounter Books, 2003). Christopher Andrew's *The Sword and the Shield* (Basic Books, 1999) and *The World Was Going Our Way* (Basic Books, 2005) documents Soviet penetration of the West during the Cold War.

[127] Meyer, *Facing Reality*, pp.55-59; on Soviet world government, see p.59.

the troubling persona of undermining American sovereignty – retreated into a more elitist camp, centralizing within a top-down structure at the expense of public membership. Even their terminology was beginning to change; the use of the label, "world government," was discouraged in light of Cold War suspicions. Lay members were fast cutting ties to the organization. At last, when the tenth anniversary of the United Nations came and went in 1955 with no clear outcome for UN empowerment, the world federalist community found itself effectively severed from the general population.[128]

The loss of public interest, however, did not mean the end of world order aspirations. Quite the opposite; the "big idea" of world organization remained active within elite circles, largely operating beyond the knowledge or concern of the public. A corollary was this: As public memory fogged with the advance of time, the notion of world government – once openly identified and celebrated – faded into our cultural background, eventually slipping into the realm of "conspiracy theory."

Ironically, as general membership within the UWF collapsed, the Suez Crisis of 1956 opened the door for an assertive development. Lester B. Pearson, Canada's Secretary of State for External Affairs at the time, successfully leveraged the Suez Crisis to create the United Nations Emergency Force. Retelling its history, Pearson said the following in 1968,

> There is a time in an international crisis when all are so frightened of what might happen that they will accept many things that they would not have even contemplated before the crisis; and indeed are unlikely to contemplate a week after it has ended. So at the time it was introduced my resolution for a police force was greeted with almost unanimous acclaim.[129]

Reinvigorated theories of world order emerged after the introduction of the Emergency Force. In England, ten Conservative Members of Parliament lobbied for a "world security authority" armed with "the most modern nuclear weapons."[130] The United States and the Soviet Union diplomatically toyed with "general and complete disarmament," a phased reduction of national

---

[128] See Baratta, *The Politics of World Federation: Volume 2*, chapter 24.

[129] Lester B. Pearson, *Peace in the Family of Man: The Reith Lectures, 1968* (Oxford University Press, 1969), pp.14-15.

[130] See *A World Security Authority?* (Conservative Political Centre, 1958).

forces in concert with the strengthening of an international authority.[131] "General and complete disarmament" was a stated policy goal and a propaganda chess piece.[132]

The Cuban Missile Crisis of 1962 demonstrated the fragile nature of the "Cold War peace." It energized academia, activists, and policy wonks to pursue an imposing bulwark against the very real threat of nuclear holocaust.[133]

131 On June 6, 1960, the Soviet Union released its three-stage plan for general and complete disarmament. Shortly after, the US State Department established the Disarmament Administration, and in 1961 the two opposing nations co-produced *The McLoy/Zorin Agreement* on disarmament. That same year the Disarmament Administration released State Publication 7277 – essentially mirroring the Soviet plan – and upped the ante by calling for a global and effective United Nations military force. For more information, see *The Soviet Stand on Disarmament* (Crosscurrents Press, 1962); *Freedom From War: The United States Program fro General and Complete Disarmament in a Peaceful World* (US State Department #7277, 1961); Lincoln P. Bloom, *The United Nations and U.S. Foreign Policy* (Little, Brown and Company, 1960); and Lincoln P. Bloom, *A World Effectively Controlled by the United Nations* (Institute for Defense Analysis, Special Studies Group, US Department of State contract No. SCC 28270, released March 10, 1962).

132 In his book *Soviet Foreign Propaganda* (Princeton University Press, 1964), Frederick C. Barghoorn, explained that the Soviet's would "put forward utopian proposals with the obvious objective of eliciting refusals. They have then denounced those refusing to accept their proposals as obstructionists and even as warmongers." By framing the disarmament debate and appealing to the consciousness of liberal Westerners, often to pacifists and religious organizations – a point made by Barghoorn in his important study – the *propaganda of peace* became a valuable tool in fermenting animosity against the West. It also elevated the Soviet position within the United Nations, particularly in the eyes of Third World leaders and Western intellectuals aliened with Soviet sentiments. An empowered UN equipped to act as the agent of "word peace" and backed by the power of world socialism, it was believed, could become the mechanism to dislodge "American imperialism." The United States countered by offering its version of "general and complete disarmament."

133 Some of those voices included Kenneth Boulding, Lincoln L. Bloomfield, Richard Barnet, Arthur I. Waskow, and Lucile W. Green. Hans J. Morgenthau, known for his political realism, also courted world order for world peace. Saul Mendlovitz created the influential World Order Models Project (WOMP) with Richard A. Falk, Carl von Weiszacker, and the input of Georges Abi-Saab. On WOMP and its contributions, see Saul Mendlovitz, "The Emergence of WOMP in the Normative Tradition: Biography and Theory," *Principles World Politics: The Challenge of Normative International Relations* (Rowman & Littlefield Publishers, 2000, edited by P. Wapner and Lester E.J. Ruiz). Before the Cuban Crisis, Glenville Clark and Louis B. Sohn were riding on their *World Peace Through World Law* (Harvard University Press, 1958), attempting to codify an international order.

Peace, it was believed, *must* be enforced through an authoritative political agency superseding the competitive tension of opposing superpowers.

Pope Paul VI was analogous in his 1965 UN address, telling his audience that the UN must *never fall but be perfected*,

> The peoples of the earth turn to the United Nations as the last hope of concord and peace... Is there anyone who does not see the necessity of coming thus progressively to the establishment of a world authority, able to act efficaciously on the juridical and political levels? Once more we reiterate Our good wish: Advance always!... Let unanimous trust in this Institution grow, let its authority increase.[134]

A few years before the Pope's speech, Thomas C. Schelling put forward a speculative yet dramatic scheme for world peace: directed coercion.

Schelling, a brilliant strategist and game-theory analyst, suggested that a world military force could use nuclear weapons against offending nations; "to inflict civil damage at a rate sufficient to induce the government to change its mind and bend to the will of the international authority."[135] Or if it wished to use non-nuclear tactics, the authority might preposition military units for ease in deployment,

> The purpose of being within the country, other than ceremonial, would be to minimize the cost and delay of invasion, occupation, or selective destruction... The force could occupy Moscow more reliably with ground forces located thirty miles away... An amphibious landing on the coast of Japan, France, or the United States would be harder than just moving troops already located within these countries.[136]

Another mode of peace-coercion would be pre-placing "critically vulnerable parts of a country's economy and essential services directly into the hands of an international force." Schelling likened this to "the landlord who shuts

[134] *Holy Father's Talk at United Nations*, October 4, 1965, speech on file.

[135] Thomas C. Schelling, "Strategy: A World Force in Operation," reprinted in *The Strategy of World Order: Volume 3 - The United Nations* (World Law Fund, 1966), p,682. Schelling's essay was also published in *International Military Force: Peace-Keeping in an Armed and Disarmed World*, edited by Lincoln P. Bloomfield (Little, Brown and Company, 1964).

[136] Ibid., p.683.

off the utilities when a tenant refuses to move." "Rather than bomb electric power installations," the strategist explained, "the force might press a key that sets off a charge of dynamite already installed."[137]

Or maybe, for the sake of efficiency – of course! – the world authority could use hostages to force change,

> If one really believed in the reliability and permanence of an international arrangement, such schemes for providing the authority with 'hostages' might be more efficient, even more humane, than providing it with bombers and shock troops. One could even go further and let the force have a monopoly of critical medicines to use for bacterial warfare on a transgressor country. As soon as it starts an epidemic, it sends its medical units in to make sure that no one suffers who cooperates. Those who oppose it – military forces, government leaders, or anyone else – are without essential vaccines and must decide for themselves whether to stay at large and suffer or to surrender to be cured.[138]

Schelling recognized that his ideas suffered from "meanness" and "probably go too far." He understood that the "more omnipotent" the world authority becomes, the more likely it would be viewed as an enemy. Lesser but still powerful national systems, he surmised, will be required to keep the international military from overpowering too quickly.

Knowing that Schelling was primarily theorizing in his advocacy of a world force, I am still left with nagging thoughts: How far is too far in the cause of global unity? Can international harmony exist without compulsion from a centralized authority? Would the *whole* tolerate opposing values and dissenting voices – be it from individual nations, identifiable groups, or single persons – and court the risk of separation and fragmentation? Is oneness sacrosanct? Are its expressions sacred?

Is the ideal of the *greater good* greater than independent freedoms? Are the visions of cohesive community – interdependence and equality – to be more valued than the liberty of individualism?

If so, then we shall ultimately have little problem accepting a version of Schelling's proposal.

---

[137] Ibid., p.683.

[138] Ibid., pp.683-684.

Fade to Green

With the rising interest in ecology during the late 1960s and early 1970s, the priorities of international visionaries began to shift. World order for world peace was still a benchmark, and remains so, but the color *green* was now added.

During the 1968 World Constitutional Convention, organized by the World Constitution and Parliament Association, Lucile Green found herself chairing its Ecology Commission – possibly the first documented merger of environmental concerns with consultations on world government.[139] Green was chosen to lead this Commission because, in her words, "I was the only one who could define the term, 'ecology'."[140] So new was the idea.

World population size and natural resource management were the prime areas of interest, with the Commission suggesting that "earth, water, air and energy" be managed for "the common good." Another recommendation was the establishment of an agency "which would act as trustee for future world parks, territories and oceans."[141]

Population control was a fundamental part of the new green thinking, and influential voices were raising the alarm that the Earth was being overrun. Garrett Hardin, a renowned American intellectual, posed and answered a troubling question: "How can we help a foreign country to escape overpopulation? Clearly the worst thing we can do is send food… Atomic bombs would be kinder."[142] *The Environmental Handbook*, prepared for the first

[139] The World Constitution and Parliament Association (WCPA) was founded by Philip Isely, a world federalist who formed the WCPA with "maximalist world federation" in mind. By the mid-1990's more than 900 NGOs from 110 countries – the majority being underdeveloped nations – had joined the WCPA Global Ratification and Elections Network. The strong support from underdeveloped countries raised a question that became a WCPA selling point: "What if the Third World begins world government?" Although Philip Isely passed away in 2012, his organization remains active.

[140] Lucile W. Green, *Journey to a Governed World: Thru 50 Years in the Peace Movement* (The Uniquest Foundation, 1991/1992), p.21 (see the text box on that page).

[141] Ibid., p.19. Note: Later drafts of the WCPA *Constitution for the Federation of Earth* listed population control, protection of the atmosphere, natural resource usage, and the establishment of wilderness areas as under the jurisdiction of the World Government.

[142] Garrett Hardin, "The Immorality of Being Soft-hearted," *Stanford Alumni Almanac*, January, 1969. As quoted in Barry Commoner's book, *Making Peace with the Planet* (New York: The New Press, 1992 edition), p.167.

Earth Day, simply said: "The goal would be half of the present world population, or less."[143] At that time the world's population was 3.7 billion.

Stanford professor Paul Ehrlich became a poster-boy for population control, equating population growth to a cancer needing to be cut out.[144] Scary scenarios reinforced Ehrlich's mandate. Nuclear war, manmade plagues, and global air pollution that would make the "planet uninhabitable" before 1990 loomed before us.[145] Climate change, due in part to human activity – especially the cirrus cloud effect from spreading jet contrails – might usher a new global ice age.[146] Overpopulation was our doom.

How would the planet, and humanity itself, be saved from the scourge of too many people?

Ehrlich suggested a number of control measures, voluntary and coercive, but he understood that it would ultimately require social change through religious and political transformation. In religion: a recognition that Zen Buddhism, the "quasi-religious" New Left, and the "Whole Earth 'hippie' movement may well help save our environment." In politics: a Planetary Regime to administer the global commons – "The Planetary Regime might thus incorporate the United Nations into a sort of International Agency for Population, Resources, and Environment."[147]

Similar thinking underscored the Club of Rome.

Founded in 1968 by the Italian industrialist Aurelio Peccei, the Club was, and remains, a diverse group of influencers acting as a catalyst for change. Breaking new ground by using computer modeling to project long-term trends, the Club concluded that human growth needed limits; population and resources were on a collision course, and environmental collapse was

---

143 *The Environmental Handbook: Prepared for the First National Environmental Teach-In, April 22, 1970* (Ballantine/Friends of the Earth, 1970, editor, Garrett de Bell), p.323.

144 Paul R. Ehrlich, *The Population Bomb* (Sierra Club/Ballantine Books, 1968, thirteenth printing, 1970), see his Prologue.

145 Paul R. Ehrlich, "Eco-Catastrophe!," *The Environmental Handbook*, pp.161-176.

146 Paul R. Ehrlich and Anne H. Ehrlich, *Population, Resources, Environment: Issues in Human Ecology* (W.H. Freeman and Company, 1972), pp.240-241. Ehrlich at least recognized that climate change was a nebulous science, and that "Climate, of course, is an ever-changing thing." Still, the Stanford professor could not help but add: "At just the time that man has populated the planet to the point of stretching his food resources to the maximum, he is almost certainly accelerating climate changes." (pp.241-242).

147 Ibid. For religion, see p.351. For politics, see p.435.

imminent. This *world problematique* would therefore require systematic world solutions. Early on, the Club proposed a World Forum of technical experts who would deliver "a dramatic 'state-of-the-world' message supported by proposed policy responses."[148] Humanity needed guidance to achieve a planned equilibrium between human development and nature. In the words of esteemed Club member Ervin Laszlo, they would "advise and proselytize."[149] Laszlo, a leading systems theorist, projected a radical transformation of planetary politics: a World Ecology Authority and World Ecology Court.[150]

It was in this intellectual milieu that the age of global environmental planning made its entrance, with the 1972 UN Conference on the Human Environment firmly pushing *green* onto the world stage. Headed by Maurice Strong, a Canadian of international reputation with solid ties to the Club of Rome,[151] the Conference linked human development to ecological imperatives. A new understanding of planetary unity was emerging.

---

[148] *The Predicament of Mankind: Quest for Structured Responses to Growing World-wide Complexities and Uncertainties – A Proposal* (Club of Rome, 1970), Annex II, p.34.

[149] Ervin Laszlo, "The Club of Rome of the Future vs. The Future of the Club of Rome," *Goals in a Global Community: The Original Background Papers for Goals for Mankind – A Report to the Club of Rome, Volume 1, Studies on the Conceptual Foundations* (Pergamon Press, 1977), p.282. In Canada, the Club's national branch flavored the International Development Research Centre (IDRC), a federal government corporation working with developing countries. And in China, two of the Club's reports were reconstructed into a mathematically formulated, scientifically validated, theory of national population; too many Chinese people, not failed government policies, had stymied prosperity and development. The result of this pseudo-scientific blame-shift was China's notorious one-child policy. For information on the IDRC connection, see Jason L. Churchill, *The Limits to Influence: The Club of Rome and Canada, 1968 to 1988* (Thesis presented to the University of Waterloo, 2006), pp.99-106. For China's one-child policy, see Robert Zubrin, *Merchants of Despair: Radical Environmentalists, Criminal Pseudo-Scientists, and the Fatal Cult of Antihumanism* (Encounter Books, 2012), pp.181-183.

[150] Ervin Laszlo, *A Strategy for the Future: The Systems Approach to World Order* (George Braziller Inc., 1974), p.176. The Authority and Court were envisioned as parts of a total world system, a "global homeostasis."

[151] In his book, *Where on Earth are We Going?* (Alfred A. Knopf Canada, 2000), Maurice Strong states he was a member of the Club of Rome's executive (p.399). However, no year is given. Strong does tell us that he read an article by Aurelio Peccei in the late 1960s and was so impressed that he flew to Rome for a meeting with Peccei: "We became friends and collaborators" (p.116). For some background on the Club of Rome's general impact on the 1972 Conference, see Wade Rowland, *The Plot to Save the World* (Clarke, Irwin and Company, 1973).

According to the Conference's unofficial report commissioned by Maurice Strong, science and specialized knowledge "has led to a new and unexpected vision of the total unity, continuity, and interdependence of the entire cosmos."[152] Strong's understanding was this,

> The central theme of our age is interdependence – the interdependence of all the elements which sustain life on this planet; the interdependence of man with these elements; the interdependence of the natural physical systems with man's needs and aspirations; and, most of all, man's interdependence with man.[153]

One result of the 1972 Conference was the formation of the United Nations Environment Programme (UNEP), an organ of the UN dedicated to environmental concerns. Strong became its first Executive Director. Interestingly, the UNEP logo conspicuously has Man in its center, sending an unspoken but powerful message: If the world is to change, ***humanity must do so first.***[154]

The real success of the Conference was not the birth of another UN agency but the placing of the natural environment on a political pedestal.[155] How the international community interpreted nature, and Man's place in it, would form guiding principals for the next phase of social evolution. This was not about creating a supra-national political authority, a point made by Strong, but about finding a mechanism through which nations could exercise their "sovereignty collectively."[156] In the decades ahead this would be re-packaged as *global governance* – the voluntary alignment of one's nation within a framework of collectively articulated values and decisions.

---

[152] Barbara Ward and Rene Dubos, *Only One Earth: The Care and Maintenance of a Small Planet* (W.W. Norton and Company, 1972), p.30. *Only One Earth* was the "Unofficial Report Commissioned by the Secretary-General of the United Nations Conference on the Human Environment." Aurelio Peccei was on the Committee of Corresponding Consultants who helped shape the document, which became an important book within the burgeoning environmental movement.

[153] Maurice Strong, Introduction, *The Plot to Save the World: The Life and Times of the Stockholm Conference on the Human Environment*, by Wade Rowland (Clarke, Irwin & Company, 1973), p.x.

[154] As explained to me by an original UNEP staff member: Source is confidential.

[155] For example: a framework document was produced to assist nations in ecological planning for global outcomes: *Report of the United Nations Conference on the Human Environment* (United Nations Publication, A/CONF.48/14/Rev.1).

[156] Strong, Introduction, *The Plot to Save the World*, p.x.

Essentially, the worldview supporting the new international consensus was to translate into national planning; a measurable response to the politicizing of nature. Humanity's relationship to the environment, and to each other, would profoundly change.

Twenty years later the world community reconvened in Rio de Janeiro. The 1992 UN Conference on Environment and Development (UNCED) – better known as the Earth Summit – was an opportunity for governments to negotiate a new and expansive set of framework documents on biodiversity, climate, and human behavior.[157] Maurice Strong, now the Secretary-General of the Earth Summit, was unequivocal about the importance of its anchor document: "*Agenda 21*, the action plan to implement the principles and agreements of Rio, is a blueprint for constructing the new world order called for at Rio."[158]

Agenda 21 and the other official texts acted as rallying flags for national, state/provincial, and municipal planning. The US Environmental Protection Agency's *Ecosystem Protection* paper of 1993, referencing the Earth Summit documents, encouraged the Executive Branch to direct federal agencies "in light of international policies and obligations" and to "amend national policies to more effectively achieve international objectives." Suggested were "human population policies" and the development of a "Green Bank Program," a federal institution to collect environmental permit fees and enforcement fines from the general public.[159]

Former principle author of the Santa Cruz County *Local Agenda 21*, Mark Edward Vande Pol, makes an astute observation: "Rules beget interpreta-

[157] Framework documents: *Agenda 21*, *Rio Forest Principles*, and the *Rio Declaration on Environment and Development*. Legally binding agreements open for signatures: *Convention on Biological Diversity*, *Framework Convention on Climate Change*, and the *Convention to Combat Desertification*.

[158] Maurice Strong, Forward, *The Earth Summit's Agenda For Change* (International Institute for Sustainable Development), available on the IISD website from 2002 until 2015 – www.iisd.org/rio+5/agenda/foreword.htm.

[159] *Ecosystem Protection* (US Environmental Protection Agency, National Performance Review, August 6, 1993), pp.9-10. Another US response was the establishment of the President's Council on Sustainable Development. In Canada, the federal government put forward national directives and reviews to achieve the goals of *Agenda 21*. Australia did likewise (see its Commonwealth document, *Our Community Our Future: A Guide to Local Agenda 21*), as did many other nations.

tions, which beget violations, which beget new rules until the system jams with conflicting demands."[160]

Mark's task was to re-constitute the UN's *Agenda 21* for local implementation, giving bureaucrats and environmental NGOs justification to directly interfere with private property in Santa Cruz County. Deeply disturbed by this process-of-control, he came away from the experience with another realization: "The last thing we need is to make a welfare case out of the planet."[161]

Returning to the United Nations, it is important to know that an extensive, behind-the-scenes process takes place before all UN summits. Preparatory conferences or *prep-cons* are first-tier events in which working-groups made up of government ministers, UN representatives, invited stakeholders, and select NGOs flesh-out the summit's goals and benchmarks. Behind this is a secondary level of activity: a matrix of government hearings and NGO consultations, expert roundtables, academic conferences, and public relation campaigns. It is within this secondary context that theoretical and ideological expressions are given ample room to maneuver.

Consider an audacious, second-tier case in point.

Two years before Rio a stakeholder event was held in Winnipeg, Manitoba. Its official theme: "Sustainable Development Strategies and the New World Order." Approximately 3,000 experts and delegates participated in nearly 200 working sessions. "Protecting the Environment – Preparing for Tomorrow" was the general motif, with "education for sustainable development" a major subject of concern. Maurice Strong was its patron.[162]

Event findings were published under the title, *Sustainable Development for a New World Agenda*, and it was expected to be a springboard for "discussion and calls to action." The report, along with the Manitoba government statement to the Earth Summit – *The Manitoba Protocol*, also written at this conference – was submitted to UNCED organizers.

---

[160] Mark Edward Vande Pol, *Natural Process: That Environmental Laws May Serve the Laws of Nature* (Wildergarten Press, 2001), p.85.

[161] Ibid., inside back cover

[162] See the outcome document, *Sustainable Development for a New World Agenda* (ICASE/STAM/CASE/ Government of Manitoba, 1990), Preface and Introduction. This event was titled the World Environment Energy and Economic Conference, also known as World '90, and was held from October 17-20, 1990. UNESCO and the International Council of Associations for Science Education, along with the Manitoba government, were primary sponsors.

Chapter two was breathtaking: "Towards A Global Green Constitution,"

> The issues are not about *if* a global politics is necessary. The question is *how* do we achieve binding agreements in Law complete with effective programs for applying sanctions against non- compliance that would oblige each nation, regardless of size, to abide by a set of principles that are required to guarantee the survival of life on this earth. Perhaps we will find that there is no other alternative to a system of rigid controls that some would equate to a police state. Unfortunately, in order to save the planet from biocide, there have to be very powerful constraints from doing the 'wrong' things. The constraints must transcend national boundaries, be world-around and enforceable. There would be a need for an agency for preventing eco-vandals from acting unilaterally.
>
> Enforcement agencies would need the power to act without being invited by the offending nation. Therefore, there needs to be an agency that is acceptable to all nation states on the planet. We can probably accept the fact that there will always be one or more nations that will not go along but there must be effective sanctions in place. If sanctions do not work, then physical occupation and the installation of a World Trusteeship would be imposed upon the offending nations.[163]

Energizing this idea was a hypothetical *Global Green Constitution*,

> The Constitution would need to be the world-around political expression of a radical new value system... governments would come to power that could most effectively formulate national policy implications of a Global Green Constitution. The United Nations would be a signator and take responsibility for the global commons... Nation states would each be signators and take responsibility for the impacts of industrial and commercial activities that occur within territorial boundaries. A Global Environmental Congress having Constitutional authority and responsibility would inspect and determine the degree of compliance of each signator nation.[164]

---

[163] Jim Bohlen, representing the Greengrass Institute, "Towards A Global Green Constitution," *Sustainable Development for a New World Agenda*, p.15, italics in original.

[164] Ibid., p.16.

Environmental protection would be humanity's highest duty. To that end, de-humanized wilderness zones must be legally enacted: "It is the human population that needs management, not wildlife."[165]

And managed we were to be through a new economic order.

Under a *Social Justice* heading, the report recommended an "assured basic income from birth to death for every woman, man, and child on Earth." Free university education, free medical and dental care, and "access to socially useful work" would hallmark an era of "global economic equality."

How could something this utopian function? Roughly assimilating the Technocracy movement from the 1930s, it was explained that an Energy Accounting system with pre-determined allotments of energy for everyone would guarantee equilibrium. Natural resources are depleting, the report said, and if Social Justice is to be attainable, then a "global policy of one child per family" would have to be implemented. This calibrated balancing of production, consumption, and population – the management of humanity for the sake of the planet – would *be* Sustainable Development.

Obviously not everyone would appreciate living under this version of world order, what "some would equate to a police state," but so what? Humanity's re-enchanted values are articulated in service to the Earth, and the planet cannot afford insubordination,

> Popular or not, green governments will oppose any culture if it proves to be prejudicial by reasons of gender, age, colour, race, religion, belief, sexual orientation, mental or physical condition, marital status, family composition, source of income, political belief, nationality, language preference, or place of origin.[166]

That this *Global Green Constitution* was a theoretical offering does not diminish the seriousness of its underlying worldview. Nor is this the only example attesting to a radical reshaping of civilization. Only a few months before the Earth Summit, the Canadian Council for International Co-operation hosted a workshop in light of Rio. "We need a unified one world order," the workshop summary said.[167]

---

[165] Ibid., p.14.

[166] For the subsection on Social Justice, including the quote on opposition, see pp.11-13.

[167] James Robertson, "Toward a New Economic Paradigm," *Sustainability: From Vision to Reality – A Summary of a Workshop on Alternative Economics* (Canadian Council for

One expert who attended the workshop proposed a *biocracy*,

> Democracy is replaced with 'biocracy,' where not people but life-sustaining systems are the central concern. Democracy remains a need within this model, at both local and global levels, but as one part of the whole system. 'Participation' becomes more than people's physical presence and deepens to contain a cultural and spiritual dimension.[168]

A new international framework did emerge from the Earth Summit, one dependent on nations voluntarily aligning domestic policies to global sentiments. The effect was subtle and substantial: Subtle in that the general public remained unaware or uninterested in the process, and profound in that it sought to re-shape citizen's behavior through regulations and campaigns. The result was an undermining of private property rights as land users faced progressively tightening restrictions. Some individuals and organizations, thankfully, spoke out in warning.[169]

International Co-operation, with funding from the Canadian International Development Agency, February 25-28, 1992), p.5.

[168] Maximo Kalaw, "A Community-based Model of Sustainable Development," *Sustainability: From Vision to Reality*, p.8. After the Earth Summit, Kalaw became Executive Director of the Earth Council – a post-Rio organization founded by Maurice Strong.

[169] A small group of individuals worked tirelessly to understand the intent and applications of the Rio agreements, along with other UN agendas, and to bring warning. Dr. Michael S. Coffman and Henry Lamb of Sovereignty International (SI) and the Environmental Conservation Organization (ECO) immediately come to mind. Both spoke to Congressional and State committees, community groups, and did interviews regarding UN activities. They also provided a platform for other voices of concern. In the 1990s and early millennial years, SI hosted conferences and ECO produced a magazine titled *eco-logic*. I attended the 1997 SI conference and was privileged to speak at its 2001 *Freedom 21* event, and *eco-logic* published some of my earlier articles. Others who labored for liberty in the face of a rising green establishment included former governor of Washington, Dixy Lee Ray, and my friend Doug Hindson. Doug worked to protect property rights in the Trent Severn watershed of Ontario, Canada. Another Canadian, Dr. Tim Ball, continues to stand against the tide of UN-initiated climate change bureaucracy. Some critical resources worth perusing on the subject are: Michael Coffman, *Saviors of the Earth? The Politics and Religion of the Environmental Movement* (Northfield Publishing, 1994); Dixy Lee Ray, *Environmental Overkill: Whatever Happened to Common Sense?* (Regnery Gateway, 1993); and James Wanliss, *Resisting the Green Dragon: Dominion, Not Death* (Cornwall Alliance, 2010). Elaine Dewar's *Cloak of Green* (James Lorimer and

Although the enshrined hope of centralized, international management did not come to pass, post-Rio literature continued to advocate total solutions. This was especially so with resources geared to young people. *Rescue Mission Planet Earth: A Youth Edition of Agenda 21* is one example.

"Written and illustrated *by* children *for* children to inspire young people all over the world," *Rescue Mission* critiqued the Rio process and *Agenda 21*. The world community simply had not gone far enough,

> The Agenda suggests no new government structures to implement even its own proposals let alone the ones it leaves out. We need a new way of governing the whole planet. The problems we face are bigger than any single country.[170]

To solve planetary problems, *Rescue Mission Planet Earth* outlined a "Global Democracy of Children." Mirroring the concept of a *soviet*, the Democracy would start with local Councils in public schools – "perhaps to organize the Local Agenda 21" – and then move upward to state, national, and continental Councils. The final stage would be an International.[171]

An explosion of youth-directed projects and campaigns emerged after Rio. Indeed, the Earth Summit ignited interest in school-based global citizenship programming and green educational outcomes. President of the European Cultural Agency, Edgar Morin, told UNESCO that the new role of education would be to "Civilize and Unify the Earth… the education of the future should teach an ethics of planetary understanding… accession to earth citizenship… for an organized planetary community."[172]

The Temple of Man was being painted green, and a generation of young people were being conditioned to see themselves as democratic representatives of Mother Earth. *Re-enchantment was being politicized.*

Company, 1995), focusing on Rio and its historical development, is a fascinating peek behind the international green agenda. Tim Ball's books, *The Deliberate Corruption of Climate Science* (Stairway Press, 2014) and the abbreviated *Human Caused Global Warming: The Biggest Deception in History* (Tim Ball, 2016) are powerful critiques.

170 *Rescue Mission Planet Earth: A Youth Edition of Agenda 21* (Kingfisher Books, coordinated by Peace Child International, with sponsorship from UNESCO, UNDP, UNEP, and UNICEF, 1994), "by children for children" from the back cover, italics original.

171 Ibid., p.84.

172 Edgar Morin, *Seven Complex Lessons in Education for the Future* (UNESCO, 1999), p.39, for "accession" and "planetary community," see p.62.

Unite Before We Destroy Each Other

Calls for a new world order resounded with the thaw of the Cold War and the Rio experience.[173]

Re-energized, the World Federalist Association participated in the Earth Summit and influenced the UN Commission on Sustainable Development, the international body charged with overseeing the Rio outcomes.[174] When the UN initiated the Commission on Global Governance, guided by a group of eminent persons – including Maurice Strong – the World Federalist Movement "steadfastly supported the Commission in its call for global governance."[175] This Commission pressed for global environmental management tools, including a Carbon Tax on energy usage.[176] Resolutions during the 1995 WFM Congress stressed environmental education, global ethics, global governance, and the formation of an International Environmental Court.[177]

Publicly recognized personalities were stepping to the plate in support of World Federalism. Former Congressman, John B. Anderson, took the WFA presidency in 1992. The next year Strobe Talbott received the WFA Global Governance Award for a *Time* article he wrote in support of world government.[178] His close friend, President Bill Clinton, sent a letter on White House stationary congratulating Talbott and wishing the WFA success.[179] One year later Talbott was Clinton's Deputy Secretary of State.

Media giant Walter Cronkite received the same accolade in 1999. Attendees at his Global Governance award ceremony, held at the United Nations,

---

[173] One example was the Wingspread Conference in Racine, Wisconsin, sponsored by the World Federalist Association. It brought together senior UN officials, members of Congress and staff from the Senate Foreign Relations Committee, distinguished professors of world law, and WFA personalities. The goal was to rethink the United Nations in light of strategies to advance world federalism and global governance. See *Rethinking Basic Assumptions About The United Nations: Conference Summary* (World Federalist Association, 1993). Conference date: December 4-6, 1992.

[174] *WFA Activist Guidebook*, Section 1, p.16

[175] *Action Report* (World Federalist Movement, May 1996), see Topic 6.

[176] *Our Global Neighborhood: The Report of the Commission on Global Governance* (Oxford University Press, 1995), p.212.

[177] World Federalist Movement, *WFM Policy: Resolutions, Proposals, and Recommendations* – Adopted at XXII Congress, San Francisco, June 1995.

[178] Strobe Talbott, "The Birth of the Global Nation," *Time*, July 20, 1992.

[179] President Bill Clinton, letter, dated June 22, 1993, copy on file. The full title of the award is the *Norman Cousins Global Governance Award*.

included UN Secretary-General Kofi Annan, actor and actress Michael Douglas and Catherine Zeta-Jones, and journalists Lesley Stahl and Ed Bradley. Cronkite, "the most trusted man in America," told his esteemed audience that the United States will have to yield up some of its sovereignty for world government, admitting this will be a "bitter pill" for many.

"To deal with world problems," the news anchor preached, "we need a system of enforceable world law, a democratic federal world government."

At one point in his acceptance speech Cronkite derided conservatives and the "religious right-wing," mimicking the belief that a humanist world order "must be the work of the devil." Cronkite mockingly added: "I'm glad to sit here at the right hand of Satan."[180]

First Lady Hillary Rodham Clinton sent her praises in a personal video message: "Good evening and congratulations, Walter, for receiving the World Federalists Association's Global Governance Award... we honor you for fighting for the way it could be."[181]

Throughout the 1990s and continuing into the new century, World Federalist events were graced by ambassadors, UN officials, prominent mayors, members of parliaments, and representatives from the House and Senate. During this time the World Federalist community had a profound affect on international developments. Bill Pace, the Executive Director of the WFM, worked behind the scenes through Canada's Lloyd Axworthy[182] and a group of Caribbean heads-of-state – maneuvering around UN Security Council objections – to successfully create the International Criminal Court (ICC). And World Federalists were instrumental in framing a new military doctrine, Responsibility to Protect (R2P), which enables the international community to militarily intervene in failing nations – a concept with real-world consequences, as demonstrated by NATO's R2P action in Libya. Both examples fit the vision of global governance; both are way markers to World Federalism.

---

[180] A copy of Cronkite's acceptance speech is on file, along with a video of his talk. As the text had extemporaneous remarks excluded, and as the video is edited to remove certain section of the speech, I have compared both for this citation. For more information see, "WFA Honors The Most Trusted Man In America," *World Federalist: The Quarterly Newsletter of the World Federalist Association*, January 2000, p.1.

[181] A copy of this video is on file.

[182] Lloyd Axworthy was Canada's Minister of Foreign Affairs from 1996 until 2000. He was also the President of the UN General Assembly from early 1999 until April 2000. For ten years he served as President and Vice-Chancellor of the University of Winnipeg.

But which system will rise to the planetary mountaintop? Will it be *governance*: this assortment of voluntary commitments? Or *government*: an international authority?

Speaking as a guest to a WFA meeting in Dallas, Maurice Strong told the assembly – myself in the mix – that governance was the way forward. Conversely, in Pope Benedict XVI's *Caritas in Veritate*, the Pontiff appealed for a "true world political authority," reforming the UN so that "the family of nations can acquire real teeth."[183] Realistically we already function within burgeoning structures of global governance, and these institutions, by their nature, point to the possibility of a grander coalescence.

In other words, it is not an either-or proposition. The modus operandi is this: Push for *governance* while striving for *government*. This dual-track was observable during the 26th International Congress of the World Federalist Movement, held in Winnipeg, Manitoba for one week in July 2012. Attending this 65th anniversary of the Movement was a gifted friend who was working on a double major in Ancient Studies and Philosophy, and yours truly.

Under the leadership of Lloyd Axworthy and Bill Pace, this distinguished assembly reviewed past achievements, re-committed to existing projects, and considered future campaigns. A letter of appreciation from Secretary General Ban Ki-moon was in our agenda package: "The old order is breaking down and we do not yet know the shape of the new. Your Movement has a crucial role to play in helping the United Nations and people everywhere to build the future we want."[184] A second note from Kofi Annan congratulated the WFM for its role in establishing the ICC and R2P doctrine.

Major agenda items for the Congress included the adoption of a *Manifesto for Global Democracy* and renewed support for the anticipated United Nations Parliamentary Assembly. The Congress also had four working commissions, each tackling different subjects of importance, with the purpose of presenting outcomes for adoption by the end of the week. My friend went to one focus group and I went a different way, attending the commission on Global Environmental and Economic Governance.

On economics, my committee talked about placing a global levy on international financial transactions and the implementing of a carbon tax on

[183] Pope Benedict XVI, *Caritas In Veritate* (Libreria Editrice Vaticana, 2009), Paragraph 67.

[184] Ban Ki-moon, UN Secretary General, Message to the World Federalist Movement on its 65th Anniversary, Winnipeg, Canada, 9-13 July 2012.

energy consumption. A truly "big idea" was the notion of a World Currency Unit to augment national reserves and to be used as a means of exchange by international monetary institutions. It was agreed that "a Summit to create a new worldwide monetary order" should be convened.

My committee also delved into "Sustainable Development Governance." For this cause we were told that an International Environmental Court was being considered, and moves are underfoot to upgrade UNEP into a "global environmental authority." The working group further considered a "supranational Democratic Climate Decision Making System" to manage global climate issues. But what would this look like? Might it be a standardizing agency, providing benchmarks for industries and nations to achieve? Could it acquire international authority over nation states? Would its pronouncements signal international intervention against a non-compliant country?

Early in the week Axworthy told us he would like to see R2P expand from its present form. Instead of a tool to be only used when a country fails to protect its citizens against genocide, it could be broadened into a powerful "new value" – R2P for poverty alleviation, R2P for natural disasters, R2P for environmental crisis, and R2P for "cultural genocide" due to climate change.

What stuck out, from beginning to end, was the repetitious reminder that a crisis is needed to move *governance* into *government*.

Could a perceived environmental crisis be the catalyst? Could threats to the Earth, real or imagined, be leveraged for world order?

A 1993 report by the Council of the Club of Rome suggested as much,

> In searching for a common enemy against whom we can unite, we came up with the idea that pollution, the threat of global warming, water shortages, famine and the like, would fit the bill. In their totality and their interactions these phenomena do constitute a common threat which must be confronted by everyone together. But in designating these dangers as the enemy, we fall into a trap... namely mistaking symptoms for causes. All these dangers are caused by human intervention in natural processes, and it is only through changed attitudes and behaviour that they can be overcome. The real enemy then is humanity itself.[185]

[185] Alexander King and Bertrand Schneider, *The First Global Revolution: A Report by the Council of the Club of Rome* (Orient Longman Limited, 1993), p.75.

Something similar but more succinct was said by a participant in the 1992 Earth Summit's Youth Movement: "UNCED also holds a broader significance. The environment was set up as a global issue in need for global action."[186]

But environmental issues are usually local or regional in nature, and seldom globally encompassing or catastrophic enough to justify demand for a world government. What about Climate Change? Certainly this is touted as a reason for international management, just as "reckless population growth" has been used as an excuse, but climate alarmism is showing its age as a theory built on faulty models and questionable assumptions. The more politicians attempt to force this narrative the less scientific the argument becomes, showing itself for what it is: an ideologically-determined agenda.

How about an *extraterrestrial encounter*?

Undeniably, the public has been culturally primed to anticipate the arrival of an "advanced race" – either alien enemies or alien saviors who impel humanity towards unification. The rich history of science fiction literature and a stream of alien-themed offerings from Hollywood have fueled imaginations and distorted the worldviews of multitudes. Arthur C. Clarke's *Childhood's End* is one literary example wherein extraterrestrials – known as Overlords and looking like medieval-styled demons – appear in the skies, and then work through the United Nations as the acknowledged center point of One World. And what a world! The Overlords guide humanity into a Golden Age: planetary surveillance destroys crime, Christianity vanishes "like morning dew" and a secular dawn brings new illumination, poverty and illness virtually disappears, the memory of war fades away, and everything is eventually absorbed into Cosmic Oneness.

Humanity is swallowed by the *Overmind*, the living consciousness of the expanding universe.[187] It is the grandest evolution.

Coming down to earth, sightings and accounts of unidentified flying objects (UFOs) by professionals – including military personnel, aviators and astronauts – have fueled interest in the topic. Rumors of government disclosure regarding the UFO phenomena make their rounds in the alternative press and on social media. Would *full disclosure* upset humanity enough to initiate some kind of world authority? Not likely. It would take something

[186] *Youth Sourcebook on Sustainable Development* (International Institute for Sustainable Development, 1994), p.63.

[187] Arthur C. Clarke, *Childhood's End* (Ballantine Books, 1953).

more dramatic – a direct intervention. This thought has spurred a new field of study, Exopolitics, which seeks to outline and disseminate the paradigm shift that would occur in politics, religion, and social behavior if a global encounter should manifest.

There is a cultural longing to collectively experience the Earth-shaking mysteries wrought by an outside intelligence: unity in peaceful cooperation, or unity against hostile intentions. We crave contact.

Former President Ronald Reagan once said the following to the UN,

> Cannot swords be turned to plowshares? Can we and all nations not live in peace? In our obsession with antagonisms of the moment, we often forget how much unites all the members of humanity. Perhaps we need some outside, universal threat to make us recognize this common bond. I occasionally think how quickly our differences worldwide would vanish if we were facing an alien threat from outside this world. And yet, I ask you, is not an alien force already among us? What could be more alien to the universal aspirations of our peoples than war and the threat of war?[188]

Reagan's "alien threat" comments are intriguing, but such speculation is of little pragmatic value in actively planning world government. This does not diminish the extraterrestrial hypothesis, but war, as Reagan rightly implied, is a force of change that is immediately tangible. It hangs over us in the present, regardless of our place in history.

But not just any kind of war threat will do; it *must* have global reach and be utterly catastrophic in its potential. This could be a regional spillover that drags superpowers into a widening conflict, escalating into an international fire storm – the ever-tense Middle East comes to mind. Or a limited nuclear exchange between Pakistan and India, or India and China. Regardless of the scenario, the threat must push the world to a tipping point.

As each successive World War birthed new international authorities, so the underlying belief is that the next global war will usher in a more advanced regime of world order. Herein was the theme we picked up on while attending the WFM Congress – *We must unite before we destroy each other*.

---

[188] Ronald Reagan, Address to the 42d Session of the United Nations General Assembly in New York City, New York, September 21, 1987, (www.reaganlibrary.archives.gov/archives/speeches/1987/092187b.htm), accessed February 15, 2017.

Olivia Chance, my friend who was interning with *Forcing Change* magazine that summer, gives us her firsthand account,

> I was struck by the glaring contradiction that echoed throughout the week. The concept, 'we must unite before we destroy each other,' was repeated in multiple forms in almost every session by various high-standing leaders of the WFM. And this is quite possibly the phrase that exemplifies the mission of world federalism, because at the movement's root it is 'not trying to build a utopia; rather it is urgently trying to prevent world-wide disaster.' Yet in every meeting where these words were uttered, an antithetical call was also issued, the hope of war.
>
> Not that the desire for war was ever expressively stated, but allusions to the need for such a disaster were scattered throughout the meetings. Those at the World Federalist Congress were very aware that other great alliances, such as the League of Nations and the United Nations, were the direct result of a war. And as their imagined global parliamentary system is a 'third attempt at world order,' it is understandable that they expect and need another globally significant war to produce the kind of international government they envision...
>
> ...all of us present at the Congress were told by Bill Blaikie that we are, 'waiting for that one historic tipping point.' It will be at that 'tipping point' when world government will seem more acceptable to the now hesitant nation-states, for it will seem more necessary to ensure human survival.
>
> I can't help but view this with horror and confusion: Horror at the thinly veiled hope for crisis, and confusion at the mixed message this sends... as the week unfolded and I heard more and more references to the need for a crisis in order to unify, I realized that the leaders of the World Federalist Movement – Blaikie, Axworthy, Pace and others – were very aware of the same issue I was: In our efforts to unite, we may have to destroy each other.[189]

---

[189] Olivia Chance, "We Must Unite Before We Destroy Each Other: A First-hand Report on the World Federalist Movement," *Forcing Change*, July 2012, Volume 6, Issue 7, pp.14-15. "Not trying to build utopia" – see Jerry Tetalman and Byron Belitsos, *One World Democ-*

Who will save us from annihilating ourselves? World Government. And if we *must* commit this gravest of sins, then who will shine a light into the dark night of our collective soul? World Government.

It could be said this way: Humanity's redemption lies in the governance of human unity, and the safeguarding of Earth is our collective holy mission.

World government is the organized, political manifestation of this ideal.

While I have heard individual World Federalists describe their Great Work as "bringing Heaven to Earth" and "ushering in the Kingdom of God," and knowing that the history of world order is laced with such language – especially from Social Gospel advocates[190] – I am compelled to ask: Which God? The King of Kings, Jesus Christ, does not require a human-derived institution to build a Kingdom. What, politically, does the one who is Holy Other have need of? Conversely, to make claim that we usher in "Heaven on Earth" is to elevate our status to that of Redeemer, or to say that God Himself is not capable without our co-redemptive intervention.

Many decades ago, Edgar C. Bundy critically examined the Federal and National Council of Churches, and the role played in promoting socialism and world government, including their interlock with politicians and foundations to that end. Spiritual politics for world order is certainly premised on a *big idea*, yet it misses the essential message of the Gospel – and it must, for the Cult of World Order offers an alternative salvation.

The core of what Bundy said in 1960 holds true today,

> They are engaged in a massive campaign to supplant the individualistic Gospel of the Galilean with a great collectivistic machine designed for political and economic ends. Where political forces move in on church affairs, the preaching of the Christian doctrine of individual salvation is of necessity silenced."[191]

---

racy: A Progressive Vision for Enforceable World Law (Origin Press, 2005), p.22. "Third attempt" – as explained in Pathways to Global Democracy, Session #1, 26th World Federalist Congress, July 11, 2012. Re: Bill Blaikie – he is a former Canadian politician who held the office of Deputy Speaker of the House of Commons.

190 For a history of the Social Gospel and World Federalism, see Martin Erdmann, *Building the Kingdom of God on Earth: The Churches' Contribution to Marshal Public Support for World Order and Peace, 1919-1945* (Wipf and Stock Publishers, 2005).

191 Edgar C. Bundy, *Collectivism in the Churches: A Documented Account of the Political Activities of the Federal, National, and World Council of Churches* (The Church League of America, 1960), p.73.

When we seek to create Heaven on Earth, the Great Commission gives way to the Great Collective. More than that, we inevitably downplay the majesty of God while elevating our own sense of collective importance.

"In other words," Bundy summarized, "the concept of the Sovereignty of God is to be abolished in favor of a more democratic concept in which man will decide whether God shall be sovereign or not."[192]

But God will not be mocked, even by our good intentions. Nor will He be dethroned by our plans and agendas, benign or malevolent.

I am reminded of Psalm 2. In this passage the people *plot a vain thing*, "the kings of the earth set themselves, and the rulers take counsel together." Why? To come against the true God and His Anointed Son: "Let us break Their bonds in pieces and cast away Their cords from us."

God's response to this declaration of definitive human mastery – the placing of the *creation* over the *Creator* – is appropriate,

> He who sits in the heavens shall laugh; The Lord shall hold them in derision. Then He shall speak to them in His wrath, and distress them in His deep displeasure.[193]

To pronounce salvation through a global political authority is to put faith in a God-substitute. It is a political religion, an organizational idolatry – an idol built in our own image.

Actress Jean Stapleton, assisting the WFA alongside John Denver, Walter Cronkite and Lloyd Bridges, understood the salvific nature of their task,

> The goal of the World Federalists is peace through unity of government. We must support their vision of oneness in diversity for it is the salvation of humanity.[194]

Nay, the Cult of World Order is not humanity's deliverance. It is only the enactment of a political priesthood in the Temple of Man, enchanted by visions of power, surrounded by laurels of green.

This, too, is another *game of gods*.

---

[192] Ibid., p.28.

[193] Psalm 2:4-6.

[194] As quoted from the World Federalist Association brochure, *What the World Needs Now has Changed*

Chapter 12

Spiritual Politics

> After intra-Protestant and intra-Christian ecumenism we have irrevocably reached the third ecumenical dimension, ecumenism of the world's religions! – Hans Küng. [1]

> The new intercourse will fructify in more inclusive, universal faiths, perhaps even a new world faith as a basis for the coming world civilization. – Paul Clasper.[2]

Foundry United Methodist is an historic church in the heart of Washington DC. Located between the Logan and Dupont circles at the corner of 16th and P streets, less than 1,500 yards due north of the White House, this congregation is bound to the rich heritage of the nation's capital. Abraham Lincoln graced its pews, as did Andrew Jackson, Calvin Coolidge, and Franklin D. Roosevelt. In the 1990s President Bill Clinton and his family attended, with the president even preaching from its pulpit.

I went to Foundry in November 1999, not to hear a Sunday morning sermon but to attend a meeting of internationalists and faith leaders. The millennium was upon us, and in the search for world peace and justice, what could religions do? Would it be possible for politics and diverse faiths to join in achieving common goals? A lead-up letter from the host said this: "Recognizing the need to work together to strengthening the United Nations, religious groups are creating a powerful voice of unity – a core principle of world federalism."[3]

---

1 Hans Küng, Preface, *The Meaning of Other Faiths*, by Willard G. Oxtoby (The Westminster Press, 1983), p.10.

2 Paul Clasper, *Eastern Paths and the Christian Way* (Orbis Books, 1980), p.108.

3 Letter from Aaron M. Knight, Director of Development, World Federalist Association (Washington D.C.), no date, copy on file.

Organized by the Chesapeake branch of the World Federalist Association (WFA), this event[4] pulled together representatives from Hinduism, Islam, Judaism, the Bahá'í and Sikh communities, and Soka Gakkai. A Catholic perspective was given by long-time World Federalist and UN reformer, John Logue. It was his talk that alerted me to Pope Pius XII's earlier endorsement of world government.[5] Protestant views came from the Foundry's own senior minister, Dr. J. Philip Wogaman, with input from the Reverend James T. Christie of Southminster United Church.[6] Christie was then council chair of the World Federalist Movement.

A Draft Summary Statement was distributed, calling for "religious and political leaders to develop a shared vision of global unity and governance for the new millennium." Noting that the United Nations had met with religious personalities the month before to focus on the "oneness of humankind and for the growth of planetary consciousness," the Statement implored a new partnership and purpose, connecting the dots between global governance and spirituality,

> Government can have spiritual as well as practical value... The gap in democratic governing institutions beyond national boundaries is a spiritual gap in an interdependent world... We call for a widening circles of dialogue and efforts, involving world religions working together constructively with trends toward the ideals of world governance, so that the unity of humankind can be brought to a new level of world reality in the millennium to come.[7]

I attended this event to better understand how *spiritual politics* was envisioned. After interacting with World Federalists, listening to speeches and panel discussions, it was evident that the prevailing motif was this: We must *redeem ourselves*. How? By creating an orderly and just society, celebrating

---

4 The event was titled *The Search for World Peace and Justice: What Can World Religions Do?* It took place on Saturday, November 13, 1999. Approximately twenty groups endorsed the assembly, including the Bahá'í Community of Washington, the Interfaith Alliance, Council for a Liveable World, the Interfaith Coalition of the Environment, United Religions Initiative, and the National Capital office of the United Nations Association.

5 See chapter 11, p.355.

6 Southminster United Church is located in Ottawa, Ontario.

7 Draft Summary Statement, *The Search for World Peace and Justice: What Can World Religions Do?* November 13, 1999. Document on file.

our diversity within a great federation of humanity – for this is our only hope to free the world of violence.

A new organization – a movement, really – I was particularly interested in had a special place at the conference. The Vice President of the United Religions Initiative (URI), William W. Rankin, was invited to deliver a keynote address and participate in a panel discussion. During lunch hour I discovered that a major reason for his involvement was to court a relationship with the WFA. Could the URI find an ally in the World Federalist community? Yes. Would the WFA uphold the URI in its development? Of course!

After all, the goal of the *initiative* was the creation of a *United Religions*.

URI for UR

In February 1993, William E. Swing, the Episcopal Bishop of California at San Francisco's Grace Cathedral, received a life-changing telephone call from the United Nations. Would the Cathedral host an interfaith assembly to commemorate the 50th anniversary of the UN?

Agreeing to the request, Bishop Swing found himself pondering the future of religion. The celebration was important for the occasion, he understood, but something more lasting was needed. The nations of the world had the UN, but religions were without a comparable structure. Framing his thoughts around the narrative of faith and *conflict*, he decided it was time to create a United Religions. Another thought struck the Anglican Bishop,

> For a second, but only for a second, I allowed myself to consider the first of the Ten Commandments. Primitive and structural! 'Thou shalt have none other gods but me.' If a religion prides itself on keeping the first of the Ten Commandments, then it will pride itself on what it does about the 'other gods.' Holy writings will be filled with the stories of how the people of the other gods were slain, and the purity of the religion was maintained against the threat of assimilation. How can history compete with the Divine command to have 'none other gods'? If the planet Earth is ever going to have a chance of continuing as a cosmic oasis in the vastness of the universe, perhaps we need to take a second look at the first Commandment.[8]

[8] William E. Swing, *A Bishop's Quest: Founding a United Religions* (XOXOX Press, 2015), pp.15-16.

Theologians and historians could argue, quite rightly, that his view of the first Commandment and the associated Judeo-Christian worldview were skewed. Nevertheless, his perspective on religion and violence – and the absence of a permanent institution for faith leaders – were sparks of inspiration: *If a United Nations, why not a United Religions?*[9]

That summer the Bishop met with officials from major interfaith groups in the hope of soliciting support for a United Religions (UR). To his dismay there was little interest in the project. The World Conference on Religions for Peace, a coalition of faith leaders, had already been issuing resolutions and recommendations since the early 1970s. The International Association for Religious Freedom, the world's oldest interfaith organization, had been building networks and fostering dialogue since 1900.[10] The Temple of Understanding in New York City was known for its spiritual influence within the United Nations. And the Council for a Parliament of the World's Religions was busy preparing for its historic gathering, the 1993 Parliament of the World's Religions.

Was there room at the table for a United Religions? Would not a "United Nations" of religions be too bureaucratic, too expensive, too risky? The very idea of the UR suggested an infringement of existing sensibilities.

Marcus Braybrooke from the World Congress of Faiths and a fellow Anglican was the only person who offered a small measure of encouragement, suggesting the UR might emerge from a youth movement.[11]

"It was abundantly clear," penned the Bishop, "that none of them wanted anything to do with the creation of a United Religions."[12]

Swing was undeterred. "I was ready to commit to be a catalyst," he wrote in his autobiography.[13] In time, some of these same organizations would come alongside the URI, and the URI would offer support in return.

Taking Braybrooke's advice, a multi-faith Youth Conference was arranged through the University of San Francisco, right on the heals of the UN anniversary. The Bishop wanted students to explore his interfaith concept, but the

---

9 Gleaned from a 1999 URI brochure, *United Religions Initiative*.

10 In 1900 the organization was known as the International Council of Unitarian and Other Liberal Religious Thinkers and Workers.

11 Swing, *A Bishop's Quest*, p.20.

12 Ibid., p.20.

13 Ibid., p.16.

university insisted on a different focus. With the goals in conflict, a group of frustrated students walked out and formed their own impromptu gathering on the campus lawn. Swing recounts the situation,

> When a large enough group arrived, they held hands and prayed and sang songs of their traditions – Muslims, Jews, Christians, Buddhists, Hindus, and on and on. Before our eyes we witnessed a grassroots display of spontaneity… I couldn't help but think at the time that in getting ready for the U.N. 50th service at Grace Cathedral, it took over a dozen people working for two years to design a liturgy that would not be offensive to some traditions, and here were these young people making it up as they went along in a matter of minutes.[14]

It was an experience that would foreshadow the URI model.

After the UN gala wrapped up, full attention was given to the UR dream. Bishop Swing traveled around the world meeting with religious personalities in the quest to raise awareness. Visiting India he spoke at the Maramon Convention, a large Christian conference annually hosted by the Mar Thoma Church. Maramon attendees responded with shock at the suggestion of interfaith universalism: *Salvation comes through Jesus Christ alone*. The Bishop was confronted with the question – "Who is Jesus Christ for you?"[15] It was a direct challenge to Swing's vision. On the other hand, some of Mar Thoma's leadership would later join the United Religions Initiative.

He spent time with Mother Teresa and Karen Singh, a prominent Hindu statesman and a giant in the field of interfaith work. He visited the Ramakrishna Ashram, the launching point of the modern Advaita Vedanta movement and the spiritual home of Swami Vivekananda. Traveling to New Delhi he went to the Lotus Temple, the impressive, marble-clad Bahá'í House of Worship with its 27 free-standing petals. In Dharamsala he visited the Temple of the Oracle before meeting with the Dalai Lama.

Pakistan, Egypt, Israel, Jordan, England, Turkey – from the headquarters of the World Council of Churches in Geneva to a meeting with Hans Küng in Tübingen to the Vatican and Pope John Paul II, Bishop Swing's "remarkable journey" became renowned within the interfaith community. Some with

---

[14] Ibid., p.27.

[15] Ibid., p.59.

whom he met were delighted; others disapproved of the UR project. Nevertheless, the religious world was now on notice and watching.

After his journey, Juliet Hollister from the Temple of Understanding and the UN's Robert Muller teamed with Swing in a public letter appealing for broad support: "You are invited to join the United Religions Initiative to help change the world."[16]

An early URI fact-sheet explained the mission,

> The mission of the United Religions Initiative is to create the United Religions – a permanent assembly where the world's religions and spiritual communities will gather on a daily basis, in prayer and meditation, dialogue, and cooperative action, to make peace among religions so they might be a force for peace among nations, for addressing urgent human need, and for healing the earth.[17]

Target deadline for United Religions: Year 2000.

Structural assistance came from unexpected sources. Management guru and designer of the Appreciative Inquiry model, David Cooperrider, offered his expertise in fleshing out the vision. Dee Hock, founder of the *Visa* credit card, was commissioned to facilitate the URI Charter writing process. Cooperrider and Hock, with other consultants,[18] guided the project away from the typical composition of other interfaith groups. Rather than a leadership driven entity, focus on the grassroots. Instead of an organization, allow it to become an *organism*.

Like the protesting students who spontaneously formed their own interfaith circle, the URI would spawn Cooperation Circles: "self-organized groups which are locally rooted and globally connected."[19] As the Charter process moved forward with a summit at Stanford University, including the input

---

[16] Letter from the United Religions Initiative, Fall 1996, signed by William Swing, Juliet Hollister, and Robert Muller, copy on file.

[17] *Mission Statement*, United Religions Initiative, no date.

[18] Joseph Prabhu was another consultant. At the time Prabhu was the Rockefeller Visiting Professor at the California Institute of Integral Studies and a visiting scholar at Graduate Theological Union. From 1988-91 he was a member of the Revisioning Philosophy project at Esalen Institute. Since 1978 he has been Professor of Philosophy at California State University, Los Angeles.

[19] *URI Cooperation Circle and Affiliate Report*, June 2000, United Religions Initiative, report introduction, no page number.

of Neale Donald Walsch,[20] and as regional URI meetings took place around the world, Cooperation Circles started forming on university campuses, in churches, and within smaller and intimate settings.

"In theory, I had anticipated that a Charter would come first, and then the Charter would give birth to a community," explained the Bishop. "What actually happened was that when we gathered to begin writing the Charter, a community broke out."[21]

The objective was still a United Religions by the millennium. On June 26, 2000 – the day the United Nations Charter was signed 55 years earlier – the URI Charter was officially launched through a Global Summit in Pittsburgh, the "city of bridges."

I attended much of the Summit, which took place on the campus of Carnegie Mellon University. So did approximately 300 others from 39 spiritual traditions and faiths: followers of Judaism, Christianity, Buddhism, Hinduism, Islam, Wicca, and Bahá'í. An "appreciative litany," acknowledging our spiritual diversity, was included in the welcome package,

> Accept a blessing from the Names we bring, hundreds, Thousands of names for what is most precious to us – *Adonai*, *Allah*, *Brahma*, *Buddha*, *the Christ*, *the Spirit*, *the Tao*, *Father Sky & Mother Earth*... Precious names, sacred names, And many, many more become our blessings for each other... We claim this site as sacred space – a furnace forging a new peace.[22]

The Summit started with an Earth Blessing, an Indigenous smudging circle on the campus lawn, followed by a reception at the towering Cathedral of Learning just a few blocks away. The next morning, June 26, began with a Sacred Opening to "invoke the sacred in any way." This was the day of the Charter signing and after lunch a long processional made its way to the Carnegie Music Hall. I remember walking behind Pagans and Buddhists and Christians, all moving to where the Charter ceremony would take place.

If you have been to the Carnegie Music Hall, you understand the sumptuousness of this locale: Rich crimson velvet, vaulted golden ceilings, and a foyer with imported marble pillars upholding a 50-foot high baroque-styled

---

20 "URI Global Conference," *URI News Update*, No. 3, Fall 1997, p.2.

21 Swing, *A Bishop's Quest*, p.124.

22 Italics in original.

canopy. To my front, on the expansive stage, rested a table with the Charter and behind this a bronze serpent posed horizontally on a stand.[23]

Music and meditations set the tone, creating an auditory backdrop for the attending dignitaries in their cultural and religious dress. It was a spectacle.

The ceremony itself included the reading of a letter from the United Nations Association of San Francisco: "We work together with you for justice and healing, for the Earth and all living things." The facilitator of the Cooperation Circle at the United Nations was supposed to connect to the ceremony through a networked telephone call routed into the Carnegie sound system. This bridge from the UN to the URI was to be a highlight, but the technology failed and the call was cancelled. However, the point was made: "The URI is connected on the ground and around the world."

An interesting situation occurred when, on that day, the *Pittsburgh Post-Gazette* announced that the Roman Catholic Church did not align with the URI vision. During the ceremony the Director of the Roman Catholic Archdiocese of San Francisco, Gerard O'Rouke, soundly rebuked the paper,

> I want to correct something that I saw in your paper today in this city. I am here officially as a member of the Catholic Church, and this is where I should be... I am officially here. It's where the Church should be right now – and it is here.[24]

At the end of the week Donald Frew from the Covenant of the Goddess performed a "traditional Wiccan foundation blessing" during the Summit's closing ceremony. Frew, who led a URI Cooperation Circle titled Spirituality of the Earth,[25] wrote-up an invocation specific for the occasion,

> We had always used fairly generic terms like 'Lady' and 'the Goddess' in our public interfaith blessings. In this one, I specifically invoked Hekate and Hermes by name, and Bishop Swing was right there raising his arms in invocation with the rest of the Circle! We have, indeed, come a long way.[26]

---

23 This same serpent was placed in the Cathedral of Learning the evening before.

24 Notes and audio on file.

25 The Spirituality of the Earth Cooperation Circle, with Elder Donald Frew as its contact, is listed in the June 2000 *URI Cooperation Circle and Affiliate Report*, p.17.

26 Elder Donald Frew, *1999-2000 Interfaith Report*, Covenant of the Goddess, July 21,

The Charter summit was bittersweet for the Bishop. On one hand the URI was asserting itself as a serious movement within the interfaith community, an undeniable organizational and personal victory. But the original hope of a United Religions was out of reach.

Swing puts this into perspective,

> On June 26, 2000, a dream died for all practical purposes… Ironically, in my pursuit of a United Religions, I had missed on the vision. I had completely missed on the response of religious leaders. I had entirely missed on the timing of events. And I totally missed on the planning that would make it happen. Nevertheless, though I flayed away blindly, I actually hit a home run… Not on my watch, but a United Religions is on its way.[27]

In considering the foundational worldview of the interfaith dream, Bishop Swing – looking through a universalistic lens – pondered the depths of Oneness: "The interfaith challenge is to grow a heart for the assumed Oneness that exists in atoms and Muslims, galaxies and Buddhists, nature and Jews, universes and Universalists."[28]

World Federalists were barely noticeable at the URI Summit. I recognized one or two faces, but no one from the WFA executive attended that I could see. Someone from the Pittsburgh branch of the WFA did attend, as their literature had been placed on a table near the entrance to the URI Meditation Room. This lack of World Federalist involvement surprised me, for the two movements had the potential to dovetail in a profound way.

Maybe like Swing's assessment, the WFA had "missed on the timing."

A Common Altar

The pedigree of the interfaith movement is the 1893 Parliament of the World's Religions, held as part of the World's Columbia Exposition. Charles Carroll Bonney, the Chicago lawyer who birthed the Parliament, did so in hopes of fighting the irreligious attitude visible in much of modern Amer-

---

2000. The CoG website with the posted report is no longer available [www.cog.org/interfaith/cogdf00.html]. A screenshot is on file with the author.

27 Swing, *A Bishop's Quest*, pp.158-159.

28 Ibid., p.190.

ica. His hope was to find a commonality that linked all faiths in a religious brotherhood, and he believed the Golden Rule would furnish this.[29]

Opening the Parliament, Bonney declared an era of spiritual progress,

> This day the sun of a new era of religious peace and progress rises over the world, dispelling the dark clouds of sectarian strife. This day a new flower blooms in the gardens of religious thought... This day a new fraternity is born into the world of human progress, to aid in the upbuilding of the kingdom of God in the hearts of men. Era and flower and fraternity bear one name. It is a name which will gladden the hearts of those who worship God and love man in every clime. Those who hear its music joyfully echo it back to sun and flower. IT IS THE BROTHERHOOD OF RELIGIONS.[30]

That the 1893 Parliament shifted the course of religious dialogue is well established.[31] Today's multi-faith milieu is an outgrowth of that venture. But other forces of thought have also contributed to this contemporary development. The idea of worshiping around a common altar – that all spiritual traditions are facets of a whole – was subtly implanted in the Western mind, in part, through the philosophic teachings of the Masonic Lodge.

Freemasonry, now at its lowest membership rate in the United States since 1924,[32] has historically been the most ingrained fraternity in the Western world. In the not so distant past every hamlet, village and town seemed to have had a Lodge. Masonic membership in 1959 exceeded 4.1 million men in the United States alone, representing the Craft's numerical highpoint in America.[33] If this population would have been amalgamated into a single city, let us call it Masonville for effect, then Masonville would have been the

---

[29] Marcus Braybrooke, "A Study Guide for Interreligious Cooperation and Understanding," *A SourceBook for Earth's Community of Religions* (CoNexus Press, 1995 – Revised Edition), p.150.

[30] Speech by Charles Carroll Bonney, "Words of Welcome," *The Dawn of Religious Pluralism: Voices from the World's Parliament of Religions, 1893* (Open Court, 1993), pp.21-22, capitals in original.

[31] See Marcus Braybrooke, *Pilgrimage of Hope: One Hundred Years of Global Interfaith Dialogue* (SCM Press, 1992).

[32] At the time of writing, the Masonic Service Association of North America listed US membership statistics to 2015. That year the Lodge was at its historical low with 1,161,253 members [www.msana.com/msastats.asp, accessed April 11, 2017].

[33] See the Masonic Service Association of North America, www.msana.com/msastats.asp.

second largest metropolis in the Untied States – bigger than Chicago with its 3.5 million at the time.

Why is this important? Because Masonic philosophy emphasizes universalistic principles, and pastors and deacons and professors and politicians and judges and fathers and sons were and are saturated in the Lodge experience, often unaware of the meaning and message underscoring its structure.

Melvin M. Johnson, "considered by many scholars to be the greatest American Freemason of the 20th century,"[34] recognized the dynamic of religious universalism within the Craft. His assessment demonstrates the crucial importance of its pluralistic spirit,

> Masonry is not Christian; nor is it Mohammedan nor Jewish nor to be classified by the name of any other sect. The power which has held it together, the chemical which has caused its growth, the central doctrine which makes it unique, is the opportunity it affords men of every faith, happily to kneel together at the same Altar, each in worship of the God he reveres, under the universal name of Great Architect of the Universe.
>
> Here, and here alone, is the real universality of Freemasonry.[35]

"Thus, and thus only," Johnson elaborated, "can we furnish to the world at large a common base upon which all civilized mankind may unite."[36]

Long before the 1893 Parliament, Masonic scholars were ascribing a unifying religious position to their Craft. Noted expert on Masonic jurisprudence, Albert Mackey, wrote the following in 1859,

> Masonry requires only a belief in the Supreme Architect of the universe... the Christian and the Jew, the Mohammedan and the Brahmin, are permitted to unite around our common altar, and Masonry becomes, in practice as well as in theory, universal. The truth is, that Masonry is undoubtedly a religious institution – its religion being of that universal kind in which all men agree...[37]

[34] *The Gourgas Medal* (Scottish Rite of Freemasonry, Supreme Council 33, Northern Masonic Jurisdiction, 2015), p.6

[35] Melvin M. Johnson, *Universality of Freemasonry* (The Masonic Service Association, 1957), Forward.

[36] Ibid., p.10.

[37] Albert Mackey, *A Text Book of Masonic Jurisprudence* (Redding & Company, 1859), p.95.

This aligns with what Albert Pike illumined in his massive tome, *Morals and Dogma*, first published in 1871. Pike had a profound influence on the Craft, and his understanding of religious universalism was a key teaching: "Masonry, around whose altars the Christian, the Hebrew, the Moslem, the Brahmin, the followers of Confucius and Zoroaster, can assemble as brethren and unite in prayer to the one God who is above all the Baalim..."[38]

Surveying 20th century Masonic scholars reveals a continuity of thought. Founder of the Philosophical Research Society, Manly P. Hall – esteemed for his knowledge of Masonic philosophy – advanced the connection between religious universalism and Freemasonry,

> No true Mason is creed-bound. He realizes with the divine illumination of his lodge that as a Mason his religion must be universal: Christ, Buddha or Mohammed, the name means little, for he recognizes only the light and not the bearer. He worships at every shrine, bows before every altar, whether in temple, mosque or cathedral, realizing with his truer understanding the oneness of all spiritual truth... No true Mason can be narrow, for his Lodge is the divine expression of all broadness.[39]

One more example will suffice.

Henry C. Clausen, when he was the Sovereign Grand Commander of the Scottish Rite, preached of a mystical tie that bound all faiths,

> [T]he One Supreme God has been known by many names to many races of men. The Sumerians, the Egyptians, the Medes and Persians, the Hebrew Kabalists, the Druids and Norsemen, the Brahmans, the Moslems, the Buddhists and the North American Indians all believed in God as the One Supreme Ruler and Creator of the Universe. This belief, held by the earliest guilds of operative masonry nearly six thousand years ago, is the same belief held by modern Freemasonry today.[40]

---

[38] Albert Pike, *Morals and Dogma of the Ancient and Accepted Scottish Rite of Freemasonry* (Supreme Council of the Southern Jurisdiction, A.A.S.R., USA, 1871/1944), p.226.

[39] Manly P. Hall, *The Lost Keys of Freemasonry* (Macoy Publishing and Masonic Supply Company, 1923/1954), p.65.

[40] Henry C. Clausen, *Clausen's Commentaries on Morals and Dogma* (Supreme Council of the Southern Jurisdiction, A.A.S.R., USA, 1974), p.161.

Freemasonry presented the "broad way" of religious universalism through the framework of the Lodge, and continues to do so. Its perennial philosophy, wrapped in allegory and the spiritual quest of perfection, was an effective conduit for interfaith acceptance.[41]

Perennial Spirituality

Another factor corresponding to the interfaith movement is the acceptance of *Perennial Philosophy* – the position that all spiritual traditions are connected to one metaphysical truth, one source of Divine Reality, and that this underlying context frames all religions and our human attempts to experience the Infinite. Man's attempt to grasp this Divine Reality, however, has resulted in the splintering of beliefs and schools of thought, and yet all of these fragments find substance in one Source. Such thinking can be traced into the eons of philosophical inquiry. It found reanimation in the Renaissance and reinvigoration in the age of Romanticism, and it blossomed within the mystical countercurrents of Modernity.

Today we hear it in clichés: "All religions are essentially the same." Or, "all religions are but pathways to the same mountain top."

The religious universalism of Freemasonry is Perennialism garbed in ritual. Theosophy put it forward as a science of religion. Pagan articulation can be found in how Gus diZerega describes the deities associated with the Pagan worldview: "Deities, like everything else including ourselves, are manifestations, or emanations, from the ultimate Source of All."[42]

Perennial philosopher and *psychonaut*, Alan Watts, offered this taking,

> I mean the conception of God as the total energy-field of the universe, including both its positive and negative aspects, and in which every discernible part or process is a sort of microcosm or hologram. That is to say, the whole is expressed in or implied by every part… This view strikes me as cleaner and simpler than monotheism.[43]

---

41 For more on Freemasonry, see Carl Teichrib, *Freemasonry: A Revealing Look at the Spiritual Side* (Lighthouse Trails Publishing, 2017).

42 Gus diZerega, *Pagans and Christians: The Personal Spiritual Experience* (Llewellyn Publications, 201), p.39.

43 Alan Watts, *Behold the Spirit: A Study in the Necessity of Mystical Religion* (Vintage Books, 1947/1971), p.xviii.

Popularizing this attitude within academia and the general public was Aldous Huxley's aptly titled anthology, *The Perennial Philosophy*. Pulling together observances from different faiths and drawing philosophical connections, his inspiration nonetheless remained grounded in the Hindu paradigm. One modern commentator on transformational culture reminds us that Huxley's metaphysics was about "translating the teachings of Ramakrishna Vedanta."[44]

Huxley asked the reader to turn away from theological separation,

> God may be worshipped and contemplated in any of his aspects. But to persist in worshipping only one aspect to the exclusion of all the rest is to run into grave spiritual peril. Thus, if we approach God with the preconceived idea that He is exclusively the personal, transcendental, all-powerful ruler of the world, we run the risk of becoming entangled in a religion of rites, propitiatory sacrifices (sometimes of the most horrible nature) and legalistic observances.[45]

Perennial philosophy has been equated to the Great Work, the Primordial Tradition, Ancient Wisdom and the Secret Doctrine. It seeks *essence*.

But as each religion is different in doctrines and histories and cosmological claims, and in their relationships to forms and functions – things like prayer, the role of priests and spiritual teachers, churches and temples and shrines, symbols and rituals, community interaction, books and creeds – how then does perennial philosophy find a practical outlet? Mystical experience; direct personal connection.

Alan Watts noted that Christianity was experientially dry, yet a vast spiritual hunger stalked the land. He charged that Protestantism had degenerated into moralism, and Catholicism's structures were for the most part incomprehensible. Mysticism, the inner feeling of union with Divine Reality, it was argued, is an ever-flowing stream of experience with the Source. Tellingly, Watts knew that the Western person who seeks "oneness with God or the universe" through contemplative practices must pull from Eastern traditions. Even our language would have to borrow from it.[46]

---

[44] Graham St. John, *Global Tribe: Technology, Spirituality and Psytrance* (Equinox, 2012), p.24.

[45] Aldous Huxley, *The Perennial Philosophy* (Chatto & Windus, 1947), p.31.

[46] Alan Watts, "Psychedelics and Religious Experience," *California Law Review*, Volume 65, Issue 1, January 1968, p.80.

There is, I believe, a natural attraction to mysticism – and certain personalities seem more intuitively drawn to it. But the methods used to achieve a numinous state are just that: *techniques* for a self-directed condition of being. A feeling of connection and expansion is encountered. I too have felt this in specific situations, and have had it induced through environmental stimuli: *It is a feeling of flow* – one linked to neurochemical changes and brain states. But as evidenced in the field of religious studies, this feeling can be associated with spiritual realities – and I believe it can be manipulated to that end, acting as a doorway into supernatural realms. Unchecked or intentionally pursuing such a state-of-being as a spiritual condition, I contest and others have argued,[47] can be psychologically disrupting and spirituality deceptive. Moreover, there are no Biblical examples or commands for the mystical approach to one's personal life. Rather, Christians are to be guided by the Spirit of God in all truth, to pray with rational thought, to be of sound mind, and through Christ Jesus to be confident in our salvation.

Feelings *are* part of our human make-up, but our standing with God is *not* dependent on how you or I feel, neither in our experiences nor in our works. It is dependent on what Jesus Christ has already done.[48]

Romans 12:2 tells us: "And do not be conformed to this world, but be transformed by the renewing of your mind, that you may prove what is that good and acceptable and perfect will of God." This is not a state of *emptying*, but of *filling* our minds with what God desires. It is relational and rational, an action centered in God's revealed Word – *proving what is good and acceptable*. It is not enigmatic and ephemeral.

The perennial philosophy of Alan Watts contributed to the infusion of Eastern mysticism into the West. Similarly, Carl Jung presented a psychologized version and Joseph Campbell – who popularized comparative religions – blending psychology, mythology, and perennialism. The intellectual and experiential influence of each of these men, including Huxley as a major

---

47 See Ray Yungen, *A Time of Departing: How Ancient Mystical Practices are Uniting Christians with the World's Religions* (Lighthouse Trails Publishing, 2006, second edition); Greg Hammond, *Mystic Seduction: Awakening Christians to a Real and Present Danger* (Gregory D. Hammond, 2014); Peter Jones, *Capturing the Pagan Mind: Paul's Blueprint for Thinking and Living in the New Global Culture* (Broadman & Holman Publishers, 2003); Dave Hunt, *Occult Invasion* (Harvest House Publishers, 1998).

48 Ephesians 2:8-10.

source of input, profoundly shaped the early years of the Esalen Institute. Huxley's perennial view encouraged religious experimentation: "In religion as in natural science, experience is determined only by experience."[49] Such Vedanta-based thinking, along with Aleister Crowley's earlier democratizing of decadence, was heady fodder for the 1960s.

In the opening year of that turbulent decade, Professor Franklin Baumer wrote, "This notion of experience is perhaps doubly appealing at the present time because of the approval it might seem to have from the natural sciences and the new science of psychology."[50]

The perennial philosophy has not been without its challengers, and some proponents have recognized the defects in its general discourse. Philip Goldberg rejects the cliché perennial mood that all religions are conceptually the same, advocating a more nuanced line to Oneness.[51] Jeffrey Kripal of Esalen grants Huxley's *Perennial Philosophy* its due, but describes the slow breakdown of the ideal within that famed community,

> The book laid the intellectual and comparative foundations for much that would come after it, including Esalen and, a bit later, the American New Age movement. By the 1980s and '90s, Esalen intellectuals were growing quite weary and deeply suspicious of what was looking more and more like facile ecumenism and an ideological refusal to acknowledge real and important differences among the world's cultures and religions. But this would take decades of hard thinking and multiple disillusionments.[52]

Not all religions are the same. Yet perennial thinking has perpetuated this alternative-fact. Differences are writ-large, including core goals: Buddhism is focused on the issue of suffering; Hinduism, the problem of reincarnation; Mormonism, the desire to attain Godhood; Islam, the admittance into an Arabic Paradise; Christianity, the need for salvation and the solution to sin through Jesus Christ. Furthermore, to demand that the fundamental

---

49 Huxley, *The Perennial Philosophy*, pp.152-153.

50 Franklin L. Baumer, *Religion and the Rise of Scepticism* (Harcourt, Brace and Company, 1960), p.285.

51 Philip Goldberg, *America Veda: From Emerson and the Beatles to Yoga and Meditation – How Indian Spirituality Changed the West* (Harmony Books, 2010), p.12.

52 Jeffrey J. Kripal, *Esalen: America and the Religion of No Religion* (The University of Chicago Press, 2007), p.87.

uniqueness of different religions somehow do not matter – that they are even frivolous – is a grave conceit. The crucifixion and resurrection of Jesus Christ is not a side event within Christianity, a hiccup after the Sermon on the Mount. Nor can it be said that Allah and the God revealed to the Hebrews are the same. They are not. Yet some Christian groups, the Mennonite Central Committee as a case in point, have pushed this progressive narrative.[53]

And when employing Dr. Peter Jones's method of interpretation between One-ism and Two-ism – reality is All One, or reality is comprised of God distinct from creation – the cosmological divide becomes unbridgeable. Perennial philosophy may have some merit when comparing Eastern religions, Sufism, Paganism and New Age beliefs, but it does not encapsulate the reality of Two-ism. *Otherness* does not fit. Ironically, while we live in a perennially accepting culture, religious illiteracy dominates. Many Westerners now understand little about basic Christianity, let alone other religions.[54]

That the perennial worldview has infused itself into the Western mind is beyond question. Rightly tying Perennialism to Hindu cosmology, Goldberg said: "Once again, 'Truth is one, the wise call it by many names.' Vedanta has so seeped into collective awareness that the spirit of this premise, if not the literal phrase, is now widely accepted in the United States."[55]

Searching for the *experiential* has encouraged a culture of spiritual sampling. Describing the occulture of society, religious historian Christopher Partridge portrays the West's new mood this way,

> Related to this basic thesis that there is a single divine reality behind the plurality of religions is a relativist philosophy and, in most cases, an eclectic syncretism which recognizes the validity of most religious belief and expression. Put simply, religious belief, wher-

[53] As taken from *What is Palestine/Israel? Answers to Common Questions* (Mennonite Central Committee, 2004 – written by Sonia K. Weaver, MCC Co-country Representatives for Palestine, Jordan and Iraq). Examples: "Christians, Jews and Muslims all believe in the same God... Christians, Muslims and Jews call God by different names depending on their native languages, but all of these terms refer to the same God" (p.32). "Jewish God-talk is sometimes more complicated than that of Christians and Muslims, but it still designates the same Supreme Being" (p.33).

[54] Encountering gross religious illiteracy in his students, Stephen Prothero – a religious professor at Boston University – was compelled to write his book, *Religious Literacy: What Every American Needs to Know - and Doesn't* (HarperOne, 2008).

[55] Goldberg, *American Veda*, p.12.

> ever it is found, is grounded in an experience of the same divine reality. Hence, it makes sense for the spiritual traveler to explore as much of the religious landscape as possible, for in so doing she is gaining a breadth of insight denied to the person who does not stray outside a single religious tradition.[56]

Tasting from a smorgasbord of traditions and beliefs thus becomes fashionable, an elevating act of self-discovery, a journey into Spiritual Alchemy.

Exaggerating for effect, let me introduce you to *Perennial Man*.

After morning yoga, Perennial Man immerses himself in the teachings of Ken Wilber and Christian mystic Richard Rohr, self-owning Wilber's Integral Theory and the flow of Rohr's Cosmic Christ. Globetrotting, he ventures as a holy nomad and loses himself in ecstatic dance on the beaches of Goa, and in Auroville he discovers intentional community before traveling to Australia for the Rainbow Serpent Festival. Tripping into the jungles of Brazil, he encounters the Plant Spirit during an ayahuasca journey. Going to the Theosophical Society headquarters in Wheaton, IL, he attends lectures on Sacred Art and discussions on Advaita philosophy, and in the quiet of the evening he contemplates inner divinity during a prayer walk in the labyrinth tucked along the west side of the grounds. In Toronto he spins-awake his mystic heart with Sufi masters, then disappears for a two-week encounter with shamans in Oregon before going to Burning Man in Nevada. Returning home, he joins a Unitarian Universalist church and celebrates the sacred harvest with its Wiccan members. He cleanses his house of negative energy with crystals purchased at the Wellness Expo, and handles workplace stress with Transcendental Mediation. Back pain is managed through Reiki, and the future is guided by Tarot cards and astrology. And traditional Christianity? This was rejected as a teenager in Sunday school and mocked in university.

Perennial Man is *spiritual but not religious*.

Seeing the writing-on-the-wall of Western civilization and the emerging of a secular spirituality, French theologian Jaques Ellul penned,

> Post-Christian society is marked by its experience of Christianity and at the same time it thinks it knows what it is turning away form...

---

[56] Christopher Partridge, *The Re-Enchantment of the West, Volume 1 – Alternative Spiritualities, Sacralization, Popular Culture, and Occulture* (T&T Clark International, 2004), p.64.

> post-Christian society is a society of men who are at the point to which Christianity brought them [in terms of social and civil development] but who no longer believe in the specific truth of the Christian revelation. At the same time, post-Christian society is convinced that it knows all there is to be known about Christianity.[57]

Rejecting the certainty of the God who is *Other* – "I am the First and I am the Last; Besides Me there is no God"[58] – the West is in a period of pluralistic integration, and it no longer knows *who* nor *what* has been discarded. This is a truism not only for the general population, but for scores of Christians as well. Seeking spiritually we find ourselves theologically adrift.

Perennial philosophy breaks down binaries and blurs differences; it can be typified as a form spiritual evolution. And like many proponents of evolutionary biology, the evidentiary focus is on *similarities* while *irreducible distinctions* are pushed aside or otherwise taken out of the equation. There is a limit to the reduction of essentials before extinction takes place. However, unlike an animal species that dies off, a degraded faith can be restored.

Perennial thinking has reshaped attitudes. Institutionally, it has been an intellectual license to organize the interfaith vision. Shining a spotlight on Perennialism, Peter Jones wrote: "The perennial philosophy, the great tradition, the old religion – all are iterations of the underlying worldview we've been calling Oneism."[59]

Doing Violence

The interfaith movement builds and brands itself around cultural memes and social justice themes: Environmental concerns, wealth redistribution, equality and social democracy, world peace, and the restructuring of institutions to fit their version of projected reality. One meme stands out: *Religion is the cause of war and conflict.*

This fashionable statement is a powerful interfaith motivator, for if religions – classically being understood as world faiths – are the primary cause of conflict then they bear the burden of responsibility to change. Are religions the chief cause of war and strife? Yes and no.

57 Jacques Ellul, *The New Demons* (Crossroad/Seabury Press, 1975 English edition), p.24.

58 Isaiah 44:6.

59 Peter Jones, *The Other Worldview: Exposing Christianity's Greatest Threat* (Kirkdale Press, 2015), p.47.

Yes, *if* we are speaking about explicit religious ideologies driving specific military actions to achieve faith-motivated goals.

For example: When examining the actions and goals of the Islamic State of Iraq and Syria, Hezbollah, al-Qaeda and the Abdullah Azzam Brigades, al-Shabaab, Boko Haram, Ansaru, the Muslim Brotherhood and the Islamic Resistance Movement known as Hamas – and other associated actors – there is a correlation between their religiously determined ideologies and violence. When one follows the trail of politicized Islam, for it *is* political – actually, a complete way of life – the religious element remains an inescapable guide to its political and social ambitions, and it gives internal legitimacy to military engagements. Furthermore, Muslim-to-Muslim conflict is often a struggle over religious authenticity. In geopolitical terms, the hostility faced by Israel from surrounding powers is firmly rooted in an Islamic milieu.

Although ideological Islam offers a headliner example of religion and conflict, more often than not the narrative turns to the Christian Crusades.[60] Occasionally someone will bring up the executions and killings during the Reformation, a shameful mark against Christendom. Rarely will anyone mention the slaughters in the Islamic Wars of Apostasy. In modern times the Catholic-Protestant clashes in the British Isles are singled out while other tensions remain overlooked: Hindu-Islamic hostilities in India, the Islamic-Christian bloodshed in Sudan, Buddhist-Hindu warfare in Sri Lanka, and Moslem-Christian fighting in Indonesia. At the same time we must remember that wars, even "religious conflicts," are usually dynamic events with multiple causes and complications.

War is seldom a simple thing.

The position that religion is the primary source, however, is an unsophisticated yet popular argument. Ken Wilber reflected this posture in a 2004 article posted on Beliefnet.com,

> Throughout history, religion has been the single greatest source of human-caused wars, suffering, and misery. In the name of God,

[60] Seldom does the person invoking the Crusades have an understanding of its broader context: the prior Islamic conquest of Christian communities in the Middle East and North Africa, hostile Islamic incursions into southern Europe in which civilians were captured and sold into the Middle East slave trade, the destruction of Christian property and crippling taxation imposed by Muslim rule, forcing Christian boys into Muslim armies, the threat of Byzantine collapse, etc.

> more suffering has been inflicted than by any other manmade cause... for every year of peace in humankind's history there have been fourteen years of war, 90% of which have been fought either because of, or under the banner of, God by whatever name.[61]

Daniel Gómez-Ibáñez, one of the founders of the 1993 Parliament of the World's Religions, asserted this narrative in an essay promoting the *Global Ethic* – an initiative launched at the 1993 Parliament,

> Religious hatred and intolerance resulted in death and destruction in almost every part of the globe. Faith inspires extraordinary allegiance: religions are among the very few causes for which people are willing to die and kill. It is no wonder that religion has been condemned by many as the cause of much of the world's strife and suffering.[62]

Atheist Richard Dawkins posited something analogous,

> Religious wars really are fought in the name of religion, and they have been horribly frequent in history. I cannot think of any war that has been fought in the name of atheism. Why should it? A war might be motivated by economic greed, by political ambition, by ethnic or racial prejudice, by deep grievance or revenge, or by patriotic belief in the destiny of a nation. Even more plausible as a motive for war is an unshakable faith that one's own religion is the only true one, reinforced by a holy book that explicitly condemns all heretics and followers of rival religions to death...[63]

The religious-war hypothesis influenced Bishop William Swing's dream of the United Religions Initiative, and it was a talking point during the 2005 United Nations Conference on Interfaith Cooperation for Peace. To save the world from the plague of religious conflict, faith leaders of the world must

---

[61] Ken Wilber, "Why Do Religions Teach Love and Yet Cause So Much War?" *Beliefnet.com*, www.beliefnet.com/wellness/2004/06/why-do-religions-teach-love-and-yet-cause-so-much-war.aspx. Accessed November 17, 2005, and again in April 2017.

[62] Daniel Gómez-Ibáñez, "Moving towards a Global Ethic," *A SourceBook for Earth's Community of Religions* (CoNexus Press, 1995 – Revised Edition), p.124.

[63] Richard Dawkins, *The God Delusion* (Houghton Mifflin Company, 2006), p.278.

unite to become a global force for good, breaking down religious fundamentalism and divisive truth claims.

President of the World Congress of Faiths, Marcus Braybrooke, sets up the narrative by providing a contrast – a choice, really: Do we accept peace or war? Do we embrace inclusive beliefs or strife? The division between what is globally acceptable and what is not, is stark,

> In my view, the interfaith vision is in tune with the character of the emerging post-modern global society. Indeed it offers the hope of a world civilization based on spiritual values, whereas the fundamentalist approach is likely only to lead to confrontation and conflict.[64]

But can the finger of guilt really point to religion as the *primary cause* of war and strife?

The 20th century is known as the bloodiest time in human history. Giving the MIT Mid-Century Convocation speech in 1949, Winston Churchill said,

> "Little did we guess that what has been called the Century of the Common Man would witness as its outstanding feature more common men killing each other with greater facilities than any other five centuries together in the history of the world."[65]

If religion is the chief factor in war and strife, then that infamous century is an essential case study. It is imperative we create a death list. However, because of the sheer number of wars and revolutions and genocides during those 100-years, we require a working casualty limit. For this brief survey our minimum death total will be 1.5 million *per event*. No doubt I will have missed some.

And we will not be able to delve into the details that make up our list. History is messy with overlapping actions and consequences; the academic will, therefore, find this index too rudimentary. Another problem is that accurate death tabulations can be difficult to ascertain. For example, the Mexican uprisings of 1910-1920 runs between 750,000 and 2 million dead, likewise the decades-old Rwanda/Burundi conflict falls into this statistically difficult range. Because of the variance in accounting I will leave out these two cases, along with many others that display complex discrepancies close to the 1.5

[64] Marcus Braybrooke, *Faith and Interfaith in a Global Age* (CoNexus Press, 1998), p.51.
[65] Winston Churchill, MIT Mid-Century Convocation address, March 31, 1949.

million mark. That said, the following death-inventory from war, genocide and democide[66] – as rough as it is – will suffice for our brief review.[67]

Prime causes will be listed, but not expanded. Alas, root factors are always more convoluted than what can be expressed in a sentence. Remember, we are looking at principal reasons. Notice how few of these mass-killing events had classical religion as its central cause.

Congo Free State (1886-1908): 8 million, with some estimates up to 13 million; control of colonial power base and economic exploitation.

Feudal Russia (1900-1917): 3.5 million – political control and consequences of revolutionary struggle.

Turkish Purges (1900-1923): 3 to 5 million – Pan Turkism and the Ottoman collapse, Islamic/ethnic factors within the context of political control and national expansionism.

First World War (1914-1918): 15 million – balance of power.

Russian Civil War (1917-1922): 9 million – political control.

Stalin Era (1924-1953): 20 million, with some estimates as high as 60 million – political control within an atheistic-Communist framework. The Holodomor, which I did not list separately, needs to be noted with its 2.5 to 7 million deaths due to government-induced starvation in Ukraine.

China Nationalist Era (1928-1937): 3 million – political control.

Second World War (1939-1945): 55 million – German/Japanese expansionism, balance of power. Sino-Japanese War (1937-1945): 17 to 24 million; Japanese expansion into China. This number may not include the Henan Famine of 1942-43 with its 3 to 4 million dead due to government exacerbation of drought conditions. Furthermore, the Sino-Japanese War blended into the Pacific Theatre of World War II after the attack on Pearl Harbor.

Bengal Famine (1943-1944): 3 to 5 million – a combination of crop failure and British government food policies in light of the Japanese military seizure of Burma.

Soviet Repatriations – Victims of Yalta (1944-1947): 1.5 to 2.8 million – end-of-war and post-war repatriation of "Soviet citizens" from Allied-controlled territory to the Soviet Union.

---

66 Democide is term coined by R.J. Rummel to differential the mass killing of civilians by the hand of their own government versus the mass killing of civilians by a foreign power.

67 Sources used include the work of R.J. Rummel, Matthew White, and encyclopedic resources. I have also consulted authors who have expertise in specific conflicts.

Post-World War II German Expulsions (1945-1950): 2.2 million with some estimating 5 million – post-war retributions and displacement of Germans from Eastern Europe, Allied policies and Soviet reprisals.

Yugoslavia (1941-1987): 1.5 to 4.8 million – political control, ethnic and religious issues are involved. The Balkan situation is especially complex and accurate accounting is difficult. The numbers given represent WWII up to the post-Tito era.

Chinese Civil War (1945-1949): 2.5 million – political control.

Mao Tse-tung (1949-1975): 45 to 70 million – political control and consequences of collectivist policies. Note: Approximately 45 million perished during Mao's Great Leap Forward due to starvation, collectivized and forced labor, beatings, and executions. The higher number of 70 million would include the death toll of the Great Leap Forward.

North Korea (1948-present): 2 to 3.5 million – political control and consequences of collectivist policies. The numbers may be much higher due to government-provoked famine.

Korean War (1950-1953): 3 million; political control.

Second Indochina War (1960-1975): 2 to 4 million – political control. The higher figure takes in the regional theater beyond North and South Vietnam, specifically Cambodia and Laos. China and Thailand are also regional players in the conflict.

Ethiopia (1962-1992): 1.5 to 2 million – political control and the exasperation of famine conditions, ethnic issues come into play.

Nigeria-Biafra War (1967-1971): 1 million, but up to 3 million due to resulting starvation; political control, religion-ethnic tensions are important.

Pakistan-Bangladesh Genocide (1971): 1.7 to 3 million – political, economic and social control over East Pakistan, plus ethnic-religious issues.

Cambodia's Khmer Rouge (1975-1978): 2.5 million – political control and collectivist policies within a Communist worldview.

Afghanistan (1979-2001, and ongoing): 1.8 million – political control, Soviet expansion, religion and tribal factors play a role in internal strife.

Second Sudanese War (1983-2005): 2 million – ethno-religious struggles played an important role, resource control and usage, government exploitation, and territorial separation.

Congo (1998-present): 3 to 5.5 million – political control and regional debasement, ethnic strife, resource and territorial control.

The sheer horror and brutality of mankind throughout the twentieth century cannot be properly demonstrated in a list. But the assertion that "religion has been the single greatest source of human-caused war" falls flat when the evidence is considered. Principal causation cannot be laid at the feet of classical religion.

In a paper contributed to the US Army Professional Writing Collection, Major John P. Conway tackled the question of war and religion,

> Most times, it can be argued that religion may play a key and significant role in the conduct of warfare on a psychological and cultural level, but is it the cause of warfare? Do nations, states and kingdoms wage war over religion? Is religion a primary cause of conflict between governments? Many have argued that it is. Another popular statement is, 'Religion has been the cause of more wars than any other factor throughout history.' This is commonly accompanied by 'people have been killing each other in the name of God for centuries.' Upon closer examination, these statements exude an element of mythology versus fact… A fundamental analysis of past wars commonly attributed to 'religion,' as the causal factor, may reveal an uninformed and reactionary misjudgment. Throughout the course of history, the cause of warfare between sovereign states, kingdoms, and governments is attributable to many factors, but can rarely be attributed to 'religion' as is so often the assertion...
>
> It becomes apparent that those who make the claim 'religion has been the cause of more wars than any other factor in history' may speak from ignorance or have ulterior motives for the assertion. Further, this type of assertion seems rooted in anti-religion posturing… Men and nations have a history of warfare and the root of conflict is power and gain… Occasionally war is fought over religion, as is perhaps the case during the reformation period in Europe. More often than not however, the cause of war can't be laid at the door of religion.[68]

[68] Major John P. Conway, "War and Religion: Is Religion to Blame?" *US Army Professional Writing Collection*, Volume 1, December 2003. This article can be accessed though the Wayback Machine at Archive.org. The full address through the Internet Archive is http://web.archive.org/web/20130415011457/http://www.army.mil/professionalWriting/ volumes/volume1/december_2003/12_03_2.html.

At the same time it must be recognized that worldviews can influence government actions that result in atrocities.

Richard Dawkins said, "I cannot think of any war that has been fought in the name of atheism."[69]

Neither can I.

But atheism unquestionably informed the worldview of governments that committed democide: the Soviet Union, Mao's China, Pol Pot's Cambodia, Samora Machel's Mozambique.[70] The last Soviet President, Mikhail Gorbachev – who knows the political expression of atheism better than Dawkins ever will – admitted to this when discussing the early years of the USSR,

> After the civil war ended, in time of peace, they [Lenin, Stalin, Trotsky, etc] continued to tear down churches, arrest clergymen, and destroy them... Atheism took rather savage forms in our country at the time.[71]

In the Soviet Union, atheism was a savagery that shook a people historically grounded in Russian Orthodoxy. In other words, atheism waged war against the religious and cultural soul of the nation, and for eight decades the people spilled their blood while living under an iron fist.

Returning to the narrative of religion equals war; it is obvious that this position lacks substance, yet it is a formidable myth, fueling the interfaith movement's quest for purpose and political legitimacy. Moreover, if the belief in uniting faiths for "world peace" rests on false assumptions, then it can be surmised that the collective peace sought will be superficial at best. Although interfaithism demands tolerance – even as it disdains Christian truth claims – the movement has the potential to assert its own dogma in a politically coercive manner, primarily through soft-law.[72]

Is there a risk that its united voice could be used to justify institutional duress against those who refuse to comply with new "social norms"? It could be argued that this happening already.

---

[69] Dawkins, *The God Delusion*, p.278.

[70] See chapter 4 to read more about Communist/atheist actions as it relates to this topic.

[71] Mikhail Gorbachev, *On My Country and the World* (Columbia University Press, 2000), pp.20-21.

[72] Soft-laws are moral and ethical codes constructed by non-governmental organizations. Through lobbying efforts, these consensus-driven recommendations become the basis for hard-law: legislation, regulations, and government enforcement structures.

Playing Politics

Mother Earth, we were told, needs to hear that we love her, so give a "prayer of gratitude" to the Earth: "Because out of Mother Earth comes all we need to live... she gives us the food, the water, the medicines, and the teachings." We were told that, spiritually speaking, "there is not only one way, there are many ways." Attendees were encouraged to go outside to the sacred fire and invoke the spirits.

As an observer to the G8 World Religions Summit (WRS) held at the University of Winnipeg in the summer of 2010, I listened as the opening ceremonies set the tone for this remarkable event. Welcoming everyone as spiritual equals, the WRS Secretary General invited us to "offer our service, and ourselves, and our lives" to the "God we know by so many names."[73]

Faith representatives had flown in from around the world, and diversity was daily on display in the colors and clothing. Hindu swamis in deep saffron, members of the Saudi Ministry of Islamic Affairs dressed in flowing desert garb, Jewish yarmulkes, crosses and clerical collars, Shinto robes, Orthodox priests in black, Salvation Army uniforms, Sikh turbans, and Baha'i leaders and evangelical Christians in business suits. They had congregated to envision planetary transformation. Even so, the world's attention was set on the G8 political summit about to take place in Toronto.

The WRS was the interfaith parallel to the political gathering.

Each year since 2005, when Jim Wallis from Sojourners and the Archbishop of Canterbury initiated the first event – an ecumenical affair[74] – faith representatives have been holding G8 assemblies. The Winnipeg meeting was suggested during Japan's 2008 World Summit of Religious Leaders.

Could select, spiritual personalities, unite to influence global politics?

---

[73] To learn more about the World Religions Summit and its back-story, see Carl Teichrib, "United Religions for World Change: The G8 World Religions Summit," *Forcing Change*, Volume 4, Issue 6, June 2010.

[74] Here is a partial list of North American participants, as taken from the 2005 report of the London Forum on G-8, *Action on Poverty Needed Now* (copy on file) – Richard Cizik, National Association of Evangelicals; Robert Davis, Executive Director of the Mennonite Central Committee; Rich Stearns, President of World Vision; Glenn Palmberg, President of Evangelical Covenant Church; Geoff Tunnicliffe, CEO of the World Evangelical Alliance; Peter Weaver, Bishop of the United Methodist Church. For the full list, see the report, *Action on Poverty Needed Now*. A digital copy can be found at www.g8.utoronto.ca/interfaith/2005-interfaith-leaders-en.pdf.

That was the hope of the 2006 Summit: "We believe that the time has come for a more systemic partnership of religious leaders with the United Nations."[75] In 2007 there was consensus to support "a world-wide protection agreement" on climate change.[76] The 2008 assembly highlighted the "mysterious giftedness of all existence," calling for "Shared Security" which has "respect for the interconnectedness and dignity of all life... that all humans live in one world... that the well-being of one is related to the well-being of others and ultimately to the earth that we all share."[77]

Another report from the 2008 Summit said that "the dharmic, pantheistic and ancestor traditions of Eastern societies remain a practical tool for mobilization in defence of the environment." The path to a sustainable planet would require the transition to a low-carbon society – changing lifestyles, consumption patterns, and social infrastructure.[78]

The Winnipeg Summit, like the others, envisioned a holistic framework. Uniting, religious leaders could guide global governance as planetary elders. There was more than just a feel of world federalism.

A clue to the internationalist agenda was discerned in those who steered the 2010 Summit. The same James Christie I met at Foundry more than a decade earlier was the WRS Secretary General. In fact, he was the one who recommended Winnipeg while in Japan. In 2010 Christie was Dean of Theology at the University of Winnipeg and served as Past President of the Canadian Council of Churches. Facilitating the Summit was Karen Hamilton, also a board member of the Canadian Council of Churches – actually, the General Secretary. Lloyd Axworthy, then president of the University of Winnipeg, generously hosted it on his campus.

Christie, Hamilton, Axworthy: These three were the Summit's heart, soul, and mind. And this trio shared an important globalist perspective – each were officials within the World Federalist Movement (WFM): Christie was the WFM Council Chair, Hamilton the WFM Executive Chair, and Axworthy the WFM President. *All for one...*

---

[75] Report of the World Summit of Religious Leaders, July 3-5, 2006, Moscow, copy on file.

[76] *Just Participation: A Call from Cologne*, Statement of the Cologne Religious Leaders Summit, Cologne, 6 June 2007, point number 5, copy on file.

[77] *Call from Sapporo – World Religious Leaders Summit for Peace*, July 3, 2008, Sapporo, Japan, copy on file.

[78] *A Proposal from People of Religion to Leaders of the Group of Eight*, Kyoto/Osaka, Japan, June 2008, copy on file. The Japan Summit took place in Kyoto/Osaka and Sapporo.

Three specific subjects were discussed at the Summit: poverty, care for the earth, and investing for peace. Impassioned speeches were given, hours of dialogue took place, and frequent calls for consensus returned everyone's attention to the preparation of an outcome document. This final report would be delivered to the political heads attending the G8 in Toronto.

Without going into extensive detail, here is a take-away from the three topic areas as gleaned from the WRS *Final Draft*, deliberations and discussions, Faith Community Response statements and other documents.

Poverty:

The Summit recommended that nations invest 0.7% of GDP in development assistance; canceling debts to poor countries, combating corruption, deterring speculation and flight capital, and fostering better conditions for small businesses. Basic access to food, water, health care, and education were reinforced. It sounded wonderful!

What was the underlying context? The scrapping of industrial-based capitalism and the formation of a new economic order. Evil oil had to end. Poverty is the result of "wealthier sectors of society," and governments must level the playing field through redistribution. We desperately need to implement a global transaction tax and empower the United Nations for global governance. As one participant said, "It's not about having a bike for each, it's about learning to share one bike in community."

Evidently, international socialism would be our economic savior.

Not every delegate was comfortable with this flavoring. The president of the Evangelical Fellowship of Canada asked that the role of government remain limited. Critically responding to the green socialism being pushed, Nick Baines from the Church of England rhetorically asked the group, "Who will pay?" *Who will give up their cell phones? Who will give up on travel?* Mr. Baines was right; we need to live in the real world.

Earth Care:

Mother Earth is being destroyed, and so we need a "communion with the planet." Human-caused global warming is bringing about more change than anything else in the past 300 million years, we were told. A representative from the Hindu Federation said, "we are the biggest parasites on Earth."

There was nothing subtle about the Green theme. Climate change is taking the planet to a point of no return, and the evil west – with evil capitalism and evil competition and evil market economies – are to blame, and by default, Western Christianity is central to the problem. The time *is now* for Earth-friendly faith expressions. One speaker proposed that all religions unite in a massive vision quest, a mystical rite-of-passage modeled after native spirituality: "It would be the biggest vision quest in the world!"

Jim Wallis echoed the need for a fresh vision.

Protection of the planet underscored the comments made by an official from the Pacific Council of Churches. Everything is interconnected, he explained, and we need to revisit the ancient religions and myths "deliberately pushed aside" by Christian missionaries. Without directly calling it such, his message was a petition to embrace a pagan cosmology. Another speaker said it was time to put aside the past dogmas of traditional faiths, meaning Christianity. The litmus test for authentic religion in this global era was interdependence and transcendent spirituality.

The Summit report read: "Faith communities see the environment through a lens of life on the planet as a unified whole, not unlike the cells of a body, infinitely differentiated in form and function yet deeply interdependent."[79]

Peace:

World peace was discussed in a general fashion, but it felt like the Summit had run out of time to address this issue in a comprehensive way. The final report condemned the arms race and called for investments in peace programs, to stop ethnic cleansing, and curtail nuclear weapons.

One mechanism to address world order was highlighted: Responsibility to Protect (R2P). I was not surprised.

The brainchild of Axworthy and the World Federalist Movement, R2P holds that the international community has a responsibility to militarily intervene in situations where national governments fail to protect their own people. From a World Federalist perspective, R2P becomes the moral justification to enable a world political authority.[80]

---

79 *A Time of Inspired Leadership and Action*, Final Draft – June 23, 2010, World Religions Summit 2010.

80 For more on R2P, see chapter 11, pp. 374-375. See also, Carl Teichrib, "Kosovo and the

Overall, the notion of world peace orbited around co-existence and interdependence, the integration into a new global arrangement. Leaders of world faiths would thus become planetary statesman.

The importance of the World Religions Summit was not so much its effect on G8 political leaders. Its real strength was the potential to turn religious leaders, and then constituents, into global change agents.

The dynamic is simple but effective: Heads of churches and religious groups are drawn into the interfaith experience as *strategic partners*. By being invited into the process they personally own the transformational agenda, for they have assisted in its construction. Leaving the meeting as proselytizers, these leaders then influence their network of religious professionals. In turn, seminaries and churches modify direction and purpose, parachurch organizations – themselves invited into the process – act as harbingers, and the new attitude moves down into the grassroots. Lay members go to the ballot box armed with emotions and slogans.

At the Summit it was acknowledged that the religious community is larger than any single, national political entity. Most of the represented faith groups had national, regional, or global followings. Some had memberships exceeding the population of the countries meeting at the G8. If harnessed, the combined religions of the world could act as a tremendous political force.

What I found especially troubling was the intentional positioning of the Christian community within the Winnipeg Summit: Canadian Foodgrains Bank, the National Council of Churches USA, Mennonite Church Canada, Salvation Army, the Evangelical Fellowship of Canada (EFC), and others.[81]

In a March 2010 interview with *ChristianWeek*, Karan Hamilton was asked if the EFC – Canada's evangelical face – would participate in the Summit.

"Not only will the EFC be here," Hamilton asserted, "but they'll be a partner in the initiative, a full partner. In fact, they could be said to have been the first partner in."

Inquiring about possible leeriness from the evangelical community, Karen

---

International Community: Just Another Pawn in the Game," *Forcing Change*, Volume 2, Issue 7, p.6.

81 For a list of participating organization and church groups, and their networks, see Carl Teichrib, "Lines of Influence: 2010, G8 World Religious Summit," *Forcing Change*, Volume 4, Issue 6, June 2010, p.19-36.

said the response from the EFC was that "Interfaith is absolutely a place were the EFC could work when we're talking about social justice."[82]

I appreciate some of the work EFC has done, but did they understand what was happening? Could they see the bigger picture?

Dr. Hamilton explained how the Summit leveraged influence,

> They come by virtue of their position and that's been a very deliberate strategy. So the Archbishop of Canterbury is invited... Jim Wallis from Sojourners is coming... The general secretary of the All African Conference of Churches will be one of the plenary speakers. His position means that he represents – institutionally, structurally, organizationally, however you want to put it – the Christians of Africa, which is half the population of Africa.[83]

Christian Problems

Christian involvement within the interfaith milieu is broad and *personal*.

Over the years I have found myself addressing Mennonite congregations regarding Mennonite advocacy of interfaith perspectives. This has not been without stress and considerable anxiety for concerned churches and denominations, participating parties, and myself. Because of such internal wrestling and my observances at global interfaith events, I have created a list of concerns regarding Christian acceptance of pluralistic transformation.

Before jumping into this list, it must be acknowledged that labels and intent can be mismatched. Interfaithism, as described in this chapter, is not about discussing religious differences with neighbors. My wife and I have shown hospitality to Mormons and Jehovah's Witnesses, and I have spent time with occultists, transhumanists, and atheists. Nor is this about engaging in debate or critical conversations with people of other faiths, publicly or privately. At times this has been labeled "interfaith dialogue," which may be a technically correct term, but it does not necessarily match the spirit of interfaith transformation. That is, to band together as diverse religions through a Perennial perspective, to cooperate for radical social change, and to become a political voice for collective ideals.

---

82 Doug Koop interview with Karen Hamilton, "World Religions summit in Winnipeg will deliver message to G8," *ChrisitanWeek*, March 26, 2010, online edition, www.christianweek.org/world-religions-summit-in-winnipeg-will-deliver-message-to-g8

83 Ibid.

Interfaithism, as demonstrated in this chapter, both generates and perpetuates a One-ist vision. It is about global unity situated in a false reality.

That said, in going through this list, you may come up with other points of contention or areas of concern. Consider this a starting line to think critically regarding the question of interfaith involvement.

1) Because interfaithism seeks a framework of "religious peace," it requires the subduing of divisive truth claims. To vocalize what the Apostle Peter said in Acts 4 is unacceptable, for it upsets inclusive sensibilities. Speaking to the Jewish leaders, we read Peter's bold words in Acts 4:10-12,

> Let it be known to you all, and to all the people of Israel, that by the name of Jesus Christ of Nazareth, whom you crucified, whom God raised from the dead, by Him this man stands here before you whole. This is the 'stone which was rejected by you builders, which has become the chief cornerstone.' Nor is there salvation in any other, for there is no other name under heaven given among men by which we must be saved.

If the goal is affirming pluralism, then declaring what Jesus said of *Himself* is objectionable: "I am the way, the truth, and the life. No one comes to the Father except through Me. If you had known Me, you would have known My Father also; and from now on you know Him and have seen Him."[84]

Interfaithism undermines the truth claim of Jesus Christ. He can only be another moral teacher or spiritual reformer, nothing more.

2) Because interfaithism implies spiritual equality across diverse beliefs, the non-believer can rightly contest that Christianity is a meaningless sect in an ocean of pointless religion. If all faiths are equally valid expressions of truth, then none of them are.

I am reminded of a surprising discussion around a coffee table at an interfaith conference in St. Petersburg, Florida. I was attending for research purposes, and I sat quietly while some of the speakers chatted about their work. The conversation amiably swirled around how all spiritual paths point to the same truths, and because of this, religions should be able to work together. But then a question was asked, and I almost spilled my coffee: "What do we do about Heaven's Gate?"

---

[84] John 14:6-7.

Only a few years before, thirty-nine members of the Heaven's Gate UFO-cult committed suicide in belief that their souls would ascend into a spaceship following the Hale-Bopp comet. Another person piped up, *Aum Shinrikyo*. Yes, how will the interfaith community accept the Japanese death-cult? Someone else asked if we would be comfortable including the Church of Satan as an equal to other faiths. *If all expressions are true...*

I smiled as the group fell silent.

3) Christian involvement in interfaithism undercuts the Biblical Great Commission: We work for inclusive peace, but end up downplaying core Biblical truths – the unique character of God, the sin nature of Man, and Jesus Christ alone as savior and redeemer. Therefore, Christian missions will tend to focus on humanitarian work and social causes, sidestepping or ignoring the salvation message central to the Bible.

4) It entrenches a status quo of intellectual silence: We will not challenge the worldview or beliefs of others, and they will refrain from challenging ours. Instead of grappling with truth claims and hard questions, we will only speak "bright blessings." We no longer contend earnestly for the faith, as there is nothing left for which we should contend.

5) Christian involvement in the interfaith movement sows confusion, mistrust, and discord in the church. Because interfaith work is seldom done by lay people (being instead an activity channeled through denominational leadership, seminaries and parachurch organizations), it usually takes time for the grassroots to discover changes in direction.

However, when the interfaith shift is revealed, it sets up a chain reaction of dissonance. This is especially true when lay members are serious about their faith and are versed in scripture, holding firm to the gospel of Jesus Christ – *which is what Christian leadership should be striving for.*

The desire for world peace, the justification of good intentions and the anticipation of social acceptance; all are factors that compel Christian organizations and churches to partner with the interfaith community. Noble and well intentioned this may appear, but persistent questions remain. Do we tolerate everything except that which fundamentally divides? Do we voluntarily stifle the truth-message of Christianity for some nebulous vision of acceptance? Have we acquiesced to Perennialism?

Are we sacrificing truth on the altar of peace?

Interfaithism is more than religious solidarity in light of social change, it is politics wrapped in a veneer of spirituality. Indeed, it could be expressed as *pagan politics*, as themes of Re-enchantment inform the movement. Pagan empowerment was something I witnessed in Salt Lake City.

Parliament of Oneness

The cavernous hall of the Salt Palace was an interfaith spectacle: Hindus, Buddhists, Zoroastrians, Bahá'ís, Sikhs, Jains, Wiccans, Muslims, followers of Judaism, and Christians. Thousands were united as one.

It was a time of worship, a place for spiritual introspection and emotional release. Multitudes lifted their voices in melodic affirmation and the enormous assembly room, with its 30-foot high ceiling and massive cement walls, pulsed with female energy.

"Remember who you are," sang out Mother Maya Tiwari. "Goddess, Mother, Shakti of this Earth."

The crowd intoned back: "Goddess, Mother, Shakti of this Earth."[85]

I was at the Parliament of the World's Religions in Salt Lake City, a five-day extravaganza in mid-October, 2015, sponsored by KAICIID – an Islamic-Vatican partnership funded by Saudi Arabia[86] – and the United Religions Initiative.[87] Friday morning was the Women's Plenary, titled *Faith in Women.*

"What if the world were a place where it was effortless to recognize our common humanity, our shared virtues and concerns, and our collective de-

---

85 *Faith in Women: Women's Dignity and Human Rights, Plenary on Women*, October 16, Halls 4&5, 10:30am-12:00pm, 2015 Parliament on the World's Religions, Salt Palace, Salt Lake City, Utah. All quotes up to footnote 86 are taken from various recordings and my personal notes from the *Faith in Women* plenary.

86 The King Abdullah bin Abdulaziz International Centre for Interreligious and Intercultural Dialogue (KAICIID), has its roots in the 2005 Islamic Summit at Mecca. Two years later, King Abdulaziz – the Custodian of the Two Holy Mosques – met with Pope Benedict XVI to discuss this interfaith vision. After more meetings within the Islamic community, and the UN Secretary General, KAICIID was formally established through an agreement with Saudi Arabia, Austria, and Spain. The Holy See would become a founding Observer. For more information, see the KAICIID timeline at www.kaiciid.org/about-us.

87 Other primary supporters: Claremont Lincoln University, the Kalliopeia Foundation, the Unitarian Universalist Association, and the Dinesh and Kalpana Patel Foundation.

votion to the Earth?" asked Rabbi Amy Eilberg. "What if the whole world, all seven billion of us, were like this?"

Heads nodded in affirmation and voices shouted in solidarity.

Ojibwe "Grandmother" Mary Lyons told the multitude: "When you breathe in, you breathe in a breath of Mother Earth. And when you exhale, those are your ancestors."

More heads nodded. *New York Times* best-selling author and New Thought personality, Marianne Williamson, wowed the audience with her charisma: "Every woman here who is a healer is a priestess. Every woman here who is a teacher or an educator is a priestess." Her call to *sacred femininity* energized the great crowd, bringing attendees to their feet again and again during her eight-minute speech.

"A Divine Goddess is not just beautiful, she's fierce," Marianne exhorted with a growl of intensity, leading to an emotionally charged call-to-action. "And when you mess with her babies... and you mess with her earth, she's had enough of that sh*t. And we're here on her behalf... you know what to do, go do it!"

The response was electrifying. Someone yelled, "Marianne for President!" It was a call that accelerated the emotional pitch: Drums around the room pounded in support. Women shouted and whistled and danced and sobbed. Others around me started to chant the presidential call. To my immediate left a woman was bowed low, weeping profusely. On my right a plain-looking, middle-aged lady was fist-pumping the air with grave intensity, lips pursed, face set like stone – a "Divine Goddess" ready to do battle for Mother Earth.

Following Williamson, Dr. Serene Jones, President of Union Theological Seminary, invited us to be "political actors" and change the world. No spectators; everyone is a social justice warrior. This is our sacred duty.

"We are strong," bridged the moderator, building on the passion of the moment. "We are woman. Make no mistake of it. We are strong."

The Women's Plenary was a rousing invocation to the goddess, but it was not a singular experience. Sacred femininity, a dominant manifestation of Re-enchantment, underscored the Parliament.

"We are one with all life," it was explained during the previous day's Inaugural Woman's Assembly. "We are one with all people. We are one with the one." Ancient goddess spirits were called to bless our gathering.

Everyone shouted back: "We are one with the one."[88]

The Red Tent Temple, a dedicated place for rituals and group discussions, had a sign that read, *Women's Sacred Space*. This scarlet room, with its flowing red draperies and red pillows and red rugs and red chairs – often described as the "womb of the Parliament" – would host a "healing Mother Earth" ritual, and prayers of gratitude "to the divinities who govern the sun." The text for one workshop read: "The Goddess/Divine/All that is, has not abandoned us and is here, accessible to reconnect us... connecting each other and the 'more than human' world."[89]

After looking at my workshop choices, I ventured down a hallway lined with banners displaying icons of the Goddess, and entered the session on the "Divine Mother." James Hurtak, author of *The Keys of Enoch*, his wife Desiree along with Audrey Kitagawa, taught on differing aspects of the feminine deity.[90] *She is the Mother of life*, came the pitch, *we are all her children*. James explained we are passing from the age of the individual to the collective; the time of the Goddess. The trio led a group meditation focusing on her images and chanting her names. It was an unfiltered message: We are entering a techno-pagan era – an alchemy of ancient wisdom, social networking, and transhuman technologies. *We are empowered by the Goddess, work in service to the Goddess, for the glory of the Goddess*.

Other themes were woven into the Parliament's tapestry. A daily Indigenous Peoples' Dialogue was held, addressing topics such as "Protection of Mother Earth" and "Indigenous Prophecies."[91] A procession of Indigenous spiritual leaders led the Parliament's Opening Ceremony, and the Indigenous Plenary reinforced the message of Mother Earth.[92]

---

88 *Women's Assembly Closing Remarks and Ceremony*, Friday, October 16, Exhibit Hall 3, 2015 Parliament on the World's Religions, Salt Palace, Salt Lake City, Utah.

89 *Program Schedule* (Parliament of the World's Religions, 2015), *Healing Mother Earth*, October 16, Room 252 AB, 8:30-1:00 AM, as found in the *Program Schedule*, p.91. "To the divinities," see *Gratitude to Nature*, October 16, Room 252 AB, 2:30-3:15 PM, *Program Schedule*, p.119. "Goddess/Divine/All," see *Keening, Greening and Finding Meaning*, October 17, Room 252AB, 10:00-11:30 AM, *Program Schedule*, p.155.

90 *Role of the Divine Mother in Religion and Interspirituality*, October 15, Ballroom B, 2:30-3:45 PM (the *Program Schedule* lists the event in Ballroom B, but I believe it was moved to Ballroom A – there were scheduling problems and room switches throughout the day, and I did not write down the Ballroom changes in my notes).

91 *Program Schedule*, p.72.

92 *Indigenous Plenary*, October 19, 2015, 10:30am-12:00pm, Halls 4&5.

A Sacred Fire was kept burning during the five days,

> The Sacred Fire is lit at the sunrise ceremony on the first day. It then burns continuously, watched over by Fire Keepers and ceremony helpers, until the end of the gathering and then is left to burn until it extinguishes itself. It is believed that a Sacred Fire holds open a direct connection to the Creator, Mother Earth, the Spirit World, and our Ancestors as we convene.[93]

Climate change was a major theme, for the United Nations' COP21 meeting would take place in Paris a few weeks later. A Parliament declaration on climate would be presented at COP21, delivered by Karenna Gore – the Parliament's Ambassador on Climate Change – daughter of Al Gore, and Director of the Center for Earth Ethics at Union Theological Seminary. The declaration, *Embracing Our Common Future*, read in part: "Earth is one interconnected whole. What we do to the Earth, we do to ourselves."[94]

The Climate Plenary started with a multi-faith children's choir, followed by opening words from Marc Barasch, founder of the Green World Campaign,

> We're here today to explore the connection between the life of the spirit and the fate of the Earth... We stand as one people under the same Tree of Life... and we are seeking, each in our own way, to harmonize a profound sense of oneness and wonder with the urgency of our times, so that Tree will continue to flourish.[95]

References were made throughout the Parliament to Pope Francis' recent encyclical, *On Care For Our Common Home*. So it was no surprise that Vatican representative, Archbishop Bernardito Auza – the Permanent Observer of the Holy See to the United Nations – gave a speech during the Climate Plenary. The Archbishop told us that, "the Earth, our Sister, mistreated and abused, is lamenting." What we need, he explained in reference to the Pope's green vision, is an "ecological conversion."

I was intrigued that Christian emergent leader, Brian McLaren, was also given a spot of importance during the Climate Plenary. After all, McLaren is

---

93 *Program Schedule*, p.33.

94 *Embracing Our Common Future: An Interfaith Call to Action on Climate Change*, printed in *Parliament Declarations and The Commitment Book: I Will Do It. I Will Lead Others To Do It!* 2015 Parliament of the World's Religions, p.4.

95 *Climate Change Plenary*, October 18, 3:30-5:00 PM, Halls 4&5.

not someone normally associated with the climate change debate. However, his brand of *Progressive Christianity*[96] beats to the drums of Oneness.

"I don't know which comes first," McLaren said. "Do I love creation because I love the Creator, or do I love God because I can't help but love the fish and the trees and the birds and the mountains and the fresh air? I don't know which comes first, but I know that the two go inextricably together."

"Our old stories often said that God gave the Earth to humans so they could use it however they wanted for their profit," preached McLaren, interpreting religious history through his Progressive Christian lens. "Those stories said that God would soon destroy the Earth, which gave powerful people a license to plunder it as if it were a store going out of business."

McLaren implored us: "Brothers and sisters, the Earth is singing to us, the Earth is crying to us, the Earth is groaning to us."

What is the Earth saying? That people of faith need to tell a new *framing story*, for "common and joint action." In other words, *embrace the myth*.

Some of my time at the 2015 Parliament was attending workshops highlighting the renaissance of Paganism. During one discussion, selections of text were read from Pope Francis' encyclical on the environment and from a Pagan declaration. Could we tell the difference? No.[97]

In a different workshop, Gwendolyn Reece, a pagan researcher and priestess of Athena and Apollo,[98] described Cosmopolis as the conscious acceptance "of the interconnectedness of all reality." A true citizen of Cosmopolis would thus recognize "non-humans" in their journey of *being*.

"As a pagan and as a witch," Reece elucidated, "I include within my immediate circle of concern invisible beings that are not necessarily invisible to quite all of us."[99]

---

96 As a socio-religious movement, progressive Christianity considers itself to be an enlightened and evolutionary approach to the faith. Typically it deconstructs Biblical narratives into suggested models for world peace, social morality, ecological sensitivity, and inter-spirituality. Generally, it takes an anti-capitalist stance, favoring visions of socialism and global solidarity. Although it fashions itself as new and cutting edge, it is neither.

97 *We are the Earth: Pagans Respond to Pope Francis on the Environment*, October 17, 3:30-5:00 PM, Room 250 A, 2015 Parliament of the World's Religions.

98 Dr. Reece was instrumental in establishing the Theophania Temple of Athena and Apollon in Washington DC, which was officially recognized in January 2016.

99 As highlighted in the workshop, *Diversity and Applied Theology in Contemporary Paganism*, October 16, 8:30-1:00 AM, Room 250 B.

In a discussion on the *Earth Charter* and the United Nations Development Agenda, Yale's Mary Evelyn Tucker elevated the Charter as a framework for evolution. Her approach reflected the core of Re-Enchantment,

> The notion we're part of a vast evolving universe; this is the first time in an international document that we have this sense we are part of an epic story of evolution... We need to light up that fire, of complexity and mystery and awe that a vast evolving universe can provide for our work. And in this sense that Earth is alive, that is clearly one of the most ancient sensibilities of humans... these are the breakthroughs of science and spirituality that this document is reflecting, of the consciousness of all of us. You see; it's picking up on the worldviews that are filtering into our midst.[100]

The official motto of the Parliament was "Reclaiming the Heart of Our Humanity," but the overarching message was *Oneness*. In fact, if we turn the motto into a question, "how do we reclaim the heart of humanity?" The answer is: *Act as One*. In this we experience our divinity, for *All is One*. But with so many religions and doctrines – approximately fifty traditions and sects were at the Parliament – how do we experience this sense of unity?

This question was the topic of a workshop titled, *Searching For Unity With Diversity: Are We Really All One?*[101] It was a subject that intrigued many, for the meeting room was full.

Philip Goldberg, author of *American Veda*, opened by saying we can find unity in many areas: common purpose, ethical principles, biology, and in environmental and ecological concerns. But real Oneness surpasses those outer dimensions.

"We are each other," Goldberg told the assembly,

> I am you, you are me... It is that level of unification and oneness that we wanted to address this morning, because, we thought, it is the most fundamental level of unity: the most fundamental level of oneness. And it's not to be found just in reasoning or in dialogue, it's to be found in the direct experience of that reality within ourselves.

[100] As discussed in the workshop, *The Earth Charter and the New UN Development Agenda*, October 17, Room 251 F, 10:00-11:30 AM, 2015 Parliament of the World's Religions.

[101] *Searching For Unity Within Diversity: Are We Really All One?* October 17, 11:45am-1:15pm, Room 251 F, 2015 Parliament of the World's Religions.

"To see the divinity in other people," he said, "that is a wonderful thing."

How does this take place? Direct experience via *contemplative mysticism*.

Demonstrating this experiential oneness, Goldberg asked us all to quiet our minds and think back to a personal, spiritual encounter; "where something happened deep within you that was, at least to some extent, transformative, where you felt an experience, a connection to divinity as you understand it." People assumed meditative postures. Heads were bowed and eyes closed; the assembly grew quiet.

After a moment of silence, he asked the audience to use a word or phrase from everyday language to express this memory. Shouts rang out across the room: "Reunion," "transcendental," "comfort," "you belong here," "peace," "interconnected," "expansion," "encounter," "joy," "love."

Could we relate? A forest of hands shot up in affirmation. And that was the point of our exercise: each could empathize, regardless of faith tradition, and nothing *separating* stood in the way – facts fade, doctrine disappears, and divergent claims recede. The *feeling* is universal, bridging the religiously minded and the secular, for the *altered state* can be found in the whirl of Sufi Dervishes, the *samadhi* of Yoga, through contemplative practices, in the ecstatic communion of a rave, or via psychedelic substances.

This workshop dovetailed with my prior research. It also reinforced a concern; a tendency in the Christian worship experience to highlight a certain feeling. "I felt God moving," or "I could feel the Spirit," are statements sometimes associated with corporate acts of devotion, and not just in charismatic congregations. There is a longing for *God feelings* within the larger Christian assembly. Years ago at a banquet, a young man described his church worship time this way: "I could feel God on my skin, I could sense Him in my scalp. With every breath I inhaled and exhaled God."

Goldberg would describe this as the *direct experience* of oneness.

Dear Christian, there is a danger in mistaking *ecstasis* for the Spirit, for in doing so, we risk exchanging Wisdom for a feeling.

Do emotions and feelings play a role in our worship? Absolutely! King David's soul-cry in Psalm 51 is a worthy example, as is the joy expressed in Psalm 32. Feelings are important, but they are not necessarily guideposts to spiritual maturity. Nor are they a reference to determine theological truths. God remains true *no matter how I feel*. Wisdom is needed to help us navigate between our very real feelings and emotions, experiences and life conditionings, and the work of God.

The *Searching For Unity With Diversity* workshop suggested that religious commonality is discovered in the mystical. This is the heartbeat of Perennialism, and it sets up the interfaith movement to become *interspiritual*. Although the 2015 Parliament stated that the goal was "interreligious harmony, and not unity,"[102] the intent and trajectory of the movement – ever since the 1893 Parliament – has been the pursuit of spiritual oneness within diversity.

An interesting speculation can be extrapolated, and I stress that this is *conjecture only*. Could a worldwide "spiritual experience" be the catalyst for global unity? If so, how might this be achieved? Might a *psychedelic agent* be designed to induce human oneness? And could this agent be in the form of a *mark*, a personal identifier permanently placed on the hand or forehead? This mark, a tangible sign of global citizenship – like a digital loyalty card – would be needed for buying and selling. Possibly this mark could be tailored to interact with one's genetics and brain chemistry, unlocking a stimulant that heightens perception and induces flow; like a manageable, *global upper* that everyone experiences together, and no one wants to be without, or opt out of. There would be no spectators in the networked planet. Everybody would be a participant in the *global myth* of a *brave new world*.

Maybe this *transhuman elixir* would be called *Soma*.

The above represents a techno-pharma-socio-political-spiritual wholeness, a total management and participant experience. It is a troubling speculation.

The 2015 Parliament of the World's Religions, with its 10,000 attendees, ended on a lofty note. The interfaith movement is growing, it was said, and this momentum needs to be maintained and advanced. To that end, resources had opened to make the Parliament more frequent. Instead of meeting every five or six years, as had been the case since 1993, the Parliament would convene every two years or so. Cheers erupted.

The Parliament was a symbol of solidarity, a place to experiment with futures, and a space for spiritual discovery – an evolutionary journey.

It was a festival.

A comment during the Closing Ceremony captured it all: "Oneness is the key. And if oneness is there, things change. Fast."

---

[102] *Program Schedule*, "Our Approach," inside front cover, p.2.

Chapter 13

Machines of Loving Grace

> We are at the beginning of a new ideological and technological revolution in which the objectives are not physical power and control of the environment, but direct intervention into the fate of man himself – José Delgado. [1]

> We are on the back of galloping technology, and we cannot dismount without breaking our necks. – James Gunn.[2]

"Did you see the robot?" I asked the porter as we passed in the dimly lit hallway of New York City's Empire Hotel.

He stopped and gave me a curious glance. "What are you talking about?"

"You passed right by a robot," I said matter-of-factly, motioning to a waiting group of people standing five doors down. "He's the one sitting."

The porter turned to look, peering at an Asian man seated on a wheeled, cart-like carrier.

"That's not a human," I emphasized. "It's a highly advanced robotic head on a mock body."

The gentleman stared, and stared some more. "No... that's a man." He sounded less convinced of what he believed than what he was seeing. "He must be handicapped, that's why he's sitting in the cart."

"Do yourself a favor," I said to the porter. "Walk up and look closely. You'll see it's not a person at all."

Pointing to an individual in the group who looked identical to the one sitting, I explained that the man standing was Hiroshi Ishiguro, a Japanese

---

1 José M.R. Delgado, *Physical Control of the Mind: Toward a Psychocivilized Society* (Harper and Row, 1969), p.246.

2 James Gunn, *Alternate Worlds: The Illustrated History of Science Fiction* (Prentice-Hall, 1975), p.13.

robotics inventor, and the "head" was his creation – a robotic double or *gemenoid* running on sophisticated software, automatically reacting to its changing environment. The porter blurted, "That can't be true!"

"Just walk by and take a look," I assured him. "It's not what you think."

Retreating down the hallway, my skeptical friend sauntered past the group, guardedly examining the person in question. Soon he was stopped, standing only a few feet away, peering closely at the life-like figure. And it was staring back at him.

Of course, the porter had pulled out his smart-phone and was taking pictures: *Technology looking at technology*.

Just a short jaunt from where this unusual interaction took place was an extraordinary gathering. For two days in mid-June, 2013, New York City's Lincoln Center was home to the Global Future 2045 International Congress (GF2045), a synthesis of Man and Machine, mind and matter, Eastern spirituality and Western secularism.

Among the mix of prestigious personalities were James Martin, the tech entrepreneur and single largest benefactor to Oxford in its 900-year history; Peter Diamandis, the creator of the XPRIZE and co-founder of Singularity University; Ray Kurzweil, Google's famed Director of Engineering; and the developer of SiriusXM Radio, Martine Rothblatt. Celebrated pioneer of Artificial Intelligence, Marvin Minsky, addressed the eager crowd through a video feed. Dmitry Itskov, the Russian media mogul who inspired the 2045 Initiative – the organizing entity behind the Congress – was in the spotlight both on and off the stage. Neuroscientists and consciousness theorists, robotic developers, post-human thinkers and religious leaders had assembled to explore the bounds of future human evolution.

Unlike global events I had attended before, my entrance to the GF2045 was made possible through a media pass. Magnum Veritas Productions, a documentary film company, had brought me on board as an advisor and interviewer. Our time at the Congress was, therefore, split between the event itself, press conferences, and conducting face-to-face interviews in the Empire Hotel.

It was an immersive and interactive experience with some of the leading minds in the transhumanist movement.

But what is *transhumanism*?

Trans-what?

An old but accurate definition can be found in the 1883 edition of *The Imperial Dictionary of the English Language*: "Transhuman (trans-hu'man), a. Beyond or more than human."[3] A contemporary description might sound like this: *Transhumanism is humanity's intentional evolution through science and technology*.

Lincoln Canon, then president of the Mormon Transhumanist Association, gave this definition in 2013: "Transhumanism is the ethical use of technology to expand our abilities from the human to the post-human."[4]

Transhumanism is thus a changeover, a stepping-stone, but not the final stage; it is a transition to a post-human potential, moving beyond what we presently are. This is a future-oriented vision, one fueled by incredible scientific and technical advances, and the possibilities they portend: greatly magnifying cognitive abilities, enhancing sensory input, genetic restructuring to permanently eliminate disease and weakness, finding ways to move our consciousness into a non-corruptible body, the extension of human life – to the point of immortality – and even *resurrecting the dead*.

A vast array of technologies and theoretical applications act like the carrot before the horse: Virtual and augmented reality, brain-computer interfacing and the anticipation of uploading one's mind into an artificial carrier, ubiquitous connection to the global network, cybernetics and chip implants, Artificial Intelligence (AI), robotics and self-replicating machines, nanotechnology, genetic manipulation, chemical switches for mood control and sharpened awareness, and cryonics for those who can afford to invest in a projected *reawakening*.[5]

Using these technologies and predicting their impact on individuals and civilization, the offering of *perfectibility* – of forging an optimal species with

---

3 John Ogilvie, *The Imperial Dictionary of the English Language: A Complete Encyclopedic Lexicon, Literary, Scientific, and Technological* (Blackie & Son, 1883, edited by Charles Annandale), p.415.

4 Lincoln Cannon, "The Purpose of the Mormon Transhumanist Association," Mormon Transhumanist Association annual meeting, April 5, 2013, Salt Lake City, UT, as taken from my notes and media from the event. This speech can be viewed on MTA's YouTube channel: https://youtu.be/iFhQf2R_IVs.

5 Cryonics is the technique of suspending a deceased person in a frozen state until such a time when science is able to resurrect the dead individual.

near infinite capacity through the works of our hands – becomes more than just a tantalizing dream. *It becomes a faith*.

The other option is to remain as we are, reside in our limitations, struggle for a few decades and die. This is unacceptable.

Thus, science becomes salvific with hope placed in the speculations of what technology may bring. Transhumanists, those who hold this promise of techno-futures, look to the Singularity with anticipation – that hypothetical point-in-time when information and technology outpaces humanity, forcing us to fully integrate into manageable matter. The Singularity will break our limitations of flesh and bone: Man, machine, and information will merge into a new creation. Post-humanity is the anticipated result, our evolution *beyond Man*: Übermensch.

Max More, founder of Extropy Institute – an early group discussing neo-human evolution – provided this explanation during an interview at GF2045,

> Transhumanism you can think of as, in some ways, an inheritor of the Enlightenment goals of fundamental progress in the human condition… But it's taking it a step beyond the humanist goal of generally improving the human condition through science and technology and good will, and it's realizing that humanity itself is limited. Because of our genetic heritage, there are certain limitations to our lifespan, to our health, to our mental well being, to our cognabilities. And it's realizing that we can take this humanist goal further and we can actually change the human condition itself.
>
> We can use science and technology to understand the causes of aging and we can learn to eliminate those causes. It's not an unsolvable problem; it's basically an engineering problem, a scientific problem. There's nothing special about the human life span. It's just an accident; an evolutionary accident... And why should we accept that? So really transhumanism is about taking control of our own human evolution, and deciding how long we want to live, how smart we want to be, how well modulated our emotions should be. It's really about turning our choices over to us rather than natural selection.[6]

[6] Max More, interviewed by Carl Teichrib for Magnum Veritas Productions, LLC., June 16, 2013, GF2045 Congress. Interview location: Empire Hotel, New York City.

Transhumanism is often understood as a secularist approach to unbounded progress, a humanist philosophy seeking Mankind's expansion, acceleration, and the overpowering of natural limitations.

Historically it draws from an intellectual lineage stretching through Modernity, and it remains a cerebral and techno-cultural movement. However, it is important to note that not all scientists and technology experts share the post-human vision. Not too long ago the mainstream scientific community, with reputations on the line, spurned those who believed in life extension and augmented futures.[7] But times have changed.

Transhumanism has stepped out from the fringes.

In terms of demographic and cultural identifiers the movement is narrow and broad: Narrow in that it is statistically and professionally predictable, as demonstrated by surveys within the transhumanist community. Variations exist from study to study, nevertheless the following 2012 survey published by the *Journal of Personal Cyberconsciousness* presents an interesting snapshot. Regarding education and occupation, 28.8% and 27.6% hold graduate and bachelor degrees, and computers and mathematics (27.8%) make up the largest fields of occupation. Most are unmarried (64.4%), ethnically white (85.4%), male (90.1%), and fall within a young professional spectrum (45.8% aged 20-29 and 21.5% between 30-39). The majority resides in large urban centers (43.8%), and less than 5% identify as rural.[8]

Broadness is found in cultural messaging. Transhuman themes have been and are prevalent in the entertainment industry: *Avatar*, the *Star Trek* series, *2001: A Space Odyssey*, *The Matrix* and *X-Men* franchises, *Elysium*, *i,Robot*, *Gamer*, *Transcendence*, *Blade Runner*, *The Island*, *Virtuosity*, *Tron* and *Tron: Legacy*, *Surrogates*, *Lucy*, *District 9*, *Ghost in the Shell*, *Splice*, and the *Terminator* series – with technology being destroyer and savior. The online gaming world is enmeshed with transhumanist identifiers, along with frequent sacralizing patterns.[9]

---

7 Brian Alexander, *Rapture: How Biotech Became the New Religion* (Basic Books, 2003), p.3.

8 Hank Pellissier and Teresa Dal Santo, "Transhumanists: Who Are They, What Do They Want, Believe And Predict?" *Journal of Personal Cyberconsciousness* (Terasem Movement, Inc, 2013), Volume 8, Issue 1, p.22-24.

9 Two studies of import: Robert M. Geraci, *Virtually Sacred: Myth and Meaning in World of Warcraft and Second Life* (Oxford University Press, 2014), and William Sims Bainbridge, *eGods: Faith Versus Fantasy in Computer Games* (Oxford University Press, 2013).

Technology's impact on industries, including the medical field, aerospace, ground transportation and agriculture, powerfully contributes to the discussion. The explosive growth of information technologies, internet based services, the smart connection of appliances and devices, and the data streams that seamlessly link society adds to the general discourse. We find ourselves in the flow of the algorithm economy, whether or not we are aware of it, and most of us have ***subjective identities*** – online profiles shaped by viewing habits and the projection of ***presence*** through virtual social platforms.

We are living in an ever changing, increasingly integrated, matrix of information and technology.

Socio-political interpretations within the transhumanist movement are diverse, but stronger pulls to the political left are noteworthy. The 2012 survey revealed that 32.7% identified as Liberal, 16.9 as Socialist, and 4.2 as Marxist. Moderates made up 15.6%, and the Libertarian approach with its limited government and free markets made up 27.4%, a sizeable minority when taken against the combined percentage of left-leaning transhumanists.[10] Surveys in 2013 and early 2017 by the Institute for Ethics and Emerging Technologies revealed a dominant leftist perspective.[11]

To the Libertarian transhumanist, science will free us to explore individual tastes and sensibilities and desires, independent of centralized authority. In the Promised Land of techno-Marxism, the post-human will operate in a perfect collectivism. Class division disappears under the revolution of evolutionary science; even gender and sex fade away in the hive existence.

Transhumanism has also been envisioned within a technocratic framework, the wiring of reality for optimal efficiency and connectedness: Algorithms and smart energy calibration will order the course of neo-humanity.

No matter how civilization is rebooted, in this *shape of things to come*, "machines of loving grace" will lead us to green pastures.[12]

---

[10] Pellissier and Dal Santo, "Transhumanists: Who Are They, What Do They Want, Believe And Predict?" *Journal of Personal Cyberconsciousness*, p.22.

[11] *Who are the IEET's Audience?* Institute for Ethics and Emerging Technologies, July 16, 2013, [https://ieet.org/index.php/IEET2/more/poll20130716]; *What Do Technoprogressives Believe in 2017?* Institute for Ethics and Emerging Technologies, February 18, 2017 [https://ieet.org/index.php/IEET2/more/hughes20170218].

[12] *The Shape of Things to Come* is the title of H.G. Wells' 1933 technocratic novel. "Machines of Loving Grace" is part of the techno-utopian poem, *All Watched Over By Machines of Loving Grace*, penned by American poet, Richard Brautigan, and published in 1967.

Philosophically the movement is rooted in Modernity's themes. Elements of Saint Simon's management-by-experts can be discerned; the Positivism of Auguste Comte pokes out from under the surface. Broad overlap exists with Karl Marx.[13] The influence of Nietzsche is visible.[14] A long line of naturalistic philosophers, men of science, and heralds of technical efficiency add their historical touch. Darwin's evolutionary paradigm is magnified as holy revelation, and eugenics – the science of human betterment through genetic selection, made infamous by the Third Reich – is a contentious association that some transhumanists recognize and others spurn.[15]

"I don't see the connection between transhumanism and eugenics," Dmitry Itskov said during an interview, explaining that his transhumanism is for everybody.[16] When I queried Max More, his immediate response was, "I don't see eugenics as having much to do with transhumanism." He was willing,

---

13 On Marxism, see James Steinhoff, "Transhumanism and Marxism: Philosophical Connections," *Journal of Evolution and Technology*, Volume 24, Issue 2, May 2014 [http://jetpress.org/v24/steinhoff.pdf].

14 Stefan Lorenz Sorgner, "Nietzsche, the Overhuman, and Transhumanism," *Journal of Evolution and Technology*, Volume 20, Issue 1, March 2009 [http://jetpress.org/v20/sorgner.pdf].

15 Eugenics was popularized in the early 20th century throughout much of the Western world. The United States engaged in positive and negative eugenics, as did England, Canada, Australia, Denmark, Sweden (which continued into the 1970s) and other nations – including colonial ruled countries. The Soviet Union worked to configure a socialist eugenics program. Nazi Germany employed eugenics within its framework as "racial hygiene," and because of this eugenics became tinctured by the horrors of the Third Reich. For more information on eugenics in narrow and broad applications, see Edwin Black, *War Against the Weak: Eugenics and America's Campaign to Create a Master Race* (Four Walls Eight Windows, 2003); Richard Weikart, *From Darwin to Hitler: Evolutionary Ethics, Eugenics, and Racism in Germany* (Palgrave Macmillan, 2004); Marc Hillel, *Of Pure Blood* (Ferni Publishers, 1979); Philippe Aziz, *Doctors of Death*, in four volumes (Ferni Publishers, 1976); Victoria F. Nourse, *In Reckless Hands: Skinner v. Oklahoma and the Near-Triumph of American Eugenics* (W.W. Norton & Company, 2008); Robert Proctor, *Racial Hygiene: Medicine Under the Nazis* (Harvard University Press, 1988); Stefan Kuhl, *The Nazi Connection: Eugenics, American Racism, and German National Socialism* (Oxford University Press, 1994); David Plotz, *The Genius Factory: The Curious History of the Nobel Prize Sperm Bank* (Random House, 2005); Andrew Kimbrell, *The Human Body Shop: The Cloning, Engineering, and Marketing of Life* (Regnery Publishing, 1997).

16 Dmitry Itskov, interviewed by Carl Teichrib for Magnum Veritas Productions, LLC., June 16, 2013, GF2045 Congress. Interview location: Empire Hotel, New York City.

however, to acknowledge an inference but emphasized, "transhumanism is really about giving us the choice of who we want to be."[17]

Anders Sandberg, a Research Fellow at the Oxford Martin School, was willing to situate the movement within *liberal eugenics* – pursuing genetic improvement without recourse to authoritative mandates. Sandberg, who has a Ph.D. in computational neuroscience, was part of the European Union Enhance Project, "looking at the ethics of enhancing humans, extending lifespans, improving mood, improving intelligence, improving bodies."[18]

The dark history of eugenics causes many transhumanists to cringe at the suggestion of commonality. At the same time, notable figures outside of the community have suggested a neo-eugenics that dovetails with the movement. Robert Edwards, the British medical researcher who developed *in vitro* fertilization, frankly supported genetic intervention: "Soon it will [be] a sin for parents to have a child which carries the heavy burden of genetic disease."[19] Nobel laureate James Watson advocated a new eugenics.[20] Dr. John Glad, an expert in Russian history who devoted his retirement to eugenic considerations, took an inclusive view of human change: "Eugenicists also perceive a need to be open to genetic manipulation, machine enhancement, and even contact with beings from other planets."[21]

---

[17] Max More, interviewed by Carl Teichrib for Magnum Veritas Productions, LLC., June 16, 2013, GF2045 Congress. Interview location: Empire Hotel, New York City.

[18] Anders Sandberg, interviewed by Carl Teichrib for Magnum Veritas Productions, LLC., June 16, 2013, GF2045 Congress. Interview location: Empire Hotel, New York City.

[19] Quoted by Natalie Ball, "Eugenics through the Eyes of Nobel Laureates: Involvement in the Intentional Improvement of Man's Inheritable Qualities from 1905-2010," *The Proceedings of the 20th Anniversary, History of Medicine Days Conference 2011: The University of Calgary, Faculty of Medicine, Alberta, Canada* (Cambridge Scholars Publishing, 2015), p.117.

[20] See James D. Watson, *A Passion for DNA: Genes, Genomes, and Society* (Cold Springs Harbor Laboratory Press, 2000).

[21] John Glad, *Future Human Evolution: Eugenics in the Twenty-First Century* (Hermitage Publishers, 2006), p.49. Glad was controversial for his endorsement of eugenics within the Jewish community, believing it was time for Jews to strengthen their genetic traits in order to remain a viable people group. He also boldly promoted sterilization and abortion programs for low-IQ women: "Abortion should be actively promoted, since it often serves as the last and even only resort for many low-IQ mothers who fail to practice contraception. Welfare policies need to be radically reexamined. Rather than simply pay low-IQ women more for each child, financial support should be made dependent on consent to undergo sterilization... Eugenic family planning services are the greatest gift

And why not seek human advancement through genetic alteration or by morphing with machines? Or if an extraterrestrial race offers us the keys to perfection, as has been suggested by some who claim alien contact – promising the mixture of genetic materials to produce an improved human hybrid – why not?[22] If all that exists is *material*, if reality is grounded in *naturalism*, if Heaven-on-Earth is a type of techno-Modernity, then civilization's operating system is pragmatism. Why feel squeamish about methods? *The ends justify the means*.

True, the pragmatic mindset is readily detected – even celebrated – but practically and philosophically this runs counter to some of the transhumanists I know. Most I have met believe in orienting change within ethically acceptable patterns, framing their perspectives through a moral compass. The Mormon Transhumanist Association (MTA) comes to mind, as does the fledgling Christian Transhumanist Association. I have personally interacted with founders and members of both groups, and I respect their good intentions: lifespan longevity, eradication of diseases, enhancing life quality, and striving to do good works. While I disagree with their cosmological worldview, they bring an important ethos to the conversation and invite critical and opposing voices to their platform. For this I applaud them.

However, the subject is more substantive than any single group. Advanced military applications – including enhancement programs through DARPA,[23] robotic assault vehicles,[24] and the race for national security Artificial Intel-

---

that the advanced countries can offer the Third World" (p.97). For his thoughts on Jewish eugenics, see his book *Jewish Eugenics* (Wooden Shore, 2011).

22 The literature on the UFO phenomena is rife with references to genetic modification. Lyssa Royal and Keith Priest in *Visitors From Within* (Royal Priest Research Press, 1992) offers channeled promises of a coming spiritual-physical upgrade in the mixing of alien and human genetics. In his book, *Abduction: Human Encounters with Aliens* (Charles Scribner's Sons, 1994), John E. Mack broached the subject of biological intervention in the abduction experience, connecting this to evolutionary processes. David M. Jacobs' troubling work, *The Threat* (Simon & Schuster, 1998), explores the topic of alien-human genetic exchange. Christian author Gary Bates explores similar themes in his volume, *Alien Intrusion: UFOs and the Evolution Connection* (Creation Book Publishers, 2004).

23 The United States Defense Advanced Research Projects Agency.

24 In April, 2017, the US Marine Corps conducted beach-landing tests to evaluate the strengths and weaknesses of an integrated non-human platform: robot amphibious assault vehicles, MUTT units, V-Bat drones, unmanned aerial vehicles, and other bots and connected devices. Other nations too are building up integrated robotic combat forces.

ligence – fits within the milieu, as does your surveillance-enabled smartphone and the web technologies we use on a daily basis. When India's Prime Minister Modi beamed himself as a life-sized, three-dimensional hologram into parts of his country during the 2014 election campaign, his *projection of presence* corresponded to transhuman models.[25] Autonomous cars and smart-cities are part of the mix. Cyborgs are no longer future fantasies, as displayed in the April 2017 edition of *National Geographic*.[26] Cloning, biohacking, genome editing and designer babies; bioethics, traditionally focusing on abortion and euthanasia, now wrestles with complex neo-eugenic issues. Technical leaps increase at a rate that feels exponential. The public struggles not only to process the speed of innovation, but is morally drifting and contextually disconnected in an age when uncanny wisdom is needed.

As humanity turns to the digital cloud for direction, will our values mirror the algorithm of the masses? *Crowd-gnosis?* Group wisdom now dictates what is acceptable and what is not.

In his write-up for the GF2045 program, Peter Diamandis expounded on *living information*, an infinitely expanding algorithm. What he was describing is the desire for a *hive-mind*,

> We humans have begun to incorporate technology inside ourselves. Humans themselves are becoming information technology. Over the last decades mankind has suddenly started changing from a loose collection of 7 billion individuals to a new kind of perpetually morphing non-physical social tissue woven from densely interconnected arrays of mobile person-nodes.
>
> In this process we – humanity – are becoming a new organism: a meta-intelligence. As a species, as this new organism, we are becoming conscious on an unprecedented new level, in a new cosmic-scale realm.
>
> As we are going through the metamorphosis of becoming this new meta-intelligence organism, we are going from evolution by natural selection – Darwinism – to evolution by intelligent direction. We are starting to direct the evolution of our biology and of our

---

[25] Lance Price, *The Modi Effect: Inside Narendra Modi's Campaign to Transform India* (Quercus, 2015), pp.131-136.

[26] D.T. Max, "Beyond Human," *National Geographic*, April 2017, Vol. 231, No. 4, p.40ff.

> minds ourselves... As we begin to liberate our thoughts, our memes, our consciousness from the biological constraints that we presently have, this will allow us to evolve far faster and ever faster.[27]

When Diamandis speaks of futures, others listen.

His work in developing space-based enterprises has elevated him as a world leader, and his XPRIZE has been a rallying point for influencers – think Larry Page, the founding CEO of Google, Ray Kurzweil, Arianna Huffington, Ratan Tata of the Tata empire of companies, and global technology strategist, Salim Ismail. In June 2017, the XPRIZE allied with the United Nations International Telecommunications Union to promote Artificial Intelligence as a revolutionary means for global good; AI for healthcare, education, poverty alleviation, and human rights. The UN Sustainable Development Goals are now a priority for AI applications.[28]

AI is reshaping industries and services. Amazon's success is linked to its AI technologies. Artificial Intelligence runs in the background of our online purchases and banking activities; self-driving cars are AI enabled; healthcare programs are utilizing AI applications. Your investment portfolio may already be managed by a robo-advisor. We hardly blink when Artificial Intelligence enters the mainstream.

Seeing the digital writing on the wall in the early years of the new century, Yale professor of computer science, David Gelernter, poetically envisioned a computer-saturated existence,

> The future will be dense with computers. They will hang around everywhere in lush growths, like Spanish moss. They will swarm like locusts. But a swarm is not merely a big crowd: Individuals in the swarm lose their identities; the computers that make up this global swarm will blend together into the seamless substance of the cybersphere.[29]

---

[27] Peter H. Diamandis, "Intelligent Self-Directed Evolution Guides Mankind's Metamorphosis into an Immortal Planetary Meta-Intelligence," *Global Future 2045 International Congress* (program), June 2013, p.15.

[28] The AI for Good Global Summit, hosted by ITU and XPRIZE – in partnership with a range of UN agencies – took place in Geneva, Switzerland, June 7-9, 2017.

[29] David Gelernter, "The Second Coming – A Manifesto," *Science at the Edge: Conversations with the Leading Scientific Thinkers of Today* (Union Square Press, 2003/2008, edited by John Brockman), p.239

Could we find ourselves in a hive-mind economy where *everything* is interconnected in a global smart grid, the perfect surveillance system, buying and selling through an AI managed crypto-currency? If so, then the gnosis of the algorithm could perceivably manage humanity as a resource in the *transformational economy*. And as the vast Internet of Things takes shape where everything from wearable medical devices to appliances to vehicles to *people* – every conceivable object, billions and billions of them – continually transmits data through embedded sensors, we may find ourselves in a world where AI dictates what is efficient and viable, and what is superfluous and in need of terminating. Remember, *global citizen*, you are the *product*.

Admittedly the above paragraph is a dark vision, but as futurist Gerd Leonhard writes, "If we, today, cannot even agree on what the rules and ethics should be for an Internet of people and their computing devices, how would we agree on something that is potentially a thousand times as vast?"[30]

Transhuman-oriented technologies are visible across the gamut of society, and no single organization has a handle on the full spectrum of change. Ramifications, benefits, and unintended consequences press into the fabric of civilization. Opportunities for great good, great evil and great confusion are before us – emboldened by the capacity of our technical creations.

Can we not just trust the experts?

Science and Society

Much to the chagrin of scientific intellectuals, technocrats, techno-elites and transhumanists, the idea of trusting the experts is met with scorn by a sizeable percentage of the populace. Lately, the response to this disparagement has been to attach a label on those who question their narratives: *you are anti-science*.

While social media has demonstrated the power of scientifically misinformed memes, the accusation of *anti-science* is generally inaccurate. Criticism is not aimed at the *scientific method*, a standard and valuable tool of inquiry, nor is it directed at science and engineering as vital fields of human endeavor. Civilization has been tremendously blessed by the beneficial results of science and the dedication of engineers and innovators, from both the private and public sectors.

[30] Gerd Leonhard, *Technology vs. Humanity: The Coming Clash Between Man and Machine* (Fast Future Publishing, 2016), p.67.

Much of the antagonism, however, rests on the ideological grandstanding of some within the scientific community, accompanied by a culture of political and economic interlock.

The dance goes something like this: Intellectual visionaries – armed with predictive models – make new claims, requiring (or demanding) public attention, along with funding and policy changes. A lobbying campaign kicks into motion. At the United Nations, action groups and academia give counsel and solidify the narrative at the global level. National governments, responding to the new pressures, invite stakeholders and experts to assist in formulating public policy. Politicians showboat on cut-and-paste proclamations and social management solutions. Budget lines are added and grants doled out; economic incentives create allegiances to the political-scientific consensus. Industries and corporations and trade associations line up with products and proposals; financial institutions monetize contracts, coordinate flow, and create markets; multilateral banking groups channel international commitments. The model has become much too big to fail. Therefore, scientific counter-claims and criticisms are downplayed while the invested narrative is continually reinforced. Globe trotting celebrities, Leonardo DiCaprio or Al Gore or Bill Gates or Bono, pompously parade the cause; *trust the experts* is shouted from the red carpet to the podium and back to the safety of private jets and yachts. Meanwhile, new winners and losers in the marketplace are determined by edict and bureaucratic compulsion; regulations and restrictions and taxes are foisted on the public.

Trust fades to contempt.

By inserting Al Gore and DiCaprio, superstar eco-grifters, I have tipped my hand to the fact that I am describing the climate change narrative. Unfortunately, the above description can be overlaid on other scientific and technical fields. Has science been ideologically weaponized for political gain, or politically weaponized for ideological revolution, or manipulated for mammon and monopoly? Aspects of science, ideology, politics and economics are ostensibly indivisible.

Will transhumanism follow suit? Garbed in a dogmatic faith-in-science and armed with loftily tantalizing promises of human perfection, the transhuman agenda cannot but find itself becoming intractably wrapped in a similar complex. It can be argued that it has already, and *always has been*.

Political control of science, and conversely, the scientific validation of political agendas, are nothing new. Segments of today's populace, however, are especially apprehensive of such interlock. And rightly so, for this complex has had profound repercussions in the public square and in personal lives.

Interestingly, the post-war decades of prosperity and protest – the 1950s to the early 1970s –revealed a techno-cultural tension that corresponds to our era of transhumanism. Human nature, it was argued in 1951, was on the threshold of being reconstituted due to scientific advancements and changing mental attitudes.[31] In those decades, optimism was placed in the transformative power of technology; the days of horse-and-buggy were still fresh in generational memory, yet trans-continental jetliners traversed the skies, satellites and spaceflights and moon landings were in the public eye, new understandings in psychology and the discovery of double-helix DNA (deoxyribonucleic acid) rewrote professions, widespread use of telephones and televisions magically bridged distances, and the industrial employment of computers and automation reshaped manufacturing. Scientists and engineers were in high demand.[32] Rising living standards foretold greater betterment.

"Will man direct his own evolution?" asked Albert Rosenfeld, *Life* magazine's Science Editor in 1965. That year, *Life* published a series of articles on the theme "control of life." The September 10th cover splashed: "Audacious experiments promise decades of added life, superbabies with improved minds and bodies, and even a kind of immortality."

Later in the serial Rosenfeld wrote,

> As scientists daily edge closer to the solution of some of nature's deepest mysteries, no idea seems too wild to contemplate. Would you like education by injection? A larger, more efficient brain? A cure for old age? Parentless babies? Body size and skin color to order?

---

31 Lawrence K. Frank, *Nature and Human Nature: Man's New Image of Himself* (Rutgers University Press, 1951). Frank was on the General Education Board of the Rockefeller Foundation and the National Resources Planning Board.

32 "The scientific and technological 'explosion' is transforming society... But the big question remains: will there be enough scientists and engineers to achieve the possibilities already within technical reach?" – Ronald Schiller, "Help Wanted: Engineers and Scientists," *The Reader's Digest*, February 1967 (Canadian Edition), p.47. For an annotative list of technical and general publications outlining scientific and engineering personnel concerns from 1965 to 1969, including workplace shortages and future industrial needs, see Frank Witham, *Scientists and Engineers in the Federal Government* (Civil Service Commission, Washington, DC, Personnel Bibliography Series Number 30, January 1970).

> Name it, and somebody is seriously proposing it... Scientists tend to agree that some of the most exciting future developments will come out of insights and discoveries yet to be made, with implications we cannot now foresee or imagine. So we live in an era where not only anything that we can imagine seems possible, but where the possibilities range beyond what we can imagine.[33]

Reviewing the potential to tinker with DNA coding and possibly create a New Man, Rosenfeld asked: "Who is that we will appoint to play God for us?"[34] A few years later he wrote the book, *The Second Genesis*, exploring what are essentially transhuman subjects.[35]

Uneasy about how technological advancements reposition human values, historian and educator John G. Burke penned the following in 1966: "As the tempo of change intensifies, one finds it increasingly difficult to maintain traditional modes of life and patterns of thought. Change itself, it appears, is sought as a way of life."[36]

Others too were expressing concern. Jacques Ellul argued that *technique* would become the guiding force in shaping the technological society, producing the "mass man."[37] C.P. Snow warned of specialization and politics, and that "trace of the obsessional" necessary in technical problem solving but problematic when applied to guiding civilization.[38] Former president of the University of Chicago, Robert M. Hutchins, critiqued the narrow scope of science and its attitudinal claim of having the corner on rational thought.[39]

---

33 Albert Rosenfeld, "The New Man: What Will He Be Like?" *Life*, Volume 59, Number 14, October 1, 1965, p.96.

34 Ibid., p.100. The sentence is worded awkwardly, but it makes the point.

35 Albert Rosenfeld, *The Second Genesis: The Coming Control of Life* (Prentice-Hall, 1969). Another book on accelerating technology and human change written in the same era is *The Biological Time Bomb* by Gordon Rattray Taylor (New American Library, 1968).

36 John G. Burke, "Preface," *The New Technology and Human Values* (Wadsworth Publishing Company, 1966/1968, edited by John G. Burke), p.iii.

37 Jacques Ellul, *The Technological Society* (Vintage Books, 1964).

38 C.P. Snow, *Science and Government* (Harvard University Press, 1961). Snow was involved in selecting technicians and scientific personnel to assist in England's military response to Nazi Germany.

39 Robert M. Hutchins, "Science, Scientists, and Politics," *The New Technology and Human Values* (Wadsworth Publishing Company, 1966/1968, edited by John G. Burke), pp.40-43.

Hutchins noted that specialization tends to assume its own importance and can misinterpret its place in the broader context. The forest is not missed because of the trees; it is missed because of the focus on a single branch.

Surveying the historical and modern interplay between technology and society, including themes of utopian futures and perfectibility, humanist Herbert J. Muller penned: "The real challenge remains that we do possess the technical means of doing almost anything we have a mind to, short of making angels of men."[40]

But could men be *controlled*?

A 1965 experiment suggested humanity could be manipulated. Yale professor José Delgado gave an impressive display of prowess over the mind when, standing inside a Spanish bullring, he demonstrated *cyborg control* over an aggressive animal. With a receiver wired into a bull's brain, the professor waited until the beast was in full charge and then, using his remote transmitter, sent a signal that abruptly stopped and turned the attacking animal. It was a startling display of biological management via an implant.

From the 1950s until the early 1970s, Delgado experimented with cerebral implants in cats, monkeys, rats, cattle, and humans. His work revealed that not only could physical movement be commanded by remote control but also moods and even feelings of euphoria. The implications were staggering. Could the mind be wired for better social integration? Do we now have the tools to shape human behavior? Are we willing to trade the illusions of personal privacy and individuality for a secure and managed existence? Have we reached the point of constructing a "psychocivilized society"?

The Yale professor pontificated on such questions in his 1969 volume, *Physical Control of the Mind*,

> Even if we agree that individual freedom should in general bow to community welfare, we enter into a new dimension when considering the social implications of the new technology which can influence personal structure and behavioral expression by surgical, chemical, and electrical manipulation of the brain. We may tolerate the practicality of being inoculated with yellow fever when visiting Asiatic countries, but shall we accept the theoretical future possibil-

---

[40] Herbert J. Muller, *The Children of Frankenstein: A Primer on Modern Technology and Human Values* (Indiana University Press, 1970), p.370.

> ity of being forced to take a pill or submit to an electric shock for the socially protective purpose of making us more docile, infertile, better workers, or happier? How can we decide the limits of social impositions on individual rights?[41]

"To outline a formula for the future ideal man is not easy," he wrote.[42]

The social implications of his experimental work reminds me of a presentation I heard during the 9th Colloquium on the Law of the Futuristic Persons, held in late 2013 at Terasem Island.[43] To be fair, it was a *projection* of myself that attended. I interacted through an avatar, a *presence of my personality* in virtual reality (VR). Terasem Island itself is a cyberspace location, a digital land parcel with a conference theater, exhibits, meeting areas, and other constructions. As a user of virtual environments since 2009, primarily through the Second Life platform, I have frequented university lectures, church services, temples and sacred spaces, festivals at BURN2 – the official Burning Man parcel – and transhumanist conferences.

A transhuman event in VR makes perfect sense, as virtual reality is one of the most important technologies underscoring the post-human ideal.

During the Colloquium, one of the lecturers expounded on the ethical aspects of BCI – brain-computer interfaces – a proven technology that connects a person's brain to a computer system, prefigured in part by Delgado's work. With advancing BCI, it was explained, humanity finds itself in need of a *trans-ethics* – a new set of values to guide "networked individuals." Questions of individual freedom, security challenges, and the use of such devices for social control need to be considered. Could a wireless BCI application include directly linking the mind to a global network, and more than that, the creation of a brain-based *personal identification* mark to enable access as planetary citizens? Is this farfetched?

Maybe, but current BCI innovation is moving from bulky gear to streamlined headsets to wireless capabilities, with the dream – wished by some, feared by others – of higher bandwidth, nanotechnology, and deep artificial intelligence integrating minds-and-machines in a cybernetic collective. Knowing that *synthetic telepathy* is already being tested, what are the ethi-

---

41 Delgado, *Physical Control of the Mind*, pp.221-222.

42 Ibid., p.253.

43 9th Colloquium on the Law of the Futuristic Persons, December 10, 2013, Terasem Island, Second Life.

cal implications of BCI enabled brain-to-brain and brain-to-machine connections? "Mind reading" is becoming *science fact*.

"Do we need government intervention toward transhumanism?" our presenter asked, noting that some kind of global "skynet" will be required to manage the system: "We need global governance... this is so dangerous."[44]

We have come a long way.

Since the 1990s, critical evaluations have been added to the discussion of science and society. The dangers of what Neil Postman called being a *technophile*, those who "gaze on technology as a lover does his beloved, seeing it as without blemish and entertaining no apprehension for the future."[45] The warnings given by Douglas Groothuis in his still relevant book, *The Soul in Cyber-Space*, that we will mistake "connectivity for community, data for wisdom, and efficiency for excellence"[46] – and that the truth of God will be substituted for the ever-changing nature of our digital idols. The father of virtual reality, Jaron Lanier, has also made a powerful case for caution, arguing that individual meaning and even creativity is being degraded in systems of cybernetic totalism.[47]

Lanier comments on the cultural elevation of information,

> But if you want to make the transition from the old religion, where you hope God will give you an afterlife, to the new religion, where you hope to become immortal by getting uploaded into a computer, then you have to believe that information is real and alive. So for you, it will be important to redesign human institutions like art, the economy, and the law to reinforce the perception that information is alive. You demand that the rest of us live in your narrow conception of a state religion. You need us to deify information to reinforce your faith.[48]

---

[44] Heikki Laakko, "Transhumanism Today and Tomorrow: Ethical Aspects and Laws Shaping Our Future," presentation at the 9th Colloquium on the Law of the Futuristic Persons, December 10, 2013, Terasem Island, Second Life. As taken from my notes of the event: Quotes are directly attributed to Laakko, while the questions are deduced from his talk. Laakko is a BCI specialist.

[45] Neil Postman, *Technopoly: The Surrender of Culture to Technology* (Vintage Books, 1992/1993), p.5.

[46] Douglas Groothuis, *The Soul in Cyber-Space* (BakerBooks, 1997), p.143.

[47] Jaron Lanier, *You Are Not A Gadget: A Manifesto* (Alfred A. Knopf, 2010).

[48] Ibid., p.29.

Important debates on technology and society are happening within the transhumanist movement. More internal criticism, however, is needed.

Tech-enterprises are likewise wrestling with ethical dilemmas, and governments will soon find themselves debating difficult boundaries. A few Christian ministries and institutions have also been discussing implications, but more review is necessary. Awareness within the Christian community is generally lacking; churches need to be informed and equipped to understand the worldviews behind the movement, bringing sober realism and wisdom to the conversation. Seminaries and apologetics ministries ought to formulate Biblical responses to the hope-in-technology, and search for opportunities to speak into the subject. Moreover, such an approach would be internally helpful as Christians navigate the maze of concerns and changing issues.

We are on the back of galloping technology…

As innovation pushes us closer to post-human promises, which way will the moral compass swing? When pragmatism clashes with ethical barriers, will transhuman goals be willingly tabled? How might the self-proclaimed "evolutionary imperative" configure in the post-human worldview? Will transhumanists claim a position of Darwinian authority; that evolution demands the strongest survive, damning those incapable of enhancement? Is the vision of techno-humanity sacrosanct? If so, then Comte's Positivism and Darwinian pragmatism will be the guiding principles – science is all that matters, and evolutionary succession is the only measure of victory.

If it can be done, or *perceived* so, will it be – no matter the cost? David Gelernter thinks so: "Everything is up for grabs. Everything will change. The Orwell law of the future: Any new technology that *can* be tried *will* be."[49]

In our attempt to be a new species, will we act less than human?

For Christians and conservative individuals, other questions need be asked: Will we shun technologies that are medically beneficial or otherwise valuable because of associations with transhumanism? I hope not. Augmentation itself is not wrong; it could be argued that eyeglasses and heart pacemakers are technological enhancements. BCI can be helpful to individuals who are physically immobilized, VR platforms are useful in communication and education, computers and internet connectivity are important tools for business and personal use. We daily use technologies linked to transhuman visions.

[49] Gelernter, "The Second Coming – A Manifesto," *Science at the Edge*, p.239, italics in original.

Discernment is required to know the difference between the techno-faith that seeks to fundamentally transform mankind into an unknown quality, and the helpful uses of innovation for present-day humanity. Will we use innovation and technology in ways that are good and advantageous? We have in the past and I trust we will continue doing so, even being trailblazers in scientific discovery and innovative development.

Transhumanism is far more than a zeal for science and technology, a fascination with digital tools and manageable matter; it is a social pressure cooker, a container heated by the intellectual forces of Modernity.

It is also an attitude of religion.

Sacred Secularism and Mystical Materialism

The 2012 survey published by the *Journal of Personal Cyberconsciousness* shared some interesting insights regarding the transhuman community and religiosity: 81.4% claimed not to be religious and 9.5% declared themselves as Christians. Judaic and Buddhist identifiers made up 1.8% each, and 5.0% came from other religions.[50]

The preponderance of non-religion was also demonstrated when the Institute for Ethics and Emerging Technologies published their findings in 2013: 49% claimed to be agnostic or atheist, 17% viewed themselves as spiritual but not religious, Buddhists represented 11%, followed by a falling range of Protestant Christians, Judaism, Pantheists, and Pagans.[51]

Founder of the Transhumanist Party, Zoltan Istvan – who traveled across America in a coffin-shaped bus campaigning as a 2016 presidential candidate[52] – consistently reminds the transhumanist community of the dominant secularist viewpoint. During the 2014 Religion and Transhumanism Conference, Istvan asked: "Does the godless lifestyle support a transhumanist lifestyle?"[53] Affirming this position, he explained that religions bind humanity with chains of morality and therefore the atheist – unencumbered by such

[50] Hank Pellissier and Teresa Dal Santo, "Transhumanists: Who Are They, What Do They Want, Believe And Predict?" *Journal of Personal Cyberconsciousness* (Terasem Movement, Inc, 2013), Volume 8, Issue 1, p.22-24.

[51] *Who are the IEET's Audience?* Institute for Ethics and Emerging Technologies, July 16, 2013, [https://ieet.org/index.php/IEET2/more/poll20130716].

[52] As I write this, Zoltan Istvan is campaigning for California's 2018 governor's election.

[53] Zoltan Istvan, "Transhumanism, Religion, and Atheism," given at the Religion and Transhumanism Conference, May 10, 2014, Piedmont, California, hosted by the Brighter

restraints – will be freer to think in transhuman terms. The troubling Biblical message of sin and salvation, and those annoying Ten Commandments, must not hinder the progress of evolution. Traveling as presidential candidate in a coffin-bus is certainly original, however, the ideological construction of a godless New Man is anything but.

Not all transhumanists agree with Istvan's tactics or politics or his atheism, which combined, became a public relation spectacle – a lightning rod for and against transhumanism. Regardless, he is not without *faith*: faith in science, faith in technology and by extension, faith in power. Within Istvan's message is a subtle but evident flavor, a *religion without revelation*.[54]

The notion of a secular faith harkens back to Saint Simon's New Christianity and Comte's Religion of Humanity. But a more direct iteration to transhumanism comes through the eugenicist and internationalist, Julian Huxley.

Back in 1927, Huxley looked forward to a coming sacred secularity as outlined in his book, *Religion Without Revelation*. This faith without recourse to a transcendent God would be predicated upon Darwinian evolution and Natural Power. Science would be the sacred force to control and direct said Power, giving rise to an interconnected and unitary system of thought and action, resulting in growth and new life. It would be a *Sacred Reality*, a phrase he used in the struggle to express his vision.[55]

Three decades later in a collection of essays titled *New Bottles for New Wine*, Huxley described the new reality to be a unifying process of progressive evolution. Man's place in this transforming universe is that of a guiding hand, a devoted trustee, an agent of change – *an embodiment*. Huxley put it this way: "man's destiny, his duty and privilege... is to continue in his own person the advance of the cosmic process of evolution."[56]

If indeed this were the case, then morality would need to be refashioned around coalescing principles and pragmatic measures. If the human population becomes too large, then to oppose control would be heinous; if cumulative knowledge is necessary for unifying processes, "then dogma is a

---

Brains Institute. His presentation was recorded and is available on the YouTube channel of the Mormon Transhumanist Association [https://youtu.be/jXOXBYr2Z7I].

54 Istvan's message has come through media interviews and conference talks, his articles and essays, and in his novel *The Transhumanist Wager* (Futurity Imagine Media, 2013).

55 Julian Huxley, *Religion Without Revelation* (Watts and Company, 1941, originally published in 1927).

56 Julian Huxley, *New Bottles for New Wine* (Harper and Brothers Publishers, 1957), p.103.

threat, and any claim to exclusive possession of the truth or to suppression of free enquiry is immoral."[57]

Notice how Huxley lumped exclusive truth claims with the prohibition of enquiry. This is misleading. Exclusive truth does not hinder the pursuit of knowledge, but places the action in a context through which to judge the *pursuit itself* and its outcome; what is acceptable and what is discarded, what is right and wrong, what is factual and what is error.

Huxley's ideology, however, rejected absolutes,

> We must accept reality as unitary, and so must reject all dualistic ways of thinking. We must accept the fact that it is a process, and so must reject all static conceptions. The process is always relative, so we must reject all absolutes... For this we must develop new methods of thinking.[58]

Sacred secularity therefore envisions Man and Evolution in a cosmic union, and our task is to embrace the non-binary, for "evolution thus insists on the oneness of man with nature."[59] From this point we can begin affirming the interdependence of the individual to the community and the cosmos. The person who accepts this paradigm "would acquire a new sense of oneness with the rest of existence."[60]

Huxley boasted: "We are perforce monists, in the sense of believers in the oneness of things, the unitary nature of reality; we see ourselves, together with our science and our beliefs, as an integral part of the cosmic process."[61]

Why is Huxley's position in *New Bottles for New Wine* important to transhumanism? First, he lays out the essential context for a scientifically justified sacred reality, a religion without revelation underscoring so much of the modern movement. Second, because it is in the pages of *New Bottles* where the term "transhumanism" comes into vogue.

Others had used the compound word before, but Huxley employed it in a way that foreshadowed magnitude. He presented a sacralizing rationale. Like a mountaineer noticing a compelling peak in the distance, being in-

---

57 Ibid., pp.103-104.
58 Ibid., p.251.
59 Ibid., p.122.
60 Ibid., p.260.
61 Ibid., pp.279-280.

wardly drawn to the summit before pondering its base, Huxley began his book with a pinnacle vision. The first chapter was titled *Transhumanism*,

> As a result of a thousand million years of evolution, the universe is becoming conscious of itself, able to understand something of its past history and its possible future. This cosmic self-awareness is being realized in one tiny fragment of the universe – in a few of us human beings.[62]

This destiny would be fulfilled by taking upon ourselves the "techniques of spiritual development," a cosmic duty to self and others resulting in the transformation of humanity,

> The human species can, if it wishes, transcend itself – not just sporadically, an individual here in one way, an individual there in another way, but in its entirety, as humanity. We need a name for this new belief. Perhaps transhumanism will serve: man remaining man, but transcending himself, by realizing new possibilities of and for his human nature.
>
> 'I believe in transhumanism': once there are enough people who can truly say that, the human species will be on the threshold of a new kind of existence, as different from ours as ours is from that of Peking man. It will at last be consciously fulfilling its real destiny.[63]

Huxley's intellectual role was significant, but his was not the only voice pronouncing an ideal state of being.

The Jesuit priest and trained paleontologist, Pierre Teilhard de Chardin, had traveled similar intellectual paths to that of Julian Huxley. In fact, the two had met in 1946 and closely followed each other's work. Huxley even penned the introduction to Chardin's influential book, *The Phenomenon of Man*. In its pages, the Jesuit reminded his readers of Huxley's principle that Man is "nothing else than evolution become conscious of itself."[64]

---

62 Ibid., p.13.

63 Ibid., p.17.

64 Pierre Teilhard de Chardin, *The Phenomenon of Man* (HarperPerennial, 1976, originally published in 1955), p.221.

Surveying human progress, Chardin noticed the persistence of unifying structures, mechanics, and movements. A "Mega-Synthesis" was evident. The "spirit of the earth" would come as world-scale spiritual forces and the genesis of our collective mind compelled transformation. This would result in a "totalisation of the world upon itself."[65] As our individual consciousness coalesced around social principles, linked together in a global network, the Earth would experience an awakening. Indeed, all consciousness would integrate into a global structure – an *earth-brain* – a state of connection and equilibrium known as the Noosphere.

Chardin noted that science, pursuing the character of evolution, will inevitably force Man to look upon himself: "Man, the knowing subject, will perceive at last that man, 'the object of knowledge,' is the key to the whole science of nature." All science will eventually focus its energies on this pinnacle of evolution,

> We find man at the bottom, man at the top, and, above all, man at the centre – man who lives and struggles desperately in us and around us. We shall have to come to grips with him sooner or later.[66]

And in searching for an understanding of Man, science and religion will unify as we reach for our higher existence,

> ...when we turn towards the summit, towards the *totality* and the *future*, we cannot help engage in religion.
>
> Religion and science are the two conjugated faces or phases of one and the same act of knowledge – the only one which can embrace the past and future of evolution so as to contemplate, measure and fulfil them.
>
> In the mutual reinforcement of these two opposed powers, in the conjunction of reason and mysticism, the human spirit is destined, by the very nature of its development, to find the uttermost degree of its penetration with the maximum of its vital force.[67]

As the very expression of evolution, humanity – wielding the energy of vital forces – will have to translate into a *new being*.

---

[65] Ibid., p.253.

[66] Ibid., p.281.

[67] Ibid., p.285, italics in original.

"What we see taking place in the world today is not merely the multiplication of men but the continued shaping of Man," explained Chardin in *The Future of Man*. "In one form or another something ultra-human is being born which, through the direct or indirect effect of socialisation, cannot fail to make its appearance in the near future."[68]

A religion of the future – "definable as a religion of evolution" – must therefore come to fruition: "a new mysticism, the germ of which must be recognizable somewhere in our environment, *here and now*."[69]

Chardin postulated that the Ultra-Human is on a convergence course with the universe itself, an Omega Point when our exalted consciousness blends with the "Cosmic Christ," the "divine in evolution." This is "an absolute direction and an absolute end."[70]

The Omega Point, percolating in the esoteric heart of humanity, *would be the full experience of Man's evolutionary unity*. Mystically speaking, it is the *divine dance* when God and Creation join as One.

How grand is the Omega Point envisioned? Mathematician Frank J. Tipler gives us a taste,

> We can say, quite obviously, that life near the Omega Point is omnipresent. As the Omega Point is approached, survival dictates that life collectively gain control of all matter and energy sources available near the Final State, with this control becoming total at the Omega Point. We can say that life becomes omnipotent at the instant the Omega Point is reached. Since by hypothesis the information stored becomes infinite at the Omega Point, it is reasonable to say that the Omega Point is omniscient; it knows whatever it is possible to know about the physical universe (and hence about Itself).[71]

Chardin peddled a mystical materialism, Huxley a sacred secularity; both are transhumanist heroes.

Although the current transhumanist community is largely agnostic or atheistic, there is interest in spirituality. Writing for *Business Insider*, Zoltan Ist-

---

68 Pierre Teilhard de Chardin, *The Future of Man* (Harper Colophon Books, 1969), p275.

69 Pierre Teilhard de Chardin, *Christianity and Evolution* (Harcourt, Inc., 1969), p.240, italics in original.

70 Ibid., p.239.

71 Frank J. Tipler, *The Psychics of Immortality: Modern Cosmology, God and the Resurrection of the Dead* (Doubleday, 1994), p.154.

van admitted that, "most transhumanists embrace some spirituality, including myself."[72]

Part of this sentiment comes from interactions with religiously oriented transhumanist groups. Another factor is the growing cultural detachment of spirituality from religion, presenting an acceptable veneer of separation from dogmas and creeds. With the postmodern slide from the hard materialism of Modernity and the subsequent social desire for re-enchantment, an aesthetically grounded sense of existence is sought after. Everyone, atheists and agnostics included, are longing for a soul-felt feeling of connection or flow – spirituality without responsibility to metaphysical truth claims.

Just before the 2015 Colloquium on the Law of the Futuristic Persons, Istvan's campaign bus stopped at the Terasem "ashram" in Melbourne Beach, Florida, and the Church of Perpetual Life – a Hollywood, Florida congregation anticipating techno-immortality. During the Colloquium he acknowledged that these interactions fostered discussions on spirituality and transhumanism, "especially the future of spirituality."[73]

Long before Istvan was on the presidential trail, however, techno-futurists and psychedelic explorers were considering the convergence of technology and spirituality. In his posthumously published book, *Design for Dying*, Timothy Leary expounded on transhuman themes and ideas of the Self made magical by science,

> Now that computer technology can personalize reality, it becomes less alien and external to use. We become one with it as a consequence of our ability to reach out and transform it... Technology

---

[72] Zoltan Istvan, "I visited one of the largest megachurches in the US as an atheist Transhumanist presidential candidate – here's what happened," *Business Insider*, Tech News section, December 2, 2015 [www.businessinsider.com/transhumanist-zoltan-istvan-visits-one-of-the-largest-megachurches-in-the-us-2015-11].

[73] Zoltan Istvan, "Transhumanism," presentation at the 10th Colloquium on the Law of the Futuristic Persons, December 10, 2015, Terasem Island, Second Life. Note: In what could be viewed as a campaign stunt he also visited Alabama's Church of the Highlands, the largest evangelical congregation in the state, where he toured the main campus and talked to one of the pastors. That is, until someone in the church did an internet search on transhumanism, and then – for better or worse – Team Istvan was escorted from the grounds. See Zoltan Istvan, "Forget Trump, Zoltan Istvan wants to be the 'anti-death' president," *Wired*, UK online edition, November 8, 2016 [www.wired.co.uk/article/the-transhumanist-age]

> extends the boundary of self... It is the age of the expanding person. This engenders a blurring of the material and 'spiritual' realms... Who are you? You are boundless. Where are you? Here, there, and everywhere.[74]

Psychonaut, social visionary and author, Terence McKenna, frequently connected psychedelic mysticism with evolution via technology. "The two concepts, drugs and computers," McKenna said in a 1988 interview, "are migrating toward each other."[75]

At an Esalen Institute workshop in 1996, McKenna spoke of cyberspace and virtual reality, nanotechnology, and the bootstrapping of information to "higher and higher levels of self-reflection,"

> It's our machines and our technologies that are now the major evolutionary forces acting upon us. It's not our political systems. It's these extra-sexual children, these 'mind children' we have assembled out of the imagination.[76]

Technology would be a handmaid to new dimensions of *experiential information*, dissolving our differences and knitting us into a global community. Virtual reality would reveal our minds to one another, opening portals to silicon-enabled psychedelic mysticism.

Technology needs an agenda, the psychonaut believed, and this is the inner evolution of humanity with accompanying outer manifestations. To McKenna, such fundamental change would require an *archaic revival*, the resurrecting of a shamanistic paradigm for our current culture. In denouncing Paganism, Christianity with its separating monotheism had stifled the flow of universal creativity, but with Christianity now on the wane, the Goddess would come alive once more. We would be transformed through our technological offerings and by an expansion of consciousness; civilization

---

[74] Timothy Leary, *Design for Dying* (HarperEdge, 1997), pp.36-37.

[75] Terence McKenna, *The Archaic Revival: Speculations on Psychedelic Mushrooms, the Amazon, Virtual Reality, UFOs, Evolution, Shamanism, the Rebirth of the Goddess, and the End of History* (HarperOne, 1991/1992), p.19.

[76] Terence McKenna, a talk given at the Esalen Institute, Big Sur, California, August 1996. An audio recording of his presentation is archived with the author. This talk, now titled *The Evolutionary Importance of Technology*, can be accessed via YouTube at https://youtu.be/0O93SEOWjE4. Using the May-October 1996 *Esalen Catalog*, I have correlated McKenna's workshop to the weekend of August 2-4, 1996.

would experience a unifying synthesis through silicon and psilocybin. Mind and matter would merge in a new planetary paradigm.

Our evolutionary development would center on an ancient-future worldview: Self-enchanting and magical re-enchantment, material and spiritual, inner and outer, as above so below – *a techno-shamanistic community*. We will be priests in the temple of the cosmos, the Earth an altar to the universe.

Technology as evolution and trans-spiritual subjects were hot topics at Esalen in the 1990s. The *Machine Dreams and Technoshamanism* workshops led attendees through mental romps,

> Is information immortal? What unexplored realms of spirit will we encounter with amazing new forms of computer and electronic hypermedia? New myths will be needed.
>
> New mysteries will be encountered. How can ancient models of mind such as shamanism, Hinduism, or voodoo help us comprehend silicon-based consciousness? Why are neuro-enhancers crucial tools for so many computer innovators? Can humans share an erotic relationship with a machine being? Are Earth spirits at play in fields of photons and electronic spin?
>
> A neo-psychedelic subculture is co-evolving with new technologies to reveal glimpses of exotic futures.[77]

In 1996, technology-futurist Douglas Rushkoff offered a similar workshop at Esalen titled *Technoshamanism: Total Immersion in Spiritual Technology*,

> To wholeheartedly embrace technology may be the only way to partake in the next phase of human evolution... Participants will experience brain machines, the Internet, computer fractals, Virtual Reality, tarot, astrology, and I Ching through computer programs, chaos math, hemispheric alignment audio, video games, and even new media... The workshop will explore the techno-vision-quest and evaluate it as an adjunct to more traditional spiritual practices. The weekend will conclude with a techno-pagan rave dance... Participants are encouraged to bring at least one item of technology...[78]

[77] Britt Welin and Ken Adams workshop, "Machine Dreams and Technoshamanism," *The Esalen Catalog*, May-October, 1993 (The Esalen Institute, 1993), p.39

[78] Douglas Rushkoff, "Technoshamanism: Total Immersion in Spiritual Technology," *The Esalen Catalog*, September 1995-February 1996 (The Esalen Institute, 1995), p.55.

On the third weekend of August 1998, McKenna and VRML[79] developer, Mark Pesce – a transhumanist influenced by Chardin's writings – held their now-famous workshop at Esalen.

The duo explored the interlocking subjects of psychedelic consciousness, virtual reality and computer simulations, nanotechnology, complexity and the organization of information, and techno-mysticism. Their workshop title was representative of the oneness believed to come through the merger of Man and Machine: *Techno-Pagans at the End of History*.[80]

The idea of techno-paganism corresponds to the cultural transformation McKenna had been pointing to for a long time. In a 1985 interview touching on the subjects of psychedelics, cybernetics and the "electronic shaman," he said, "We cannot travel much further with definitions of humanity inherited from the Judeo-Christian tradition."[81]

Seduced by the imagination we have bestowed upon our machinery, humanity is attempting to write a new definition of what it means to be human. We want to make ourselves in the image of our works. It is an act of sacred secularism, a journey to mystical materialism.

Perfectibility and Singularity

Perfection underscore the human longing for order out of chaos.

We long for ideal social and political relationships. We desire the perfect day, the perfect mate and perfect children, the perfect career, and perfect knowledge. Ever-higher aspirations and peak experiences may fit within this greater model, along with a host of other subjects: body images and views of biology, the perfecting of artistic endeavor, ethical and moral expectations, religious duties, ethnic and cultural traditions, and feelings of spiritual arrival. In a way this embodied desire for perfection erodes the common

---

79 Virtual Reality Markup Language is a standard file describing 3-D imaging for virtual reality applications in the World Wide Web. Today the word "Modeling" replaces "Markup."

80 Mark Pesce is well known as a techno-pagan, interacting with cybernetics through a decidedly Pagan lens. See Eric Davis, "Technopagans: May the astral plane be reborn in cyberspace," *Wired*, online edition, July 1, 1995 [www.wired.com/1995/07/technopagans]. See also, Eric Davis, *TechGnosis: Myth, Magic and Mysticism in the Age of Information* (Harmony Books, 1998), pp.192-193. Davis, a contemporary of Pesce and a fellow traveler with McKenna, is himself a psychonaut and visionary futurist who lectures at Esalen and is well known within the Burning Man community.

81 McKenna, *The Archaic Revival*, p.165.

belief in humanity's inherent goodness. Why seek improvement if we are good already? That we *do* good things and are often well intentioned is not disputed; that we *are* good is another matter. *Imperfection is the norm.*

Transhumanism seeks to find practical paths to human perfectibility – or at least betterment that, when compared to our normal existence, appears radically superior and ultimate.

As techno-pagan Mark Pesce elucidated,

> Men die; planets die, even stars die. We know all this. Because we know it, we seek something more, a transcendence of transience, translation to an incorruptible form. An escape, if you will, a stop to the Wheel.
>
> We seek, therefore, to bless ourselves with perfect knowledge and perfect will, to become as gods, take the universe in hand, and transform it in our own image, for our own delight. As it is on Earth, so it shall be in the heavens, the inevitable result of incredible improbability, the arrow of evolution lifting us into the Transhuman, an apotheosis through reason, salvation attained by good works.[82]

Biblically, the problem of the human condition is not biological or cognitive or technical limitations, but *positional* separation from God our creator.

This *relational severance* occurred when Mankind chose to pursue aggrandizement, to be more than Man. It was an act opposed to the position God set on noble human existence, to be His representatives or image bearers on Earth. Humanity chose, rather, to find a new identity via technique, the intentional transgressing of God's stated limitations.[83] *We would represent ourselves*. This act of disobedience immediately became inherent and is known as the problem of *sin*,[84] with moral and physical consequences plaguing every person; we naturally seek to be masters and saviors of our destiny, doing what is right in our own eyes. Whether inwardly or outwardly *I lie*, you lie; *I steal*, you steal; *I murder*, you murder; *I commit adultery and idolatry*, and you do the same. It is not that *we are one*, but that *we are all broken*.

---

[82] Mark Pesce, *Becoming Transhuman*, a presentation given at Mindstates, Berkeley, California, May 2001; transcript of talk, p.10.

[83] Genesis 1-3.

[84] Romans 5:12.

When compared to the transcendent standards of Holy God, our natural state is immediately exposed. In the Old Testament, the prophet Isaiah tells us that even our deeds of justice – our proclaimed righteousness – are "like a menstrual cloth," and our sins sweep us away as the wind blows the withered leaf.[85] In the ancient Jewish world such "filthy rags" were illustrative of being spiritually unclean, an appropriate picture as menstruation cloth could be washed but would never become perfectly clean. The more such rags were hand-scrubbed, the more the fabric would degrade until it became worthless and discarded. It is an apt picture of our inability, by our own works, to attain *positional perfection* – to be viewed by God as righteous.

In the New Testament the Apostle Paul reminds us that Jews and Greeks, all mankind, has fallen under the curse of sin. In reiterating the words of the Psalmist, Paul points to the true state of our hearts,

> The LORD looks down from heaven upon the children of men, to see if there are any who understand, who seek God. They have all turned aside, they have together become corrupt; There is none who does good, no, not one.[86]

Positional perfectibility remains out of our hands; because of our sinful nature we are incapable of fixing this dire situation on our own. In fact, that is the point. Yet we long for perfectibility, a return to our previously unfallen state but without recourse to God's exclusive mandate – *salvation through Jesus Christ alone*.[87] So we continually seek ways to save ourselves and reclaim Eden for our own greatness.

Looking back over the history of technology and religious thought, activist Professor David F. Noble made an astute connection,

> Over time, technology came to be identified more closely with both lost perfection and the possibility of renewed perfection, and the advance of the arts took on new significance, not only as evidence of grace, but as a means of preparation for, and a sure sign of, imminent salvation.[88]

---

85 Isaiah 64:6, Lexham English Bible (Logos Bible Software, 2011).

86 Psalm 14:2-3.

87 Acts 4:12.

88 David F. Noble, *The Religion of Technology: The Divinity of Man and the Spirit of Invention* (Penguin Books, 1997/1999), p.12.

Perfectibility is an inescapable feature of religious philosophy.

Confucianism seeks *self-attained perfection* through the deliberate engagement of ethical character development, right duty and actions, virtue through education, and social etiquette. Or consider Hinduism as a process, a quest for perfection in the undifferentiated Atman; or the steps of perfection, transformation, and the going beyond as a Great Being in the Buddhist tradition; or the Sufi's journey to union through the passing of stages, becoming Perfect Man in the flow of God. The Mormon faith emphasizes perfection, impelling the believer to strive for exaltation through proper behavior, temple requirements, and priesthood duties.

The examples in the above paragraph are paths of *practical perfection*: Do these things, focus on these principles, act this way, or follow these spiritual techniques. Salvation is dependent on your active participation.

Esoteric beliefs add another dimension to the perfection theme. The Hermetic Order of the Golden Dawn, arguably one of the most influential occult groups in the Twentieth Century, encouraged its members through rituals and experimentation "to be more than human, to transcend physical limitations" – "to be more than human, and thus gradually raise and unite myself to my Higher and Divine Genius."[89] A spiritually cryptic version of evolution promised a path to ascension and perfection, degree-by-degree.

Presenting a Masonic interpretation, W.L. Wilmshurst penned the following in his classic, *The Meaning of Masonry*,

> From grade to grade the candidate is being led from an old to an entirely new quality of life. He begins his Masonic career as the natural man; he ends it by becoming through its discipline, a regenerated perfected man. To attain this transmutation, this metamorphosis of himself, he is taught first to purify and subdue his sensual nature; then to purify and develop his mental nature; and finally, by utter surrender of his old life and losing his soul to save it, he rises from the dead a Master, a just man made perfect...
>
> This – the evolution of man into superman – was always the purpose of the ancient Mysteries, and the real purpose of modern

[89] Israel Regardie, *The Original Account of the Teachings, Rites and Ceremonies of the Hermetic Order of the Golden Dawn* (Llewellyn Publishing, 2003, first published in 1937), pp.10,135.

> Masonry is, not the social and charitable purpose to which so much attention is paid, but the expediting of the spiritual evolution of those who aspire to perfect their own nature and transform it into a more god-like quality. And this is a definite science, a royal art.[90]

Henry C. Clausen, while Sovereign Grand Commander of the Supreme Council of the Scottish Rite of Freemasonry, hinted at a coming techno-spirituality,

> Science and philosophy, especially when linked through mysticism, have yet to conquer ignorance and superstition. Victory, however, appears on the horizon. Laboratory and library, science and philosophy... outstanding technicians and theologians are now uniting as advocates of man's unique quality, his immortal soul and ever expanding soul.[91]

Theosophy with its blend of Eastern religions and Western occultism, taught that perfectibility could be achieved through directed, spiritual evolution. Those who have so advanced are known as "Adepts or Supermen."[92]

According to C.W. Leadbeater, an early Theosophical authority, these Supermen maintained physical bodies far exceeding normal men in terms of longevity and capacity. It was also claimed that these Adepts could transition from body to body, temporarily possessing others to achieve a purpose.

Leadbeater presented a general argument for these Perfected Men,

> The existence of Perfected Men is one of the most important of the many new facts which Theosophy puts before us. It follows logically from the other great Theosophical teachings of karma and evolution by reincarnation. As we look round us we see men obviously at all stages of their evolution – many far below ourselves in development, and others who in one way or another are distinctly in advance of us. Since that is so, there may well be others who are very much further advanced; indeed, if men are steadily growing better and better

[90] W.L. Wilmshurst, *The Meaning of Masonry* (Gramercy Books, 1980, originally published in 1922), p.47.

[91] Henry C. Clausen, *Emergence of the Mystical* (Ancient and Accepted Scottish Rite of Freemasonry, Southern Jurisdiction, 1981), p.92.

[92] C.W. Leadbeater, *The Masters and the Path* (The Theosophical Press, 1925), p.3. Other names ascribed to advanced soul beings include, "Great Ones, the Planetary Spirits, Great Angels, Karmic Deities, Dhyan Chohans, Buddhas, Christs and Masters." (p.200).

> through a long series of successive lives, tending towards a definite goal, there should certainly be some who have already reached that goal.[93]

This evolution into Perfect Men, it was believed, is part of the drama of incorporation into the Universal Over-Soul, the "great unit consciousness" or *Brahma* in which the oneness of all exists.[94]

The transformation of religion and society through a worldizing process is considered another dimension of this same Great Work. Universal consciousness and human evolution, rising from the lower to the higher, provides the background for an obscure statement in an 1891 edition of *Lucifer*, a Theosophical magazine. In this text, the transmutation was described as passing from "the lower kingdoms of nature, up to the divine trans-human realisation at the close."[95] Roughly twenty years later Russian theosophical thinker, P.D. Ouspensky, described "cosmic consciousness" as "trans-humanizing a man into a god."[96]

What was being described from an esoteric position was a type of Singularity, a point when spiritual technique ushers in a planetary transformation, and a time when Man ceases being human on the evolutionary path. Such a pinnacle moment has also been portrayed as a great *convergence* or *emergence*. The transhuman version, however, sees this primarily as a technical and informational convergence: Machine intelligence exceeding human capacity, which will spur an exponential rate of artificial cognition and force humanity to transform into a Great Being. But debate within the transhuman camp continues as to what the Singularity will be like and what it entails. It is a future oriented prediction with passionate believers and questioning skeptics. Nevertheless, it fits with Chardin's idea of the Omega Point, that supposed period when science and spirituality blossom into the evolution of Cosmic Consciousness and the arrival of the Ultra-Human.

---

93 Ibid., p.1.

94 The concept of the Universal Over-Soul plays out in Terence McKenna's idea of the Overmind. It is visible in the Rosicrucian and esoteric model of the Cosmic Christ, and in the New Age notion of Cosmic Consciousness. Each speaks to the same value: All is One.

95 H.A.W. Coryn, "Consciousness," *Lucifer*, Vol. 9, No. 50, October 15, 1891, p.125.

96 P.D. Ouspensky, *Tertium Organum: The Third Canon of Thought, a Key to the Enigmas of the World* (Alfred A. Knopf, 1922, second edition, originally published in Russian in 1912), p.318.

Google's Ray Kurzweil, a rock-star in the transhumanist community, correlates the Singularity to a human-machine transcendence. Kurzweil is religiously agnostic and although his approach is prophetically scientific, his concept amounts to a spiritual translation through technology. The post-human journey approaches a *god-point*, producing an existence that would appear deified when compared to our present situation. A few lines from his *New York Times* bestselling book, *The Singularity is Near*, helps us connect the dots behind his big idea,

> As a consummation of the evolution in our midst, the Singularity will deepen all of these manifestations of transcendence...
>
> ...the matter and energy in our vicinity will become infused with the intelligence, knowledge, creativity, beauty, and emotional intelligence (the ability to love, for example) of our human-machine civilization. Our civilization will then expand outward, turning all the dumb matter and energy we encounter into sublimely intelligence – transcendent – matter and energy. So in a sense, we can say that the Singularity will ultimately infuse the universe with spirit.[97]

Zoltan Istvan passionately expressed his thoughts on the Singularity to those attending the 10th Colloquium on Terasem Island,

> I am a person striving to achieve and reach the Singularity... Who doesn't want to know what the Singularity really is? Who... wouldn't press a big red button and say 'I want to go there right now' and discover everything there is that far into the future; whether it's omnipotence, whether it's just omniscience, whether it's a perfect hive mind... whether it's a complete immersion into one, single entity where, one doesn't even recognize himself anymore.[98]

I believe the *unexplainable idea* of the Singularity and the transhuman quest to reach this fuzzy future is flawed.

Can it be attained or even recognized if we are unsure of what it is, especially something apparently so vast and potent and all-encompassing? Reality

---

[97] Ray Kurzweil, *The Singularity is Near: When Humans Transcend Biology* (Penguin Books, 2005), pp.388-389.

[98] Zoltan Istvan, "Transhumanism," presentation at the 10th Colloquium on the Law of the Futuristic Persons, December 10, 2015, Terasem Island, Second Life. Recording of the event on file.

cannot be condensed into an algorithm, let alone a formula that equals or surpasses the human experience; machines – even Artificial Intelligence – remains locked in utilitarian functions, and to push beyond intended capabilities often results in damage and degradation; information is not the same as life; we are unable to define what *thought* is, and understanding consciousness remains out of reach.

Consciousness and so much of the human experience cannot be qualified nor quantified in the material. To be human is more than just occupying "meat space." There is an immaterial side to existence; our spirits and souls, and the free will associated with relationships, beliefs, values, and our unique personalities. We are not material entities only, but a complex of biology, spirit and soul. *We are fearfully and wonderfully made*.[99]

Dressed in material mysticism – that it is our destiny to somehow awaken the material universe with our material proficiency – the Omega Point or Singularity is an attempt to sell an accelerating technological future based on a model from a non-existent past. It aims to translate what has never been proven: The evolutionary change from one species into an entirely new species, and not just any Darwinian transformation but the arrival of self-deified Man through the perfecting of information.

But might we encounter a type of Singularity, the unification of technologies, religions, politics and ideologies, all squeezed into a world system? This would only be possible under the right international conditions of extreme conflict or social tension, providing a planetary *gestalt* experience and the opportunity to fundamentally restart civilization. The person or entity that pulled off such a feat would be hailed as a world savior, a guiding force to administer evolution. The Singularity would be embodied as the image of the New Man.

Historical patterns give some latitude to speculate as to what an ultimate *image of Man* may look like. Models could include an enhanced United Nations or a replacement institution with far-reaching powers, or a "planetary king" as suggested by Yermentay Sultanmurat.[100] Theosophists anticipate a coming Perfected Man, the "World Teacher" who is to coalesce all things in the Great Work. Maybe a self-proclaimed Higher Intelligence from another

---

[99] Psalm 139:14, "I will praise You, for I am fearfully and wonderfully made; Marvelous are Your works, and that my soul knows very well."

[100] See chapter 11.

dimension would be the *ambassador of Oneness*, an extraterrestrial messiah laying claim to the evolutionary imperative by announcing that ***his race*** seeded Mankind on Earth. Or possibly the image is something we manufacture to be subsequently highjacked; an Artificial Intelligence possessed and "made alive" by a malevolent spiritual entity. All of this is conjecture, the stuff of movies. The Bible, however, describes a coming Man of Lawlessness.[101]

Using the vernacular of psychological warfare, could it be that the Singularity is a spiritual PSYOPS, the last Great Deception reflecting the first Great Deception?

The future, grounded in the distant past, races into our present.

Techno-Religiosity

Modern transhumanism has resurrected a marginalized philosophical religion, birthed a "trans-religion," and energized a subset of the Mormon faith.

For transhumanists in Russia, the ideas of Nikolai Fedorov and Cosmism have been renewed. Fedorov, who died in 1903, was a quiet librarian who advocated a synthesized philosophy constructed from Russian Orthodoxy and technical progress. Looking upon the resurrection of Jesus Christ as an example to follow, Fedorov held that God intended humanity to engage in *self-resurrection*.

In other words, if Jesus could rise from the dead, then Mankind must find a technical way to likewise achieve this eminent goal. Given enough time, everyone from the past, present and future would be raised to immortality through the spiritual application of technology.

David F. Noble merges his commentary with Fedorov's thoughts,

> Federov combined the ideals of Russian Orthodoxy, the Russian aristocracy, and the Russian peasant commune into a doctrine of what he called 'the Common Task,' the unification of all humanity and the 'removal of all the obstacles that prevented the evolution of man's humanity toward its last stage, the stage of self-creation, immortality, and God-likeness'... This transformation, which entailed the reconstitution of the bodies of past humans, demanded mankind's complete mastery and control over the universe, including space.[102]

[101] 2 Thessalonians 2:1-12.
[102] Noble, *The Religion of Technology*, p.121.

Early Russian Cosmists also incorporated Theosophical and occult ideas, Perennial philosophy and Gnostic approaches, self-organizing complexity and chaos theory, Russian cultural sentiments, and mystical science – "higher magic partnered to higher mathematics."[103]

While Fedorov discouraged some of the esoteric teachings of his contemporary futurists, the Cosmist worldview opened wide the doors of philosophical imagination. Cosmism also fit within the Russian tendency for totalitarian solutions. In his book, *The Russian Cosmists*, George M. Young explained that it placed the "good of the whole community above the freedom of the individual to go his or her own independent way."[104]

Konstantin Tsiolkovsky – a friend and protégé of Fedorov – believed all matter consists of life, which flows from lower states to ever-higher orders of being. His thought was that as we climb the ladder of material existence, expanding into the universe and reaching the pinnacle of material development, we will finally break free of our physical bodies and move into an era of Gnostic-like spiritual perfection.[105]

Laboring in his homemade laboratory, Tsiolkovsky put his Cosmist and scientific concepts to paper. His ideas were groundbreaking; astronautic theory, multi-stage rockets and spaceflight, artificial gravity and space-based solar energy.[106] He also designed space colonies that could sustain up to 100 people, containers wherein the social elite would move upward while laborers worked for the collective good.[107] His technical papers formed an intellectual path that eventually culminated in the launching of Sputnik 1. Today you can see a prominent statue of Tsiolkovsky, the world's father of modern rocketry and a Soviet hero, sitting under the 107-meter tall Monument to the Conquerors of Space in Moscow. Cosmism then and today looks to space for salvation.

A Cosmist contemporary of Tsiolkovsky worth noting is Vladimir Ivanovich

---

[103] George M. Young, *The Russian Cosmists: The Esoteric Futurism of Nikolai Fedorov and his Followers* (Oxford University Press, 2012), p.3.

[104] Ibid., p.25.

[105] Ibid., pp.145-154.

[106] Marina Benjamin, *Rocket Dreams: How the Space Age Shaped our Vision of a World Beyond* (Free Press, 2003), p.122. See also Young, *The Russian Cosmists*, p. 148-149 and Noble, *The Religion of Technology*, p.120-121.

[107] Ibid., p.123. Tsiolkovsky also believed in self-perfection by weeding the human population of defective individuals. See Young, *The Russian Cosmists*, pp.151-152.

Vernadsky. Certainly not a household name in the West, his thoughts have nevertheless soaked into our spiritual milieu and the transhuman project.

Vernadsky's importance lies in his theory of the Earth evolving an intelligent biosphere. Others before him had similar ideas and Chardin's belief in the Noosphere, a consciously awakening planet, may have been formulated after attending a lecture by Vernadsky. The Russian, however, was able to press this hypothesis into a synergistic philosophy: *matter has life*.

George M. Young writes, "He was one of the first scientists to emphasize that the exchange of matter leads to a basic unity of the planet, its human inhabitants, and the cosmos."[108]

All things, according to this creed, share a unity of life. In expounding on Vernadsky's theory, Young contextualized it in a remarkably familiar way,

> We are, in a very deep sense, related to all on our planet – to animals, vegetables, and minerals, as well as to other human beings, and as the rational component of the biosphere, we have a responsibility, literally, to all.[109]

In light of this we are all considered Global Citizens, and our allegiance *must* be to the Earth – and not just as an inanimate object, but personified as thinking matter. We could call this the image of Gaia, *the living planet* or Mother Earth. Young writes: "As inhabitants first and foremost of the cosmos and the planet, human beings owe allegiance to the biosphere more than to any other nation, ethnic entity, economic class, or system."[110]

Cosmism today is fashionable.

In my 2013 interview with Dmitry Itskov, the founder and host of the Global Future 2045 International Congress, he explained that Tsiolkovsky was "definitely the person who inspired me." Specifically, it was Tsiolkovsky's vision of "radiant mankind and this transformation from this material body to the energetic form of a human body, it is spiritual transformation."[111]

Dmitry, whose evolutionary mission began with an experience of spiritual transformation, invoked Tsiolkovsky's name and dream during his opening

---

[108] Young, *The Russian Cosmists*, p.156.

[109] Ibid., p.157.

[110] Ibid., p.158.

[111] Dmitry Itskov, interviewed by Carl Teichrib for Magnum Veritas Productions, LLC., June 16, 2013, GF2045. Interview location: Empire Hotel, New York City.

speech at the GF2045. It was not the first or only time I would hear Tsiolkovsky mentioned.

The Cosmist goal of unlimited transhuman freedom – escaping the bonds of Earth – was also visible in the GF2045 introductory video: The planet is on the brink of global collapse and we must either choose a new dark age or a new paradigm in human evolution; a complete technological and social revolution is therefore required if Man is to survive; BCI, artificial intelligence, and simulated worlds will point the way forward; and with this revolution will come a new ideology, ethics, psychology and culture, and even a new metaphysics. By creating manageable matter, we will move our consciousness into an *artificial carrier* and upload our personalities into a series of nearly immortal avatars. Then we can reach for the universe and ascend to the stars. The new gnostic man, unencumbered by Earth and limiting matter, will then be devoted to "spiritual self-improvement."[112]

GF2045 is certainly not the only example of Cosmism within the transhumanist movement. Much of the community has, in broad or specific ways, adopted some elements of the Russian philosophy. Giulio Prisco, a former analyst with the European Union Space Agency and past director of the World Transhumanist Association,[113] is a modern day apostle. I have personally spent time with Prisco while attending a conference of the Mormon Transhumanist Association, and our avatars have crossed paths in Second Life. Prisco is devoted to the post-human cause and advocates a new Cosmism: "Science and religion, spirituality and technology, engineering and science fiction, mind and matter. Hacking religion, awakening technology."[114]

Ben Goertzel is another modern Cosmist, noting that science requires faith as we look beyond the data points to seek a holistic future. Recognized for his brilliance in artificial intelligence, cognitive robotics and perceptual psychology, Goertzel holds a Ph.D. in Mathematics and is the author of *A Cosmist Manifesto*.[115] His volume bridges science and psychedelics, technology and philosophy, Carl Jung's Collective Unconsciousness and mathematics.

[112] *2045: A New Era for Humanity* (2045 Initiative, released in 2012 as a lead-up to GF2045). This video is available online.

[113] The World Transhumanist Association later morphed into Humanity+, an influential transhuman think tank.

[114] The quote comes from a sidebar paragraph in Giulio Prisco's Turing Church blog [http://turingchurch.com], accessed June 2, 2017.

[115] As taken from his online CV [http://goertzel.org/Goertzel_resume.pdf].

In his discussion of the "global brain," a subject he specializes in, Goertzel offers two possibilities. First, the merging of individuals within the collective intelligence, "sacrificing much of the individuality we currently associate with being human, but gaining a feeling of oneness with a greater mind." Or a system that retains a certain level of individuality without complete immersion, "connecting to the global brain could be more like using the Internet today – but an order of magnitude more pervasive."[116]

"Assuming a free society, interacting with the global brain would be optional," he wrote, "but nearly everyone would take the option, just as so many other highly convenient, inexpensive technologies have been adopted by nearly all people given the chance."[117]

He is correct. Humanity will opt in.

Trans-humanism has also birthed a trans-faith. In 2002, Martine Rothblatt officially launched the Terasem Movement, a self-described *trans-religion*. Terasem – meaning "earthseed" – incorporates teachings on technical immortality and mind uploading, prayers, rituals, and Kundalini yoga. It is a fusion of spirituality, visionary creativity, and a secular faith in technology.

But what does it mean to be a trans-religion?

Gabriel Rothblatt, Martine's son and a Terasem pastor, gave an explanation during the 2013 Mormon Transhumanist Association's annual conference: "Trans-religion means transcending religion. It means encompassing all religions. Essentially, secularism." Core traits of the techno-faith, Gabriel explained, are joyful immortality, unity, and diversity – "the self-fulfilling prophecy of creation."[118] Terasem's central beliefs: life is purposeful, death is optional, God is technological, and love is essential.

Martine Rothblatt argues that classical religions will eventually conform to the technological extension of humanity. Of special interest to the Terasem founder is the religious acceptance of *mindcloning*. By uploading massive amounts of personal information – creating what they call *mindfiles* – it is hoped that when some future technology comes online, these databases can

---

116 Ben Goertzel, *A Cosmist Manifesto: Practical Philosophy for the Posthuman Age* (Humanity+ Press, 2010), pp.235-236.

117 Ibid., p.236.

118 Gabriel Rothblatt, speech titled *Terasem Movement Transreligion*, given during the Mormon Transhumanist Association annual conference, April 5, 2013. A video copy of his presentation is posted on the MTA YouTube channel [https://youtu.be/BcQqFYXeFDo].

be reconfigured into the "conscious prostheses of ourselves."[119] Rothblatt expects that this digital personality will then desire spirituality, and trusts that traditional religions will recognize the copied soul of the virtual human double as valid. Equating the soul to consciousness and then extrapolating the mindclone to the function of an organ, Martine writes,

> No classical view of religion believes you transplant a soul when you transplant a heart. Nor can you kill a soul by killing the body. Hence, the mindclone continues to radiate the soul of its person whatever may have occurred to the associated body. Beautifully, this is consistent across atheism and theism...
>
> ...Mindcloning will be viewed as a medical technology, analogous to organ transplants, a life-extending technology embraced by even the most classically minded adherents to Judaism, Christianity, and Islam.[120]

Important to this story is Rothblatt's personal life.

Having been born as Martin in 1954, the global communication and satellite expert announced being trans-gendered at the age of forty. The following year, 1995, Rothblatt's revolutionary volume, *The Apartheid of Sex*, argued for gender fluidity and trans-genderism as a social norm.[121] *The Apartheid of Sex* played a major role in promoting the concept of gender as a social construct; labels of male and female are acts of injustice, as sex is a complex continuum; and creative expression is negated when we constrain sex and gender to binary roles. Gender, like humanity itself, would be *trans* in the spin-cycle of social transition.

In the 2011 edition of *The Apartheid of Sex*, re-titled *From Transgender to Transhuman*, Rothblatt recounts the non-binary position, adding the following in the Preface,

> In a similar fashion I now see that it is also too constraining for there to be but two legal forms, human and non-human. There can be limitless variations of forms from fully fleshed to purely software,

---

[119] Martine Rothblatt, *Virtually Human: The Promise – and the Peril – of Digital Immortality* (St. Martin's Press/Picador, 2014), p.270.

[120] Ibid., pp.268-269.

[121] Martine Rothblatt, *The Apartheid of Sex: A Manifesto on the Freedom of Gender* (Crown, 1995).

> with bodies and minds being made up of all degrees of electronic circuitry between. To be transhuman one has to be willing to accept that they have a unique personal identity, beyond flesh or software, and that this unique personal identity cannot be happily expressed as either human or not. It requires a unique, *transhuman* expression.[122]

Terasem is obscure outside of the transhumanist community. However, to post-human thinkers and techno-utopians, this new secular religion is a beacon of enlightened progressivism.

Transhumanism has also energized the creation of a Mormon-based organization, the Mormon Transhumanist Association (MTA). Unlike Terasem, the MTA is not a religion in itself but a network to advocate transhuman goals with an unapologetic Mormon stance: "Mormonism mandates transhumanism."[123] In other words, rapidly advancing technologies point to a fulfillment of the Mormon teaching that man is to strive for exaltation, to become as God. Although the majority of its membership is Mormon, mainly affiliated with the Church of Jesus Christ of Latter-day Saints, it is not exclusive to Mormons. Atheists, agnostics, and progressive Christians are part of its demographics. Gabriel Rothblatt has been a member of the MTA. Cosmist Giulio Prisco, an atheist transhumanist who adopted a religious position due to his MTA involvement, is a member.

Responses to the 2014 MTA *Members Survey* offer some extra details as to the composition of its body. In terms of Cultural Politics and Economic Politics, 53% and 31.8% see themselves as Progressives; 75% are married and have never been divorced; 85.7% are male; and 42.2% have earned a post-graduate degree.[124] Interestingly, as transhumanist organizations go, the MTA has experienced relative longevity. Other groups have started and then fragmented or faded away.[125]

---

[122] Martine Rothblatt, *From Transgender to Transhuman: A Manifesto On the Freedom Of Form* (Martine Rothblatt, edited by Nickolas Mayer, 2011), p.xiv, italics in original.

[123] Lincoln Cannon, then president of the MTA, made the statement during the 2013 MTA conference (April 5). For more on the connection between Mormonism and transhumanism, see Allsop et al, "Complementary Aspects of Mormonism and Transhumanism," *Parallels and Convergences: Mormon Thought and Engineering Visions* (Greg Kofford Books, 2012, edited by A. Scott Howe and Richard L. Bushman), pp.67-92.

[124] *Mormon Transhumanist Member Survey 2014 Summary*; on file.

[125] From what I have gathered, most have failed due to internal tensions and clashes.

Formed in 2006 with 14 people, the MTA had close to 600 members ten years later. But numbers are always less important than narrative and reach, and in both it has demonstrated success: first in moving the conversation past secularist boundaries, and then in projecting the post-human theme beyond its membership. Indeed, much of the recent transhuman shift from secular approaches to religious contexts have come through MTA input. And in terms of reach, the association's voice has touched a broader audience. In 2015 the journal *Theology and Science* published an essay on Mormonism and transhumanism, and articles broaching the two showed up in *HuffPost UK*, *Mail Online*, *The Daily Dot*, and *iDigital Times*. *The New Yorker* published a piece the following year, and the popular online tech-site, *New Atlas*, ran a story in early 2017. From 2010 onward the Mormon group has been mentioned in various works exploring transhumanism,[126] and the MTA itself collaborated on a book, *Parallels and Convergences: Mormon Thought and Engineering Vision*.[127]

However, the MTA's annual conference has raised its reputation as a platform to explore techno-ethics and to bolster post-human speculations. Transhumanists and futurists like Natasha Vita-More, James Hughes, Giulio Prisco, Aubrey de Grey, Eric Steinhart, and Robin Hanson have shared the podium. Likewise Mormon historians and authors, and MTA members – many with professional backgrounds – have presented papers and theories. And sometimes critics have been invited to speak.

I traveled to Salt Lake City in 2010 to attend the MTA conference, *Transhumanism and Spirituality*. Held on October 1st at the University of Utah, this

[126] The MTA is mentioned in the following works: Robert M. Geraci, *Apocalyptic AI: Visions of Heaven in Robotics, Artificial Intelligence, and Virtual Reality* (Oxford University Press, 2010); Gregory R. Hansell and William Grassie (editors), *H+/-: Transhumanism and Its Critics* (Metanexus Institute, 2011); Catherine Wessinger (editor), *The Oxford Handbook of Millennialism* (Oxford University Press, 2011); Maxwell J. Mehlman, *Transhumanist Dreams and Dystopian Nightmares: The Promise and Peril of Genetic Engineering* (John Hopkins University Press, 2012); Morgan Luck (editor), *Philosophical Explorations of New and Alternative Religious Movements* (Routledge, 2012); Calvin Mercer and Derek F. Maher (editors), *Transhumanism and the Body: The World Religions Speak* (Palgrave Macmillan, 2014); William Sims Bainbridge, *Dynamic Secularization: Information Technology and the Tension Between Religion and Science* (Springer International Publishing, 2017).

[127] A. Scott Howe and Richard L. Bushman (editors), *Parallels and Convergences: Mormon Thought and Engineering Vision* (Greg Kofford Books, 2012).

event explored religious and technological boundaries. The MTA president outlined his *New God Argument* and Terryl Givens connected mythology and the human-divine struggle in his presentation, *Fear and Trembling at the Tower of Babel*. Others talked of humans and spiritual entities locked in a struggle for scarce resources; that all life is interconnected in the quest for spiritual perfection; and that transhumanism should be a next-gen religion intent on unifying humanity. One speaker suggested it was time for faith communities to evolve perceptions of God and spirituality, shifting theology to embrace paradox and replace dogmas with questions: "Part of evolving spirituality is paying attention to how we image God."[128] Giving a keynote, Max More contrasted atheist transhumanism against the "petulant child... cosmic sadist" of the Old Testament.

"I should tend to want to discourage talking of gods in transhumanism," More said. "I think we can probably do better than that..."[129]

Evangelical Christianity was not given high marks.

I penned an article about the meeting and published it in my magazine, *Forcing Change*. Later this was circulated within the Mormon transhumanist community and elsewhere. Many months afterwards Lincoln Cannon, a co-founder of the MTA, contacted me.

Would I be willing to attend the 2013 conference to give a Christian critique of religious transhumanism?

I was surprised by the request but thankful for the opportunity, and appreciative that the organization would consider bringing a critic to the table. This was an open door and I agreed to participate.

When I arrived at the venue in Salt Lake City, Cannon – a perceptive and eloquent spokesperson for Mormonism and transhumanism – immediately shook my hand and said, "You're brave to be here." I understood the sentiment, for my evangelical beliefs and worldviews stood in contrast to those around me. But Cannon was taking a risk too. By inviting an outside critic he was courting a level of uncertainty, and with it, the potential for pushback from his own community. It was a gutsy move on his part and by the MTA board, who treated me with courtesy and respect.

---

[128] Quoted by Carl Teichrib, "The Rise of Techno-Gods: The Merging of Transhumanism and Spirituality," *Forcing Change*, Volume 4, Issue 10, October 2010, p.10-11, as drawn from audio recordings and research notes from the conference.

[129] Ibid., p.11.

Having only fifteen minutes to make a case, the standard time given to most of the presenters, my talk had to be concise yet meaningful. This was far from easy. For days I had struggled over my task and sleep had been elusive. My desire was to communicate in a way that was heartfelt and loving, honest and truthful. The potential for misrepresentation and miscommunication was ever on my mind, and I wrestled with this responsibility up to the moments before my name was called.

What did I say?

The speech is publically available,[130] but the basics are thus: An acknowledgment that Christianity is not opposed to human betterment through technology, however it is the issue of salvation that is at the core of its tension with transhumanism. After giving a brief survey of the Biblical perspective of God's relational design in Genesis 1, that all things were created by Christ Jesus as the Author of Life (John 1:3), that humanity broke fellowship with God and therefore chose the path of death, and that Jesus Christ entered the world of men – experiencing death but defeating this enemy in a finalizing act – I closed by focusing on Christ's crucifixion, specifically the one thief hanging by His side.

Allow me to expand on this.

In preparing for my talk, I was struck by what took place at the cross. Jesus, hanging naked and scourged and beaten, was being publicly executed between two thieves. Consider the narrative from the Gospel of Luke,

> Then one of the criminals who were hanged blasphemed Him, saying, 'If You are the Christ, save Yourself and us.'
>
> But the other, answering, rebuked him, saying, 'Do you not even fear God, seeing you are under the same condemnation? And we indeed justly, for we receive the due reward of our deeds; but this Man has done nothing wrong.' Then he said to Jesus, 'Lord, remember me when You come into Your kingdom.'
>
> And Jesus said to him, 'Assuredly, I say to you, today you will be with Me in Paradise.'[131]

---

[130] Carl Teichrib, *A Conservative Christian Critique of Religious Transhumanism*, speech given to the Mormon Transhumanist Association, April 5, 2013. Posted on the MTA YouTube channel: https://youtu.be/VFxDVZjyjeE. You can also read a copy of the speech in *Forcing Change*, Volume 7, Issue 4, April 2013, pp.14-18.

[131] Luke 23:39-43.

Specifically, it was what was *missing* that caught my attention.

Notice that Jesus did not tell the man he would be saved by doing good works – in fact, the thief was dying because of his crimes. Good works were out of the question. Nor did He say to the thief, "Find a technical or scientific solution to your problem of death." Neither did He say to join the priesthood, or follow temple obligations, or start a charity, or go to church, or even be baptized. There was no eight-point path to enlightenment, no constructing "Heaven on Earth," no postures for liberation, no chants or spells or rituals. The thief was being executed *now* and could do *nothing practical*.

And this returns us to our present state-of-affairs. Like the thief, there is nothing technical to be done on our part. For us, the problem is *positional*. Just as one man's act of disobedience to God, Adam in the Garden, became representative of the human race, condemning us to death without our say in the matter, so our salvation could only come through one Man being obedient, without guilt, having the ability to overcome death – without our say in the matter.

This would require none other than the Author of Life to directly intervene. It would have to be *His perfecting act* given as a gift. The Apostle Paul put it this way: "For by grace you have been saved through faith, and that not of yourselves; it is the gift of God, not of works, lest anyone should boast." The implication is clear: plusses are not going to work. It cannot be Jesus Christ *plus* technology *plus* politics *plus* religious rites and obligations, plus, plus, plus. The plusses are never ending and never good enough.

In John 14:6 we read the words of Jesus: "I am the way, the truth, and the life. No one comes to the Father except through Me." There may be some temporary good in the plusses, but they are incapable of saving. The real question is this: Will we trust in Jesus Christ for our salvation?

Belief and trust in Jesus Christ was all the robber had left, and that the thief recognized his own sin demonstrates a contrite heart.[132] Belief opens the door to relationship, repentance to forgiveness, trust to expectant hope. Jesus Christ said to him, "Today you will be with Me in Paradise." For it

---

[132] A great example from the Old Testament is King David in Psalm 51. "For You do not desire sacrifice, or else I would give it; You do not delight in burnt offering. The sacrifices of God are a broken spirit, a broken and a contrite heart – these, O God, You will not despise" (Psalm 51:16-17).

would be Christ, by the power in Himself, in God the Father and the Holy Spirit – the Deity-in-trinity[133] – through which death would be conquered three-days later. As the Apostle Paul said in his letter to the early Christians, Jesus Christ is the "firstborn from the dead, that in all things He may have the preeminence."[134]

The thief's soul was safe in the *perfect position* of the Redeemer.

For those who, like the thief, admit our inability to save ourselves – who believe and repent, entering into a relationship of trust with the Author of Life – a New Man is born.

This is not the New Man of Marx or Lenin. This is not the Supreme Being of Comte or the Übermensch of Nietzsche or the Master Race of Nazi Germany. Neither is this the Perfected Man of Theosophy or the "Good Man Made Better" of Freemasonry or Chardin's UltraMan. It is not Exaltation through the rituals and obligations of Mormonism. Nor is it the neo-human dream of eugenicists or the post-human vision of transhumanists.

No, the New Man in Christ – the person whose salvation is placed in the *already resurrected* Messiah – is *new* in a different way. Redeemed in the position of Christ, the person is now spiritually aware and awake. The ancient letter to the church in Ephesus illustrates what this looks like: to no longer walk in the futility of a darkened understanding, a person alienated from God, living a life of self-gratification and greed. Instead, walking in the truth of Jesus Christ, to discard our former conduct, "the old man which grows corrupt" and to renew the spirit of our mind, "that you put on the new man which was created according to God, in true righteousness and holiness."[135]

The character of the New Man is to be established on the image of God, graced with tender mercies, kindness and humility, expressing power with reservation and gentleness – the meaning of meekness – to be longsuffering,

---

[133] Consider who raised Jesus from the dead: Jesus Himself – "No one takes it from Me, but I lay it down of Myself. I have power to lay it down, and I have power to take it again. This command I have received from My Father" (John 10:18); God the Father – "whom God raised up, having loosed the pains of death, because it was not possible that He should be held by it" (Acts 2:24); And the Spirit – "But if the Spirit of Him who raised Jesus from the dead dwells in you, He who raised Christ from the dead will also give life to your mortal bodies through His Spirit who dwells in you" (Romans 8:11).

[134] Colossians 1:18.

[135] See Ephesians 4:17-23.

"bearing with one another, and forgiving one another." The New Man is to put on love, "which is the bond of perfection" and to "let the peace of God rule in your hearts." We are to be thankful to God, acknowledging Jesus Christ in our words and actions.[136]

We are saved through faith, but after salvation the New Man is to exemplify this in what we say and do. The new life is active, not passive. Faith without works is a dead religion.[137]

I will be honest. While my salvation is in the finished work of the Messiah, the Old Man in me battles with the New Man I am supposed to be. A day is coming however, when those in Christ will be raised by Him in spirit and body: *Resurrection to life*.[138]

Vacation Death

What the Bible says about trusting Christ for perfection and a coming resurrection is dismissed by atheist transhumanists, even as they strive for perfection and resurrection. Religious transhumanists, on the other hand, tend to add plusses to what Christ accomplished. Of course, if what the Creator of Life did was insufficient, then Mankind as a created being is even more helpless. The problem cannot be the solution.

Scientifically escaping personal extinction and re-animating the dead are inescapable themes in transhumanism. It was manifest at GF2045.

Dmitry Itskov put this into a utopian framework, telling me that racial and national tensions will cease, and war will become impossible "because there will be no death."[139] By 2045, Itskov and others contest, our minds "will become substrate-independent." In other words, our *transferable* consciousness will be able to choose its own body types, shape shifting nano-robotic forms or "body holograms featuring controllable matter."[140] Peter Diamandis projected his idea of an "immortal planetary meta-intelligence," writing

---

[136] See Colossians 3.

[137] See James 2:14-26.

[138] See Romans 6:9.

[139] Dmitry Itskov, interviewed by Carl Teichrib for Magnum Veritas Productions, LLC., June 16, 2013, GF2045. Interview location: Empire Hotel, New York City.

[140] "Future Prospects of 2045 Initiative for Society," *Global Future 2045 International Congress* (official program), June 2013, p.5.

in the Congress program: "We will no longer have to die a physical death, enabling who we are... to continue for a far longer time."[141]

While at GF2045, I had the opportunity to interview Natasha Vita-More, the wife of Max More and a transhuman designer passionate about "whole body prosthetics." She speculated what death might look like in a *post-terminal* existence,

> Death ought not to just have one express definition... we will be redefining death the more and more we develop the sciences and technologies to intervene with death. So, we have to look at death from various perspectives. You may want vacation death. You may want partial death. You may want to be put into cryonic suspension or another type of preservation unit... and then come back and revisit life again. So there are all sorts of alternatives to this finality of death.[142]

Examples of the transhuman dream of death-suspension and future resurrection abound.

Before transhumanism became the intellectual movement it is now, American writer Alan Harrington offered a survey of immortality. His perspective demonstrated the anti-God sentiment of the 1960s cultural shake-up,

> Death is an imposition on the human race, and no longer acceptable. Men and women have all but lost their ability to accommodate themselves to personal extinction: they must now proceed physically to overcome it. In short, to kill death...
>
> Our survival without the God we once knew comes down to a race against time. The suspicion or conviction that 'God is dead' has lately struck home not merely to a few hundred thousand freethinkers but to masses of the unprepared. Ancient orthodoxies may linger, but the content of worship has begun to collapse. This is what makes our situation urgent: around the world people are becoming increasingly less inclined to pray to a force that kills them.[143]

---

[141] Diamandis, *Global Future 2045 International Congress* (official program), June 2013, p.15.

[142] Natasha Vita-More, interviewed by Carl Teichrib for Magnum Veritas Productions, LLC., June 16, 2013, GF 2045. Interview location: Empire Hotel, New York City.

[143] Alan Harrington, *The Immortalist* (Celestial Arts, 1969/1977), p.3.

Years later, mathematical physicist Frank Tipler postulated a naturalist theory of Eternal Life in his book, *The Physics of Immortality*.

According to the Tulane University professor, the Christian belief in a spiritual being called God and the non-material idea of the soul are faulty but not beyond redemption. God, Heaven, and life evermore can be manifested through quantum mechanics in a coming Omega Point. The monotheistic faiths, he argued, are expressions of mathematical constructs: "The key concepts of the Judeo-Christian-Islamic tradition are now scientific concepts. From the physics point of view, theology is nothing but physical cosmology based on the assumption that life as a whole is immortal."[144]

Tipler's Eternal Life Theory, riding the Cosmist theme of *material resurrecting material*, understandably received pushback from his academic peers. However, what was once ridiculed as scientific absurdity is chic philosophy – the allure of *mystical materialism*.

But something else needs to be considered: Just because techno-elites are serious about scientific immortality does not mean their naturalist dream is within reach. At GF2045, one transhuman philosopher told me that he had been striving for resurrection most of his adult life. Quieting his voice in sober reflection, he acknowledged that for almost thirty years this had been his primary pursuit and yet, with all the technical advances of the past three decades, he was not one day closer to immortality. The irony did not escape me. I too believe in a coming resurrection and look forward to that glorious day, but our faiths are placed on different foundations: One in the shifting sands of silicon, the other the Rock of Ages; one in the endless toil of fallible hands, the other in the Author of Life – *who already proved Himself by walking out of the tomb*.

Breaking the death barrier is the hope of famed innovator Ray Kurzweil. In his bestsellers, *The Age of Spiritual Machine*s and *The Singularity is Near*, the technologist proposed that our memory information – our *mind files* – could be the keys to immortality. Correlating the human body to computer hardware, he advocated for backing up our personalities,

> Up until now, our mortality was tied to the longevity of our hardware. When the hardware crashed, that was it... As we cross the divide to instantiate ourselves into our computational technology,

[144] Tipler, *The Psychics of Immortality*, p.17.

> our identity will be based on our evolving mind file. *We will become software, not hardware*...
>
> As software, our mortality will no longer be dependent on the survival of the computing circuitry. There will still be hardware and bodies, but the essence of our identity will switch to the permanence of our software. Just as, today, we don't throw our files away when we change personal computers – we transfer them, at least the ones we want to keep. So, too, we won't throw our mind file away when we periodically port ourselves to the latest, even more capable, 'personal' computer...
>
> Our immortality will be a matter of being sufficiently careful to make frequent backups.[145]

Kurzweil is equating *information with life*.

"Ultimately software-based humans will be vastly extended beyond the severe limitations of humans as we know them today," he writes.[146] And in evolving away from personal extinction, he muses, we will no longer need to rationalize our demise. Death will be defeated by data.

The Terasem Movement embraces the mind file concept by encouraging its members to partake in *mindcloning*, the creation of a digital double that will supposedly live beyond biological death through virtual reality. Mind file dossiers are constructed by having Terasem members submit as much personal information as possible, as often as possible: pictures and other media, documents, and journal entries detailing one's experiences and emotions. Terasem can also bank samples of your DNA and in the unknown future when science supposedly catches up with the dream, your mind file memories will be uploaded to a reconstructed body.

What is important to keep in mind is this: Everything being described is driven by a determined worldview. Consider the words of Giulio Prisco,

> We will develop spacetime engineering and scientific 'future magic' much beyond our current understanding and imagination. Spacetime engineering and future magic will permit achieving, by scientific means, most of the promises of religions – and many amazing

---

145 Ray Kurzweil, *The Age of Spiritual Machines: When Computers Exceed Human Intelligence* (Penguin Books, 1999/2000), pp.128-129, italics in original.

146 Kurzweil, *The Singularity is Near*, p.325.

> things that no human religion ever dreamed. Eventually we will be able to resurrect the dead by 'copying them to the future.'[147]

Zoltan Istvan offered an imaginative scenario during his 2015 Terasem Island talk, suggesting that the Christian "heaven" could be constructed in virtual reality. Or through "quantum archeology," a *time-magic technology*, we might "come up with a way to resurrect every single human being that ever lived, at any time in history, and give them a chance to live again, if they want – or give them a chance to just be dead." This "Jesus Singularity," he believed, would fulfill Christian prophecy.[148]

Aging and death: if these two fundamental problems could be overcome, then tensions between people and conflict between nations could be resolved. Such thinking lies behind RAAD Fest, a project of the Coalition for Radical Life Extension. Located in beautiful San Diego, California, RAAD – Revolution Against Aging and Death – is an immersive and collaborative transhuman gathering designed as the "Woodstock of radical life extension."[149] Part conference, part festival, RAAD brings together leading thinkers, tech-innovators and scientists, futurists and artists and musicians in celebration of immortality. Together through the power of our knowledge we can live forever, together we reach for something more.

If this is a type of Second Genesis, it is not a re-creation but a *re-fall*.

In reviewing the contemporary transhuman theme of immortality, I am reminded of Alan Harrington's earlier prediction of a transitional generation. After examining the state of 1960's medical knowledge and the promise of cryonics, he forecast a coming period that would lie between the dying society and the rise of immortalists,

> Members of the transition generation will almost surely not live to experience the immortal state. Knowing this, we will have to psych ourselves, like athletes, into a superior performance. We can begin with a self-congratulatory religion rather than a humbling one, spreading abroad a new faith, honoring our race instead of punish-

[147] Giulio Pisco's mini-manifesto has been reprinted in Ben Goertzel's book, *A Cosmist Manifesto* (Humanity+ Press, 2010), pp.10–11.

[148] Zoltan Istvan, "Transhumanism," presentation at the 10th Colloquium on the Law of the Futuristic Persons, December 10, 2015, Terasem Island, Second Life.

[149] The first RAAD Fest took place August 4-7, 2016 and August 9-13, 2017.

> ing it for an imaginary primal crime. Through our efforts we honor the human species by helping to turn it into the divine species.[150]

Some contemporary transhumanists might see themselves as the transitional generation, what Harrington described as "the heroes and heroines of the evolutionary process."[151]

For others, hope and trust is centered on finding a technological solution to death before their passing. From either perspective, however, to be truly post-human requires mastery over mortality – to enter the realm of divinity, *to be as God*.

Being and Becoming

Transhumanism is the quest to move from *being* to *becoming*: from being human with all of its mortal flaws to becoming divine-like in knowledge and capacity. God-talk, regardless of how individual transhumanists frame deity, is rife within the community. It runs three ways: We become gods, or our machines become gods, or by our techno-evolution we awaken the universe to its god-state. All three speak to one boast – *Man is God*.

The Mormon view often communicates the first position. In *Parallels and Convergences: Mormon Thought and Engineering Vision* – co-sponsored by the Mormon Transhumanist Association – we read the following,

> The end point of engineering knowledge may be divine knowledge. Mormon theology permits us to think of God and humans as collaborators in bringing to pass the immortality and eternal life of man. Engineers may be preparing the way for humans to act more like gods in managing the world.[152]

Lincoln Cannon's opening speech during the 2013 MTA conference followed a similar pattern,

> The Mormon Transhumanist Association stands for the proposition that we should learn to become Gods, and not just any kind of God, not the God that would raise itself above others, but rather the God that would raise each other together. We should learn to become

[150] Harrington, *The Immortalist*, p.273.
[151] Ibid., p.273.
[152] Richard L. Bushman, "Forward," *Parallels and Convergences*, p.vi.

> Christs, saviors for each other, consolers and healers, as exemplified and invited by Jesus.[153]

Obviously I fundamentally disagree with this assertion.

However, Lincoln's attitude is much different than Richard Seed's approach, and I compare the two only to show the range of thinking found within the broad community. While Lincoln hopes for a mutually beneficial god-state, Seed, the physicist who made national news for supporting human cloning in the late 1990s, allowed hostility to show in an interview for the documentary, *TechnoCalypse*,

> We are going to become Gods. Period. If you don't like it, get off. You don't have to contribute; you don't have to participate. But if you're going to interfere with me becoming God, we're going to have big trouble. Then we'll have warfare.[154]

Seed went on to say, "the only way to prevent me is to kill me; and you kill me, I'll kill you."[155]

It would be easy to dismiss Seed's rhetoric as hubristic nonsense, especially in that before the national spotlight turned on him for his cloning advocacy, he was a little-known figure. Seed's words, nevertheless, play into a contextual reality: The history of Man "playing God" is one of deepest subjugation and destruction. We proclaim the good but are unable to break from that which is evil; we are incapable of resisting the allure to become a god *made in our fallen image*.

When Kevin Kelly, then editor of *Wired* magazine, wrote his 1994 book *Out of Control*, he openly dabbled in god-talk. Considering the direction of virtual reality and the possibilities of a techno-hive, Kelly recognized the appeal of human deity through technology,

> Stripped of all secondary motives, all addictions are one: to make a world of our own. I can't imagine anything more addictive than being a god... Godhood is irresistible.[156]

---

[153] Lincoln Cannon, *The Purpose of the Mormon Transhumanist Association* (presentation), Mormon Transhumanist Association annual meeting, April 5, 2013, Salt Lake City, UT.

[154] Richard Seed, *TechnoCalypse*, written and directed by Frank Theys (Votnik, 2006).

[155] Ibid.

[156] Kevin Kelly, *Out of Control: The Rise of Neo-Biological Civilization* (Addison-Wesley

Could our technical creations be set loose to discover their own sovereignty? Might our innovations make some future attempt at *becoming*?

Kelly toyed with these underlying ideas,

> ...as we unleash living forces into our created machines, we lose control of them. They acquire wilderness and some of the surprises that the wild entails. This, then, is the dilemma all gods must accept: that they can no longer be completely sovereign over their first creations.
>
> The world of the made will soon be like the world of the born: autonomous, adaptable, and creative but, consequently, out of our control. I think that's a great bargain.[157]

John Glad pondered something similar: "Will the computer have a God? Will God have a God?"[158]

Comparing "carbon-based technology" – human beings – to computational technology, it was clear to Glad that the human brain was too restricted by its size and speed and time needed for learning. Limitless machines would therefore win the day,

> Any effort to improve the human brain is targeted at an instrument which is inherently limited in its capacity. The machine brain, on the other hand, will be something like God.[159]

Ben Goertzel wrestled with ideas of *evolving mind* and *building god*,

> Whether or not transhuman minds now exist in the universe, or have ever existed in the universe in the past, current evidence suggests it will be possible to create them – in effect to build 'gods.' As well as building gods, it may be possible to become 'gods.' But this raises deep questions regarding how much, or how fast, a human mind can evolve without losing its fundamental sense of humanity or its individual identity.[160]

Publishing, 1994), p.233. The book was also published under the title, *Out of Control: The New Biology of Machines, Social Systems, and the Economic World*.

[157] Ibid., p.4.

[158] Dr. John Glad, interviewed by Carl Teichrib for Magnum Veritas Productions, LLC., February 19, 2013. Location: John Glad's apartment, Washington, D.C.

[159] Glad, *Future Human Evolution*, pp.104-105.

[160] Goertzel, *A Cosmist Manifesto*, p.29, italics in original.

Ray Kurzweil offered a "God" viewpoint through his Singularity model, the reaching of a universal divine-state through the expansion of our technological stepchildren,

> ...we can consider God to be the universe... The universe is not conscious – yet. But it will be. Strictly speaking, we should say that very little of it is conscious today. But that will change and soon. I expect that the universe will become sublimely intelligent and will wake up...[161]

Mark Pesce asserts the immortalist divinity of Man,

> ...once the genome was transcribed, once we knew what made us human, we had, in that moment, passed into the Transhuman.
>
> Knowing our codes, we can recreate them in our so-called synthetic worlds of ones and zeroes: artificial life.
>
> Now that we have discovered the multiverse – where nothing is true, and everything permissible – we will reach into the improbable, resequence ourselves into a new being, debugging the natural state, translating ourselves into supernatural, incorruptible, eternals.
>
> There is no god but Man.[162]

Upon the Tower of Technology we erect idols to ourselves.

At the end of *The Phenomenon of Science*, Soviet cybernetic visionary and mathematician Valentin Turchin pondered the interconnecting paths of evolutionary futures. Looking at humanity from outside itself to gain the "scientific knowledge of reality," he closed with these chilling words,

> We have constructed a beautiful and majestic edifice of science. Its fine-laced linguistic constructions soar high into the sky. But direct your gaze to the space between the pillars, arches, and floors, beyond them, off into the void. Look more carefully, and there in the distance, in the black depth, you will see someone's green eyes staring. It is the *Secret*, looking at you.[163]

---

161 Kurzweil, *The Singularity is Near*, p.390.

162 Pesce, *Becoming Transhuman*, transcript page 12.

163 Ben Goertzel's *A Cosmist Manifesto* is dedicated to Valentin Turchin, quoting Turchin's closing paragraph from *The Phenomenon of Science*; italics in Turchin's original text.

The Future is Past

Cybernetic medicine, brain reverse engineering, neural-dust-enabled BCI, gemenoids and telenoids and robot heads; GF2045 was a showcase of the *already* and the theoretical. But not everything worked out.

"Dmitroid," the android head of Dmitry Itskov – a robotic copy – failed to materialize. Designed by the renowned robotics inventor David Hanson, Dmitroid was supposed to be introduced on the first day of the Congress, but technical glitches kept the android from its public debut. For many participants this was a disappointing turn of events, as Hanson's robots are world-known for their life-likeness.

But it was not the technologies that caught my attention; it was the politics and religion – and the reiteration of crisis to promote the transhuman cause.

To this end, the GF2045 program outlined the need for a new development strategy to address global challenges, and Itskov spoke of bringing lasting world peace. Evolutionary transhumanism would end competition and the struggle for survival, thus the *new human* could bathe in spiritual enlightenment.

Dr. James Martin,[164] the man who literally wrote the book on computers and networking, outlined a series of burgeoning world crisis: overwhelming climate change, an out-of-control human population, resource scarcity, the destruction of agricultural capacity, and massive economic imbalances. All of this, he explained, will require a total transformation of human nature and the reshaping of our future before it arrives. Coal-fired power plants would thus have to be shut down and the world's number of domestic cattle lowered to 200,000 from roughly 1.5 billion. Solar powered "climate change

[164] I interviewed James Martin at GF2045 on June 16, 2013. After the interview, Dr. Martin and I walked from the Empire Hotel back to the Lincoln Center, and during our chat I discovered that he, like myself, grew up on a farm. This commonality immediately created a sense of connection, and he invited me for a meal and a chance to talk off-the-record. It was a fantastic opportunity, but unfortunately I had to decline as another interview was scheduled in the next few minutes. He expressed interest in a future meeting and we reluctantly parted. But I never talked to him again. A few days later on June 24, a kayaker found Dr. Martin dead in the Bermuda Sea not far from his private island. Upon hearing the news of his passing it felt like a fifty-pound weight had hit me. The sobering yet enduring words of Isaiah 40 rings true: "All flesh is grass, and all its loveliness is like the flower of the field. The grass withers, the flower fades, but the word of our God stands forever."

cities," he said, would sprout in the far northern and southern regions of the globe.[165] He noted, with some accuracy I believe, that Russia and China may be better positioned to survive world upheavals. And he predicted the necessity of an international technocracy to manage global society by 2045.

Transhumanism and technocracy; one is a nail and the other a hammer.

One goal of GF2045 was to compel the United Nations to take a leadership role in future human evolution. Itskov wrote in the program book: "I believe that the new evolutionary strategy should be considered at the level of large public and transnational organizations and government leaders."[166] An open letter was sent to then UN Secretary-General Ban Ki-moon, beseeching his support and calling on the United Nations to promote a "strategy for the transition to neo-humanity."

Ban Ki-moon never showed at the Congress, but the petition to consider a transhuman politic demonstrated a growing political awareness.

Religion too was expressed.

From the opening speech to the last day's interfaith panel, spirituality and religion were intertwined within the techno glitter. Cosmism was on display, it was true, but Itskov had opened the door for other spiritual paths. Tibetan Buddhists and Hindu Monks and spiritual sojourners joined in discussing evolutionary transformation.

Quantum activist Amit Goswami argued for the *ground of all being*, the oneness of science, spirituality, and psychology. Transcendent consciousness *is* reality, he explained, calling for a reconfiguration of human nature and the evolution into a quantum society. A one-world soul is encompassing mind and body, matter and consciousness – *we are all one*.[167]

Swami Vishnudevananda Giri, the founder of a Russian yogi school, promoted an evolutionary model beyond the technological. *Transcendent transhumanism* is the goal; science united to spirituality, and the intentional recognition of our God-like nature. He reminded us that the first transhumanists were yogis and spiritual masters, and that our task is to form a

---

[165] Solar powered cities in the far north and distant south infer tie-in to a global energy grid, for the shortened sunlight hours in winter would drastically reduce solar production during months when energy use would be the highest and most critical.

[166] Dmitry Itskov, "On the Path to a New Evolutionary Strategy," *Global Future 2045 International Congress* (official program), June 2013, p.1.

[167] As taken from my notes of the event.

God-like civilization and become immortal God-men – controlling thought and time, and possessing immortal bodies located in multiple realities: "Fantasy will become reality."[168]

Hindu yoga master, Mahayogi 'Pilot' Baba, a former Wing Commander in the Royal Indian Air Force, said something similar: "You are the light, you are the truth, you are the beginning, you are the end."[169]

I recognized where Mahayogi Baba pulled those words. He had borrowed the sayings of Jesus Christ, creating a montage of self-serving spirituality in the place of the Messiah's exclusivity. Baba had combined John 14:6 and Revelation 22:13,

> Jesus said to him, 'I am the way, the truth, and the life. No one comes to the Father except through Me. (John 14:6)
>
> I am the Alpha and the Omega, the Beginning and the End, the First and the Last. (Revelation 22:13)

The words of Jesus Christ in Revelation 22 parallel God's powerful declaration as found in Isaiah 44. Indeed, Jesus Christ is the Redeemer, "the Lord of hosts," declaring Himself as "the First and the Last,"

> Thus says the Lord, the King of Israel, and his Redeemer, the Lord of hosts: I am the First and I am the Last; Besides Me there is no God... Is there a God besides Me? Indeed there is no other Rock; I know not one. (Isaiah 44:6,8b).

The writer of Ecclesiastes famously said there is "nothing new under the Sun."[170] And he was right. *You will not surely die... you will be like God... knowing good and evil.*[171]

Social critic Neil Postman is spot-on: "'Thou shalt have no other gods before me' applies as well to a technological divinity as any other."[172]

Yearning for technical oneness through our "machines of loving grace," transhumanism is Man becoming what we worship.

It is just another *game of gods*.

---

[168] Ibid.

[169] Ibid.

[170] Ecclesiastes 1:9.

[171] Genesis 3:4-5.

[172] Postman, *Technopoly*, p.165.

Chapter 14

Celebrating Oneness

> The mutation is a success, Doctor. The culture war is over. WE WON! – Timothy Leary.[1]

> Our greatest power is in the group; our greatest power is in the group. – Paradox Pollack.[2]

Lasers skimmed across the 15-acre pond, striking the beach near the main sound stage before moving up to spray dancers and flow artists with reds and greens and blues. Behind our gathering, a heavy wall of trees – poplar and oak – absorbed the kaleidoscope, dissipating the beams into the shimmering darkness of the deep foliage. Basslines energized the night air; the ever-present beat absorbing and infusing everyone, then moving outward to be transformed by distance into a dull sounding *doof, doof, doof, doof, doof.*[3] Drops and builds plunged and peaked the mood, cascading and escalating the emotion of the music. Bodies moved and flashed under the effect of strobes. Poi and hoop artists spun in the changing colors.

People drifted through the blurry zone of darkness and light: friends and lovers and strangers. Pungent smoke wafted from the shadows.

---

1 Timothy Leary, *Design for Dying* (HarperEdge, 1997), p.95, capitals in original.

2 Paradox Pollack, acting as High Priest in Pepe Ozán's opera, *The Return of Empress Zoe*, performed on August 31, 1996 at the Burning Man festival in Nevada's Black Rock Desert. "Our greatest power is in the group" was part of a chant given around a small fire with other members of the opera. Video on file with the author; a copy can be found online at https://youtu.be/xkD772SgMuA, *The Return of Empress Zoe*, uploaded by Paradox Pollack. Pollack was co-founder of the San Francisco-based Dream Circus and Mystic Family Circus, and is an actor, director, producer, and choreographer.

3 In Australia, the ever-present thump associated with Electronic Dance Music would come to be known as *doof*.

This fusion of sound, movement and light continued until morning, when the summer sun washed over the stage, the beach, and the tents scattered along the forest trails. The lasers were no longer effective, and most of the partiers were stumbling to their sleeping bags, exhausted or otherwise incapacitated. Disc jockeys (DJs), however, continued to mix songs under the rising orb, playing for the remaining stragglers, but mostly for themselves.

It was July 2015, and I was attending an art and music festival tucked inside a 320-acre tract of woods and meadows. Trails and rough bush roads crisscrossed the property, with the main attraction being an old gravel pit converted into a recreational area, including a private swimming lagoon and beach. It was the perfect hideaway for a weekend of electronic dance music (EDM), conscious experimentation through psychedelics, and for participants to let loose and party.

Admittedly the gathering was smaller than expected. Pre-event interest on social media indicated about 600 people would be attending Dimensional Rift,[4] but the actual number was less than half that. Nevertheless, it was a brief glimpse into what is known as a Temporary Autonomous Zone (TAZ).

Made famous by Hakim Bey, TAZ is an anarchist approach to cultural, social, and political liberation. Recognizing an overlap between civil uprisings and the free flow encountered in festivals and experimental communities, TAZ is viewed as a *liminal* region – an evolutionary space between yesterday's world and tomorrow's dreams, "a moment of cultural disorientation"[5] – where novel experiences take on a transformational quality. Here, participants connect in a co-creative theater of social and spiritual insurrection. Festivity, therefore, acts as *liberating illegality* – that is, the intentional transgressing of normalized culture and formal boundaries.

In the TAZ, the individual encounters a sense of tribe, a temporary utopia where organic community is discovered in a synergy of sights and sounds. It is a *vibe* shaped by the party actors who are influenced, in turn, by *set and setting*. Coming in contact with a range of syncretistic experiences and the feeling of *communitas*, the spectator is transfigured into a participant, an interconnected member of the hive – a node of energy within the net-

---

4 The 2015 Dimensional Rift festival, July 3-5, took place near St. Laurent, Manitoba.

5 Andrew Johner, "Transformational Festivals: A New Religious Movement?" *Exploring Psychedelic Trance and Electronic Dance Music in Modern Culture* (Information Science Reference/IGI Global, 2015), p.60.

work. New social information is generated and absorbed; then, once the event is over and everyone disperses, the experience is re-transmitted into the "default world," soaking into the cracks and pores of civilization.[6]

One way to consider it is this: "heresy as cultural transfer."[7] Dimensional Rift, a minor bush rave, was but a small taste.

My task was to conduct social surveys, talk to partiers and volunteers and sound artists, and try to better understand the broader cultural movement being mirrored in this event. Wearing my Outback hat, equipped with a gnarled walking stick, and armed with a clipboard, I approached participants with a two-page sheet of questions and worldview statements.

Between lunch hour on Saturday – when people were starting to rouse from a night of activities – and late afternoon when a string of supercell storms devastated the event, I was able to conduct a small sampling of surveys.[8] Most who took the time to fill out the form did so amiably, and this opened up space to chat about experiences and expectations. Only a few turned down my request, and one girl was too stoned, slowly handing back her empty paper with an equally empty look.

Although the overall number of questionnaires completed was too low for my satisfaction, they did yield interesting information. Nearly half who filled out the forms claimed to be Christians *in the past*. Based on conversations, it was apparent this was not simply a cultural identifier – rather, there were strong hints of hurt and disillusionment from a former church life. Turning from the Christian faith, they had gravitated to Buddhism, Wicca, New Age, Atheism or Agnosticism, and/or Transhumanism.

---

6 The concept of TAZ was expounded by Hakim Bey, *T.A.Z: The Temporary Autonomous Zone* (Pacific Publishing Studio, 2011, originally published in 1991), pp.67-98. Hakim Bey is the pen name of Peter L. Wilson, a controversial social critic, poet, and anarchist philosopher who spent time studying Tantric and Sufi traditions.

7 Eric Davis, *Nomad Codes: Adventures in Modern Esoterica* (YETI, 2010), p.37. This quote is part of an essay on Peter L. Wilson and the cross-pollination of cultures.

8 2015 was the last year for the annual Rift as the damage caused by the thunderstorms effectively wiped out the operation. Because of the deluge I left the festival early, hoping to make it through the bush road before it became impassable. Others had already exited during the storms, heavily rutting the trail. Bouncing along with my windshield wipers on high and water up to my floorboards in places, my truck's exhaust system snagged something, ripping off the muffler and tailpipe. It was a long drive home; soaked from packing gear in the downpour, and wearing my earmuffs to deaden the noise – the same I wore to catch a few hours of sleep during the festival… *doof, doof, doof.*

When confronted with the statement, "God is separate from nature and me," the vast majority *disagreed*. To the line, "Humanity is valued above nature," most rejected this assertion. "Earth is a living organism" was met with a resounding *yes*.

The responses correlated with the festival theme: *Together. We Are One*.

Unpacking the Visionary Picture

Evolutionary culture, also couched as transformational culture, is an indicator of the West's acceptance of a new outlook: The rejection of the Christian claim, and the desire for enchantment. It is aesthetic and experiential, exploring and shaping – even transgressing and repackaging – the attitudes aligned with Post-modernism, the Self of human potential, and New Age spirituality. Evolutionary culture, grounded in revolutionary social moods, reflects and refines the worldview *already embedded in society*.

While popular culture has done much to facilitate the shift into a new spirituality,[9] the idea of evolutionary culture goes beyond the usual construct of movies and literature. Instead of placing the message within the medium, transformational culture brings it to the forefront with little-to-no pretext or guise. The visionary paintings of Alex Grey falls under this category, and his psychedelic-inspired temple – *Entheon* – located 65 miles north of New York City, exemplifies *spiritual art* as evolutionary religion.[10] Large art installations such as *Aluna* with its depiction of cosmic unity, and *Ilumina* with its message of universal oneness, fits the concept of transformational culture.[11] Publicly accessible Pagan theater, such as Edinburgh's famed Beltane, can be considered in this light.

A range of modes and features can be found, but one expression is of special interest: *transformational festivals*.

---

9 For a sweeping survey, see Christopher Partridge, *The Re-Enchantment of the West: Alternative Spiritualities, Sacralization, Popular Culture and Occulture*, 2 Volumes (T&T Clark International, 2004/2005).

10 Drew Zeiba, "In upstate New York, a DMT-Inspired psychedelic temple rises," *The Architect's Newspaper*, June 13, 2018 [https://archpaper.com/2018/06/psychedelic-art-temple-entheon]. For more on the temple and Alex Grey's spiritual community, see *CoSM: Chapel of Sacred Mirrors – Vision Plan, 2018*. CoSM's Council of Advisor's includes Ken Wilber, Deepak Chopra, Jean Houston, and Matthew Fox.

11 *Aluna* and *Ilumina* were large at installations at Burning Man, 2017.

Media producer and artist, Jeet-Kei Leung, who popularized the phrase "Transformational Festival,"[12] offers this descriptive taste,

> The emerging culture of transformational festivals builds around electronic music's core ritual of ecstatic dance, to incorporate visionary art and performance, workshop curriculums in a spectrum of new paradigm subjects, the creation and honoring of sacred space and ceremony, and a thriving social economy of artisans and vendors.[13]

One academic offered this explanation,

> The entire festival is a playground for amplifying extrasensory experience in an aural world of empathic pleasures. The psychedelic amalgam of music, dancing and other forms of ecstatic entertainment are a sonic entanglement in visceral chemical rapture... The multiplex of out-of-mind, and out-of-body experiences generated through the event's chemical and technological expertise allow attendees to explore an experimental and temporary social hybrid of entertainment, community, and spirituality.[14]

Describing the scene can be problematic.

An expanding library of scholarly literature on the subject exists, but the offering is relatively small. Well-framed Christian critiques are practically absent; as of this writing, a few researched articles are in circulation, primarily on one event – Burning Man – but beyond that, there is little to nothing published on the topic. As far as I know (and I could be wrong), my 2013 essay in *Forcing Change* magazine, clumsy as it was, represented the first Christian critique of the movement as a global phenomenon.[15] But this lack of comparative literature is not what makes a description difficult.

---

[12] Jeet-Kei Leung, interviewed by Saphir Lewis, *The 2013 Festival Guide: Gatherings for Cultural Transformation* (Festival Fire), Issue No.1, p.13.

[13] Jeet-Kei Leung, as stated in the video documentary, *The Bloom: A Journey Through Transformational Festivals – Episode 1, Fundamental Frequencies* (Producer: Jeet-Kei Leung and Ancient Future Now, released 2013).

[14] Andrew Johner, "Transformational Festivals: A New Religious Movement?" *Exploring Psychedelic Trance and Electronic Dance Music in Modern Culture*.

[15] Carl Teichrib, "Celebrations for Transformation: From Burning Man to Tomorrowland and Beyond," *Forcing Change*, August 2013, p.1.

As transformational events are sensory oriented, psychologically powerful, social and spiritual – all at the same time – it is hard to define or explain in just one or two sentences. Like other abstracts such as Post-modernism, the New Age and Re-enchantment, the overall concept has a nebulous quality. Part of the reason is due to being individually empirical; people attend for different reasons, and take away insights that are unique to them. No central authority offers guidance or doctrine, although a general ethos is evident.

In the TAZ, personal and formal identities may be shed, replaced with transient personas. This could be as benign as a temporary name, either made up by oneself for the purpose of play or given by somebody else, usually as a way to remember the person in question. For example, when I was at Burning Man in 2017, a neighboring camp dubbed me *Deer Killer*, for reasons that will become apparent later in the chapter. Alternative personas, however, can be more complex – even psychologically destabilizing, blurring the line between fantasy and reality.

Take, for instance, how an attendee of a particular genre of festival described the challenge of the "real self" to Sarah M. Pike, a professor of Comparative Religions,

> Many – or most – of the social boundaries that these people work with in their ordinary lives are torn apart, melted away and otherwise disrupted in 'festival space.' I think that this is one of the most virulent aspects of liminal space – that it disrupts the ordinary boundaries and definitions, causing new ones to arise.[16]

This accounting of festival space, Pike recognized in the attendees' response, points to "a kind of violence to festival goers' sense of self."[17] This can be a powerful tool for psychological restructuring. By striping away personal boundaries, the individual is vulnerable to *social reassembly*; losing oneself in the moment opens oneself to be restructured by the group experience.

Overall, self is explored within a dynamic context. Participants co-create and share in the flow, "the holistic sensation when we act with total involvement, when action and awareness are one."[18] Outlining this experience of

---

[16] Sarah M. Pike, *Earthly Bodies, Magical Selves: Contemporary Pagans and the Search for Community* (University of California Press, 2001), p.207.

[17] Ibid., p.207.

[18] Victor Turner, *The Anthropology of Performance* (PAJ Publications, 1986), p.133.

communitas within the carnival and parade, anthropologist Victor Turner wrote what is a telling parallel to the contemporary festival encounter,

> ...just as a river needs a bed and banks to flow, so do people need framing and structural rules to do their kind of flowing. But here the rules crystallize out of the flow rather than being imposed on it from without.[19]

Personal and social transformation is consciously pursued within a set-and-setting conducive to *suggestibility*.

Neurochemical changes occur as the sharing of the EDM experience brings a *feel* of connection, sensory overload impresses the mind, and allowance for transgression reframes previous sensibilities. Boundaries shift, and a palpable social mood is generated. The atmosphere evokes anticipation of what *will be* and what *could be*, and the *carnivalesque*[20] – a collective relationship "whose net effect is social leveling"[21] – is lived out within the temporary community. The festival is marked by immediacy and participation, encouraging personal experimentation within a new set of group norms. A scaffolding for social engineering is erected.

There are no spectators in the TAZ.

Room is given for spontaneity and sacrilege and sexuality, thus a non-judgmental and inclusive approach is upheld and celebrated. Traditional and conservative moral standards are traversed, overlapping the social history of raves with its sensual acceptance and blurring of orientations.[22] Depending on the event, clothing may be optional. Space and time to explore models of social and sexual license are not unusual. This may be in the form of workshops and lectures, or theme camps designed to accommodate certain experiences, such as open relationships and polyamory. Sensuality and sexuality is accentuated.

Radical tolerance is the buzz-phrase.

---

19 Ibid., p.133.

20 See Mikhail Bakhtin, *Rabelais and His World* (Indiana University Press, 1984). See also, Victor Turner, *The Anthropology of Performance* (PAJ Publications, 1986) and Graham St. John, *Technomad: Global Rave Countercultures* (Equinox Publishing, 2009).

21 Graham St. John, *Global Tribe: Technology, Spirituality and Psytrance* (Equinox Publishing, 2012), p.219.

22 Jimi Fritz, *Rave Culture: An Insider's Overview – A Primer for the Global Rave Phenomenon* (SmallFry Press, 1999), pp.160-167.

Music is a vital element, with EDM soundscapes being centralizing experiences. Everyone is on the same level, and everyone is connected into something bigger. It has been called the *planetary dance*, a timeless and universal feeling of dropping one's ego and collectively tuning in. One producer put it this way: "Its one thing if you're dancing alone in your room, and it's another experience altogether when different individuals are experiencing oneness through music."[23]

In this respect, DJs become digital shamans and sound-technology becomes a vehicle of felt-transcendence. As explained in the early days of rave by sound artist Goa Gil, a key figure in Goa trance: "I'm basically just using the whole party situation as a medium to do magic, to remake the tribal pagan ritual for the twenty-first century."[24]

Core patterns are discernable from event to event: Communitas and flow, the awareness of an immersive vibe, expressed human potential, social cohesion within the tribe, and reinforcing messages of oneness. The culture oozes sacred secularity, the desire for connection and mystery, and the longing for enchantment.

There is the feeling of a *new homeland*.

And as most festivals are set within natural environments – deserts, meadows and forests, mountain valleys, ocean beaches – there is a sensation of closeness to nature. In fact, the event's physical site undergoes a metamorphosis as colorful structures and stages are erected, artwork and costumes add vibrancy, and performance and play infuses energy. The collective imagination imposes a new meaning on the location itself, with the natural environment acting as both canvas and frame. Sights and sounds merge. Art becomes life; life becomes art.

The *virtual* manifests in the *real* as a "lived utopia."[25]

Spirituality is an important component. Depending on the festival, you may encounter shrines, sacred spaces and temples, religiously charged ceremonies, visionary artwork depicting spiritual evolution, yoga and other forms of holistic participation, and the pursuit of the mystical. Psychedelic

---

[23] Adil Kassam, as interviewed in the documentary, *Electronic Awakening* (Producer: AC Johner with Keyframe-Entertainment and the Federation of Earth, 2012).

[24] Goa Gil, 1994, as quoted by Erik Davis, *Nomad Codes*, p.52.

[25] Graham St. John, *Technomad: Global Raving Countercultures* (Equinox Publishing, 2009), p.121.

substances are part of the panorama, either in the philosophical tapestry or acknowledged as a direct enhancer.

The event itself may be described as *ritual*, and this is accurate.

In this light, transformational gatherings are referred to as *Dionysian*, recalling the ecstatic festivals given in honor of the Greek deity of wine and dance. Attendees of those ancient assemblies would enter a trance-state in which "all borders were dissolved – between the sexes, between classes, between nature and culture, and between man and the gods."[26]

Overlapping myth and ritual within rave culture, one academic writes,

> Here it is not the ritual that finds meaning through mythical re- enchantment, but rather it is the mythological symbolism which acquires depth and significance through the ritual event. In other words, it is not the mythical framework that interprets the ritual gesture, but rather the experience that gives meaning to an imaginary mythological landscape.[27]

Speaking to the religious flavor within psytrance gatherings – a key genre in the broader movement – cultural researcher and scholar, Graham St. John, labeled it as "mystical-based perennialism."[28] Unpacking the layered undercurrents, he described the scene as *technoccult*; a blending of psychedelics, digital soundscapes and cyber networks, ecological mysticism, human potential, and New Spirituality.

Variations of occulture are integrated,

> ...a host of therapeutic, artistic, and spiritual pursuits, illustrate that psytrance inhabits a new spiritual milieu. Itself a network of deviant and hidden knowledge and practice, from magick, prophecies, and shamanism, to astrology, esoteric Christianity, UFOs, and alien abductions, psytrance constitutes a discernable field of contemporary occultism.[29]

---

26 Assaf Sagiv, "Dionysus in Zion," *Azure* (Spring 2000), p.156. Graham St. John brings out the Dionysian aspect in his book, *Global Tribe*, p.200-201. See also Des Tramacchi, "Entheogenic dance ecstasis: cross-cultural contexts," *Rave Culture and Religion* (Routledge, 2004, e-book version, edited by Graham St. John), p.138.

27 Francois Gauthier, "Rapturous raptures: The 'instituant' religious experience of rave," *Rave Culture and Religion* (Routledge, 2004, e-book edition), p.69.

28 St. John, *Technomad*, p.168.

29 Ibid., p.169.

The One-ist orientation of evolutionary culture is readily acknowledged and celebrated. It is not an overstatement to say that this is, indeed, the point. One-ism holds the center: "Now you know that you, me, everything is one, or God as you wish to call it."[30]

In the rave-festival documentary, *Electric Awakening*, the separating nature of traditional religions – specifically Christianity – is contrasted with the holism expressed in transformational gatherings. Event organizer, Liana Sananda, outlines the fundamental difference between the two paradigms using a One-ist lens,

> That's what established religions have done; is said, God is separate, God is other, God is outside of you. And this is what I think has been the great fall from grace, is humanity disconnecting from the experience of spirituality. Part of what we are doing at these gatherings is regaining our natural, intuitive wisdom and redeveloping this deep experience of the divine.[31]

In considering the spiritual facet, allow me to share a brief story.

During a trip to California in February 2015 – ironically, to give a talk on transformational festivals at a TruthXChange conference – I found myself, for a short time, sitting beside a young lady in the Minneapolis airport. She was carrying a performance hula-hoop, and there was something about her mannerism that struck me.

"Are you a flow artist?" I asked as she made herself comfortable. "Yes!" was her immediate response, excited that someone recognized her art form.

"Which transformational festivals have you been to?"

She named several in the eastern United States, including Pennsylvania's EvolveFest, noted for its Ascension Temple, and now she was traveling west to participate in more. Her commitment was obvious, so my final question before separating was simple, yet revealing: "What links all of this together? What binds the movement?"

"It's all spiritual," she answered without hesitation. "It's all very spiritual."

Transformational festivals are *spiritual containers*, dedicated spaces to explore and shape an *ancient-future worldview*. It is where the mythical and mystical coalesce with the technological and digital. Evolutionary culture, it

[30] Federico Sommariva, rave promoter and DJ, as quoted by Jimi Fritz, *Rave Culture*, p.188.

[31] Liana Sananda, as interviewed in the documentary, *Electric Awakening*.

could be argued, is a *new religious movement*. Festival acts as the Church of Re-enchantment.

These events are also *social containers*, zones where the "default world" is pushed aside for a different version of reality. Often it is a hybrid of libertarian self-expression and self-morality within a group driven sense of unity-in-experience. Festival acts as a *sandbox* for social engineering: "These events are temporary visits to the future we are building."[32]

So who goes? Counter to the stereotype, these are not "hippie gatherings." I have met university students and software developers and nurses and construction workers and business owners and retirees... the list is long. Occupations aside, here is a glimpse of education levels of those who attended Freezer Burn in 2017, a regional Burning Man event annually held near Ponoka, Alberta. That year I surveyed 10% of the festival population, and of the 86 forms filled out, 20 participants had some college or university, 34 held a Bachelors degree, another 12 had their Masters (two listed double Masters), and one had a Doctorate. In other words, those attending are the people in your neighborhood.

Evolutionary culture is a reflection of the shift occurring around you.

265 Pins

In considering transformational culture, it is essential to recognize that this movement can be viewed narrowly, or through a more ample lens.

Narrow, in that there is a specific genre known as *Transformational Festivals*, the letters capitalized as a term for gatherings like Ohio's Rootwire and California's Lightning in a Bottle, British Columbia's Shambhala and New Brunswick's Evolve, Australia's Rainbow Serpent, Costa Rica's Envision, Brazil's Universo Paralello, and Malta's Earth Garden. The above-mentioned assemblies – a small sampling – are blends of electronic dance music, yoga and energy healing, visionary artwork, connection and spirituality, workshops, play performance, and intentional community. Personal and social transformation is expected.

Earthdance certainly fits the mold as a global celebration of social justice and planetary activism, wrapped in EDM, Gaia-consciousness, and community ritual. Hundreds of planetary-synchronized Earthdances have taken

32 Saphir Lewis, "It's 2013. Post Apocalyptic 2012, We Are In the New Era and It's Teeming With Life," *The 2013 Festival Guide*, p.4.

place since 1997.[33] Today, the movement is aligned with the United Nations International Day of Peace.

But a wide range of festival modes fits within the interpretation, for the concept infers a level of broadness and flexibility, producing what could be categorically referred to as (small-letter) *transformational festivals*. A variety of social, cultural, and spiritual strands are tied into this framework. And while EDM serves as the musical core for so much of the culture, diverse forms and themes exist beyond the music.

Employing this wider lens, the following groupings have been noted for their change qualities: Yoga festivals and other Hindu-based gatherings calibrated for Western consumption, like Colorado's Hanuman Festival and the Holi Fest at Utah's Sri Sri Radha Krishna Temple; celebratory events geared to the Pagan community,[34] such as Starwood and Pagan Spirit Gathering in the US Midwest; and mythical festivals catering to fairy and folk lore, such as Oregon's FaerieWorlds. Eclectic events such as the long-running Oregon Country Fair and Saskatchewan's Ness Creek Festival, incorporating nature and spirituality, art and music, communitas and mutual story, can be included under the umbrella.

Raves, and especially psytrances, are foundational to the overall scene, having long been recognized for their spiritual and social properties.[35] The Sacred Earth Open-Air psytrance festival, annually held in the US Midwest, offers this about itself: "Our gatherings are about transformation and becoming. Whatever your sense of spirituality is, you bring that to the event."[36]

Germany is host to a plethora of psytrance gatherings, and Portugal's bien-

---

[33] The idea of a synchronized, global dance festival for world unity and Earth consciousness came to musician, Chris Deckker, through a vision while he was inside the King's Chamber of the Great Pyramid in Giza. In 1999, the Earthdance operation moved to San Francisco and the event was coordinated with the UN International Day of Peace: "From its psy rave roots, Earthdance has grown to become one of the largest globally synchronized music and dance events, having been held in over 1,000 locations in 80 countries." – Earthdance, *History* [www.earthdance.org/story], accessed June 5, 2018.

[34] For a detailed examination of Pagan festival from the perspective of participant observer, see Sarah M. Pike, *Earthly Bodies, Magical Selves: Contemporary Pagans and the Search for Community* (University of California Press, 2001).

[35] See Jimi Fritz, *Rave Culture* (SmallFry Press, 1999); Graham St. John, *Technomad* (Equinox, 2009) and *Global Tribe* (Equinox, 2012).

[36] *Sacred Earth Open-Air: About the Experience*, [www.sacredearthopenair.com/ experience], accessed May 29, 2018.

nial Boom Festival – the mothership of psytrance – attracted 40,000 people in 2014. Boom's 2018 vision statement reads,

> At Boom, music is sacred. The dancefloors are temples for transcending ordinary states of perception and the limitations of our egos. Through dance and music, we can reconnect to our own individual divine essence, while in synch with the beating heart of the whole tribe. All in One!... Boom's ultimate aim is to facilitate individual and collective transformation.[37]

Graham St. John describes the Dance Temple at Boom as "a place where all of one's senses are accounted for and rearranged."[38]

In his words, the Boom experience was akin to "passengers aboard a transdimensional lightship," where "participants behave as altered sensory lifeforms."[39] The language St. John uses reflects the blending of occulture elements and themes: *remixticism*, *media shamanism*, *techgnosis*.

Psytrances offer a "techno-logic towards re-enchantment."[40]

Flow art events, tribal convergences, goddess gatherings, and solar festivals like the 2017 Oregon Eclipse, which brought together 30,000 people for seven days to celebrate the Sun; all find placement within the larger milieu of transformational culture.

Some music extravaganzas like Belgium's TomorrowLand demonstrate an overlap, a commercialized concentration of social energy. Described as "the United Nations of festivals,"[41] this EDM mega-event is one of the hottest parties on the planet. Brussels Airlines, partnering with ID&T – the company behind TomorrowLand – provides special flights from dozens of countries.[42]

But this is more than just a global blowout; participants are absorbed into a magical mythos. From its thematic legends to its immersive staging and artwork, like the 25-meter abstract of the Goddess Nike – the centerpiece of

---

37 *BOOM Vision*, [www.boomfestival.org/boom2018/vision/boom-vision].

38 Graham St. John, *Mystery School in Hyperspace: A Cultural History of DMT* (Evolver Editions, 2015), p.184.

39 Ibid., p.184.

40 St. John, *Global Tribe*, p.133.

41 Clodagh Kinsella, "Put the Needle on the Record," *bthere magazine* (Brussels Airlines' Inflight Magazine), Issue 92, July 2014, p.30.

42 Brussels Airlines made 236 TomorrowLand flights in 2017. The Brussels Airlines/ID&T partnership is a remarkable example of joint product branding.

the One World bridge[43] – the layered message of TomorrowLand is global unity, communitas, and oneness. Performing DJs frequently refer to this event as sacred, and the festival site itself is officially called *Holy Grounds*.

More than 400,000 people attended the 2017 installment.

Purists would argue that colossal dance events like TomorrowLand are business enterprises, capitalizing on the scene, and thus taking away from the intention of authentic transformation. This is partially true: ID&T is a leading EDM entertainment provider. A million people annually attend its festivals and events, economically participating in the brand.[44] But TomorrowLand sells more than a world-renowned vibe. It preaches: we are *people of tomorrow... we are one*.

So how large is the phenomena of transformational culture? How many *containers of change* dot the landscape? It is difficult to say. The Electronic Dance Music industry, in aggregate, was valued at $7.4 billion US in 2017, a 3% year-over-year increase.[45] Of course, transformational events featuring EDM would constitute a percentage of that total number, and festivals outside the EDM scene would not be counted at all. At the moment, I am unaware of any study that has captured and analyzed the movement's total economic footprint, taking into account EDM and non-EDM assemblies. However, I can provide a rough snapshot of its regional scope.

Desiring to gauge the placement and popularity of transformational culture in the United States and Canada, I started a Google Earth mapping project in 2014. The interpretation I chose in selecting festivals was based on the broader understanding, so Pagan gatherings and significant yoga events like Wanderlust were added. Then, using online sources and print materials, I took the time to assess each event as I found it. When a festival met the criteria to be considered as transformational or represent a major element toward that end, I would pin the exact location and include a short description. Annual, frequent, and single events from 2013 were mapped, along with a handful from the previous year or two that were of special interest.

---

[43] "The Mysterious Sculpture," *TomorrowLand Today*, Sunday, July 24, 2016, p.7. The 2016 theme was The Elixir of Life.

[44] From the ID&T company website: www.id-t.com/company/about (accessed January 13, 2018). ID&T offers more events than just TomorrowLand.

[45] Kevin Watson, *IMS Business Report 2017: An annual study of the Electronic Music Industry* (Danceonomics.com, 2017).

Some gatherings were tiny, that is, less than 100 attendees. Most had hundreds or thousands, and some in the tens of thousands, and more.[46] In terms of geography, the American west coast and British Columbia were splattered with dots. A heavy concentration was found in Colorado. Texas had a fair number, as did Alberta. The eastern seaboard states were lit up, and the Midwest had strong representation – especially with Pagan festivals.

Research and pinning continued into 2016. However, with a sizable list of events still to be vetted, I closed the project down in early autumn. The task had become overwhelming. I already had 265 pins on the map.

In Their Own Words

I have talked with participants inside the TAZ who have only come for the party, to de-stress in an environment wholly other than their day-to-day setting. "To let my hair down, to get out of my skin," as one retired professional told me during Burning Man, 2017.

That the party is an important attraction is without question. In fact, it is probably safe to say that the majority attend for this reason alone, irrespective of social change themes or spiritual inclinations. At Burning Man – arguably the most recognized transformational gathering on the planet – the spectacle itself is a major draw, and the abstract ideas of evolutionary culture may not enter the person's thoughts at all. A retired couple from Ottawa told me they annually attend for the uniqueness of the place; like taking an *Alice in Wonderland* vacation. One Montrealer bragged how he was just there for the sexual adventure. All of this, of course, has the capacity to incite personal change at some level.

I also talked to people who fully embraced its transformational qualities. And I spent time attending workshops and networking events, listening to and asking questions of those who came as social change agents, culture shapers, and visionary tech-entrepreneurs. Not only did they understand the shift, they were engineering it.

[46] For those who might be wondering, urban raves were not included on the map. Nor did I pin Coachella (99,000 daily attendance in 2016), Electric Daisy Carnival (134,000 in 2016), Miami's Ultra Music Festival (165,000 in 2016), or Chicago's Lollapalooza (estimated at 400,000 in 2016). Tennessee's Bonnaroo (45,000 in 2016, a drop from the 2013 high of 90,000) was added for its incorporation of transformational elements, and Georgia's TomorrowWorld (150,000 in 2014) because of its brand link to TomorrowLand.

Reasons for attending transformational festivals vary, and purpose may be more defined in certain settings. Going to a Pagan assembly like Rites of Spring in Massachusetts has an obvious function: to specifically engage in Pagan interaction. For those participating in other festival genres, like Burning Man, the reasons may be more generic in terms of self and community.

Consider how participants responded to my survey at the 2017 Freezer Burn when I asked why they were attending: "Friends and connection," "to give and receive joy," "fun and meet people," "exploration," "curiosity," "art and visual pleasure," "try and forget about the world," "collective participation," "to love myself," "connection and expression," "to broaden my horizons," "add to the party," "socialization and introspection," "seeking unique experiences," "to open my mind," "be in a space of magic and love," "relax my spirit," "to love and be loved."

One woman in the 55-64 year-old bracket explained that she came to spend time with her daughter, and to find healing. Her answer to the question of religious identification: "Broken hearted."

In other words, those attending were hoping to meet some personal need, or contribute to that end: the longing to do something with purpose and value, the desire for novelty, the craving for meaningful interaction, and love. Many came for the party, others gravitated to the spiritual, and some understood the transformational aspect and sought this end.

One artist scribbled on my survey, "To make a sacrifice to the art gods in gratitude for my creative energy." Others wrote, "We are all one," and, "Collective will and intention." Someone else penned on the bottom of her page: "This is about community... We all share a connected consciousness, people working together to build a space of synergy, symbiosis."

Strong themes of collective and personal transformation can be gleaned from the broader culture,

> What we're trying to do, all of us here – everyone of us – is developing our personalities and our spirituality to go to higher dimensions.
> – Raja Ram, sound artist.[47]

> The rave experience is about coming together with a unified vision and one-mind. It's about raising a huge amount of collective energy

[47] Raja Ram, sound artist, speaking at Psy-Fi, Netherlands. *Psy-Fi Official Aftermovie 2017*, published on January 24, 2018, available to be viewed at https://youtu.be/P84aXN4H0zQ.

for an intensely spiritual experience. And that is more powerful than any drug. – Kim Stanford, Toronto Raver Information Project.[48]

Within a few days, it permanently expanded my sense of what humanity could become... The festival was an initiation, in itself. – Daniel Pinchbeck, author.[49]

These festivals are really doorways to open a whole, life altering change, and that leaves a real door open for the person [who comes] for the music act, and then they find a whole another world of spirituality... And then it takes them into a whole another journey in life that they never expected. – Debra Giusti, festival producer.[50]

I know a lot of people have the same story, but the experience of Burning Man was just so overwhelming and so powerful that it literally set my life on a 90-degree turn from the direction it was heading, and I never looked back. – Jesse Flemming, festival producer.[51]

Simply the most extraordinary spiritual and political and cultural thing that has ever happened to me, and it, of course, completely affected the rest of my life. – John Rinaldi, event promoter.[52]

What's happened is that we've now gone into what I think is a process, what some people call Re-enchantment, where into this void [of disenchantment] people have started to create their own sense of the sacred, and of myth and legend. – Jason Pfizl-Waters, programming director, FaerieWorlds Festival.[53]

In the 2017 *Black Rock City Census*, an annual survey designed to reflect the entire population of the temporary city that makes up Burning Man,

48 As quoted by Jimi Fritz, *Rave Culture*, p.43.

49 Daniel Pinchbeck, *How Soon is Now? From Personal Initiation to Global Transformation* (Watkins, 2017), p.4.

50 Interviewed in *The Bloom: A Journey Through Transformational Festivals – Episode 1.*

51 Interviewed in *The Bloom: A Journey Through Transformational Festivals – Episode 1.*

52 As interviewed in the video documentary, *Dust and Illusions: 30 Years of Burning Man* (Madnomad Films, 2009). Rinaldi is known as "Chicken John" in the San Francisco arts-and-Burning Man community.

53 As interviewed in the video documentary, *The Bloom: A Journey Through Transformational Festivals – Episode 3, New Ways of the Sacred* (Producer: Jeet-Kei Leung and Ancient Future Now, released 2013).

22.3% said they "absolutely" had a transformational experience that year. Another 22.6% answered "somewhat" to the question of personal transformation. Only 10.5% said "not at all."[54]

Surveys are important tools for analyzing an event's composition and the scope of impact, in this case, transformational qualities. But data-points cannot capture the myriad of personal experiences. Everyone has a story.

I am reminded of a young man at the Dimensional Rift festival who was describing to a small group how the night's combination of drugs, music, and lights had set up his mind for ecstatic visions. In the tent next to mine, sound artists were structuring their psychedelic intake to achieve desired moods and effects. On a very different spectrum, while in the Temple at Burning Man, I watched as people poured out their grief and pain, longing for healing and cathartic transformation. At Freezer Burn, one middle-aged couple – clean and sober, *for the festival is the drug* – explained how the event had imparted a new sense of wonder and purpose.

The festival, the couple insinuated, was their church.

Transformative Backdrops

Music, dance, art, celebration, community; in this, transformational culture is constructed on common features of the human experience. Regarding its modern history, however, the broader movement has its roots in the soil of the 1960s, and in points of contact paralleling that era's cultural and social revolution. It draws from the Post-modern attitude, from the human potential movement, from the Perennial mood, and from a longing for connection – to each other, and to the Earth. There is a distinct and profound psychedelic backdrop, and that the movement would even exist without this context is doubtful.

Today's transformational culture is tethered to the modern past.

Taken together with what has been written in previous chapters, the following information adds to the overall picture. The first part touches on the spirit of the age, the second on the role of art, then the psychedelic road trip of 1964, and the celebration of a growing counter-culture. Each is a snippet from a complex era. Finally, we will sample the ripple effects that followed.

---

[54] *Black Rock City Census: 2013-2017 Population Analysis* (BRC Census Lab, 2018), p.139.

Do What Thou Wilt:

During the 1950s and early '60s, disillusionment with "Establishment government, Establishment religion, even Establishment philosophy" resulted in a cultural yearning for alternatives.[55] Rationalism and materialism, the "atomic age" worldview, was being "jettisoned in favor of the ancient belief in magic, myth, and the mystical."[56] One man's occult philosophy was of special importance in setting the tone for generational rebellion.

Aleister Crowley, who lived from 1875 to 1947, was a British magician and socialite of infamous reputation. His involvement with esoteric societies, the Hermetic Order of the Golden Dawn and the Ordo Templi Orientis,[57] thrust him into the occult currents of Europe and America. Crowley's own mystical quest incorporated yoga, ceremonial magic, hashish, and sex rituals; and he developed a series of rites around the use of mescaline to "induce religious ecstasy."[58] Renowned for his bi-sexual appetite and many mistresses, his penchant for public attention and his larger-than-life personality, the newspapers dubbed him the "wickedest man in the world."[59] Crowley referred to himself as the Beast 666.[60]

In 1904, Crowley and his clairvoyant wife went in Cairo, Egypt, where "a messenger from the forces ruling this earth" gave a spiritual transmission.[61] The result was a handwritten tract, *The Book of the Law*, spelling

---

[55] Hans Holzer, *The New Pagans* (Doubleday and Company, 1972), p.xi.

[56] Gary Lachman, *Aleister Crowley: Magick, Rock and Roll, and the Wickedest Man in the World* (Jeremy P. Tarcher/Penguin, 2014), p.325.

[57] Aleister Crowley attended Cambridge University before joining the Hermetic Order of the Golden Dawn, an esoteric society focused on magical rituals. He later formed the A.·.A.·., a spiritual college designed around Kabalistic teachings, and he was the most noted personality in the history of the Ordo Templi Orientis. Of his thoughts on Christianity, Crowley wrote the following in relation to his early life: "I did not hate God or Christ, but merely the God and Christ of the people whom I hated. It was only when the development of my logical faculties supplied the demonstration that the Scriptures support the theology and practice of professing Christians that I was compelled to set myself in opposition to the Bible itself... The sum of the matter is that Judaism is a savage, and Christianity a fiendish, superstition." Aleister Crowley, *The Confessions of Aleister Crowley* (Arkana/Penguin, 1989), p.73.

[58] Colin Wilson, *The Occult: A History* (Random House, 1971), pp.363-364.

[59] Richard Cavendish, *The Black Arts* (G.P. Putnam's Sons, 1967), p.41.

[60] Aleister Crowley, *The Confessions of Aleister Crowley* (Arkana/Penguin, 1989), p.387.

[61] Aleister Crowley, *The Book of the Law* (Weiser Books, 1976), p.5.

out a spiritual-moral philosophy known as *Thelema*. The essence of this Law embodied the desire of Will under the maxim, "do what thou wilt." True Will, the alignment of Self and cosmic purpose, would be discovered through "magick," the technique of Power applied to Will.

"What is a Magical Operation?" asked and answered Crowley. "It may be defined as any event in Nature which is brought to pass by Will."[62]

His outlook was decidedly One-ist. Speaking of the magician who seeks to exert influence, the Beast 666 wrote, "*as a Mystic*, he knows that all things are phantoms of One Thing... that all things are in himself, and that he is All-One with the All."[63]

Crowley had essentially connected Nietzsche within an esoteric framework. Or as *Playboy* editor and counter-culture guru, Robert Anton Wilson, said of this anti-Christian philosophy, it was a "blend of Nietzschean Super-manism and anarcho-fascist Darwinism."[64]

Sin, to Crowley, was only that which is restrictive.[65] "Do what thou wilt shall be the whole of the Law," was the epicenter of his morality-shaking worldview.[66] In his ritual, *The Mass of the Phoenix*, the Selfist credo was reinforced within the context of pursuing one's own pleasures: "There is no grace: there is no guilt: This is the Law; DO WHAT THOU WILT!"[67]

The *idea* of Crowley as a trend-setting *transgressor* found favor in the 1960s. Jim Morrison of the Doors and Jimmy Page of Led Zeppelin drew from his antinomian creed, and Mick Jagger of Rolling Stones was reported to be interested.[68] In an interview, John Lennon said: "The whole Beatle idea was to do what you want... do what thou whilst, as long as it doesn't hurt somebody."[69] And a young David Bowie sang of affinity to the Golden Dawn, being "immersed in Crowley's uniform of imagery."[70]

---

[62] Aleister Crowley, *Magick: In Theory and Practice* (Dover Publications, 1976), p.107.

[63] Ibid., p.120, italics in original.

[64] Robert Anton Wilson, *Cosmic Trigger: The Final Secret of the Illuminati* (Pocket Books, 1977), p.61.

[65] Crowley, *The Book of the Law*, p.23.

[66] Ibid., p.50.

[67] Crowley, *Magick*, p.330, capitals in original.

[68] See Gary Lachman, *Aleister Crowley* (Jeremy P. Tarcher/Penguin, 2014).

[69] Quoted by Lachman, *Aleister Crowley*, p.326.

[70] David Bowie, "Quicksand," *Hunky Dory* (RCA Records, 1971).

Crowley's philosophical fingerprints were discernable through the music, movies, and literature of that era.[71] The Beast 666 was a cultural icon.

Timothy Leary, the Harvard psychologist and LSD visionary, said that "do what thou wilt" was the "theme of the Me-generation." He went on to say that while Crowley was "not around to receive the credit he deserves, he is surely smiling in the Thelemic cosmos he now inhabits."[72] The magician's great genius, explained Leary in *Design for Dying*, was that he democratized decadence.[73]

Rebellion, wrapped in moral relativity, was Crowley's gift to the 1960s. Break the rules, go beyond convention, pursue your carnal passions, be your own master, exert your Will: *transform through transgression*.

Changing Art:

In the early years of the 20th Century, new artistic styles and attitudes reflected disenchantment with modernist assumptions. Art forms were pushing against accepted boundaries. Cultural and social norms, and political and economic structures, were being reinterpreted through a radical lens.

Dada, a literary and visual genre pulling from Cubism and Futurism – and drawing from the emotional and material wreckage of World War I – turned the art world on its head by accentuating the absurd, ridiculing social sensibilities, re-assembling the random, and mocking the rational. Capitalism and nationalism were objects of artistic scorn. Dada tended to warp the normal, twisting the mundane into non-meaning. Although overlap exists between Dadaism and Surrealism, the latter focused on the creative unconscious while the former pushed absurdity and chance.

Art historian Peter Conrad writes,

> Dada existed to destroy preconceptions: its motive was what [Tristan] Tzara called 'the Satanic insistence' on asking 'What for?' – the same quizzical imprudence that drives Milton's fallen angel. Through their capricious teasing, the Dadaists gave vent to 'the chaotic wind of creation'... Creativity was breezy, irregular, a chaotic disruption of the atmosphere.[74]

---

[71] Lachman, *Aleister Crowley*, see chapter 11.

[72] Timothy Leary, *Changing My Mind, Among Others* (Prentice-Hall, 1982), p.192.

[73] Leary, *Design for Dying*, p.94.

[74] Peter Conrad, *Creation: Artists, Gods & Origins* (Thames & Hudson, 2007), p.479.

Art scholar, H.R. Rookmaaker, described Dada as the killing of high value,

> It was Dada that tried to laugh away all that is of value in our world, a nihilistic, destructive movement of anti-art, anti-philosophy, yet with mystic overtones akin to Zen Buddhism. It could well be seen as a new gnosticism, proclaiming that this world is without meaning or sense, that the world is evil – but with no God to reach out to, as God is dead by now...
>
> It used all art forms and tried to break all taboos, all norms for art, all sacred and non-sacred traditions. Dada was a nihilistic creed of disintegration, showing the meaninglessness of all western thought, art, morals, traditions. It destroyed them by tackling them in an ironic way, with black humour, by showing them in their absurdity, by making them absurd.[75]

New Dada-inspired artistic attitudes surfaced after World War II. The Beat Movement, like Dada, expressed dissatisfaction with social conventions.[76]

A nomadic-mystical and risqué nature underscored the Beat, which incorporated poets and writers, musicians, and artists within urban enclaves. Moral permissiveness and sexuality as identification was part of the culture.[77] The movement was one of questioning: "The Beat Movement was one of the earliest manifestations of postmodernism."[78]

The Happenings Movement, a free-play theater style connected to the Beat, added another dimension by involving the viewer as an immersive participant in the act of creation, anarchy, and destruction. Happenings were chaotic settings, "where our own psychological reaction is a part of the effect."[79] Rookmaaker noted that Happenings frequently stepped beyond art, acting as a "new form of political demonstration... and often a new kind of religious rite, or an orgiastic, mystical, atheistic, or rather nihilistic, cult."[80]

A space to project restlessness and transgression had been opened. Revolutions in art portend social change.

---

75 H.R. Rookmaaker, *Modern Art and the Death of a Culture* (IVP, 1973), p.130.

76 M.A. Caws, "Dada," *Encyclopedia of American Poetry* (Routledge, 2001), p.170.

77 Mark Hamilton Lytle, *America's Uncivil Wars: The Sixties Era from Elvis to the Fall of Richard Nixon* (Oxford University Press, 2006), p.51.

78 Paul Varner, *Historical Dictionary of the Beat Movement* (Scarecrow Press, 2012), p.2.

79 Rookmaaker, *Modern Art and the Death of a Culture*, p.181.

80 Ibid., p.181.

Road Tripping:

The summer of 1964 witnessed a strange, American road trip. Ken Kesey, author of *One Flew Over the Cuckoo's Nest*, assembled a group of friends and followers – his Merry Band of Pranksters – and together, in a wildly painted 1939 International Harvester school bus, they tripped across the United States. It was "the great freak forward."[81]

Four years earlier Kesey was a student at Stanford University, writing his novel. Looking to make extra money, his friend Vic Lovell told him about a drug trial at a veteran's hospital in Menlo Park. Volunteers were paid to be guinea pigs, then plied with mescaline, psilocybin, and LSD. It later turned out that the clinical study was part of the Central Intelligence Agency's MK-ULTRA program, a covert mind-and-drug project.[82] But as the story goes, the test subjects turned the tables.

Kesey quickly took a night job in the same hospital, gaining access to the psychiatric ward's supply of substances. A new Bay Area scene took shape around Kesey's liberated LSD. The now successful author quickly became the central figure in a vortex of Pranksters and psychedelic experimenters.

---

81 Martin A. Lee and Bruce Shlain, *Acid Dreams: The Complete Social History of LSD: The CIA, The Sixties, and Beyond* (Grove Press, 1992), p.121.

82 Peter Conners, *White Hand Society: The Psychedelic Partnership of Timothy Leary and Allen Ginsberg* (City Light Books, 2010), p.166. On MK-ULTRA and mind control, see John Marks, *The Search for the Manchurian Candidate: The CIA and Mind Control – The Secret History of the Behavioral Sciences* (W.W. Norton & Company, 1979/1991); Don Gillmor, *I Swear By Apollo: Dr. Ewen Cameron and the CIA-Brainwashing Experiments* (Eden Press, 1987); and Harvey Weinstein, *A Father, a Son and the CIA* (James Lorimer & Company, 1988). The United States General Accounting Office published the following in *Human Experimentation: An Overview on Cold War Era Programs* (GAO/T-NSIAD-94-266): "our review... identified hundreds of tests and experiments in which hundreds of thousands of people were used as subjects. Some of these tests and experiments involved the intentional exposure of people to hazardous substances such as radiation, blister and nerve agents, biological agents, LSD, and phencyclidine. These tests and experiments were conducted to support weapon development programs, identify methods to protect the health of military personnel against a variety of diseases and combat conditions, and analyze U.S. defense vulnerabilities. Healthy adults, children, psychiatric patients, and prison inmates were used in these tests and experiments" (p.3). On page 6: "from 1953 to about 1964, the CIA conducted a series of experiments called MKULTRA to test vulnerabilities to behavior modification drugs. As part of these experiments, LSD and other psychochemical drugs were administered to an undetermined number of people without their knowledge or consent."

A host of personalities entered Kesey's circle. Allen Ginsberg and "Zen lunatic"[83] Neal Cassady, both influential Beat personalities, were part of the group. Timothy Leary's partner Richard Alpert was associated, as was journalist Hunter Thompson. Stanford and Berkley intellectuals rubbed shoulders, as did the Hells Angels, who partied with the Pranksters.[84] Jerry Garcia and his band of musicians, The Warlocks, were in the mix. Music history was made when The Warlocks were re-introduced as the Grateful Dead at a Prankster event in 1965.[85]

What solidified Kesey's place in the nation's cultural history, however, was a monumental Happening. A core group of his Pranksters did the unthinkable; they took the psychedelic experience to main-street USA. In 1964, the great American road trip became the outrageous American acid trip.

Starting in La Honda, California, Kesey and his Pranksters set off across the country in their kaleidoscopic-painted bus – arguably, the first *art car*. On the back was a sign, "Caution: Weird Load," and on the front was the misspelled word, "Furthur."[86] Already outfitted with beds, kitchen and restroom, the bus was upgraded with an external loudspeaker, a roof-mounted sitting deck with an access port, and copious amounts of mind altering drugs. New names and personas were assumed, and the rowdy crew followed the experience where it took them. It was a TAZ on wheels, and the United States was the set-and-setting.

Parading into small towns and big cities with the loudspeaker blaring and public antics to match, the Merry Pranksters would inevitably draw a crowd. Such a sight had never been seen before; such ideas were novel and shocking. People were stunned by the spectacle, having been, in effect, psychologically jolted. A film camera captured the coast-to-coast craziness, and the Pranksters lived within *their own movie*. It was a pressure-cooker experience: Drugs, sex, rock and roll, and shock-induced insanity in a multi-colored, rolling can. The gospel of acid had been preached.

The trip itself had been a circuitous route: Phoenix, Houston, New Orleans, Pensacola, and then up to New York City. They stopped at Timothy

[83] Lee and Shlain, *Acid Dreams*, p.123.

[84] Ibid, pp.119-126.

[85] Andrew Grant Jackson, *1965: The Most Revolutionary Year in Music* (Thomas Dunne Books/St. Martin's Press, 2015), p.252.

[86] Tom Wolfe, *The Electric Kool-Aid Acid Test* (Picador, 1968/2008), p.71.

Leary's mansion-commune in Millbrook, where the East-coast guru had set up his League for Spiritual Discovery.[87] Turning westward, they traversed the US Midwest before angling up to Alberta where the Pranksters attended the Calgary Stampede. There, they picked up a 15-year old girl, deceived the police who were looking for the run-away, and took her to California. Soon after returning to La Honda, a jaunt was made to the Esalen Institute where their leader gave a seminar titled, "A Trip with Ken Kesey."[88]

America had been initiated into the psychedelic '60s.

Happenings of Change:

A cultural crossover was happening in the Haight-Ashbury district of San Francisco. What had been a local haven for Beats was now feeling the influx of the burgeoning Hippie movement. Energized by the music scene emanating, largely, from Los Angeles' Laurel Canyon and Sunset Strip, and turned-on by the Bay Area's psychedelic wave, the Hippie attitude was one of "good times and good feelings."[89] The Hippies celebrated in the "spirit of medieval fairs," while the Beats tended to isolate themselves; the Beats listened to folk and jazz, but the "Hippies wanted to dance."[90]

And dance they did.

On October 16, 1965, in San Francisco's Longshoreman's Hall, a concert party organized by Chet Helms and his art commune, Family Dog, managed to produce a kind of social magic. Pranksters, psychedelic rockers, Beats and Hippies, gelled in a trance-state of dance and drug-induced ecstasy.

"Those in attendance that night sensed that the forces of the Haight scene had converged into something powerful," writes historian Mark H. Lytle. "Kesey saw in that gathering a way to further his quest to turn on the masses."[91]

Kesey put in motion his brainchild, the Acid Tests, to be the method through which the *feeling* could be reproduced. From late 1965 until the end of March 1966, the Pranksters conducted Acid Tests in the Bay Area, Portland, and Los Angeles. These were semi-public LSD parties advertised with the challenge: "Can you pass the Acid Test?" LSD was not yet an illegal substance.

---

87 Tom Wolfe describes the Millbrook encounter in a negative light. However, Graham St. John offers a congenial version in his *Mystery School in Hyperspace* (pp.59-61).

88 Wolfe, *The Electric Kool-Aid Acid Test*, p.119.

89 Lytle, *America's Uncivil Wars*, p.204.

90 Ibid., p.204.

91 Ibid., p.205. For more on this event, see Lee and Shlain, *Acid Dreams*, pp.142-143.

In *White Hand*, a history of Timothy Leary's relationship with Beat poet and Prankster, Allen Ginsberg, author Peter Conners gives this explanation,

> The Acid Tests were LSD-fueled sensory assaults of music, dance, art, and extravagant weirdness that were meant to, as the title implies, 'test' the trippers' psyches under extreme conditions. Unlike Leary's experiments, the Acid Tests weren't about visionary revelation or self-realization for the participants: they were more about releasing cosmic tension and upending the confines of constricting societal mores.[92]

"The Acid Tests were one of those outrages," penned Tom Wolfe in his famous telling of the Kesey episode, "one of those *scandals*, that create a new style or a new world view."[93]

The Acid Test extravaganza, the one that set the counter-culture in high gear, took place on the second-last weekend of January 1966. This was the Trips Festival held in Longshoreman's Hall, near San Francisco's Fisherman's Wharf. Hosted by the Pranksters and their friend, Stewart Brand – who, like Kesey, had been turned-on to LSD through MK-ULTRA, and who later published the *Whole Earth Catalog* – Trips was a three-day blowout attended by 6,000 to 10,000 people.

It was a drug-induced, multi-media, sensory-overloaded, display of boundary dissolving insanity,

> ...with just about every sight and sound imaginable: mime exhibitions, guerrilla theater, a 'Congress of Wonders,' and live mikes and sound equipment for anyone to play with. Closed-circuit television cameras were set up on the dance floor so people could watch themselves shake and swing. Music blasted at ear-splitting volumes while Day-Glo bodies bounced on trampolines. At one point Kesey flashed from a projector, 'Anyone who knows he is God please go up on stage.'[94]

Jerry Garcia of the Grateful Dead tried to describe the madness: "Thousands of people man, all helplessly stoned, all finding themselves in a room of

---

[92] Conners, *White Hand Society*, p.34.

[93] Wolfe, *The Electric Kool-Aid Acid Test*, p.250, italics in original.

[94] Lee and Shlain, *Acid Dreams*, p.143.

thousands of people, none of whom any of them were afraid of. It was magic, far out beautiful magic."[95]

The Trips Festival was not a concert. Trips was, rather, an immersive experience combining media technologies, music and dance, art and performance. It was celebration, transgression, and absurdity with a spiritual feeling of connection. In terms of Western evolutionary culture, Trips was the first transformational festival – a counter-culture TAZ.

One year later, on January 14, 1967, San Francisco's Golden Gate Park was home to the Human Be-In. Unlike Trips, this festival was an outdoors event, portrayed as a *gathering of the tribes*; the idea being that Western civilization must embrace a tribal system,[96] and counter-culture factions – Berkeley activists, Beats and Hippies – needed to merge in a "new and strong harmony."[97] Exact number of attendees remains unknown, but it is estimated that 20,000 to 30,000 people came for the *love-in*.

It was a poorly planned and loosely assembled event. Organizers were debating the night before over how much time should be given to speakers such as Timothy Leary, and one person suggested moving it from Golden Gate Park to the beach for a "groovy naked swim-in."[98] It stayed in the Park, and the music was provided by the likes of Jefferson Airplane and the Grateful Dead. Eastern spirituality and political activism were sermonized for the crowds. Most of all, the Be-In was about *being together*: being in solidarity, in community, and being present in the change.

The Los Angeles Free Press, covering it's own city's much smaller Be-In, also published a report describing the San Francisco vibe,

> 'Welcome,' said a calm voice from the platform. 'Welcome to the first manifestation of the Brave New World.' And a kind of collective sigh came over the audience. Could this be true, could it be really true? Here we were 20,000 blown minds together – gathering for nothing more than love and joy, to celebrate our oneness...[99]

Beat-Prankster-Hippie-Activist, Allen Ginsberg, played a major role in setting

95 Quoted by Lee and Shlain, *Acid Dreams*, pp.143-144.

96 Oliver Johnson, "Pow-Wow," *The Los Angeles Free Press*, January 20, 1967, p.3.

97 "The Beginning is the Human Be-In," *Berkeley Barb*, January 6, 1967, p.1.

98 Conners, *White Hand Society*, p.201.

99 Oliver Johnson, "Pow-Wow," *The Los Angeles Free Press*, January 20, 1967, p.3.

the spiritual tone. He was poetical, experimental, and mystical.[100] Timothy Leary famously roused the masses with his signature motto: "The only way out, is in. Turn on, tune in, and drop out."[101]

Beat poet Lenore Kandel imparted Eastern philosophy to the gathering,

> The Buddha, who will reach us all, through love: not through doctrine, not through teachings, but through love. And, as I'm looking at all of you – all of us – I feel more and more that Maitreya is not this time going to be born in one physical body, but born out of all of us... This is an invocation for Maitreya, may he come: To invoke the divinity of man, through the mutual gift of love...[102]

Ron Thelin, co-owner of The Psychedelic Shop in Haight-Ashbury, the first retail outlet for drug paraphernalia in the United States, described the Pied-Piper effect of the Be-In: "It was like this calling, like a conch shell blowing, 'Hey' – from an ancient time – 'Come out, come back, re-appear; all you Gods and Goddesses, you divine people, home, come'."[103]

Not all shared the hype. The *Berkeley Barb* was critical in its follow-up, saying the Be-In was a waste of time; "the worst thing of all was the emptiness of the speakers, the lack of anything going on."[104]

Although the event was an organizational mess, it sparked a vision. The Be-In *was* a conch shell blowing, and tens of thousands of young people flocked to San Francisco in what became the Summer of Love.[105] Potent drugs, too, flooded the streets of Haight-Ashbury. A dramatic increase in violent crime marked the "acid ghetto," and in the ugly wake of the "good vibes" was a trail of human wreckage.[106]

---

[100] See the event video at *Open Culture*, "Rare Footage of the Human Be-In, the Landmark Counter-Culture Event Held in Golden Gate Park, 1967," (www.openculture.com/2014/09/rare-footage-of-human-be-in.html). Peter Conners' *White Hand Society* details Ginsberg's organizational role.

[101] Conners, *White Hand Society*, p.204.

[102] Excerpted from video footage of the Human Be-In.

[103] Ron Thelin, interviewed in the documentary, *Sgt. Pepper: It Was Twenty Years Ago Today*, aired on KCET Los Angeles, 1987, video on file.

[104] "The Beginning is the Human Be-In," *Berkeley Barb*, January 6, 1967, p.4.

[105] Jean-Francois Revel writes, "In 1967... the hippie population of San Francisco was about 300,000, and San Francisco's total population at the time was less than 750,000." Revel, *Without Marx or Jesus* (Doubleday and Company, 1970/1971), p.208.

[106] Lee and Shlain, *Acid Dreams*, pp.186-193.

A string of concert festivals emerged after the Human Be-In, each a container of celebration for the growing counter-culture. The Fantasy Fair and Magic Mountain Festival incorporated Happenings and music acts, and the Monterey Pop Festival set a new standard for large concert gatherings. The iconic event of the 1960s, of course, was Woodstock with 400,000 partiers.[107]

One historian writes,

> If the music brought the fans to Woodstock, the crowd stole the show... So widespread was the sense of community that people began to see themselves as the 'Woodstock Nation,' suffused in peace and harmony.
>
> Many people came away persuaded that Woodstock signaled a revolution in consciousness. The counterculture was winning the struggle for the nation's soul.[108]

However, a few months later the Altamont Free Festival – a West coast attempt at the Woodstock vibe – turned violent and deadly. As the Rolling Stones performed *Sympathy for the Devil*, 18-year old Meredith Hunter approached the stage with a gun and was subsequently stabbed to death by a member of the Hell's Angels security team. Altamont graphically signaled the result of a "do what thou wilt" society. One observer wrote, "Woodstock is the potential but Altamont is the reality."[109]

The Acid Tests had set minds and spirits in motion. Trips energized the mood. The Human Be-In had rooted the movement, and music festivals functioned as celebratory and transgressive models of realignment.

The counter-culture remained in motion after the 1960s, but it was changing – in part because of the negative impact of the drug scene, the commercialization of the vibe, an eroding national economy, and domestic dissent over the Vietnam War.[110] San Francisco was still home to novel artistic expres-

---

[107] Sheldon Chartier, a personal friend, wandered into Woodstock from the event's backside. He was 14-years old, visiting a neighboring farm, and could hear music from across the field. Curious as to what was happening, he – with his 9-year old brother in tow, and all following the farmer's teenage daughter – walked through the crops and into the festival. Sheldon described his multi-day experience as terrifying, chaotic, and magical.

[108] Lytle, *America's Uncivil Wars*, p.335.

[109] As quoted by George McKay, *Senseless Acts of Beauty: Cultures of Resistance since the Sixties* (Verso, 1996), p.14.

[110] Lytle, *America's Uncivil Wars*, p.338.

sions, radical social ideas, and alternative lifestyle communities. Many early participants, however, transitioned into mainstream society. Others stayed within the scene as it shifted in the years that followed. Some die-hards looked elsewhere to find a familiar groove.

With the backdrop of the 1960s in mind, French social critic and theologian, Jacques Ellul, made the following observation,

> Music, drugs, incense, violence, sexual freedom: festival... The desire is to get one's bearings, and to establish an intervening space foreign to the rest of the world, an ocean in which to plunge without restraint, so as to blot out everything which is not the festival. The festival, greatly longed for by all the contestants as a way of putting down modern society, is acclaimed as an ought-to-be, and as the revolutionary means par excellence.
>
> Here it is, put into actual practice. It is already experienced, sometimes as a way of creating the new life, sometimes as a political method...[111]

Modern Dionysian Man transgresses moral sensibilities while affirming an alternative set of final values: "This call for festival is nothing more or less than a deep religious seething discharging its lava."[112]

America's counter-culture was primarily a spiritual revolution.

Planet Dance:

Tremors from San Francisco's explosive culture pulsed around the world, birthing local and regional flavors. These new expressions morphed and spread, evolving and coalescing.

In Great Britain an underground club scene developed in parallel with America's social revolution. The most notable establishment was London's UFO Club, featuring music acts like Pink Floyd and Jimi Hendrix. The UFO Club was short lived, but it became an iconic outpost in the city's psychedelic skyline. It also embedded an *alien* motif within the counter-culture: We are

---

[111] Jacques Ellul, *The New Demons* (The Seabury Press, 1975), p.142.

[112] Ibid., p.143. Around the same time, Jean-Francois Revel wrote, "a 'revolutionary situation' exists when, in every cultural area of a society, old values are in the process of being rejected, and new values have been prepared, or are being prepared, to replace them." Revel, *Without Marx or Jesus* (Doubleday and Company, 1970/1971), p.9.

all travelers in the cosmic carnival, each having a close encounter or *contact* with our *alien selves*, a theme that seeped into psytrance.[113]

The United Kingdom also witnessed a free festival movement, multi-day music and art gatherings without commercial attachment. These drew large crowds and the negative attention of public authorities.[114] Soon, a nomadic-hippie movement known as the New Age Travelers took shape. Essentially, the Travelers congregated into makeshift caravan communities, moving to and from free festivals. Many Travelers accepted a mythical approach: "a return to the land and to indigenous mysteries associated with the land: ley lines, faery culture, spirits of place, the power of ancient sacred sites, and so on."[115] The world famous Glastonbury Festival has its roots in this milieu.[116]

In line with the New Age Travelers and free festivals, and building on the techno-sounds of the 1980s, was the development of *teknivals*. These were loosely amalgamated techno-carnivals made up of independent sound camps converging on one location. Based on the rave experience, and acting as an alternative response to state restrictions on club/rave gatherings, these multi-day teknivals operated on the margins of society. Free to attend, the movement, however, utilized a *gifting economy* that circumvented commercial interests. But it did more: By embracing the gifting principle, a social framework of participation was created, and expected.

"The party-as-gift, the gift of music, makes demands," explains Anne Petiau, a cultural sociologist. "It calls on each one to contribute and commit oneself to the collective event."[117]

Due in large part to legal pressures, the UK teknival scene pushed outward, spreading into continental Europe and beyond. But teknivals are not just an artistic back-story. Unauthorized techno-carnivals still take place in the UK, Bulgaria, Spain, and Romania. Approximately 60,000 people attended FrenchTek 2018, in spite of legal prohibitions. Teknivals are a facet of today's transformational culture.

---

[113] St. John, *Global Tribe*, pp.203-205.

[114] For one example, see George McKay, *Senseless Acts of Beauty* (Verso, 1996), p.26.

[115] Christopher Partridge, *The Re-Enchantment of the West*, Volume 1 (T&T Clarke International, 2004), p.159.

[116] Ibid., pp.160-162. See also, St. John, *Technomad*, p.35

[117] Anne Petiau, "Free Parties and Teknivals: Gift-Exchange and Participation on the Margins of the Market and the State," *DanceCult: Journal of Electronic Dance Music Culture*, 2015, Volume 7, Issue 1, p.126.

Something else was in motion on the other side of the world. Toward the end of the 1960s, multitudes of die-hard hippies from America and Europe filtered into South Asia, "trying to find themselves in a country where it's easy to get lost."[118] Goa, the former Portuguese colony on the west coast of India, became a counter-cultural haven: A location with lax laws, white sand beaches, psychedelic drugs, all-night parties, and radical self-expression.

San Francisco transplant, Gilbert Levy – better known as Goa Gil – stands out as the quintessential Goa DJ. Gil spent time in Haight-Ashbury with the Family Dog collective during its heydays, but by 1969 he left for Europe, and then made his way overland to India. There he entered the world of the *sadhus*, Hindu monks, and soon Gil was mixing mysticism with music.

By the late 1980s, Gil was producing a hippy-techno-Hindu groove; an amalgamation of yoga mysticism and trance dance – an East-West techno tribal rhythm. It was a *direct experience*, a feeling of timelessness and communion. Graham St. John described it as, "a spiritual carnival of dance in which Shiva, in the androgynous form of Nataraj, Lord of the Dance, became an iconic figurehead typically ripped from Hindu context and pressed into service as a psychedelic superhero."[119]

Goa trance, as Professor Christopher Partridge explains, provided a "sense of transcendence; a sense that the music was connecting the raver to that which was beyond the mundane and the entertaining; a sense that the dancers were gathering as a spiritual community."[120]

Goa Gil gave this interpretation in a 2001 interview,

> The party is Holy! It is the Old Time Religion! Since the beginning of time mankind has used music and dance to commune with the Spirit of Nature and the Spirit of the Universe... we go beyond thought, beyond mind, and beyond our own individuality, becoming One in the Divine Ecstasy of union with the Cosmic Spirit.[121]

Trance became a spiritualized sound technology. Dionysus and Shiva merged under tropical skies: "It's just oneness and unity."[122]

[118] Eric Davis, *Nomad Codes: Adventures in Modern Esoterica* (YETI, 2010), p.45.
[119] St. John, *Global Tribe*, p.202.
[120] Partridge, *The Re-Enchantment of the West*, Volume 1, p.167.
[121] Quoted by St. John, *Global Tribe*, p.85.
[122] Goa Gil, as interviewed in the documentary, *Electronic Awakening*.

Other locations, too, were music hotspots. The Spanish island of Ibiza was the go-to place for European partiers. Young Israelis, on the other hand, favored Goa. After completing their obligatory military service, many Israeli youth would break for the Indian state. Here they would "enter other holy-lands, and entertain experimental post-service identities."[123]

Trance thus found its way to the Jewish nation, and Israel subsequently became a psytrance steamroller, consuming and producing at a level no other country had before.[124] "Trust in trance" was heard in the Holy Land.[125]

Goa influences were also adopted in Australia, spinning a doof culture; bush raves built around psytrance. It moved into European and North American settings, blending with the newer rave scenes – zones of techno and transgression, oneness and expression. Styles changed and splintered and evolved, but the power of Goa in creating the global psytrance phenomena is unmistakable: "techno is the sound of one world shrinking."[126]

Drug interests, too, shifted with the rave environment. MDMA,[127] or Ecstasy – a drug known to produce sensations of empathy – became the substance of choice, amplifying the impression of communitas on the dance floor.[128] With MDMA, this first generation of *global citizens* would feel themselves as interrelated nodes in a cosmic network.

As psytrance became transnational, picking up new flavors, alternative spiritual ideas were also incorporated. A techno-Perennialism was visible, acting as a stage upon which a range of spiritual worldviews could be sampled: "neo/technopaganism, techno/neoshamanism, New Age, Goddess spir-

---

123 St. John, *Global Tribe*, p.237.

124 Ibid., p.234-247. Also, Assaf Sagiv, "Dionysus in Zion," *Azure*, Spring 2000; J.I. Schmidt, "Full Penetration: The Integration of Psychedelic Electronic Dance Music and Culture in the Israeli Mainstream," *DanceCult*, 2012, Vol.4, Is.1; and Graham St. John, "The Vibe of the Exiles: Aliens, Afropsychedelia and Psyculture," *DanceCult*, 2013, Vol.5, Is.2.

125 Joshua I. Schmidt, "Full Penetration: The Integration of Psychedelic Electronic Dance Music and Culture in the Israeli Mainstream," *DanceCult: Journal of Electronic Dance Music Culture*, 2012, Volume 4, Issue 1, p.47.

126 Davis, *Nomad Codes*, p.52.

127 3,4-Methylenedioxymethamphetamine.

128 Jimi Fritz writes that, "Ecstasy is to the rave what LSD was to the psychedelic movement of the sixties. But whereas the sixties were about opening our minds, rave culture is about opening our hearts. With LSD, we may *think* about the nature of love but with ecstasy we are more inclined to feel it as a direct experience." *Rave Culture*, p.138, italics in original. I would argue that love is not a chemically derived feeling but an act of choice.

ituality, Sacred Ecology, Music religion, etc."[129] Psytrance itself functioned as a "synchretic alternative spiritual movement in its own rite."[130]

Counter-cultures in the United States, too, assumed new forms in the post-1960s environment. One of the more eclectic movements, the Rainbow Family of Living Light – a loose network of hippies, folk artists, Pagans, and peace activists – congregated in 1972 for the Gathering of Tribes. Turning their backs on "Babylon," the default world of consumerism, approximately 20,000 Rainbow people trekked into Roosevelt National Park.[131] Their purpose: to "express peace on earth, harmony among all people," "to hold open worship," and honor positive evolution.[132]

It would be a hippy-folksy utopia in a wilderness setting.

With the trappings of Babylon abandoned for makeshift shelters and campfires and primitive living, the Rainbow Family would, for a short time, experience the "New Jerusalem Mandala City."[133] All faiths were welcomed,

> The plan for the city will be an interwoven mandala expressing all aspects of human efforts and achievements, modelled [sic] after plans laid down in the Bible for [the] New Jerusalem (Rev 8,21,22) and corresponding visions in the Vedas, the Koran, the Book of Kells, the vision of Black Elk, the New Mexico Sun Sign, and many other religious texts and visions. They all depict the Holy City and the harmonious coming together of all peoples and races and beliefs to share the differing aspects of varying lifestyles and common communion with the Lord resulting in the reblossoming or rebirth of the Tree of Life and the entrance into the New Age.[134]

Following the 1972 Gathering the Family has annually converged in a national forest somewhere in the United States. Over 13,000 people entered the Malheur National Forest during the 2017 event, and in 2018 they grouped

---

[129] Psyence Vedava, "Exploring Psytrance as Technognosis: A Hypothesis of Participation," *Exploring Psychedelic Trance and Electronic Dance Music in Modern Culture* (Information Science Reference, 2015, e-book edition), p.172.

[130] Ibid., p.172.

[131] Michael I. Niman, *People of the Rainbow: A Nomadic Utopia* (The University of Tennessee Press, 1997), p.32.

[132] *The Rainbow Oracle of Mandala City* (July 1, 1972), inside front cover.

[133] *The Rainbow Oracle of Mandala City* (July 1, 1972), p.15.

[134] Ibid., p.7.

in the Chattahoochee National Forest. The Family's footprint has expanded with regional events and World Rainbow Gatherings.

Part of the mystique is the wilderness itself, a compelling setting for the Romanticized notion of eco-community. Re-enchantment is lived in a social and aesthetic connection with the natural environment,

> The physical space of a Rainbow Gathering, in a natural environment, is itself considered sacred... Nature is not just a sacred object; nature is mother, nature is Gaia, and nature's rhythms represent more possibility and potential than anything created by the humans of Babylon.[135]

Capitalism is disparaged, yet the fact remains that Gatherings are dependent on the resources supplied through the default world. Nevertheless, sharing and de-commodification are important principles in the Rainbow community. Personal change is anticipated, and the Rainbow Gathering has been listed as a transformational event.[136]

While Rainbows offered an eco-hippy, back-to-nature tribalism, other subcultures flowed into America's social stream. Clubs in Chicago and Detroit went from playing Disco to spinning electronic dance music, and Ecstasy made its appearance on dance floors in Dallas.[137] By the late 1980s, the UK rave phenomena had jumped the Atlantic, landing in California.

In his history of rave, Jimi Fritz explains,

> On the West Coast the ethos of the rave scene blended nicely with the hippy mentality and values that had been well established in California since the sixties. In no time at all, the spiritual aspects of rave culture were enhanced and amplified by a new generation of techno-hippies. From California rave spread eastward back across America and in a remarkably short time every state in the union had been exposed to this new cultural sensation.[138]

Psytrance influences converged as well. California became the melting pot.

---

[135] Chelsea Schelly, *Crafting Collectively: American Rainbow Gatherings and Alternative Forms of Community* (Routledge, 2016), p.123.

[136] *The 2015 Festival Guide: Gatherings for Cultural Transformation*, Issue 3 (Festival Fire, 2015), p.48.

[137] Fritz, *Rave Culture*, pp.31-32.

[138] Ibid., p.36-37.

The Moontribe Collective, a techno-community that spun out of Los Angeles' rave scene, took the dance into the Mojave Desert, holding free, Full Moon parties. Jeet-Kei Leung relates how these outdoor parties connected participants to nature. And then something shifted,

> Wiccan, Pagan, New Age and eco-feminists influences saw us intuitively timing our gatherings with the full moons, the solstices, honoring them with some kind of ritual – opening circles, closing circles – in this way, there was a realignment with natural and cosmic cycles, a tuning-in with the Mother, a reconnection and restoring of a relationship full of honor... as urban, technological humans, we had stumbled back upon the most ancient of tribal rituals.[139]

"This is also a future culture," Leung elucidated. "This is the counter-culture of the internet, of the web 2.0 generation."[140]

Evolutionary culture is assembling an ancient-future mythos: A Dionysian impulse lived in the present, with visions of tomorrow. It pulls from the forces of change that shaped America, and the world, during the 1960s. It draws on the ethos of *do what thou wilt* and the social power of transgression, the revolutionary side of art, the psychedelic-fueled experiments in social engineering, and the feedback loop of assimilating subcultures.

Transformational festivals are the shop floor, so to speak, to tinker with radical engines of social change. They are spiritual Happenings.

Playa Fire

On the evening of the summer solstice, 1986, a handful of friends carried a wooden, 8-foot tall human effigy to the shoreline of Baker Beach, a strip of oceanfront along the southwest side of the Presidio in San Francisco. A small but curious crowd assembled to watch as the figure was raised, set in place, and then doused with gasoline. At sunset the effigy was torched.

From its humble beginnings, Burning Man has become an annual, world-recognized gathering that starts on the last weekend of August and ends on Labor Day. Attendance has dramatically increased: less than two dozen in

[139] Jeet-Kei Leung, *Transformational Festivals and the New Evolutionary Culture*, talk given at TEDx Vancouver, November 27, 2010. This presentation may be viewed online at the TEDxVancouver YouTube channel: https://youtu.be/Q8tDpQp6m0A.

[140] Ibid.

1986, 300 in 1989, 1,000 in 1993, 10,000 in 1997, and over 25,000 by the Millennium year. More than 69,000 people attended in 2013, and since 2015 the number of *paying* participants has been capped, officially, at 70,000.

Beyond the growing numbers, the artwork and cultural footprint of Burning Man has become legendary, so much so that in 2018 the Smithsonian dedicated its entire Renwick Gallery to the Burn experience. Academic researchers study its ethos and cultural spread, and social engineers and change agents use the platform to cross-pollinate ideas.

Personnel from technology companies flock to the Burn. This makes sense as the West Coast tech sector is interlocked with the 1960s counter-culture.[141] So much so, that the tech industry carved out its own TAZ, the annual Digital Be-Ins, a cyber-psychedelic spin-off of the 1967 Human Be-In, with presentations by Timothy Leary and sponsorship from Apple, Microsoft, and Yahoo.[142] During the 1997 Digital Be-In, Larry Harvey – the co-founder of Burning Man – compared his event to the digital world, painting the Burn as a "compelling physical analog for cyberspace."

His was an appeal for a new kind of social network,

> Both Burning Man and the Internet make it possible to regather the tribe of mankind, to talk to millions of dispersed individuals in the great diaspora of our mass society. Living as we do, without sustaining traditions in time and ungrounded in a shared experience of place, it is yet possible to transcend these deficiencies. We must use technology to create space stations here on planet Earth, islands of intense and living contact. It is time to come home.[143]

And *come home* they did.

The following year, a new internet search engine – Google – clearly aligned itself with Burning Man. Days before the company was incorporated on September 4, 1998, Google splashed its first doodle on their webpage, the Burning Man symbol. It went up on the 30th of August, hours before the

---

[141] See Fred Turner, *From Counterculture to Cyberculture: Steward Brand, the Whole Earth Network, and the Rise of Digital Utopianism* (University of Chicago Press, 2006).

[142] See the Digital Be-In official webpage: www.be-in.com/ events/past-events.

[143] Larry Harvey, *Burning Man and Cyberspace*, 1997. His speech notes can be found at: https://burningman.org/culture/philosophical-center/founders-voices/larry-harvey/cyber.

event started, sending a message to Silicon Valley that the very week the company would be incorporated, the team would be at the Burn. In its early years, Google headquarters was decorated with Burning Man images and the company ran a free shuttle-bus to the event,[144] and in 2007 the corporation produced an internal video for employees going to the desert festival.[145] One Google milestone is of special importance, the hiring of Eric Schmidt as CEO. After reviewing fifty candidates, Schmidt's résumé floated to the top. Why? Schmidt had been to the Burn. The clincher was taking Schmidt to Burning Man so he could be observed in a wild and complex social environment.[146] If he passed this test, he would get Google. He did, and the world changed.

Other personalities gravitating to the Burn include Facebook co-founder Dustin Moskovitz, a multi-year attendee, and Jeff Bezos of Amazon. Philip Rosedale, creator of Second Life – the first virtual world accepted by the mainstream – was inspired by the 1999 Burn.[147] Elon Musk of Tesla Motors brought his Roadster prototype to the Burn in 2007. While at the 2014 HBO premier of the television series, *Silicon Valley*, Musk chastised the producer and cast, saying they had missed the mark: *Burning Man is Silicon Valley*.[148]

Transhumanism, too, has points of connection. In the weeks before the 2018 event with its art focus on robotics, a *Burning Man Journal* article reflected on the interplay of man and machine,

> Much as we teach our robots to be like us, we robot creators play God, creating something in our own appearance and liking. It is only a matter of time before our creation will eat the apple, and know the difference between good and evil. Silicon Valley replays Christianity like an annual pageant.[149]

---

[144] S. Kotler and J. Wheal, *Stealing Fire: How Silicon Valley, the Navy SEALs, and Maverick Scientists are Revolutionizing the Way We Live and Work* (DEY St., 2017), p.19.

[145] Fred Turner, "Burning Man at Google: A Cultural Infrastructure for New Media Production," *New Media & Society*, Volume 11, Issue 1-2, February/March 2009, p.75.

[146] Kotler and Wheal, *Stealing Fire*, pp.20-21.

[147] Philip Rosedale interview, "Why Build A Virtual World?" *NPR TED Radio Hour*, September 18, 2015 (www.npr.org/templates/transcript/transcript.php?storyId=440302192).

[148] Nellie Bowles, "At HBO's 'Silicon Valley' Premier, Elon Musk Has Some Notes," *Recode.net*, April 3, 2014 (www.recode.net/2014/4/3/11625260/at-hbos-silicon-valley-premiere-elon-musk-is-pissed).

[149] Misa Rygrova, "I, Robot – We, God," *Burning Man Journal*, August 7, 2018 (https://journal.burningman.org/2018/08/philosophical-center/the-theme/i-robot-we-god).

Why is this desert gathering so important to the tech world?

It is a setting where sensory overload boils over into new ideas, even products.[150] Burning Man is the tech industry's creative commons, its unofficial United Nations; a place for networking and envisioning the future.

Urban planners also have their eyes on Black Rock City (BRC), the temporary community built around the Man effigy. BRC was highlighted during the 2018 winter meeting of the US Conference of Mayors, as civic leaders looked to find correlating inspiration for American cities.[151] Then during the 2018 Burn, members of the US Conference of Mayors – including the president of the Conference – took a trip to BRC for a first-hand look.

And BRC *is* a city. It has streets and plazas, a federally approved airport with hundreds of flights during the week, a post office and newspaper, emergency services, and a radio station. To note: there are no vendors with the exception of ice and coffee sales in Center Camp. Citizens of BRC bring everything needed for a week in the desert, and the event's internal economy is based on gifting, one of the Ten Principles forming the ethos of Burning Man.[152] And as the event is "leave no-trace," people pack-out their own trash.

"A true city arises, develops, evolves, catches fire, then disappears," wrote journalist Brian Doherty, "built on a back-drop of nothing, imbuing it with a rich metaphorical resonance..."[153]

BRC is an evolutionary city with an evolutionary culture, and Burning Man is the premier, transformational event of our time.

Since 1990, the Burn has been held in the Black Rock Desert of northern Nevada,[154] an enormous region with a 200-square mile playa – a flat, alkaline lakebed (playa means beach in Spanish). Daytime temperatures can exceed

---

[150] The Burn has been a test site for Google Earth tools. See Fred Turner, "Burning Man at Google: A Cultural Infrastructure for New Media Production," *New Media & Society*, pp.89-90. Another inspired development is SolarCity, one of America's largest solar installation companies, conceived by Elon Musk and Lyndon Rive during the 2004 Burn.

[151] *Draft Agenda: The 86th Winter Meeting of The United States Conference of Mayors* (January 24-28, 2018, Washington, DC, Capital Hilton Hotel).

[152] The Ten Principles: Radical Inclusion, Gifting, Decommodification, Radical Self-reliance, Radical Self-expression, Communal Effort, Civic Responsibility, Leaving No Trace, Participation, and Immediacy. An unwritten eleventh principle is Consent.

[153] Brian Doherty, *This is Burning Man: The Rise of a New American Underground* (BenBella Books, 2006), p.3.

[154] In 1997 it took place in Hualapai Flat.

100-degrees Fahrenheit, and fierce winds drive massive dust storms across the city, choking out the air in whiteout conditions. The sheer size of the playa compels a response to scale; colossal-sized temples, huge art installations, and of course, the Man – a towering human effigy, some years standing over 100-feet tall – the central figure of Black Rock City. At the end of the week, the Man is burnt to the ground as tens of thousands party around the inferno, an explosive outpouring of celebration. On the following day, the Temple – gigantic and complex structures, in 2011 it was 120-feet tall with a 200-foot diameter – is razed as thousands watch in silence. After each burn, naked dancers and fire spinners move among the red hot coals.

Other shrines and temple-art pieces are erected. In 2015, some of Timothy Leary's ashes were brought by actress Susan Sarandon, deposited in the temple-like, 5-story Totem of Confessions, and torched. Other installations included the House of Enlightenment in 2017, and the 70-foot-tall, all-metal Flower Tower, a flame-shooting "Cathedral Devoted to Happiness."

At the end of the week BRC breaks apart as people leave, and the Black Rock Desert returns to its barren state – until next year.

Describing Burn Man is notoriously difficult. Is it a festival? Is the Burn an experiment in social cohesion, or a model of libertarianism? Is it about art and play? Is it hedonism, nudity and debauchery, or introspection and spirituality? Yes and no, all at the same time.

One contributor to BRC's newspaper expressed it this way,

> It is our palette and canvas, to create the world we can't enjoy at home... It's pagan. It's anti-religious. It's a Trojan horse... It's a chance to get out of town and hang with some good chaps. It's sex and drugs and trance music. It's artistic expression. It's a week of survival on chips-and-salsa... It's Utopia-On-A-Stick.[155]

It is the "largest act of ephemeral collective creativity man has ever known," explained Brian Doherty, "in an atmosphere largely free of imposed meanings or behavioral norms – [it] has no real parallel."[156]

Part of the alchemy that makes Burning Man hard to categorize is the participant driven nature of the event. Every sculpture and painting, each camp

---

[155] S. McKenzie, "Utopia-On-A-Stick," 3 Sept. 1998, in *Burning Man Live: 13 Years of Piss Clear – Black Rock City's Alternative Newspaper* (RE/Search Publications, 2009), p.58.

[156] Doherty, *This is Burning Man*, p.4.

program, and all daily offerings – from raves to art cars to personal costumes – are voluntary creations. This means the Burn is constantly shifting, minute-by-day-by-year. A general theme is announced months in advance, giving overall direction and philosophical perspective, but this is a guideline only.[157] In 2018, the theme had a transhumanist orientation, *I, Robot*, while the Temple – a massive, spiral structure titled *Galaxia* – was built to represent Isaac Asimov's "superior form of Gaia... the ultimate network, the fabric of the universe connecting living beings into one entity."[158]

Meanwhile, hundreds of encounters take place simultaneously without any reference to the theme whatsoever. It is a montage of experiences within one convergence. Burning Man is an oversized, full-sensory Happening.

It is important to understand that Burning Man is not a single event, but a container for an array of interests and experiences. The definitive guide to what transpires is the annually published *What, Where, When*. Handed to participants upon entering the city, this book lists the daily lectures, discussions, rituals, and other activities. From 2011 to 2016, the *WWW* was 160 pages long, and in 2017 and 2018 it was 191 pages, with each page averaging ten descriptive listings – keep in mind, this *only* reflects the accepted *WWW* listings.[159] Everything under the sun is open to explore, from the serious to the silly, the sexual to sociable, the spiritual to sacrilegious.

The following ten activities are a sampling. Camp names are in brackets:

> **Journey Into Gender** – Enter this coming of age at any age ritual to redefine gender and reclaim past rites. Bring open heart, mind, soul, desire, objects, and costumes to share. (Gender Blender)[160]

> **The Great Work: Holy Guardian Angel** – Aleister Crowley believed knowledge and conversation with one's Holy Guardian Angel should be the preeminent goal of every magician. Learn more! (Sacred Spaces Village)[161]

---

[157] The first official theme was *Inferno* in 1996. Playing off this, a theatrical production titled *HELCO* – featuring Satan and the selling of souls, including spoof TV commercials – was produced in anticipation of the Burn. *HELCO* became that year's premier art installation.

[158] *The Galaxia Story*, Temple Galaxia webpage [https://templegalaxia.org/temple].

[159] In 2017, over 3,600 events were submitted for inclusion in the *WWW*. In 2018 the number jumped to more than 4,300. Note: due to circumstances, not all listed events take place.

[160] *What, Where, When: 2011 – Rites of Passage* (Burning Man, 2011), p.55.

[161] *What, Where, When: 2012 – Fertility 2.0* (Burning Man, 2012), p.59.

Fire Dodgeball – Make new friends, and throw a ball of fire at them. Please wear fire-safe clothing. (!Zoom!)[162]

Building a Mainstream Psychedelic Movement – Daniel Jabbour, founder of the Psychedelic Society of San Francisco discusses the ethics and strategy for building a mainstream psychedelics movement. (Soft Landing)[163]

Slut Celebration Play Party – Young sluts unite. Come play in the sluts' five bedrooms. No monogamous couples or single guys. (Sensual Playhouse)[164]

Reiki Shamanism – Weaving Reiki energy medicine with ancient shamanic journeying, illuminate your pathway to spiritual insight, channeling spirit guides, rescue souls. (Shamandome Camp)[165]

Carnal Healing: The Circle of Sexuality – Join us for a night of Sexual Magic as we cast a circle to invoke and honor global sexual deities and ask for their healing and support. (Diva Nation)[166]

The UN's Agenda 2030 & Sustainable Development – Learn about increasing our impact through international & national initiatives. Explore ways to be a local and global citizen. (Earth Guardians)[167]

AI & Man's Quest to Invent God – The story of our development of an Artificial Intelligence being and how will we grow with it. (Red Lightning)[168]

Holy Sacrament of The Man – It is time to drink the kool-aid. Come for communion to receive the body and blood of The Man & reflect on The Man's sacrifice for us. (Bhudda Bank)[169]

The spiritual dynamics are significant.

The BRC census from 2013 to 2017 revealed interesting data points. When asked about Spiritual Identity, approximately half of the participants consid-

---

[162] Ibid., p.127.

[163] *What, Where, When: 2013 – Cargo Cult* (Burning Man, 2013), p.104.

[164] *What, Where, When: 2014 – Caravansary* (Burning Man, 2014), p.99.

[165] Ibid., p.110.

[166] *What, Where, When: 2015 – Carnival of Mirrors* (Burning Man, 2015), p.99.

[167] *What, Where, When: 2016 – Da Vinci's Workshop* (Burning Man, 2016), p.53.

[168] Ibid., p.73.

[169] *What, Where, When: 2017 – Radical Ritual* (Burning Man, 2017), p.106.

ered themselves "Spiritual, Not Religious." Roughly one quarter identified as Atheist, 15% Agnostic, about 7% responded with "I Don't Know," 6% as Religious, and less than 1% Deist.[170] In the category of Religious Denomination, the breakdown for 2017 was: No Religion, 71.8%; Catholic, 7%; Jewish, 6%; Christian (other), 4.1%; Other 3%; Protestant, 2.6%; Buddhist, 1.9%; Pagan, 1.4%; Pastafarian,[171] 1.2%; Muslim, 0.6%; and Hindu, 0.4%.[172]

Burning Man itself is a platform to explore alternative spiritualities.

Re-enchantment, occulture, and myth are ingrained in many of the activities and artwork. Messages of cosmic oneness are prevalent, along with workshops on Yoga, shamanism, goddess rituals and sacred femininity, tarot, and esoteric philosophy. An earlier reference to the mythic was Pepe Ozan's famed operas. From 1996 to 2000, the Argentine sculpture orchestrated large theatricals for Black Rock City.[173] These were primal, ritualized operas embellishing Pagan themes: Satan's amusement with Empress Zoe, the marriage of the Mesopotamian deities Ishtar and Dumuzi, a Dravidian Fire Ceremony, a Haitian Vodou story, an Atlantean pyramid ritual.[174] Regardless of the medium, the concept of *spirituality as experience* is a central component. Diverse religious practices and beliefs are thus accepted. In the great American search for higher meaning, Burning Man "has become a ritualized space for those who seek spirituality but not religion."[175]

Christianity, however, is mocked. Irreverence for all things is expected, but in terms of religious messaging, Christianity is seriously derided.[176]

Christopher Partridge writes: "it is clear that the spirituality encouraged at Burning Man is explicitly non-Christian... when it makes use of Christian symbolism it almost always does so negatively, as parody."[177]

---

170 *Black Rock City Census: 2013-2017 Population Analysis*, p.28.

171 Pastafarian is a parody religion mocking Christian beliefs, creationism in particular.

172 *Black Rock City Census: 2013-2017 Population Analysis*, p.29.

173 Other operas took place in 2002 and 2003, but were of lesser renown.

174 For more on Ozan's operas, see *The Burning Man Opera*: www.burningmanopera.org. See also, Lee Gilmore, *Theater in a Crowded Fire: Ritual and Spirituality at Burning Man* (University of California Press, 2010), pp.83-87. The documentary, *Dust and Illusions* (Madnomad Films, 2009), also outlines the story of Pepe Ozan..

175 Lee Gilmore, *Theater in a Crowded Fire: Ritual and Spirituality at Burning Man* (University of California Press, 2010), p.67.

176 The back issues of *Piss Clear*, BRC's newspaper from 1995 to 2007, amply demonstrates that ridicule of all sorts is common to the culture – including mockery of the Burn itself.

177 Partridge, *The Re-Enchantment of the West*, Volume 1, p.164.

The Man itself is an object of mythic interpretation. Although no explicit meaning is assigned to the effigy, Burning Man insiders and academic observers recognize a ritualistic persona.[178] Stewart Harvey, brother of Larry Harvey – the visionary behind Burning Man – describes the annual event as a "ritual of destruction and renewal."[179] As he put it,

> ...a deceptively simple and incredibly moving reenactment of destruction and rebirth... The Man is consumed by fire and yet lives to be reborn the following year. The ritual feels both timeless and yet utterly immediate, and it takes place in an environment that is at once otherworldly and oddly familiar.[180]

"Although Burning Man channels many of the ceremonial aspects of religious ritual," Steward Harvey writes, "it does so without an accompanying dogma."[181]

Larry Harvey places the Man within a setting of secular divinity,

> The Man we've made, of course, is not a god, nor is the burning of the temple evidence of supernaturalism. Energy did not flow from the Man into a group of followers. Rather it was their energy, their full-hearted participation that created the Man.[182]

After the 2017 Burn with its theme, *Radical Ritual*, Larry told an audience at the Nevada Museum of Art,

> The moral of our theme, in fact, was that it doesn't really matter what you believe, it's what you experience... The whole point, this year, was to convince people that Burning Man is a spiritual movement. It's not a religion, but it's a spiritual movement. And you know it when you see it.[183]

---

[178] One academic work of note is Lee Gilmore's *Theater in a Crowded Fire: Ritual and Spirituality at Burning Man* (University of California Press, 2010).

[179] Stewart Harvey, *Playa Fire: Spirit and Soul at Burning Man* (HarperElixir, 2017), p.6.

[180] Stewart Harvey, "Black Rock Dawn," *Playa Dust: Collected Stories from Burning Man* (Black Dog Publishing, 2014), pp.30-31.

[181] Harvey, *Playa Fire*, p.6.

[182] Larry Harvey, "Forward," *Playa Fire: Spirit and Soul at Burning Man*, p.viii.

[183] *Larry Harvey in Conversation with David Walker: Reflections on the Growth of Burning Man*, hosted by the Nevada Museum of Art, October 12, 2017. The selection quoted can be accessed here, beginning at the 11:16 mark: https://youtu.be/NYPJoRGKMSk.

Larry Harvey, who passed away on April 28, 2018, was an avowed atheist with a penchant for metaphysical philosophy. He was fond of reversing the religious world order, to flip the question of which supernatural Being is supreme by saying, why not "simply say that being is supreme?"[184]

Harvey's background and the genesis of Burning Man are important in understanding the worldview context. Although this history is both complex and vague, we will briefly focus on a few factors.

Larry was a product of his generation, and his own internal struggles. His father was a staunch Freemason with an interest in sacred symbolism, and Larry himself gravitated to reading studies of comparative religion as a teenager. Both men had a hard time relating to one another, a fact Stewart Harvey brings out, noting their clash of sensibilities, yet recognizing that "Larry and our father were the same man."[185] To his parent's consternation, Larry started exploring his "own quest for pharmaceutical revelations... [becoming] a proto-hippie."[186]

In 1967, Larry went to San Francisco and experienced the Summer of Love. He left briefly, returning for a time in 1968 to "get a second dose of hippie heaven." Then, in the mid-1970, he took a place on Ashbury Street "just a few blocks from the Grateful Dead house."[187]The utopian glow left over from the1960s, and the continued artistic vibrancy of the Bay Area, offered a cultural milieu that was amiable to Larry's sense of identity.

Years later, in the summer of 1986, Larry was reading James G. Frazer's classic text, *The Golden Bough*. First published in 1890, Frazer's book was instrumental in the early field of comparative, mythological study – influencing the thinking of Sigmund Freud and Carl G. Jung.[188] A section in *The Golden Bough* outlines the history of fire festivals and the ritualistic torching of effigies, including midsummer burns, interpreting these as acts of magical protection against evil and witches.[189] According to Jerry James, the carpen-

---

[184] Larry Harvey, "Forward," *Playa Fire*, p.viii. He often repeated this phrase.

[185] Stewart Harvey, *Playa Fire*, p.11, see also p.14.

[186] Ibid., p.10.

[187] Ibid., pp.9-12.

[188] John B. Vickery, *The Literary Impact of The Golden Bough* (Princeton University Press, 1973), pp.94-95.

[189] A revised edition of the classic text was published as *The New Golden Bough* (Criterion Books, 1959, edited by Theodor H. Gaster). For the section on fire festivals and effigy burns, see pp.610-647.

ter who built the first Man, Larry was into *The Golden Bough* when he called James to construct the figure.[190]

Is this the reason the first Man was burnt on Baker Beach, to play-act an ancient ritual – a mythic stepping-stone in human evolution? Larry had been to other solstice fires, a not uncommon happening along the shores of San Francisco.[191] Stewart Harvey, too, points to *The Golden Bough* story, but adds that Larry wanted to create "a more personal gesture of fiery expression," and not imitate some "hoary legend from the distant past."[192]

It is an intriguing angle, but the meaning behind the initial Burn remains unclear. When asked about its genesis during an on-stage interview at *Le Web*, Europe's largest tech conference, Larry responded by saying, "Well, I've made up seven or eight stories about it, because people want a myth, and they're all true." He remembers calling his friend about building the effigy, but nothing before that: "Like so much that's creative, it just came out of the black water, just materialized in front of me, probably largely due to subconscious processes."[193]

Stewart Harvey comments,

> Creative inspiration is rarely delivered in a tidy package... but in Larry's case the road is especially twisty, because he is a person who has spent most of his life trying to make sense of human existence, and he is voraciously well read on the topic. Human evolution is absolutely at the heart of Burning Man.[194]

By the 1987 Burn, Jerry James could sense that something ritualistic was taking shape. Others, too, could see potential.

Members of the recently formed Cacophony Society, "culture jammers" with ties to the defunct Suicide Club – a secretive, San Francisco prankster group – were part of the early Burns. Both Suicide and Cacophony were

---

190 Jerry James, "In the Beginning," *Playa Dust: Collected Stories from Burning Man* (Black Dog Publishing, 2014), p.20.

191 Jerry James references Larry's prior attendance at solstice burns, and Stewart Harvey details San Francisco's solstice history. See James, "In the Beginning," *Playa Dust*, p.20; Stewart Harvey, *Playa Fire*, p.13.

192 Stewart Harvey, *Playa Fire*, p.14.

193 Larry Harvey interview, *Le Web London*, 2013. A video of this talk is online at: https://youtu.be/ufQncdmuHlw.

194 Stewart Harvey, *Playa Fire*, p.9.

artistically rooted in the neo-Dada movement, the Beats, and the Happenings.[195] Each were extensions of the city's earlier counter-culture, and Cacophony dubbed itself the "Merry Pranksters of the 90's."[196] Larry never joined Cacophony, but the group played a role in the annual event.

After local police stopped the Burn on Baker Beach in 1990, it was obvious a new location was needed. Cacophony suggested taking the Man to the Black Rock Desert in September of that year. The rest, as they say, is history, and it has been a roller-coaster ride with accidents and deaths, organizational dramas, and colorful encounters with authorities and local residents.[197]

One internal tension point was over EDM and the development of a rave encampment a mile from the Burn. In 1996, three ravers were seriously injured when a speeding car hit their tent. The following year, anti-ravers in a flaming art vehicle – shooting 70-foot streams of fire – threatened to burn down the rave camp. Goa Gil, who was performing that night, found himself squared-off in front of the mutant vehicle. The art car backed down and "ravers gained a foothold at Burning Man."[198]

In time, the other elements of today's Burn were added; a stronger emphasis on art, theme-based encampments, a full slate of workshops, and a Temple in the year 2000. Information technologies and the internet itself were maturing, and Burning Man paralleled this development – moving from its "wild west" persona of the 1990s into a defined cultural movement.

As the Burn grew in popularity and size, a Regional movement sparked to life. Regional Burns now take place across the United States, in Canada, and around the world. For example, Israel hosts the Mid-Burn gathering where an effigy of Adam and Eve is torched, and AfrikaBurn takes place near Tankwa Karoo National Park in South Africa. The virtual world of Second Life is home to BURN2, the only official Regional held in a completely digital environment. Unofficial gatherings like Washington DC's Catharsis on the Mall are rooted in the Burn, and many transformational festival are directly influenced by the desert convergence.

---

195 Gilmore, *Theater in a Crowded Fire*, p.26.

196 *Rough Draft*, Issue #48, September 1990, the newsletter of the Cacophony Society.

197 Brian Doherty's, *This Is Burning Man* (BenBella, 2006), details some of this history.

198 Graham St. John, "Begoggled in the Theatre of Awe: Electronic Dance Music Culture at Burning Man," *Playa Dust: Collected Stories from Burning Man* (Black Dog Publishing, 2014), p.148.

The Burning Man organization, too, has gained an international voice. Staff members are sought after for media interviews, speak at major conferences, and lecture in academic settings. Global Leadership Conferences and European summits are hosted by the organization, and it interacts with foundations and think tanks, such as the Esalen Institute and Steward Brand's Long Now Foundation.

Burning Man is far more than a party in the desert. It is a *planetary TAZ* with global implications.

Essentially, the Dada-Crowley-Kesey effect of the 1960s has been reshaped for our global context. Stewart Brand, co-host of the 1966 Trips Festival – and an important figure in the development of the internet, popularizing the term *personal computer* – understood the cultural-social connection,

> Burning Man, they have surpassed in every way the various things we were attempting with the Acid Tests and the Trips Festival, Burning Man has realized with such depth and thoroughness and ongoing originality and ability to scale and minimalist rules, but enough rules that you can function, and all the things we were farting around with, Larry Harvey has really pulled off. I don't think that would have come to pass without going through whatever that spectrum of the '60s was, the prism of the '60s, the spectrum of bright colors that we espoused for a while. It all got exacerbated by the Internet and sequence of computer-related booms, but I think it flavored a whole lot of the basic nature of Burning Man.[199]

One participant interpreted the Burn experience this way,

> I think of Burning Man as the first extraterrestrial city on earth. It completely integrates technology and visionary art with neo-tribal ritual... The playa is a portal, preparing us for the cosmic dance party everyone's waiting for.[200]

"Burning Man is a self-service cult," Larry Harvey once famously remarked. "Wash your own brain."[201]

---

[199] Stewart Brand, "Summer of Love: 40 Years Later," *SFGATE*, May 20, 2007, [www.sfgate.com/news/article/Summer-of-Love-40-Years-Later-Stewart-Brand-2559651.php].

[200] As quoted by Jonathan Talat Phillips, *The Electric Jesus: The Healing Journey of a Contemporary Gnostic* (Evolver Editions, 2011), p154.

[201] Quoted by Brian Doherty, *This Is Burning Man*, p.290.

Camp of the Unknown God

We were on a collision course, and I was oblivious to it until the impact.

Halfway through a 30-hour road trip to Black Rock City, I found myself 60 miles north of Idaho Falls on I-15. The sun had set an hour ago, and I never saw the deer – which must have been running full-tilt – until our paths irreversibly intersected, and my trip changed in the blink of an eye. Although I was able to drive a few more miles, finding an exit ramp to park on, it was obvious my 20-year-old truck was done.

Waiting for the State Trooper, I posted the following message on social media: "Well, I hit a deer north of Idaho Falls. Truck. Is. Totalled."

I had killed the deer, and the deer had destroyed my ride.

It was 2:30 AM when the State Trooper kindly dropped me off at a hotel in Idaho Falls. I went to bed discouraged and exhausted, overtired from previous days of very little sleep, and unsure how to coordinate my return home. The best option, it seemed, was to dump my camping gear and catch a bus to North Dakota, having my wife travel down from Manitoba to pick me up. Three hours later we were sorting out an exit strategy over the phone; Burning Man 2017 looked to be a dead-end.

At breakfast a friend from Ohio private messaged me. What was needed to make this trip work? Before lunch another friend reached out from Missouri, then Oklahoma and Alberta. Each pledged to help in some way; a rental vehicle was in the picture. Thanks to Christian believers who were willing to give sacrificially, Burning Man was back on the map.

After more late-night road adventures, mercifully with nothing damaged but my sense of direction and pride, I found my way to a ranch in northern California near the backside of the Black Rock Desert. Here I rendezvoused with Robert Worley, a friend who had been reaching out to the Burn community since the mid-1990s, attending, back then, with gifts of bottled water and Living Water.[202] And here, too, was Christian hospitality as our ranch hosts graciously opened up their home to us, and to me as a stranger – and then adding blessings that would allow the continuation of this book.

In all of this there was an important lesson: Such acts of Christian love, which happen daily to people around the world in small and large ways, are

[202] Jesus said: "If anyone thirsts, let him come to Me and drink. He who believes in Me, as the Scripture has said, out of his heart will flow rivers of living water." – John 7:37-38.

an extension of the two Great Commandments as given by Jesus Christ: "You shall love the LORD your God with all your heart, with all your soul, and with all your mind.' This is the first and great commandment. And the second is like it: 'You shall love your neighbor as yourself'."[203]

God's children are recipients and participants in the true, gifting economy.

Unlike the fleeting city in the desert, the *ultimate gift* is established and eternal. Consider the words of Jesus Christ, which cuts to the heart when you realize He was talking about Himself as the ultimate gift – a gift that would remove the condemnation of sin for those who would trust in Him,

> For God so loved the world that He gave His only begotten Son, that whoever believes in Him should not perish but have everlasting life. For God did not send His Son into the world to condemn the world, but that the world through Him might be saved.[204]

On Sunday, August 27, Bob and I drove onto the playa and made our way to Black Rock City. Hundreds of campers had already lined up, and for the next four hours our vehicles crawled-and-stopped through the 101-degree heat. If anything, this opened time to visit with those around us: adventurers from Australia, members of theme camps, and virgin Burners. When we reached the gate at sunset a layer of alkaline dust coated everything.

At the entrance we received our *What, Where, When* guide, a BRC map, and a brochure on Zendo and the Bureau of Erotic Discourse. Zendo works with people experiencing a bad psychedelic trip and offers "a safe place to reconnect with yourself." The Bureau reminded everyone of sexual consent, and explained what to do if you are raped or otherwise sexually assaulted.

Our purpose in attending was two-fold: Research to better understand the movement and points of impact, and engage in a model of outreach.

I spent time going to workshops and discussions, talking to artists, visiting theme camps, and considering the artwork. At the Palenque Norte lectures I heard two differing perspectives. On Tuesday, Republican tax reformer, Grover Norquist, presented a libertarian view of government and talked about building left/right coalitions for liberty around issues of principle. On Wednesday, psychedelic futurist Daniel Pinchbeck advocated a new "global operating system." What we need, he explained, is a collective-

---

[203] Matthew 22:37-39.

[204] John 3:16-17.

shamanistic initiation to shift our consciousness and save the planet – and Burning Man is important to this process of social-spiritual evolution.

I attended a presentation on virtual reality and the re-wiring of the brain; another on the difficulties in designing the *Tower of Voices* – the national memorial to Flight 93 – a talk given by one of its engineers; and still another on the metamorphosis of Christianity, with a consensus that doctrine must give way to radical inclusion and social justice. Later I walked into Camp Play-Alchemist during a panel on polyamorous relationships, reinforcing consensual non-monogamy and the push for the next phase of contractual unions.

At Shamandome, Bob and I sat through an interactive talk on shamanism, psychedelics, and neuroscience. Acceptance of ayahuasca by many professionals, we were told, was allowing this psychedelic to cross-pollinate with progressive ideals. The plant deities were being awakened; the mind and nervous system was being opened to ancient, spiritual entities. This harmonized with the acknowledgement of ayahuasca as a "global spiritual movement" during the 2015 Parliament of the World's Religions.

I also happened upon Reverend Billy's "Famous Sunday Sermon." Dressed in a white suit, black shirt and clerical collar, Reverend Billy – a well-known personality in the Burn culture – preached a message of Re-enchantment. The following is a paraphrase from my notes,

> We have fired the God who claims to be all knowing, and because of that, we have entered the age of mystery. Now that we are alone in the universe, where do we turn? Science? It knows far less than the persona it projects. So we must turn to our experiences, our realities, and our sense of Self. And we turn to the sacredness of the Earth, for we are made from the Earth. We can therefore trust the Earth, even in our death – which is just part of life – for it is the Earth that sustains and embraces us. Earth-allelujah!

Camp Mystic, "a beacon of humankind's evolution,"[205] had a full slate of workshops, panels, networking events, and performances. Technology lead-

---

[205] Excerpted from Camp Mystic's *Manifesto* at https://campmystic.org/mystic-manifesto. Under the section Radical Evolution, the text reads: "We do this through exploring evolutionary love, evolutionary relationship, evolutionary civilization, evolutionary entrepreneurship, evolutionary leadership, evolutionary sex, evolutionary masculinity, evolutionary femininity, evolutionary community, and more."

ers and social change agents converged on Camp Mystic's open floor, surrounded by goddess shrines and banners devoted to the sacred feminine. One afternoon I walked in during a poetry reading affirming divine unity: *Your truth is the same as Jesus, Buddha, and Krishna* – "You are Yahweh."

In terms of social engineering, I was especially intrigued by two panel discussions: "Building a Permanent Burning Man," and "Digital Currency and the Economics of Unity." Both workshops were about projecting forces of change into the default world. Could the creation of a *secret country* provide the necessary leverage?

In the first panel, Ryan Allis – founder of Hive.org and former National Co-Chair of Tech for President Obama's campaign – spoke of how two social-economic models were before us. The present model is *Game A*: capitalism, scarcity, patriarchy, white privilege, and individualism. *Game B* is where Burning Man's "mercenaries of light" need to take us: the sharing economy, the sacred feminine, the psyche of inner space, and group generated norms. How will we arrive at Game B? Blockchain and distributed ledger technologies, the structures upon which Bitcoin and digital tokens are created.

The panel on "Digital Currencies and Economic Unity" asked us to broaden our horizons. Distributed ledger technologies could be used to re-tool macro systems: economic models, legal norms, and governance itself. Blockchain, we were told, has the potential to enable Initial Country Offerings, that is, to create *virtual nations* with networked citizens sharing a common ideal. Bear Kittay, Burning Man's Global Ambassador, reminded us that the Burn prototypes an emerging civilization. It was argued that blockchain and Burning Man, fused in a partnership of social license and liquid democracy – *a decentralized hive of unity* – could incite large scale change.

Taking the time to explore the artwork yielded interesting conversations and observations. One artist told me how a double dose of mescaline had brought inspiration by opening the doorway of her mind to a visitation by the Goddess. At the Mayan Warrior art car, a massive truck-based sound-stage pumping 70,000 watts of power, a DJ began his set by talking about interfaith unity through music and dance, and connecting our divinity – the "oneness within us all" – through this "sacred ritual." A few blocks from our camp, and not far from the Orgy Dome, was a statue of Pan with his chest ripped open to reveal a flaming heart; a small bowl was set before him for offerings and tokens. After the Temple burn on Sunday evening, marred by the tragedy of the night before,[206] Bob and I found ourselves walking beside a 20-foot marionette. She was returning to her oversized bed for the night and telling everyone how magical the Temple was, for it showed "we are all one."

It was in this spiritual-pagan-secular environment in which Bob and I borrowed from an ancient example of Christian outreach.

In Acts 17:16-34 we read of the Apostle Paul in Athens, specifically at the Areopagus – a rocky hill adjoining the Acropolis. It was a highly charged religious setting. Established on the Acropolis was Athena's Parthenon, the imposing temple dedicated to the Goddess. Next to it was the Temple of Athena and Poseidon, and on the same grounds, but closer to the Areopagus itself, was the smaller Temple of Athena Nike. Numerous shrines, monuments, and sacred spaces were set along the bottom of the hillside, including the Sanctuary of Pan. To the southeast stood the massive Temple of Zeus. And to the north of the Areopagus was the Agora, a colonnaded building for community markets and assemblies, and noted for its own deity shrines. The Areopagus itself was significant, as this was a meeting place for the Areopagus Council, an esteemed court overseeing matters of religion and custom. This was the setting Paul found himself in.

In Acts 17, Paul has assessed the spiritual culture of the city. He then went to the Jewish synagogue so as to reason with Jews and God-fearing Greeks, and he frequented the marketplace to proclaim the resurrection of Jesus Christ. At the Agora he encountered Epicurean and Stoic philosophers, and these men considered Paul to be a thought beggar, someone picking up religious scraps and reassembling them to fit a personal narrative – a babbler without context. Others stepped in to say, "He seems to be a proclaimer of foreign gods." So Paul was taken to the Areopagus for questioning.

Standing before the Council – the cultural gatekeepers – Paul noted their social-spiritual situation, telling them he even found an altar with the inscription: "TO THE UNKNOWN GOD." Using this as a jumping point, Paul described the Unknown God in terms of positional uniqueness; God is Lord of heaven and earth, the author and source of life "who does not dwell in temples made with hands." He also talked about God's relational disposition

---

[206] As the Man was engulfed on Saturday evening, 41-year old Aaron Mitchell raced past the fire safety officials and ran into the inferno. Firefighters pulled him out seconds before the blazing timbers collapsed, but with burns covering 97% of his body, he died a few hours later. Alcohol and drugs were ruled out. His death was labeled a suicide.

to mankind, reminding the Greeks that their own philosophers have wrestled with this, but that the Divine Nature is not devised by art or invention. The time for spiritual ignorance, Paul contended, is over. The only honest response is to repent, for God will judge humanity through the righteousness of Jesus Christ – established by the fact that He rose from the dead.

To condense this as a model for outreach: Paul entered their setting, he analyzed the city's spiritual culture – understanding it before going to Athens, for he exhibited a respectful knowledge of their worldview – and then he found a point of contact by which he could communicate the good news of Jesus Christ. Those of the Areopagus Council responded in three ways: some mocked, others wanted to hear more later, and a few people – including a Council member – became believers.

What does this have to do with our time at Burning Man?

The week before leaving for Black Rock City, a friend suggested we put up a sign at our tent with the words, "CAMP OF THE UNKNOWN GOD." This was a breakthrough, for earlier in the summer Bob and I had been discussing approaches for outreach. Borrowing from Acts 17 seemed appropriate.

How big was our footprint? Minuscule: one tent, one sign, and two dusty men. But the outreach model was viable. People stopped to talk.

"Where did this camp name come from?" asked an atheist. Another time an esoteric artist paused and inquired, "Who is the unknown God?"

These were open doors, and they happened throughout the week. Our response? Offer a chair in the shade of the tent, give them liquids and food, and then ask about ***their*** story. Allowing our guests to talk first demonstrated we were interested in who they were as individuals; we genuinely wanted to know them, and desired to understand where they were coming from. Having them talk first also created, for ourselves, mental placeholders – return points we could jump back to if the conversation stalled. And when our time together closed, we could often find a way to reinforce the conversation by referring to something we learned about them previously.

Next, we would explain Paul's time in Athens, his interaction in the *spiritual marketplace* – the BRC parallel did not escape our guests – and how Paul presented the "Unknown God" as both knowable and relational through the righteousness of Jesus Christ. Only once did someone leave when Jesus' name came up. Everyone else wanted to hear more, and some asked if they could return to continue the conversation later, and some did.

Remember, this is Burning Man, with no practical end of carnal outlets and entertaining adventures. Yet, here we were, discussing matters of eternal importance. It was a reminder that although Western culture has pushed Christianity aside, people are still longing and seeking. This, too, dovetailed with what Paul told the Council: We seek and grope for Him, hoping to find Him, "though He is not far from each one of us."[207]

Talk with our visitors would turn to the Ten Commandments, God as moral lawgiver, and that we are all lawbreakers in need of a Savior. At times Bob would expand on the prophetic message of the Bible, including the role of Israel, showing that Jesus Christ was and is the fulfillment of prophecy. And he would regularly say to our guests: You are my *Brother in Adam*, my *Sister in Eve* – but my real hope is that you will become my *Brother in Christ*.

When the esoteric artist visited, our starting line was a comparative illustration between the idea of spiritual oneness and the God who is distinct.

"Are you saying that *your* value is equal to your art?" I asked.

"Of course not," he responded. "I am of more value than my art."

Agreeing with his observation, I gestured to the sky and the distant mountains. "God is the ultimate artist," I said. "Are you telling me…?"

"I see where you're going with this," he interjected. "The artist is always greater than his artwork. God has to be of more value. He must be different."

True spirituality, I explained, has to be grounded in an unchanging God who is exalted – positioned higher, of infinitely greater value – than the sum of the created universe. To affix our soul in anything or anyone lesser is to settle for a *temporary spirituality*.

"This *is* temporary," he quietly affirmed. "*The Man burns*."

I have met some of the nicest people at transformational festivals; Burning Man especially. Friendships have been kindled, and I look fondly on my time with those whom I have interacted with on the playa. Like Bob, it is my hope that an even deeper relationship will take place.

Burning Man is more than just a social-spiritual movement. It is a mission field. After all, the Burn is but a reflection of the world, and we as believers in Jesus Christ are His witnesses to the "ends of the earth."[208] We are to be truth-tellers, loving representatives of God from BRC to your back yard.

---

[207] Acts 17:27.

[208] Acts 1:8b.

BRC is a wake-up call to the Christian community. In listening to those who participate in transformational culture, it is evident that for many, deep hurts exist in relationship to encounters with Christians and church life. Yes, Christians can be harsh, unloving and unforgiving – our hope is in Christ, but our actions can be betraying. Do we shoulder some of the responsibility for our culture's turning? Is there a correlation between the church's loss of its first love, and the yearning for a new spirituality?

The rise of evolutionary culture and its claim to creative expression reveals another concern: the realm of art. Generally speaking, we have failed to understand its role, either outside or within the Christian context. There is an historic tension within the church over art and those gifted in its creation. For the sake of strengthening the full body of believers, and for reclaiming the wonder of art for the glory of God, I believe we need to seriously reconsider this gifting. If anything, the impact of evolutionary culture may yet force us to review and acknowledge the importance of art.[209]

The above "take aways" reflect thoughts I wrestled with on my return from BRC in 2017. Other gleanings have been sprinkled in the previous chapters. Indeed, research into transformational festivals and my time at Burning Man were crucial in developing key concepts in this book.

The fact remains that Black Rock City is symbolic of our shifting, global epoch – a blending of the spiritual Self and sacred secular. Stripped of its party reputation, what we find is a cosmopolitan experience at the crossroads of religion, philosophy and ideology, a place where modern forces of change merge with ancient forces of spirit.

Burning Man epitomizes the Temple of Man in the Age of Re-Enchantment. *It is a foreshadowing.*

[209] Two small books worth considering as a starting point for a Christian discussion of art: Philip G. Ryken, *Art for God's Sake: A Call to Recover the Arts* (P&R Publishing, 2006), and Hans R. Rookmaaker, *Art Needs No Justification* (Regent College Publishing, 2010).

Part V

Transformation

If God is not dethroned and his laws not revoked, he represents an important rival to the despot's authority, living in millions of hearts. If he cannot be driven out of hearts, total control by the state is impossible.
– Peter Hitchens, *The Rage Against God.*

Fear God and keep His commandments, For this is man's all. For God will bring every work into judgment, Including every secret thing, Whether good or evil.
– Ecclesiastes 12:13b-14.

Chapter 15

Choosing Freedom

> Christians are people of hope. We long for the day when the kingdom of God will be fully revealed, when Jesus will return in glory, and when death itself will be conquered. This is our hope, the hope of Christians past and present. – Stewart E. Kelly. [1]

> Yes, if Christianity is true, it is clearly not a theory. It is a love affair with life and its author. It is reality. – Mary Poplin.[2]

Forecasting the future is risky business. We experience the now, can peer into the past, but the future remains murky. We see through a glass dimly.

The practical means of considering tomorrow, then, is to decipher historical patterns and trends. Objects in the mirror are closer than they appear, precisely because the past frames our present. This also means our future pulls from the back-story. *Game of Gods* has labored with this in mind.

Patterns exist. Foundations have been laid and pieces are being assembled. What, then, does the future entail as we erect this Temple of Man?

Might oneness be institutionalized into a world union? Could we see a substantially reformed United Nations, or maybe a new body, to supersede the aging assembly? Will this represent a practical synthesis of East and West, of mysticism and management?

Lucile W. Green endorsed such a blending in 1977,

> The view of the world as seen from space is 'a beautiful blue planet,' not a patchwork of pink, yellow and purple blotches separated by dotted lines. A wholistic, one-world view is emerging

---

1 Stewart E. Kelly, *Truth Considered & Applied: Examining Postmodernism, History, and Christian Faith* (B&H Publishing, 2011), p.325.

2 Mary Poplin, *Is Reality Secular? Testing the Assumptions of Four Global Worldviews* (IVP Books, 2014), p.265.

> from space travel and other miracles of modern technology and from communication. A new consciousness is also emerging from a growing awareness in the West of the wisdom of the Eastern world-view. Buddhism, Hinduism, Taoism and Shinto, while they differ in many respects, portray the world as a multi-dimensional, organically interrelated eco-system of which man is one of many inter-dependent parts. Perhaps we can learn through them to see the world whole, as it really is, and together – West and East – begin to build the foundations of a new world order.
>
> The most urgent item on the planetary agenda is to set the limits of freedom and order in supra-national, global affairs. A constitution for the world is needed which combines the achievements of both hemispheres: that is, constitutional limitations and a bill of rights from the West and a spacious world-view from the East.[3]

The allure of world government still tugs humanity.[4]

It is unlikely, however, that a future planetary system will be a secular construct – it will reflect the occulture of its age, and build upon the myth of Re-enchantment presented at the time. Religious leaders, too – explored in chapter 12 – have a history of interfacing with global political visionaries, and the interfaith community is a voice for progressive internationalism. The two movements already walk hand-in-hand, acting as joint fulcrums for change. Could there be an authoritative merger, a synthesis of pragmatic politics and established religions? This would require a dominating, global impetus: A crisis of magnitude. The notion may seem fanciful in times of relative peace, but this can change in the flash of atoms splitting over a city.

How will transhumanism be embodied? What are we willing to trade for the fruit of technological assimilation and its promise of near-immortality? Are we drinking an elixir to a better life, or ripping the lid from Pandora's box? Might our digital tools, wrapping the world in an ever-tightening web, become the definitive vehicle for coexistence and interconnection? Will we give up autonomy for hive-mind convenience; that Marxist dream of perfect

---

3 Lucile W. Green, *Journey to a Governed World: Thru 50 Years in the Peace Movement* (The Uniquest Foundation, 1991), pp.34-35.

4 A 2018 survey of ten nations concluded that, "Seven adults in ten (69%) think that a new supranational organization needs to be created to respond to global risks." *Attitudes to Global Risk and Governance Survey, 2018* (Global Challenges Foundation, 2018), p.6.

productivity as the means to equality? This portends a revolutionary period. In that case, will our digital tools be used as silicon bludgeons to beat into submission those who question the prevailing ideology?

What will techno-oneness look like?

I am reminded of a workshop attended while I was at Burning Man, 2018. The subject was artificial intelligence, crypto-currencies and psychedelic spirituality. The discussion was led by a major personality in the field of smart contracts, and digital governance was on the table. Implied was a new civilization built on four interlocking blocks: 1) a new spirituality inspired by shamanic techniques, 2) the new ethos being constructed, in real-time, at Burning Man, 3) a digital means of exchange, tied into and validating the new social contract, and 4) artificial intelligence as the management system. Being described was a scalable, techno-pagan, social-spiritual synthesis.

How will our new myths unravel? As we embrace the gospel of global citizenship with its stipulation of planetary loyalty, what will we sacrifice in service to Gaia? Pagan practices of old conjure gruesome images. Will we find ourselves looking down from the blood soaked platform of a Mayan temple, or see children sacrificed in the fire-red arms of Molech? Might we legitimize such morbid rites of fertility and seasonal cycles? No. We are too sophisticated for such primitivism; just ask any one of the 50 million human babies aborted *every year*.[5] Are there comparative differences between the two? Of course: this is not argued. Abortion, nevertheless, is absolutely recognized as a means to maintain Earth's sustainability.[6] In fact, during the

---

5 *Fact Sheet: Induced Abortion Worldwide* (Guttmacher Institute, March 2018), p.1.

6 Safe abortions – couched as reproductive rights – are linked to sustainable population control. See *World Survey on the Role of Women in Development, 2014: Gender Equality and Sustainable Development* (United Nations, 2014), chapter 5: "Ground sustainable population policies in sexual and reproductive health and rights, including the provision of universally accessible quality sexual and reproductive health services, information and education across the life cycle, including safe and effective methods of modern contraception, maternal health care, comprehensive sexuality education and safe abortion" (p.114). In 2009, the case was made for an abortion action-plan specific to developing nations in terms of the "twin challenges of rapid population growth and environmental degradation." See J.J. Speidel et al., "Population Polices, Programmes and the Environment," *Philosophical Transcriptions of The Royal Society, Biological Sciences* (The Royal Society, 2009), p.3060. For an older but critical review of population policies, including abortion, see Julian L. Simon, *Population Matters: People, Resources, Environment, and Immigration* (Transaction Publishers, 1990).

Global Citizenship 2000 Youth Congress, Robert Muller boasted how policies he helped to develop had *prevented the births of 2.2 billion children* – for the sake of Mother Earth. Maybe the two, Molech and the modern world, are not so far removed after all.

A more supernatural angle must also be considered. Are we approaching a future in which the Pagan deities of ancient times become more to us than just symbols of nature and enlightenment? The Bible, a book revealing the supernatural world, outlines the fact that unholy entities exist. Christians accept the supernatural reality of God, and we acknowledge that satanic hosts are active – that Satan was the accuser before Job in the Old Testament,[7] and that the Devil is like a lion searching for prey[8] – but as products of modern thinking, we tend to downplay the serious nature of Pagan spirituality as found in Scripture. If the Pagan past is being conjured to project our future, then we face a troubling thought: that the spiritual personalities who enchanted the minds of men *then* may have a role in re-enchanting us *now*.

More questions arise. How might the Islamic monism of Will – submission, not choice – intersect with visions of Oneness? Islam has a definite structure that frames Muslim identity, informing political, economic and social life; it is more than just a faith. The influx of Islam has added new stresses to Western civilization, already internally cracking as the Christian ethos is undermined. How this unfolds in the face of other emerging changes remains a question of significance.

Pages could be filled with mounting queries and scenarios. The *personal* side, however, must be considered. How has Oneness shaped your beliefs? Are there spiritual practices you employ that are grounded in Oneness? Have you wrestled with its varied ideological expressions? Or maybe you have accepted the more secular approach, that Man is the measure of all things – the Humanistic, atheistic perspective. If so, what are the applications and outcomes? I am reminded of what secularist and mathematician, David Berlinski, wrote in his critique of *atheism and its scientific pretentions*: "We can say nothing of interest about the human soul. We do not know what impels us to right conduct or where the form of the good is found."[9]

---

[7] Job 1:6-7.

[8] 1 Peter 5:8.

[9] David Berlinski, *The Devil's Delusion: Atheism and Its Scientific Pretentions* (Basic Books, 2009), p.xv.

How has Oneness manifested in your home, workplace, and church? Where and how has this overarching paradigm intersected with your life?

Conversely, have you considered the implications of God being categorically other? This means His standards exist beyond time and matter, and cannot be annulled. His role as moral lawgiver and judge are irrevocable. This is sobering. The writer of Ecclesiastes rightly says, "Fear God and keep His commandments, for this is man's all. For God will bring every work into judgment, including every secret thing, whether good or evil."[10]

Added to this is the Biblical understanding that we are created as His image bearers on Earth,[11] literally designed to be God's representatives; not because of our abilities, but as a status bestowed to the human race by His decree.[12] Our value, therefore, is eternally established – this is not based on our personal merit or the dictates of man, but grounded in God's word. And this was further demonstrated in that God loved us enough to take upon Himself the sin of humanity, fully tasting pain and agony in the act of redemption: "For God so loved the world that He gave His only begotten Son, that whoever believes in Him should not perish but have everlasting life."[13]

How might the realization that God is *other*, and that we are designed as His image bearers, change your perspective – your life?

A General Response

As the Christian ethos in the West slips away, One-ist alternatives become increasingly emboldened. What should be our response?

Notice I did not ask, *what should our reaction be*? There are times and places when a hard reproach is necessary, but this can also incite counter reactions and the entrenching of polar views. A response, in contrast, is measured and tempered, seeking to change hearts and minds in a constructive manner. This requires highlighting what is true in a way that is respectful. I will be the first to admit my failings in this regard; it is easier to react and let the bridges burn, but seldom is this beneficial.

---

[10] Ecclesiastes 12:13-14.

[11] Genesis 1:26.

[12] Michael S. Heiser, *The Unseen Realm: Recovering the Supernatural Worldview of the Bible* (Lexham Press, 2015), pp.42-43.

[13] John 3:16.

Some *general* thoughts come to mind, applicable to anyone interested in upholding liberty and engaging in worldview issues.

First, we need an understanding of the two paradigms – Oneness and Otherness – and to know our own positions. Take the time to study, and to grow in knowledge and wisdom. A noisy world of information is at our fingertips; seek that which is of higher value.

Second, recognize where and how worldviews intersect in your life, and let your voice be heard. When relevant, document and exposit in such a way it respectfully deconstructs the perceived reality. Every circumstance will be different as we experience challenges in the workplace, school, church, or home – acumen and clear judgment are essential. Allow me to give an example, a unique situation, shared in the hopes of stirring our thoughts.

I have a friend who departed from his Christian heritage many years ago. For a decade-and-a-half he studied in the Kabbalah, then Native American spirituality before wandering into the camp of Tibetan Buddhism – *it seemed I was fighting for my sanity*. But God led him to the clarity that Jesus Christ is the indisputable way maker.

My friend owns a shop, and sometimes the topic of Buddhism comes up with clients. His visitor's knowingly smile with notions of blissful spirituality. My friend then asks if he can read a text from an eminent Bön Buddhist, a piece of writing illuminating the heart of the Eastern path. *Of course!*

> It is at this stage that we become free. Nothing disturbs us and we act according to 'crazy wisdom.' As the text says, we 'behave like a pig or a dog' who has no dualistic considerations. Good, bad, clean, dirty, everything is perceived as having 'one taste.' Another text says that at this stage we become 'like a little child who does not know anything and will do anything,' who is without any preferences or concepts of good or bad, so there is nothing to accept or reject…
>
> Nothing can disturb us any longer, everything arises in its own way and is liberated in its own way. If we do something, it is fine; if we do not do it, it is fine. There are no longer any rules to follow.[14]

His client's eyes widen with sudden realization. *Really?*

[14] Tenzin Wangyal Rinpoche, *Wonders of the Natural Mind: The Essence of Dzogchen in the Native Bon Tradition of Tibet* (Snow Lion, 2000), p.143.

For those who will see, this Buddhist teaching is more than a road to nowhere, it is a way of destruction.

What my friend did was simple yet effective: allowing the other person to recognize the folly. How else can a change of heart and mind begin?

Lastly, we must demonstrate a tangible and positive alternative. It is not enough to reveal error; a constructive way forward is essential. Confront the challenge, yes, but present something better. Be willing to point out another path; the value of individual life, liberty and responsibility, the importance of private property, freedom and flourishing, right and wrong.

One more point needs to be made: We tend to think that large and organized movements are needed to effectively engage in worldview issues, that challenges to liberty and the Christian faith are best handled through agencies and groups dedicated to those causes. There is a place for such, but personal responses are needed. It is the teacher tactfully asking valid questions when the curriculum demands global citizenship; the healthcare worker who raises concerns when One-ist spiritual practices are sold as medicine; the pastor challenging denominational leaders on interfaithism; the student offering alternatives to the professor's leftist ideologies; the landowner standing up to the encroachment of overbearing green policies; the engineer and specialist reigning in technocratic tendencies in their chosen fields; the politician working on behalf of constituents while curbing the tide of statism. It is the parent showing love, and sharing in knowledge and wisdom. It is the friend who cares for a friend, and who extends a hand to the stranger.

What we need are truth tellers who act in love, men and women who credibly stand in the gap.

Options For Christians

Professing Christians have three primary response options.

First, we can ignore the worldview changes around us, thinking we are somehow unaffected. The fact you are reading this, however, demonstrates that this is not your position; with knowledge comes responsibility. Nevertheless, there is a tendency to close our eyes to the challenges, even ignoring the very forces of change that are reshaping our immediate setting.

To be fair, there are many Christians who simply have not considered the unfolding worldview revolution. Sometimes it is hard to see what is in front of us, especially when day-to-day struggles consume so much energy and attention. God grant us the wisdom we need.

But an indifferent approach will only last so long. As manifestations of Oneness become more evident and rooted, we will inevitably find ourselves in a situation hostile to the Christian message of absolutes, of sin and salvation, and of the need for an exclusive Redeemer. We will become increasingly marginalized and even demonized as the dangerous *other*.

The second option is problematic and seriously troubling: To accept and embrace tenants of Oneness, merging its associated ideals with Christian concepts. The modern story of Western Christianity abounds with examples, pulling from both secular and mystical visions.

Blending faith messages with dreams of internationalism, the Social Gospel movement promised Heaven on Earth through collective efforts – a religious endorsement of socialist world federalism. Many churches and ministers subsequently drank from the fountain of collectivism. Corresponding is the popular social justice movement, its roots in the dual history of Catholic common-good teachings and Marxist-based class warfare.[15] When stripped of its platitudes, social justice – today, an immersion in identity politics – has a flavor akin to the Marxist-centric idea of oppression and oppressors. The individualistic nature of the gospel, that individual persons are afforded salvation, is overshadowed with a message of social redemption through values modification and class struggle.

Or we follow mystical inclinations, like the universal flow-state sold by ecumenical teacher Richard Rohr and contemplative Christian transhumanist, Mike Morrell – that *everything is holy* in the divine flow of wholeness.[16] All you need to do is see it that way, and participate, embracing the *spiritual path*. Individual salvation is replaced with the *feeling* of cosmic flow, and the Holy Spirit becomes a *mythic force* we tap into.

This does not mean all things described as mystical necessarily points to Oneness. Are there instances of metaphysical experiences in the Bible? Yes, we find many examples of visions and dreams, of angelic visitations, and of supernatural happenings wherein God communicated in a spiritual man-

---

[15] On the history of social justice, see Carl Teichrib, "The Fallacy of Social Justice: All for One, and Theft to All," *Forcing Change*, September 2010, Volume 4, Issue 9.

[16] Richard Rohr and Mike Morrell, *The Divine Dance: The Trinity and Your Transformation* (Whitaker House, 2016), see pp.186-191.

ner. However, in those cases God Himself initiated the experience for very specific reasons; they were not instigated or pursued by man, or practiced as a technique to achieve connection or enlightenment, nor were they of a private interpretation. I believe God still intervenes in extraordinary ways, but not in a manner that contradicts Himself. God's ways are not our ways.

Another example bridging into the second option was the Emergent Church movement. Originally touted as a conversation about how to live the gospel within a Postmodern setting, the movement itself adopted the Postmodern attitude, leading to theological revisionism. Social justice was confused for missions. Christians needed to be more inclusive – that is, to declare Biblical truth claims as exclusive was a mark of arrogance. The road to redemption was broader, the story more open.

Brian McLaren, a leading voice in the Emergent community, cast a negative shadow on personal salvation,

> Sadly, in too many quarters we continue to reduce the scope of the gospel to the individual soul and the nuclear family, framing it in a comfortable, personalized format – it's all about personal devotions, personal holiness, and a personal Savior. This domesticated gospel will neither rock any boats nor step out of them into stormy waters. We have in many ways responded to the big global crisis of our day with an incredible, shrinking gospel. The world has said, 'No thanks.'[17]

McLaren was wrong. For two millennium the gospel message has been rocking souls, because God Himself rocked eternity by defeating the tomb.

A shrinking gospel? No, it is a saving gospel, and while some say yes to the Good News, the history of humanity is soaked in the consequences of continually saying, "no thanks." Indeed, this is the *game of gods* – to say "no thanks" as we strive to save ourselves, either as individuals or in our communal towers of Babel. Without a personal Savior there is no hope for personal salvation, and ultimately no hope for the world.

So what did McLaren suggest as a response to "big global crisis"?

Do you remember Jim Garrison, the man behind Mikhail Gorbachev's State of the World Forum, as outlined in chapter 6? Garrison has a long

---

[17] Brian D. McLaren, *Everything Must Change: Jesus, Global Crisis, and a Revolution of Hope* (Thomas Nelson, 2007), p.244.

history of promoting world governance and the mythic qualities of Earth spirituality.[18] McLaren suggested we follow Garrison's model of global governance, along with the economic ideas of David Korten from the Club of Rome. We would thus construct a "framing story that envisions an interdependent, mutually committed, global community of communities."[19]

Although many Emergent lay-followers, I am sure, would not have considered global governance to be part of their story – the movement was not unified – McLaren's recommendations demonstrated a reconfiguration of priorities. The redemption of individual souls was downplayed in his collective vision. *Vive la révolution.*

The Emergent movement itself moved on, fading and transitioning.[20] New games, however, are always in play as attempts are made to remake the faith in the world's image. *Progressive Christianity* claims an "experience of the Sacred and the Oneness and Unity of all life."[21] *Evolutionary Christianity*, another movement of sorts, pushes cosmic evolution in a way that dovetails

---

18 Re: World government. In 1995, Garrison gave an interview advocating a new world order, saying, "Over the next 20 to 30 years, we are going to end up with world government. It's inevitable... There's going to be conflict, coercion and consensus. That's part of what will be required as we give birth to the first global civilization." – Jim Garrison, "One World Under Gorby," *San Francisco Weekly*, May 31, 1995. Re: Earth spirituality. Garrison said in a promotional video that, "the Earth herself is the bedrock... there is something like geo-mythology; there's a mythology that came from the ancient peoples, there is also a mythology that emanates from the Earth herself." Garrison continued on about the primordial goddess and the primordial mind, inter-species communion and eco-spirituality, and about our search for Earth Wisdom. Video title: *Earth Wisdom & the Primordial Mind at Wisdom University: Indigenous Mind, Interspecies Connection, EcoSpirituality* (Wisdom University, no date, video on file).

19 McLaren, *Everything Must Change*, pp.262-263.

20 The influence of the Emergent Church is undeniable in shifting many Christians, including young pastors, into viewing the Bible through a Postmodern lens – even a post-truth framework. In 2008, *Christianity Today* published an article titled "R.I.P. Emerging Church." In the years that followed, the movement went into decline as a vocal force. The reasons are numerous, including a revisionist handling of Scripture, which compelled some of its leaders to denounce the movement publicly. Some lay-people who embraced Emergent thinking returned to more orthodox positions, while others moved in different directions, including Progressive Christianity.

21 "The 8 Points of Progressive Christianity," *ProgressiveChristianity.org* (https://progressivechristianity.org/the-8-points). Progressive Christianity is a loose movement that blends leftist social activism, the transgression of traditional sexuality, eco-spirituality and environmentalism, and collective salvation.

with spiritual transhumanism. Of course, the interfaith movement is also before us, compelling churches and denominations to take the wide road.

To mirror the world and call it "Christian" is our second option.

Option number three is to be *in the world* but not *of the world*, and in so doing, to take seriously our Biblical call to be Ambassadors for Christ. But what does this mean?

The Apostle Paul used various illustrations for the Christian life. He likened the sharing of the Good News to that of co-laboring in a field or garden; someone sows, another waters, but God makes things grow.[22] Later he used the metaphor of an athlete, as one who disciplines his body for competition, striving for a prize. We, too, are to be diligent and disciplined in the faith, running the race well.[23]

Then when Paul encouraged his friend, Timothy, to be "strong in the grace that is in Christ Jesus," he used three illustrations: a committed soldier who is willing to endure difficulties, an athlete competing according to the rules, and a hardworking farmer who partakes of his crop.[24] Even if you have never been a soldier, athlete or farmer, those roles are relatable.

Paul also used another illustration. In 2 Corinthians 5:20-21 we read,

> Now then, we are ambassadors for Christ, as though God were pleading through us: we implore you on Christ's behalf, be reconciled to God. For He made Him who knew no sin to be sin for us, that we might become the righteousness of God in Him.

Being an ambassador is not something we normally consider. What does this entail? An ambassador is the *official* and *legal* representative of one's government to a foreign nation. In the era of monarchies, this would be an emissary of the king. We will use this royal designation, for as Christians we have been commissioned by the King of Kings.

Being an ambassador means we know the power and position of our King. We represent His interests, and have aligned our own priorities with the mission of being in the King's diplomatic service. We are trained in His ways, and we are cognitive as to how our actions reflect His character, for we are His image bearers in a foreign territory.

---

[22] 1 Corinthians 3:6-9.

[23] 1 Corinthians 9:24-27.

[24] 2 Timothy 2:1-6.

The culture and traditions of the place we find ourselves in are not unknown to us. We are set apart from their customs, but we are not uninformed regarding the character or composition of the nation. In fact, like the Apostle Paul in Athens,[25] we know the setting and beliefs well enough to engage with a level of competency and discernment.

As a royal diplomat our task is twofold. First, to effectively communicate the King's message, regardless if the land is hostile or friendly. Second, we are to be vigilant to the schemes of foreign powers, recognizing challenges to the King's interest. Then as an ambassador should, we petition for intervention while alerting others in His service to areas of concern.

Being an emissary is a serious undertaking: "Now then, we are ambassadors for Christ, as though God were pleading through us: we implore you on Christ's behalf, be reconciled to God."

Our calling is best summed by Jesus Christ,

> You are the light of the world. A city that is set on a hill cannot be hidden. Nor do they light a lamp and put it under a basket, but on a lampstand, and it gives light to all who are in the house. Let your light so shine before men, that they may see your good works and glorify your Father in heaven.[26]

Choosing Freedom

"God remains dead!" Nietzsche declared. "And we have killed him!"[27]

Nietzsche was *partially* correct. God was killed, but the Author of Life is not bound by the curse of death. In the words of Jesus Christ,

> Do not be afraid; I am the First and the Last. I am He who lives, and *was dead*, and behold, I am alive forevermore. Amen. And I have the keys of Hades and of Death. [28]

In this declaration is the promise of *real transformation*. Not a techno-Pagan, Marxist-socialist, global-political, Perennial-communal-spiritual New Man – not a refashioning of ourselves from the images we desire or project – but

---

[25] See Acts 17.

[26] Matthew 5:14-16.

[27] Friedrich Nietzsche, *The Gay Science* (Cambridge University Press, 2001/2008), p.120.

[28] Revelation 1:17b-18, italics for emphasis.

the assurance of being fully restored by Him who created us. Death has been defeated, and this portends a reality *beyond the grave*. We can therefore live with assurance and certainty, having our hope grounded in someone who is unmoved by the changing forces of nature or the schemes of man.

It is a revolutionary revelation.

Indeed, the Christian message of otherness – the distinction of God, the finished work of Jesus Christ, and the value of the individual above nature and systems – is thoroughly counter-cultural. As Lloyd Billingsley said,

> The Christian faith has indeed shown that it can 'turn the world upside down.' It is, in a very real sense, revolutionary. So are the free political and economic arrangements that have in the past accompanied Christian faith. They are the exception, not the rule, in history. Free people are the true revolutionaries. They can expect resistance.[29]

Jesus Christ once said to a group of Jewish believers: "If you abide in My word, you are My disciples indeed. And you shall know the truth, and the truth shall make you free."[30]

The freedom offered was not economic, political, or social freedom – wonderful byproducts that have flowed from the Christian worldview. His freedom was, first and foremost, the liberty of our soul from the bondage of sin and death,

> Most assuredly, I say to you, whoever commits sin is a slave of sin. And a slave does not abide in the house forever, but a son abides forever. Therefore if the Son makes you free, you shall be free indeed.[31]

Oneness promises a pseudo-freedom by compelling you to become nothing. Christ offers freedom by giving Himself so we are no longer in the grip of sin; and sin is based upon the notion we can justify and save ourselves.

Oneness says our purpose is ultimately meaningless. In Christ, however, we are one in His purpose; not that we become God, but that we are received

---

[29] Lloyd Billingsley, *The Absence of Tyranny: Recovering Freedom in Our Time* (Multnomah Press, 1986), pp.173-174.

[30] John 8:31-32.

[31] John 8:34-35.

as sons and daughters of the King. Value and meaning flows from an eternal source – not from some nebulous, cosmic force, but from the personal Creator of the cosmos.

But in the spirit of freedom, which can only exist if reality is constructed on distinctions, you have to choose.

What will you put your faith in? The cult of world order? Spiritual politics? Technology? Will you look for meaning in a mystical feeling? Are you trusting in an ancient-future vision? Will you, as a compliant global citizen, proclaim the myth of Re-enchantment?

The Temple of Man beckons; come, *let us build our Babel – let us play our game of gods.*

Or will you place your hope in Someone who is eternally greater?

> Thus says the Lord, the King of Israel, and his Redeemer, the Lord of hosts: 'I am the First and I am the Last; besides Me there is no God.'[32]

[32] Isaiah 44:6.

INDEX

Where "n" is bracketed, the person/subject is found in a footnote on that page. Where "n" is not bracketed, the person/subject is found within the main text *and* a footnote.

A

B

E

F

G

J

K

L

M

N

O

P

Q

R

U

V

W

Y

Z

About the Author

Carl Teichrib is a researcher, writer, and lecturer focusing on the paradigm shift sweeping the Western world, including the challenges and opportunities faced by Christians. Over the years he has attended a range of political, religious, and social events in his quest to understand the historical and contemporary forces of transformation – including the Parliament of the Worlds Religions, Burning Man, and the United Nations Millennium Forum.

Since the mid-1990s, Carl's research has been utilized by numerous authors, media hosts and documentary producers, pastors, professors and students, and interested lay people. From 1997 to 2001, he was the Director of Research for author Gary H. Kah. Then, in 2007 Carl founded the monthly magazine, *Forcing Change*, an online digest that ran until the end of 2015. The full-time writing of *Game of Gods* commenced in January 2016.

Carl continues to engage on worldview issues.

More Information

This book's bibliography can be found at **www.gameofgods.ca**.

For nine years Carl Teichrib produced a monthly journal titled *Forcing Change*, focusing on worldview issues and transformational movements. To access all *Forcing Change* back issues, and to receive updates on new articles, interviews, speaking engagements, research projects and more, go to **www.forcingchange.org** and sign-up for this free service.

To book media interviews or speaking engagements, please go to **www.gameofgods.ca** or **www.forcingchange.org**.

Made in the USA
Lexington, KY
24 April 2019